An Altar for Their Sons

An Altar for Their Sons

The Alamo and the Texas Revolution in Contemporary Newspaper Accounts

Gary S. Zaboly

With Photographs from the Phil Collins Collection

State House
Press

Buffalo Gap, Texas

Library of Congress Cataloging-in-Publication Data

Zaboly, Gary S., 1950-
    An altar for their sons : the Alamo and the Texas Revolution in contemporary newspaper accounts / Gary S. Zaboly.
        p. cm.
    Includes bibliographical references and index.
    ISBN-13: 978-1-933337-46-3 (hardback : alk. paper)
    ISBN-10: 1-933337-46-X (hardback : alk. paper)
    1. Texas—History—Revolution, 1835-1836—Sources. 2. Alamo (San Antonio, Tex.)—Siege, 1836—Sources I. Title.

F390.Z33 2011
976.4'03—dc23

2011020903

State House Press
P. O. Box 818
Buffalo Gap, Texas 79508
325.572.3974 • 325.572.3991 (fax)
www.tfhcc.com

Printed in China.

Distributed by Texas A&M University Press Consortium
800.826.8911
www.tamupress.com

ISBN-13: 978-1-933337-46-3
ISBN-10: 1-933337-46-X
10 9 8 7 6 5 4 3 2 1

Original art by Gary S. Zaboly
Book designed by Rosenbohm Graphic Design

Bright was their fortune, and sublime their doom,
Who perished at the Alamo—their tomb
An altar for their sons—their dirge renown!
—from "The Heroes of the Alamo"
New Orleans Bee, July 25, 1836

This book is dedicated to my wife Cora

. . . and to the early influences in my life that got me to this point, especially the Disney TV series, *Davy Crockett*; the movies *The Last Command* (1955) and *The Alamo* (1960); and the first books, Olga W. Hall-Quest's *Shrine of Liberty: The Alamo*, Robert Penn Warren's *Remember the Alamo!*, William Weber Johnson's *The Birth of Texas*, John Meyers Meyers's *The Alamo*, Lon Tinkle's *13 Days to Glory*, and of course, Walter Lord's *A Time To Stand*.

Contents

Introduction   1

A Chronology   14

1   Spanish Texas   17

2   The Leaders Emerge   29

3   Road to Revolt   45

4   First Battles   69

5   Crockett Goes to Texas   103

6   "The Enemy Is Advancing on This Post"   121

7   The Alamo Encircled   143

8   Assault   191

The Alamo during the 1836 Siege (after page 246)   S1–S64

9   Retreat and Massacre   281

10 San Jacinto and the First Year of the Texas Republic   317

11 Memories, Legends, and Legacy   371

12 Contemporary Alamo Poetry   427

Notes   433

Sources and Acknowledgments   445

Afterword   447

Index   449

Introduction

Few writers have ever better explained, and in so few words, the true meaning of the Alamo story than did John Myers Myers at the end of his 1948 book, *The Alamo*: "The Alamo isn't a structure now; it is a symbol of valor in the minds of men. It can never fall again."[1] If the newspaper accounts presented here do anything, they certainly prove Myers's point: that the Alamo almost instantly transcended the *facts* that were reported and became, for most Americans, the heroic epitome of courage and resistance in the face of overwhelming odds. Just why this relatively small-scale battle in an isolated southwestern prairie town achieved such sudden legendary stature across the entire nation, and not just in Texas and neighboring regions, is not difficult to understand once these newspaper reports are read.

For the majority of Americans in 1836 the annihilation of the Alamo garrison was viewed not as the bloody suppression of rebellious expatriates in a foreign land but as genocide committed on fellow citizens by an "unprincipled and blood-thirsty tyrant," in the words of the *New York Evening Star*.[2] Reports that the Mexican army had mutilated the slain defenders only sharpened the country's thirst for vengeance. When news came of the systematic liquidation of the surrendered Texian garrison at Goliad three weeks after the Alamo's fall, there was no longer any doubt of the enemy's barbarousness. According to the *New York Herald*, "Under the form of a legitimate war, Santa Anna has perpetrated deeds more atrocious than those of the pirate on the high seas—of the wandering, houseless Arab of the desert. . . . Is it possible to hold terms at all with such a race of miscreants as these Mexicans have proved themselves to be? . . . let the Mexican embassy be drummed out of the country. They only represent a band of savages worse than the Seminoles."[3]

The *Washington Globe* agreed with this analogy: "The Indians were never known to butcher *all* their prisoners. They decimate their victims and satisfy their revenge, by putting a few to death. Santa Anna has introduced a new code of national law on this continent."[4] Apparently even noncombatants were not exempt from this "new code"; one letter from Texas claimed that the Mexican leader was "committing the most horrid cruelties, putting to death every one he meets, without regard to sex, age, or condition. The females are usually given up to the brutal passions of the soldiers, and afterwards butchered."[5] Susanna Dickinson, wife of one of the slain Alamo lieutenants, was said to have "suffered from the Mexican officers the most odious pollution that ever disgraced humanity."[6] Such frightful accounts could not be bettered as emotional calls-to-arms, and they worked; fired-up volunteers began flocking to Texas from every corner of the nation.

General Antonio López de Santa Anna had only himself to blame; by adopting a no-quarter policy against the US "pirates" who were attempting to wrest the northern state of Coahuila y Tejas from Mexico, he had, in the words of the *New York Herald*, roused up "a spirit of noble vengeance throughout the United States". It was a spirit "only to be paralleled by the sensation produced in ancient Greece on the fall of Leonidas being known throughout her smiling land."[7] Some even viewed the stand at the Alamo as unprecedented. "No history, either ancient or modern," declared the *Richmond Enquirer* of April 29, 1836, "neither the pass of Thermopylae, nor the battlefield upon which our progenitors have fallen, presents the remembrance of a more unequal and obstinate engagement."

It was understandable hyperbole, especially in light of the exaggerated reports of the battle that initially streamed out of Texas. For instance, casualties inflicted on the waves of assaulting Mexican troops by the tiny garrison were at first thought to have been sensationally huge: "between two and three thousand men," according to the *New Orleans Bee* of March 28, 1836, or, anywhere from eleven to sixteen killed or wounded Mexicans for every defender. The martial prowess of the defenders—"almost superhuman," as the *Richmond Enquirer* put it—became a key element in the legend.[8] Indeed, *all* Americans could be proud because approximately half the fallen were not Texas settlers but recent volunteers from the states—"bone of our bone and flesh of our flesh," as one paper put it.[9] These heroes had "determined to conquer or die," noted the *Arkansas Gazette* of May 3, 1836. "Every man fought to his last breath."

The valor of the Alamo defenders was underscored by reports that considerably magnified the strength of the attacking enemy columns: "1,508 desperate convicts placed in the Van Guard and forlorn hope by Santa Anna, with the bayonets of 3,300 regular infantry, and the swords of 2,200 cavalry at their backs," according to the

Rochester Daily Democrat.[10] A letter from Texas in the *Frankfort Commonwealth* raised the number to "8,000 troops."[11]

That the Texian garrison, then thought to have numbered only 150 able-bodied fighters out of about 187, had not flinched in the face of such incredible odds was deemed only natural.[12] "In physical strength, one American is equal to three Mexicans, hand to hand," claimed "a Citizen of the West, intimately acquainted with the situation of Texas."[13] David Crockett alone was said to have shot down "twenty-three of the colored hireling slaves of Santa Anna."[14] In a toast at a festival in La Grange, Tennessee, in May, E. J. Moody called Crockett "a second Samson—who piled his enemies heaps upon heaps, but with a different instrument."[15] Another report had Alamo commander William B. Travis, despite a mortal head wound, rising up from the fire-step to kill a Mexican officer by "running him through with his sword."[16] Even the grievously ill Jim Bowie, according to some accounts, had summoned forth a final spark of energy to smite the "cowards" attacking him:

> Lying in bed he discharged his pistols and with each discharge brought down an enemy. So intimidated were the Mexicans by this act of desperate and cool bravery, that they dared not approach him, but shot him through the door, and as the cowards approached his bed over the dead bodies of their companions, the dying Bowie, nerving himself for a last blow, plunged his knife into the heart of his nearest foe at the same instant that he expired.[17]

No matter that conflicting rumors were printed suggesting that the Alamo leaders had died less than courageous deaths—that Travis had stabbed himself; that Bowie had shot himself or had been "murdered in his bed, sick and helpless"; or that Crockett and five or six others had surrendered, only to be immediately executed—few chose, or wanted, to believe them.[18]

In less than an hour of combat, the defenders of the Alamo had been transfigured into the kind of hero archetypes who, in the words of Carl Jung, can "set the tone of a whole society."[19] And despite the frequent physical defacements it would suffer from later military and commercial interests, the battle site became a shrine, a holy ground for generations of Texans. One anonymous, early and prescient poet grasped the full mythic meaning of the event in his "The Heroes of the Alamo," published in the *New Orleans Bee* in July 1836:

Bright was their fortune, and sublime their doom,
Who perished at the Alamo—their tomb
      An altar for their sons—their dirge renown!

Their epitaph nor rust shall ere efface,
Nor Time, that changes all things else debase—
      Nor later ages in their pride disown!

Their tomb contains, enshrined beside the dead,
A mighty inmate.—Her for whom they bled—
      Their country's unforgotten fame.

Witness the heroic Travers, who in death
Did win high valor's more than Pythian wreath,
      A crown unfading—an immortal name![20]

The Texas "sons" of the Alamo heroes have never forgotten them. Early in his presidency Lyndon B. Johnson defended sending US troops to assist the South Vietnamese army by explaining, "It's just like the Alamo. Somebody damn well needed to go to their aid. Well, by God, I'm going to Vietnam's aid and I thank the Lord that I've got the men who will go with me." Johnson even fabricated a personal connection with Travis, Crockett, and Bowie by declaring to US soldiers at Korea's Camp Stanley, "My great-great-grandfather died at the Alamo."[21] If some pessimistic civilian observers were likening the Marines's stand at Khe Sanh in early 1968 to Dien Bien Phu, Johnson was calling it "another Alamo" and saved the base by airlifting thousands of reinforcements and tons of materiel to it, and by cluster-bombing the surrounding North Vietnamese positions.[22]

Starting in the mid-1960s, Texas governors such as John Connally and George W. Bush championed vigorous, if unsuccessful, efforts to persuade Mexico to return the only Alamo flag known to have survived the battle, the company colors of the New Orleans Greys. Three Mexican flags captured by Sam Houston's army at San Jacinto on April 21, 1836—those of the Toluca, Matamoros, and Guerrero battalions—were even offered in exchange. One officer of the US Embassy in Mexico City, whose great-great-great-great-uncle was Alamo casualty Daniel Cloud, devised a scheme to bring the flag back as part of a traveling exhibition that would later conveniently become indefinitely extended. But all these attempts came to naught.[23]

Non-Texan politicians have not forgotten the Alamo and its defenders, either. Manhattan-born Theodore Roosevelt resigned his post as Assistant Navy Secretary in May 1898 to co-command the First United States Volunteer Cavalry regiment—the "Rough Riders," as the public called them. Recruits were trained in a San Antonio park, and "were glad," observed Roosevelt, "that our regiment had been organized in the city where the Alamo commemorates the death fight of Crockett, Bowie, and their famous band of frontier heroes." After arriving in Cuba in June, this unlikely brew of cowboys, gamblers, outlaws, Ivy League athletes, miners, firemen, and Fifth Avenue swells proved itself gallant while winning victories despite heavy resistance and casualties. The war over, Roosevelt returned to New York, where that fall his well-earned martial fame easily won him the governorship. Two years later he was chosen as McKinley's vice president. An honor guard of Rough Riders attended his first Inaugural speech in 1904, and the following year he returned to San Antonio to address a reunion of the regiment, and swarms of citizens—in front of the Alamo, of course.[24]

During the 1960 presidential campaign, candidates John F. Kennedy and Richard M. Nixon both stood in front of the Alamo on different occasions to "attack" their rivals, state their policies, and secure the vote of Texans.[25] In a piece published that October titled, "Alamo as Backdrop," the *Dallas Morning News* complained that the shrine should not be used "for partisan political purposes in 1960."[26]

But the Alamo was far too potent a symbol of guts and determination *not* to be employed to underscore partisan points in the news media, and other politicians without Texas birthrights continued to recognize this. In October 1968, South Dakota-born Vice President Hubert H. Humphrey spoke before the Alamo to blast his Republican rival, Nixon, for the presidency.[27] In 1976, Nebraska-born President Gerald Ford stood at a lectern in front of the old church to counter criticism from his own party that the United States had fallen behind the Soviet Union militarily. Ford noted that the Alamo had been conquered by an army "of superior size and strength. In global terms, America must never give any such advantage to any potential enemy—and we never will."[28] With the "altar" of Texas liberty photographed behind him, how could anyone dare question his resolve?

On January 21, 1985, in his second Inaugural address, Illinois-born President Ronald Reagan asked Americans to cooperate with one another in their common "journey," reminding them of those who have traveled before us. . . . Now we hear again the echoes of our past: a general falls to his knees in the hard snow of Valley Forge; a lonely President paces the darkened halls, and ponders his struggle to preserve the Union; the men of the Alamo call out encouragement to each other. . . . It is the American sound. It is hopeful, big-hearted, idealistic, daring, decent, and fair.[29]

As this collection of newspaper accounts will demonstrate, the Alamo story from its inception, with all its iconic and allegoric power, has indeed been an *American* story. The dust jacket to the first edition of Walter Lord's superb *A Time to Stand*, published in 1961, included the subtitle: *The Epic of the Alamo Seen as a Great National Experience.*[30] This referred not to how the event had evolved in the American consciousness and culture over the intervening decades, but how it quickly became, in *1836*, a catalytic moment that galvanized most of the nation. San Jacinto, the vastly more important Texas Revolution battle, ironically remains little known, if at all, to the average citizen outside Texas, but say the word "Alamo" and there is generally instant recognition. Another poet of 1836, writing for the *New York Evening Star*, beseeched his countrymen in "The Massacre at Bexar":

> Say ye of North, East, South or West,
>   Friends! Kindred of the slain!
> Shall the blood of the murder'd brave,
>   For vengeance cry in vain?
> Remember Bexar![31]

When Travis urged his "fellow citizens [to] assist me now," in his letter from the fort of February 24, he was not only addressing "the People of Texas," but "All Americans in the world." A *Memphis Enquirer* editorial boldly emphasized this point: "SIXTEEN HUNDRED of the Mexicans killed in the siege, is the imperishable monument left to their memory by the ONE HUNDRED AND EIGHTY-SEVEN Texians—we may say AMERICANS."[32] In Buffalo, New York, on April 23, resolutions were read at a meeting organized to "aid and support the Texians," because Texas had been "settled by those who have a common origin with ourselves, many of them being either acquaintances, friends, or relatives of us or our fellow-citizens."[33] Comprising the two volunteer companies of

"New Orleans Greys," for instance, were men from eighteen states as well as at least six foreign countries.[34]

The Mexicans themselves also saw the Texas revolt largely as a scheme inspired and assisted by recent US arrivals and expansionists. Along with his postbattle report expressed to his ministers back in Mexico City, Santa Anna sent the captured flag of the New Orleans Greys, noting, "by looking at it yourselves you will know better the true intentions of the traitorous colonists, and their cooperators of the ports of the United States of the North."[35]

Until the middle of May 1836, when word of Santa Anna's defeat at San Jacinto arrived in Mexico City, most Mexican newspapers utilized prose—and poetry—no less purple and jingoistic than that of US presses to express their country's euphoria over the victory at the Alamo. "What enthusiastic exultation and happiness was to be seen yesterday on the face of every good Mexican," observed the *La Lima de Vulcano*, "when he learned the splendid news." Echoing the intense animus against the enemy found in newspapers in the United States, Mexican editorials rejoiced that the rebels "have bitten the earth they profaned, their impure blood has flowed in atonement of their great insults, and between the fire and steel of our valiant men, their black souls have expired, nourished in immorality and profligacy."[36]

Santa Anna, in the words of a poet in the *El Santanista Oaxaqueño* of March 23, had wielded his "proud and noble sword" to free Mexico from "the ungrateful, vile, and mean foreigners."[37]

A letter written by a Mexican officer who had taken part in the March 6 assault was published in *El Mosquito Mexicano* in April; it reveled in the fate of the Texian "wretches," a fate brought about by their "foolish temerity." Though willing to allow that most of the defenders had put up a "tenacious resistance," the officer added that one of their leaders, "the perverse braggart Santiago [James] Bowie, died like a woman, almost hidden under a mattress."[38] Another paper sneered: "Poor James Bowie. How quickly your stupid, inane arrogance is dissipated. These fools do not know Mexicans."[39]

By taking the Alamo, the courageous *soldados* had also avenged the humiliating capitulation of the army of General Martín Perfecto de Cos at San Antonio the previous December "ETERNAL PRAISE TO THE INVINCIBLE ARMY OF MEXICO," blared the *El Nacional* of March 2, "Renown, honor, and glory to the brave honor of the fatherland," proclaimed *La Lima de Vulcano*.[40] The anonymous officer in *El*

Mosquito Mexicano noted that the Mexican soldiers had attacked the fort with "dauntless constancy."

> I assure you that all ideas of fright or terror were removed at the sight of so many valiant men who by ladders, over batteries, through embrasures and even upon one another, clambered over the entrenchments. . . . Eternal praise to the immortal SANTA-ANNA and to the chiefs, officers and troops who so heroically have avenged the outrages inflicted upon our great nation!"[41]

The *generalissimo* himself did not stint when it came to publicly applauding the valor of his men, who had been seen "fighting individually, each one disputing for the most heroic action." If accounts appearing in US newspapers had exaggerated the number of fallen Mexicans, Santa Anna was not above inflating the Texian body count either. "More than 600 bodies, all foreigners," lay sprawled across the Alamo's "fosses and entrenchments," he wrote in his March 6 report, which was published fifteen days later in *Supplemento al Diario del Gobierno.* Furthermore, there was "an additional number not yet accurately known; these, endeavoring to escape the bayonets of the infantry, fell beneath the sabers of our cavalry." His own troops, he claimed, had suffered far fewer casualties: "70 men dead and 300 wounded, amongst whom are two chiefs and 23 officers."[42]

For his apparently decisive achievement, the Mexican leader was compared in the press to Napoleon, even Hercules.[43] "Oh great Santa Anna," gushed one newspaper poet, "the invincible, the immortal Santa Anna."[44] The anonymous Mexican officer also extended "praise eternal to the brave General Cos, who at the head of the attacking column, has vindicated himself of the unfounded and coarse accusations of his unjust enemies."[45] All in all, the accounts of this and other recent Mexican victories in Texas, as *El Nacional* saw it, recorded "deeds whose intrinsic glory and heroism words cannot amplify."[46]

For all the sublime rhetoric bombarding newspapers in both Mexico and the United States in 1836, opinion about the Alamo and about the Texian revolt in general was hardly monolithic in either camp. In the United States, the introduction of the double-cylinder press four years earlier had led to an explosion of cheaply priced dailies and weeklies, with some, like the *New York Sun*, selling for just a penny.[47] The result was skyrocketing circulation, and a democratization of both content and readership as the focus shifted from the needs of the mercantile elite to that of the broader, market-based public.[48] These "penny presses" offered customers not only hard news (and plenty of gossip), but also a glut of conflicting, strongly worded editorial views on all serious issues—political, regional, societal, commercial, military, and religious. And these swirling waters were made muddier by publishers and correspondents who freely employed distortions and slander, even vicious lies, to advance those views.[49] For many of them, Texas proved an abundant source of highly serviceable fodder.

Abolitionist papers, of course, were among the most strident and hostile. "As scurvy a set of ingrates and straggling political adventurers as ever disgraced humanity," is how the *Republican Monitor* summed up the Texians. As for their objectives:

> If the "heroes" who are fighting for liberty (i.e., the *liberty* to hold men in *slavery*) in Texas, had remained in the United States, they would not have been "murdered" by Santa Anna. . . . Away with the sickly sensibility that would involve our nation in a quarrel with another, to sustain such a cause as this![50]

To the *Boston Atlas*, Sam Houston was nothing more than "a miserable vagabond and brawler," while his men were fugitive US "murderers, swindlers, and horse thieves."[51]

Jacksonian papers like the *Daily National Intelligencer*, of Washington D.C., took a kindlier, if still critical stance.

> We mourn over the fate of Col. CROCKETT and of all those of his degree of merit who have become victims to their own daring, in defending, at a distance from their own firesides, what they considered the cause of freedom. But we cannot shut our eyes to the fact that the citizens of the United States who have entered the Mexican territory (of which TEXAS was as much an integral part as the city of MEXICO itself) in hostile array, with arms in their hands, have done so at their own peril, and have themselves only to blame for the consequences.[52]

For some newspapers, the Alamo's fall swept away previous apprehensions about the revolt against Mexico. Although admitting "we have been opposed to this Texian War from first to last," the *Memphis Enquirer* of April 12 added:

Gen. Santa Anna is now defending his own country, but he should defend it as a soldier—not as a tyrant; we say we have *been* against the war; but our feelings we cannot suppress—some of our own bosom friends have fallen in the Alamo. . . . We would avenge their death, and spill the last drop of our blood upon the altar of Liberty. "Down with the Tyrant!"

Even before news of the Alamo's capture reached it, the Democratic *New York Times* conceded that

Davy Crockett . . . is a good man in his way, and albeit we have spoken harshly of some of his antics, we will do him the justice to say, that we have full confidence in his valor and willingness to fight on all proper occasions. We doubt not that his rifle will speak volumes among the Mexicans.[53]

Another New York paper, the *Sun*, although expressing its "sincere hopes, of the success of our Texian brethren [that] are founded upon their bravery and perseverance," cautioned that the "massacre" at the Alamo was not necessarily an unprecedented "violation of the strict law of arms." To support this viewpoint, it cited previous examples such as the bayoneting of surrendered American troops by the British at Paoli in 1777 and the slaughters committed in conquered towns during the Peninsular War.[54]

Published opinion in Texas itself also reflected a diversity of views, often stoked by extreme anger, much of the latter of course directed at Santa Anna. But not a little of it was also aimed at "the backwardness of some of our fellow citizens, in turning out in defense of their wives and children," as noted in the *Telegraph and Texas Register* on March 5, 1836. Captain Moseley Baker warned that, if the Alamo fell, all of Texas would be lost, and no one would be left to "tell the dreadful tale—or to reproach those that remain for their supineness, or their cowardice." After the Mexicans captured the Alamo, traveler William Fairfax Gray tried to convey in a letter published in a Kentucky newspaper the bitterness many Texians felt over the slaughtered garrison, "sacrificed by the cold neglect—the culpable, shameful neglect—of their countrymen."

Like their northern counterparts, when it came to the Alamo, Mexican newspapers also reflected a variety of opinions. Although Santa Anna headed an antiliberal, centralized form of government, one that mercilessly suppressed rebellions, it was not his usual policy to shut down dissident presses. His opponents were allowed to register their criticisms in editorials, handbills, and books, although an excessively sarcastic personal attack might result in the author being suddenly escorted into the office of an irritated *presidente*.[55]

None of the Mexican papers sided with the Anglo American rebels, however, and all of them initially applauded the recapture of San Antonio. But as time passed and other accounts of the battle reached Mexico (some from imported US newspapers), Santa Anna's Alamo field report was increasingly seen, especially in federalist circles, as a document filled with exaggerations intended to inflate his image and justify his autocratic goals.[56]

Toluca's *La Luna* declared in its April 2 issue that even though "the invaders [Texians'] pride was humbled, [and] the valor of Mexican soldiers proved," the fact that General Cos had broken the parole of his 1835 surrender treaty by returning to Texas with Santa Anna cast "discredit" on the nation's honor. Indeed, this should persuade "thoughtful men that the victory at the Alamo has not been a real gain." Other papers, such as Mexico City's *El Cosmopolita* and *El Republicano*, added their voices warning of the generalissimo's regal ambitions.[57]

At the beginning of his eyewitness narrative of the 1836 campaign, *Zapadore* (Sapper) battalion captain José Enrique de la Peña indicated that his purpose in writing it was to rectify "the accumulation of lies told to falsify the events, published in national as well as international newspapers, but especially in the latter, and the cheap adulation the former have rendered to the men least deserving of it."[58] In fact, here and there in his account Peña supports his views by quoting or referring to "various printed articles," most often those written by fellow officers who agreed with him that their commander had failed the army, and thus the nation, on so many counts. Some of the Mexican newspaper articles criticized Santa Anna's strategy; others noted how insufficient provisions and medical supplies had led to horrible suffering and death among the soldados.[59] One of them condemned the 1835 *pronunciamiento* issued by Santa Anna and minister José María Tornel decreeing that "any foreigners invading the Republic be treated and tried as pirates whenever found armed." Peña emphasized the point that the decree had led to the "barbarous sacrifice" of surrendered Texians at Goliad and other settlements, acts that "focused the shocked attention of the civilized world, presenting us Mexicans as Hottentots, as savages who do not know how to respect any right."[60]

Former *Washington Post* publisher Phil Graham once said, "Journalism is the first rough draft of history," and for both Americans and Mexicans of 1836, newspapers provided the major, and at times the only, source for tidings from the outside world. That reports of the Alamo battle were often colored by censorship and exaggeration springing from a host of impulses and agendas, from political to racial, does not negate the true value of most of the selections presented in the following collection. For out of such factional, frequently passionate points of view arose military and geopolitical decisions that affected all of North America, and eventually the world. And beyond the usual bulletins and summaries of events, there are other, more numerous newspaper extracts of rare historical import included here: letters from the war front and elsewhere in the Southwest and Mexico, official documents, republished broadsides and decrees, field reports, diary excerpts, interviews with battle survivors (such as the extraordinarily detail-rich account of the slave Joe on page 219), passages from books and magazines of the period, and subsequent memoirs by participants in the war. There is also a section devoted to the Alamo-inspired poetry of the day.

To attempt to fully annotate every misspelling, or vague or erroneous item as reported in these accounts would require a multivolume work, so footnotes have been kept to a bare minimum, inserted only when deemed most necessary or illuminating. A concise, interweaving narrative has been added to clarify or explain each quote in its historical or biographical context.

When the idea of this book was first conceived, it was thought to limit the newspaper extracts to those that directly concerned the siege and battle. But because the Alamo story cannot be fully understood without knowing the "big picture"—the hows and whys that led to the event as well as all its immediate repercussions—it was decided to enhance the book's value by adding a generous number of newspaper reports dealing with developments in Texas long before, and long after, the events of February and March 1836. Some of these actually concern events at the Alamo itself; others, occurrences in the lives of the men who would play major roles in the Texas Revolution (such as Bowie's participation in the bloody Sand Bar Duel in 1827 or Santa Anna's fluctuating fortunes in Spanish Mexico and the early Mexican republic). And scattered throughout the central and main current of 1835–1836 newspaper copy are a few extracts published in later years, sometimes decades, that offer valuable amplification, in terms of facts and details, of the earlier ones.

New translations of important Mexican newspaper accounts have also been made, correcting some mistranslations found in previous printings, especially regarding military terminology.

One of the surprising things discovered during the compilation of these accounts was the truly widespread extent of the celebrity of David Crockett—"Davy" as he was more affectionately known then—even at a time when his political star had faded. Despite being denied a fourth term in Congress in 1835, when he began his journey to Texas to reinvent himself shortly after the election, it became major news all across the country. In most of these newspaper reports one finds amusing allusions to the half-horse, half-alligator, bear-hunter image he had himself perpetuated at the beginning of his career as a politician, to his later regret. The publication of the first *Davy Crockett Almanack* in 1835 only added to the sealing of that image in the public consciousness, just as the world was about to lose him.

The primary function of this book is to serve as a *source work*—for scholars, buffs, and general readers. On the other hand, one can also read these accounts for the sheer pleasure and immediacy they evoke as contemporary windows into a time of great upheaval, passion, challenge, violence, and human drama.

Aside from theories and conclusions put forth in some of the captions to the illustrations and footnotes, in the main no attempt has been made to take sides on such fiercely debated Alamo topics as how Crockett really died, if Travis actually drew a line in the dirt with his sword, and so on, but where possible more fuel *is* thrown on a few controversial fires, so to speak, to shed new light on some of these arguments.

Naturally it would be impossible to collect *all* the Alamo-related newspaper reports of the time, both US and Mexican, into a single book; instead, what has been done here is to assemble the most historically essential, significantly known ones, along with many perhaps not so significant but which nevertheless offer rare color and insight into the period, conflict, and people involved.

NUMBER OF NEWSPAPERS PUBLISHED IN THE WORLD.—A German paper says, "In Spain there are twelve newspapers; in Portugal seventeen; in Switzerland thirty six; in Belgium sixty two; in Denmark eighty; in Austria eighty two; in Russia and Poland eighty four; in Holland one hundred and fifty; in Great Britain two hundred and seventy four; in Prussia two hundred and eighty eight; in the other Germanic States three hundred and five; in Australia nine; in Africa twelve; in Asia two; and in America, *eleven hundred and thirty eight*—from which it will be seen that there are more than half as many newspapers published in America (with the exception of France, which the writer has left out, and well he may, for she has so completely muzzled the press, that there might as well be none, and cast a stain on her escutcheon which it will be difficult to wipe off,) than there is in the whole world put together, and with not one fortieth of the population." It is no wonder then that this country bears the reputation abroad of being not only the happiest, but the freest nation of the earth, when the press, which we consider to be the sentinel on the watch tower, is left free, not only to guard us against all encroachments on our rights, (if it acts up to its profession,) but to diffuse information far and wide over the country; for wherever knowledge is, there will freedom also be found.

—*Gloucester Telegraph*, January 27, 1836

A Chronology

The following list of dates and events, published in the *Macon* [Georgia] *Weekly Telegraph*, attempted to delineate the history of the Anglo American role in Texas up to the formal recognition of the Texas Republic by the United States. It is not without the inevitable exaggerations and many egregious errors in names, places, and dates, but it is useful as a contemporary glimpse at the perceptions Americans held of the new nation at their southwestern borders.

Remarkable Events in the History of Texas.
1821–2.—Gen. Stephen F. Austin establishes a colony in Texas.
1832.—The colonists first take up arms against Mexico.

June 26, 1832.—Battle at Velasco, in which John Austin commands the Texan forces, and Ugortechea the Mexican; Texans victorious. The Texans espouse the cause of the Liberals in Mexico. Convention at San Felippe to frame a Constitution for the "State of Texas."

April, 1833.—Gen. Austin appointed Commissioner to Mexico. He is imprisoned.

Sept., 1835.—Gen. Austin returns. The Texans declare for the Federal Constitution of 1824.

Oct. 2, 1835.—Battle of Gorgole, and Costonada defeated by the Texans, under Col. Moore. Gen. Samuel Houston arrives, and is appointed General of Department. Lorenzo de Zonala, formerly Governor of Mexico, appointed Chairman of the Committee of Safety.

Oct. 8, 1835.—Fort at Goliad taken by the Texans under Captain Collingsworth. Delegates meet at San Felippe. Gen. Austin appointed Commander-in-Chief. Gen. Houston elected a member to the Consultation from Nacogdoches, joins the army.

October 27, 1835.—Battle of Conception, under the command of Fannin and Bowie—the Texans lose one man only, and the enemy one hundred.

Nov. 1835.—Consultation meet and organize at San Felippe, and Dr. Branch T. Archer is chosen President.

Nov. 7, 1835.—The Consultation declare for the Constitution of '24, and elect Henry Smith, Governor, and J. W. Robinson, Lieut. Governor.

Nov. 8, 1835.—The Texans gain a victory over the enemy at Bexar.

Nov. 25, 1835.—Gen. Burleson succeeds Gen. Austin in command.

Dec. 5th, 1835.—San Antonio stormed and taken under the command of J. Milam and Neil, with great loss to the enemy.

Dec. 7, 1835.—Col. Milam killed.

Dec. 9, 1835.—The enemy, under Gen. Coss, capitulates.

Dec. 12, 1835.—Gen. Houston issues his Proclamation. Commissioners are appointed to the United States, to solicit aid in support of the Texan cause.

Dec. 10, 1835.—The Provisional Government of Texas orders a Convention. The Orleans Greys, the Tennessee, and Alabama, and Georgia volunteers arrive in Texas.

1836.—Col. Grant and Col. Johnson, with a small party on their way to Metamoras, are cut off and destroyed.

1836.—Santa Anna swears to take Texas or lose Mexico. Marches against Texas with 10,000 choice troops, few of whom ever return.

March 3.—San Antonia besieged.

March 6.—Storming of the Alamo, under the command of Santa Anna; 4,000 well disciplined troops opposed to 140 raw Texans; fifteen hundred Mexicans were killed. On this occasion the gallant Travers, Bowie, Crocket, and Evans, were barbarously murdered after their capitulation.

March 2.—The Convention at Washington, Texas, unanimously decree a Declaration of Independence. Gen. Houston appointed Major General and commander-in-chief of the army.

March 11.—Captain King, with 23 men, overtaken by 1,000 Mexicans, and in an open prairie at Refugio barbarously shot. Ward gains a victory over the enemy, and afterwards attacked by 1,600, is obliged to surrender.

March 18.—Battle of Fanning and Urrea near Goliad, in which 700 Mexicans are killed, and only 7 Texans; a flag of truce is sent to the Texan camp, and an armistice is signed by Fanning and General Urrea; the Texans deliver up their arms, are marched to Goliad, and 400 are treacherously and barbarously shot.

April 21.—The memorable and glorious battle of *San Jacinto*, in which Santa Anna and his forces are all destroyed or taken prisoners; the Texans had two killed and six mortally wounded—the Mexicans 630 killed and 730 taken prisoners; General Santa Anna and all his Staff are made prisoners, *more than double the whole effective force of Texas!*

September.—General Houston elected by the People, first President of the Republic of Texas, and General M. B. Lamar Vice President.

October 3.—First Congress assembled at Columbia.

December.—Santa Anna is released, and goes to Washington, U. S. The independence of Texas acknowledged by the United States, France, England, Belgium and Holland.

1840.—Treaty of Commerce, &c., ratified between England and Texas, by the United States and Texas.

—*Macon* [Georgia] *Weekly Telegraph*, January 1, 1844

1
Spanish Texas

The mission town of San Antonio de Valero was ironically cofounded by a Canadian-born double agent, Louis Juchereau de St. Denis, in the employ of New Spain to help build Spanish posts in the unsettled Texas country. In 1716, he rode north from Mexico City with Captain Domingo Ramón and an expedition of some seventy-three others, including cavalrymen, brown-robed padres, herdsmen, women, and children. When they arrived at San Pedro Creek, Father Ignacio Espinosa agreed with St. Denis that it indeed marked a fine location for a mission. By 1718, a presidio was founded on the nearby San Antonio River and the mission site moved closer to its protective walls. Colonial American newspapers during the first half of the eighteenth century took almost no notice of the formation of this new Spanish settlement. It was not until 1840 before any paper, in this case the *Austin City Gazette*, endeavored to outline in some rather flowery detail the story of the founding of the town that would play so crucial a role in the birth of the Texas Republic. Naturally its author had few kind things to say about the Spanish/Mexican overlords from whom Texas had been recently declared independent, among other points of criticism, observing that the enforced Indian labor that built the San Antonio missions had reduced "fellow creatures to a state of abject slavery."

EVENTS IN THE HISTORY OF
SAN ANTONIO DE BEXAR.
By David L. Wood,
Written in compliance with a promise made by him to Professor J. L. Riddell, of New Orleans.
SAN ANTONIO DE BEXAR, which town we propose making the subject of a brief history, is indebted for its founding to religion.—Welding the insidiousness of the sinister and sordid motives of secularizing their insignificant services to ill-directed purposes of the State and Church, which are inseperable in Mexico, with the plausible and philanthropic intentions of converting the savages to the Catholic faith, the vice regal government established the military station of Bexar in 1718, which, at first, was held by only fifty men under the command of a captain. It will be observed, that up to that period the natives of the eastern provinces of the colonial dominions of Spain, were a wild, rude, unreclaimed, and inoffensive race of beings, living in primitive ignorance alike of the cultivated arts of peace and war; and but a shade better conditioned were these subjects, inhabiting the sections of the country under the jurisdiction of the laws in the east, from whom agriculture, and some few other of the employments of civilized man, received a trifling attention. Descendants from the same barbarian parentage and having advanced no farther along the road to civilization than constrained by necessity, the fruitful mother of invention amongst every people, those aboriginal husbandmen and simple graziers, dwelling in rudely constructed huts about the more civilized portions of the Mexican frontier, lived upon reciprocated terms of intimacy with the less reclaimed wanderers of the forest— presenting, in the extraneous avocations of a semi-barbarous life, a precarious state of existence between civilization and barbarity.

Carrying out the original designs and having previously represented to the papacy in visionary colourings the enlargement of power derived to the church by extending the diocesal authority in that quarter, and having obtained therein the papal concurrence, the legate to the see of Mexico, a restless prelate, urged upon the Bishop (inasmuch as the Indians in the other sections of his majesty of Spain's dominions had been profitably converted to religion and the nefareous uses of the clergy) the necessity of taking speedy measures to adopt a course calculated to secure the services of the pagans in the unreclaimed province of Texas. The unwearying exertions of such devoted enthusiasm achieved the commencement, in 1727, or more probably soon after, of several Catholic missions in Texas, under the protection afforded by the military station of Bexar. Massive and rude as are those gothic structured edifices, they produce an agreeable interruption to that monotonous sameness of denuded hills presented to the tourist by the surrounding country, and the mission San Jose, finished in 1732, and the front of which is handsomely decorated with intaglia work, may be esteemed the only one of them possessing claims to symmetrical architecture and sculptural beauty.

The liturgy of the holy Catholic faith was enjoined upon the unprepared natives, and those who were formerly scrupulous about becoming uncompromising proselytes to the new doctrine of deity and immortality, were coerced into religion by the ready swords of the bigotted soldiery. Primitive ignorance, with its concomitant beauty of unaffected simplicity, was esteemed no apology for the dissentient, and with the most intolerant zeal, thousands were annually condemned to the laborious and toilsome penance of preparing mortar and carrying stones with which to prepare the "houses of God." Tradition hands down, that 1200 at one time were thus employed during the progress of San Jose, who were forced with whips and by the gloomy dread of certain death, if resistance was manifested, to pack upon their shoulders the ponderous materials from a quarry several miles distant. Thus, by the means of an arbitrarily exercised authority to support an avaricious conduct of the most reprehensible

selfishness in reducing unfortunate fellow creatures to a state of abject slavery, the stupendous structures of those fortified missions were mainly erected. It should not be a matter of surprise, in this enlightened period, when we reflect that such has been the oppressive course of papacy and monarchy combined in every age of church history; but it is really more the cause of wonder that its devotees should ever be induced to believe (with abundance of evidence to the contrary) otherwise than that religion becomes unrobed of its amiable humility when propagated by violence.

Subsequent to the period of these events the northern Indians, tempted by the prospects of pillage, began to make predatory incursions into the settlements of San Antonio de Bexar and Labahia, and being joined by many of those unruly savages, by whom clerical thraldom was born with stubbornness, disturbed, for a length of time, the tranquility of the inhabitants, and finally threatened the very existence of those places as frontier fortresses or stations. Plunder, rapine, and depradation became common occurrences, retaliation but exasperated the Indian foe, and deeds of atrocity were eagerly enacted as though but to glut the thirsty vengeance of the infuriated barbarian. Such was the critical state of affairs, about this part of the frontier of New Spain, when the supreme Government fitted out and despatched the celebrated expedition against the Comanches, commanded by General Ubalde, a brave officer and skillful Indian fighter. It had for its object the protection of the exposed citizens and the chastisement of the enemy.

General Ubalde arrived in time to engage and disperse a large body of Indians, who had taken up the line of march to attack Bexar, where the citizens of the surrounding country had entered into fortifications to be prepared against surprise. They fought bravely, but military skill and efficiency, which must ever predominate, prevailed. Being defeated with great loss and routed, they fled and were pursued to their place of refuge, a valley laying along the Rio Frio, surrounded by a chain of precipitous hills and having to it but few entrances, which are very rugged and difficult of passage. Those passes are narrow clefts in the rocks, seldom wider than two or three feet, and wind through craggy cliffs and around rocky prominencies several hundred feet in height. It has been related by some, upon traditionary authority, that the Indians obstructed pursuit into the valley by casting into the cavity of one of the passways a number of the carcasses of horses; but the real truth is, that General Ubalde entered the valley, and not being cunning to discover their places of concealment and able to ferret them out, returned. The valley, in commemoration of the services of so successful a chieftain, was thence afterwards called Canon de Ubalde.—This signal discomfiture thwarted the attempts of the enemy, destroying their main hopes, infused in them a proper dread of the arms of their neighbours, and restored tranquility to the country.

Bexar underwent many reverses of fortune until the year 1730, about which time, says a current report, the settlement of the place recommenced; but the visit of the Marquis de Aguayo, the eminent patron of the place, is, with much more certainty, referable to an earlier though indefinite period. This enterprising pioneer, to whom was entrusted the regulation of the different settlements around the frontier of the colonies, correctly considered the place an excellent trading station, but for the people dwelling along the Rio Grande and the populous tribes of northern Indians, vast members of whom, by this time, had been converted (if we may be allowed the expression) to christianity, and reduced to cultivators to some degree of the soil in various parts of the country. A petition was presented to his majesty that four hundred families might be sent out as colonists to San Antonio, a town founded near the military station on the opposite bank of the river and named San Antonio de Bexar, from the patron saint of that portion of the country. The policy of Aguayo was to attract attention as eagerly as might be and to elicit as extensive an interest in the newly created city as would be practicable. He solicited that two hundred of the emigrants be selected from the Indians of Tlaxcala, and the remainder from Galicia in Spain and the

Canary Islands, conferring what rank of *hidalguia*[a] upon such families as would embark in the undertaking as an inducement to enlistment. It has been asserted that the whole number was obtained in the Islands, but without justifiable foundation. Of the four hundred families who engaged in the enterprise and started, it appears that only fifteen reached their destination, the expense of whose transportation and settlement amounted to 72,000 dollars, a considerable part of which was defrayed by the munificent Marquis. This attempt having so far miscarried, the indefatigable Aguayo besought that the prisons of the province of New Spain be emptied of their inmates, who were sent to supply the deficiency, and to share with the newly created nobles the glory of being the founders of a city.

Notwithstanding these contrarious elements the settlements progressed rapidly, and the community prospered, the place commanding extensive facilities for trade, and the country around being admirably adapted to the purposes of grazing and tillage. San Antonio de Bexar, from being the resort of expatriated people and the Botany Bay of Mexico, became the important mart of border traffic upon the verge of the territory, and at one time presented the appearance of a magnificent city of the wilderness, with all the hum, the bustling, and the brisk business avocations pertaining to the inhabitants of such. Its population has been estimated to have been 12,000, during this period of its highest prosperity.

During the revolution which gave birth to the independence of Mexico, San Antonio de Bexar was sometimes the scene of battle, and experienced uncertain vicissitudes in being variously occupied by the belligerent parties. Not far from the place is shown the field where General Toledo was defeated in 1813, in a battle signalized for having been stoutly and dubiously contested. The authenticated particulars connected with this sanguinary engagement, like many interesting incidents interwoven with the history of our subject, must remain unavailable until a peace be established between Texas and

[a] Nobility.

Mexico, and the archives of the latter country are unclasped to be consulted by the historian. The city, indeed, since the effect of the severe punishment inflicted by Ubalde upon the Comanches had subsided, did not enjoy a year's uninterrupted tranquility while subject to the dominion of distracted Mexico. The inefficient protection afforded after that era in its history was too precarious and imbecile, and Indian hostilities filled up the intervals between those revolutions which frequently led the combatants to decide there the intestine contests.

- With the year 1832, when the struggle commenced in Texas for liberty, begins a brighter and more important era in the history of San Antonio de Bexar. The best and the richest flower in the flosculous wreath of celebrity with which circumstance has encircled this eventful place, was entwined there by the martyred and godlike heroes of the encrimsoned Alamo. There reigned in Texas no Spartan law to which they owed from love of country implicit obedience; but, prompted by those hallowed principles which elevate man to an enviable amplitude with his God, and enshrines his deeds upon the grateful remembrance of ages to come— the noblest immortality—they preferred death to a retreat, which, while it wounded deeply the Mexican military presumption, elicited the admiration of all patriots and philanthropists in Christendom.

—*Austin City Gazette*, June 17, 1840

In the late 1760s, a French naval officer with an extreme travel compulsion, Pierre Marie François de Pages, rode west from Nachitoches, Louisiana, to the Texas mission towns of Nacogdoches, San Antonio, and "Labadie" (La Bahía, or Goliad). His impressions of the Spanish and other inhabitants of the region merit inclusion here, as summarized in a review of his book, *Travels Round the World in the Years 1767, 1768, 1769, 1770, 1771*, published in France in 1782.

Unspeakable were the hardships to which good M. Pages was reduced, and indeed willing, to suffer, in his passage through the vast and uncultivated country of the sons of nature:

a bear-skin was his bed, a bear-skin his roof, and a bear-skin his wardrobe and kitchen. Hunger, thirst, fever, and fatigue, were his constant companions, from Natchitoches to San Antonio, to which he traveled through Adaisses and Naquadoch,[b] where he found a great number of Spaniards, half savage, hunting for their subsistence, but (as they had either fallen back from civilization, or had not arrived at it) brave, humane, compassionate and hospitable. In his passage from San Antonio to New-Mexico, he found great errors in the accounts that have been given of the Spanish posts in that vast region; and he has composed a map of New-Mexico, which (according to the reports of the commissaries of the academy) contains several things entirely new with respect to the geography of that country. In this voyage our author observed, that malignity and perfidy were in a visible progressive proportion to rank and birth, and that morals diminished in the same proportion, so that of the savage, the Indian, the Creole, and the Spaniard, the latter was always the least sociable and virtuous.

—*Pennsylvania Packet*, January 6, 1784

If the missions of San Antonio had enjoyed a modicum of prosperity during the middle decades of the 1700s, there had always been serious challenges to their growth, from the elements, epidemics, raids by the Apaches and Comanches, and especially from the declining number of Indian converts, for the latter problem made it impossible to employ sufficient manpower to finish the construction of the churches and their attached compounds. Then, in 1793, a royal decree secularized all the missions in Texas. The baptized Indians were given the church lands for tillage and pasturage, and most of the priests returned to Mexico. In the wake of this abandonment the once-disciplined religious communities fell into poverty, and the church buildings themselves went to weed.

In 1803, one hundred cavalrymen of the Second Flying Company of San Carlos de Alamo de Parras quartered themselves within

---

[b] Los Adaes and Nacogdoches.

the compound of Mission Valero. Eight years later, in Mexico, a country friar named Hidalgo led a brief, unsuccessful revolt against French-allied Spanish aristocrats. But one of Hidalgo's followers, a landowner named José Bernardo Gutiérrez de Lara, decided to enlist US aid to revive the revolution, and he happily found many willing men east of the Sabine River. Augustus Magee and Samuel Kemper organized the "Republican Army of the North" and, with Gutiérrez, entered Texas on August 8, 1812.[1] Three days later the mixed force of five hundred, composed of "principally the desperate riflemen, hunters, and outlaws of the southwest," as one observer later recalled, and of French, Italian, and Spanish volunteers from Louisiana and Texas, captured Nacogdoches.[2] On November 7, it seized La Bahía , a community comprising a town and fort destined to play major roles in the Alamo story of 1836. The following letter mistakenly calls "Lavardia" a seaport, but it does provide a rare early description of the presidio there as the filibuster army found it.

Extract of a letter, dated Natchitoches, November 29, 1812.

M'Gee's party have taken Lavardia, a seaport, on the Gulph of Mexico, and six days' journey to the West of St. Antonia. Letters from the party of the 14th instant, have reached here—they met with no opposition, the Spaniards evacuated previous to their arrival. It is a square stone work, with two bastions, the side of each angle measuring three hundred feet, a stone church and barracks; they got possession of two eighteen-pounders.— Report says, that there are several thousands of Spaniards and Indians around them; there is nothing to substantiate this but rumor. They have had but one or two small skirmishes with the Spaniards, in one of which there were eight Spaniards killed; the latter have always fled; as to the booty acquired at Lavardia, I have no knowledge, but certain it is, that present circumstances do not justify former reports relative to the people of that country being in favor of the revolution.

—*Green Mountain Farmer* (Vermont), February 17, 1813

Published a day later in another Vermont paper, this letter provides additional specifics regarding La Bahía and its presidio.

PRIVATE CORRESPONDENCE.
Alexandria, Louisiana, December 4.

Letters have been received from Colonel M'Gee, up to the 14th [illegible]. He had taken Labadre on the Bay of St. Bernard about 25 leagues south of St. Antonia, and about 15 leagues East of the Port of Matagorpa. The town contains about 150 houses, a fort of 100 yards square, including some strong buildings. The resistance was very feeble; and only seven or eight Spaniards killed and as many wounded. They took three pieces of cannon—were near 1000 strong—in health and well supplied with provisions. They march direct to St. Antone, when they expect a more firm defence, and from whence I expect shortly to hear some very interesting news.

—*Bennington News-Letter* (Vermont), February 18, 1813

A week after its occupation of the presidio, Magee's army suddenly found itself besieged there by a Royalist force.

LATEST FROM THE MEXICAN PROVINCES.
Extract of a letter dated Natchitoches, December 3, 1812.

The revolutionary army is said to consist of 1000 to 1200 men. On Saturday last we received intelligence that they were surrounded in the Fort of Labadie about 70 miles from St. Antonia, by 5000 Spanish troops and Indians commanded by Governor Salcedo and Colonel Herera. The same day we had letters from Magee, dated Labadie 19th October, stating that he was intrenched there, and that the enemy about 600 strong were in sight, but would not be brought to a battle.—That Captain Slocum at the head of 18 men attacked and put to flight 150 of them. From these contradictory accounts we can draw no certain conclusions. (If 18 could drive 150, why should 1200 intrench themselves before 600?). The courier who brought the last news heard firing of cannon for three hours the morning before he left Labadie.

—*Bennington News-Letter* (Vermont),
January 27, 1813

Kemper was made colonel of the force inside La Bahía following Magee's death. After finally engaging the surrounding enemy and driving them off, Kemper and Gutiérrez (sometimes referred to as "Bernardo"), buttressed by reinforcements, marched north to attempt a seizure of San Antonio. As would occur twenty-three years later, atrocities stained the campaign, including a mass execution of prisoners despite the promise of mercy.

FROM MEXICO
Private Correspondence, NATCHITOCHES, May 17.
Last evening arrived here from the city of St. Antonio, Mr. Roberts, the bearer of dispatches from the revolutionary army at that place. I have seen several letters, and conversed with Mr. Roberts and several other persons, who all agree in the following statement of facts:

That the revolutionary army, commanded by Don Joseph Bernardo Goteros, after the battle at Labardie on the 10th of March, in which governor Salcedo lost 150 killed and wounded, 61 prisoners, and above 100 who deserted and came over to the revolutionary army, raised the siege of Labardie and marched to St. Antonio; Bernardo left Labardie on the 22nd of March, with about 800 men, including Americans, Spaniards and Indians; on the 29th, was met about 8 miles from St. Antonio by general Herrera with 1200 men and six pieces of cannon—a battle ensued, which continued about an hour, good part of the time with bayonets and sword in hand—the two armies all mingled togther—the result was Herrera was completely defeated with the loss of all his cannon and much baggage, about 100 dead on the field of battle, and got back to St. Antonio in the greatest disorder. The next day Salcedo sent proposals to Bernardo of capitulation, which were refused; on the 1st of April he surrendered at discretion, and Bernardo with his army

entered the city; about 300 of the soldiers with colonel St. Bruna and his brother, made their escape, and have got over the River Grand into the province of Quahuilia, where the soldiers came from. General Bernardo, advised by the principal inhabitants of St. Antonio, caused Salcedo, Herrera, and all the principal officers to be imprisoned.

The next day it was reported that there was a small vessel at Matagorda, about 150 miles below St. Antonio in a south-easterly direction, in which 14 of the prisoners were to be shipped off for the United States. They were accordingly marched out under a guard of Spaniards, and taken about six miles to a creek, where they were all put to death: amongst them were governor Salcedo, general Herrera, and his brother the major; captain Areos, a very rich inhabitant of St. Antonio, and his two sons; captain Domingus, late Inspector General; captain Pegart late Commandant at Chacogdothes.[3] The others I did not know personally, but were from beyond River Grand. Colonel Monterey, of the Royal army, was killed in the battle of the 29th of March. The Spanish officer who had the charge of these prisoners justifies himself, that Salcedo had caused his father and two brothers to be beheaded in St. Antonio, their heads dragged by mules to Montclova and through the streets of that city—and several other similar acts. It is said that Bernardo consented to their execution in compliance to the wishes and entreaties of the Spaniards.—the Americans who were there knew nothing of it. General Toledo, unfortunately had not arrived. It is said that Bernardo found in St. Antonio near 3000 men, and that one half of them had been disarmed by Salcedo: Bernardo has since formed about 1000 of them into a regiment.

The province of Texas is proclaimed free and independent, by name of the state of Texas. Confiscation of near 200 of the best houses in St. Antonio has taken place, and a great deal of public property. Bernardo lost in the battle of the 29th of March, five Americans killed, four Spaniards and two or three Indians; amongst the killed was William Owens, formerly of Baltimore, lately a merchant in this town, and a Mr. Snodgrass of the Mississippi Territory.

Bernardo is governor of the new state at present, and commander of all the troops; but Toledo will probably command the army after his arrival, which will be in eight or ten days. It is believed that by October, an army of 5 or 6000, well appointed and equipped, will be ready to march from St. Antonio towards Mexico, and that the three next provinces will surrender without opposition, most of the principal officers being taken at St. Antonio. A regular mail, once a week, is to be immediately established between St. Antonio and this place, and in a short time will no doubt be extended to Mexico. This town is like Pittsburg, becoming an immense thorough fare, being the point of landing and departure to and from the Spanish country.

—*Universal Gazette* (Washington D.C.),
June 11, 1813

Word of the developments in Texas and of the fat promise of its lands began to attract the attention of many across the United States.

Extract of a letter from Attakapas (Louisiana) dated September 1, 1813, to a gentleman in Boston.

The Spanish or Mexican country is becoming a very interesting subject of conversation here. The little band of Republicans, that collected first on the River Sabine, to the number of 300, increased as they moved on towards the capital of the Province of Texas (St. Antonio) to the number of 3000. They were like a rolling snowball.

St. Antonio has surrendered to the Republicans—consequently the whole Province of Texas, a vast extent of country, of the richest soil, and most healthy and pleasant climate, and probably many mines.

—*Bennington News-Letter* (Vermont),
October 26, 1813

Shocked by the butcheries they had witnessed during the campaign, many of the Americans returned to Louisiana.[4] Command of the volunteers who remained at San Antonio fell to a Cuban, José Álvarez de Toledo y Dubois. Marching north to give him battle was Spanish colonel Ignacio Elizondo, whose forces were totally defeated. An unidentified

Royalist prisoner (simply signing his name as *N*), managed to escape from San Antonio and pen his opinions of the engagement as well as noting conditions within "that unhappy town."

NEWS FROM MEXICO
Nachitoches, Aug. 8, 1813.

I was imprisoned at St. Antonio, and condemned to death by the insurgents when Elisondo advanced with a considerable detachment of Spanish regulars and militia. The notice of his arrival threw that unhappy town into confusion, and overwhelmed the presumptuous crowd of rebels with dismay; so that I found no difficulty to make my escape, and reach the Spanish field. But, alas! I cannot recollect without sorrow the unfortunate events of that day! The bold and proud, though unexperienced Elisondo, seems to have brought the most spirited and gallant warriors to an unavoidable route; who, under a sage leader, might have put down the insurgents, and their heterogenous band of followers. He acted contrary to the orders of Aredondo; and without waiting to be joined either by him, or by the main division of the Spanish army, which was then near Rio Grande, fifty miles from St. Antonio, he advanced towards that place, and encamped with boasting and vain parade; and, losing time, he has been assailed impetuously, and in spite of the undaunted bravery of his troops, has been obliged disgracefully to retire. Thus he frustrated the noble enthusiasm and courage of the Spanish warriors under his command. I thought it proper to take refuge in this place, until affairs change at Texas, for I am convinced that they cannot fail to change soon, to the destruction of the insurgents. St. Antonio is plunged in general distress, famine, and misery; there is nothing but desolation. Neither flour, nor any other food is to be found there, except some maize at eight dollars a bushel and some loaf sugar at four dollars a pound. I don't speak of other minute objects of common necessity; it must be sufficient to assure, that you would look in vain for even a grain of salt or an article of clothing in that mournful country; and the absolute want of money increases the general consternation. Confined to such a melancholy prospect of calamities, those mutineers are brought to despair, and the foreign adventurers who have been so blind as to follow them, begin to disband. How can it be possible to dwell longer, without money or provisions, in a vast desert, surrounded by ragged mountains, where we are only to meet with wild beasts, or some scattered bands of savage Indians? Such would be considered as the highest degree of human insanity. N.

—*Alexandria Gazette* (Virginia),
October 14, 1813

The Spanish Army was not yet done with the revolutionists. General Joaquín de Arredondo advanced toward San Antonio with more than eighteen hundred troops and eleven cannon. Toledo moved south to meet him, but eventually found himself decoyed into a well-arranged and very bloody ambush at the Medina River.

From the *Red River Herald*—Extra.
Defeat of the Revolutionists. Extract of a letter from a gentleman of the first respectability, dated, NATCHITOCHES, September 4, 1813.

I am sorry to inform you, that the Republican Army of Texas, were, on the 18th ultimo entirely defeated, 20 miles beyond St. Antonio, by the army of ARRADONDO. General TOLEDO attacked them in their camp, a well chosen position, with a force of about one to three. The Royalists (mostly regular troops from the interior) were at first beaten and driven some distance with the loss of three pieces of cannon and many killed.—General TOLEDO, suspecting an ambuscade, organized his troops to halt and form on a better ground, but the Americans, with an indescribable enthusiasm and impetuosity in despite of every exertion of their officers, rushed into the ambuscade, where many pieces of cannon of the enemy were opened on them by which they were mostly destroyed—such as were not retreated in confusion leaving everything behind them. General TOLEDO, Colonels Kemper and Perry, with about 60 others, have arrived at Nacogdoches, and report says as many more are at Trinity. W. B. Wilkinson, who

was in the battle acting as aid to General Toledo, arrived here yesterday and returned this morning with annunciation to enable such as were at Nacogdoches to make a stand, and as far as possible cover the retreating remnant of the army, who are hourly coming in.

Three hundred families had left St. Antonio and La Bahia for this place, 200 of them women on foot escaping from the bloody vengeance of Arradondo who at Atlimeo and Saltillo distinguished himself by putting women and children to death.

It is probable 300 Americans are lost, and the whole country between Rio Grande and the Sabine will be desolated. We can yet form nothing like a list of the whole numbers killed. From persons who are hourly arriving here we are led to believe we shall in a few days have several hundred of the most wretched of human beings fleeing from their country and their homes to save their lives.

Doctor Forsythe is safe at Nacogdoches. William Slocum, the two Gormley's and Caston of the Mississippi Territory are missing.

How safe we are here is doubtful; a short time will show us.

—*New Hampshire Gazette*, October 12, 1813

Arredondo and Elizondo were even more ruthless with their Spanish-blood prisoners than Gutiérrez had been. There to witness—and perhaps participate in—the butchery was a nineteen-year-old Royalist lieutenant named Antonio López de Santa Anna. But unlike the 1836 Texas campaign, on this occasion most of the captured Americans were spared.

Alexandria (Louisiana), September 24.

The unfortunate sufferers are coming in daily, it appears that much to the astonishment of all, Elesondo has liberated the Americans taken prisoner in and after the action. No parole was required; he advised them never to take up arms against the Royalists again unless by approbation of the American government, of which he spoke with much respect and intimated that an expedition under the patronage of government, would have his co-operation.—He treated the

Americans with humanity and supplied them with provisions for their return home; but most of the Spanish prisoners were shot.

—*Green Mountain Farmer* (Vermont),
November 2, 1813

The next grandly ambitious scheme concocted by private Americans to seize Texas from Mexico was that of Dr. James Long, a surgeon who had served with Andrew Jackson's army at New Orleans in 1815. He led his filibuster army (composed of "robust country fellows," according to an eye-witness at the Natchitoches gathering place) across the Sabine River in early June of 1819.[5] Among their number was the twenty-three-year-old Louisianian James Bowie.[6] During the first days of their adventure the men exuded high confidence, which is conveyed in the following letter. Also contained in the letter is a rare early reference to the "weak fortress" of San Antonio—namely, the Alamo.

Extract of a letter from an officer in the patriot army, to his friend in Portsmouth, dated "Western side of the Sabine, province of Texas, June 23, 1819."
We did not cross the Sabine on the 10th, as I calculated when I wrote you last. It was necessarily deferred until the 12th. Our force has considerably increased since crossing, and numbers daily join our standard, which was hoisted as soon as we reached the shores of Texas, under a salute of 21 guns. Our march has been delayed, in consequence of not having received a supply of powder, which we are in hourly expectation of. You may expect my next letter to be dated from St. Antonio, Labodie, or Monterey; the former of which has a weak fortress manned by a few worn out troops. We expect nothing from either of these places but what we may pretty generally from Spaniards—tame submission.
—*Litchfield Republican* (Connecticut),
August 12, 1819

After occupying Nacogdoches in late June, Long declared Texas a republic. Attempting to enlist allies, he visited the Galveston Island headquarters of pirate Jean Laffite, but his appeals for help were politely refused, even though the rest of Texas seemed ripe for the picking.

Nacogdoches, (TEXAS), August 4.
On the 19th instant the detachment under the command of General Long, met a Spanish woman 40 miles west of Nacogdoches, by the name of Maria El Garma Freminia. . . . She states that she left Labadie a few weeks ago in company with two men, both soldiers in the service of the King of Spain . . . when she left Labadie, that place was in a very unpleasant situation—the garrison being in a state of total defection, having in it not more than 20 soldiers at the time of her leaving the place, the most of whom watched only for an opportunity to run away;—that they are not well supplied with provisions; that the Camanche Indians, their eternal enemies, harass them and keep them continually annoyed on every side, so that they cannot go more than one mile in safety from the place. The commandant of San Antonio cannot assist them.
—*New Hampshire Gazette*,
October 23, 1819

The inevitable Spanish army, this time under Colonel Ignacio Pérez, marched north to challenge Long. In October, Long's force was engaged piecemeal and, with Pérez in hot pursuit, its remnants driven back across the Sabine.[7] Spanish and US soldiers then faced one another on opposite banks of that river.

AFFAIRS AT TEXAS.
NEW-ORLEANS, NOV. 27—By a letter from the Sabine, we learn that on the 31st ult. Col. Perros commandant of San Antonio, with 300 Spaniards, appeared on the bank of that river and that Capt. Beard, with a detachment of American troops, was preparing to dispute his passage into the territory of the U. States, when the Spanish officer sent in a flag of truce, with assurances of his friendly views, and deprecating all ideas of open hostilities. The Spaniards had previously captured all the Americans whom they fell in with, not only the soldiers of General Long, and the Camanche traders, but those who had peaceably settled in Texas, as cultivators of the soil. By the return of the flag, Capt. Beard transmitted a letter, demanding from the Spanish commander the release of

all his American prisoners, except such as had violated the laws of nations. This demand was immediately complied with, and permission was given to the Americans to secure their property. An American officer was despatched to see the arrangement completed.—It is understood that this party of Spaniards, having cleared the province of Long's men, and those who had been engaged in unlawful trade, will return to the Trinity, where they have 1000 men, intended to act against the Camanche Indians.

—*Boston Gazette*, December 27, 1819

The pugnacious Dr. Long was only temporarily stymied by this setback; the following year he reentered Texas with a smaller, and apparently loud, band of frontier followers.

GEN. LONG.—The following is an extract of a letter received at Nackitosh, from Dr. James Hewitson, dated

ST. ANTONIO, NOV. 4, 1821

On the night of the 3d of October, General Long, with 50 men of all nations, entered the town of La Bahia, producing the greatest consternation by their horrid yells. (I happened to be there at the time). They put to flight the centinels and took possession of the Fort and artillery without opposition. As soon as intelligence of this reached St. Antonio, the governor dispatched col. Ignacio Paris with 150 men, with orders to retake the place and make prisoners of Long and his party. He arrived near La Bahia and sent to Long requesting to see him, to ascertain the cause of this unfriendly visit. Long met him and stated his object was to establish the independence of these provinces.—Col. Paris replied that their independence was already achieved, and it was unnecessary for him to give himself any further trouble about it; but if he was an independent republican, as he stated, why not let such occupy the Fort, for they were the proper persons to hold it. Long would not give it up. This interview was at 8 o'clock in the morning, and half after eleven, Col. Paris made the attack, a warm firing was kept up for twenty-four hours—Long's artillery did no execution, and he finally surrendered at

discretion. Long and his party were brought prisoners to St. Antonio, and from thence were sent to Santillio to take their trial, which will be a hard one, being regarded as public robbers and pirates.

On the 17th of October the entry of Yturbide[c] into Mexico was announced here, and the Independence of the Empire ratified. This news was received with great rejoicings, and since this city has been in a constant uproar, by illuminations, te deums, and fandangoes.

—*Arkansas Gazette*, February 19, 1822

Dr. Long would never see the United States again; while allegedly engaging in disruptive behavior he was shot to death by a sentry in Mexico City.[8] Ironically another, more successful—and nonviolent—American "invasion" of Texas was being undertaken even while Long's company of adventurers was still on the march. In January 1821, Moses Austin had been granted a permit by the Spanish government to settle three hundred families in southeastern Texas; a settlement Spain saw as the perfect buffer against the troublesome Comanches. But Moses's death placed the enterprise in the hands of his son, Stephen, who traveled to San Antonio in late summer of 1821 to meet with Governor Antonio Martínez. Terms for the new colony were worked out, but with the news of Mexico's declaration of independence from Spain, Austin was forced to journey south to Mexico City to treat with the new rulers. It was not until February 18, 1823, that the land grant contract was finalized and signed.[9]

US opinion about Texas, however, was divided, often discouraging, as evidenced by the following account originally published in an Arkansas newspaper—which also happens to mention the condition of the underequipped presidial garrison of the Alamo.

From Texas.—A gentleman who has lately been on an exploring tour in the Province of Texas, passed through Arkansas, and has communicated the following interesting facts relative to the situation of that country. He represents the

---

[c] Agustín de Iturbide, who was proclaimed emperor of independent Mexico in May 1822.

condition of the people as miserable in the extreme; industry is scarce known among them; and business of every description is at a stand.— Although possessed of one of the finest and most fertile portions of the globe, yet agriculture is entirely neglected, and, to a person accustomed to a civilized life, they present a picture literally bordering on starvation; bread stuffs are very scarce and dear, and, like the natives of the forest, they depend almost entirely on the chase for a scanty subsistence. At St. Antonio, a place which has once been a wealthy and populous city, nothing but wretchedness was visible.—That place is garrisoned by about 75 soldiers, who are nearly destitute of ammunition. The people of that place have once been in a state of ease and affluence, but in consequence of the soldiers of the Spanish and Republican armies having been quartered on, and pillaging them, for several years, together with their own indolence, they are now reduced to the most abject state of poverty. The remark is also applicable to La Bahia and the other principal posts which our informant visited.

—*Ark. Gaz.*
—*Vermont Journal*, July 1, 1822

Another cautious US appraisal of Texas was published the following spring.

CHARLESTON, April 25.—The Spanish Country.—Settlements were commenced in Texas as early as 1660. It had an independent Spanish Government two years before New Orleans was established by the French; at different times for thirty years before, the French had menaced the whole country. How slow the progress of settlement has been in this vast country! A country 300 leagues in length, and more than 100 in breadth. A few years ago, in its whole extent, there were but three towns (called by the Spanish posts) and three missions of Indians.

The towns of San Antonio, LaBahia, and Nacogdoches, since 1812, have gone rapidly to decay. There may once have been in the whole of Texas, 6000 souls, but it is doubtful if there were 4000 in 1820—not as many inhabitants of fixed domicil as some of the townships have to

the middle and eastern states, where the population is dense. Within the last year some two or three thousand souls have gone to Texas: how they will make out the ensuing winter is uncertain.—The supplies will have to be sent them, for they cannot crop sufficient this season for subsistence.

From all accounts the temperature is healthy. The air possesses extraordinary purity, so much so that is said you may jerk and save beef there in the same manner that they do in La Plata. It is well watered; when we say so we mean relatively; you must not expect to see many of those running brooks, purling streams, and gushing fountains, to be found in Pennsylvania, east of the mountains, upper east Jersey, Connecticut and Massachusetts. There are, however, some fountains and excellent streams of water.

Pasturage, in some parts, is scarce, in others it is abundant. On the route from Nacogdoches to St. Antonio, the eye meets with but little that is inviting. It would, in many cases, remind one of Madam De Stael's description of the Russian Ukraine: "The country appears like the image of infinite space, and to require eternity to traverse it." The lovers of the chace can have a rich treat, game is most abundant. In the northwest part of the territory, horses, deer and buffalo, are countless. But this part of the territory is infested with the Camanches, an expert race of savages, who know the use of the bow and arrow, and the musket, and the lance. They some times deal Parthian like with their enemies.

The good folks of Missouri, Illinois, Indiana and Kentucky, suffering under evils, God knows afflicting enough, had

"Better bear the ills we have,
Than fly to others that we know not of."

They had much better wait and hear the accounts that will be given by those who have gone before them. Two or three years hence the country will be much better understood, and persons can then remove with greater safety, and not run the risk they now do of suffering vastly from the total destitution of every thing like comfort in the country, and even of such things as are essentially necessary to those accustomed to privations.

We intend no injury to Mr. Austin—we wish him success; and believe he is influenced by laudable feeling, and in the fair prosecution of his own interest. He is generally spoken of as a man of integrity, and if we have misrepresented the country, we shall be happy to correct any erroneous statement we have made respecting it, when pointed out to us.

The country will be desirable in many points of view a few years hence, and the government of the United States will lastingly regret not having procured it from Spain by some means or other. Mr. Austin's settlement is much more likely to succeed by a moderately vigorous growth, than by such precocity as the late emigration must have produced.—*Arkansas Gazette.*

—*Boston Weekly Messenger*, May 15, 1823

Not for another twenty-two years would the United States, "by some means or other," finally procure Texas.

The Leaders Emerge

Eight years after his participation in Dr. James Long's first disastrous attempt to seize Texas, frontier land speculator James Bowie found himself in the trees along a sandbar in the Mississippi River near Natchez about to witness a duel of honor between his friend, Samuel Wells, and Dr. Thomas Maddox. A complex series of confrontations and insults had led to this moment, and the irony would be that in the ensuing—and grisly—"Sand Bar Duel" of September 19, 1827, neither Wells nor Maddox received any injury. Wells himself soon thereafter described what had happened.

From the New-Orleans Argus, Sept. 28.
The following is an extract of a letter addressed to the editor of the Argus, containing a statement of the late bloody affair, near Natchez, by a party from Alexandria, via Rapide:

CONCORDIA, Sept. 24, 1827.

Dear Sir—I was invited by Dr. Maddox, not long since, to an interview without the limits of the state. I met him at Natchez, on the 17th inst.; on the 18th I was challenged by him; I appointed the 19th for the day, and the first sand beach, above Natchez, on the Mississippi side, for the place of our meeting. We met, exchanged two shots without effect, and made friends. Myself and my friend Major M'Whorter, and my surgeon Dr. Cuney, were invited by Dr. Maddox and his friend, Col. Crane, and surgeon, Dr. Denney, to the woods, where his friends, who were excluded from the field, were stationed, to take some refreshment; when about half way, we were met by my friends, Gen. Cuney, Mr. James Bowie, and my brother, who had

accompanied me from Red River, and who were also excluded from the field, and had taken their station in the woods, about two hundred yards from the field. Gen. Cuney, on meeting us, enquired of me how the matter had been settled; I told him that Dr. Maddox and myself had exchanged two shots and made friends. He then turned to Col. Crane, who was near me, and observed to him that there was a difference between them, and they had better return to the ground and settle it, as Dr. Maddox and myself had done. Dr. Cuney and myself interposed, and stated to the General that that that was not the time nor place for the adjustment of their difference; the General immediately acquiesced, and his brother had turned to leave him, when Crane, without replying to Gen. Cuney, or saying one word, fired a pistol at him, which he carried in his hand, but without effect. I then stepped back one or two paces, when Crane drew from his belt another pistol, fired it, and wounded Gen. Cuney in the thigh; he expired in about fifteen minutes. As Crane presented his second pistol, Gen. Cuney placed his hand on the breach of his but did not draw until he had received Crane's second fire, and as he was falling, Gen. Cuney did not fire a pistol on the ground. In addition to the above, I will state, on the authority of Dr. Hunt, of Natchez, that Crane had said to his friends, in Natchez, that if Gen. Cuney made his appearance on the ground, he, Crane, would kill him—and that at all events, he intended to kill him the first opportunity—and well has he kept his promise. Dr. Denney has since informed me that Crane had made the same declaration previous to his leaving home. Dr. Hunt called at Dr. Cuney's quarters the evening previous to the meeting, with the view of communicating Crane's intention, but unfortunately Dr. C. was not at his lodgings, or otherwise this premedited murder would have been prevented.

Your obedient servant.

SAM'L. L. WELLS.

Further particulars relative to this affair furnished us:

Mr. Bowie upon seeing Gen. Cuney fall, drew his pistol; Crane, after shooting Gen. Cuney, drew a third pistol; Bowie and himself exchanged shots simultaneously, but without effect: Crane fled. By this time Major Wright and the two Blanchards, from Red River, came running down from the wood with drawn pistols, when Wright stopped, took aim at Bowie, fired and missed him; he then advanced three or four paces, drew another pistol, presented it at Bowie, who observed to him that he was unarmed, but that if he was a man, to shoot. Major M'Whorter, who was near Bowie, placed an arm into his hand—they both fired; Wright one or two seconds first, and both with effect. Mr. Bowie was shot through the breast, Wright was struck in the side, but the ball did not enter. Wright then fled. Bowie drew a knife and pursued him, and when within about ten feet of him, he received a simultaneous fire from the two Blanchards; one of the balls took effect in his thigh and cut him down; observing which, Wright wheeled, and he and Blanchard drew their sword canes, rushed on and commenced stabbing Bowie, who was prostrate. Bowie scuffled for some seconds, until he gained his seat; he then reached up, caught Wright by his coat, drew him down on to him, and at one stab dispatched him; Mr. M. Wells, who had been attending on Gen. Cuney, after he had fallen, observing Bowie's situation, ran to his relief, fired at Blanchard, but fortunately only wounded Blanchard in the arm. The combat here ended. Crane had three pistols, Major Wright and the two Blanchards two each. The gentlemen from Natchez, and its vicinity, who had accompanied them, and who were on the ground in the affray, were armed—some with one, and others with two pistols. There was also brought to the field a double barrelled gun, and other arms were near at hand. In all, they numbered fifteen or twenty pistols and one shot gun—the other party had five pistols.[1]

—*South-Carolina State Gazette and Columbia Advertiser*, November 10, 1827

A rebuttal by an "eye witness," possibly Robert Crain, appeared in the *Louisiana Argus* four days after the above letter was first printed in the September 28 issue of the *Argus*.

From the *Louisiana Argus*.

NEW-ORLEANS, Oct. 2.

Mr. Editor—I observed a statement in your paper of the 1st inst. of the bloody affair near Natchez, which to say the least of it, is very much misrepresented, and my regard for truth has induced me to come forward and make a plain statement of the facts as they really occurred, which if it should be necessary, can be authenticated by several respectable citizens of Natchez. Dr. Maddox invited Mr. S. L. Wells, without the limits of the State of Louisiana; they met at Natchez on the 17th ult.; on the 18th Wells was challenged by Maddox, the 19th was appointed for the day of combat, and the first sand beach above Natchez, on the Mississippi side, for the place of meeting; they met, exchanged two shots without effect, and made friends; while the combatants and friends, on each side, were retiring from the ground, Wells invited Maddox, his friend Col. Crane, and surgeon Dr. Denny, to the woods, where his friends, who were excluded from the field, were stationed, to take some refreshments.— Crane objected, stated as his reasons, that there were certain men among them that he could not meet. Wells then assented to go where Maddox's friends were stationed in the woods, who were also excluded from the field. When about half way they were met by the friends of Wells viz.—Mr. Jas. Bowie, Gen. Cuny, and Mr. T. J. Wells. Gen. Cuny, on meeting them, observed to Col. Crane that it was a good time to settle their difference: Crane had a pistol in each hand, which he was carrying to the woods; he immediately put himself in an attitude of defence; he observed Bowie with a drawn pistol, he therefore shot him first, wheeled round and shot Cuny. Bowie did not fall, but Cuny did, and expired in about fifteen minutes. Bowie exclaimed, Crane you have shot me, and I will kill you if I can. They both fired simultaneously; Bowie's fire was without effect.—After Bowie made the above declaration to Crane, he drew a large butcher knife and endeavored to put his threats in execution, but was prevented by a blow from Crane with the butt of his pistol, which brought him to his knees; before he recovered, Crane got out of his way. Bowie then discovered Major Wright, who had arrived from the woods to the scene of action, in company with the two Blanchards, exclaimed to Wright, you d----d rascal don't you shoot; Wright observed that he was not afraid of him and levelled his pistol—they both fired; Bowie's shot struck Wright in the right side which went through him; Wright's fire was without effect, it struck a snag behind.— After firing, they both advanced on each other; Wright with a sword cane, and Bowie with a large butcher knife; Bowie stabbed Wright through the arm in two places, he then left him, and went to Alfred Blanchard, made three stabs at him, one of which struck him in the left side; he then left Blanchard and returned to Wright, and gave him a stab in the breast which went to his heart—he died instantly. Bowie was fired at twice by A. Blanchard, and once by C. H. Blanchard;—one of the shots struck him in the thigh, which brought him down—he fell a short distance from Wright. A. Blanchard was shot through the arm by T. J. Wells.—Maj. M'Worters signalised himself by taking a deliberate shot at C. H. Blanchard when he was disarmed, 7 or 8 paces distance; but it was without effect. The only injury Bowie received from Wright was one or two slight wounds with a sword came.

AN EYE WITNESS.
—<i>Village Register and
Norfolk County Advertiser</i>, November 8, 1827</div>

Although these and other accounts of the Sand Bar Fight were reprinted in many newspapers across the nation, Bowie's name was hardly a household one yet. Only with his later fame as co-commander and casualty of the Alamo did articles begin to appear purporting to trace his life and his supposed prowess with the knife that bore his name. The following piece from an 1837 issue of the *Arkansas Advocate* (reprinted from the *Red River Herald*), is typical.

The Bowie Knife.—This weapon, of which too much has been said of late, is longer and heavier than a butcher's knife, and equally calculated for cutting or thrusting. It was invented by Col. James Bowie, who was killed by the Mexicans at the capture of the Alamo, in Bexar. The circumstances which gave rise to this name, was about as creditable as the purposes which it has since subserved. Some twelve or eighteen months ago, three brothers by the name of Bowie, in the State of Mississippi, had a deadly conflict with seven other persons, armed with every species of weapon, among the rest, with a large knife of which we are now speaking. This was handled by the brothers with such dexterity as to decide the conflict in their favor, although numbers were against them—and it has since been called by their name, "the Bowie knife".—It is made to carry under the coat, and now very generally worn by "gentlemen stabbers" in the South and West.

(New York paper).

The above account of the origin of the famed "Bowie knife," taken from a New York paper is entirely inaccurate. The first weapon of this description which has attained such a dreadful celebrity, was manufactured in the Parish of Rapides, in the State of Louisiana, near the plantation of Capt. Charles Mulhollan on Bayou Boeuf in 1820. This knife was made according to the instructions of Col. James Bowie, then known by the appellation of Big Jim Bowie.

It is originally intended to answer the double purpose of blazing trees, and of a hunting knife. The Colonel carried this weapon for five or six years, when the dreadful conflict, yet fresh in the recollections of many, took place in the State of Mississippi, a circumstance which at once gave it an unrivalled reputation among the *amateurs* of [illegible]. All the steel in the country was immediately converted into Bowie knives.

The Col. "in himself a host" never counted the number of his enemy, when a fight was on the *lapis*. His battle cry was always, "come boys, let us jump them; we must conquer or die," and these we are told were his last words to his brave compatriots Travis, Crockett and others who fell in the siege of the Alamo. *Red River Herald.*

—*Arkansas Advocate,* February 3, 1837

On the day Bowie was wielding his "large butcher knife" on the Mississippi sandbar, west Tennessee frontiersman David Crockett was planning his journey to Washington, D.C., where he would begin serving his first term as representative of his state's Ninth Congressional District. If his political skills left much to be desired, his charisma, wit, and rustic artlessness made him a conspicuous anomaly in Washington almost from the start. It also made him an easy target for his sneering foes, especially when, after his 1829 reelection, he began to oppose many of the bills supported by Andrew Jackson.

The Jackson (Tenn.) Statesman contains a communication, offering a reward for Col. Crockett, Member of Congress, from which we make the following extract:

"Strayed or stolen from the Jackson ranks, a certain Member of Congress, from the Western District, named *David Crockett.* Davy is upwards of six feet high, erect in his posture, and has a nose extremely red, after taking some spirits. He possesses vast bodily powers, great activity, and can leap the Ohio, wade the Mississippi, and carry one steam and two flat boats upon his back. He can vault across a streak of lightning, ride it down a honey locust; grease his heels, skate down a rainbow and whip his weight in wild cats and panthers. Davy took the bounty in the Western District, enlisted in the Jackson ranks, and performed prodigies of valor, in divers engagements, between the Jacksonites and the Adams boys. He defeated and put to flight the celebrated John C. Wright, by comparing him to a Monkey with spectacles

on—demolished the Little Prince, by telling him that the people in the Western District danced all their toe-nails off at Saturday night frolics; and grinned a panther to death at Washington City, (as he says.)"

—*New-Hampshire Patriot and State Gazette,* May 23, 1831

Defeated in his 1831 run for a third term, Crockett nevertheless saw his celebrity boosted in early 1833 when the book, *The Life and Adventures of Colonel David Crockett of West Tennessee,* was published in Cincinnati. Although its authorship is still debated by scholars, it was almost certainly drawn, to no small degree, from anecdotes Crockett himself had told to a number of his friends, especially Mathew St. Clair Clarke, clerk of the House of Representatives. The book sold like hotcakes. (Subsequent printings were retitled *Sketches and Eccentricities of Colonel David Crockett of West Tennessee.*)[2] One scene in the book described a visit made to the Crockett family cabin, Crockett himself walking out,

in plain homespun attire, with a black fur cap on, a finely proportioned man, about six feet high, aged, from appearance, forty-five. His countenance was frank and manly, and a smile played over it as he approached me. He brought with him a rifle, and from his right shoulder hung a bag made of raccoon skin, to which, by means of a sheath, was appended a huge butcher's knife.[3]

A few extracts from *Sketches and Eccentricities* inevitably made their way into the newspapers and helped seal Crockett's backwoods persona in the popular imagination. The following, from the *Baltimore Gazette and Daily Advertiser,* is an unadorned, graphic account of one of his many bear hunts, which vividly describes what a cold, wet, dirty, bloody, and even sad business they sometimes were. It is told in Crockett's peculiar vernacular, according to the writer. Here, too, "Davy" is dressed in, what some modern scholars often see as fanciful or purely showy attire, but in the grubby reality of the west Tennessee forest was quite common—the hunter's utilitarian "deer skin clothes."

The Messrs. Harpers, of New-York, have published a volume entitled "Sketches and Eccentricities of Colonel David Crockett, of East Tennessee." Every body knows, or ought to know, David—Douce Davy, or rather the Hon. David Crockett; his fame is abroad. The following is the Hon. Gentleman's account of a
BEAR HUNT.
"I was going 'long," said he, "down to a little *Hurricane*,[a] 'bout three miles from our tent, where I knew there must be a plenty of bear. 'Twas mightily cold, and my dogs were in fine order, and very busy hunting, when I seed where a piece of bark had been scratched off the tree, I said to my companion, there is a bear in the hollow of this tree. I examined the sign, and I knew I was right. I called my dogs to me; but to git at him was the thing. The tree was so large 'twould take all day to cut it down, and there was no chance to climb it. But, upon looking about, I found that there was a tree near the one the bear was in, and if I could make it fall agin it, I could then climb up and git him out. I fell to work and cut the tree down, but, as the devil would have it, it lodged before it got there. So that scheme was knocked in the head.

"I then told my companion to cut away upon the big tree, and I would go off some distance to see if I couldn't see him. He fell to work, and he hadn't been at it long before I seed the old bear poke his head out; but I couldn't shoot him, for if I did, I would hit him on the head, and he would fall backwards; so I had to wait for him to come out. I didn't say any thing: but it wan't a minute before he run out upon a limb and jumped down.

"I ran as hard as I could, but, before I got there he and the dogs were hard at it. I didn't see much of the fight before they all rolled down a steep hill, and the bear got loose and broke, right in the direction of the Hurricane. He was a mighty large one, and I was 'fraid my dogs would lose him, 'twas such a thick place. I started after him, and told my friend to come on. Well, of all the thick places that ever

you did see, that bear carried me through the thickest. The dogs would sometimes bring him to bay, and I would try for my life to get up to 'em, but when I would git most there, he would git loose. He devilled me mightily, I tell you. I reckon I went a mile after the bear upon my hands and knees, just creeping through briers, and if I hadn't had deer skin clothes on, they would have torn me in pieces.

"I got wet; and was mightily tired stooping so much. Sometimes I went through places so thick that I don't see how anything could get through; and I don't *believe* I could, if I hadn't the dogs fighting just before me. Sometimes I would look back and I couldn't see how I got along. But once I got in a clear place; my dogs, tired of fighting, had brought the bear again to bay, and I had my head up, looking over to get a shoot, when the first thing I knew I was up to my breast in a sink hole of water. I was infernal mad that I had a notion not to get out; but I began to think it wouldn't spite any body, and so I scrambled out. My powder was all wet, except the load in my gun, and I didn't know what to do. I had been sweating all the morning, and I was tired, and I looked rather queer with my wet leather clothes on; but I harked my dogs on, and once more I heard 'em fighting. I run on, and while I was going 'long I heard something jump into the water. When I got there I saw the bear going up the other bank of the Obion river—I hadn't time to shoot him before he was out of sight—he looked mighty tired.—When I come to look at my dogs, I could hardly help from crying. Old Tiger and Brutus were sitting upon the edge of the water, whining because they couldn't git over; and I had a mighty good dog named Carlow,—he was standing in the water ready to swim; and I observed as the water passed by him it was right red,—he was mighty badly cut. When I came to notice my other dogs, they were all right bloody, and it made me so mad that I harked 'em on, and determined to kill the bear.

"I hardly spoke to 'em when there was a general plunge, and each of my dogs formed a streak going straight across. I watched them till

---

[a] A "hurricane" referred to a tangle of fallen trees, knocked down by a storm.

they got out on the bank, when they all shook themselves, old Carlow opened, and off they all started. I sat down upon an old log. The water was right red where my dogs jumped in, and I loved 'em so much it made me mighty sorry. When I come to think how willingly they all jumped in when I told 'em, though they were badly cut and tired to death, I thought I ought to go and help 'em.

"It was now about twelve o'clock. My dogs had been running ever since sunrise, and we had all passed through a hurricane, which of itself was a day's work. I could hear nothing of my companion, I whooped, but there was no answer; and I concluded that he had been unable to follow me, and had gone back to the tent. I looked up and down the river, to see if there was a chance to cross it; but there was none—no canoe was within miles of me. While I was thinking of all these things, my dogs were trailing; but all at once I heard 'em fighting. I jumped up—I hardly knew what to do, when a notion struck me to roll in the log I had been sitting on, and cross over on that. 'Twas part of an old tree, twelve or fifteen feet long, lying on a slant. I gave it a push, and into the water it went. I got an old limb, straddled the log, with my feet in the water, and pushed off. 'Twas mighty ticklish work: I had to lay the limb across, like a balance pole, to keep me from turning over, and then paddled with the hand that wasn't holding the rifle. The log didn't float good, and the water came up over my thighs. After a while I got over safe, fastened my old log to go back upon, and as I went up the bank I heard my dogs tree. I run to 'em as fast as I could; and, sure enough, I saw the old bear up in a crotch.—My dogs were all lying down under him, and I don't know which was the most tired, they or the bear.

"I knew I had him, so I just sat down and rested a little; and then, to keep my dogs quiet, I got up, and old Betsey thundered at him. I shot him right through the heart, and he fell without a struggle. I run up and stuck my knife into him several times up to the hilt, just because he dev-illed me so much; but I had hardly pulled it out before I was sorry, for he had fought all day like

a man, and would have got clear but for me.

"I noticed when the other dogs jumped on him to bite him, old Carlow didn't get up. I went to him, and saw a right smart puddle of blood under him. He was cut into the hollow, and I saw he was dying—nothing could save him. While I was feeling 'bout him, he licked my hand; my eyes filled with tears; I turned my head away, and to ease his sufferings, plunged my knife through his heart. He yelled out his death note, and the other dogs tried to jump upon him; such is the nature of a dog. This is all I hate in bear hunting. I didn't git over the death of my dog in some time; and I have a right to love him to this day, for no man ever had a better friend."

—*Baltimore Gazette and Daily Advertiser*, November 15, 1833

Crockett's ubiquity in the national media served him well in 1833, for that August he was reelected to Congress. The following month *Niles' Weekly Register*, a Whig paper, both defended and embraced Crockett by editorializing on the veracity of his character.

COL. CROCKETT. A great deal has been said in the newspapers concerning col. Crockett, who has been again elected a member of Congress from Tennessee. It was the misfortune of the colonel to have received no school education in his youth, and since to have had but little opportunity to retrieve that defect; but he is a man of strong mind, and of great goodness of heart. The manner of his remarks are so peculiar that they excite much attention, and are repeated because of their originality; but there is a soundness, or point, in some of them which shews the exercise of a well disciplined judgment—and we think it is not easy for an unprejudiced man to communicate with the colonel without feeling that he is honest. We have had some opportunity of knowing the calibre of many members of congress for 25 or 30 years past, and have met with many, very many, far less capable of ascertaining truth than col. C—much less attentive to the duties of their place—and of no real use than would be one of *Maelzel's* automatons so constructed as to pronounce the words aye and no. But the colonel does not thus say a yea or no—for, whether right or wrong, *the vote is his own.*

We have been oftentimes asked "what sort of a man is colonel Crockett?" and the general reply was—"just such a one as you would desire to meet with, if any accident or misfortune had happened to you on the high way."

—*Niles' Weekly Register*, September 7, 1833

Almost three years later—and less than four months after the death of David Crockett—*Niles' Weekly Register* offered up a character analysis of another key player in the Alamo story: Antonio López de Santa Anna. It provides some brief biographical information but focuses mainly on his Machiavellian military career in Mexico during the turbulent 1820s.

SKETCH OF SANTA ANA.

Some particulars of this personage, which we have derived from gentlemen intimately acquainted with him, may be interesting to the public.

Santa Ana is about 42 years of age, and was born in the city of Vera Cruz. His father was a Spaniard of old Spain, of respectable standing though poor, his mother was a Mexican. He received a common education, and at the age of 13 or 14 was taken into the military family of the then intendant of Vera Cruz, gen. Davila, who took a great fancy to him and brought him up. He remained with gen. D. until about the year 1820. While with Davila he was made a major, and when installed he took the honors very cooly, and on some of his friends congratulating him he said, "Si mihi ciera dios qui siera estar algo mas." (If you were to make me a God, I should desire to be something greater.) This trait developed at so early a period of his life, indicated the existence of that vaulting ambition which has ever since characterized his life.

After serving the Spanish royal cause until 1821, he left Vera Cruz, turned against his old master and benefactor, and placed himself at the head of some irregular troops which he raised on the sea coast, near Vera Cruz, and which he called Jaroches in their language,

and which were denominated by him his Cossacks, as they are all mounted and armed with spears. With this rude cavalry he besieged Vera Cruz, drove Davila into the castle of San Juan d'Ulloa, and after having been repulsed again entered at a subsequent period, and got entire possession of the city, expelling therefrom the old Spanish troops, and reducing the power of the mother country in Mexico to the walls of the castle.

Subsequent to this Davila is said to have obtained an interview with Santa Ana, and told him he was destined to act a prominent part in the history of his country, and now, says he, I will give you some advice: "Siempre vayis con los muchos," (always go with the strongest party). He always acted up to this motto until he raised the *grito*, (or cry), in other words took up the cudgels for the friars and church. He then overturned the federal government and established a central despotism, of which the priests and the military were the two privileged orders. His life had been from the first of the most romantic kind, constantly in revolutions, until the last fatal rencontre.[b] His manners are extremely affable; he is full of anecdote and humor, and makes himself exceedingly fascinating and agreeable to all who come into his company; he is about 5 feet 10, rather spare, has a moderately high forehead, with black hair, short black whiskers, without mustaches, and an eye large, black, and expressive of a lurking devil in his look; he is a man of genteel and dignified deportment, but of a disposition perfectly heartless, but has never evinced a savageness of character except in the massacres in which he has been implicated in Texas. He married a Spanish lady of property, a native of Alvarado, and through that marriage obtained the first part of his estate called Manga de Clavo, 6 leagues from Vera Cruz. He has three fine children, yet quite young.

The following striking anecdote of Santa Ana illustrates his peculiar quickness and management: during the revolution of 1829, while he was shut up in Oxaca, and surrounded

---

[b] A reference to the Battle of San Jacinto on April 21, 1836.

by the government troops, and reduced to the utmost straits for the want of money and provisions, having a very small force, there had been in consequence of the siege and firing every day through the streets, no mass for several weeks. He had no money, and hit upon the following expedient to get it; he took possession of one of the convents, got hold of the wardrobe of the friars, dressed his officers and some of the soldiers in it, and early in the morning had the bells rung for mass. People delighted at having again an opportunity of adoring the Supreme Being, flocked to the church, where he was and after the house was pretty well filled his friars showed their side arms and bayonets from beneath their cowl; and closed the doors upon the assembled multitudes. At this unexpected denouncement there was a tremendous shrieking, when one of his officers ascended the pulpit and told the people that he wanted $10,000 and must have it. He finally succeeded in getting about $6,500, when he dismissed the congregation.

As a sample of Santa Ana's pious whims we relate the following:

In the same campaign of Oxaca, Santa Ana and his officers were there besieged by Rincon, who commanded the government troops. Santa Ana was in a convent surrounded by a small breastwork. Some of the officers one night to amuse themselves took the wooden saints out of the church and placed them as sentries, dressed in uniforms, on the breastwork. Rincon alarmed on the morning at this apparent boldness began to fire away at the wooden images, supposing them to be flesh and blood, and it was not until after some of the officers who were not in the secret had implored Santa Ana to prevent this desecration that the firing ceased. Many similar facts are related of Santa Ana. We have no room at present to say more than there is no man who has filled the space he has that is so little understood. In short, he is all things to all men. He never was out of Mexico, and the likeness exhibited of him in this city bears no resemblance to him.

—*Niles' Weekly Register*, June 25, 1836

The man who would defeat Santa Anna in Texas in 1836, Sam Houston, was, in early 1829, rocked by the sudden and complete breakdown of his weeks-old marriage to Eliza Allen. Swearing he would not reveal what had happened "to a living person," Houston resigned his governorship of Tennessee and left to seek mental and moral solace among his old friends, the Cherokees, in their new homes west of the Mississippi.[4]

The case of Gov. Houston of Tennessee, is most extraordinary. He was yet comparatively a young man, not we presume exceeding 25—of a noble and commanding figure, uncommonly handsome, sprightly and of a gay disposition. Though not very learned or profound, he was a bold animated speaker. His conduct in the Indian war under Gen. Jackson had raised him to distinction. In the duel with White,[c] it was said that, after avoiding the contest to the utmost point that was possible, consistent with the usages of the country, and retain his standing, he turned and met the danger with fearless bravery and coolness. When White fell, supposed mortally wounded, Houston took his hand, expressed his regret, and told W. he had brought the evil on himself, to which the wounded man assented. Called by the voice of the people from Congress to the elevated and dignified station of Governor of Tennessee, it seemed as if nothing, but a wife, to ensure his domestic bliss, and to share his honors, was necessary to as perfect happiness, as human nature is capable of enjoying.—He leads to the altar a woman lovely to the eye. Suddenly we behold him plunged deep in woe—speaking of his wretched condition. He resigns the high place he held, and rushes like Timon—from civilized society, and seeks oblivion in the wilds of the savage.—*Pa. Village Record.*

—*Farmer's Cabinet* (Amherst, New Hampshire), June 6, 1829

When Houston boarded a packet at Clarksville, his appearance left little doubt that he was indeed fleeing civilization.

---

[c] General William A. White, shot by Houston in a duel in 1826.

It is stated that previous to his leaving Nashville, Gov. Houston equipped himself *in an Indian dress*, and went away with the determination of associating himself and residing among the savages. His age is 35, not 25, as before stated.

—*Eastern Argus* (Portland, Maine),
June 5, 1829

Houston's political enemies, and the malicious scandalmongers who could always find a venue for their dirt in newspapers, went straight for the jugular. Perhaps the most intriguing part of the following attack is that it gives Texas as Houston's destination, three years before he actually went there.

Governor Houston.—Extract of a letter from a gentleman in Nashville to his friend in Pittsburg, dated May 8th, 1829.
"Samuel Houston, Gov. of Tennessee, and a candidate for re-election, and who was recently married to Miss Allen, has parted from his wife, and endeavored to fix a stigma of the blackest kind upon her character—he accused her of infidelity, and of illicit intercourse with *negroes*! and charged her with other gross and disreputable actions. His wife would have nothing to say to him after the first intimation of what he had done. This, it is said, brought him to a sense of what he was about. After entreating her to make it up, which she would not do, he left Nashville for Texas. Mrs. H. is an amiable young lady; the whole family are respectable, and many of her brothers are public men. Such an insult was not to be borne lightly, and there is little doubt that if the Governor had remained, they would have made him repent his baseness. Rumors are astir that this was a deep laid scheme of villainy by the Governor, that he might have a pretext for leaving his situation and friends for Texas, where he expects to receive a commission, and make some revolutions. Time alone will decide the truth or falsity of this matter."

—*New-Hampshire Gazette*, March 30, 1829

In less than a year after leaving Tennessee, Houston was traveling back east, this time to Washington, D.C., as an ambassador of the Cherokees, seeking to present tribal grievances regarding reneged government annuities, and to protest the excessive amounts of liquor being peddled to the Indians by traders.

A paragraph which we copied a day or two since from the *National Intelligencer*, announced the arrival in Washington of Gov. Houston, formerly of Tennessee; the *Shawneetown* (Illinois) *Gazette* of the 2nd inst. thus notices the object of his visit, and his personal equipment.
"On board the steamboat Amazon which left here on Tuesday last, was General Houston, late Governor of Tennessee, accompanied by three Cherokee Chiefs, forming, it is rumoured, a detachment from the Indians to the general government. Gen. Houston was equipped with his leather hunting shirt, bullet pouch and scalping knife, in true Indian style."

—*Republican Star* (Maryland),
February 16, 1830

In 1829, twenty-year-old Alabama resident William Barrett Travis had a lot on his plate: supporting a wife and child by practicing law and tutoring part-time, and editing and printing his own newspaper, the *Clairborne Herald*, a four-page weekly he had launched the year before.

Immediately upon his acceptance to the bar in February 1829, Travis had posted a proud advertisement in his paper.

WILLIAM B. TRAVIS has established his Office for the present at the next door above the Post Office, where he may be found, at all times, when not absent on business.

—*Clairborne Herald*, February 27, 1829[5]

But by March 1831, Travis was deep in debt, his businesses failing and his marriage suffering from the effects. Sued by creditors, he was found guilty, and an order for his arrest was pending. Travis chose to mount his horse and flee to Texas, far from the reach of the Alabama authorities. In time, once he was relocated and solvent, he could send for his wife and child.[6]

By that March, James Bowie had not only been permanently settled in Texas for a year but had also married the teenaged Ursula Veramendi, daughter of Don Juan Martín de Veramendi, one of the wealthier and more important citizens of San Antonio de Béxar. That November the ceaselessly entrepreneurial Bowie raised a party of eleven adventurers, including his brother Rezin, to seek the legendary Los Almagres silver mine near the long-abandoned San Saba mission and presidio, 120 miles northwest of Béxar. Rezin penned a vivid, suspenseful account of what proved to be the unanticipated high point of the expedition: the frontiersmen's battle with a much larger band of Indians. The account first saw publication in a Philadelphia newspaper, *Atkinson's Saturday Evening Post and Bulletin* of August 17, 1833, and was subsequently reprinted in many other papers.

The following interesting narrative of a fight with the Waccos and Tawachanies,[d] Indians in Texas, amounting to 164, and a party of the Americans, nine men and two boys, eleven in number—is related by Razin P. Bowie, Esq., one of the party, now in this city.

On the 2d of November, 1831, we left the town of St. Antonia de Baxar for the silver mines on the St. Saba River, the party consisting of the following named persons—Razin P. Bowie, James Bowie, David Buchannan, Robert Armstrong, Jesse Wallace, Mathew Doyle, Cephas R. Hamm, Corriell, Thomas M'Caslin, Gonzales and Charles, servant boys. Nothing particular occurred until the 19th, on which day about ten a.m., we were overhauled by two Camancha Indians and a Mexican captive, who had struck our trail and followed it. They stated that they belonged to Isaonie's party, a chief of the Camancha tribe, sixteen in number, and were on their road to St. Antonia, with a drove of horses, which they had taken from the Waccos and Tawackanies, and were about returning them to their owners, citizens of St. Antonia. After smoking and talking with them about an hour, and making them a few presents of tobacco, powder, shot, &c, they returned to their party, who were waiting at the Ilano river.

We continued our journey until night closed upon us, when we encamped. The next morn-

ing, between day light and sunrise, the above named Mexican captive returned to our camp, his horse very much fatigued, and who, after eating & smoking, stated to us that he had been sent by his chief, Isaonie, to inform us we were followed by 124 Tawackamie and Wacco Indians, and forty Caddos had joined them, who were determined to have our scalps at all risks. Isaonie had held a talk with them all the previous afternoon, and endeavored to dissuade them from their purpose; but they still persisted and left him enraged, and pursued our trail. As a voucher for the truth of the above, the Mexican produced his chief's silver medal, which is common among the natives in such cases. He further stated, that his chief requested him to say, that he had but sixteen men, badly armed, and without ammunition—but if we would return and join him, such succour as he could give us he would. But knowing that the enemy lay between us and him, we deemed it more prudent to pursue our journey, and endeavor to reach the old fort on the St. Saba river before night, distance thirty miles. The Mexican then returned to his party, and we proceeded on.

Throughout the day we encountered bad roads, being covered with rocks, and the horses feet being worn out, we were disappointed in not reaching the fort. In the evening we had some difficulty in picking out an advantageous spot where to encamp for the night. We, however, made choice of the best that offered, which was a cluster of live oak trees, some thirty or forty in number, about the size of a man's body. To the north of them a thicket of live oak bushes about ten feet high, forty yards in length and twenty in breadth. To the west, at a distance of thirty-five or forty yards, ran a stream of water.

The surrounding country was an open prairie, interspersed with a few trees, rocks and broken land. The trail which we came on lay to the east of our encampment. After taking the precaution to prepare our spot for defence, by cutting a road inside the ticket of bushes, ten feet from the outer edge all around, and clearing the prickly pears from amongst the bushes, we hobbled our horses, and placed sentinels for the night. We were now distant six miles

---

[d] Waco and Tawakoni.

from the old fort above-mentioned, which was built by the Spaniards in 1732 for the purpose of protecting them while working the silver mines, which are a mile distant. A few years after it was attacked by the Camancha Indians, and every soul put to death. Since that time it has never been occupied. Within the fort is a church which, had we reached before night, it was our intention to have occupied to defend ourselves against the Indians. The fort surrounds about one acre of land, under a twelve feet stone wall.

Nothing occurred throughout the night, and we lost no time in the morning, in making preparations for continuing our journey to the fort; and when in the act of starting, we discovered the Indians on our trail to the east, about two hundred yards distant, and a footman about fifty yards ahead of the main body, with his face to the ground, tracking. The cry of Indians was given, and all hands to arms. We dismounted, and both saddle and pack horse were immediately made fast to the trees. As soon as they found we had discovered them, they gave the war whoop—halted and commenced stripping preparatory to action. A few mounted Indians were reconnoitering the ground; amongst them we discovered a few Caddo Indians by the cut of their hair, who had always previously been friendly to the Americans.

Their numbers being so far greater than ours (164 to 11) it was agreed that Razin P. Bowie should be sent out to talk with them, and endeavour to compromise rather than attempt to fight. He accordingly started with David Buchannan in company, and walked up to within about forty yards of where they had halted, and requested them, in their own tongue, to send forward their chief as he wanted to talk with them. Their answer was—"how de do! how de do!"—in English, and a discharge of twelve shot at us, one of which broke Buchannan's leg. Bowie returned their salutations with the contents of a double barrelled gun and a pistol. He then took Buchannan on his shoulder, and started back to the encampment. They then opened a heavy fire upon us, which wounded Buchannan in two more places slightly, and

piercing Bowie's hunting shirt in several places, without doing him any injury.—When they found their shot failed to bring Bowie down, eight Indians on foot took after him with their tomahawks, and when close upon him, were discovered by his party, who rushed out with their rifles and brought down four of them—the other four retreating back to the main body. We then returned to our position, and all was still for about five minutes.

We then discovered a hill to the north-east, at the distance of sixty yards, red with Indians, who opened a heavy fire on us with loud yells. Their chief, on horseback, urging them in a loud and audible voice to the charge, walking his horse perfectly composed. When we first discovered him our guns were all empty, with the exception of Mr. Hamm's, James Bowie cried out, "who is loaded!" Mr. Hamm observed, "I am." He then was told to shoot that Indian on horseback. He did so, and broke his leg and killed his horse. We now discovered him hopping round his horse on one leg, with his shield on his arm to keep off the balls. By this time, four of our party being reloaded, fired at the same instant, and all the balls took effect through the shield. He fell, and was immediately surrounded by six or eight of his tribe, who picked him up and bore him off. Several of these were shot down by our party. The whole body then retreated back of the hill, out of our sight, with the exception of a few Indians, who were running about from tree to tree out of gun shot.

They now covered the hill for the second time, bringing up their bowmen, who had not been in action before, and commenced a heavy fire with balls and arrows; which we returned by a well directed aim with our rifles. At this instant another chief appeared on horseback, near the spot where the last one fell. The same question of who was loaded, was asked; the answer was, nobody; when little Charles, the mulatto servant, came running up with Buchannan's rifle, which had not been discharged since he was wounded, and handed it to James Bowie, who instantly fired, and brought him down from his horse. He was surrounded by six or eight of his tribe, as was the last, and bore off under our fire.

During the time we were engaged in defending ourselves from the Indians on the hill, some fifteen or twenty of the Caddo tribe had succeeded in getting under the bank of the creek in our rear, at about forty yards distance, and opened a fire upon us, which wounded Matthew Doyle, the ball entering in the left breast and on the back. As soon as he cried out he was wounded, Thomas McCaslin hastened to the spot where he fell, and observed, "where is the Indian that shot Doyle." He was told by a more experienced hand not to venture there, as, from the report of their guns, they must be riflemen. At that instant he discovered an Indian and while in the act of raising his piece, was shot through the centre of the body, and expired. Robert Armstrong exclaimed, "damn the Indian that shot McCaslin, where is he!" He was also told not to venture there, as they must be riflemen; but on discovering an Indian, & while bringing his gun up, he was fired at, and part of the stock of his gun cut off, and the ball lodged against the barrel. During this time our enemies had formed a complete circle around us, occupying the points of rocks, scattering trees and bushes. The firing then became general from all quarters.

Finding our situation too much exposed among the trees, were obliged to leave it, and take to the thickets. The first thing necessary was to dislodge the riflemen from under the bank of the creek, who were within point-blank shot. This we soon succeeded in, by shooting the most of them through the head, as we had the advantage of seeing them when they could not see us.

The road we had cut round the thicket the night previous, gave us now an advantageous situation over that of our enemy, as we had a fair view of them in the prairie, while we were completely hid. We baffled their shots by moving six or eight feet the moment we had fired, as their only mark was the smoke of our guns. They would put twenty balls within the size of a pocket handkerchief, where they had seen the smoke. In this manner we fought them two hours, and had one man wounded, James Correll, who was shot through the arm, and the ball lodged in the side, first cutting away a bush,

which prevented it from penetrating deeper than the size of it.

They now discovered that we were not to be dislodged from the thicket, and the uncertainty of killing us at random shot; they suffering very much from the fire of our rifles, which brought half a dozen at every round. They now determined to resort to stratagem, by putting fire to the dry grass in the prairie, for the double purpose of routing us from our position, and, under cover of the smoke, to carry away their dead and wounded, which lay near us. The wind was now blowing from the west, and they placed the fire in that quarter, where it burnt down all the grass to the creek, and then bore off to the right and left, leaving around our position a space of about five acres that was untouched by the fire. Under cover of this smoke, they succeeded in carrying off a portion of their dead and wounded. In the mean time our party were engaged in scraping away the dry grass and leaves from our wounded men and baggage, to prevent the fire from passing over it; and likewise, in pulling up rocks and bushes to answer the purpose of a breastwork.

They now discovered they had failed in routing us by the fire, as they had anticipated. They then re-occupied the points of the rocks and trees in the prairie, and commenced another attack. The firing continued for some time, when the wind suddenly shifted to the north, and blew very hard.—We now discovered our dangerous situation, should the Indians succeed in putting fire to the small spot which we occupied, and kept a strict watch all round. The two servant boys were employed in scraping away dry grass and leaves from around the baggage, and pulling rocks and placing them around the men. The remainder of the party were warmly engaged with the enemy. The point from which the wind now blew being favorable to fire our position, one of the Indians succeeded in crawling down the creek and putting fire to the grass that had not been burnt, but before he could retreat back to his party, was killed by Robert Armstrong.

At this time we saw no hope of escape, as the fire was coming down rapidly before the wind, flaming ten feet high, and directly for the spot we occupied. What was to be done—we must either be burnt up alive, or driven into the prairie amongst the savages. This encouraged the Indians; and to make it more awful, their shouts and yells rent the air; they at the same time firing upon us about twenty shots a minute. As soon as the smoke hid us from their view, we collected together, and held a consultation as to what was best to be done. Our first impression was, that they might charge on us under cover of the smoke, as we could make but one effectual fire—the sparks were flying about so thickly that no man could open his powder horn without running the risk of being blown up. However, we finally came to a determination, had they charged us, to give them one fire, place our backs together, and draw our knives, and fight them as long as any one of us was left alive. The next question was, should they not charge us, and we retain our position, we must be burnt up. It was then decided that each man should take care of himself as well as he could, until the fire arrived at the ring around our baggage and wounded men, and there it should be smothered with buffalo robes, bear skins, deer skins, and blankets, which, after a great deal of exertion, we succeeded in doing.

Our thicket now being so much burnt and scorched, that it afforded us little or no shelter, we all got into the ring that was made round our wounded men and baggage and commenced building our breastwork higher, with the loose rocks from the inside, and dirt dug up with our knives and sticks. During the last fire, the Indians had succeeded in removing all their killed and wounded which lay near us. It was now sundown, and we had been warmly engaged with the Indians since sunrise, a period of thirteen hours; and they seeing us still alive and ready for fight, drew off at a distance of three hundred yards, and encamped for the night with their dead and wounded.— Our party now commenced to work in raising our fortifications higher, and succeeded in getting it breast high by ten p.m. We now filled all our vessels and skins with water, expecting another attack the next morning. We could distinctly hear the Indians, nearly all night, crying over their dead, which is their custom; and at daylight, they shot a wounded chief—it being also a custom to shoot any of their tribe that are mortally wounded. They, after that, set out with their dead and wounded to a mountain about a mile distant, where they deposited their dead in a cave on the side of it. At eight in the morning, two of our party went out from the fortification to the encampment, where the Indians had lain the night previous, and counted forty-eight bloody spots on the grass where the dead and wounded had been lying. As near as we could judge, their loss must have been forty killed and wounded.

Finding ourselves much cut up, having one man killed, Thomas M'Caslin—and three wounded, D. Buchannan, Matthew Doyle, and James Corriell—five horses killed, and three wounded—that we re-commenced strengthening our little fort, and continued our labors until one p.m., when the arrival of thirteen Indians drew us into our fort again. As soon as they discovered we were still there, and already for action and well fortified, they put off. We after that remained in our fort eight days, recruiting our wounded men and horses; at the expiration of which time, being all in pretty good order, we set out on our return to St. Antonia de Bexar. We left the fort at dark, and travelled all night and next day until afternoon, when we picked out an advantageous spot and fortified ourselves, where we remained two days, expecting the Indians would again, when recruited, follow our trail; but, however, we saw nothing more of them.

David Buchannan's wounded leg here mortified, and having no surgical instruments, or medicine of any kind, not even a dose of salts, we boiled some live-oak bark very strong, and thickened it with pounded charcoal and Indian meal, made a poultice of it, and tied it round his leg, over which we sewed a buffalo skin, and travelled along five days without looking at it, when it was opened, the mortified parts had all drop off, and it was in a far way of healing, which it finally did, and his leg is as well as it ever was. There was none of the party but had his skin cut in several places, and numerous shot-holes through his clothes.

On the twelfth day we arrived, in good order, with our wounded men and horses, at St. Antonia de Bexar.

—*Saturday Evening Post*
—*Baltimore Gazette and Daily Advertiser*,
September 7, 1833

The weary men received a heroes' welcome in San Antonio, and James Bowie was soon encouraged to lead another party out to finally crush the Towakoni.

New Orleans, Jan. 14.

THE TEXAS INDIANS. We are indebted to a friend for the Texas Gazette of the 27th December, from which we copy the following:—

Extract of a letter from a respectable citizen, dated December 7.

"Mr. Bowie arrived here last night from San Saba, having had a fight with 160 Indians, on the 21st November. Among them were 40 Caddoes. He fought from 8 o'clock in the morning with only five men (4 others being wounded at the beginning, one having died) till half past 6 o'clock P.M.—saw fall 21 Indians, mostly Caddoes—fortified themselves at night, and remained 8 days after the battle at the fortification.

"We have been informed, from an undoubted source, that the party of troops that went from Bexar, to attack the Tauacana Indians in their towns, when on their return to Bexar, fell in with a party of 27 Indians, and killed 23 of the number, four only escaped."

EXPEDITION   AGAINST   THE TAHUAKANOS INDIANS. Permission having been granted by the Political Authorities of the country, to Mr. James Bowie to make an expedition against this horde of thieves and marauders, of our frontier, a volunteer corps, to be commanded by officers of their own election, will go out in the coming month of January. The present is believed to be a favorable moment to strike a final and fatal blow to these disturbers of our peace; as they have lately been considerably damaged by an expedition from Bexar, in which they lost two hundred and fifty horses, and afterwards in a desperate fight with Mr. James Bowie. It is stated that they still have two thousand horses in their possession, which may be taken. Information has been received that the Tahuakanos intend to make a campaign against DeWitt's colony, for the purpose of destroying it; if this be the case their next blow will be directed against this colony. All that feel disposed to go and chastise these murderers of our property are invited to meet at Gonzales, on the 20th of next month, the time and place appointed for a general rendezvous whence they will proceed on the campaign.

—*New London Gazette and*
General Advertiser, February 15, 1832

Bowie's company eventually numbered thirty-eight, composed of whites and friendly Indians. But despite a ten-week circuit of the country to the north the main Tawakoni band was not found.[7]

In 1832, Sam Houston was Texas-bound, ostensibly as a US agent for Indian affairs, but his real reason for migrating there was probably manifold: the prospect of land ownership, a revived political future, and perhaps even a future in a Texian republic seized from Mexico. Fifty-four years later, an anecdote concerning this fateful ride of Houston's was printed in a South Dakota newspaper.

Sam Houston's Abstinence Pledge.

Col. Elias Rector, of Arkansas, used to tell a good story about his riding some miles with Sam Houston, then on his way to Texas to take part in the war of Independence. Houston rode a pony, was dressed in a buckskin suit, and with his rifle stretched across his shoulder he looked every inch the hunter. He drank freely from a bottle. At length they arrived at the fork of the two trails, one of which led to Fort Smith, where Rector was going, and the other to Texas. Houston held up his bottle in the air, and was about proposing a parting drink, when young Rector checked him and said if Houston would not consider it impertinent in a young man he wished to make a request.

"What is it?" said Houston. "It is," replied Rector, "that you here pledge yourself never to take another drink of intoxicating liquors." "All right, my boy," said Houston, "I'll do it," and raising the bottle above his head he dashed it to the ground, wetting the ground with its contents. "Now," said Rector, "as a slight gift in memory of me, I will give you my razor," it being the custom of the people in those days to carry their razors and shave themselves. Houston accepted the gift, and on extending his left arm, whetted the razor on his leathern sleeve, and with an exulting tone remarked: "I'll keep this razor and shave me with it when I become president of the republic." He put spurs to his bobtailed pony, and the friends parted. Houston kept his word, he kept the razor until he became president of the republic of Texas.

—*Aberdeen Daily News,* November 30, 1886

3
Road to Revolt

By the end of 1825, Stephen Austin was no longer the only US-born empresario of a colony in Mexican Texas (in his case, on the Brazos River). There was, for instance, Green DeWitt's grant on the Guadalupe River with Gonzales as its central town. Just west of the Sabine River sat the lands granted to Colonel Haden Edwards. For the time being the Mexican government was pleased with the North Americans, who were indeed living up to their promise, industriously building homes and farms, and at last dealing sternly with the aggressive Indians in their neighborhoods. But the war for independence from Spain had left Mexico in a state of heavy debt, factional strife, and deprivation on every level. As a result, its garrisons in Texas suffered, especially the one occupying the Alamo.

> A letter from St. Antonio, Texas, dated 24th October, states that provisions were very scarce in that province, so much so that the few troops there were put upon short allowance. The troops were nearly in a state of mutiny on account of their pay and clothing, not having received any of either for the past year. The commandant finds it impossible to borrow funds, and no remittances have been made from Mexico. Should the troops refuse duty and disperse, it is feared the settlements will be in danger from incursions by Indians, who have already lately evinced a disposition to be troublesome.
> —*Richmond Enquirer*, January 24, 1826

It was not the threat from Indians, however, that soon turned Mexico's attention more seriously toward its northernmost province. As leaders of the Nacogdoches-based colony, Edwards and his brother Benjamin proved to be overly imperious in expressing their demands to see proofs of land ownership from the Mexican and other settlers already living there. In October 1826, Mexico revoked the Edwards's grant; but the Edwards brothers would not go quietly, and in November they raised the flag of revolt.

> NATCHITOCHES, DEC. 26
> *Declaration of Independence in Texas.*—We are credibly informed by several persons, who have lately arrived from Texas, that on Saturday the 16th inst. the united forces of the Districts of Nacogdoches and the Aysh Bayou, declared the Province of Texas, free and independent of the United States of Mexico, and hoisted a Flag at Nacogdoches, with the words "Liberty and independence" on it. We are not informed whether Austin's Colony participates in the affair, but we presume from the intimacy that exists between many of the settlers there, and the leading characters who have gone thus far, that there must be an understanding between them in the affair.
>
> It is said, that a few days previous to the declarations being made, six Indian Chiefs of the nations in the vicinity of the Province, held a council and promised to assist the new party.
>
> Many, no doubt, will think these patriots to be the remnant of Don Quixotte's band of heroes, but, if there is any union between those who compose the different settlements, which have lately been made in the Province, and the Indians, it will be a serious affair to the adjoining province, if not to the Mexican Government.
>
> The Mexican Government has heretofore paid very little attention to this part of the

Province of Texas, leaving those who were there previous to the introduction of the colonists and the colonists to govern themselves, without any knowledge of the laws or officers who were qualified to administer justice. The only officers are Alcaldes and Sheriffs.

JANUARY 2.
By a gentleman from Nacogdoches, we learn that 200 Indians, principally Cherokees, joined the Independent Republicans, on Friday last, at Nacogdoches.

We likewise understand that this new Republic has been christened the "Republic of Fredonia," and that their flag, as we mentioned last week, consisted of a stripe of red and white, being emblematic of Union between the Red and White men, and all in favor of the new born infant, had mounted red and white cockades, as an indication of favoring the Union.

We have also received an address from the Committee of Correspondence of the Republican Army at Nacogdoches, and a Treaty entered into between the Nacogdoches Independents and the Chiefs of twenty-three Tribes of Indians.

There are different reports in circulation relative to Colonel Austin's Colony—some say it will readily join, while others contradict the assertion. We presume however the Empresado will keep clear—many no doubt, within his jurisdiction, will join in the campaign fitting out to besiege St. Antonio, where there is 400 regular troops of the 9th Regiment, well armed, and a large quantity of Artillery and Military stores. If the "Fredonians" should get to St. Antonio, before they have time to recruit from the adjacent posts, (the nearest of which is 300 miles) they may probably take St. Antonio. How long can they retain possession, is a query.

A National Congress is to assemble at Nacogdoches, on the first Monday in February, to form a Constitution and appoint Executive Officers.—The following gentlemen have been elected: Col. H. Edwards, B. Edwards, Esq., H. B. Mayo, Esq., Colonel Legon, Mr. Thompson, J. Sprowl, Esq., and Doctor J. A. Huber.
—*South Carolina State Gazette*,
February 10, 1827

But Stephen Austin deemed Edwards and his rebellious cohorts "totally wrong" in regard to their reasons for launching a rebellion and leagued himself and his own militia with the cannon-armed Mexican detachment from San Antonio that marched east to crush the Fredonians. When they reached Nacogdoches, they were met with no resistance.[1]

Texas.—Extract of a letter from Natchez, Feb. 13, to the editors of the Baltimore Chronicle:
"The republican party calling themselves Fredonians, have ceased to exist, and the Mexican party have quiet possession of the province of Texas. They have taken ten prisoners who have been put in irons, and marched on to Nacogdoches from the Aysch-bayou, where they were taken for trial.—They probably will suffer death. They are strongly escorted by 70 or 80 men (Spaniards) well mounted—to escape is impossible. It is rumored in this town that the Cherokees have murdered Fields, one of the signers of the declaration of Fredonians. Dr. Hunter's life is said to be jeopardized.

"Col. Edward's family have escaped from Nacogdoches, with the exception of his son in law, Mr. Harrison, who is in irons, a prisoner."
—*Brattleboro Messenger* (Vermont),
March 30, 1827

With recent events recalling the filibuster days of Augustus Magee, Samuel Kemper, and Dr. James Long, a new wariness arose in the minds of Mexican officials about the intentions of the Anglo American colonists. And the fact that Texas was drawing new immigrants from the United States at an alarming rate—many of them of a lawless stripe—heightened their concerns. A Louisiana newspaper tried to put a positive spin on the situation.

We have lately seen a former resident of this district, who, who has just returned from the adjacent Mexican province of Texas. He reports that the country is fast filling up with Americans, and that several sections of it have been well settled. The state of society is almost entirely pastoral, and an individual's wealth is rated by the number of his horses, mules, and horned cattle.—Four lawyers are already settled at San Felipe—and courts are regularly held there.—Several fugitives from the United States have been given up to our authorities, and, transgressors against their own laws, are rigidly punished.

This account of order and good management is truly consolatory for us who reside so near their limits. It will not hereafter be an asylum for our fugitives from justice. *Attakapas Gazette.*
—*Providence Patriot*, April 24, 1829

Equally confident—and typical of the many glowing newspaper accounts that enticed even more Americans to move to Texas—is the following capsule history written by one of Austin's colonists about the colony and how it continued to thrive.

AUSTIN'S SETTLEMENT, (TEXAS.)

We have been induced to republish the following article, upon the assurance of a friend, that it is from the pen of a gentleman in whom every confidence may be placed.

———

Impressed with a belief that a brief description of Austin's Colony in Texas will not be uninteresting to many of our readers, I am induced to furnish the following, which is formed from a personal knowledge of its history and situation; as also, by a residence of the last seven years.—The settlement of American families in Texas, was commenced by Col. S. F. Austin under the authority of the Mexican Government, in the autumn of the year 1823, although many families has been residing there for nearly two years prior to that time. In the year 1820, the commandant General of the eastern internal Provinces, granted permission to Moses Austin, the father of Col. Austin, to establish 300 American families in Texas. Mr. Austin died previous to making a commencement in the location of families, leaving his son Stephen charged with the fulfillment of the contract, for which purpose, in the year 1821, he proceeded to Bexar, the capital of Texas, to receive from the authorities of that place, a legal acknowledgment of his power as the agent of his deceased father. On the arrival of

Colonel Austin at Bexar, he found the country in a state of revolution, on which account the government of the Province advised him to go to Mexico; accordingly he left Bexar for that place, and arrived there in the year 1821; Iturbide was crowned Emperor shortly after the arrival of Col. Austin in Mexico, and as soon after that event as prudence and policy dictated, he presented the permission obtained by his father from the Spanish Commander, and solicited its confirmation, which, after the delays that generally attend Spanish tribunals, and the then unsettled state of the Government would admit, was sanctioned in February, 1823.

After receiving from the Emperor his documents, Col. Austin, fearing the Emperor would not maintain himself long upon the throne, concluded to delay his departure from Mexico for a time, and remained long enough to witness his dethronement and the installation of the Congress which had been dissolved by Iturbide; this induced the Col. to solicit from Congress their approbation to all the former proceedings in his business; this, they gave by a decree dated 11th of April, 1823. Thus authorized, Col. Austin departed from Mexico for Texas, where he arrived in August, 1823, and as before stated commenced the organization of the Colony and the location of the emigrants that fall. The limits of the Territory designed by the Mexican Government to Col. Austin, for the settlement of the families introduced by him has for its eastern boundary, the upper road leading from Bexar to Nacogdoches; its western, the river Labacca; southern, the sea coast or shore of the Gulf; and lies between the 28th degree 30', and 31st degree of north latitude, and 94 degrees 30', and 96 degrees 30', of west longitude, from Greenwich.

The Brassos and Colorado rivers are the principal that run through the Colony, the former discharges its waters into the Gulf, and the latter into the Matagorda Bay; there are several large creeks that discharge their waters into the Bay and Gulf, although they do not merit the character of rivers, besides which, there are numerous creeks emptying into the Brassos and Colorado, that are permanent in their waters, being supplied by springs. The soil of the Margins of the Colorado and Brassos, is generally alluvial and covered with timber, consisting of ash, elm, cotton wood, hackberry, sycamore, live oak, &c., interspersed with very large cane brakes, and is by planters considered equal to any soil in the world, for the cultivation of Cotton and Sugar.—The prairies are covered with grass, affording an inexhaustible range for cattle and horses during the whole year, while the soil of them is cultivated in cotton and corn to a very great advantage to farmers in the prairies, as they thereby avoid clearing the cotton lands, and are enabled to cultivate a much larger quantity in a much shorter space of time.

The population of the colony is from 3000 to 4000 inhabitants, which with some few exceptions, are Americans. The majority of the inhabitants are agriculturalists, while others devote much of their time to stock raising; this latter branch of industry is one that yields to the grazier a handsome income, as the stock is maintained without any other expense than occasional herding, the whole year round; indeed, it is a positive fact, that it is less expensive to raise a cow beast of 3 years old than to raise a chicken one year old. The prospects of the crop in the middle of last month was very flattering, and it was estimated that 1,000 bales cotton, 150,000 bushels of corn, and from 130 to 150 hhds. sugar (experimental), would be made. It may be well here to remark, that the luxuriant growth of the cane in the Colony presents the planter the most flattering prospects for the application of his force to the cultivation of it, while the section of the country which from its local situation, soil and climate is congenial to the growth of cane, is very great.

The local Government of the Colony is administered by officers who are elected by the settlers, and consist of an Alcade, who has civil and judicial jurisdiction, two Regidores (Aldermen), and one Syndic, forming in conjunction with the Alcade as president a municipal body styled an Ayunmeinto. The Alcade and one of the Aldermen are elected annually, and cannot be re-elected until two years after they have retired from office. Justice is administered

in a prompt and summary manner, few crimes are committed, and generally speaking, there is less disorder than in sections of the western countries of the United States. The climate is remarkably healthy, and salubrious, springs abound in the margins of all the creeks, and the water is good.

Land can be obtained by emigrants with great facility from the Empressairo (founder of the colony), and the commissioner of the Government under the colonization law, which authorizes the grant to families, who are actual settlers of one league Mexican measures equal in English to 4446 acres superficial surface, and unmarried men can obtain the fourth part of that quantity the expenses of which will not amount to four cents per acre. The same law requires that emigrants should be furnished with testimonials of good character from the last place of residence.

At San Felippe de Austin, the capital of the Colony, there is a very good school, presided by a teacher of first rate literary acquirements, from the State of New York; there are several other small schools in various parts of the Colony. There are seven cotton mills, and one steam saw mill nearly ready to go into operation.

Matagorda and Galveston Bays afford fine harbors and safe entrance, there being never less than twelve, and at times fifteen and sixteen feet water on the bars. At present the principal part of the trade of the Colony is carried on in small vessels, which enter the Brassos river, where there is a bar about 30 yards wide, over which 6 feet water can only be calculated on with certainty, although there is often 7 to 9 feet water. The cotton raised in the Colony is eventually sent to New Orleans for a market, and the surplus corn, beans and sweet potatoes, are sent to Matamores, Tampico and Vera Cruz.

—*Daily National Intelligencer*,
December 7, 1829

Meanwhile, conditions in Mexico continued to be chaotic, and Spain saw its chance to regain its lost North American kingdom. In July 1829, an expeditionary force of nearly three thousand men under Spanish General Isidro Barradas was sent from Cuba to attempt that reconquest and landed at Tampico. Displaying his personal quality of never dawdling when action needed to be taken—a characteristic that would propel him to victory as well as defeat in 1836 Texas—Antonio López de Santa Anna without authority immediately gathered a force of two thousand local militia at Veracruz, seized all the ships in the harbor, and set sail for Tampico. Luck was on his side; yellow fever broke out among the Spanish force, and Barradas split his troops into several different positions. A New Hampshire newspaper published Santa Anna's own account of his attack on Barradas at Tampico.

A vessel has arrived in New-Orleans, which left Vera Cruz on the 3d ult. but brought no later advices from Tampico. Our New-Orleans correspondents have forwarded us the following official bulletin of Gen. Santa Anna, announcing his attack upon Tampico on the 20th of August, which agrees essentially with the particulars hitherto published.

"On the 19th of August, I arrived at my quarters in this village, when I learnt that the enemy had made some movements on Altamira. Notwithstanding the small number of my troops, I was determined to surprise the enemy in his quarters at Tampico Tamaulipas, in which he had left 600 men. I effectually crossed the river on the night of the 20th, in spite of the vigilance of the Spanish gun boats, with 400 regular troops and some militia, and advanced to the fort within gun shot, when the soldiers fired on the enemy, it being impossible to restrain their enthusiasm; and by this means destroyed my hopes of taking the castle by surprise. At this moment it was impossible to do any thing but advance; and at 2 o'clock in the morning I entered the village under a brisk fire of the enemy, which obliged him to destroy some of his positions, and to concentrate his forces into two fortified points, which was supported by the fire of a gun boat from the river.

"The firing lasted till two o'clock in the afternoon, when the enemy hoisted a flag of truce, requested to capitulate, and offered to deliver up his arms.

"We were formed when Gen. Barradas presented himself with his army, and notwithstanding the superiority of his force, I was disposed to resist, when he requested an interview, and begged me to repair to my general quarters, where we would enter into negotiations.

"My position at this moment was critical, and I retired with pride, bartering him a favor which necessity imperiously demanded; taking advantage, I marched out thro' the Spanish troops with flying colors and beat of drum.

"If Gen. Garza had attacked the enemy on his retrograde march from Altamira, the 21st of August would have been the last of the existence of the vanguard of the Spanish army; but it unfortunately did not occur.

"The loss of the enemy consisted of 82 men, in killed and wounded, and ours in 54 wounded and 17 killed.

"The advantages gained by this glorious day is incalculable, as it has taught the enemy how to appreciate Mexican valor. He has lost, and for ever, Altamira, and we have reduced him to the only point which he now occupies, and from which he cannot proceed without surrendering.

"The division which fought in this action, distinguished itself in an extraordinary manner; it was impossible to know whether the soldier, the officers or the chief displayed the most patriotism. All this I communicate to your excellency for your satisfaction.

"God and Liberty—Head Quarters at Pueblo Viejo of Tampico, August 24, 1829.

ANTONIO LOPEZ DE SANTA ANNA."

—*New Hampshire Gazette*, October 20, 1829

During the negotiations for the final surrender of the Spanish army, Santa Anna was certain to underscore that that surrender must be unconditional; otherwise a massacre of the besieged would ensue.

FROM MEXICO.

A Vera Cruz paper of September 26th, has been received by a house in New York, by way of Havana. It contains the correspondence between BARRADAS and SANTA ANNA previous to the capitulation, and the articles of the capitulation as already published. General ST. ANNA had arrived at Vera Cruz, where he was received and entertained with the highest honors.

Of the correspondence, which we have not time to give at length, the first is a letter from St. Anna to the Spanish General, dated Pueblo Viejo, Sept. 8th, in which he tells the latter, that he has ventured to come with a small band of adventurers to oppose eight millions of inhabitants who have sworn to die rather than be made slaves, and that if BARRADAS did not surrender in forty-eight hours all the forces in Tamaulipas, he would admit of no terms, and give no quarter.

To this BARRADAS replies, that having fulfilled the object of the King, and being desirous of saving the blood of both parties, he concludes to accept the proposals, and requests that persons may be appointed for this purpose; but that the communication between Tampico and La Bavra may be left uninterrupted.

ST. ANNA replies to this by saying that his orders are imperative, and that the demand must be unconditional, or he shall proceed to destroy them without exception; but that he has given orders to suspend hostilities until the forty-eight hours have elapsed.

BARRADAS rejoins, on the 9th, that it is not weakness, but the desire of saving life, that has induced him to open negotiations and to reply to the foregoing note, and he objects to having his soldiers, who have won so many battles, called slaves and adventurers.

ST. ANNA replies, there will be soon 20,000 Mexicans at his command, but that it was not because he was strong, and the others so weak, that he had given them these terms, but because invaders deserved nothing better, and that they have only to decide on the fate that awaits them. He concludes by saying, that the note of the date previous must be enforced, and the armistice must terminate at 8 o'clock the next morning.

The sixth letter is from Barradas in reply, in which he names the persons authorized to settle the capitulation, on the terms proposed by St. Anna.

We subjoin the proclamation of St. Anna, announcing the result of the invasion.

PROCLAMATION OF GEN. SANTA ANNA.
The General in Chief of the Army of operations to the Troops under his command.

COMPANIONS IN ARMS! The happy moment has at length arrived in which we desired to see the inveterate enemies of our country yielding and humiliated. Our country is free forever: thanks to your magnanimous exertions! Her independence has been firmly established: thanks to the constancy and valor you have exhibited. Your efforts have been great—my voice is not powerful enough to express my admiration. They are, it is true, the productions of that love of country which animates your hearts. For it, in the hour of battle, you showed a heroism most worthy of praise, and despising the enemies' forces, and their entrenchments, you advanced calmly on to claim the victory.

My Friends! What sacrifices you have made! How much blood has been shed by your comrades! But they have been necessary, that we may secure the important object that we proposed in honor of the Republic; the magnitude of the triumph also required it; the country is, this day, conqueror by herself alone; and will reap the fruit which you have sown with your blood. Finally, you have concluded the war. Future generations will bless you, the present will bear you the tenderest affection in their hearts.

Soldiers! In the name of the nation, and especially in my own, receive the most cordial and unreserved thanks; for all your ardent exertions, for the good order you have so strictly preserved, be assured that the Republic and the whole world will be deeply impressed with your prowess, and the civic virtues which distinguish you; by the former, you have made your enemies admire you; by the latter you have acquired days of glory and happiness for the country, which your friend and General will ever cherish in his memory.

Head Quarters, Pueblo Viejo, Sept. 12, 1829.
ANTONIO LOPEZ SANTA ANNA.
—*Daily National Intelligencer,*
November 9, 1829

Exhilarating as this victory was to Mexicans, the country remained politically tattered; by late 1829, its president, Vicente Guerrero, had been replaced by vice president Anastasio Bustamante. Both Guerrero and Bustamante had planted seeds of future turmoil in Texas; the former by announcing the emancipation of all slaves throughout Mexico—which the slave-owning Texians feared would ruin their economy, as well as being a challenge to their property rights—and the latter by approving passage of a law that would not only encourage more Mexican families to move into Texas to offset the burgeoning Anglo American population there, but that would also outlaw new immigration from the United States and create eight military garrisons to further "Mexicanize" the province. Additional colony laws included an order to deport all squatters; another would establish a customshouse at the Texan port of Anahuac.[2] Commanding the new Mexican garrison at Fort Anahuac—many of its soldiers convicts—was Colonel John ("Juan") Davis Bradburn, a Kentucky-born expatriate whose hardknuckles adherence to the letter of the Mexican law soon made him a villain to the Anglo Texians.

William Barrett Travis had moved to the town of Anahuac after leaving Alabama in 1831 and became part of a highly vocal anti-Bradburn faction, especially after some drunken *soldados* committed outrages on the town's civilians, including an attempted rape, in April 1832. A small riot ensued, followed by anonymous threats against the garrison three weeks later unless runaway slaves protected by Bradburn were released. At this, Bradburn ordered the arrests of three suspected ringleaders: two of them being Travis and his fellow lawyer, Patrick C. Jack.[3] All this was occurring during a time of violent civil strife in Mexico, when Santa Anna himself was waging military campaigns against the Centralist Bustamante administration.

From the New Orleans Patriot
DISTURBANCES IN TEXAS.—A gentleman who arrived in this city on Sunday evening last, overland from Anahuac, (the principal military station of Mexican troops in the province of Texas,) informs us that disturbances of rather a serious nature have recently occurred between the government troops stationed at that place, under the command of Col. Bradburn, and an organized party of disaffected citizens of that province.

It appears that three individuals charged with conspiracy against the government, had been arrested by Col. Bradburn and committed for trial before a martial court; whereupon the friends of the prisoners demanded of Col. B. that they should be given up to the civil authority, which requisition was refused.

On Sunday, the 10th June, a party of about 120 mounted men, armed with rifles, pistols and knives, arrived within seven miles of the town of Anahuac, when they halted and sent messengers to the garrison making the peremptory demand of three American prisoners, menacing an immediate attack in case of noncompliance, but Col. B. still refused to deliver them over. In consequence of which the party, about 3 or 4 o'clock in the evening entered the town; considerable firing took place during the night, but without effect. The next morning Col. B., by way of conciliation, proposed that if the invading party would remove to a designated point distant about five miles from the town, he would on the following day, at 10 o'clock, deliver the prisoners over to the civil authority, which terms were agreed to, and part of the invaders retired, though many still remained with their arms in consequence of which Col. B. considered the treaty broken on the part of the opposition, and not only refused to deliver up the prisoners, but marched into the town & dispersed those who had remained there, and took several prisoners.—On the day of the party's entering Anahuac some 10 or 15 individuals who were considered friendly to the person of the commandant, were seized and placed under guard, but were released upon the removal of the party. Our informant remained at Anahuac some 8 or 10 days after the retreat, and was informed that the revolting party had assembled again about seven miles from Anahuac, and had increased their force to between 3 and 400 men, that they had openly declared themselves hostile to the government and in favor of Santa Anna. He further states that Col. B. had sent to Natchitoches for a reinforcement of 200 men, which was daily expected. It was anticipated that the opposition party would endeavor to cut them off and in the event of their success they will no doubt afterwards storm the fort at Anahuac.

The troops of the garrison at Anahuac under the command of Col. Bradburn, are said to amount to about 300 effective men.

—*Brattleboro Messenger* (Vermont),
August 4, 1832

One party of armed Texians sailed down the Brazos River intent on capturing the Mexican fort at the port of Velasco.

TEXAS.—We have accounts which show, that 150 men from different parts of the colony, recently presented themselves in arms at Anahuac, demanded the release of the three prisoners, and obtained from Bradburn a promise that they should be delivered up if the colonists would withdraw to a certain distance. A few of the latter, however, who were afterwards seized in the town, were accused of violating their promise; and the prisoners were not released.

On the 27th of June the fort of Velasco, at the mouth of the Brassos, and fort Anahuac, on Galveston Bay, were attacked, and, after several hours fighting, taken, with the loss of several lives. The following is an account we copy from the Louisiana Advertiser.

"In consequence of these reasons, the fort of Anahuac on the Bay of Galveston, and the fort of Velasco, at the mouth of the Rio Brasses, on which the flourishing town of Brassoria is situated, were both closely invested. On the morning of the 27th June, before day light, the fort of Velasco was attacked by the American colonists under the command of Capt. John Austin,[a] with a force of 120 men, armed with rifles and pistols, and a small schooner fitted up hastily for the occasion with three six pound guns. The land forces advanced in two divisions to within thirty yards of the ditch, and commenced, in conjunction with the schooner, a heavy and well directed fire. The fort mounting one long brass 9 pounder and 90 men, was ably and well defended, but after a severe contest of four hours, surrendered with a heavy loss, that on the part of the assailants amounted to 5 killed and 18 wounded. By the articles of capitulation the prisoners are to be sent to Matamoras at their own expense.—Thus was secured the key to all the Southern possessions of Austin's colony.

"In the meantime the fort Anahuac was closely invested by a force of 300 American colonists. Here a negotiation again took place of the resort to force, and by a treaty entered into by the contending parties, it was stipulated 'that Col. Bradburn (who had been superseded in his command by a senior officer) should be tried by a military court. The imprisoned Americans enjoyed all the benefits of the civil laws, and the runaway negroes from the United States delivered to their owners.'

"A meeting of the inhabitants of the colony was then called to assemble in general convention at San Felipe, the seat of government, on Saturday, the 7th July, to deliberate on the existing state of the affairs of the colony, and to adopt such measures for future security as may be deemed expedient in the present emergency.

"It is supposed that one of the effects which may be produced by this convention will be to send a special messenger to the seat of the general government, the city of Mexico, to represent the erroneous policy of keeping armed troops among the inhabitants, which, from the nature of things, must ever be a fruitful source of collision; and pledging themselves and all that is dear to them, that they will support and protect the civil authorities of the republic, who may be sent among them, in the full discharge of all their constitutional duties."

—*Richmond Enquirer*, August 7, 1832

Four years before he wrote his famous letter from the Alamo "To The People of Texas & All Americans in the World," which was printed in numerous newspapers throughout the United States, Travis penned an account of his imprisonment by Bradburn and of related events. But this letter saw publication in

---

[a] Apparently a distant Connecticut-born relation of Stephen F. Austin.

only a few papers, and the writer was not identified by name.

TEXAS.

Extract of a letter from a gentleman in Texas to his friend in this City, dated July 8.

Dear Sir—Your letter dated New-Orleans, May 18, found me a prisoner in the Fort of Anahuac, and was opened by a Mexican officer attached to the Fort, before I was allowed permission to peruse it. It may be necessary that I should relate to you a detailed account of my imprisonment and the cause. On the 17th day of May last, myself, (a lawyer by profession) and another of the profession were arrested and thrown into the Fort, on the grounds of a supposition of our political opinions, and private ideas being contrary to the general government and disapproved of by the military commandant, Col. John D. Bradburn, at this place. We were in close confinement until the 2d of July, and were released by a glorious victory obtained over those tyrants, by the American settlers in this colony.—Shortly after our imprisonment, by great efforts, I succeeded in smuggling a letter, by means of my servant, to the colonists, to inform them of my imprisonment, and to appeal to them for redress, which shortly followed. 150 volunteers immediately marched to our relief, and took possession of the town of Anahuac, but not the Fort. On this occasion, Col. Bradburn entered into an arrangement with the colonists, to exchange us for 15 cavalry men, whom the Americans had made prisoners. On the ratification of the treaty the Mexican prisoners were delivered up to Bradburn; but immediately on obtaining them, he broke the treaty by refusing to set us at liberty. The colonists, inveterate at such conduct from a man whom they had always abhorred as an usurper, flew to arms, and to the number of 300, marched against him. By this time Bradburn had obtained reinforcements, and erected additional fortifications to withstand an encounter.

The colonists besieged him by sea and land, about the last of June, when Col. Piedras marched to his assistance with 150 regular troops and some militia, but found himself, before aware, in the power of the colonists. Commissioners were despatched by Col. Piedras to enter into a treaty with their captors, in which we were to be released, together with all our citizens prisoners, the government to pay for all property destroyed by their troops; Col. Bradburn who created these disturbances to be removed from office for his unconstitutional conduct,—all of which have been complied with. We were released honorably on the 2d inst. and on the same day the tyrant Bradburn was arrested. In addition to the 200 colonists who were engaged in the neighborhood, Capt. Austin of Brazoria, was on the march to this place with 250 men and 2 pieces of cannon; it was found necessary to bring the cannon by water through the mouth of the Brasos, at which place stands a fort of great strength. In passing it the schooner Brazoria, containing the cannon, was fired on by the fort, at which she dropped below and opened a heavy cannonade, but without effect as the walls were of great thickness; but the conquest over, it was achieved by the colonists on shore.

The country is now restored to tranquility and peace. The Americans have gained every thing which they claimed, and for which they assembled; the predominance of the civil authority, and the protection of their rights against a military usurpation, as tyrannical as it was unjust, illegal and unconstitutional. The Mexicans have been taught a lesson which they will not soon forget, that *Americans know their rights, and will assert and protect them;* and that constitutions, laws, and sacred guarantees, are not things to be broken and trampled under foot at the will and pleasure of every petty tyrant, who may be invested with a "brief authority." Having, as I before said, gained every thing for which we have contended; good order and obedience to the laws and constituted authorities, which would do honor to an older and organized country, reign in every point of the colonies—There is every prospect that this happy state of things will have a long and prosperous duration. The liveliest vision of hope, which the colonists of Texas have ever entertained, seems now about to be released. The odious law of the 6th of April, 1830, has been virtually repealed; grants of extensive portions of the country, which have been for a long time suspended, have been lately confirmed.

Every barrier to the colonization of the hardy, enterprising and venturous sons of North America, has been broken down and removed; the tide of emigration to this country from the United States will again act through its accustomed channels. The high and unequal tariff with which we have been for some time oppressed, and under which the country was drooping, will be suspended so far as it operates on Texas, for several years to come. The infamous Fisher, and the still more infamous Bradburn, have been removed from the office, and their places are filled by a single individual, of the highest integrity and honor, senor Don Juan Costina.[b] The season has been much better than common, and the most sanguine hopes of the farmer have been more than realized, by the finest crops of corn and cotton, that have been raised in this country since its first settlement. The crops of each of the abovementioned staples will be at least 100 per cent more than of any former year. In short, every inducement is now held out to the industrious emigrant from the north. Under the influence of a correct and impartial administration of the laws, Texas must shortly be one of the most flourishing spots upon the face of the globe, and be entitled to assume that high and important standing, for which nature evidently designed her.—*Louisiana Advertiser.*
—*Baltimore Gazette and Daily Advertiser*,
August 14, 1832

Coincidentally, another future Alamo commander had played an important role in the minirevolt of 1832, yet one whose name went equally unheralded in the newspapers, James Bowie. After Colonel José de la Piedras returned from a pacified Anahuac to his post at Nacogdoches, Americans in nearby communities began planning to attack him; after all, was he not, like Bradburn, a proponent of Bustamante's harsh anti-Anglo laws? On August 2, a skirmish erupted in the town square resulting in casualties on both sides.

That night Piedras withdrew his two hundred soldiers and began a westward retreat. But at the Angelina River, Bowie and twenty men opposed their crossing, wounding several of the Mexican cavalrymen.[c] The next day Piedras reluctantly directed a subaltern to treat for terms with Bowie, and the surrendered Mexican column was escorted back to Nacogdoches by the twenty-one Texians.[4]

Mexico had been too distracted by the bloodshed within its own immediate borders to pay much attention to these recent frays north of the Rio Grande, and not until December 1832, with the ousting of Bustamante, did civil hostilities end. Bustamante was replaced by Manuel Gómez Pedraza, who served as acting chief executive until Santa Anna was elected president in May 1833. Santa Anna assured the people that his ambition was "restricted to beating my sword into a ploughshare."

That April, Texian leaders, including a recently arrived Sam Houston, held a convention at which they decided to present a petition to the now supposedly liberal Mexican government. It would request the repeal of Bustamante administration laws that had, among other things, prohibited further immigration by Americans into Texas and had imposed high duties on much-needed imports. They also wanted to propose that Texas be allowed to sever its union with the state of Coahuila and become a separate state under the Mexican banner to achieve a more localized and efficient government. Because he had already personally dealt with officials in Mexico City, Austin was chosen as the logical delegate to deliver the petition.[5]

For Bowie, it soon proved a time of enormous emotional pain. His wife, Maria Ursula, along with a sibling and her parents (and possibly at least

---

[b] Lieutenant Juan Cortinas of the Anahuac garrison.

[c] This small ambush, along with some elements of the 1835 "Grass Fight," was recreated in the 1955 motion picture *The Last Command*, but it was moved ahead three years and set during the time the Texians were besieging General Martín Perfecto de Cos's army in San Antonio. It was also expanded into a small-scale battle with hand-to-hand combat and dozens of Mexicans falling and their ammunition wagon catching fire and blowing up. Oddly, in the film Bowie (played by Sterling Hayden), had twenty-five men and the Mexican detachment only one hundred, much better odds than the real Bowie had faced in 1832.

one child of the Bowies), all died of the "Asiatic cholera" in Monclova, Mexico, where they had ironically gone to escape the epidemic then plaguing Texas.[6]

It is stated as a remarkable fact, that of the deaths by cholera in Mexico four fifths were females.—Although the epidemic had been most fatal among the lower classes, many respectable inhabitants had been its victims. In the city of Mexico, eight members of Congress, two or three Judges of the Supreme Court, and the collector of the customs, had died.
—*Vermont Independent Inquirer*, November 2, 1833

By the first month of 1834, disheartening news arrived of how Austin had fared in Mexico.

From the New Orleans Bulletin. We deeply regret to learn that an adverse feeling towards Texas still prevailed in the Mexican government. It is not to be admitted as a state, and troops were to be marched thither to overawe the people. Col. Austin and the deputation had left the capitol in disgust.
—*Providence Patriot*, January 18, 1834

Then came worse news: during his return journey to Texas, Austin was arrested; a letter he had written to the predominantly Mexican town council of San Antonio, expressing his opinion that Texas should nevertheless declare itself independent from Coahuila, had been sent back to Mexico City, which infuriated Santa Anna and his administrators. From his Mexican prison cell, Austin wrote letters to Texians imploring them "not to be excited on account of my arrest, and strongly urged and begged they would be faithful to the Mexican republic."[7] He advised them to "remain quiet—populate the country—improve your farms—and discountenance all revolutionary men on principle." Yet he did envision Texas as one day separating entirely from Mexico, as "a gentle breeze shakes off a ripe peach. Can it be supposed that the violent political convulsions of Mexico will not shake off Texas as soon as it is ripe enough to fall?"[8] For the most part, Texas stayed calm, and relations with Mexico proved generally untroubled during his incarceration.

Far to the northeast, in New York City, and at the end of April 1834, Congressman David Crockett was just beginning a tour designed not only to bolster his reputation and political stance—thus enabling him to publicly rail against that "superannuated old man," Andrew Jackson—but also to promote his recently published and mostly autobiographical *A Narrative of the Life of David Crockett of the State of Tennessee.*

DAVID CROCKETT.

The Hon. David Crockett arrived in New York on the 30th ult. He was waited upon by a committee of Whigs who accompanied him to his lodgings at Congress Hall—where arrangements were made for him to see his friends. He is apparently about fifty years of age, middle sized, stoutly built, dark hair, rather sharp features, with an extremely pleasing cast of countenance, in which humour and eccentricity are strongly portrayed. He addressed a few sentences to those around him, which excited a great deal of laughter,—not so much by the matter of his observations, as the peculiarly droll manner in which he delivered them.

GENTLEMEN: I had no idea of addressing you; but as some important subjects have lately arisen under curious circumstances, I shall make a few observations to you. As to the Bank of the United States, the President believes that he has conquered "the monster;" and what will his next march be? He will make war upon the Senate for having done its duty; and the next thing he will do, will be to put his foot on it and tell them to go. It is, however, as enlightened a body as ever existed, and I hope the time will come when the people will be satisfied that that body has done its duty. Only one year back we had the best currency in the world; the farmer, the manufacturer, the tradesman, every one in short, was busily employed and received profits, but within the last seven months, how sadly are things altered! I speak from the allegations contained in petitions. You now see labourers going about offering to work for their victuals. And this is all to gratify the ambition of a superannuated old man. I don't believe that the currency can ever be restored to the state it was, for we have lost confidence in each other, and every thing like confidence is at an end.

—*The Portsmouth Journal and Rockingham Gazette* (New Hampshire), May 10, 1834

A week later, Crockett was in Boston, savoring an equally appreciative reception.

DAVID CROCKETT. This celebrated Western Tennessee member of Congress, was in Boston last week, and a supper was given to him at Gallegher's by a party of young men. The Transcript says—

On the removal of the cloth, "the Twelfth Congressional District of Tennessee" having been proposed as a toast, Col. Crockett rose and addressed the company in a very happy speech of nearly half an hour's duration—in which he expressed his gratitude for the unexpected honors which had been paid him—referred to the prominent events of his political life—spoke of the conduct of the present administration in terms of decided disapprobation—thanked the company for the honor they had done him, in plain, honest, and simple expressions, and sat down amidst bursts of reiterated applause.

Colonel Crockett is an uncommonly fine looking man, to use the current Yankee phraseology. His face has an exceedingly amiable expression, and his features are prominent and striking. He wears his hair, which is black, (with a light shade of brown) parted from the centre line of his head, combed back from his temples, and ending in a slight natural curl at the neck—not unlike the simple manner of many of the clergy. The stories that have been told of him are ridiculous and wanton exaggerations. He is an entirely different man in appearance, conversation, and address, from the familiar image of "Davy Crockett," of which, as the ideal representation of the Colonel, every one flatters himself he has a perfection conception.

There are very few persons, who have as little reputation for eloquence as Mr. Crockett, who could have made a better speech, than was made by him at Gallegher's last evening. His language was chaste and pure, and his manner calm, subdued, and fascinating. We acknowledge, for ourself, that we have been much mistaken in our apprehension of his personal appearance, and general intelligence; and in so saying, we believe we can express the opinion of all his young friends, who supped with him last night.

—*American Advocate* (Maine), May 14, 1834

By early July, Crockett was boarding the steamboat *Hunter* at Pittsburgh, following his busy and eventful "Tour to the North and Down East." He was going home to Tennessee to visit family and friends for several months while Congress was in recess. Inevitably, the voyage ahead of him—two weeks of traveling down the Ohio River and a section of the Mississippi River—would provide him with additional opportunities for self-promotion, telling stories, and engaging in the humor-laden political discourse in which he so delighted. He swapped yarns with Captain Stone and his crew and gave speeches to the applauding citizens of the stopover ports of Wheeling, Cincinnati, and Louisville. *The Cincinnati Mirror and Western Gazette of Literature and Science* of February 21, 1835, included an article that touched upon the Ohio leg of Crockett's journey.[9] The writer recorded his impressions of Crockett in a rare and unusually descriptive pen portrait, which reveals that on occasion when Crockett was in more familiar frontier surroundings, he was not adverse to dressing like a frontiersman.

This was col. Crockett . . . he was about six feet high—stoutly built—his hands and feet were particularly small for a man of his appearance and character. . . . His complexion was swarthy; his cheek bones high; his nose large, and designed to favor as an Indian's. His hair was long, dark, and curly-looking rather uncombed than carefully attended to. His pantaloons, which were fashionably cut, developed an extremely handsome limb, and his loose calico hunting shirt, ruffled around collar, cape, cuffs, and skirt, full and flowing, set off his person as the rough and untutored woodsman, to peculiar advantage.

—*Cincinnati Mirror and Western Gazette of Literature and Science*, February 21, 1835[10]

In early 1835, in San Felipe, Texas, William Barrett Travis took advantage of the calmer state of affairs in the province to concentrate on his law practice and engage in a partnership.

Law—

W. BARRET TRAVIS & WILLIS NIBB, have united in the practice of law. They will attend to any business entrusted to their care, in the jurisdiction of Austin and Columbia.

—*Texas Republican*, February 14, 1835

In Mexico, the fires of the next big "political convulsion" had been lit when Santa Anna decided to let his vice president, Valentín Gómez Farias, essentially run the country while he, the Hero of Tampico, retreated to his Veracruz hacienda. Under Farias, the radical liberals ran rampant, attacking church privileges, secularizing education, and reducing the size of the regular army. In April 1834 Santa Anna, reacting to the outcry of conservatives and the largely religious populace, exiled Farias and overturned the radical laws of the past year. Ignoring the Constitution of 1824, which was loosely patterned after the US Constitution and allowed Mexican states a certain amount of autonomy, he stripped state civic militias of their power and ordered the establishment of a professional regular army.[11] These changes kindled shock, outrage, dissent, and, in many quarters, violent opposition.

REVOLUTION IN MEXICO.—The ship Congress 18 days from Vera Cruz, reports that a revolution had broken out, & four States had already pronounced the measures of Santa Anna illegal, and declared in favor of the Vice President, Don Gomez Farias. The President left his farm near Vera Cruz, on the 6th April, for the capital, where great excitement prevailed. A bloody war was expected.

—*Vermont Phoenix*, May 1, 1835

Meanwhile, Texas continued to flourish in many respects; more Americans continued to settle in the province, many of them drawn there by glowing newspaper accounts of its fertile lands, such as this extraordinarily detailed one, which covered everything from ecology to the Comanches' buffalo hunting methods to transportation.

TEXAS.

[General Wavel,[d] an English officer, whose account of Texas is contained in the appendix to Ward's Mexico, gives the following interesting description of that fine country:

"Texas contains about one hundred and sixty millions of English acres. In the northern part, the climate differs but very little from that of the south of Europe, of Buenos Ayres, and the Cape of Good Hope. To the south the white settlers from the United States experience no ill effects from exposure to the sun. Few countries possess so large a proportion of rich land, or are so capable of supporting a dense population.

"The coast is low, and during the rainy season, it becomes unhealthy. It is skirted by a number of islands, separated from the main land by narrow straits. The most considerable of these is San Luis or Galveston, the easternmost point of which shelters the harbor of that name.

"The bay of Espiritu Santo is the next harbor of importance; and this, from the numerous shoals, cannot be frequented by vessels drawing more than eight or ten feet of water.

"The anchorage is generally good, and as the water shoals gradually, vessels approaching the coast may be guided entirely by the lead.

"Few countries are better supplied with navigable rivers, streams and rivulets, than Texas. The rivers, at a short distance from their mouths, are generally narrow, deep and clear, with a moderate rapid stream.

"They abound in fish, to which the North American settlers have given the English names, trout, carp, tench, &c. although what I saw differed widely from the fish of the same name in Europe.

"Steamboats run from New Orleans to Natchitoches, 300 miles above the junction of the two rivers, once or twice weekly; except during the autumn, when a chain of rocks prevents their passing higher than Alexander, 120 miles lower down. About 150 miles above Natchitoches, is the Great Raft, i.e., an accumulation of drift timber, which for many miles

---

[d] Arthur Goodall Wavell.

forms one connected mass all across the bed of the river, and obstructs the navigation except when the water is very high. Keel boats already proceed some hundreds of miles above the raft; and there appears to be no doubt, that, when this obstacle is removed, the river will be navigable to a very considerable distance; indeed, it is generally believed, almost as far as New Mexico. The government of the United States directed captain Birch, together with another officer, to examine accurately the Great Raft, and to ascertain the possibility of removing or avoiding it.

"From their report, it appears that by merely cutting a canal at an estimated expense of 30 or 40,000 dollars, boats may pass through the Caddo, a chain of smaller lakes, not only avoiding the raft, but also a distance of 100 miles. The object which the government of the United States had in view, was to open a channel for communication with New Mexico, and for the Indian traffic.

"Some branches of this trade have already proved very lucrative; for, in addition to small quantities of precious metals, copper, wool, and very valuable hides, and peltries, have been obtained, in exchange for articles of little value. The Indians require but few things; beads, small looking-glasses, common guns and rifles, a kind of baize, red and blue, called by the North-Americans, strouding; knives, awls, vermillion and ammunition.

"Of spirits they are passionately fond, and will make any sacrifice to obtain them; but to supply them with these, which act almost as a poison, and have not unfrequently given rise to assassinations and other atrocities, is prohibited by law. The hides and skins, and peltries obtainable, are those of the buffalo, horned cattle, horse, panther, leopard, bear, deer, antelope, raccoon, black fox, muskrat, and beaver; and they are of the best quality.

"The Nueces, Trinidad, and San Antonio, are fine streams, and in size about equal to the Sabine, which forms the boundary. The Navasota, Angelina, and Neches, San Jacinto and Arroyo de Cedros, are navigable to a great extent, except at certain periods; and the

Arroyo de la Vaca, (or Lorilaco river), which runs but a short distance into the interior, has, it is stated, nine feet water upon its bar. The rivulets and inner streams are innumerable. As in Devonshire, almost every valley has its stream or brook; and judging from the small fish which I observed in them, I should conceive the greater number to be perennial. The low lands, which extend along the coast, are admirably adapted to the cultivation of rice. In some parts, sugar, and in other parts cotton, may be produced similar to that of the Sea Islands. The central part of Texas is prairie, nearly level, and abounding with a most luxuriant vegetation; the banks of the rivers being lined with timber or skirted by ground gently undulating, and covered with trees. Here the depth of rich alluvial soil is very considerable; and cotton, wheat, barley, rye, Indian corn, indeed every production, both of more temperate climates and of Europe, is raised in equal abundance and perfection. The prairies, in their natural state, afford a constant supply of excellent pasture.

"The valley of the Red River is stated by the numerous North American settlers, to contain some millions of acres, exceeding in fertility even the celebrated Mississippi bottom, the valley of the Roanoke, or indeed, any lands to be found in the United States. They have styled it the "Garden of the West," and the cotton which it already produces, far excels the Alabama, Tennessee, or indeed any, excepting that of the Sea Islands. I here ought to remark, that growing cotton possesses one great advantage.— Children, so young as to be unable to engage in any other occupation, can be employed in picking cotton, and at the age of nine or ten, probably do as much as grown up persons. Every species of grain thrives admirably in this fertile tract, and it is thought that the ribbed sugar cane, lately introduced from the Phillippines, and which arrives at maturity a month sooner than the common sort, would answer well there. In the vallies is found the red, or pencil cedar of the largest growth, also a great quantity of the Bois d'arc, of which the Indians make their bows. It is of a beautiful yellow color, susceptible of the highest polish, not heavy, but exceedingly tough and elastic. In addition to these, trees of all varieties which flourish in the United States are to be met with—white, red, dwarf, or scrub, and post oaks (of the former of which staves are made; while the latter is so strong, hard and tough, that it is frequently employed in lieu of iron to make the screws of cotton presses); together with iron-wood, hickory, and many other woods admirably adapted for the lathe. The sugar maple is also very valuable. An auger hole being bored in its trunk, in the spring of the year, a small spout is inserted, and the liquor, which is subsequently evaporated to a consistency, is caught in a vessel.

"A single tree has been known to yield one hundred and fifty pounds of sugar; the average daily produce being from three to four or six pounds. I found its flavor very pleasant, but do not think it is nearly so sweet as the common sugar.

"Humboldt's prediction, that carriages would pass from Washington to the city of Mexico, has been verified.

"North Americans have, in their convenient and light Dearborn or Jersey wagons, repeatedly passed into the interior of Mexico from the United States. Roads are very easily made through Texas, as the country is either flat or gently undulating.

"To clear away the wood costs little trouble; and although the rivers are numerous, being generally narrow and deep, they oppose no obstacles but such as can be easily surmounted.

"That fact that Mr. Couci, an enterprising Frenchman, with about forty others, nearly all his countrymen, passed through Texas with several large wagons laden with goods, in June, 1826, is the best proof of the facility with which every difficulty, such as those which are usually met with in a new country, is here overcome. The Dearborn or Jersey wagon, just mentioned, is admirably calculated to journey through countries where rivers or other natural impediments may render it necessary that each part be speedily reduced to a small size or weight, so as to be rendered portable, and taken to pieces with the greatest ease, and a raft formed of a few trunks, or the larger branches of trees,

which suffice to convey it across the rivers, or the whole is progressively passed by hand over any other obstacle.

"Those who have settled in Texas a few months, really enjoy more comforts (and these, in addition to the opportunity of realizing a handsome property) than any peasantry with which I am now acquainted. One act of liberality and hospitality, which is constantly practised by all his neighbors towards a new comer, whose character is found unexceptionable, would do honor to the most civilized people. They all assemble at the spot which he has fixed upon for his residence, with their axes and draught oxen, fell the timber, and build for him his log-house. This generally consists of three apartments, one for sleeping, another for eating, both closed in all around, while in the centre, which is left open on both sides, he keeps his saddles and tools, and takes his meals during the hot weather.

"The kitchen (also a log hut) is usually separated from the house, and so is also the smoke-house, where the meat is smoked and kept.

"The log-house is by no means an inconvenient residence; indeed, some of them are roomy, neat and durable, very strong, and well calculated to afford protection from every inclemency of the weather.

"The wild animals to be met with in Texas are the buffalo, or the bison, known in this country as the bonassus, which enters Texas from the north in vast herds during the winter; the panther, leopard, bear, otter, beaver, antelope, deer, raccoon, black fox., &c. Turkies abound; there are two species of the partridge; swans often arrive in great numbers, together with immense flocks of wild ducks and geese. The flesh of the buffalo, especially its humps, is excellent, and generally prized far above beef; the bear's ham is also considered a great delicacy.

"By far the most interesting animal is the wild horse from Barbary, which the Arab transplanted into Spain, passing from thence to the New World, and being turned loose by the first European settlers, it has peopled the rich plains of Texas with droves innumerable. The mustang, or wild horse, is not often large or heavy, but shows blood; it is well made, hardy, active, and if caught young, very docile, although whenever an opportunity offers, it is apt to rejoin its wild brethren. The piebald, light brown, chestnut, and dun colors prevail.

"Their defect is the tenderness of the hoof, which is too frequently to be met with amongst them, as they are bred on soft ground; whereas, throughout Mexico, those which are reared on a hard rocky soil, have a solidity of hoof which renders shoes unnecessary even to the fore feet; the hind feet are seldom shod. The mode of catching them is similar to that by which wild elephants are caught in India.

"A space sufficiently large to contain a drove is enclosed with stakes, trunks, and branches of trees; the entrance is narrow, but gradually widens outwards, and a herd is driven, or decoyed into it by a horse trained for the purpose. I have seen instances of attachment, on the part of a young colt thus caught, to a careful master, far stronger than I before witnessed in a horse.

"The country of the Camanches is the mountainous district of San Saba, which they cross both in the spring and autumn, and where they deposite their families occasionally during their long expeditions. These Indians generally kill the buffalo with their bow and arrow, their horses being trained to carry them close to it, and on its right side. Sometimes they pursue and, with a sharp iron (crescent shaped) passing its left flank, sever the ham string of the right leg, when the animal falls away from the horse; they sometimes almost shoot it with the rifle. The scent of the buffalo is, however, so acute, that it can be only approached from the leeward side: it is timid till wounded, but then its impetuosity is irresistible, and its attacks are repeated until it falls. Being both active, and from its vast bulk very powerful, the charge of an old bull is described as tremendous. The long shaggy hair which covers its head and breast, gives it a terrific appearance, and it rushes headlong at whatever it perceives (after the smoke of the rifle) blowing and snorting with astonishing loudness.

"Should it discover and throw down its antagonist, it gores, and tramples upon him until (if desperately wounded) it falls dead by his side. The horns of the buffalo are short, but very sharp pointed, although thick at the base. Being very hard and black, they are highly prized for cups and other purposes. Its flesh when fat is excellent, especially the hump; the skins, covered with an excessively thick hair, nearly approaching to wool, are much used in the northern parts of the United States, more especially as a wrapper upon travelling in the sledges or sleighs over the ice and snow. The Indians give a softness and pliability to these skins greater than that of the buck or even doe-skin of Europe. The following is, I believe, the process adopted. After tanning with sumac and bark, the skin is stretched over a hole in the earth and smoked; the brains of the animal and alum are also rubbed into it. It is subsequently painted in cheques, diamonds, and similar figures, the colors being very durable.

"The first person who took effectual measures to carry into effect extensive schemes of colonization in Texas on their own private account, was Mr. Austin, an inhabitant of Louisiana; and after he had traversed this vast country near the coast, he fixed upon the spot between the rivers Brazos and Colorado, where he obtained a very extensive grant from the Spanish government.—Embarrassments, owing to the failure of a large proportion of the banks of the Western States, together with the revolution, prevented his reaping the fruits of his exertions.

"His eldest son, Stephen Fuller Austin, succeeded to the claims, and to the indefatigable and enterprising spirit of his father, who died about the year 1820 or '21. In 1823, he obtained from the first Independent Congress the recognition of the grant; and through inundations, which there were no reasons to anticipate, have twice done serious injury to the infant colony, he has the merit of having succeeded in peopling a wilderness, and providing a number of industrious families with an ample subsistence, as well as with the means of acquiring not only comforts, but wealth.

"The only persons who have examined the country, or indeed, it may almost be said, have visited it, except momentarily, are settlers from the United States. So very considerable a portion of the population of the adjacent districts has flowed into Texas from the United States, that there are now at least ten times as many inhabitants as there were only four years ago. Indeed, from the neighboring territory (Arkansas) alone, as one of its most respectable land proprietors assured me, 10,000 out of 46,000 persons have quitted it in order to establish themselves there. Along a very considerable part of the road that leads from Natchitoches to San Antonio de Bezar, better lodging and provisions are obtained, in greater abundance, and at a lower price, than on many of the principal roads in Spain. The hospitality of all is most meritorious, and the usual price of each meal (which consists almost invariably of pork, eggs, bacon, butter, maize cakes, hot coffee, and sometimes venison and other meats,) is only one shilling. This country might easily absorb all of the surplus population of Great Britain, a nucleus being formed by the settlement of about one hundred industrious agriculturalists, who, after the first year, might supply grain for at least ten times their number. Cattle, and more especially pigs, will increase most rapidly, almost without any care or trouble, in the woods. Thus each successive year would, by affording increased sustenance, allow the number of settlers to be tripled, to say the least.

"Nature has evidently given to Texas commercial advantages, which she has denied to almost every other part of Mexico; indeed, few countries, if any one, are more favorably situated for carrying on an extensive and lucrative foreign and domestic traffic.

"The principal export doubtless will be cotton, which grows in the greatest abundance, and is in quality inferior only to that of the Sea Islands. As the capital employed in raising it is very inconsiderable, the Texas colonist will be able to undersell every competitor in foreign markets. His healthy lands, cultivated by free and cheap labor, cost him comparatively nothing: whilst the North American and West Indian require an interest on a large sum employed in the purchase of property and slaves, subject to many contingencies.

"Pot and pearl ashes will be obtained in clearing the lands.

"Texas will supply the West Indian Islands with timber, salted provisions, flower, and whatever else they now require from the United States, at least equal in quality, and at a lower price, than they can be obtained from thence. Mules and horses will also be exported to Cuba and the Antilles.—The southern parts of the United States are already supplied from thence, and Coahuila, with both; but more especially the former, which are sometimes embarked at the Brazos de Santiago, close to the mouth of the river Bravo del Norte, but more generally conveyed by land. It is thought that Texas may prove well suited for the growth of the merino wool, both on account of the climate, and the extent of uncultivated land, over which they may be allowed to graze at liberty. The North Americans have exported wool from Coahuila, but I have been informed, that although the staple is long, it is by no means fine, and there is a burr in it which it requires much trouble to extract. The latter disadvantage will not be met with in Texas, except possibly among the mountains of San Saba, for I have observed throughout Mexico, that wherever the land is arid, burrs and thorny plants of every description abound; although wherever water is abundant, they are scarcely to be found.

"Swamps, stagnant water, and a rank vegetation, together with the disorders arising marsh-miasmata, render a large proportion of the southern parts of the United States little better than a sickly desert. A circumstance that I have nowhere else observed increases the inundations, which are the real causes of these evils, to a very great extent. The ground is so level, that not only do the more considerable rivers overflow, but by their reflux into the smaller tributary streams, produce the same effect on both sides to a very considerable distance. This I remarked more particularly when ascending the Red River. A current from the Mississippi ran up it, not much less than one hundred miles. Nearly all the rivers of Texas, on the other hand, are "encaisses," and except near their mouths, seldom, if ever, produce inundations prejudicial

to either property or health. Nevertheless, during the rainy season, there is a sufficient rise in the rivers of Texas to render even the smaller branches navigable, and afford opportunities of conveying the produce of the interior by water carriage to the coast."
—*Commercial Bulletin and Missouri Literary Register*, June 15, 1835

Although Texas would soon bubble again with cries for revolt, in Zacatecas, the Mexican state immediately south of Coahuila, blood was already being spilled in renewed civil fighting. It was a conflict sparked because Santa Anna's order decreeing that Zacatecas's powerful militia force be reduced in size had been ignored, and as a punishment, he marched an army north in the spring of 1835 intent on crushing all who would dare defy his authority.

INTERESTING FROM MEXICO.
SEVERE BATTLE AND VICTORY
OF SANTA ANNA.

On the 11th May early in the morning Santa Anna attacked in several directions, with a force of 3400 men, the position of Don Francisco Garcia, the revolutionary chief, who was at the head of 5000 men, with a large train of artillery. After an obstinately contested battle, which lasted two hours, Santa Anna gained a signal victory, killing and wounding hundreds, and taking many prisoners. The loss on his side was one hundred in killed and wounded. He states in his official report that the field of battle offered a frightful and heart rending spectacle. He has completely destroyed the hopes of the enemies of the present government. Their cannon, small arms and ammunition, are all in the power of Santa Anna. The battle took place on the plains of Guadaloupe near Zacatecas, in which latter place Santa Anna has established his headquarters.

Gen. Parres has been sent with 500 cavalry in pursuit of those of the enemy who escaped.

It is stated by Captain Cunningham, that a law is now before the congress of Mexico the object of which is to prohibit the introduction of American (*Mentz*) cotton. It is rumored that it would probably pass.

Another law is in discussion to exempt from an postage or duty foreign as well as domestic periodicals.

El Diario states that Colonel Butler, who was charged with negotiations from the United States of America to the Mexican Government, was preparing to set off on his return, having obtained a temporary leave of absence to that effect. It further says that the relations of friendship between the two countries were well maintained by this functionary, and that his conciliatory manners and open communications with the secretary and the chiefs of the executive, as well as his personal qualities, had rendered him extremely popular; therefore, concludes by wishing him a prosperous voyage, but above all, his speedy return.

The following is Santa Anna's official account of this battle:—

HEAD QUARTERS, Zacatecas.

I have to inform his excellency the minister of war, and of the marine that yesterday the 11th May, at 9 A.M. the troops of the general government of the union obtained a splendid triumph over the forces commanded by Don Francisco Garcia, exceeding 5000 men; and pressing a grand train of artillery. Two hours of a very bloody action on the plains of Guadaloupe sufficed to secure us a victory that our enemies had hoped to obtain by their warlike appearance; and the manouvres they performed on the field where they had the hardihood yesterday morning to establish their camp. At 5 o'clock, I attacked them at various points not having with me more than 3,400 men of all the troops composing my army of operations; and although I could have procured a greater number of troops, yet I chose to offer battle with those I met at Aguascalientes, that my operation might not be delayed. All has fallen into my power: cannons, arms, artillery, and about 800 prisoners. The field of battle presented a most dreadful spectacle. On our side there were about 100 men killed and wounded. Torrents of blood flowed by the caprice of Don Francisco Garcia, and the other guilty chiefs—who blind and obstinate refused to comply with the proposals that I had made them at the same time that they uttered the contained printed document, and the gross reply (annexed) that they made me. Soon as this triumph was obtained, I marched rapidly without losing a moment to try to seize immediately all the fortifications, magazines and depots; and as many prisoners as possible of those who were prepared to offer no resistance: and I have taken possession of the whole city.

His excellency general Parres, at the head of 500 cavaliers, will continue this afternoon his march on Frenile and Sombrerete. I am desirous of giving you a detailed account of all my operations, and I shall also give you more minute details of the affair of this day, when I shall have more leisure. The generals, officers and all the troops under my command have performed their duties; and all merit the highest praise.

I can now do no more than congratulate the government on a triumph which must consolidate the peace and welfare of the republic, and express my regret for the loss of those Mexicans, who had been sacrificed in the defence of the sacred cause of their country, but the chiefs, the prime movers in this unjust rebellion, must render an account to God and the nation for the evils they have occasioned.

Please sir, inform his Excellency the president *pro tem* of all, for his own satisfaction, and accept the assurance of my perfect respect.

God and liberty! Head Quarters, Zacatecas, 12th of May, 1835.

ANTONIO LOPEZ DE SANTA ANNA.

P. S.—Since the above was written, I have made 2,700 prisoners of the enemy.

A. L. DE SANTA ANNA.

I submit the above for your knowledge and satisfaction—and I request you meantime to give the greatest possible publicity to the news—that these who regard the good order and prosperity of the nation may rejoice with us in a triumph which must contribute powerfully to maintain that order and prosperity: that the anarchists may learn their feeble power, and that the republic has to fear nothing from their destructive projects.

—*Baltimore Gazette and Daily Advertiser*, June 16, 1835

It was a victory tainted by more than "torrents of blood," as related in this account of the looting and rapine that followed the fighting.

The Atrocities of Santa Anna.

A correspondent of the Courier & Enquirer writes from Vera Cruz, under date of the 22d ult:—

The excesses committed by the victor Santa Anna and his troops in Zacatecas and vicinity, are without parallel in the history of civilized nations. It appears that all strangers were exposed to their diabolical rage; the only American in the place was basely assassinated in presence of his wife, who was afterwards stabbed to the heart, stripped of her clothing and thrown exposed into the street. The English Minister has made a peremptory demand for indemnity to his majesty's subjects for the injuries done to their property, which they will doubtless obtain. We have no Minister at this Court to make a similar demand for the injuries done our citizens, and if made by our late Charge des Affaires, it would doubtless be unavailing, as in all previous ones. The impropriety with which the authorities of this country have outraged both the persons and property of our citizens, renders them peculiarly obnoxious to future abuse from the authorities during their civil commotions, of which the country has been abundantly prolific for the last ten years.

—*Philadelphia Inquirer*, July 16, 1835

Santa Anna also ordered the fort at Anahuac to be reoccupied by a Mexican garrison and that the collection of import duties be reimposed there to prevent any more revenue being lost in the extensive contraband trade. Once again tensions flared between the town's citizens and the soldados, and two Anglos were arrested in a customs-related incident. This time, in late June, Travis led the rescuing force of twenty-five armed men and a six-pound cannon "mounted on a pair of sawmill truck wheels."[12]

TEXAS.

The New Orleans Bulletin of the 18th ult. has the following notice of the movements in Texas:

"Capt. Moore, of the schooner Shenandoah, in a short run from Brazoria, reports that the Texonians had seized upon the fort of Anahuac, garrisoned by one hundred men, whom they captured, and sent to San Felipe. A portion of the people thought this step was pushing matters to extremities, and one that was uncalled for, but all were determined to maintain their just rights, should they be assailed by Mexican powers."

The following are additional particulars—

"The people of Anahuac, on the 7th inst. rose upon the Mexican soldiers, quartered in that place, and captured their fort, which was no sooner done, than they offered to desert Santa Anna, and join the Texonians, but instead of receiving them the people drove them far into the prairies, towards Nacogdoches—and also reports that the people on the Brassos river were organizing a military force to proceed immediately to the defence of the town of San Antonio. Great excitement prevailed among all classes of the inhabitants.

—*New London Gazette*, August 12, 1835

Many "Texonians," however, condemned Travis's bold seizure of the fort at Anahuac. The criticisms grew so sharp that he felt it necessary to post an ad in the *Texas Republican*.

W. Barrett Travis requests a suspension of public opinion in regard to the Capture of the Fort of Anahuac, until he can appear before the public with all the facts and circumstances attending the Capture of that Fort.

—*Texas Republican*, July 18, 1835

Although Travis did write an account explaining the reasons for his actions, it never saw publication. But he had his supporters; Texas war party proclamations issued at San Felipe on June 21 and 22 called for armed opposition to the Mexican force that General Cos declared was on its way to garrison the province.[13] Cos replied to such clamors by sending copies of a letter to the three political chiefs of Texas, and it was published in the *Texas Republican* of August 22, 1835. In it he cautioned that "some badly disposed persons have been able to induce the belief that the Mexican Government has no right to send its troops to those places where they think it necessary." He advised the disgruntled "inhabitants" to take legal, not martial steps, to express their objections.[14] But news—and rumors—of war party plans had already spread far and wide.

Alexandria, La., August 6. We were informed by a gentleman a few days ago, direct from Texas, that James Bowie, formerly of this place, ex-Governor Houston, and the notorious, if not celebrated, Robert Potter, are organizing the militia of Texas to oppose the Mexican troops. Present appearances seem to favor the notion that the citizens of Texas will have to do some fighting or continue to suffer many of their grievances.

—*Arkansas Gazette*, September 1, 1835

In a carefully worded letter, Houston attempted to deny that any violent resistance was in the works.

The following is a copy of a letter from ex-Governor Houston, to the editor of the Red River Herald. It will be perceived by reference to it that the reports which have reached this place, of a probable disturbance between Texas and the Government of Mexico, were entirely unfounded—and he strenuously denies ever having been concerned in organizing the troops of Texas.

NACOGDOCHES, TEXAS
Aug. 15, 1835.

Sir:—An article published in the "Planter's Intelligencer," printed at Alexandria on the 5th inst. has just met my notice. The newspaper is published by R. SMITH. The first *initial* may be *significant*, for aught I know of the individual. I should not notice articles of this character, if they only alluded to me personally, but as they refer to the country of my adoption, I deem it proper to contradict such unfounded rumors as, if believed, are calculated to produce, in the interior of Mexico, an excitement against the citizens of Texas. The article to which I allude says, that "We were informed a few days ago by a gentleman direct from Texas, that James

Bowie, formerly of this place, ex-Governor Houston, and the notorious if not celebrated Robert Potter, are organizing the militia of Texas to oppose the troops of Mexico." &c. Some *individual* from Texas may have made the above statement, but I aver that no *gentleman* could have done so, for the reason that it is not true in fact!! Intelligence and veracity constitute the first attributes of a gentleman, and if this individual made the statements on his own authority, he either did not understand the matters of which he spoke, or understanding, he chose to misrepresent them!! Col. Bowie and Col. Potter are so capable of attending to their own matters, that I will refer them to their own notions of adjustment. It is true that Col. Bowie came from the Brazos to Nacogdoches, for the avowed purpose of raising men to unite with him and march in pursuit of some hostile Indians, who had been depredating on the frontier of Austin Colony. He marched a few days since with a small detachment, and expected to be joined by the young warriors of some friendly tribes of Indians.

This is the only true intelligence which could have reached R. Smith. No recent excitement has induced the organization of the militia of Texas. As early as last spring, an order was received by the Political Chief from the Supreme Executive of Coahuila and Texas, directing him, and, through him, the subordinate authorities, forthwith to organize the Civic militia of the Department of Nacogdoches, which embraces all the country laying between the Trinity and Sabine rivers. Owing to various causes, and, among others, the changes daily occurring in the interior, prevented the organization being completed. But so far as it has progressed it has been by authorities of the country and not by individuals.

The situation of Texas has been peculiar, though, at this moment, I think her *tranquil*, and it is to be hoped we shall have no difficulty. The number of Federal troops within the limits of Texas (proper,) does not, I presume, exceed 500 men, rank and file; and these troops are stationed exclusively within the Mexican population.

It is impossible to conceive any plausible pretext for the *invasion* of Texas by Federal troops, inasmuch as her citizens have maintained, at all times, their integrity to the laws and Constitution of the Republic!!!

It has been, to some extent, unfortunate for Texas, that individuals have passed through her territory, and on their return to the United States, have, from ignorance of other causes, misrepresented the feelings and disposition of her citizens. These things have induced speculations upon the *present and future political relations of Texas*—when expressed in the newspapers of the day, were well calculated to embarrass the true interests of the people of Texas, if accredited by the Supreme Government of Mexico, and on its part induced suspicion and vigilance towards the North American population in Texas.

I am, with great respect,
   Your obedient servant,
        SAM. HOUSTON.
To the Editor of the Red River Herald.
   —*Arkansas Advocate*, September 25, 1835

In early September, Stephen F. Austin, at last released from his incarceration and subsequent detention in Mexico, returned to Texas and allied his voice with those who also espoused that the rights of "Texans" should not be trampled upon. Yet he did not call for armed revolt until word arrived that General Cos had landed at Copano near Refugio with some four hundred troops in mid-September. By that time, New York and other East Coast cities were already receiving news of the sparks flying around the Texas tinderbox, the indecision of much of its populace, and the Indian troubles mentioned by Houston.

The settlers, however have had to encounter difficulties of a formidable character, arising from the hostile incursions of the Indians into the settlements, who have stolen and carried off many horses and cattle, and murdered a number of travellers. These inroads had compelled the inhabitants to arm and embody for the purpose of punishing the unprovoked savage aggressors. But before an expeditionary force could be sent against them, intelligence arrived, that the American born members of the Legislative bodies of Coahuila and Texas, together with the governor, had been imprisoned by the military, and that that functionary with several citizens of Texas, were in close confinement.

It is also announced that Santa Anna contemplated sending a powerful military force into Texas, to coerce the citizens into compliance with his wishes, to make himself Dictator, on pain of expulsion from the country. This news threw the colonists into commotion at once, and while some were for marching immediately to San Antonio to seize the depot of artillery and small arms and ammunition there, others considered it too hasty a measure and a plausible excuse for Santa Anna to act.

Every man capable of bearing arms was however enrolled as a necessary measure of precaution. Officers were chosen to command them, and blockhouses and other places of strength were erected for the safety of the women and children, and for the repulsion of the invaders, should any arrive. A great excitement was got up, meetings of the citizens in favor of warlike measures were held, and handbills issued of a corresponding character.

Others, however, were for submission to Santa Anna for the sake of peace, and all orderly government being suspended, discord and anarchy reigned among the people, who without any concert, knew not how to act. Col. Austin was daily expected in the province, when it was believed measures would be adopted calculated to quiet the apprehensions of the people, and restore the chaotic mass to order, unanimity and peace.

—*New York Sun*, September 19, 1835

For a Mexican view of the deteriorating relations between Texas and Mexico, the *Philadelphia Inquirer* reprinted an editorial originally published in *El Mosquito Mexicana*. In it, the incursions of "savage Indians" became the ostensible reason Mexican troops were being sent into Texas.

Santa Anna Versus Texas.

The New York Commercial Advertiser gives the following as a free translation of an editorial article in a late number of *El Mosquito Mexicana*—a paper that is supposed to speak the sentiments of the party with which Gen. Santa Anna has recently identified himself. From all the information that has reached us upon the subject, we feel confident that Santa Anna cherishes a desire to act towards Texas in the same tyrannical spirit that he recently conducted himself towards Zacatecas—but he is somewhat apprehensive that the people of Texas will not yield so readily as did those of Zacatecas, and hence he deems it expedient to pursue a more cautious policy.

"The evidence increases daily upon us that it is the Americans of the north who have excited and directed the savage Indians in their attacks upon this republic—instigating them to visit the interior states with every species of outrage and cruelty, in order that the nation may be prevented from constituting and consolidating itself under an efficient system—that they may be enriched with the spoils transmitted to them by the Indians after each incursion—and enabled to make themselves masters of Texas, the object of their insatiable cupidity. We are convinced that owing to the perfidy which marks the character of these pernicious neighbors of the Mexican republic, it will not be easy to put a stop to these barbarous aggressions, and that to effect the desired object, it will be necessary to inspire those *apostles of liberty* with a better sense of morality than they now exhibit, in order that they may learn to respect the rights of other nations and treaties solemnly executed—their government must be taught to confine within its own territory those savage hordes, who never leave it except to pillage from their neighbors, confident of that impunity which is afforded to them by *the flag of the freest country in the world*, and by the weakness of the despoiled—and finally the Mexican government must maintain upon the frontier a sufficient force which shall chastise the Indians, penetrate to the remotest confines of the states, from which the North Americans should be driven, and carry into effect *against them* those extraordinary measures recently decreed against the Indians, which are so justly condemned by

the Gazeatte of Zacatecas.—Against these boasting pretenders to liberty and enlightenment the most prompt and rigorous means should be adopted to restrain them in their career of vandalism and perfidy—not against savages, wanderers and hunters by nature, and instigated to aggression by the Americans, who make use of them merely as instruments, to gain the coveted prize, unchecked and unpunished by their government."
        —*Philadelphia Inquirer*, September 29, 1835

Three days after the preceding article was printed in Philadelphia, the shots of the first real engagement of the Texas Revolution were fired.

4

First Battles

The anticipated final blowup between Texas and Mexico began on September 29, 1835, when more than one hundred mounted Mexican troops from San Antonio arrived on the outskirts of the town of Gonzales on the Guadalupe River. Their leader, Lt. Francisco Castañeda, had been sent by Béxar commandant Col. Domingo Ugartechea to demand that the Texian citizens hand back a brass six-pound cannon that had been given to them as a defense against Indians. Capt. Albert Martin, in command of the eighteen Gonzales militiamen who stood ready to meet Castañeda, responded to the Mexican demand by requesting time to consult with absent town officials; in reality, Martin needed the time to allow outside volunteers to arrive and reinforce his puny ranks. The next day, Martin wrote a letter that was eventually printed in the *Texas Republican*.

> Gonzales, Sept. 30, 1835.
> *Fellow citizens of San Felipe & La Baca*:
> —A detachment of the Mexican forces from Bexar, amounting to about one hundred and fifty men, are encamped opposite us; we expect an attack momentarily. Yesterday we were about eighteen strong, to-day one hundred & fifty, and forces continually arriving. We wish all the aid, and despatch, that is possible to give us, that we may take up soon our line of march for Bexar, and drive from our country all the Mexican forces. Give us all the aid and despatch that is possible.
> Respectfully, yours,
> Captain ALBERT MARTIN,
> "   R. M. COLEMAN,
> "   J. H. MOORE.
> —*Texas Republican*, October 10, 1835

The cannon—actually an unmounted tube—was dug up from its hiding place and affixed to a pair of cart wheels and scrap metal was chopped up for ammunition. The Texians then made the first move, as explained in this letter written by a Committee of Vigilance and Safety official and published across the nation.

> GONZALES, Oct. 3, 1835.—Your letter of September 27 has been received, and we rejoice to see that volunteers are on their march to our assistance. The Rubicon is crossed, and it is now of vital importance in Texas that we should be immediately reinforced. About 12 o'clock on the 20th, the military, about two hundred in number, arrived on the western bank of the Guadaloupe, and attempted the passage of the river, but were repulsed by eighteen men, (the whole force then in the place;) and then encamped on the mound at DeWitt's. On the 1st of October, about 12 o'clock, they took up their march and encamped about seven miles above this place, in a very strong position. Suspecting that their object in this movement was either to wait for a reinforcement from San Antonio, or to cross at the upper crossing, about fifteen miles above, it was determined to attack them before their plans could be carried into execution. Accordingly, on the same night, the whole force, on foot, amounting to about 160 men, from Guadaloupe, Colorado, and La Baca, commanded by Col. J.H. Moore, crossed the river, attacked the enemy about daybreak, and put them to flight without the loss of a single man. Inasmuch as we expect a formidable attack from Ugartechea, should the forces long remain idle, the determination is to attack San

Antonio, as soon as we can receive reinforcements, to prevent this country from becoming the battle ground. This committee, therefore, earnestly desire that you would use your influence to send to this place, as soon as possible, as many reinforcements as possible. Respectfully yours,
W. M. FISHER, Chairman.
—*New-Bedford Mercury*, November 20, 1835

Gonzales had been little more than a glorified skirmish, and everyone knew that the real military threat—General Martín Perfecto de Cos and his command—was advancing north from Copano Bay to reinforce Ugartechea at San Antonio. Word that Cos was carrying a fortune in coins also spread rapidly, via a letter from Port Lavaca.

From the Red River Herald, October 20.
Latest from Texas.
Extracts from a letter written by a gentleman of unquestionable veracity, dated La Baca, October 1, 1835.

"The new officers who came with the arms, said, that as soon as General Cos should reach Bexar, it would be the signal of march for San Felipe de Austin.

"Cos is about to pass on to Bexar. He has a guard of thirty men with him, and the Morelos battalion of lancers is close at his heels. Cos has about $60,000 in specie, for the purpose of paying off the troops. He informed the Alcalde of the Nueces, that he intended to overrun Texas, and establish custom-houses and detachments of his army where he thought fit."

A letter from Bexar says, "The people must either submit, or prepare for defence; as the intention is to march into the colonies, and regulate the land affairs, and a great many things, by military force; also, to clear the country of what they choose to call vagrants, &c."
—*Arkansas Advocate*, November 20, 1835

By the time the following two letters were written, Cos had already arrived at Béxar.

BRAZORIA, (Texas,) Oct. 6
"We learn by Mr. Hoffman, who has just arrived from San Felipe, that information

had just reached that place, that Gen. Samuel Houston would be in the town of Washington on yesterday at 10 o'clock, with one thousand troops from East of the Trinity.[a] In addition to this, it is estimated from the numbers already gone, that there will be 1,000 men in the camp at Gonzales. The patriotism, chivalry and gallantry of the citizens of Texas cannot be surpassed, &c.
JOHN A. WHARTON,
Acting Chairman of the Committee of Safety.

Correspondence of the Philadelphia Gazette.
NACOGDOCHES, TEXAS,
5th Oct. 1835
Since I wrote you the 13th September, we have been constantly engaged in organizing the country, by communications of the different Committees of Vigilance and Safety of the different Municipalities, public meetings, &c. On the 1st inst. we elected delegates to the convention of all Texas, to be held on the 15th of this month, (seven representatives from each Municipality) making seventy members. On the 27th ult. our committee met that of *Ayish Bayou*, as I intended. Yesterday an express arrived here from Colonel S. F. Austin and the Committee of San Felipe, communicating to us the arrival of Gen. Coss, with his troops at Bexar, where he joins the forces under Col. Agotheche, with a determination of making a forced march immediately on the colonists, and doing us all the injury in their power, in hopes of finding us unorganized and unprepared. The Americans have raised en masse on the Colorado and Brazos. The committee of San Felipe sent to us to march and join them immediately in repulsing the enemy, and urging on us the necessity of a general turn out. On Thursday next, our citizens take up their march from our place, to join the forces of the west. We despatched a courier to the Ayish Bayou for the same purpose yesterday, and the troops of Santa Anna will be driven beyond the Nueves before our return.

---

[a] In October, Sam Houston was the acting general in chief of the Department of Nacogdoches.

Our town is all alive to the cause of liberty. In going round to-day, I find all engaged in preparing their arms. Enough only will remain at home to protect our families and property from the tribe of Spanish Indians who live here, and who are now very impudent. They are great rascals, and nothing but fear keeps them from doing mischief.

The great council held by the North American Indians of Texas, which I alluded to in my last, broke off without their coming to any hostile intentions towards us, but rather friendly—their having more confidence in our doing them justice than in the Mexican Government. Yesterday the two Cherokee Chiefs, civil and military, with several of the principal men of the nation, held a talk with our committee. They represented, by agreement at their late council, all the other North American Indians of Texas, and they agreed, by our invitation made to them while they were in council, to accompany our delegates to the convention on the Brazos, and gave us the most solemn pledges of friendship. So we have much less uneasiness on account of them at this moment than when I last wrote you.

We are at war with the military party, and a war in which we support the constitution we have sworn to, which the military have trampled upon; and in this cause we risk our property and our lives, in preference to being degraded by submission to a military tyrant. We trust our friends abroad will look on our cause with that interest they have not denied to foreign countries. We feel much the want of muskets. There are none to be had in New Orleans. We have a number here without cocks, left by the Mexican soldiers when they were whipped off three years ago by the American colonists; and they knocked off the locks and burned them, that their enemies might not have the use of them.[b] What a treat would an arrival of a good quantity of muskets be to us at this moment. We have sent to New Orleans for rifles, the only arms to be had there, and the supply of them is deficient.

It is expected that Gen. Coss will attempt to attack the convention while in session; but we will try to bring men enough in the field to disappoint him in taking our representatives as easily as he did those of Coahuila and Texas at Monclova. We shall be forming a state in the midst of war, and the military movements of our enemy only stimulate us to action and union, trusting in the glorious result.

—*Mercantile Advertiser and New York Advocate*,
November 9, 1835

During that first week in October, Texian volunteers from several towns joined Captain George Morse Collinsworth's small detachment as it marched west from Matagorda on the Texas coast, bent on capturing the Mexican presidio at La Bahía (Goliad) and perhaps even Cos himself.[1] The last man to join them was to become the first true hero of the Texas Revolution—Ben Milam.

Correspondence of the *New-Orleans Bulletin.*
BRAZORIA, (Texas) Oct. 22, 1835.
DEAR SIR—

While all eyes were directed with intense anxiety towards the military operations near Gonzales—supposing *that* to be the only point from whence we might expect important news—we were astonished by receiving information of the capture of the fort and town of Goliad, (La Bahia) by a party of colonists. These were volunteers from the transcendently fertile banks of the Caney and from the town of Matagorda, a place destined to become an important city.

Before this party entered the field, most of the volunteers were at Gonzales—and fearing that the harvest of honors would be reaped before they could arrive there—they struck off from La Baca with the daring determination of taking Goliad by surprise.

Goliad is situated on the southwest side of the San Antonio river, thirty leagues below Bexar, and it is fifteen leagues from Copano, the landing place of Aransas bay, and about the same distance from the La Baca end of Matagorda bay. The fort is built upon the point of a very steep and high hill, formed of rock, with a deep ravine upon one side and a low prairie upon

---

[b] These weapons had been surrendered by the Mexican garrison at Anahuac in 1832.

the opposite—while a broad elevated prairie extends towards the southwest.

The walls of the fort are of stone, and lime, and bear in places the marks of the storms of an hundred winters, but are still proof against any thing less than the batterings of heavy artillery.

A long forced march brought the van-guard of the colonists to the San Antonio river fording below the town at 11 o'clock on the night of the 9th inst. Here they halted for the main body and to make arrangements for the attack. A very small party were sent into town, and they brought out, with the utmost secrecy, a worthy citizen friendly to the constitution of 1824. And by his assistance guides were procured, perfectly acquainted with the place.

The main body of the colonists missed their road in the night, and before they found out their mistake, were at the upper ford, immediately opposite the town. They then struck across, for a short cut, to the position occupied by the van-guard. Their route led through a *muskeet* thicket. The muskeet is a tree of the locust family, full of thorns, and at a little distance resembles the common peach tree in size and appearance. While the parties were treading their way through this thicket, the horse of some of them started in affright at an object beneath a bush. The rider checked his horse and said, "who's there." A voice answered in Spanish. One of the party supposed that he recognized in the voice an old acquaintance of La Bahia—and asked if it was not such a one, mentioning the name. "No," was the reply, "my name is *Milam*."

Col. Milam is a native of Kentucky. At the commencement of the Mexican war of Independence he engaged in the cause, and assisted in establishing the Independence of the country. When Iturbide assumed the purple, Milam's republican principles placed him in fetters—dragged him to the city of Mexico, and confined him in prison until the usurper was dethroned. When Santa Anna assumed the Dictatorship, the republican Milam was again thrust into the prison at Monte Ray. But his past services and sufferings wrought upon the sympathies of his hard hearted jailors.

They allowed him the luxury of the bath. He profited by the indulgence and made arrangements with an old compatriot to place a fleet horse suitably equipped upon the bank of the stream at a time appointed. The colonel passed the sentinel as he was wont to go into the water—walked quietly in—*mounted the horse and fled.*

Four hundred miles would place him in safety. The noble horse did his duty; and bore the colonel clear of all pursuit to the place where our party surprised him. At first he supposed himself in the power of his enemy—but the *English language* soon convinced him that he was in the midst of his countrymen.

He had never heard that Texas was making an effort to save herself. No whisper of the kind had been allowed to pass to his prison. When he learnt the object of the party, his heart was full. He could not speak—*for joy.*

When the company arrived at the lower ford they divided themselves into four parties of twelve men each. One party remained as a guard with the horses. The other three each with a guide, marched by different routes to the assault.

Their axes hewed down the door where the colonel commanding the place slept—and he was taken a prisoner from his bed. A sentinel hailed—and fired. A rifle ball laid him dead upon the spot.—The discharge of fire arms and the noise of human voices now became commingled. The Mexican soldiers fired from their quarters and the blaze of their guns served as targets for the colonist riflemen.

The garrison were called to *surrender*, and the call was translated by a gentleman present who spoke the language. They asked for terms.

The interpreter now became the chief speaker. "No," answered he. They say they will massacre every one of you, unless you come out immediately and surrender. Come out—come out quick. I cannot keep them back—come out if you wish to save your lives—I can keep them back no longer. "*O do* for God's sake keep them back," answered the Mexicans in their own language—"We will come out and surrender immediately"—and they rushed out with all possible speed and laid down their arms.

And thus was the fort at Goliad taken—a fort, which with a garrison of three hundred and fifty patriots in the war of 1812-13 withstood a siege of an army of more than two thousand Spanish troops and force them to retire—discomfitted.

At the capture of the fort three Mexican soldiers were killed and seven wounded, and one colonel, one captain, one lieut. with twenty-one petty officers and privates were made prisoners—others of the garrison escaped in the dark and fled.

In the Fort were found two pieces of Brass cannon, 500 muskets and carbines, 600 spears with ammunition and provisions.

One of the colonists was wounded in the shoulder.

Col. Milam assisted in the capture of the Fort, and then he spoke: "I assisted Mexico to gain her independence. I have spent more than twenty years of my life, I have endured heat and cold, hunger and thirst, I have borne losses and suffered prosecutions. I have been a tenant of every prison between this and Mexico—*but the events of this night have compensated me for all my losses and all my sufferings.*"

The colonists were commanded by Gen. M. Collinsworth—but it would be difficult to find in the company a man not qualified for the command.

Goliad is of vastly more importance in a military point of view than Bexar, as the latter is in a valley upon the banks of the river and commanded by the hills on each side—and is therefore indefensible.

The main army under Col. Austin marched from Gonzales on the 13th inst. against Bexar.

When provoked, there is in Col. Austin the courage of the lion: and there is in him, *at all times,* the caution of the fox. With him in command, if we do not hope for a speedy victory we at least do not fear a defeat.

I send this by a soldier (Captain John Duncan, lately of Mobile.—*Ed. B.*) Who fought at the capture of Goliad, and if there be any error in my statement, you will have the means of correcting them before you.

Your obt. Servt.   S.
—*Southern Patriot,* November 21, 1835

Two days after the capture of Goliad more than three hundred Texians marched out of Gonzales under the command of Stephen F. Austin. Their object: surround Cos's army at San Antonio de Béxar and force him to surrender his troops and the town. The slow-moving news concerning these and previous events took, on average, about a month to reach East Coast cities, and by the time it did it was often garbled or replete with wild rumors amidst a handful of facts. The following, however, offers at least one prescient observation regarding the superiority of Mexican cavalry against frontier riflemen in open country.

Texas.—New Orleans papers of the 24th ult. contain advice from Texas up to the 8th, at which time the landing of a large body of Mexican forces was momentarily expected on the coast, near Brazoria. Gen. Cos was in La Bahia with a strong force, and 800 pair of iron hobbles intended for the benefit of the Texians.

The latest accounts from Gonzales state that the two parties arranged on each side of the river—the enemy 200 strong—but no battle had taken place.

Two thousand Mexican troops were expected to land at the mouth of the Brazos by the 25th ult.

A private letter in the *N. O. American,* contradicts the statement of an engagement having taken place at Gonzales. But another letter, of October 8th, states that Gen. Houston, with 1000 men, has captured San Antonio, and seized a convoy of $60,000 belonging to Gen. Cos. The Mexican despot, says the letter, rules a million of men— Texas has 7000 with American hearts and courage and determined to be free. The enemy have a well appointed cavalry, who are volunteers. The infantry is composed of convicts, who are placed in the army as a punishment for their crimes. Our riflemen are a deadly species of troops, as all the world knows, but in the prairies they will be powerless against cavalry. Bayonets and lances are what are, therefore, most needed by American volunteers.

—*New York Sun,* November 9, 1835

Two and a half weeks later, the same paper finally received positive news of Austin's army, not Sam Houston's, having taken positions around San Antonio.

> *From Texas.*—New Orleans papers, of the 10th last, contain a little additional information from Texas. Gen. Houston had left San Felipe, to join Col. Austin, near San Antonio, and had been joined by the volunteers from Natchez and Nacogdoches—the former including a fine corps of cavalry, and the latter consisting of about 150 men well provided, and in fine health and spirits. Cos's army was 1700 strong, and he was in daily expectation of a reinforcement of 400 Mexicans. The forces of the volunteers nearly equal them in number, are better soldiers, and do not fear their enemies.
>
> *Still Later.*—The *N. O. Union* learns, from a gentleman that has just arrived, by land, from Texas, that the Texians had been able to surround Gen. Cos and his small army of 1700 men, and that all chances of escape was shut out from him. The Texians speak confidently of an easy victory.
>
> —*New York Sun*, November 26, 1835

In the wake of Austin's march, other volunteers continued to rendezvous at Gonzales. One novice soldier there communicated to a friend the news that the Mexicans had strongly fortified San Antonio—even mounting an artillery piece atop San Fernando Church.

> In Camp, Gonzales, Oct. 25
> Dear Sir. The company of volunteers to which I belong, is now in three days march of our main army, and we will leave to-morrow to join them; they are encamped six miles this side of San Antonio, and have been there six or eight days, waiting for reinforcements, which are daily coming in, and our cannon, to the number of five or six pieces, which will be there in six days. What is to be done you will learn hereafter; now, I am not able to inform you. I shall be in your city about the middle of November.
>
> San Antonio is garrisoned, a strong fortress commanding most of the town, and the streets barricaded and defended by cannon; cannon on the church, which is stone. Most of the houses are of stone, and occupied by the military, all the families having left. A number of Mexicans have joined our army. Gen. Cos says he is ready to fight.
>
> —*New London Gazette* (Connecticut), December 16, 1835

Prior to making his final push on San Antonio, Austin had first encamped his army on Salado Creek, about five miles east of the town. On October 27 he assigned Col. James Bowie and Capt. James Walker Fannin the task of choosing a suitable site for the army's next encampment on the outskirts of Béxar.

> An Extract of a letter from a Member of the Convention to Colonel John Forbes, of this place, (Nacogdoches, Texas.)
> An express arrived here last night from Camp with the important news, that our army, under the command of Gen. Austin, gained a victory over the enemy, one mile and a half from San Antonio, in which our loss was one man wounded only, the enemy lost 50 wounded, and 10 men left dead on the field of battle, and information from the town says 24 died of their wounds, making 40 of the enemy killed in all, and one 6 pounder, and a number of small arms, &c. taken; our army remaining complete victors of the field. Our troops were 90 men under the command of Colonel James Bowie, our brave townsman, who had taken possession of the post, the Mission of Concepcion, 12 hours before the fight. The enemy by means of spies, had an accurate account of their numbers, and sent 400 of their choice troops and two six pounders, commanded by Col. Ugartechea to take them.
>
> The Nacogdoches troops, under Capt. Rusk, and the San Augustin under Capt. Agustin, we met two days march from camp, and hurried them on. We learn that from 150 to 180 men under Col. Sublette, are on the way, 64 men have arrived from N. Orleans in complete uniform and armed.
>
> Our army when I left, Gen. Austin informed me was 600 men—I suppose it is now 8 or 900

men; and 4, 6, 18, and 32 pound cannon are on their way to San Antonio for our army, and the place is closely besieged, and will be taken by starvation or storm if it must.

The enemy are said to expect aid, and it is of the greatest importance that the fort should fall before their arrival; therefore, I pray you, do forward all the volunteers in your power, let all come who can come, and come quickly, and you will be organized for a short and glorious campaign.

An armed Mexican vessel has appeared off Velasco, and letters of marque and reprisal have been granted to five vessels in the port at the mouth of the Brazos river, who will give a good account of the Black Pirate.

East of the Trinity, the men are all gone or going, let not Red Landers[c] be behind in the glorious struggle for LIBERTY. What I say first, I say last, let all the men come that can be spared from home, those that go will be amply rewarded, and those that refuse to come will feel the bitter consequences of not acting as becomes freemen.

To the Committee of Vigilance and Safety at Nacogdoches.

SAN FELIPE DE AUSTIN, Nov. 1, 1835.

Gentlemen—As it is our duty to keep you properly apprised of the affairs of our country we will send you an extract from Colonel Austin's letter of the 28th October.

Head quarters, Mission of Concepcion, 1 ½ miles from Bexar—Oct. 28, 1835.

To the President of the Consultation of Texas.

I have the honor to inform you that the enemy, to the number of three hundred cavalry and one hundred infantry, as nearly as could be ascertained, with two pieces of artillery, at sunrise this morning attacked a detachment of Col. Bowie and Capt. Fanning, composed of ninety men who were posted at this place, and after a warm engagement of three hours, were repelled with the loss of one piece cannon, a six pounder, and about thirty muskets; sixteen men left dead on the ground, and from

all accounts as many more were carried off; the wounded we can only conjecture, with the exception of two that remained on the field; it is with great regret that I say that on our side we had one man, Richard Andrews, wounded, I fear mortally; but we have sustained no other loss except a few horses.—The main body of the army came up about thirty minutes after the enemy had retired.

S. F. AUSTIN

The most of the members of the consultation have returned from the army, and we are in hopes that there will be a quorum here by tomorrow.

There was an armed vessel made its appearance on our coast, attempted to land at Velasco, fired one shot at the town, it was manfully returned by the citizens of the place from an eighteen pounder, and after firing four shots at her, she stood off, and has been more shy; so says an express from that place. The United States Volunteers, from New Orleans, are all mounted and on their way to the army.

We have the honor to be, Yours, &c.

R. R. ROYALL, President.

S. HOUSTON, Secretary.

—*Arkansas Gazette*, December 15, 1835

Another report, originating in a New Orleans newspaper, added more details of the engagement at Concepción.

NEW ORLEANS, November 30.

LATER FROM TEXAS.—A gentleman just arrived from Texas, states that on the 28th of October, James Bowie, with 90 men, being in advance of the main army, took possession of a church, a mile and a half from San Antonio. The Mexicans, 400 strong, under the command of Col. Utaracher, sallying out from the city, made an attack upon Bowie's forces, and after an engagement of three hour's duration, were repulsed with the loss of one piece of artillery and forty muskets, leaving 18 men dead upon the field.[2] The entire Mexican forces within the wall of San Antonio, number now only 800, while the Texian army without are 2500 strong, well armed, and in good spirits. The garrison

---

[c] The Red Lands was the largely lawless region sandwiched between Louisiana and Texas.

The Battle of Concepción, October 28, 1835

Sent ahead by Gen. Stephen F. Austin to scout for a suitable campsite for the Texian army, Col. James Bowie with his second in command, Capt. James W. Fannin, led ninety mounted men to a horseshoe bend of the San Antonio River about five hundred yards from the Mission Concepción. On the foggy morning of October 28, Col. Domingo de Ugartechea challenged Bowie's arrival with a detachment sent by General Martín Perfecto de Cos consisting of some three hundred cavalry, infantry, and artillery.

Bowie's men, dug in along the high riverbank and shaded by pecan trees, took a large toll of the charging enemy with their rifles. It was a fight that began around 8:00 a.m. and ended only when the battered Mexicans retreated in the early afternoon, long after the fog had cleared. They left behind on the prairie a brass six-pounder, a battle standard, and twenty-three dead and wounded. Forty-two wounded *soldados* were taken off the field, of whom fifteen eventually died.[1] The Mexican infantry—about one hundred of the Morelos battalion, nicknamed the "Invincibles"—had fought bravely, but the hidden Texian sharpshooters were too much for them. Of Bowie's force, only one man was killed and one wounded.[2]

Bowie's attire on this glorious day for the revolutionists was never described, although it might have been a hunting shirt or a similarly practical combat dress, or perhaps the black coat shown here; when an inventory was made of Bowie's personal property over a year and a half after his death, among the items were two black cloth coats.[3] Bowie's weapons at the time included a double-barreled shotgun.[4] About forty Mexican muskets were picked up from the battlefield.[5]

---

1. Stephen Hardin, *Texian Iliad: A Military History of the Texas Revolution* (Austin: University of Texas Press, 1994), 33; Diary of Samuel Maverick, October 28, 1835. Available at www.tamu.edu/ccbn/dewitt/bexarmaverick.htm.
2. Alwyn Barr, *Texans in Revolt: The Battle for San Antonio, 1835* (Austin: University of Texas Press, 1991), 26.
3. J. Frank Dobie, "James Bowie," in *Heroes of Texas* (Waco: Texian Press, 1966), 46.
4. William C. Davis, *Three Roads to the Alamo: The Lives and Fortunes of David Crockett, James Bowie, and William Barret Travis* (New York: Harper Collins, 1998), 431.
5. *Richmond Enquirer*, December 17, 1835.

is almost without provisions, their beeves having been captured by the Texians. They are now confined strictly within the walls of the city, and all their sentinels being shot by the besieging army, the moment they venture without. A declaration of rights has been published, under the Constitution of 1824.

—*N. Orleans Post.*
—*Richmond Enquirer*, December 17, 1835

In faraway Boston, news of developments in Texas was mixed with reports of efforts elsewhere to come to the aid of the revolutionaries, along with editorial opinion that weighed the possibility of annexation against that of an independent republic.

The New York Journal of Commerce says that very considerable numbers of men are leaving various parts of our country for Texas, taking with them the arms and ammunition necessary for war. Some hundreds will leave the Atlantic coast within ten days, and a still larger number will go from the West. The Journal thinks that "Santa Anna will find the Kentucky riflemen bad troops to contend with, in such a war as will be waged in Texas, and it would not be strange if, take it all in all, he should find this the hardest job he ever undertook."

Major B. Hammatt Norton, who has become a resident in Texas, and is deeply interested in the prosperity and independence of that delightful country, has made an appeal, through the columns of the papers, to the Bostonians, whom he calls upon to assist and protect their fellow countrymen who are threatened to be driven from Texas by a War of Extermination. We doubt, adds the editor of the Transcript, if the Major's appeal will produce much effect here, although we understand that one of our citizens has promised the Major to furnish dragoon equipments in full, from stirrup to holster, for a hundred horses. The Texanians must trust chiefly for assistance, in time of need, to the border States.

It is probable (says the New York Times) that the next news from Texas will give an account of a battle between the Texanians under Austin and Zavala,[d] and the Mexicans under Cos. In the event of a regular war, the issue cannot be doubtful. The inhabitants of Texas are mostly Americans, more hardy, more enterprising and more intelligent than the Mexicans. They hold out strong inducements to adventurers to join their standard—inducements such as will not be resisted. If they succeed in establishing the independence of Texas, they will have ample wealth in their large and fertile public domain to reward the services of all who are willing to join them. Under such circumstances, men will flock to their standard, and they will soon be able to present a numerical force equal to any that can be brought against them. We shall not be surprised to learn that the hardy yeomanry of the southwest are resorting to Mexico in great numbers. Success to the Texanians.

A meeting of the citizens of New Orleans has been called, to consult upon measures to be adopted in this emergency. But although individuals may hasten to the assistance of their friends and countrymen in peril in a foreign land, the general Government cannot interfere in their behalf. If this Republic were not already too unwieldy, we could wish that Texas might, by a treaty be annexed to the United States. If by any combination of fortuitous circumstances, the settlers in Texas should succeed in their contest with the Mexicans, they will probably declare themselves independent—and thus lay the foundation of a powerful nation.

—*Boston Post*, October 31, 1835

And what of Mexican president, Antonio López de Santa Anna, now that General Cos had gotten himself into such a predicament at Béxar? The *Arkansas Advocate* offered its wishfully thought opinion.

There is much speculation as to the probable result of matters in Texas. Our impression is, that Santana will have his hands too full at home, to attend to her, that other states will follow the example of Guadalajara and Samaulipas, which

---

[d] Lorenzo de Zavala, former Mexican politician turned Texas settler, who in March 1836 was elected ad interim vice president of the Republic of Texas.

have already risen against him, and that Texas will just be left alone. If the republicans conquer him, Texas will be made a free State—if he conquer them, he will be willing to sell it to the United States—as it will always be more plague than profit to a monarch.

—*Arkansas Advocate*, November 20, 1835

A New Hampshire paper reported a potpourri of news from the southwest, including mention of the siege of Béxar and of a Texian position situated within artillery range of "the fort"—the Alamo.

TEXAS. A provisional government has been completely organized in this country, to whose affairs recent events have given uncommon interest, a bill of rights adopted and Henry Smith appointed Governor and J. W. Robinson, Lieutenant Governor. The present state of the war will be understood from the following paragraphs from Niles' Register:

There has been some fighting—and the "Texas Register" of Nov. 11, says—

"The latest information from the seat of war, [at Bexar,] although by no means discouraging, is not of the most flattering character. The strength of the army, from the best information, was between six and seven hundred; they had five pieces of artillery. A detachment was stationed within cannon shot of the fort, in a position where the bank of the river served to protect them from the fire of the enemy. There has been no important action since the 28th ult. The army is yet in good spirits, and most of them have pledged themselves to remain sixty days longer, if necessary. They are still calling for heavy cannon and reinforcements, to enable them to reduce the garrison at that place, and insist upon the necessity of accomplishing that object before abandoning the campaign."

A powerful diversion is spoken of in other provinces. But Mexico was taking measures to throw a strong force into Texas—some say 15,000 men.

The people of Texas do not, however, appear discouraged. They have succeeded in several small affairs. Gen. Houston is appointed commander of their regular army. Gen. Cos had not surrendered, as was reported—but his troops, it was said, had been reduced to the necessity of eating their mules.

—*New Hampshire Patriot*, January 11, 1836

Details of the military situation at Béxar that found their way into the papers were not always as explicit as they were in the following, which mentions several of the artillery pieces that would eventually help defend the Alamo during those fateful thirteen days in 1836.

Correspondence of the New Orleans Bulletin.

BRAZORIA, (Texas) Nov.14, 1835 DEAR SIR:—Bexar has been fortified by Gen. Cos, who now occupies the place with 700 Mexican troops. The town has been surrounded with ditches five feet in depth and near twelve broad, and the earth from them has been thrown up inside—so as to form an efficient defense. The ditches have been filled with water from sluices which were employed to irrigate the fields. Artillery are mounted upon the top of the great church and other advantageous positions. The garrison have twenty-eight pieces of cannon.

The main army of the colonists, under the command of Gen. Stephen F. Austin, and numbering near one thousand men, are now besieging the place; but they have but five pieces of cannon, and none of them exceeding six pound calibre. The whole army are now waiting the arrival of a twelve pound gun-ade, which it is hoped will be sufficient to knock down the enemy's defenses.

The long eighteen-pounder which came from New Orleans, unfortunately was not accompanied by any shot fitting its calibre, and this oversight will cost the country a delay and expense greater than the cost of fifty guns. And this is not all—for if the twelve pounder should not prove sufficient to demolish the enemy's works, the place must be taken by assault, at the expense of the lives of many brave men, whom both humanity and policy call upon us to save from the sacrifice.

Travis's Horse Raid

"I have taken a position on the Alamo Canal, at the mouth of a dry gully about one mile from town," wrote Stephen F. Austin, commander of the Texas Army, to Col. James Bowie and Capt. James W. Fannin on October 31, 1835. Austin was beginning his siege of the Mexican force under Gen. Martín Perfecto de Cos, a force occupying both the town of San Antonio de Béxar and the nearby Alamo fort. He added, "I have certain information that all the surplus [enemy] horses, except about 150 or 200, are started to Laredo last night. . . . I have dispatched Captain Travis, with 50 men, to overtake and capture them. He has guides, and I have no doubt will succeed."[1]

Travis, at least on this occasion, did not succeed, and returned in such a discouraged mood that he tendered his resignation on November 6.[2] Thus, he was only a private when he went out again the following day with another party in a renewed search for the Mexican horses. Twelve of the men, however, decided to elect *him* captain of the expedition. Among these men were the scout Erastus "Deaf" Smith and Tejano leader Juan Seguín.[3] They found the *caballado* watering on San Miguel Creek more than forty miles south of Béxar. A surprise charge into the Mexican camp achieved a bloodless victory; the approximately three hundred mounts (including ten mules), which Travis described as "gentle Spanish horses," were captured and herded north.[4]

On November 14 Austin penned a circular to "the people of Texas," describing the army's progress; this was published in the *Telegraph and Texas Register* a week later. He included the news of Travis's bold capture of the herd, although admitting that they were "poor horses."[5] Printed reports of the raid soon spread across the country, and for the first time the name William Barret Travis received national notice.

Although he was an officer in the Texas regular cavalry, that establishment had not yet received uniforms. The illustration shows Travis, at far left, wearing speculative field dress—common but rugged clothing of the type then available in Texas: a simple roundabout jacket, a black neck stock for a martial look, buckskin pants, vaquero-type leather leggings, and a white beaver hat similar to the one worn on campaign by Colonel Henry Dodge of the US Army, who had led his First Dragoon Regiment on a circuit of Comanche country the year before. Strapped over Travis's shoulder is a favorite arm of the Texian soldiers: a double-barreled shotgun, along with belted twin shotgun pouches. His horse equipment is essentially Spanish and similar to that of Juan Seguín, shown

(continued)

here in black top hat and buckskin shirt (based on a circa 1828 watercolor of a typical "Ranchero de Texas" by Lino Sánchez y Tapia). Seguín's rifle is also strapped over his shoulder, protected from the elements in a fringed buckskin case.

At far right rides Deaf Smith, far removed from his Dutchess County, New York, birthplace; Smith was an accomplished scout whom Travis dubbed "the Bravest of the Brave in the cause of Texas."[6] During the siege of Béxar, Smith was described as "a hard-featured backwoodsman in a green hunting shirt." His horse's rig was also Tejano—the best type for the country he was operating in.[7]

Because the mounts were in poor condition, Austin ordered Travis to leave them at Seguín's ranch, where they could be grazed back to health, and then to return to San Antonio for new orders. Seguín himself was kept busy looking for additional Mexican mounts.[8]

1. Stephen F. Austin to Colonel James Bowie and Captain Fannin, October 31, 1835, Frank W. Johnson, *A History of Texas and Texans* (Chicago: American Historical Society, 1914), 282.
2. Archie P. McDonald, *Travis* (Austin: Jenkins Publishing Company, Pemberton Press, 1976), 133–134.
3. William C. Davis, *Three Roads to the Alamo: The Lives and Fortunes of David Crockett, James Bowie, and William Barrett Travis* (New York: Harper Collins, 1998), 466; "Personal Memoirs of John [sic] N. Seguin" (circa 1858), in Todd Hansen, ed., *The Alamo Reader: A Study in History* (Mechanicsburg, Penn.: Stackpole Books, 2003), 193. Seguín's memoir places the capture of the horse herd *after* the siege of San Antonio, a forgivable mistake considering he wrote the memoir almost a quarter-century after the fact.
4. McDonald, *Travis*, 137.
5. Circular, "Letter from Head Quarters, November 14, 1835," *Telegraph and Texas Register*, November 14, 1835.
6. Lt. Col. William B. Travis to Governor Henry Smith, Béxar, February 15, 1836, in Wallace O. Chariton, *100 Days in Texas: the Alamo Letters* (Plano, Tex.: Wordware Publishing Co., Inc., 1990), 235.
7. Herman Ehrenberg, *With Milam and Fannin: Adventures of a German Boy in the Texas Revolution*, ed. Henry Smith (Dallas: Tardy Publishing Co., 1935), 67.
8. Davis, *Three Roads to the Alamo*, 468; Seguín in Hansen, *The Alamo Reader*, 193.

A party of hostile Indians have killed Lieut. Collinsworth in the vicinity of Goliad. He was a brother of the commander of the gallant band who took Goliad; and for courage and skill as a marksman, he had no superior in the colonist army.

Four hundred men from the garrison of Bexar made a sortie upon a party of colonists—not one fourth of their numbers—but were defeated with loss. Major Fanum, who commanded a company of the party assailed, took from the enemy a brass six pounder after a desperate struggle—the Major having killed a soldier of the famous Morelos battalion while in the very act of spiking the gun—by a weapon which was sent to him by Mr Toby of your city.

S.

—*New Hampshire Sentinel*,
December 31, 1835

Other details of Cos's defensive works found their way to the press via a letter dated San Augustine, December 6, 1836.

[Following the clash at Gonzales] the Mexican troops then centered at San Antonio (or Bajar or Bexar): fortified, and block up the streets and burn the wood buildings, leaving nothing standing but stone. The place is strongly fortified with a wall from three to five feet thick.

—*Philadelphia Saturday Courier*,
January 9, 1836

If Cos's soldiers "had been reduced to the necessity of eating their mules,"[3] soon the besieged Mexicans would be short three hundred of their horses. On November 14, Austin penned a letter to the members of the Consultation at San Felipe de Austin, briefly summarizing recent events concerning the siege, including a foray by cavalry captain William Barrett Travis that had seized a large Mexican army horse herd.

HEADQUARTERS BEFORE BEXAR,
November 14, 1835.
TO THE CONSULTATION OF TEXAS,

I have the satisfaction to inform you that since my last, some important advantages have been gained over the enemy. Captain Travis has taken three hundred head of horses, that were sent out of Bejar to Loredo. They are poor horses; and were taken about forty miles from this place. The enemy is closely shut up in Bejar, and more and more discouraged every day. All we need is perseverance, and re-inforcements to keep up the army. I entreat the Convention to hurry on re-inforcements, with all possible despatch, and the campaign will soon end.

There is very little prospect that the enemy will get any aid from the interior.

Respectfully your obedient servant,

S. F. AUSTIN.

—*Telegraph and Texas Register*,
November 21, 1835[e]

General Cos's side of the situation at Béxar, at least up to the first week in November, was culled from Mexican newspapers and offered in the following New York paper report. Noted, too, were Santa Anna's energetic maneuvers toward raising funds—and a big army—with which to finally crush the Texians' revolt.

IMPORTANT FROM MEXICO.

By the ship Mexican we have received our regular files of Mexican papers.

In relation to Texas, the organization of an expedition so long talked of, is carried on but slowly. About 1500 men and fifteen pieces of artillery had arrived at San Luis Potosi, under the command of General Ramirez Sesma, and two more regiments were detained at Queretaro by the want of funds. It is now expected that a great part of these troops will be ordered to Tampico, where Santa Ana himself was expected to arrive towards the 6th instant, having left the city of Mexico on the 28th ultimo for San Luis.

In the absence of official reports from General Cos, who commands the Mexican troops in Texas, we give the following extract of a letter written by his second in command, Colonel Ugartechea, and inserted in the Censor of Vera Cruz.

The colonel writes from Bexar, the 2d of November, that General Cos, at the head of 400 infantry, was fortifying that town, whilst he himself was stationed at Alamo, with 300 cavalry, that both positions were so closely beset by the troops under Colonel Austin, that not a day elapsed without some skirmishing taking place. In alluding to that of the 28th October he pretends he had killed or wounded 76 Texians, having lost on his side but fourteen men. He concludes his report by stating that their position becomes daily more and more critical, having already 50 men on the sick list, and being in great want of provisions of all kinds. General Cos was anxiously expecting Colonel Jose Juan[f] with the reinforcement sent from Mexico in order to make an attack on the besiegers.

General Santa Ana, previous to leaving the city of Mexico, had made a forced loan of one million dollars to defray the expenses of the war, and had taken with him 300,000 dollars.

The governor of Vera Cruz, Colonel Vazguez, had made another loan of 30,000 dollars to arm a flotilla against Texas. At the last dates the merchants of that town had voluntarily

---

[e] The *Telegraph and Texas Register* was a brand-new paper; its first issue printed at San Felipe de Austin on October 10, 1835. By mid-December, it claimed a circulation of five hundred.

[f] Lt. Col. José Juan Sánchez Navarro.

subscribed about 20,000 dollars for the expenses of the war.
—*Morning Courier and New York Enquirer*, December 28, 1835

By mid-November, Austin's army had been reinforced by two companies of the volunteer New Orleans Greys, arriving about a week apart, under captains Thomas H. Breece and Robert C. Morris. Their earlier progress had been noted in an Arkansas newspaper.

From the Alexandria (La.) Intelligencer, Oct. 28.
The steam-boat Ouachita arrived at this place yesterday, from New-Orleans, having on board a company of sixty volunteers, on their way to Texas. One other company embarked on board of a vessel, a few days since, for Brazoria. Two more companies are expected from New-Orleans, in the course of few days, for Texas, to assist the citizens of that country in their struggle for liberty. God send them speed.
—*Arkansas Advocate*, November 20, 1835

The *Telegraph and Texas Register* eventually republished a circular originating out of Nacogdoches that noted the entry of Breece's company into Texas.

First company of Texian Volunteers from New Orleans.
You cannot pronounce the word "liberty" but it is sure to find a warm response from the United States. When Mexico and the republics of South America were struggling with their Spanish oppressors, the blood and treasure of the United States was freely and unhesitatingly poured out for their defence. Greece and unfortunate Poland were also cheered on in their strike for freedom, by the warm regards and prompt succor of the older born freemen of America. But now that Texas sends out the cry of oppression, our brethren in the United States, who are "bone of our bone, and flesh of our flesh," have acted with even more than their wonted energy and decision. If proof were needed, the fine company of volunteers from New Orleans, consisting of fifty-four men, under the command of captain Thomas H.

Breece and lieutenants John J. Baugh and Geo. Washington Main, which arrived in town yesterday morning, and will leave early to-morrow morning, for the seat of war, must satisfy the warmest expectations of the most ardent friends of Texian liberty.

They are mostly athletic mechanics, who have abandoned their homes and lucrative employments for the disinterested purpose of sustaining the righteous cause of freedom. Their very appearance must convince every Texian that they will either "do or die." Besides this fine corps, we are also apprized that two companies of riflemen have already left New Orleans by sea, for Brazoria; and that another company of heavy cavalry was to follow immediately. Other companies were being raised there, and, it is expected, will soon be in the field. In fact, we are assured that the pulsation, from Maine to Louisiana, is universal in favor of Texas, and that volunteers may be expected from all quarters of the Union.

The first company of Texian volunteers from New Orleans was received and entertained by our citizens of Nacogdoches, in a manner which was creditable to their liberality, and which must have convinced the members of the corps of the gratitude which the Texians know how to feel for such disinterested services.

A fine company of volunteers, raised in San Augustin and its vicinity, consisting of forty men well mounted and equipped, under the command of captain Bailey Anderson, also arrived here this morning, and was escorted into town by the New Orleans company. They will leave this evening for the seat of war, carrying with them the best wishes and fondest hopes of our citizens.
—*Telegraph and Texas Register*, December 2, 1835

Despite plummeting morale and a lack of adequate provisions, the Texians kept wearing away at the besieged Mexican force, as described in this New York City newspaper report pieced together from accounts in New Orleans papers.

The siege of Bahar goes bravely on. The Mexicans have shut themselves closely within the walls of the place; but the arrival of heavy cannon was daily expected by the Texians, and by this time the place had doubtless been forced to surrender. In fact, on the 24th ult. even with the small pieces the besiegers had with them, they had already made a small breach in the church of Bahar, which the Mexicans have converted into a citadel.

A troop of Texians under Capt. Travis have taken about 300 head of horses from the enemy, these will be of the greatest utility in organizing companies of cavalry.

On the 18th ult. a company of Texian cavalry, numbering 35 men, under Captain Bird, fell in near Bahar with a squadron of about 150 Mexican cavalry. Capt. Bird retreated to a ravine, and there defended himself so effectually against the superior forces opposed to him, that in a few minutes they retreated precipitately, leaving five men killed on the ground, and a number wounded. It is said that the Mexicans showed more cowardice in this than in any previous action.

The Indians in several instances, have attacked the Texians. Lieut. Collingswood was fired upon by a party of them near Goliad, and killed.

The Mexican governor of San Patricio, has been obliged to surrender to a party of Texians which took the place, after a severe action in which the Mexicans suffered considerable loss.

—*New York Sun*, December 23, 1835

The next large-scale fight for control of San Antonio de Béxar took place on November 26, when a Texian detachment, led by Bowie and scout Erastus "Deaf" Smith, intercepted a Mexican army mule train attempting to deliver fresh hay to Cos's cavalry units at the Alamo. As reported in a Nashville paper, news of this engagement was followed by word of a failed attempt launched from New Orleans and spearheaded by anticentralist exile José Antonio Mexia to seize the Mexican port of Tampico.

LATEST FROM TEXAS.

Our previous accounts from San Antonio were to 25th. By an arrival at New Orleans we have information two days later from the seat of War in Texas.

Our informant states that a detachment of Gen. Cos' Cavalry, out procuring grain for the horses, were attacked on the 27th ult. by a party of Texians, and by them defeated with a loss of thirty-five horses, and suffering in killed and wounded, to the number of fifty men. The loss of the Texians—three men slightly wounded. Cos' detachment of Cavalry consisted of about 150 men, which, before the engagement was concluded, were re-inforced by 150 infantry; the party of Texians employed in the assault amounting to about the same number.

General Austin has been elected Commissioner, together with Messrs. Archer & Wharton, to the United States, with plenary power to negotiate loans, &c. Edward Burlisson has been elected by the army, to fill the place vacated by Gen. Austin. Gen. Burlisson is therefore at the head of the Volunteer Army of Texas.

Gen. Houston has been appointed by the General Council of the Provisional Government of Texas, to the command of the regular Army to be raised.

GEN. MEHER DEFEATED AT TAMPICO

Intelligence has been received in New Orleans by a member of Gen. Meher's corps, who came passenger in the schooner Halcyon, that the schooner Mary Jane (which took Gen. M. and his company to Tampico) was lost on the Bar, in attempting to get in. The crew and company arrived safe on shore. The General then marched to the fort at Tampico, which he took possession of without opposition, and attacked the town at night, but was repulsed with the loss of several killed and twenty-two taken prisoners—the remainder, including Gen. Meher, escaped and took passage on board a vessel for Brazoria, where they safely arrived— many of whom are waiting an opportunity to return to New Orleans.

—*Nashville Banner & Nashville Whig*, December 28, 1835

Reports of the progress of Austin's army at San Antonio remained optimistic, yet always looming overhead was the shadow of Santa Anna's vengeful hand.

NATCHEZ, Dec. 17.

TEXAS.

Some of our fellow citizens have returned from Texas. They represent every thing in that country as progressing as prosperously as the friends of Texas could wish.

A Courier has been intercepted from Santa Anna to Cos. Santa Anna writes to Cos to hold on to the garrison until March when he will come to his relief with from 5000 to 10,000 men. San Antonio must fall before then, and is in all probability, already in the hands of the Texians. The eighteen pounder, purchased at New Orleans, was on the way, together with a five horse wagon load of balls. With the aid of the eighteen pounder, the work will be soon accomplished.

—*Nashville Banner & Nashville Whig*, January 1, 1836

Included in the following article—reflecting a variety of news from the Texas war front—was the insinuation that Cos's soldiers had forced women of Béxar into prostitution.

LATEST FROM ST. ANTONIO.

Mr. Winston arrived here on Tuesday last, having left St. Antonio on the 28th ultimo. He informs us that Gen. Cos had barricaded that town, and planted cannon upon the church, which occupies its square and centre, and is three hundred feet above its level. By this position, Mr. Winston further states, the Mexicans are enabled to rake all the streets in the place—there being only four.

Gen. Cos has 800 troops under his command at that point, while a part of the Texian army, about 200 in number, are in possession and stationed at some mills one-half mile above St. Antonio, and the remainder of it stationed at several advantageous points for the purpose of cutting off all manner of recruits to Cos.

On the 27th, the day previous to Mr. W.'s departure, a report had reached the Texian forces that a reinforcement of 400 Mexicans were on their way to join General Cos. Col. Fanning, (of Ga.) a gallant soldier and a skillful

officer, was despatched with one hundred men to meet them and cut them off.

On the 29th, the Texian army were to have received a large field piece, with one hundred and one balls. As soon as they arrived they designed to assault the town, and from their favorable situation at the mills, it was expected to break down the walls and storm the town, without even the loss of lives or bloodshed.

The brave and intrepid little Texian army have bantered General Cos with the odds of four to one, if he would dare march out and give them a fair fight in the open prairie; but the courageous General could not muster courage enough to show fight with his eight hundred Spaniards against two hundred Texians!

The republican Mexicans of St. Antonio are much enraged at the brutal conduct of Gen. Cos, in prostituting female virtue to the licentiousness of his soldiery, for which it is supposed that he cannot possibly ever leave the town.

Houston has been appointed major-general of the regular troops, and was, on the 28th ult., recruiting. By this time he is with the main army at St. Antonio. Gen. Austin has resigned his command; Col. Fanning was solicited to take it, but, because his company, who went with him to that country, insisted that he should remain their commander, he declined.

In all probability the town of St. Antonio, by this time, has been made a conquest by the Texians. If this be the case, they have declared themselves free and independent, and Texas is, by conquest, theirs. Each common soldier will be entitled to 640 acres of land in addition to wages.—*Memphis Gazette*, Dec. 10.

—*Richmond Enquirer*, January 5, 1836

The following intimate account of an "incident" during the siege of Béxar, as recalled by Gonzales veteran Richard H. Chisholm, was published in a Texas newspaper sixteen years later and was written somewhat in the style of a folksy memoir. It contains, amidst some possible errors of memory, a few rarely noted details that are verified in a handful of other accounts, such as Mexican rockets fired from the Alamo and from San Fernando Church and the huge flag flying over the "black flag battery."[4]

For the Advocate.
An Incident in the Siege of San Antonio.

"Well, Uncle Dick," we all cried, as we sat round the fire one cool evening, not long since, in the building which is called, in this newly established town of his, The Hotel. "Well, Uncle Dick, come tell us a story of the war of Texian Independence." Richard H. Chisholm, or as he is more familiarly called, Uncle Dick, had fought all through the war—had seen the first flash of gunpowder which was burnt in it—and had forged, in Gonzales, with his own hands, the first cannon ball with which the Texians charged their cannon, to hurl death and defiance into the embattled hosts of Mexico, and which hissed in their ears in voices of thunder, that these were the sons of sires who had fought, bled and died in the old American Revolution, had built up a nation the most glorious in the world, and which Imperial Jove, himself, well might have called the Eternal. With his own hands he had wrought from common blacksmiths' iron, forty large round shot, and had cut up five hundred pounds of the same iron into grape shot and slugs. This composed, at the time, the whole of the Texian store, with only two small cannon to shoot them from. With this small force in artillery, and having only 900 effective men, armed with rifles and bowie knives, they undertook the siege of San Antonio, and with these, they compelled the well trained regulars of Mexico to evacuate the town.

Upon our call, the old man cast his eyes upon the rafters, and seemed to be endeavoring to collect his thoughts. A faint smile then broke over his countenance, and he thus began a story of the Siege of San Antonio:

"It was at the siege of San Antonio, and we were camped at the old mill,[g] situated above the town, when one night there was a call made for volunteers to go and assault the town. This was intended as a feint by the commanders, though we (the men) were kept in entire ignorance of that fact, and thought that the attack was to be made to carry the town in earnest. Well, the call was made, and of the company commanded by

Captain John Alley, (of which I was a member,) every man volunteered. The object really was to discover (as I learned afterwards) the situation of a marked battery which it was supposed the Mexicans had planted, in case of an assault, to rake us fore and aft. The weather was very cold and bad, and each man took his blanket or overcoat and sallied forth, silent and in darkness, rifle in hand and knife at belt.—The attack was to have been made on the four sides of the town at once. Burleson commanded our division, and Cols. Travis, Neille, Fannin and Bowie, the others. The signal of attack was to be three guns from the division of Travis, (who had charge of the force engaged,) fired one after the other in quick succession. When these arrangements were made, the word was passed, and we marched forward. Spies, also, were sent in advance, to guard us against discovery. Two and two we moved forward, sometimes crawling on our hands and knees and sometimes half bent, until we crept within two or three hundred yards of the church, and here our passage was impeded by a brush fence. Then came the word along the line in whispers, from the commander, passed from man to man: Let every man be ready; cross the fence one at a time; lay flat on the ground as soon as you get over, and crawl slowly and cautiously forward. I suppose somewhat near half had crossed in this manner, when it came to the turn of a Dutchman (Sam Shoupp was his name) to cross. He did not exactly understand the order, and thinking that fighting was to be done right off, had cocked his musket. In crossing, his foot become entangled in the brush—he fell over, and his gun went off, very near killing two or three, and making a tremendous report. Halt, and lay close! now ran along the line. Down fell every man in the grass, and up went the rockets from the walls of the Church and Alamo, illuminating everything around, and *sentinella alerto* rang from the walls in quick, loud and startled tones, that made the cold air of the night vocal with its echoes. Occasionally a rocket would alight near us, but was scarcely on the ground before some of the men had bounced upon it and extinguished it. I have often thought of that time, and wondered

<hr>
[g] Most accounts refer to it as a sugar mill.

we were not discovered. The rockets were very brilliant, and sometimes they would fall very near us. Thus we lay for a considerable length of time, until the tumult in the town had somewhat subsided, and again we moved forward, laying close to the ground, and moving more like beasts than men. A short distance before us, the picket-guard fire, which we were slowly nearing, blazed cheerily and brightly up, and often I wished I was by it. Behind it lay the town, and in the street we were approaching there was a fandango house, and the dancing was going on at a rapid rate. From where we lay, we could see the men and women whirling round in the waltz, and hear the notes of the violin, played most beautifully. It appeared, too, that the same scene was also being enacted in three other parts of the town, from the sounds we could hear. Our course lay along a ditch about four or five feet deep, and more than half full of water. Silently we moved forward along its banks, and soon the body of the picket-guard sentinel loomed up in the darkness, between us and the light of the fandango house. Just then the dogs of the town scented us, and came tearing out towards us, up to the place where the sentinel stood, who was stationed about fifty yards in advance of us. Around him they stopped, howling and barking at such a rate that any one less watchful than himself would have suspected the vicinity of something unfriendly. We heard his rough voice bid the dogs be-gone, in his own tongue, and then call out toward us, who goes there? who goes there? Again he would endeavor to quiet the dogs, and again call out to us in Spanish, "who goes there?" We could plainly see that he was anything but comfortable! We had halted when the dogs first came out, and were laying flat on the ground and watching. Myself and my companion were the two foremost men.—He was Sam High Smith, well known to most of the old settlers of the West as a brave and good man. He remarked in a whisper to me—Uncle Dick, I see that fellow. I see him, too, said I, in the same tone. Sam then raised himself up and pointed his gun towards the sentinel, and said, "I could fetch him down as pretty!" Well, said I, I could too;

but don't shoot, or old Ed Burleson will be as mad as the devil. But I could bring him down so pretty that it would be a pity not to do it, said he. I heard him cock his gun. For God's sake, Sam, said I, don't shoot; old Ed will be as mad as hell, if you do; for he told us not to fire until we heard the three signal guns, and if we break his orders he will be as mad as the devil. But the temptation was too strong for Sam. Whilst I was yet speaking, almost, I saw a stream of fire issue from his rifle simultaneously with a sharp report, and the Mexican took to his heels, the dogs went howling after him, and all ran towards the town. Now you've played hell, said I. Well, I missed him, said Sam; but just hark how the damned scoundrel is running—just listen! Sure enough, we could hear his heels rattling among the gravel beautifully. Now, said Smith, old Ed will be round here directly, and we will tell him that it was the Mexican fired at us. You need not do that, said I; old Ed knows too well the difference between an escopette report and the crack of a rifle. He will tell you so too. Just then Capt. Swisher came up, and demanded of me who it was that fired. I told him I believed it was some of the boys on my right. No, said Sam, it was the damned scoundrel fired at us. The fandango was still going on, and the only effect of the shot was, that the sentinels on the walls of the Church and Alamo sent up a double quantity of rockets, and filled the air with cries of *sentinella alerto*. About the time that the conversation above related occurred, some fellow from behind fired at the fandango room. Immediately we heard screams, curses in Spanish, and groans—the light was immediately put out, and we broke up that fandango. Simultaneously with the report of the gun, the command was given to fall into the ditch, which was instantly obeyed. Every man jumped into it, up to his hips, in water as cold as ice.—The cannon from the walls of the Church and Alamo then bellowed forth, and the balls came flying and tearing the ground up and throwing dirt all over us. The rocks, too, where the balls would strike, flew into fragments, which filled the air.—I was in the war from the beginning to the close, and have been in many

From the Phil Collins Collection

East India Musket with Bayonet

This beautiful musket is quite rare because it is complete with bayonet and bayonet scabbard and all are in excellent condition.

According to the engraving on the tail of the lock plate, it was produced in London by Mr. Ramsay Sutherland. He produced flintlock pistols, coach guns, and muskets from the late 1700s until the 1830s, and though he may only have produced the locks, the markings suggest it's probable that he was responsible for the complete musket.

Due to the historical background of muskets of similar origin, it could well be that this one was first used during the Napoleonic Wars, but as there are no unit markings present, it cannot be proven. During those wars, a staggering 2.8 million of these Brown Bess muskets were produced for the British government. They obviously thought they were going to be busy not only building the empire but also enforcing it.

When the wars ended in 1815, there was a considerable surplus, so in 1823 when the Republic of Mexico needed replacements for its poor weapons, a contract was agreed upon to purchase the surplus firearms for Mexico. The

This gives you an idea of what the Baker bayonet scabbard throat might have looked like if intact.

predominant weapon was the East India Brown Bess and many of Sutherland's muskets were among those sold, finally ending up in Texas and used at the Alamo, Goliad, and San Jacinto.

This sale from England to Mexico continued until 1835.

The accompanying bayonet is the standard British 1750 pattern, its blade triangular in shape. The leather scabbard with brass throat is intact except for the brass tip.

This gives you an idea of what the Baker bayonet scabbard throat might have looked like if intact.

In all, I believe it is a great example of the most used weapon by the Mexican forces in the Texas Revolution. –PC fights and cannonades, but I never heard nor saw such an one before or since. They pealed incessantly, and the balls struck closely, too, considering that it was in the dark, and we in a ditch! Our men fired back, but could do no injury, being a good way off and having to fire upon the lights only, though they fired upon every one that showed itself.—About this time, Travis fired his three signal guns, and then the cannon turned upon him—then it was first at him and then at us, until about 3 o'clock, the weather as cold as the polar regions, and we standing in the water. About 3 o'clock we managed to get out of the water and return to camp, which we reached about the dawn of day. I then laid myself down to snatch a nap of sleep, and slept, I suppose, an hour or two, (the cannonading continuing all the time, now being on the mill, where we were.)—I had slept, as I said before, an hour or two, when I was aroused by the sweetest music I thought I ever heard— French horns, fifes and drums. The Mexicans were marching out to attack us in our position in the mill. They filed out in beautiful order. Six hundred infantry and four hundred cavalry, marching out to attack us, 140 in all, concealed behind the walls of an old mill! The infantry deployed to the right and the cavalry to the left—they marched to a little open prairie, about 200 yards in our front, and halted. There they stood, the officers riding up and down the lines, beating them with the flats of their swords, and sometimes riding half way to us. But the men stood stock still; no threats, blows, entreaties or promises, could induce them forward. We could hear the officers swear and carajo and strike, and then they would start towards us and cry out in Spanish, to come on. But no! the dastardly soldiers would not budge! One of our men (old Deaf Smith, of burning bridge memory) jumped on the walls of the old mill, and waving his hat round his head, beckoned them forward—but they thought themselves near enough, and would not come. In a few moments the music, which came out so gaily, struck up a doleful air, and we could see them turn slowly around and take up their march back to the town. Back they went, these fine picked soldiers

of Mexico, whose iron heels were to tramp out the struggling liberty-spark that yet blazed in Texas—one thousand in number, returning without striking a blow, before 140 of the ragged, untrained soldiers of Texas! There arose a shout from our ranks, wild tumultuous and derisive—hats were flourished, and the laugh and jest went gaily round at the expense of the bold Mexicans. But still the cannonading continued, and the balls occasionally cut very close. I had cooked a pot of beans, and was just about to commence eating them—I had taken the pot off the fire, and invited my mess to come and eat. Boys, come and take some beans, said I. As I spoke, I stooped to sit down; and as I stooped to sit down, a cannon ball bounded over the wall, grazed my head hard enough to knock me heels-over-head, passed on, and tore a hole in the ground large enough to throw in a good-sized ox. I lay on the ground awhile, then arose and put my hand on my head to see if there was much of a hole in it, rather uncertain about whether I was dead or alive. Boys, said I, you can eat them beans, for that damned Mr. Cos's ball has taken away my appetite. Two young men had climbed two pecan trees, to look over into the town and see what they (the Mexicans) were at. Presently we saw smoke from one of their cannons rise high in the air. We knew very little about war, less about cannon, and did not care a snap of the fingers for anything. So one of the men in the trees called out to the other— By the Lord, their old cannon snap'd that time! But before he was done speaking, the ball hustled through the tree and tore off some limbs so close in his vicinity, that he and the others hustled down in much quicker time than they went up, and then the laugh went round against them; and, boys, I believe Mr. Cos was trying to hit you, some of them said. Another man was stooping down by a projecting wall, filling his gourd-bottle with water; a ball came and tore away the wall, turned him a somerset, and he alighted on his back. He got up, felt to see that no bones were broken, and then in an angry tone called out—That Mr. Cos is damned rascal. If I could get a crack at him, I'd stop them pop-guns! I'll kill two of his men anyhow, to pay for that scare! Such were the soldiers of Texas! Thus they scorned danger and cracked their jokes amidst the rattle of musketry and the boom of cannon! It was thus that the day wore on. We brought out our two little pieces of cannon, and began to return the fire from the town. We had but few balls, and consequently had to collect those fired from the town, to keep up our fire, and as soon as a ball would strike the ground, a dozen men would jump towards it, and as soon as it was cool enough to ram down without burning the powder in the cannon, back it went to make its return to the camp from whence it came.[5] About half an hour before sundown, Cos raised a large black flag, seeming to cover nearly half an acre of ground, and when the breeze would unfurl its sable folds we could see painted in large yellow letters, on either side, the words—*The war of extermination!* Immediately we knew our terms—victory or death! And between his clenched teeth, each one swore a solemn oath to make that ground his resting place, and to let the wolves of the prairies fatten on his flesh, and his bones bleach exposed in the sun, ere his face should be turned from the enemy! The cannon and rifles were instantly turned upon this horrible flag, and soon we had the pleasure of seeing it torn and riddled into fragments.—That night it hung drooping in the "moonless nie;" and though the breeze blew, it of itself seemed reluctant to be seen even in the night; and that shame which never yet tinged the Mexican face for the most dastardly deed, seemed instinctively to possess and oppress their horrid flag. It was thus we continued fighting—sometimes with rifles and in close quarters, and always cannonading—for five days and nights. In the meantime, Gen. Austin resigned, and Burleson took command. The fifth day we entered the town in triumph, and with pleasure saw the warriors of Mexico—superior in numbers and discipline—evacuating the town; here and there the dead bodies of their comrades bleaching in the sun. I would to tell you of many deeds that were done, and many men who fought in the siege. Milam, than whom no better nor braver man ever lived, whose noble bosom now rests beneath the sod

he fought for! and the Lockhart boys, too, and various others. But I am tired now, as I expect you are, and will give you the story at another time. For the present, let us retire to rest."

GEO. M. REID

December 15, 1850.
—*Texian Advocate*, February 20, 1851

Richard Chisholm's reminiscence of the attempted Mexican attack on the old mill is verified in the following 1835 report originally published in the *New Orleans Bee*. Also included is news of the long-awaited Texian offensive into Béxar itself. Just as the Texian army was about to abandon the siege because of diminishing provisions, insufficient clothing, and bad weather, a middle-aged man stepped forward and addressed his comrades, "Who will follow old Ben Milam into San Antonio?" The next day, December 5, two divisions of volunteers, totaling about three hundred men, began what would become a grueling five-day assault.

NEW ORLEANS, December 21
IMPORTANT FROM TEXAS.—On Saturday a gentleman who recently left Texas, called at this office to inform us that on the 29th ult. about 350 Mexicans in a sortie made an attack on a detachment of the Texian army at that part of the entrenchments near the mill in the neighborhood of San Antonio; and that between fifty and sixty of the enemy were killed, while on the part of the Texians, there were only one killed and three wounded. The gentleman informed us that the Texians kept the enemy completely at bay with their rifles, which they used calmly and deliberately in operation: hence the disparity of number killed on both sides.

But yesterday the arrival of the Julius Caesar from Brazoria, whence she sailed on the 14th inst., affords us additional information more interesting and important, as concentrating the incidents of the Texian struggle towards the denouement. Early on the morning of the 5th inst., the Texians under Capt. Milam made an assault on the town of San Antonio. We have not ascertained the particulars of this attempt, but are informed that after a hard contested strife with the besieged, which continued unremittingly for 36 hours, the assailants succeeded in obtaining possession of three stone houses, where they secured themselves, and from which they were enabled to silence three of the enemy's guns commanding important positions. The express that brought the intelligence to Brazoria had left about 4 P.M. on the 6th; and at that period the fight continued to thicken on all sides. The Texians had then 2 killed and 12 wounded; and although the loss of the enemy could not be ascertained—as they carried off as many of the dead as they could, the destruction was considered great, as not less than 17 corpses were counted around one of the guns that had been silenced.

Since writing the above, a passenger called to inform us, that the latest advices received from San Antonio, were that Cos had been obliged to evacuate the town and retire into the fort with the forces left him; and that there appeared little doubt of his being compelled shortly to capitulate, or be put hors de combat. Separate victories may stimulate the Texians to accomplish a final one; and this being effected, Texas will probably be declared free of the Mexican people and confederacy. "To this complexion must it come at last."

—*Richmond Enquirer*, January 7, 1836

Then arrived news that most Americans and Texians had long expected: Cos had surrendered!

GLORIOUS NEWS FROM TEXAS.
"Freedom's battle once begun
Bequeathed from bleeding sire to son
Tho' baffled oft is surely won."
St. Antonio, the last fortress of the despot Santana, in Texas, has fallen!

The valor and perseverance of the colonial troops were irresistible. This ever to be remembered event took place on Thursday, Dec. 10th. On the Saturday previous (the 5th) 300 of the Colonial troops entered the town of San Antonio, under the command of Col. Benj. R. Milam. They could not at first get possession of the public square owing to the walls and ditches across the mouths of the streets, each of which was likewise defended by two pieces

of artillery, and in consequence of this, they occupied some buildings and tops of houses adjacent. Here they remained battling unceasingly night and day, until Wednesday the 9th when they forced their way into the square and drove the enemy across the river into their fort called the "Alamo."

In these relative situations the battle continued until Thursday 10th, when the enemy capitulated.

By the capitulation, upwards of 1000 yielded to less than 300. The town itself was surrendered with 24 pieces of brass artillery, 1900 rounds of powder, ball, grape and canister, with the public stores of every description.

This glorious conquest was achieved, with a loss on the part of the conquerors of only 3 killed and 30 wounded, while the loss of the enemy in killed is variously estimated, at from 60 to 150.

But the joy of triumph was sadly diminished by the circumstance that the brave Milam, the dauntless leader of the storm, was numbered among the slain. He fell by a ball through the head while fearlessly animating his men to victory. Long! long will Texas and the friends of liberty remember and lament his fall. Among the gallant band who stormed the town were more than 100 volunteers from the US, of the north. The New Orleans Grays and Blues constituted a great majority of these, and the remainder were from different parts of the state of Mississippi. The whole of them were among the first and foremost where the battle raged hottest; and displayed throughout the undaunted bravery of disciplined regulars.

—*New Orleans Bee*, January 4, 1836

Milam became the first of many martyrs of the Texas Revolution, and fifty years later his death was recalled by a veteran during an interview with a correspondent, one "A. J. S." of the *Galveston News*, who had visited San Antonio.

From the Alamo I wandered to Soledad street, and entered the old Veramendi house, famous in Texas history as the place where the gallant Milam lost his life when the Texans under him stormed the city in 1835. From Mr.

Pleasant McAnneily, who was an eye-witness, I learned the particulars of Milam's death. He says that after they had worked their way to the Veramendi house, Deaf Smith, the spy, ascended to the roof and shot a Mexican near the plaza, but was in turn fired on and severely wounded, and had to be brought below. The Mexicans then commenced a heavy fire through the doors fronting the street; the men sheltered themselves the best way they could and commenced digging port holes through the walls. Franklin Harvey, while crossing the yard in the rear of the building, was killed, and in a few minutes Milam came, and, seeing a great many balls lying on the ground, stooped to pick one up, when one of the men exclaimed: "Look out, colonel;" but at that instant a ball struck Milam in the head, and he fell forward. Several brave men, however, went to him and conveyed his body into a room. Near the spot where Milam fell there is a mound of earth and stones about three feet high, where, some say, he is buried; but others say his remains lie on the west side of the San Pedro, with a flat stone to mark the spot.
—*Texas Siftings*, October 10, 1885 (reprinted from *Galveston News*)

Milam's last moments were also related by the granddaughter of Texas Revolution veteran John Ingram. She took down his oral memoir specifically for an 1895 issue of the *Dallas Morning News*.

In a few Days Colonel Milam called for volunteers to "go in and take San Antonio." Three hundred men stepped out, grandfather among the number. This act was not approved by General Burleson. They went into the town the latter part of the night, took possession of two houses, Veramendi being one, and opened fire on the enemy again at daybreak. The Mexicans had their cannon so arranged that they were exposed to the Texans in reloading. As fast as they came out to reload the Texans would shoot them down, therefore they had to abandon the use of their cannon.

The Texans took the town house by house the third day. Their gallant leader, Captain Milam, was killed. Each man stayed at his post as Milam had ordered. The fourth morning the enemy had a black flag floating from the Alamo. This meant no quarters. This so excited the Texans that they came near charging the Alamo, but the Mexicans drew the flag down the next day, being the fifth day of the siege and the 9th day of December, 1835. A white flag was raised and the companies surrendered. The Texans then sent for General Burleson, who was at camp about one-half mile away. The general immediately came and arranged the condition of the surrender. Grandfather was talking to Colonel Milam a few minutes before he was killed. He saw him buried in Veramendi's back yard, the place where he was killed. He was shot from the cupola of the church. The Texans got their cannon, which had been dismounted, and placed it on a rock wall. Captain Dickinson sighted it for the cupola of the church and another man took a long pole and touched it off.[6] It is needless to say there was no more shooting from the cupola.
—*Dallas Morning News*, April 14, 1895

The terms of Cos's surrender were summarized in a February 1836 issue of *Nile's Register*.

FROM TEXAS.
Capitulation of San Antonio.

Articles entered into between general Cos, of the Mexican army, and gen. Burlison, of the army of Texas, on the 10th of December, 1835.

General Cos, is to retire in six days with his officers, arms, and private property, on parole of honor. He is not to oppose the re-establishment of the constitution of 1824.

The infantry and the cavalry, (the remnant of Morale's battalion), and the convicts to return taking with them 10 rounds of cartridge, for safety, against the Indians.

All public property, money, arms and ammunition to be delivered to gen. Burilson, of the Texian army.

Private property to be respected and the citizens to be protected in their persons.

The sick and wounded to be provided for.

No soldier to be molested on account of his former political opinions.

Prisoners of war. To be set at liberty.
—*Nile's Register*, February 6, 1836

Cos Surrenders

"St. Antonio, the last fortress of the despot Santana, in Texas, has fallen!" cheered the January 4, 1836, edition of the *New-Orleans Bee*. Faced with increasing casualties, desertions, and a chaotic situation within the Alamo—jammed with hundreds of besieged troops, horses, and noncombatants—General Martín Perfecto de Cos grimly decided to treat for the best possible terms with the surrounding army of rebel Texians. On the morning of December 9, 1835, three figures left the fort, heading for the town of San Antonio de Béxar, where a brave but tiny contingent of the Mexican army still held on. As shown in the illustration (left to right) these emissaries were: Don Ramón Múzquiz (his face based on a later portrait), a leading Bexareño whom Antonio López de Santa Anna would appoint the town's "Jefe Politico" the following year; Lt. Col. José Juan Sánchez Navarro, the officer in charge of this duty; and First Lt. Don Francisco Rada, of the Second Company (Activo) of the Nuevo Leon battalion. They walked across ground battered by several "exceedingly cold and wet" days of almost "continuous rains."[1]

The Mexican eagle still flew over the old church; not until the next morning would a white "parley" flag be raised there.[2] And on that day—December 10—the capitulation terms were finally agreed upon, the paper itself signed on December 11.[3]

---

1. Frank W. Johnson to General Edward Burleson, San Antonio, 1835 (no date), in Wallace O. Chariton, *100 Days in Texas: The Alamo Letters* (Plano, Tex.: Wordware Publishing Inc., 1990), 16; C. D. Huneycutt, *At the Alamo: The Memoirs of Captain Navarro* (New London, N.C.: Gold Star Press, 1989), 5, 14.
2. Huneycutt, *At the Alamo,* 20.
3. Francis Johnson, *A History of Texas and Texans* (Chicago: American Historical Society, 1914), 1: 358–360.

Long before word of San Antonio's fall arrived in Mexico, troops were already beginning their march northward to assist Cos and exterminate the upstart Texians.

From the New-York Daily Advertiser
LATE AND IMPORTANT FROM MEXICO. GREAT EXCITEMENT AGAINST THE AMERICANS—SANTA ANNA IN QUIET POSSESSION OF THE GOVERNMENT— TWO MILLIONS OF DOLLARS

APPROPRIATED, AND AN ARMY ON THEIR MARCH AGAINST THE TEXIANS
The packet ship Montezuma, captain Davis, arrived yesterday, having sailed on the 6th inst. The news is of the most interesting character. A friend who possesses the best sources of information, has obligingly furnished us with the following summary of news from his private letters, dated Mexico, 1st, and Vera Cruz to the 6th, which is much later than has been received via New Orleans.

The excitement against the Americans in the whole republic was so great, in consequence of the capture of the *Correo* and the proceedings of the Texians, that serious apprehensions were entertained for the safety of the person and property of the former.

The popular party have made some demonstration to disturb the public tranquility; but the government was informed in time of their maneuvers, and several of the leaders were arrested. On the 1st, tranquility prevailed in the whole republic.

Two thousand infantry were already on their march to Matamoras and four hundred cavalry to Monterrey. General Fortazar was to take the command of the infantry, and Gen. Montezuma that of the cavalry. Santa Anna was to leave his seat for Mexico on the 7th inst. He has greatly enlarged the army for the last two months. The bishops of Puebla and Mexico have put at his disposal two millions of dollars, for the purpose of putting down the rebellion in Texas. It was confidently expected that Santa Anna would go to Texas immediately after the promulgation of the new Constitution.— The basis of it had already been published under the title of *acta constitutiva*. We shall give more details as soon as we get our papers.
—*Saratoga Sentinel*, December 12, 1835

Back in Béxar, the victorious Texians counted their spoils.

INVENTORY,

Of military stores delivered in conformity with the capitulation entered into on the 11th of December, 1835, between general Martin Perfecto de Cos, of the permanent troops, and general Edward Burleson, of the colonial troops of Texas.

IN BEJAR.
30 useless muskets.
5 boxes ammunition.
4 drums.
4 boxes with 66 hats and 49 blankets, of the company of lancers.
1 bale with 12 dozen blankets.
1 four-pound cannon, mounted.
1 chinesco.
2 trumpets.

2 clarions.
1 large clarion.
2 cymbals.
IN THE ALAMO.
2 four-pound cannon, mounted.
2 small brass ditto.
1 four-pound field piece.
1 ditto three-pounder, complete.
1 rammer.
1 cannon, four-pounder, with carriage and rammer.
1 iron culverine, of 9-inch calibre, mounted.
1 howitzer of 5-inch calibre.
1 cannon, six-pounder.
1 field piece, four-pounder.
1 cannon, three-pounder, mounted.
1 ditto six-pounder, mounted.
257 carabines and muskets.
IN THE ARSENAL.
11,000 musket cartridges.
2 cartouch boxes.
10 bags grape shot.
9 ditto with cartridges.
18 swivel worms.
8 howitzer ditto.
100 small cannon cartridges.
18 packages musket cartridges.
10 port fires.
16 swivel worms.
40 swivel cartridges.
1 bag containing one hundred pounds of powder.
50 packages cartridges.
16 ditto ditto
1 box cartridges, damp.
1 box musket cartridges.
1 box powder.
1200 musket cartridges.
1 ammunition box with twenty cannon balls.
10 quick matches.
1 box howitzer worms.
3 boxes musket cartridges.
2 ammunition boxes with forty cannon balls.
1 match cord.
1 box howitzer worms.
1 box cartridges.
2 ditto ditto.
7 empty ammunition chests.

17 muskets.
1 bugle.
2 boxes ammunition.
1 rammer.
1 lanthorn.
4 large cannon.
2 swivels.
1 four-pound cannon, mounted.
1 box 26 stands of grape.
1 box musket cartridges.
1 bag of powder.
1 bag of gun flints.
1 drum.
15 carabines, out of order.
11 packages cannon ball.
1 piece small ordnance.
        Delivered by Manchaca.
67 muskets.
15 coats.
9 gun locks.
49 duck jackets.
1 bunch of wire.
3 bars of steel.
1 small ditto of iron.
1 bunch flax thread.
15 skeins sewing silk.
63 duck jackets.
2 barrels containing one hundred and sixty-six
        bayonets.
9 aparejos.
58 lances.
1 pair scales with weights.
1 piece of linsey.
50 muskets with bayonets.
13 lances.
Bexar, December 13, 1835.
        Delivered by
JUAN CORTINA,
J. FRANCISCO DE RADA,
FRANCISCO HERRERA.
        Received by
JAMES CHESHIRE,
WILLIAM G. COOK,
W. H. PATTON.
Copy.
        F. W. JOHNSON,
        Colonel Commanding.
—*Telegraph and Texas Register*, January 2, 1836

The condition of Texas as it stood at this cross-roads in its history was summed up in a letter written by a Texas resident and printed in a New Hampshire newspaper.

FROM TEXAS.
Extract of a letter from a Gentleman residing at Matagorda, Texas, January 12, 1836, to a correspondent in Portsmouth.

The report that St. Antonio with Gen. Cos and his army, consisting of 1300 men, has surrendered to the Texans, is correct; and after a solemn oath from both officers and soldiers, that they would not again take up arms against Texas, they were allowed to go home with a few arms, ammunition, and some stores sufficient to last ten days.

This shows the magnanimity and generosity of the Americans. Our army consisted only of between 3 and 4 hundred men, and by this conquest gained a strong fortress, and the only one of note on our borders.—A large quantity of stores, arms, ammunition, horses and heavy artillery were taken.

Gen. Cos was severely wounded, and very many of his men killed, on our side Col. Milam was killed; and 6 others only, having from their favorable situation a good cover from the enemy.

When Cos sent into our Camp his white flag, our little army had but one keg of powder, besides a few rounds in their pouches. There was a singular providence in this, and it seems a proof that the arm of the Almighty had been stretched forth to give us the victory. We have now volunteers pouring in from all quarters, expecting another attack in the spring from Santa Anna, although many think he will not attempt it; but if he should, he will find no boy's play, as we can compete with any force he will dare to send from home; a counter revolution in Mexico, and a constant desertion of soldiers from his army, will prevent his sending a large force.

If Santa Anna knows what is for his good, he had better let us enjoy the Constitution of 1824, unmolested, otherwise, I have no doubt Texas will declare her Independence.

The company of volunteers who have just arrived, is commanded by a gentleman of high standing, who has been a member of the legislature of Alabama, has a considerable fortune, and a family residing in Courtland, Alabama. His officers, and part of his soldiers are young men of fortune, who are desirous of signalizing themselves, and have volunteered in a good cause.—When such men come to our aid, with heaven's blessing we are strong. There are, of course, many others of desperate character, who have all to gain, and nothing to lose.—Our standing army is recruiting fast.

The present state of things reminds me of the history of our own country in its infancy;—the bustle of arms and soldiers, and the busy scenes that constantly present themselves. Our cause is in fact the same which induced our Fathers to take up arms against Great Britain.

We have been deprived of the rights under which every man settled in the country, the laws of which were guaranteed by the Mexican nation to emigrants.—When troops began to enter the borders of our peaceful and quiet country under false pretences (while the inhabitants of Texas thought themselves safe from any invasion,) they, as true Americans, thought it time to demand their rights and privileges at the point of the bayonet; as they have done of late most gloriously. The death of those 28 poor fellows who were shot at Tampico,[h] has created a most deadly and determined hatred towards the Mexicans, in the hearts of all Texians, and woe be to those who enter her borders as enemies.

It is supposed the other states of Mexico, favorable to the Liberal constitution of 1824, seeing the success of Texas, will rise en-masse, and put Santa Anna down. His speedy dethronement is generally expected.
—*Portsmouth Journal of Literature and Politics*, February 20, 1836

However, not all of Cos's surrendered troops had joined him in the long march back to Mexico.

---

[h] A reference to the US prisoners who were executed after José Antonio Mexia's failed attempt to take the port of Tampico in November.

Extract of a letter to the Editor of the *Philadelphia Gazette*, dated,
NACOGDOCHES, (Texas,) Dec. 27.
Our town is generally like a fair,—soldiers passing to the field of action, emigrants coming into the country in immense numbers, the war notwithstanding; and for the last three or four days a number of the volunteers who went out at the commencement of the war, returning after the fall of San Antonio; and with those returning to-day, are several Mexican soldiers, who, after the surrender, requested to be allowed to come home with the Texonians, as servants. They cut a droll figure in the Mexican uniform, and their faces were nearly as black as negroes.
—*Phoenix Civilian*, February 2, 1836

The Mexican government, burning for revenge, promised it would deal with the rebels like the "pirates" they really were—a promise that would figure disastrously large in the events to come.

From the Diario of the 5th.
"We have the pleasure to announce that the expedition offered from Yucatan to protect Matamoras and Santa Anna de Tamaulipas, has arrived in safety, having parted company only with the schooner Jacinta with one hundred men on board, and that schooner is hourly expected at the latter place."

The official account of the capture of Bexar by the Texans is published in the Diario of the 2d, together with a letter from General Cos, dated at Salinas, twelve leagues from Bexar, on the road to Laredo. The Diario of the 3d thus comments upon the capture:—

"The fall of Bexar is lamentable, but the effect will be prejudicial to those perfidious colonists; they will speedily be punished by the valiant bands who are now marching to revenge their brethren in arms, and to take satisfaction for the outrages which have been committed by a people who ought to have better shown their gratitude for innumerable favors, of which they have proved themselves so unworthy.

"We do not deceive ourselves in predicting that the affairs of Texas will terminate favorably for Mexico, and that what now appears a

66

misfortune, will prove in reality a benefit, since it will become the means of establishing tranquility on durable grounds in that interesting portion of the republic."

General Cos writes that in his retreat from Bexar, he is accompanied by more than 500 men.

The collector at the port of Mazatlan has given up to the government half of his salary for one year, in aid of the expedition against the Texians; which act of patriotism is duly lauded in the *Diario del Goberno*.

The Nacional of the 1st contains a proclamation by the supreme government, dated the 30th December, of which the following is a translation.

1. All foreigners who shall land at any port of the republic, or arrive within its boundaries by land, being armed and having hostile intention against our territory, shall be treated and punished as pirates, and considered as belonging to no nation with which the republic is at war, and fighting under no recognized flag.

2. In the same manner will be treated all foreigners who shall land at any port; or introduce over land, arms and munitions of war, being intended to be used at any place in rebellion against the government or to be placed in the hands of its enemies.

The same journal announces the march of General Sesma with 2400 men for Bexar, and that 6000 more were at San Luis, waiting only for money to follow in the same direction.

El Cosmopolita of the 2d, announces that general Santa Anna set out that morning from San Luis Potosi for Leona Vicario, (formerly called Saltillo,) where he expected to arrive in three days.

The papers are filled with complaints and reproaches touching the movements in the United States for aiding the Texans; our government is censured for not preventing them, and the judicial opinion elicited from the District Court of the U.S. for this district, some time ago, is very severely commented on.

N. Y. Com.

—Baltimore Gazette and Daily Advertiser,
February 3, 1836

General Cos had been humiliated, and the honor of Mexican arms had to be restored. And to that end, as reports in another Mexican newspaper claimed (via translation by the US press), Santa Anna's new army was nearing ten thousand in number.

NEW ORLEANS, Feb. 9.—We have been favored with a file of the Tamaulipas Gazette to the date of the 7th of January, and give the following extracts:

"MEXICO, Dec. 25.—It has been officially announced to the Supreme Government, that on the 10th ult., the town of St. Antonio de Bejar was occupied by the rebel settlers of Texas, after eight days' consecutive attacks, and that the brave defenders of this post yielded only from a want of ammunition. His Excellency the General in-chief of the operations, Don A. S. Santa Anna, feeling, as every true Mexican ought, the disgrace thus sustained by the Republic, is making every preparation to wipe out the stain in the blood of those perfidious strangers. It is calculated, that on the 22d of the present month, he will begin his march upon Bejar, with an armament of 8,000 men and 25 pieces of artillery."

"JANUARY 10th.—His Excellency, the commander-in-chief, has succeeded, in the short space of little more than a month, in levying an effective army of from 9 to 10,000 men, which have commenced their march to San Luis de Potosi, firmly determined to conquer or die in the holy cause of avenging the outrage offered to the Mexican name and institutions. The sloop of war, general Bravo, is scouring the coast of Texas, to intercept the supplies of arms and provisions destined for that point. The ports of Tampico and Matamoras have been garrisoned with troops, sent for that purpose from the State of Yucatan, with a view to prevent any surprise from some better combined expedition than that misled by the adventurer Mejia."

It will be seen, that, like Jonathan's snake, the Mexican army destined against Texas, enlarges at every mention. In the extract we gave yesterday, it was stated at 6,600, on the 25th December, it grew into 8,000, and on the 10th of the January following has swelled into

9 or 10,000! The great discloser of all truths, Time, will show.

—*Richmond Enquirer*, February 27, 1836

For David Crockett, the first half of 1835 had been a time of keeping his sights aimed on the biggest game of the year: getting reelected in August to a fourth term in the US Congress. On the one hand, he continued to exploit his popular image as a frontier curio, and on the other, he never stopped raging against what he saw as President Andrew Jackson's tyranny, and the possibility that the "political Judeas," Martin Van Buren, might follow Old Hickory into the White House in 1837. If that ever happened, he had sworn in December 1834, "I will go to the wildes of Texes."[7]

Crockett had been nurturing his own presidential aspirations but saw some key supporters begin to fall away from him as his record of failed legislation, unending vitriol against political opponents, and heavy debt made him less attractive as a candidate. And two recent books (largely ghostwritten) with his name attached to them—*An Account of Col. Crockett's Tour to the North and Down East, in the Year of Our Lord One Thousand Eight Hundred and Thirty-Four* and *The Life of Martin Van Buren*—had met with poor sales. It seemed to him, and to many others, that his political star was dimming.

Major Downing and Davy Crockett appear to be getting out of vogue. The New York Times says—"In Col. Crockett, there is nothing but vulgarity, bald, barren slang, and stale jokes revamped in a dialect half yankee and half backwoodsman. In his last book there is not one title of redeeming humor." The Richmond Compiler remarks—"We must confess our want of taste to appreciate this family of books, in which vulgarity, cant phrases, and local barbarisms of speech, take the place, and what is worse, gain the applause of wit and smartness.

The truth and justice of these remarks cannot be denied. The merit of political satires should be their wit; the principal attraction of the works referred to is the vulgarity and slang of their dictions.

[*Phil. Gaz.*]

—*Baltimore Gazette and Daily Advertiser*, April 25, 1835

Crockett could still be charming at elite Washington affairs, yet he never fully detached himself from his roots as a man of the people.

The gossip of the Washington letter-writers, is far more amusing latterly than the proceedings of Congress. A correspondent of the Boston Gazette says:

A few evenings since, Matthew St. Clair Clarke, Esq. late Clerk of the House of Representatives, gave a splendid soiree, to which the members of Congress were invited without distinction of party. Davy Crockett was in attendance, and received the flattering testimonials of the ladies. Davy, with all his rudeness, is not destitute of an occasional grace of manner, and action, or something else, which commends him to the smiles of the fair, and some of the anecdotes he relates to them are abundantly ludicrous and amusing. In the course of the evening, a young widow from the North, who is celebrated for her wit and beauty, after all her fund of humor had been exhausted, incidentally asked Davy where he boarded? Davy replied, that he had previously boarded at Brown's Hotel, but had left the establishment for a day or two, on account of a political gala that was then approaching. I do not board in the place my predecessor did, said Davy, for I never could endure the fare to which he submitted. And where did he board?—enquired the lady. Oh, he boarded with a blacksmith, replied the colonel, and slept in the coal yard, and paid his board by blowing and striking, and shoeing horses, after the House had concluded each day's business!

—*Vermont Phoenix*, February 13, 1835

In July, the *Arkansas Advocate* reprinted the following speculation, originally appearing in a Tennessee newspaper, on the upcoming race for the congressional seat between the Whig Crockett and the Democrat Adam Huntsman, a bright, peg-legged lawyer and political writer cut from nearly the same waggish cloth as Crockett.

From the Jackson (Ten.) Truth Teller.
CONGRESSIONAL ELECTION.

The canvass for a seat in Congress from this district is daily increasing in warmth and interest. Two old campaigners—Col. Crockett and Mr. Huntsman—are in the field single handed. The latter of these gentlemen has never been beaten in a popular election, while past events prove that the former, in a backwoods phrase, is "hard to head." 'Tis a handsome race, and such an one as we like to see. When last heard from, the two candidates were in Henry county, speechifying the people—David, it is said, among other things, collecting materials for his anticipated work, the "Second Fall of Adam," while "Black Hawk," with his accustomed sagacity, it is said, is daily made to grieve at seeing his competitor's labor thrown away—feeling every confidence that he will be enabled to put him "up a tree," at the polls on the first Thursday.

We are gratified to learn that the canvass continues to progress with perfect harmony and good humor between them.

—*Arkansas Advocate*, July 10, 1835

Evidence of Crockett's "good humor," if now laced with a slightly bitter tang, can be seen in the following campaign confrontation between himself and Huntsman, as reported by the Whig *Advocate*.

We learn from one of the Tennessee papers, that while Col. Crockett, a few days ago, was addressing the people in Wesley, a pert political opponent, with the view of confounding him, handed him a 'coon skin asking him if it was good fur. The speaker, instead of flying into a passion, deliberately took the skin, blew it, examined it, and turning to the owner, dryly remarked, "No, sir, 'tis not good fur; my dogs wouldn't run such a 'coon, nor bark at a man that was fool enough to carry such a skin." The poor fellow slunk away, and has not been heard of since.

—*Arkansas Advocate*, August 28, 1835

Early election results in west Tennessee's Carroll County were leaning Davy's way: "Crockett, 816 — Huntsman, 650." Elsewhere the count ran closer.[8] It was beginning to seem quite possible that Crockett might return to Washington, D.C., to serve another two years in Congress. And if Van Buren should happen to be elected president in 1837, well, then Davy would probably pack up his kit, as he had threatened, and move to Texas.

5

Crockett Goes to Texas

A. Huntsman is elected to Congress from the 12th district of Tennessee, beating the buffoon, Davy Crockett, by about 300 majority.
—*Arkansas Gazette*, August 25, 1835

Thus did one newspaper announce newcomer Adam Huntsman's defeat of Whig candidate David Crockett in his run for a fourth term in the US House of Representatives. The Jacksonian press was ruthless in its sarcastic glee.

"GO AHEAD." Davy Crockett, it appears, by the latest returns, has been *treed* by his opponent *Huntsman*. David has lost his election, his opponent having received a majority of more than two hundred votes; whereat we shall have one universal yell of despair from the Wigs and Wiglets from Maine to Florida and from Cape Cod to Terrahaute. The *buffoon* may now play his antics to the *varmints* of the forest, or join a caravan and *grin* for the amusement of the "lookers on."
—*Eastern Argus* (Maine), September 9, 1835

The development, in fact, was tailor-made for punning jabs.

A HUNTSMAN BEATEN, YET VICTORIOUS.—The Hon. DAVID CROCKETT, of hunting fame renowned, has at length been *beaten* on his own *beaten* track, and by one of his own kith, bone and persuasion. A. Huntsman, Esq. Has been elected member to Congress from West Tennessee, vice DAVID CROCKETT, Esq. "grinned off."
—*Commercial Bulletin and Missouri Literary Register*, August 24, 1835

Determined to brave a new start in rebellious Texas, the forty-nine-year-old Crockett himself issued a statement explaining the defeat as he saw it and, incredibly, mentioned the very man—Mexican general Antonio López de Santa Anna—who in less than six months would be personally responsible, by some accounts, for ordering Crockett's execution.

COLONEL CROCKETT. This gentleman has published a letter in the National Intelligencer, complaining indignantly of the base arts which were resorted to by the administration party, for defeating his election to Congress. He says,

"I had to contend against the whole popularity of Andrew Jackson and Governor Carroll, and the whole strength of the Union Bank. I have been told by good men that the managers of that Bank offered twenty-five dollars a vote for Mr. Huntsman. I had no bank to aid me: I expected to have a fair race; but when the time came, and the polls opened, I found all Huntsman judges, and, in nearly all cases, Huntsman officers to hold the election. In fact I am astonished that I came so near beating him as I did. Men that were out of their County could vote for Mr. Huntsman, and, at the same place, when they offered to vote for me, they were refused by the same judges.—In fact, I see no hope. The people have almost given up to a *Dictator*. Andrew Jackson has franked loads of the Extra Globe to every Post Office in this District, with a prospectus to get subscribers for it. Now I wish to ask the world a question, or the oldest man living, if ever they or he knew any President to serve out his time, and then to set down to open electioneering for his successor? The very paper franked by him, states that Judge White has sold himself to the Bank, and that there are no Jackson-White-men. I have come to the conclusion, when the People will sanction the like of this, we have but little to hope for. I do believe Santa Anna's Kingdom will be a paradise, compared with this in a few years. The People are nearly ready to take the yoke of bondage, and say "Amen! Jackson done it—it is all right."

—*Salem Gazette* (Massachusetts),
September 8, 1835

Some Whig papers also opined that political chicanery had foiled Crockett's return to Congress but held out hopes for his political future.

The tories raise as loud a shout at the defeat of David Crockett as that worthy would in *treeing* a panther. Davy is a hard customer, and they are no doubt glad to get rid of him. To effect that object all sorts of means were put in requisition. Even Gen. Jackson himself did not scruple to step into the ring to assist in flooring the backwoods man. A Tennessee paper states that fabricated documents, in the hand writing of Major Donalson, and *franked by the President*, giving an account of the mileage charged by Crockett, were circulated among the people, with the view of defeating his election! It is stated that he lost his election by a few hundred votes only. Huntsman who was elected over him, however, is opposed to Van Buren, so that the result is not material. Davy we hope will be more fortunate the next heat.–*Dov. Enq.*

—*New Hampshire's Portsmouth Journal of Literature and Politics*,
September 12, 1835

One paper offered a reason to explain how "Timber Toe" Huntsman had won: the sheer force of his personality.

CROCKETT'S SUCCESSOR. It is well known that Davy Crockett did not regret his defeat as a candidate for Congress so much, as he did being beaten by one Adam Huntsman. A correspondent of the Baltimore Patriot says,

that Adam is not to be sneezed at. "He made his debut on the 25th inst. (says that writer), and the members more generally crowded round him than they have ever been known to crowd around John Quincey Adams—ADAM spoke low, it is true; but then, when he bro't his grinning powers into full play, and bro't his heavy hickory iron shod leg—for you must know that the hero who beat CROCKETT, besides being short and thick, has a powerful wooden leg— down upon the floor in confirmation of a position, he produced an astonishing effect. From the distance where I stood I was unable to hear what he said; but from the crowds he drew about him, and from the peals of laughter which evident suppression only prevented from reverberating through the Hall, he is destined to become a lion like his predecessor." From the peculiar facility with which both these gentlemen distort their phizzes, we are inclined to think that to grin well must be the chief qualification of candidates in their district.—*Albany Advertiser.*

(Huntsman punctuates and *expounds* his speeches by his wooden stump. He is a greater *stump* orator than Davy Crockett, who was unable in pugilistic strife to knock Huntsman *off his pins*. Quintilian enumerates among the arts of rhetoricians the *supplosio pedis*, and *percussio femoris*, but he was a stranger to the modern "mortal pestle *pound* ye." Salem Gazette).

—*Salem Gazette*, February 2, 1836

A commentary in the *Louisville Advertiser* underscored the seeming lack of capable leadership in the Whig party and suggested that Crockett be picked as a vice presidential running mate for the November 1836 election.

The *Harrison, White, Webster, "any man"* Whig PARTY, appear to be in a deal of trouble about a *head*. If they should finally settle down upon Gen. Harrison, it is probable they will be equally at a loss for a *tail*. It may be well to suggest one for them, therefore we name for their consideration, Col. *Davy Crockett*, the most celebrated of the Whig fraternity. Now that he had been beaten for a seat in Congress, may be he will consent to play second fiddle to the *"Hero of the North Bend!"* The Whigs would be well fitted out with such a ticket. What the one failed to accomplish by his *commanding* talent, might be effected by the *grinning* faculty of the other.

We take the above advice to the Whigs from the Brookville (Ia.) Inquirer; it is very good, but unfortunately impracticable; Davy has become disgusted with this country since his defeat, and has determined to move to Texas, stock, lock, and barrel.—*Louisville Advertiser.*
—*Vermont Gazette*, October 6, 1835

"And good riddance!" is how some papers viewed Crockett's planned Texas journey.

We see by some of the papers that David Crockett, the Congressional buffoon, contemplates a removal to Texas. In his own language we say "go ahead."
—*Patriot and Democrat* (Connecticut), October 10, 1835

Col. Crockett is going to migrate to Texas.—There is a man in this city, called Sawney Bennet, whom Davy should take with him for his private secretary.[a]
—*New York Sun*, October 15, 1835

On November 1, Crockett left his home in Weakley County, Tennessee, en route with a brother-in-law, a nephew, and a neighbor for the potentially greener pastures of Texas. They all understood that dangers galore lay ahead of them; most of Texas was still a raw wilderness; the belligerent Comanche Indians remained unconquered; and it was by now old news in the United States that Mexican president Santa Anna was planning to send "a powerful military force into Texas, to coerce the citizens into compliance with his wishes, to make himself Dictator, on pain of expulsion from the country."[1] Word that that force—and in effect, the expected war—had already arrived in Texas, had been received by Tennesseans a week earlier, via a report in the *National Banner and Nashville Whig* of October 23.

---

[a] "Sawney Bennet" was a swipe at James Gordon Bennett, Sr., publisher of the *New York Sun*'s rival *New York Herald*, which professed a politically autonomous stance. "Sawney" was a synonym for foolish, weak, or silly.

WAR IN TEXAS.
IMPORTANT.—In the New Orleans Union of 13th inst., we find the following, taken from an extra of the Red River Herald, just received. A meeting of the friends of Texas was called on that evening in New Orleans, to adopt measures for the assistance of our brethren in Texas
HIGHLY IMPORTANT FROM TEXAS.
War in Texas—Gen. Cos Landed near the mouth of the Brassos with 400 men.
Isaac Parker has just arrived from Texas, bringing the Intelligence that Gen. Cos has landed near the mouth of the Brazos with 400 men, with the intention of joining the 700 federal troops stationed at San Antonio de Bexar, and marching upon the people of Texas. He has issued his Proclamation, "declaring that he will collect the revenue, disarm the citizens, establish a military govern't, & confiscate the property of the rebellious." Messr Johns & Baker bore the express from San Felipe to Nacogdoches. Steph S. Austin has written to several citizens of Nacogdoches, that a resort to arms is inevitable.
They have hoisted a flag with "The constitution of 1824," inscribed upon it and 200 freemen gathered around it, determined to stand or fall with it.
We subjoin the following letter from General Houston to the gentlemen who brought the intelligence:
SAN AUGUSTINE TEXAS,
Oct. 5th 1835.
DEAR SIR: —At your request I hand you a memorandum, that you may be informed of our situation—*War in defence of our rights, our oaths and our Constitution is inevitable in Texas.!*
If *Volunteers* from the United States will join their brethren in this section, they will receive liberal bounties of land. We have millions of acres of our best lands unchosen and unappropriated.
Let each man come with a good rifle and a hundred rounds of ammunition—and come soon.

Our war-cry is "Liberty or Death." Our principles are to support the Constitution, and *down with the Usurper!!!*
Your friend,
SAM. HOUSTON.
To Isaac Parker, Esq. Present.
We have no time to make any comments. The people of the United States will respond to the call of their brethren in Texas!

So Crockett well knew that he would be riding into a hornet's nest. But as an arena for the swift restoration of both his ego and his political life, and in which to build a new home for his family, Texas, by its proximity and current predicament, could hardly be bettered. Outside volunteers were needed, and he and his men would eagerly add their rifles to the cause. The rewards of victory—"liberal bounties . . . of our best lands"—would be huge.

A seven days' ride from Weakley County brought Crockett's little company to Memphis.

Extract of a letter dated Memphis, (Tenn) Nov. 7, 1835, to a gentleman in this city.
"Davy Crocket arrived here to-day with his rifle and dog, on his way to Texas."
—*Albany Journal*, December 2, 1835.

Other newspapers also reported his arrival and his cause.

Colonel Crockett—The *Jackson* (West Tennessee) *Truth Teller* of the 13th inst. states this distinguished legislator passed through Memphis a few days since on his way to Texas, where he is going to join the American forces against the Mexicans.
—*New York Transcript*, November 28, 1835

On November 2, Crockett's party left Memphis, taking the ferry across the Mississippi.[2] Well-worn trails then led them through a seventy-mile stretch of forested landscape in eastern Arkansas, which gradually gave way as "the Big Prairie" opened up.[3] They rode past tiny, scattered settlements and isolated cabins, and if the situation allowed, the great man was invited to spend the night. One such respite was recalled some five months later.

The following anecdote of him [Crockett] was communicated to us, last fall, by a highly respectable emigrant from North Carolina, who, with his family, passed a night in the same house with Col. Crockett, in the Big Prairie, when the latter was on his way to Texas. On being introduced to the lady of the gentleman, and telling her that he was going to Texas merely to have an opportunity of indulging in his favorite propensity for fighting, she asked him what he had done with his family, to which he dryly replied: "I have set them free—set them free—they must shift for themselves."
—*Arkansas Gazette*, May 10, 1836

Could Crockett have really uttered so coldhearted a statement regarding the fate of his family? It is certainly possible; people sometimes say things they do not really feel and perhaps later regret. But because his intention was to build a new home in Texas for his family, perhaps something was lost in translation by the time the quote reached the ears of William Woodruff, editor of the vehemently anti-Whig *Arkansas Gazette*. In fact when the preceding report was published, the Alamo's fall was already two months old; did editor Woodruff feel that enough water had passed under the bridge since Crockett's death for his paper to resume denigrating him, however subtly?

By the time Crockett and his little company entered Little Rock on November 12, their numbers had doubled since leaving Tennessee. The following day Albert Pike, editor of the Little Rock–based *Arkansas Advocate*, a Whig organ, inserted a terse but heartfelt notice of the storied ex-congressman's arrival.

We shall die contented. We have seen the HONORABLE DAVID CROCKETT—who arrived in this place last evening, on his way to Texas, where he contemplates ending his days. A supper was given him at Jeffries' hotel, of which many citizens partook. No room for further remarks.
—*Arkansas Advocate*, November 13, 1835

The following week, Woodruff managed a mostly polite report, if tinged with the inevitable touch of wryness, and not without a dig at the enthusiasm of the *Advocate*'s editor. (Notably missing was the epithet "buffoon," which the *Gazette* had employed so casually in August.)

> *A rare treat.*—Among the distinguished characters who have honored our City with their presence, within the last week, was no less a personage than Col. DAVID CROCKETT— better known as DAVY CROCKETT—the *real critter* himself—who arrived on Thursday evening last, with some 6 or 8 followers, from the Western District of Tennessee, on their way to Texas, to join the patriots of that country in freeing it from the shackles of the Mexican government. The news of his arrival rapidly spread, and we believe we speak within bounds, when we say, that hundreds flocked to see the wonderful man, who, it is said, can whip his weight in wild-cats, or grin the largest panther out of the highest tree. In the evening, a supper was given him, at Jeffries' Hotel, by several *Anti-Jackson-men*, merely for the sport of hearing him abuse the Administration, in his outlandish style, and we understand they enjoyed a most delectable treat, in a speech of some length with which he amused them. Having no curiosity that way ourselves, we did not attend the *show*. But our neighbor of the Advocate was there, and so delighted was he, that he says he can now *"die contented."* Happy man!
>
> The Colonel and his party, all completely armed and well mounted, took their departure on Friday morning, for Texas, in which country, we understand, they intend establishing their future abode, and in the defence of which, we hope they may cover themselves with glory.
>
> —*Arkansas Gazette*,
> November 17, 1835

Three days later, the *Advocate* offered a rebuttal to the somewhat sarcastic reportage of the *Gazette*.

> We have a single word to say for Colonel Crockett. He was honored and hospitably received here—not because "he can whip his weight in wild cats, or grin a panther out of the highest tree"—(as the Gazette says)—because there are plenty of Arkansas *boys* who can do the same—but because he is an honest man, and a true friend to Hugh L. White.[b] Neither was the supper given by several *anti-Jackson* men. As well men of one party as of another joined in it. Neither did he *abuse* the Administration in an outlandish style. His remarks were few, plain, moderate and unaffected—without violence or acrimony. He spoke against the Administration and against the *heir apparent*—but he did it by quietly detailing facts. His remarks were far from outlandish. He neither aimed at display or eloquence—and was simply rough, natural, and pleasant.
>
> We have lost our partner.[c] He has shouldered his rifle and taken up the line of March for Texas, in company with five or six young men, desirous "to stain with hostile blood their maiden arms." Success to them all, and him in particular.
>
> —*Arkansas Advocate*,
> November 20, 1835

Seven weeks after Crockett's arrival in Little Rock, the *Arkansas Advocate* remarked on a report of the event made in yet another paper with a contending political view.

> The Kentucky Gazette says that Col. Crockett has made a speech of *some hours* length here, against the Administration, and started in the morning armed cap-a-pie,[d] amid the huzzas of men, women, girls and boys. The editor of that paper is good at *stretching* a story. He must have had some hand in Emmons' life of Van Buren.
>
> —*Arkansas Advocate*, January 1, 1836

Later that month, the *New York Sun* made note of a particularly ironic boast of Crockett's.

---

[b] Judge Hugh Lawson White (1773–1840) of Tennessee was one of three candidates the Whigs would unsuccessfully pit against Andrew Jackson's chosen successor, Martin Van Buren, in the election of 1836.
[c] Charles E. Rice, coeditor of the *Arkansas Advocate*.
[d] Head to foot.

Crockett's Speech at the Little Rock Dinner

A high point in David Crockett's journey through Arkansas while en route to Texas was a supper given to him at Little Rock's Jefferies Hotel on the evening of November 12, 1835. Feting the famed congressman were a number of town notables, including Albert Pike, editor of the Whig *Arkansas Advocate*, Col. Robertson Childers, several "anti-Jackson-men," and even a few men of the opposing political party. "They enjoyed a most delectable treat," wrote the editor of the Jacksonian *Arkansas Gazette*, "in a speech of some length with which he amused them." The *Little Rock Times* noted the "stamping and applause of his audience."[1]

That night Crockett, by all accounts, voiced his political opinions "without violence or acrimony." Like Will Rogers he depended on his characteristic humor to charm, captivate, and persuade his audience.[2] According to the unpublished autobiography of editor Pike, one of the stories Crockett told that night was one he had often related, and it was frequently recorded in the memoirs of some of his contemporaries.[3] The anecdote appeared, for instance, in an 1867 issue of *Harper's New Monthly Magazine*:

> ONE of Judge Wright: Many years ago the famous Colonel Davy Crockett and Governor M'Arthur, one of the first governors of Ohio, were in a menagerie in Louisville, Kentucky. Colonel Crockett, looking at a large baboon, remarked to his companion that there was a wonderful likeness between the brute and their friend Judge W. Looking around at the moment he saw his Honor the Judge standing between M'Arthur and himself. Taking off his hat, and looking first at Judge W. and then at the baboon, he said, "Gentlemen, I owe *one* of you an apology, *but I do not know which.*"[4]

---

1. *Arkansas Advocate*, November 12 and 20, 1835; *Arkansas Gazette,* November 17, 1835; *New York Times,* January 12, 1836, quoting from the *Little Rock Times* of November.
2. *Arkansas Advocate,* November 20, 1835.
3. Manley F. Cobia Jr., *Journey into the Land of Trials: The Story of Davy Crockett's Expedition to the Alamo* (Franklin, Tenn.: Hillsboro Press, 2003), 42.
4. *Harper's New Monthly Magazine*, 35, no. 209 (October 1867): 675.

David Crockett has gone to Texas, and he says that he will "have *Santa Anna's* head, and wear it for a watch-seal." Davy was honored with a public dinner at Little Rock, Arkansas, where there were many fine things said to the western coon hunter, and as many returned.— Two such men as Ex-Governor Houston and David Crockett will probably handle the Mexicans rather roughly.
—*New York Sun*, January 29, 1836

Even before any of the eastern newspapers had received word of Crockett's brief sojourn in Little Rock, there had been occasional editorializing about his search for a new horizon, and much of it was guardedly supportive and optimistic.

Davy Crockett has actually gone to Texas, with his "rifle, and a hundred rounds."[e] His farewell letter to his quondam constituents, states that he left his native state and country in consequence of a determination long ago formed and expressed, of expatriating himself in case Martin Van Buren should be elected president—strong *premonitories* of which event he now begins to see. Davy also has discovered, he says, that our politicians are inconsistent, selfish, and insincere; and he brings Miss Martineau forward to prove the charge.[f] Perhaps he will find more sincerity amongst the Texians, and less of party intrigue; and we are quite certain he will find there fewer political mountebanks. Reminding Davy of his story of the "bear and alligator," we advise him to take care of his *paws*; and also recommend to him his motto, "be sure you're right, then go ahead," which will carry him safely through his Texian adventures. If there be, however, such a thing as a faro-bank to be found in

Texas, we fear Davy will forget all his prudential maxims.
—*New York Sunday Morning News*, December 6, 1835

Within a week, another New York paper also speculated on his chances.

Colonel Crockett who has recently gone to Texas is probably one of the best shots in the world. One hundred men like Crockett would be of immense service to the Texians at this time— if you could only make them believe that their enemies were *bears*, instead of men.—Crockett has been known to send a rifle ball through the same hole nine times in successive fire.
—*Albany* (New York) *Journal*, December 11, 1835

Riding out of Little Rock on the morning of November 13, Crockett and his followers resumed their journey through the southwestern quarter of Arkansas, eventually arriving on the banks of the Red River. From this point their precise route of travel is uncertain and attempting to trace it is no small challenge, considering the wealth of local traditions that have Crockett meandering all over northeastern Texas during the last five weeks of 1835. One of the strongest of these traditions claims that he and his men did not immediately cross the river, but took the military road paralleling the north bank of the Red and followed it some seventy miles westward to Fort Towson. This ran through Choctaw land, part of the Indian Territory (present-day Oklahoma) into which that tribe had been removed just a few years earlier. South of the fort, a ferry took Crockett and his companions across the river to old Jonesboro (which no longer exists), located in what was then still part of Arkansas Territory (and soon to be absorbed into the Texas Republic).[4]

It was but a sparsely settled region, yet it seemed that wherever Crockett went he found transplanted Americans who met him with open arms, either old friends or settlers only too happy to entertain the illustrious Tennessean.[5] It was also a land brimming with game, and on at least one occasion he was invited to go on a bear hunt.[6] On another, with a different party of homesteaders and presumably those

---

[e] This is a direct quote from Houston's call for volunteers of October 5, 1836.

[f] A reference to Harriet Martineau's views in her *Illustrations of Political Economy* (1832–1834) and other writings. Martineau, a reform-minded English critic of all things social, economic, and political, was in early 1836 just completing a lengthy tour of the United States, which she later described in *Society in America* (1837), and *Retrospect of Western Travel* (1838).

of his own men who were still with him, Crockett rode westward in search of buffalo. Their route took them across Bois d'Arc Creek, which runs into the Red River through today's Fannin County and beyond the creek onto a prairie bordered in the west by the long north-south line of woodlands called "Cross Timbers." The northwestern sector of this prairie was pierced by Choctaw Bayou, which also ran into the Red.[7]

For Crockett, as he expressed it in a letter to his children, it was "the richest country in the world, good Land and plenty of Timber and the best springs . . . and game plenty. It is the pass where the Buffalo passes from the north to south and back twice a year, and bees and honey plenty." Here, he felt, he could easily settle himself and his family.[8]

Although no documentation has been found to tell us how his luck fared on this hunt, a report reprinted from the *Arkansas Gazette*, noted this interruption in Crockett's plans.

> *Davy on a new scent.*—We understand, the celebrated DAVY CROCKETT, who passed through this place [Little Rock], some weeks since, on his way to take part with the Texians against their Mexican oppressors, took a new scent on reaching Red river, and has gone on a *Buffalo hunt.* Davy is as fond of hunting as fighting.
>
> —*Arkansas Gaz.*
> —*Commercial Bulletin and Missouri Literary Register*, February 9, 1836

Following this interlude, Crockett and his men headed eastward again to avoid, by some traditions, a rumored Comanche war party lurking in the south and rode all the way to the small settlement called Lost Prairie on the west bank of the Red River just below the sharp bend the river makes as it begins its southward course to the Gulf of Mexico. Here they made another overnight stop. This respite is of particular interest because out of it was born a letter written by Lost Prairie resident Isaac N. Jones, addressed to Crockett's widow and published in the late summer in many newspapers after first appearing in the *Jackson* (Tenn.) *Truth Teller.*

LOST PRAIRIE, Ark's. 1836

Mrs. David Crockett,

Dear Madam.—Permit me to introduce myself to you as one of the acquaintances of your much respected husband, Col. Crockett. Of his fate in the Fortress San Antonio, Texas, you are doubtless long since advised. With sincere feelings of sympathy, I regret his untimely loss to your family and self. For if amongst strangers, he constituted the most agreeable companion, he, doubtless, to his wife and children, must have been a FAVORITE, *peculiarly* prized. In his loss, Freedom has been deprived of one of her bravest sons, in whose bosom universal philanthropy glowed with as genial warmth as ever animated the heart of the American citizen. When he fell, a soldier died. To bemoan his fate, is to pay tribute of grateful respect to Nature—he seemed to be her son.

The object of this letter, is to beg that you will accept the watch which accompanies it. You will doubtless know it when you see it. And as it has his name engraved on its surface, it will no doubt be the more acceptable to you.

As it will probably be gratifying to you to learn in what way I became possessed of it, permit me to state, that, last winter (the precise date not recollected by me,) Col. Crockett, in company with several other gentlemen, passed through Lost Prairie, on Red river, (where I live).[g] The company excepting the Colonel, who was a little behind, rode up to my house and asked accommodations for the night. My family being so situated, from the indisposition of my wife, that I could not accommodate them, they got quarters at one of my neighbors' houses. The Colonel visited me the next day and spent the day with me. He observed whilst here, that his funds were getting short and as a means of recruiting them, he must sell something.—He proposed to me to exchange watches—he priced his at $30 more than mine, which sum I paid him, and we accordingly exchanged.

---

[g] By Jones's indication that Crockett had visited him "last winter" and considering the evidence that has Crockett arriving in Nacogdoches about 130 miles south of Lost Prairie by January 5, it is probable that his visit to Jones had taken place no earlier than the third week of December.

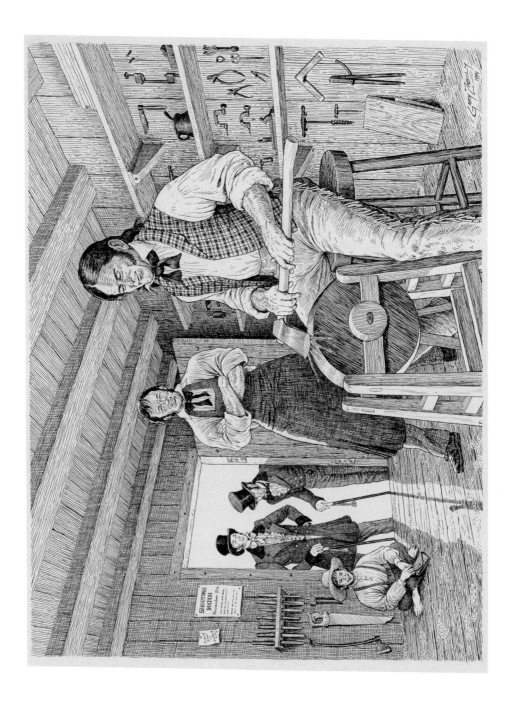

His Honor Grinding an Axe

An extract from the Jacksonian *Little Rock Times* marking David Crockett's stopover visit to that city was republished in the *New York Sun* almost two months later on January 12, 1836. It includes an amusing, if revealing, vignette of the man's essentially homespun nature:

> *Colonel David Crockett.*—This gentleman and party, consisting of six or eight comrades, arrived in our city on Thursday afternoon last, on his way to join the Texians in arms. A supper was given him by a number of our citizens, (the Colonel not wishing to remain with us but for the night) at which he made a very amusing speech, as we should judge from the stamping and applause of his audience. We are told that he "used up" the Administration "head and tail." We had some curiosity to see this celebrated man, and our eyes were gratified with a sight of him on Friday morning last—and reader where—not in the hall of legislation, not in the bar room of a tavern, neither was it in a lady's chamber—but in a carpenter's shop *grinding an axe*. Oh! "what a falling off was there." His Honor grinding an axe.

With his open frankness, his natural honesty of expression, his perfect want of concealment I could not but be very much pleased. And with a hope that it might be an accommodation to him, I was gratified at the exchange, as it gave me a keepsake which often reminds me of an honest man, a good citizen and a pioneer in the cause of liberty amongst his suffering brethren in Texas.

His military career was short. But though I deeply lament his death, I cannot restrain my American smile at the recollection of the fact that he died as a United States soldier should die, covered with his slain enemy, and, even in death presenting to them in his clenched hands, the weapons of their destruction.

We hope that the day is not far distant, when his adopted land will be freed from a savage enemy, and afford to yourself and children, a home rendered in every way comfortable, by the liberal donations of her government.

Accept, dear madam, for yourself and family, the most sincere wishes for your future happiness, from

Your most ob't servant and friend,
ISAAC N. JONES
—*Jamestown* (New York) *Journal*,
September 7, 1836

By January 1, 1836, reports had reached as far south as Washington-on-the-Brazos that Crockett's company had paused to hunt buffalo somewhere to the north. In a letter of that date written in Washington by Maine tourist Edward Warren mention is also made of an early rumor of Crockett's death.

You may have heard that David Crockett set out for this country with a company of men to join the army. He has forgotten his avowed original

intention and stopped some 80 or 100 miles to the north of this place to hunt buffalo for the winter! For a long time it was feared that he and his party had been destroyed by the tribes of wild Indians through which he intended to pass; but, at last, it is ascertained that he is at his favorite amusement.
—*Bangor* (Maine) *Advertiser*,
March 19, 1836

Whatever the origin of the rumor of Crockett's death, word of it leapfrogged across the country.

The Washington correspondent of the *Journal of Commerce* under date of the 17th instant says: —"A letter was read today by a member of Congress from Brownsville, Tennessee, in which it was stated that intelligence had been received there of the death of Col. David Crockett, in Texas, soon after his arrival in that country."
—*Rhode Island Republican*, February 24, 1836

David Crockett is no more! He died on his way to Texas. Alas, poor Yorick!
—*New-Hampshire Gazette*, February 23, 1836

A month later the nation's presses offered cheerier tidings.

DAVY CROCKETT NOT DEAD.—We are happy to state, on the authority of a letter from Tennessee, that the report of the death of the eccentric Davy Crockett, is not true. "He started (says the letter) on a hunting expedition to the Rocky Mountains, and then dropped down into Texas; but we expect him home early in the Spring."
—*New York Mercury*, March 24, 1836

Indeed, Crockett had not died in northern Texas, nor had he traveled several hundred miles west to the Rockies, but instead was leading his company south from Lost Prairie and down Trammel's Trail to the old Spanish town of Nacogdoches, where they arrived on January 5. There, the famous man was generously feted and applauded. Four months later the *Arkansas Gazette* printed one of the speeches he was heard to make in that town.

Col. Crockett.—The following anecdote is so characteristic of this very eccentric man, that we have no doubt it is literally true:

A gentleman from Nacogdoches, in Texas, informs us, that, whilst there, he dined in public with Col. Crockett, who had just arrived from Tennessee. The old bear-hunter, on being toasted, made a speech to the Texians, replete with his usual dry humor. He began merely in this style: "I am told, gentlemen, that, when a stranger, like myself, arrives among you, the first inquiry is—what brought him here? To satisfy your curiosity at once as to myself, I will tell you all about it. I was, for some years, a member of Congress. In my last canvass, I told the people of my District, that, if they saw fit to re-elect me, I would serve them as faithfully as I had done; but if not, *they might go to hell, and I would go to Texas.* I was beaten, gentlemen, and here I am." The roar of applause was like a thunder-burst.
—*Arkansas Gazette*, May 10, 1836

Another piece of Crockett dialogue supposedly uttered at Nacogdoches appeared in a New York paper.

Davy Crockett's last.—When the gallant Colonel passed through Nacogdoches on his way to join the Texian army, before the capture of the Alamo by the Texians, he carried with him the celebrated rifle which was presented to him in Philadelphia two years ago, and which he familiarly called his "Betsey." On leaving the town, he was surrounded by a number of persons to whom he made a short address, in the course of which he used this expression: "I will die with my Betsey in my arms—No—I will not die. I'll grin down the walls of the Alamo. The Americans will *lick up* the Mexicans like *fine salt.*" this prediction was verified. The Alamo was taken, and the Mexicans expelled for a short time. The disastrous re-capture of the fort, however, showed that the walls of the Alamo would not stay *grinned down.*
—*New York Sun*, May 10, 1836

The reference to the Alamo still being held by Martín Perfecto de Cos's force at this time is of course entirely apocryphal, at least as far as the speech having been made in Nacogdoches is concerned because San Antonio had been captured by the Texian army back on December 10, and news of this was already known as far east as New Orleans by January 4. But the quote is in texture typical Crockett and was oddly enough partially echoed elsewhere.

> Colonel Crockett, whose death was reported some time since, is said to be alive and kicking. He has expressed his determination to *grin* all the Mexicans out of Texas.
> —*New York Sunday Morning News*, March 27 1836

By January 9, Crockett left Nacogdoches for a trip east to San Augustine, where he was given another grand dinner and where he observed that his overall stock in the prenatal republic was quickly rising.

> DAVY CROCKETT.—This eccentric genius, it seems by the following paragraph, is now in the Province of Texas, and is about trying his luck for a seat in the convention. That latitude is better suited to his capacities, and probably he will be more fortunate than he was in Tennessee:
> "Col. Crockett visited San Augustine and met with a very warm and cordial reception from the citizens of that place, who earnestly solicited him to become a candidate to represent them in the next convention. His reply was that he came not to this country for office but to fight her battles and help gain the liberties of the people. At the same time stated that he would rather be a member of that convention than be in the U.S. Senate. Therefore we may expect the Colonel to occupy a seat in the convention."
> *Texian and Emigrants Guide.* [Nacogdoches] —*Mississippi Free Trader and Natchez Gazette*, March 4, 1836

Back at Nacogdoches, Crockett and his men enlisted as six-month volunteers in the Texian army and took the oath of allegiance to the planned government, as recalled more than two years later by administering judge Col. John Forbes.

Col. Forbes has recently related to us an interesting anecdote of the celebrated Crockett. At the commencement of the war the latter arrived at Nacogdoches accompanied by several volunteers. Soon after their arrival they proceeded to the office of Col. Forbes, (who was then first judge of that municipality) to take the oath of allegiance. The Colonel [Forbes] immediately wrote out the following form:

> "I do solemnly swear that I will bear true allegiance to the provisional Government of Texas, or any future Government that may be hereafter declared, and that I will serve her honestly and faithfully against all her enemies and oppressors whatsoever, and observe and obey the orders of the Governor of Texas, the orders and decrees of the present or future authorities, and the orders of the officers appointed over me according to the rules and articles for the government of Texas, so help me God."

Upon offering it to Crockett, he refused to sign it, saying that, he was willing to take an oath to support any future *republican* Government, but could not subscribe his name to this form as the *future* government might be despotic, the Colonel [Forbes] therefore inserted the word republican between the words future and government, and Crockett readily signed the instrument. The original has lately been deposited in the office of the Secretary of War, in which the word republican appears *interlined* and beneath it is the autograph of David Crockett.
> —*Telegraph and Texas Register*, April 28, 1838

Following this, Crockett's party leagued itself with a small number of other newly signed volunteers and began preparing themselves for the 270-mile ride across south central Texas to San Antonio. But a curious newspaper entry seems to imply that Crockett was in no particular hurry and that he was once again temporarily setting aside the serious business of the world to indulge in his favorite recreation.

> Col. Crockett, with 300 men, has gone into the interior to hunt buffalo, during the cessation of hostilities.
> —*Arkansas Advocate*, February 19, 1836

Crockett's Big Buffalo Hunt

While traveling through northeastern Texas en route to the scene of conflict, David Crockett was reported, in at least one newspaper account, to have gone on a buffalo hunt, according to the February 9, 1836, edition of the *Commercial Bulletin and Missouri Literary Register*, reprinted from the *Arkansas Gazette*. In typically snide fashion—when it came to writing about Crockett—the *Gazette* noted:

> *Davy on a new scent.*—We understand, the celebrated DAVY CROCKETT, who passed through this place [Little Rock], some weeks since, on his way to take part with the Texians against their Mexican oppressors, took a new scent on reaching Red river, and has gone on a *Buffalo hunt.* Davy is as fond of hunting as fighting.—*Arkansas Gaz.*

After leaving Nacogdoches in the second week of January, 1836, he apparently engaged in another buffalo hunt, on a vaster scale.

> Col. Crockett, with 300 men, has gone into the interior to hunt buffalo, during the cessation of hostilities.
> —*Arkansas Advocate,* February 19, 1836

The intriguing part of this report is its fuzziness regarding precisely when and where the hunt took place—if indeed it ever did. Allowing about three weeks for the news to have reached Little Rock would suggest that the hunt was launched during the last two weeks of January. But where did those three hundred men come from? If reflecting a true number, some accounting for the three hundred might be found in the fact that upon Crockett's arrival in Nacogdoches the town was full of visitors: other volunteers from the states, and men who had arrived to attend the feast being held for Don Augustan Viesca, an avowed foe of Antonio López de Santa Anna and the ousted governor of Coahuila y Tejas.[1] In addition, many of the Texian soldiers from the victory at San Antonio had recently returned to their homes, and it is not unlikely that a good number of them would have flocked to Nacogdoches to see the living legend from Tennessee. On February 2, long after Crockett's departure, 407 men voted in the general election there for members to the new Convention, so clearly the town continued as a bustling gathering place.[2]

1. Manley F. Cobia Jr., *Journey into the Land of Trials: The Story of Davy Crockett's Expedition to the Alamo* (Franklin, Tenn.: Hillsboro Press, 2003), 95, 99.
2. Paul Lack, ed., *The Diary of William Fairfax Gray, from Virginia to Texas, 1835–1837* (Dallas: William P. Clements Center for Southwest Studies, Southern Methodist University, 1997), 80.

From the Phil Collins Collection

Kentucky Horse Rifle and Pistol

This Kentucky horse rifle and belt pistol are in wonderful condition. The rifle measures 42 inches overall with a 28-inch barrel. It was made in Pennsylvania and converted from flint to percussion in the 1840s. Made of curly maple wood, these rifles were preferred by the Tennessee horsemen and carried across the saddle. It's thought that rifles like these and long rifles would have been favoured by David Crockett's men.

Likewise, the well-preserved Kentucky belt pistol was known as being the "common soldier's friend" and was also favoured by the Tennessee horsemen riding with Crockett. The pistols were reasonably cheap, easy to come by, and paired with the Kentucky horse rifle, the owner could feel safe, protected, and well armed. This example is made of oak and has an English Richards lock and stock. With the exception of the ramrod, everything is original.

I remember a childhood illusion being shattered one day when I saw a programme on TV saying that most of the cowboys and frontiersmen were not the sharpshooting characters we were being fed by the movie industry. Now many years later, with a large collection of weapons from that period, I can understand why!

The muskets, long rifles, pistols, and such were either extremely heavy, making them difficult to use quickly or were just plain unreliable—or both!

The idea of such weapons being fired with one arm whilst holding a horse's reigns was almost impossible. With flintlocks relying on powder, you took your own life in your hands before you attempted to snuff out the enemy. Many beards were singed! –PC

On February 2, long after Crockett's departure from Nacogdoches, 407 men voted in the general election there for members to the new convention,[9] and Crockett's name had been placed on the list of aspirants.

> The election of members to a Convention to form a system of Government, was held on the 1st inst., and the Convention was to meet on Wednesday last. Among the Candidates were the notorious Robert Potter, and Col. Crockett.[h]
> —*Arkansas Advocate*, February 19, 1836

But Davy, who had only recently arrived in Texas, failed to receive a single vote as one of the four delegates who would represent San Augustine at the upcoming consultation on independence.

The route taken by Crockett's group from Nacogdoches to San Antonio—the latter town seen by most as the immediate object of Santa Anna's army—was not described in any newspaper account. But the country lying between Nacogdoches and Washington-on-the-Brazos, the first leg of the trip, had been traversed just a few weeks earlier by tourist Edward Warren from Maine and limned by him in lushly romantic terms in a letter dated January 1.

> For the last four days we have been travelling over one continuous prairie, sometimes level for miles and at others rolling and uneven. At one time you will observe small islands of trees for shelter and fuel—while at another as far as the eye can reach you behold nothing but one sea of waving grass. The country we passed over the last day of our ride was by far the most beautiful. Towards evening we ascended a very high swell, from which we could see the country some twenty miles in every direction. The sun was just going down and the sky had assumed that grandeur of appearance peculiar to the climate. The country was undulating

more than usual, and the long swells with the deep green verdure at their feet and about their base, looked not unlike the successive folds of an immense garment, or drapery with evergreens woven in between. The sun was setting before—the moon rising behind—while on either hand was stretched out this beautiful landscape. The scene was beautiful beyond description.
> —*Bangor* (Maine) *Advertiser*, March 19, 1836

To fill in the gaps of the parts of Crockett's progress in Texas that went unreported, the press resorted to its usual politically charged commentary.

> Col. David Crockett is yet alive and kicking. Information has been received from him very recently. He had been a Coon hunting among the Rocky Mountains, and is expected home soon. We would recommend him to the whigs of this state as an "available" candidate for the Presidency, seeing they cannot agree upon any that have as yet been brought forward.
> —*Stamford* (Connecticut) *Sentinel*, March 28, 1836

Another paper took several potshots at the supposedly "distinguished" men of Texas, Crockett among them, whose backgrounds were deemed too checkered to be respectable.

> DAVY CROCKETT, it seems, is enacting wonders in Texas. It does not appear that he makes long speeches on political subjects, as he used to do, when he starred it with JAMES CROW, Esq. through the Atlantic cities; but he makes the woods of Texas resound with his alligator voice, and the conversation of his rifle. Texas can certainly boast now, of possessing in her midst several *distinguished* men:—ROBERT POTTER, whose domestic exploits will live on the historic page: HOUSTON, ditto, and CROCKETT, ditto. The course of this last "stupendous man," is somewhat more eccentric than that of his crusading compeers. We heard him say once, as he stood before the humming crowd under the semi-circular row of pillars at the Exchange—"I love my

---

[h] Like Crockett, Robert Potter had moved to Texas in 1835 to turn over a new leaf or two, abandoning a political career in North Carolina tainted by his tendencies toward violence and gambling. He would be killed in Texas in 1842 during the Regulator-Moderator War in Harrison County.

country.—if I don't I wish I may be shot!" but he has left her, and gone to Texas. What can be done without him?

—*Philadelphia Public Ledger*,
April 5, 1836

Only a few days before news of the slaughter at the Alamo arrived on the East Coast, the *New York Times* put in a few good words for the "wag of the canebrakes," and for his newfound role as a soldier in a faraway revolution.

Davy Crockett is fighting like a wildcat in the cause of the Texians. He is a good man in his way, and albeit we have spoken harshly of some of his antics, we will do him the justice to say, that we have full confidence in his valor and willingness to fight on all proper occasions. We doubt not that his rifle will speak volumes among the Mexicans—It is said he has had poor sport among the buffaloes on the Arkansas prairies. He will make up for lost time in Texas, and do some execution among noble game.

—*New York Times*, April 7, 1836

6

"The Enemy Is Advancing on This Post"

Tourist Edward Warren from Bangor, Maine, had certainly picked the most interesting of times to visit Texas. He had arrived at Washington-on-the-Brazos in late December 1835 and, on January 1, 1836, wrote a letter to his uncle, one of a series of letters eventually published in the *Bangor Commercial Advertiser*. In it he mentions meeting Sam Houston.

> I have just been introduced to General Houston, the Washington of Texas. He is a fine looking man, something over six feet high, large and of a commanding appearance. He wears buckskin trowsers, which were once of a light color, but from long use have become much soiled; the nature of this article after being wet is to shrink, and as the General's have seen much wet weather they have become not only very tight but short, coming but little below his knees. But this peculiarity among the people he has to command, is much in his favor. You recollect the character of the man the Texians have elected their chief—once a member of Congress, governor of Tennessee, and an adopted son of an Indian chief.—As a commander he seems possessed of sufficient decision, and will in my humble opinion, conduct the Texians to victory and independence. I am informed by

> his most intimate friend, Mr. Hockly, that he intends to strictly imitate Washington!
>
> —*Bangor Commercial Advertiser*, March 19, 1836

Unlike George Washington, however, Houston saw his presumed command of the Texian army fractured by the Matamoros expedition, an adventure originally assigned to his leadership in mid-December by Governor Henry Smith. Its object was the capture of the supposedly wealthy Mexican border town of Matamoros, and it was hoped that the expedition would also arouse the Federalist-leaning states of northern Mexico into another revolt against Antonio López de Santa Anna.

Many viewed it as a convenient way to hold onto the over seven hundred idle volunteers remaining at Béxar, Goliad, and elsewhere, the majority of whom were getting especially homesick now that Martín Perfecto de Cos had been defeated. About two-thirds of the three hundred men stationed at San Antonio had, in fact, already begun their march southeast to Goliad, the expedition's rendezvous point, on December 30.[1]

Taking personal and immediate command of this "volunteer army" were colonels James Walker Fannin, Frank W. Johnson, and James Grant. Houston was easily shunted aside because he was still in central Texas trying to raise a regular army. But he saw the expedition as nothing more than a waste of precious men and materiel; it had stripped San Antonio of most of its provisions and supplies, leaving behind only a skeletal garrison under the command of Lt. Col. James C. Neill. Dangerously exposed and undermanned as they now were, these few men nevertheless made a pact to hold both the town of Béxar and the Alamo.

At a meeting of the troops now in the garrison of Bejar, on the 31st of December, 1835, the following resolutions were adopted.

Resolved, That this be a meeting to ascertain the rights of volunteers.

Resolved, That we approve and recognize colonel Neill as commander-in-chief, and unanimously accord in the sentiments expressed by that gentleman in his letter to us.

Resolved, That we consider it highly essential that the existing army remain in Bejar.

Resolved, That we have at all times the privilege of electing our own company officers, and for the commander-in-chief to recognize the same.

Resolved, That we consider the above highly essential for the unity and interest of the existing volunteer army in Bejar.

Resolved, That the thanks of this meeting be given to major Jameson,[a] for his prompt, communicative, and kind attention to this meeting.

Resolved, That a copy of the proceedings of this meeting be addressed to the Convention at San Felipe.

WM. BLAZEBY,
Chairman.
JOHN JONES,
Secretary.

The adoption of the third resolution was occasioned by the marching of two-thirds of this volunteer army for Matamoros, putting the safety of Bejar in jeopardy, and taking with them the ammunition, clothing, and provisions, intended for the winter supply of this garrison.

W.B.
—*Telegraph and Texas Register,*
January 23, 1836

[a] Green B. Jameson, who was made engineer of the Alamo's fortifications.

Despite the inheritance of considerable stores of arms, ammunition, and other military supplies after the fall of Béxar, the Texian army on all fronts remained fearfully deficient in most of the basic items required for effective offensive and defensive actions. Two weeks before the capture of San Antonio, a list of such necessities had been drawn up by the General Council, and it was published in the first issue of the *Telegraph and Texas Register* to appear in 1836.

AN ORDNANCE AND DECREE.
To purchase Munitions of War, Provisions, Arms, &c., for the Army of Texas, and defence of the Sea Coast.

Be it ordained and decreed, and it is hereby ordained and decreed by the General Council of the Provisional Government of Texas, that the following items and articles contained under the heads of munitions of war, provisions, arms, &c., scientific instruments, books and stationery, are, and they are hereby declared necessary for the use of the army and defence of the sea coasts of Texas: and the said articles are hereby ordered and decreed to be purchased accordingly.

MUNITIONS OF WAR, ARMS, &c.
4 twelve-pounders, mounted for field service.
4 twelve-pounders, mounted for fort service.
3 eighteen-pounders, mounted for fort service.
6 twenty-four pounders, mounted for fort service.
6 thirty-two pounders, mounted for fort service, with 100 round shot for each cannon.
2 thirteen-inch howitzers, with two hundred bomb shells.
2 pair of shovels and pokers for hot shot.
1000 kegs cannon powder, 300 yards flannel, together with all the necessary implements and accoutrements for field service for the above cannon.
300 yagers, 3 feet in barrel, 1-4 twist with moulds, &c.
600 muskets, with bayonets, straps, cartridge-boxes, &c.
200 sergeants' swords, with belts, &c.
200 pair horseman's pistols, with holsters, moulds, &c.
200 kegs rifle powder, FFF.
4000 musket balls.

8000 lbs. bar and pig lead.

1000 butcher knives, and 1000 tomahawks well tempered, with handles.

20 drums and fifes, and 10 bugles (6 Kentish).

6 stand regimental colors.

1 stand general colors.

160 Spanish Oppelousas saddle-trees, with red blankets.

100 pr. Stirrups.

100 " spurs.

100 surcingles.

100 bridles and cabristras.

A complete assortment of camp equipage and cooking utensils for one thousand men, with officers' marquees or tents for 65 officers.

1 Grand Marquee and General's Marquee, equipage and fly.

10 baggage wagons with gear for 60 horses.

150 axes.

150 spades.

50 mattocks.

3 sets carpenters' tools for field service.

6 sets blacksmiths' tools.

1 set gunsmiths' tools, with anvil, bellows and portable forge.

200 soldiers' tents.

1,200 blankets, 3 1-2 point, French colored.

20 sets corn mills, or patent hand mills.

2,000 brogans, from 6 to 12.

2,000 suits grey uniforms, with proper number Sergeants' Corporals' &c.

2,200 colored cotton shirts.

2,200 yarn socks.

5 army medicine chests.

1,000 canteens, last improved shape and size.

225 coffee pots (part greques.)

PROVISIONS.

350 bbls. flour.

200 " fine ship bread.

20,000 lbs. middling bacon.

50 bbls. mess pork, inspected.

15,000 lbs. coffee.

15,000 " brown sugar.

20 bbls. cider vinegar.

5 " whiskey.

3,000 lbs. Kentucky chewing tobacco.

120 gallon French Brandy.

120 " Port Wine.

INSTRUMENTS, BOOKS AND STATIONARY.

3 Thermometers (Farenheits) with cases.

1 Chronometer with case.

6 Army Telescopes.

4 Spirit Levels.

100 copies Scott's Infantry Drill, or the last improved work.

26 copies Crop's Discipline and Regulations.

7 " M'Comb on Courts Martial.

36 " " School of the Soldier and other improved works on Courts Martial, and Tactics on Fortifications, and Gunning, &c., together with Instruments.

An assortment of blank forms of returns of Field, Staff and Company Officers, blank muster inspection and pay rolls, which can be had at any garrison in the United States.

3 portable Writing Desks with wax, wafers, quills, stationary, &c.

Passed at San Felipe de Austin Nov. 27, 1835.

JAMES W. ROBINSON

Lieut. Gov. and ex-officio President of the General Council.

E.M. PEASE,

Sec'y of Gen. Council.

Approved, Nov. 30, 1835

HENRY SMITH, Governor.

C. B. STEWART, Sec'y to Executive, Recorder, &c.

—*Telegraph and Texas Register*,

January 2, 1836

In mid-January, James W. Robinson became acting governor of Texas after Henry Smith's vocal opposition to the plundering aims of the Matamoros expedition led to his impeachment. In a proclamation published in the *Telegraph and Texas Register*, Robinson summarized an urgent letter he had just received from Colonel Neill and added a high-flown appeal to arms that prophesied that the coming conflict would lead to the birth of an eternal "monument in the affections of your countrymen, and of the world."

PROCLAMATION.

EXECUTIVE DEPARTMENT, SAN FELIPE DE AUSTIN, JANUARY 19, 1836.

FREEMEN OF TEXAS.—Yesterday an express arrived here from San Antonio de

Bejar, bringing despatches from J. C. Neill, lieutenant-colonel commandant of that post, communicating the important intelligence that a force of two thousand five hundred men were a short time since at Laredo, and that one thousand five hundred of them had advanced as far as the Rio Frio, eighty miles from San Antonio, and that an immediate attack was expected: and also communicated the alarming fact, that only seventy-five men were in the Alamo under his command, and that provisions were scarce. Under these circumstances they ask for your aid, to defend the fortress against the enemy. *Will you go?* I regret to call upon you at this time of year, when your domestic affairs demand your care and attention; but I am constrained by the imminent danger that threatens your brethren in arms, and by the danger in which the frontier inhabitants would be exposed by neglecting to defend them, and by the disgrace and ruin of the country, consequent upon delay.

Rally, then, my brave countrymen, to the standard of constitutional liberty, and join your united energies, and spread the mantle of your courage over your defenceless country. Your homes, your families, your country call, and who can refuse to obey? Your homes and your firesides are assailed; will you refuse to defend them? The unprotected orphan makes the silent, but irresistible appeal: the prattling child, unconscious of its danger, makes its holy invocation: the tender mother, the kind sister, and the beloved wife, cling to you with a fond hope and unshaken confidence in your patriotism and unshaken bravery. March, then, with the blessings of your household Gods, to the western frontier, where you will be organized for a short, but glorious campaign. March, then, where victory awaits you, and the genius of freedom spreads her banners, and will crown her sons with imperishable laurels. Roll back the crimson stream of war to its source, and make the tyrant feel the fiery sun of blazing, burning, consuming war; and since he has driven you to take up arms in your defence,

give him "war to the knife, and the knife to the hilt." Let him know how freemen can die, and how freemen *will live*—that one day of virtuous liberty is worth an eternity of slavery, that if there is a boon, an offering held dear to heaven,

"'Tis the last libation liberty draws
From the heart that breaks and bleeds
    In its cause."

March, then, united, and without delay, and you will erect a monument in the affections of your admiring countrymen, and of the world, that will stand as firm as the pyramids of Egypt 'mid surrounding ruins, that shall continue while time shall last, and only perish "amid the war of elements, the wreck of matter, and the crash of worlds."

The God of war guide you to victory, honor and peace.

I remain,
    Your much obliged fellow-citizen,
        JAMES W. ROBINSON,
            Acting Governor.
            —*Telegraph and Texas Register*,
                January 23, 1836

Colonel Neill's letter of January 14 was printed in the same issue of the *Telegraph and Texas Register.*

COMMANDANCY OF BEJAR,
JANUARY 14, 1836.
To the Governor and Council, San Felipe de Austin.

SIRS,—I beg to refer you to my official communication, under date of yesterday, since when, I am sorry to inform you, that our situation becomes such as to be compelled to acquaint you of it by express. There can exist but little doubt that the enemy is advancing on this post, from the number of families leaving town to-day, and those preparing to follow; among which, is that of John W. Smith, who has this evening engaged wagons to remove his family into the colonies.[b] We

---

[b] Bexar merchant John W. Smith, after bringing his Mexican wife and children to the safety of Gonzales, would return to San Antonio and play an important role in the Alamo story.

are informed that the advance of the enemy is on the Rio Frio, and so situated are we, for want of horses, that we cannot, through our own exertions, gain any information, not being able to send out a small spy company. The volunteers that entered for two or four months, under Burleson or Johnson, did so with an understanding that they were, for that period, to be paid monthly; which not having been complied with, has weakened me very much, as several left yesterday and to-day, and I have not now more than seventy-five men fit for duty, and afraid that number will be considerably reduced in a few days. Unless we are reinforced and victualled, we must become an easy prey to the enemy, in case of an attack.

My frequent repetitions of the subject of our distress, and the apprehensions of an enemy, arise partly from the interest I feel for my country, and a wish to preserve those lands she has acquired in the infant stage of her campaign; and being well convinced as above stated, that the enemy may be nearer than rumored, without a power of ascertaining it through our own men on whom we may depend, and would, if necessary, ascertain the movements of the enemy, however distant, had we but a few horses.

In this extremity I will assure you, that as far as our strength goes, we will, till reinforced, use it both in spy service, and if drawn within the walls, will defend the garrison to the last.

I beg leave to subscribe myself,
Your obedient servant,
J. C. NEILL,
Lieutenant-colonel, commanding.
P.S.—The bearer of this takes a requisition to the chairman and members of the committee of safety, at Gonzales, to assist me with as many men and horses as possible, until I can receive reinforcements through orders of the government, from some other quarter, for which I have applied, and hope to receive soon, at the same time putting them in possession of my situation, and my cause of apprehension.

I shall not again make application for aid, as considering it superfluous, but wait the result of either receiving aid or an attack before it should arrive; in which case I will do the best I can with the small force I have.
—*Telegraph and Texas Register*,
January 23, 1836

Six days after Neill's letter appeared in the *Telegraph and Texas Register*, a letter from Mexico—evidently written by a merchant—was published in the *Morning Courier and New York Enquirer* (the paper disavowing any support for the opinions expressed therein). It was dated December 4, 1835, but it was a reminder that Neill's concerns about his command becoming "an easy prey to the enemy, in case of attack," were well founded.

Extract from a letter dated Mexico,
Dec. 4, 1835.
My dear Friends—It is with gratitude that I embrace the kind offer of our friend C. D., to have a letter transmitted for me, via Tampico and New Orleans, in the anxious hope that it will reach you with dispatch, to relieve your minds about me here, and explain why no letter reached you last packet. The policy of this Government demands that for the present, all communication with North America should be closed; but that only to prevent intelligence of their movements being conveyed to Texas. This is forced upon the Mexican Government by the hostile movements, and acts, of the merchants and other citizens, of New York, New Orleans &c. Such unaccountable folly and manifest injustice on the part of Americans appears to us here in the most heinous light.

Your public press, are bold and loud about their country's honor, &c. regarding *France* and the indemnity; but where is their honor, and honesty in respect to Texas? Is America not at peace with Mexico? Why then does the American Government allow public committees, and men and arms &c. to be shipped openly from her ports in violation of existing treaties, not only to fight against Mexico, but to assist rebels. Two thirds of all those that assume the designation of *Texians* are smugglers, which we, as well as many others can prove; but suppose that they were *Mexicans*, what right have *Americans* to interfere? Would they have submitted to Mexicans going rifle in hand upon American ground, in troops in like manner to assist any party of their citizens similarly situated? They are not only doing what is unjust, but are endangering the lives of thousands of their own countrymen, whose blood, *if shed shall assuredly be on their own head.*

Great activity prevails throughout this republic. Large loans, voluntary and otherwise, have been made to the Government, and *Santa Anna* left this city eight days since for *Texas*. When concentrated, his forces will amount to 9000 foot, and 1700 well mounted horse at least; such is the statement as given by those whom, I believe have the best information. I have seen 300 of the cavalry, and in my opinion they are excellent troops. *Santa Anna* is decidedly popular with two thirds of this republic; and even the liberals are at this moment making voluntary loans, considering it their duty to do so, taking up the quarrel in a national point of view.

I pity the *Texians,* first because they are wrong, and secondly because they will meet with little *mercy.* The infatuation is great; the very Constitution of 1824, which they now make their war cry, was never adopted by them; but on the contrary, opposed and trampled under foot, and any attempt by the Government to collect the revenue according to that Constitution was violently resisted,— and yet such acts are approved and supported, by men professing moral principles, the leading men of your city.

We remain as yet in quietness,—but God alone knows how long. I advise, without fail, that you ship the annexed order per first packet, as no interruption is anticipated to imports.

—*Morning Courier and New York Enquirer,*
January 29, 1836

Calls by the Texian leaders for military assistance, however, were not going unanswered in the United States.

Texas—Fifty fine looking fellows, from Newport Ohio, in full uniform, completely equipped, we perceive, have arrived in Louisville, Kentucky, from Cincinnati on their way to Texas. They are under Capt. Sherman,[c] and the Louisville Journal, speaking of their soldier-like appearance, says "they looked as if they could whip five times their weight of Mexicans." They had a benefit the other night at the theatre at Cincinnati, and returned their thanks the next morning in a card to the editors, which they requested them to publish, and "charge it to the account of Santa Anna." We imagine these accounts will accumulate so fast about these times that the Dictator will become bankrupt to those numerous debtors who call upon him for payment, among not the least formidable of whom will be the General Houston of San Antonio and the manes of the murdered youths at Tampico.

—*New York Evening Star,* January 18, 1836

On the Brazos River, another detachment of volunteers raised one of the several variants on the US flag that had suddenly appeared in rebellious Texas, as described by a New Hampshire–born foot soldier.

ADOPTION OF A FLAG BY THE TEXIANS.
We have seen an extract of a letter from a young gentleman (now a volunteer in Texas) to his father, in Exeter, dated at "Camp Fannin, Rio Brazos, Jan. 28, 1836," which states as follows:—

"Yesterday our Battalion was paraded, marched into town, drawn up in line opposite to the Flag-staff, and at the firing of a signal cannon, a flag containing a single star and the stripes, and the word *Independence* was run up by the hands of Mr. HARTWELL WALKER, (son of Wm. Walker, Esq. of Portsmouth, N.H. and grandson of our friend Col. Seth Walker,) a distinguished member of the New Orleans

---

[c] Captain Sidney Sherman, later appointed lieutenant colonel in Col. Edward Burleson's regiment. He became an active participant in the defeat of Santa Anna and in the politics of the new Texas Republic.

Greys, who took so conspicuous a part in the capture of San Antonio de Bexar. He is now commissioned as sailing master of the Schooner of War Invincible, lying off the harbor, waiting to take a part of us to Copano. He is a fine fellow, and will never *haul down* the flag he has been the first to raise. At the moment the flag was run up, our battalion presented arms, and fired a volley in salute. Meantime the steamboat Yellow-Stone, 14 days from New-Orleans, crowded with volunteers, appeared in the offing, and under charge of the Pilot, came up the river as the flag was hoisted. We counter-marched and formed a line on the beach, and as they passed, presented arms, fired a volley and cheered: as a cannon from the shore and the boat, and three cheers from the passengers answered and joined in the *salute and welcome*."

—*Portsmouth Journal of Literature and Politics*, March 5, 1836

On January 17, Houston sent Col. James Bowie and some thirty men to San Antonio. Their object, as the general wrote ex-Governor Smith, was to demolish all of the Mexican fortifications built in the town and, if deemed feasible, "blow up the Alamo, and abandon the place, as it will be impossible to keep up the station with volunteers."[2] Houston also realized that the Matamoros expedition had to be terminated now that a Mexican invasion force was on its way north. At Goliad and Refugio, he attempted to talk the volunteers out of marching south into Mexico; without unity, the scattered Texian troops would be destroyed piecemeal. Nor could they depend on friendly Mexicans for allies, he warned, no matter how much the latter hated Santa Anna. Despite his pleadings, the best Houston managed to achieve was a delay in launching the expedition, although small advance elements did begin probing southward on scouting and horse-hunting adventures.[3]

One of the men riding to Béxar with Bowie was a young second lieutenant of the Texas cavalry, James Butler Bonham. Over two weeks earlier the *Telegraph and Texas Register* had published a notice announcing Bonham's new law practice in Brazoria.

Shortly after his arrival at San Antonio, Bowie conferred with its commandant, Colonel Neill, over Houston's somewhat discretionary order regarding the demolition and abandonment of the defensive works there. General Houston thought that the Anglo settlements in the east could be better defended at their border, where Texian forces would have the advantage of interior lines and swifter concentration of forces. But Bowie and Neill agreed that the war had to be waged at Béxar, far west of the vulnerable settlements, and more especially because the cannon divided between the town and the fortress of the Alamo—some twenty-one pieces—could not be hauled eastward due to a lack of sufficient ox teams.

The slowness of news dissemination in those days meant that papers throughout the United States often received a mixed bag of conflicting information concerning developments in Texas. The following slew of reports, brought together on one page in a late February edition of the *Richmond Enquirer*, is typical, offering contradictory, and mostly rose-colored, information regarding the Texians' political situation, the progress of Santa Anna's northward-advancing divisions, and the chances the Texian army had to repel them.

(From the New York Courier and Enquirer.)
TEXAS.—Accounts have been received from Galveston Bay to the 25th, and from the river Brazos to the 31st December. From these we are much gratified to learn, that the state of affairs in Texas is such as to warrant the expectations entertained by the friends of free Government here of the ultimate success of the settlers in effecting their separation from the despotic government of Santa Anna, and establishing a free and independent Republic.

Judging from the various decrees and decisions which we find in the Telegraph, which is published at San Felipe, the Government of Texas is assuming a regular form—the members of it direct all their exertions towards the organization of the various branches of internal administration, placing at the same time the army and the navy on such a footing, as to baffle any new attempt on the part of the Mexicans again to invade with the least prospect of success, any portion of the territories of Texas, properly so called.

In consequences of advices received by the government, that a Mexican force under General Sesmas had entered the province of Coahuila, probably with the intention of forcing its way into Texas, active measures were immediately taken to send an army of 1500 men to Goliad to defend that important point, and to oppose the progress of the enemy into the interior of the colony. At the same time San Antonio de Bexar was to be placed in the best possible state of defence, and supplied with four months' provisions, so as to render it almost impracticable for the Mexicans again to take possession of this important point, without a long siege, which it is obvious they will never be able to sustain for want of supplies.

It had already been ascertained, that Sesmas' soldiers were in every respect inferior to the hardy, strong and brave Texians; that the Mexicans encountered such difficulties in crossing the extensive prairies of Coahuila, owing to the bad state of the roads, want of provisions and transports, that their progress scarcely exceeded five or six miles a day. Sesmas, it appears, boasted that he would secure the communication by sea between Matagorda or Copano, and Metamoras, by which means he calculated to receive all the supplies for his army by water, and thus avoiding the transport by land, from the internal provinces, a distance of 600 miles. But in this he was disappointed, as the two first mentioned ports are blockaded by the Texian cruisers; and the strength of this blockade is about being increased and extended to most of the Eastern Mexican ports, the government of Texas having purchased two large and substantial steamboats, which are to be armed and employed in protecting the extensive coast of the colony.

Advices from Matagorda, state that Goliad, although garrisoned only by 200 men, could easily stop for three months the march, and resist the attacks of 2000 Mexicans.

The arrival of volunteers from the Western States, as well as from Louisiana and Alabama, was uninterrupted; so that the Texian Government expected to organize an active division of 3000 Riflemen by the 1st of February, besides providing the necessary garrison for Bexar, Galveston bay, Los Brazos, Goliad and other points on the coast.

We would almost hazard the opinion that Texas will not again be troubled with a Mexican army; but if it should, there can be but little doubt that it would fall an easy prey to the Texian forces.

LATER FROM TEXAS.—The New Orleans Bulletin, of February 2d, contains a public document, dated Goliad, Dec. 22d, and signed by a great number of names, chiefly Americans, declaring Texas "a free, sovereign and independent State."

The declaration enters somewhat at length into the conditions of Texas, deplores the leniency of the Texian Government in permitting Cos to capitulate, and affirms that many officers, civil and military, are more ambitious of emoluments than the good of the country. It is furthermore stated, that there is more danger from the corrupting influence of Santa Anna's gold than from his bayonets. The necessity of forming an independent sovereign State immediately, in order that all her energies may be concentrated, is pointed out with great force.

[*N. Y. Gazette, Feb. 17.*]

TEXAS.—Brazoria papers of the 13th and St. Philip of the 9th of January, have been received at N. Orleans. The chief intelligence is the ordering of troops and volunteers to encamp on the western frontiers, to prevent Cos and his forces or the hostile Indians from entering Texas. They were to have rendezvoused at San Patricio on the 27th inst., by order of the general council and commanding officers. The campaign under general Houston will commence on the 1st of March—that under Santa Anna somewhat earlier.

NEW ORLEANS, Feb. 8—We have read a letter dated Matamoras, January 18th, which states that the fall of San Antonio de Bexar has served to stimulate the Mexicans as well as the Texians; and that armies from all parts were preparing to start for that place. On the 12th, Santa Anna had arrived at Saltillo, with 10,000 men well armed, and 25 pieces of artillery; Ramirez Lesinia had 2,500 men under his command; the troops at Lipantillon and Bahia had moved towards Bexar; and about 3 or 4000 men would be ready to start from Mexico, Zacatecas and Queretana, should occasion arise. D. Vital Fernandez was then at Matamoras, as commander-in-chief, with about 800 men under him, which he had brought from Campeachy.—*Bee.*

TEXAS.—Advices from Brazoria to the 13th and from San Felipe to the 8th Jan. have been received at New Orleans. General Cos has certainly forfeited his parole and is busily engaging in recruiting. The tone of the Texians is very decided, and they seem to entertain very little fear that they will be in a condition to meet Santa Anna wherever he may attack them.

—*Richmond Enquirer*, February 27, 1836

Santa Anna's personal determination to deal a devastating blow to the Texian rebels, despite an unending array of obstacles, was evinced in a letter he wrote from his Leona Vicario (Saltillo) headquarters on January 11 to Minister of War José María Tornel.

To His Excellency the Minister of War—
    The first division of this army, under the command of General Ramirez Sesma, arrived at Guerrero on the 12th instant; the division commanded by General Cos will occupy Monclova on the 16th; and the remaining troops are arriving at head quarters. The difficulties which are encountered on procuring provisions for the troops, in consequence of a deficiency in the means of transportation, and many other unavoidable operations, will possibly retard our

march a few days on San Antonio de Bexar, but nothing will be spared to overcome this difficulty of a march through a desert, and we shall begin very soon operations.

Head Quarters of Leona Vicario,
    11th of January, 1836.
Signed, ANTONIO LOPEZ DE SANTA ANA.
    —*Morning Courier and New York Enquirer*,
February 27, 1836

The *generalissimo* had also ordered the creation of a special military order and medal, both designed to inspire his soldiers to exert themselves to their fullest in the coming arduous campaign. Tornel penned the announcement, which was published in at least one Mexican newspaper.

Attention! Civil Wars are always bloody. Our soldiers ever aspire to shed the blood of foreigners who seek to take away from us our rights and menace our independence. This war is righteous, and should be without remorse; and this nation will adorn with flowers the tombs of its defenders. Remember, soldiers, in civil war triumphant victory must always be accompanied by the mourning and by the tears of widows and orphans. It is in the face of such reflections that our brave troops start out on a campaign, so full of privations, to retrieve the disasters at Bexar. So many misfortunes have already been suffered, and so many more may come that the Supreme Government is supremely indignant and ardently desires vengeance. It, therefore, esteems it very fitting that it should enact the following law:

Art. I. The war against Texas is national;

Art. II. To reward services that the army will make in this campaign and in wars of like nature, there is established a military order to be called the *Legion of Honor*;

Art. III. In order to be admitted to this order it is necessary to have made the Texas campaign or to serve in Tampico, or other points of foreign aggression. The general-in-chief of the army himself will record the merits of each one. [Here, eight rules of procedure regarding the actual decoration ceremony follow].

Bowie's Parley with the Comanches

When James Bowie heard in July 1835 that the Indians along Texas's northern borders were being stirred up by "renegades," he realized he had to lead a party there to put a lid on that potential explosion. Doing so was doubly important because most Texians anticipated that a Mexican army would soon arrive to give the settlers enough trouble.

Bowie first went to see Chief Bowl of the Cherokees. Whether he visited other tribes, including the Comanches, is not known. Because reports of his actions and whereabouts were so scanty, rumors began circulating about his fate. The *Louisiana Advertiser* of September 16, 1835, noted: "Col. James Bowie was killed by a party of Camanche Indians about six weeks since."

In fact, Bowie was alive, and dealing with a crowded schedule: after conferring with the Indians he traveled east to Louisiana, this time on a variety of personal and business-related matters.[1] Returning to Texas in the fall, he took part in the ousting of Gen. Martín Perfecto de Cos from San Antonio. Eventually, in mid-January 1836, Sam Houston assigned Bowie to go to Béxar to begin withdrawing troops and artillery from that post. But deciding that the town needed to be held, not abandoned, Bowie began to consolidate its defenses.

Now arises a heretofore unasked question: during the five weeks that remained before the Mexican army showed up, on February 23, did Bowie leave San Antonio on a mission to placate the Comanche Indians? According to a report originally appearing in the *Charleston Patriot*, "particulars" received from "a gentleman recently in the Texan naval service who left Victoria on the 8th of February" seem to suggest he did. After noting that things were quiet in Texas, the report stated: "Col. Bowie had gone to hold a talk with the Camanche Indians, and keep them quiet if possible."[2]

Alamo commandant James C. Neill had, on January 8, written to Governor Henry Smith that the Comanches were "in an attitude of hostilities toward us," but were willing to hold peace talks.[3] Four days later garrison member William R. Carey wrote that "the Savage Camanche Indians is near at hand we expect soon to have a fight with them."[4] This is confirmed in the letter written by Maine tourist Edward Warren, who, while encamped on the San Antonio River between Goliad and Béxar on January 14, heard that "some two or three hundred Camanche had come to the town and others were hanging about the country, that their intention undoubtedly was to put the Americans there to

(Continued)

death and pillage the town."[5] On January 14 Neill wrote that a Comanche had arrived in town, suggesting April 20 as a date for arranging the treaty talks.[6] (Also on January 14, Alamo defender David Cummings wrote his father that "the northern Indians have joined to our assistance"—a vague, but possible reference to this Comanche offer of a treaty, although it probably referred to Houston's talks with the Cherokees, Creeks, and Choctaws.)[7]

Since he had left Victoria on February 8, the "gentleman" of the "Texan naval service" would certainly have had enough time while there to hear news of these developments in San Antonio. And because Bowie's movements in San Antonio in the weeks between his arrival (January 18) and that of the Mexican army (February 23) were not recorded on a strict day-by-day basis, and because that thirty-six-day time frame would have easily allowed him the opportunity to ride out of town on such an important mission, it is within the realm of possibility that he *could* have gone to confer with the Comanches at their nearby camp or village, "to keep them quiet if possible." Still, solid evidence to confirm this terse newspaper report has not yet come to light.

George Catlin noted that the Comanches he saw in Texas in 1834 were, "in stature, rather low, and in person, often approaching to corpulency." He depicted their warriors as almost universally wearing long hair, in a few cases with braids.[8] War chiefs often wore buffalo horn headdresses and carried lances and buffalo hide shields like their warriors. Those who owned guns protected them in fringed skin cases. Bows were made from bois d'arc wood.

As drawn here, the sign-talking Bowie (his fingers saying "lies") is attired in a deerskin coat similar to one worn by his brother Rezin in an oil portrait attributed to G. P. A. Healy, now in a private collection.

1. William C. Davis, *Three Roads to the Alamo: The Lives and Fortunes of David Crockett, James Bowie, and William Barret Travis* (New York: Harper Collins, 1998), 428–430.

2. *New York Evening Star*, March 25, 1836.

3. J. C. Neill to Gov. & Council of Texas, January 8, 1836, in Wallace O. Chariton, *100 Days in Texas: The Alamo Letters* (Plano, Tex.: Wordware Publishing, 1990) 114.

4. Wm. R. Carey to Dear Brother & Sister, January 12, 1836, in Chariton, *100 Days in Texas*, 137.

5. *Bangor Commercial Advertiser*, March 22, 1836.

6. Neill to Houston, January 14, 1836, in Chariton, *100 Days in Texas*, 145.

7. David Cummings to his father, San Antonio de Béxar, February 14, 1836, in Todd Hansen, ed., *The Alamo Reader: A Study in History* (Mechanicsburg, Penn: Stackpole Books, 2003), 675.

8. George Catlin, *Letters and Notes on the North American Indians* (North Dighton, Mass.: J. G. Press, 1995), 2:72–77.

Art. IV. The candidate for the honor must kneel and swear: "I swear to be faithful to the country, the Government, and to honor and do all that constitutes the duty of a reliant loyal gentleman of the Legion of Honor." The soldiers and the sergeants then swear together to fight with extraordinary valor on the day of battle.

The insignia of the Legion of Honor shall be a cross or star with five radiants. The center shall be surrounded by a crown of laurel; at one side shall be the national arms, on the other the motto, *Honor, Valor, and Country*. On the reverse side of the medal in the center shall be the name of the campaign or action for which the decoration is awarded with the words *Republica Mexicana*. This cross shall be of silver for the cavalrymen, but gold for all officers. The Grand Crosses will bear a band with red border on each edge across the right and left shoulders. This is a purely military order and shall be considered the highest honor the Mexican soldier can merit. None besides soldiers ought to obtain it.

—*El Mosquito Mexicano*, January 22, 1836

Arriving fairly late at the Alamo, on February 3, two weeks after Bowie got there, was cavalry Lt. Col. William Barrett Travis. In early December, he had been elected by the Texas Council as "first major of Artillery in the regular Army of Texas."[4] It was an honor he politely refused, even though, judging by Richard H. Chisholm's account of the Texian army's nighttime probe against Cos's defenses in November,[d] Travis had indeed briefly led a detachment that included an artillery unit. Preferring to serve on horseback, he gladly accepted when appointed an officer in the newly created Legion of Cavalry on December 20.[5] On January 21, Governor Smith, who had refused to relinquish his authority despite his impeachment, ordered Travis to collect one hundred willing riders and reinforce San Antonio. But it proved a depressing journey for the young officer because less than a third of that number had answered the call, and as a lieutenant colonel, he justifiably felt the command was too small

for his rank. While he rode west, the *Telegraph and Texas Register* ran an advertisement he had posted concerning his law business.

LAW NOTICE

THE PARTNERSHIP heretofore existing between Travis & Nibbs, has been dissolved by limitation. The unfinished business entrusted to them will be attended to by Travis & Starr.

W. B. Travis and Franklin J. Starr have associated themselves in the practice of law, and will attend to business in the courts of San Felipe, Washington, and the adjoining municipalities. One or both of them will be constantly found in San Felipe.

—*Telegraph and Texas Register*, January 23, 1836

Travis's arrival in San Antonio went unnoticed by the newspapers, as did Colonel Neill's leave of absence beginning on February 13—for family reasons, as he said—which only exacerbated the conflict over command that had already begun between Bowie of the volunteer army and Travis of the regular army. What the papers did report about Béxar's situation, as briefly mentioned in the following two extracts, concerned its undermanned and underprovisioned condition.

LATEST FROM TEXAS.

We are indebted to an officer lately in the Texian Naval Service, who arrived in this city[e] on Friday last via New Orleans, and who left Victoria, a port in Texas, on the 8th ult.,[f] for several particulars in relation to the state of affairs in that Territory. Our informant states that Gen. Houston arrived there from the Mission de Refugio, (which at that time was Head Quarters) on way to San Felippe, the seat of Government, some difficulty having taken place between Governor Smith and the Provincial Government, who had not, however, resigned. The Troops were concentrating at Copeno. They were to move on the 1st March, and the forces consisted, as well as can be

"The Cavalry Are the Choice Troops from the Interior"

For his invasion of Texas in 1836, Antonio López de Santa Anna brought, along with his infantry regiments, the following *Permanente* (line) cavalry units: 321 troopers of the regiment of Tampico, 280 of the regiment of Dolores, 180 of the regiment of Guanajuato, 148 of the regiment of Cuautla, 30 of the regiment of Coahuila, and 9 of the regiment of Veracruz. Sixty-one presidial cavalry also accompanied the expedition.[1] Each permanente cavalry regiment had eight companies, composed of lancers (ninety-six per regiment), heavy cavalry, dragoons, and hussars.[2]

The uniform varied by specialty, but many of the line troopers wore a scarlet tailcoat faced with green, either single or double-breasted depending on the year of issuance, grey riding pants with red stripes on the side seams and reinforced with black buckskin. The helmet was of tanned cowhide, with brass shield, comb and chinstrap, and a black goat pelt.

Information received in Texas from friends who observed the Mexican army gathering along the Rio Grande warned that "the cavalry are the choice troops from the interior, they are armed, every one with lance, musket, pistols and sword."[3] A merchant in Mexico had also commented, "I have seen 300 of the cavalry, and in my opinion they are excellent troops."[4]

The lances averaged nine feet in length with red pennants. The "musket" was generally a carbine, and the pistols were usually carried in saddle holsters. The "sword" was a brass-guarded saber. Helmet covers and either ponchos or cloaks were worn to protect uniforms from trail dust and bad weather.

Lt. Col. José Juan Sánchez Navarro, at Laredo in January with the gathering forces, described the cavalry under Gen. Joaquín Ramírez y Sesma as "overflowing with conceit, good clothes, shoes, excellent equipment, and with very gorgeous horses."[5] Of "Senor Gen. Don Joaquin Ramirez y Sesma," who would have both his great highs and deep lows as a cavalry commander in the upcoming campaign, the *Richmond Enquirer* reprinted a brief appraisal of him from a Mexican newspaper:

> The Mercurio pompously speaks of him as a "cabellero," who unites rare qualities for the situation, and is besides a man of affluence, "cuya ambicion no haya cosa que

(Continued)

pueda ecsitar sino es el anhelo de adquiri gloria sirviendo a su patria." (A man whose ambition can have no other object than the aspiration to acquire glory for his country.)

—Richmond Enquirer, January 28, 1836

The Mexican horse soldiers were respected by their enemies, even after the disastrous day at San Jacinto on April 21, 1836, as noted in the following extract from a US newspaper in July:

The division of Mexicans lately defeated at San Jacinto, mostly infantry, is not a fair specimen of Mexican soldiery.—Their best troops are cavalry, and inhabit that tract of country which lies between Guanzuato and the capital, called El Bahio. This was the great theatre of war during the revolution, from 1810 to '21. General Mina was killed there. Their weapons are principally the broadsword, lance and lasso, or rope. When they fell in with the Spanish infantry, the lassadores made the first onset. They rode two and two, some distance from each other—one end of the rope fixed to the pummel of one saddle, and the other to that of another—made a desperate rush, and the intervening rope was made to drag against the column. Close upon the company of lassadores, came the lancers, and encountering the infantry thus thrown into confusion, made great slaughter. How this mode of warfare would do against the Texians, I cannot say. Should they (the Texians) confine themselves to the woods, as they ought, the Mexicans would not find it practicable.

—New-Bedford Mercury, July 7, 1836

1. Richard G. Santos, *Santa Anna's Campaign against Texas, 1835–1836* (Waco: Texian Press, 1968), 14–17.
2. Rene Chartrand, *Santa Anna's Mexican Army, 1821–48* (Oxford: Osprey Publishing, 2004), 13.
3. *Albany Evening Journal*, March 25, 1836.
4. *Morning Courier and New York Enquirer*, January 29, 1836.
5. C. D. Huneycutt, *At the Alamo: The Memoirs of Captain Navarro* (New London, N.C.: Gold Star Press, 1989), 37.

recollected, of the following: at the Missions, 180; at Labadie, 110; at Copeno, 210; at Bexar, 80. 100 men had landed at Dimmot's point from North Alabama about the 10th February; 180 sailed from New Orleans about the 23rd. They are the troops that left New York and were carried into Nassau, N.P.; Col. Fanning commands the forces at Copeno. The gallant Corps of Volunteer Greys from New Orleans had generally returned, disgusted with the service, saying that they would no longer fight to *enrich a few land speculators*; they went to establish the

LIBERTY of the Country. The general supposition in Texas was, that there would be no fighting until the summer was far advanced, as the insurrection of the two Generals of St. Anna's, occasioned a division of his forces, which at no time amounted to more than 8000 troops. Col. Bowie had gone amongst the Camanche Indians to have a Talk, and he will endeavor to keep them quiet.

Elections were going on at the time our informant left for members to the New Convention, which was to assemble on the 1st March. On the 4th March, the Texian *Declaration of Independence* was to be made at San Felipe and the Provisional Government under the new order of things instituted.

The Texian Banner was the same as that of the United States, with the exception of a single *Star* in the centre, instead of the *Thirteen.*
—*Charleston Patriot*, March 14, 1836

RANDOLPH, Tenn., March 1. Volunteers are returning from Texas. As we heretofore predicted, they have found any thing else there than food for a frolic, and report very discouragingly of the inhabitants of the country. In the camp, at San Antonio, the troops had been entirely out of bread-stuffs some days before our informant left, their food being Spanish beef. We wish not to cast a damp feeling upon the spirit of those disposed to see Texas free from the Mexican Government, our own opinion being what it may. We are a friend to liberty any where and every where, in its pure sense; but any information whatever it may be, from Texas, we feel bound to give. Many that have returned from that country speak of the land as being rich and productive. But of its inhabitants they give a miserable account.—They are said to be very poor, and care not a fig under what Government they live. We speak of them generally: doubtless there are exceptions. The volunteers even have to pay for the food for the horses; say that there is no money there excepting what the volunteers take with them, and that the majority of them are returning. The principal object of the majority of the inhabitants

that fight is plunder and pillage. The country is now free from Mexican troops, but Santa Anna is expected in the spring with a powerful army. The inhabitants are said to be indolent, and quite contented. The only lands that can be given to volunteers are upon the head waters of the stream, and back in the interior, the fine lands on the navigable streams being included in the grants to companies by the Government. The weather during the winter has been a continual stream of sunshine—no rains for two or three months.
—*Recorder.*
—*Albany Evening Journal* (New York), March 23, 1836

With too few men left in San Antonio to defend both the town and the Alamo—as Cos had attempted in 1835—the Texians transferred all the cannon still in Béxar into the mission fort. Sometime between February 5 and 10, another man arrived whose name would forever after be connected with the Alamo: David Crockett. Accompanying him were only about a dozen men, but his charismatic presence gave the garrison a major morale boost. (He had arrived in time to meet Colonel Neill just before the latter rode east for a stated three-week leave.) Crockett's entry into San Antonio, like Travis's, was not noted in the newspapers, nor would his presence there be recorded until after Santa Anna began his siege. What the papers continued to report, however, were dire tidings of a substantial Mexican army creeping northward, as witness this collection of accounts published in sequence in an upstate New York newspaper.

From the *Natchez Daily Courier*, March 4.
TEXAS—BY EXPRESS
Information has been received at Nacogdoches that Santa Anna's forces are on their march to the frontiers of Texas. His advance, consisting of about 3500 men, are advancing on San Antonio and the different posts below that place.

The Texians, although not so well provided with supplies as is necessary for a protracted campaign, have no doubt but that they can maintain those posts until reinforcements arrived to their assistance, even if the whole force of Santa Anna should advance more rapidly than is anticipated. But little doubt now exists that the campaign will be protracted, as the war on the part of the Texians will for the present be entirely defensive. This will give time for emigrants to the country to arrive and participate in the final struggle. The Texians are united for the same purpose; some difference of opinion has existed as to the expediency of an entire declaration of Independence, or an adherence to the Constitution of 1824. But both parties have the same object in view, which is a resolute determination to resist the military despotism of Santa Anna.

The report that Gen. Houston has been removed from the command of the army, is unfounded. The Convention met on the 1st of this month, at Washington, on the Brazos.— There is little doubt that they will declare entire Independence, and take the most energetic steps for the defence of the country. Those who join them at the present period, when they are struggling for their freedom, and even for their existence, will be cordially received, and liberally recompensed. The natural resources of the country are unbounded, and they who assist in their defence and development, will be richly rewarded.

The foregoing information has been received from Lt. Stansbury, who has just arrived from Nacogdoches, and brings authentic information as to the state of affairs. He further states, that the Camanches are quiet, and general Houston is engaged in treating with them.

SAN PATRICIO, Feb. 6, 1836.
Dear Sir—Don Placido Benavides has just arrived, and brings disagreeable intelligence. Gonzales' command is entirely dispersed, and twenty-two men were taken prisoners.[6] 300 cavalry and 300 infantry have arrived at Matamoras, which, in addition to the garrison, makes the effective force now there 1000 men, and more are expected shortly. Cos and all his officers from Bejar, are raising troops to march on Texas. 1000 men are already on the Rio Frio. 1000 more on the march near the Rio Grande, destined for some point of Texas; and forces are gathering rapidly in all directions for the same object. It is believed that an attack is intended on Goliad and Bejar simultaneously.

Roderigus has broken his parole since 5 o'clock this evening, and as I have but 18 effective men here, and no horses, I could not pursue him.

The inhabitants of Tamaulipus are generally in favour of (1824) but are so much oppressed by the military, that many of the principal men have been arrested; they are completely fettered. Santa Anna caused a report to be set afloat that he was with the troops at Matamoras, but it is ascertained beyond all doubt that he is on his way to the Rio Grande, for the purpose of pushing on those forces.

Don Placido deems it of the utmost importance troops be sent to Bejar, as well as others retained in this direction, and also assures me that Santa Anna wishes to draw the troops of Texas out to Matamoras, in hopes to throw a strong force in their rear, while he makes his attack on the upper part of the Colonies. This information he received from the first alcalde of Matamoras.—He has been within 20 leagues of the town, and corresponded with him.

Cos is actually with Sesma and Ugartechea. They have 1000 spare horses, and a large number of Pack mules.

It is with regret, but I am absolutely obliged to give Dr. Holt your horse to carry him, with this.

Yours, most sincerely,
ROBERT MORRIS.

The people of Tamaulipas as well as those of the Rio Grande, complain much of Dimitt's Proclamation; and would have acted with more decision were it not for that act, but they fear it is now almost impossible; but are still anxious for the cause. The cavalry are the choice troops from the interior, they are armed, every one with lance, musket, pistols and sword, and Santa Anna has sworn to take Texas or lose Mexico!

Dr. Grant has been out two days with thirty men. I feel very anxious about him. I intended to have sent you more wagons to-morrow morning early, and in fact had the oxen yoked to start before day-light, but shall now await your further orders.

P.S. To raise funds and provisions, Cos causes each man to give an inventory of all he possesses, with valuation on each article, on which he demands one per cent, every twenty days; he then sends two men to make the appraisement over, and if he finds that they make a return higher than the owners, he demands three per cent in lieu of one, and each family has to furnish a fanega of corn also every twenty days, and even causes the women to grind, without respect to station. His soldiers have assassinated many of the most influential citizens, and whose wives and daughters are prostituted—the whole country is given up to the troops to induce them forward.

R. M.

Extract of a letter to a gentleman in Philad. dated NACOGDOCHES, Feb. 14—We feel here as if we were on a powder magazine: and if the spark once takes, there is no retreat. Let the Indian war whoop be here once sounded, and a worse tale would be related than the late massacre by the Seminole Indians in Florida.[g] We have lately been convinced by our neighbouring tribes, the Cherokees, Shawneees, Kickapoos, &c. that they can raise fifteen hundred warriors, and are at any moment prepared for action, being well armed, and keeping an ample supply of ammunition.

—Philad. Gaz.
—Albany Evening Journal, March 25, 1836

The Indian problem, and the threat of Mexican influence among the Texas tribes, brought General Houston to Nacogdoches, where he attempted to throw water on the "powder magazine."

TEXAS. It was reported at Nacogdoches, on the 18th instant, that Santa Anna was daily

expected, and that the Mexicans had defeated two small parties of the Texians—one commanded by Colonel Grant, consisting of thirty men; the other, much larger, by Colonel Gonzales, who lost twenty-two, taken prisoners. General Houston was holding a talk at Nacogdoches with the chiefs of the Choctaws, Creeks and Cherokees, and it was expected they would join the Texians.

—Boston Daily Courier, March 31, 1836

Houston himself communicated developments at Nacogdoches and elsewhere to a friend in Tennessee. His letter was published in that state's major newspapers.

From the Nashville Republican of yesterday.

TEXAS. We have been favored, by the gentleman to whom it was addressed, with the following extract from a letter from Gen'. SAM HOUSTON. It is dated Nacogdoches, 19th of Feb. 1836. As he makes no allusion to his removal from the army, but in fact, speaks of his return to it in a few days, we may conclude that the report of his having been removed, is untrue.

Extract of a Letter from Gen. Sam Houston.

I am here to hold an Indian Treaty, and when that is done, I will return to the army. I intend it shall end on the 24th or 25th inst. The Indians are our neighbors, and we must keep them friendly. Our Campaign will commence next month, and we may have some warm work. Until the grass rises the Mexicans cannot advance, unless it is by sea—the Mexicans only advance on horses or by water.

The Convention will meet on the first of next month, and I doubt not but *Independence will be declared.* Our cause is the cause of all mankind—tis the cause of human Liberty!!! We can only look to the United States for aid. We regard them as our kindred; and in the hour of our peril, *they will not forget that we are brothers.*

Our cause must triumph—It is so recorded in fate! Despotism cannot chain the minds, or manacle the limbs of Freedom! Our struggle will cost us the lives and blood of brave men, but we will *nerve* for the combat and meet

---

[g] A reference to the ambush of Major Francis L. Dade's command of 150 US regulars in Florida on December 28, 1835. Only three men survived.

it—the brave can die but once; cowards die ten thousand deaths.

Your heart will be with us—I do not ask your person—I would forbid it—but where are the young men of Tennessee? the generous sons of valorous Fathers? The field to wealth, to fame and honor, is presented to them in Texas. If any should come, let them engage during the war. Our greatest misfortune is, that men who have arrived, (or the greater part of them) have volunteered for no definite period. Some quit the army when they please, and return to the United States with reports unfavorable to us and our cause—this they believe will justify *their* conduct. Let men who wish to aid us, embark during the war, or for two years. Our pecuniary resources are few—at present, we lack means such as men.

Salute my friends in Nashville who have contributed to our aid, even in good wishes, for our success.

—Nashville Banner & Nashville Whig,
March 18, 1836

Houston was not the only Texian leader who surmised that there was not enough new grass between the Rio Grande and San Antonio to support the advance of Mexican cavalry. Sixty-nine years later, José María Rodríguez, son of Bexareño Ambrosio Rodríguez, recalled how Colonel Travis remained convinced that Santa Anna would not try to march so early over such a barren country.

Travis slept in town almost every night. He walked to the Alamo in the morning and returned in the evening. He traversed the path that passed the door of Rodriguez and led to the footlog across the river.[7] He often stopped to visit with his friend Ambrosio Rodriguez. And the boy listened to the talks and remembered. Rodriguez all during the winter after the killing of Ben Milam, continued to tell Travis that he was foolhardy in staying with a handful of men. He insisted that he had definite information that Santa Anna would be in San Antonio with seven thousand men in the spring. Travis did not believe it. That he later came to think that he would be able to hold out. He was expecting

reinforcements. He was urged by Rodriguez to go into the interior of the state and recruit his troops. But he stayed with the Alamo.

—Daily Express, May 5, 1905

An independent Texas republic was the goal of most of the men under colonels Travis and Bowie—who had agreed to conduct a joint command of the garrison—not a reunion with the kind of Federalist nation Mexico had originally declared itself to be in 1824. In a late February issue of the *Telegraph and Texas Register*, an anonymous writer who dubbed himself "Jefferson" penned an essay titled, "Shall We Declare For Independence?" He listed all of the grievances Texians held against the current Mexican government, which, he noted, echoed closely those that had inspired the American revolutionists of 1776. He also made the racially charged point that white Texians must

separate from a people one half of whom are the most depraved of the different races of Indians, different in color, pursuits and character; and *all* of whom are divided from us by the insurmountable barrier which nature and refined taste have thrown between us—a people whose inert and idle habits, general ignorance and superstition, prevents the possibility of our ever mingling in the same harmonious family; and if possible, could only be done by self-degradation.

—Telegraph and Texas Register,
February 27, 1836

In the same issue of the *Register*, another article appeared that warned of Santa Anna's near approach (in fact, by the time this edition was published in San Felipe, the siege of the Alamo was already four days old!). It also urged all able-bodied Texians to prepare for the final martial conflict that was expected some time in March.

HIGHLY IMPORTANT INFORMATION.

We lay this week, before our readers the substance of the information brought by Mr. Pantillion and Mr. Smith, relative to the movements of general Santa Ana.[h] Of the correctness

---

[h] Isadore Pantallion, a Tejano, and John W. Smith of Béxar.

of this information, not the least doubt can be entertained; and the people of Texas must arouse from lethargy, and prepare to encounter the enemy of liberty, the invader of their country; and they have to encounter him with a determination to "conquer or die."

Mr. Pantillion is direct from Matamoros, and brings intelligence that one thousand troops had arrived at that place, and were expecting shortly to be joined by others; and that early in March, they would move forward to Texas, for the purpose of attacking Goliad.

He also states that about one thousand men, under the commands of generals Filisola and Cos, are stationed on the Rio Grande, awaiting the arrival of five hundred more troops; after which they intend to move on to Texas, for the purpose of attacking Bejar.

He further states that the army under the immediate command of Santa Ana, consisting of about six thousand men, commenced their march from Saltillo to Monclova, on the 27th ult.; and that Santa Ana himself left, with the last division, on the first inst. His plan of operations, as communicated to Mr. Pantillion by intelligent friends of Texas in Matamoros, was to push at once for the heart of Texas, with that part of the army under his immediate command, while the other two divisions make a simultaneous attack on Bejar and Goliad. Santa Ana, it is said, has been furnished by the clergy with one million of dollars which has greatly assisted him in preparing for the expedition; so that he is now well provided, and comes with a train of thirty pieces of artillery, swearing to "conquer Texas or lose Mexico."

Mr. Smith, who was the active and faithful pilot of the American army at Bejar, has been within a few miles of Rio Grande, and corroborates the information of Mr. Pantillion. He says the army on the Rio Grande is busily engaged in mounting cannons, and preparing for the campaign; and that in March, we may expect to be invaded by the whole Mexican force.

Citizens of Texas, the hour is fast approaching when your valor and patriotism are again to be tested. The friends of freedom will now ascertain whether you are deserving their sympathy and assistance. Show that they have not been deceived: convince them that their exertions in your favor have not been directed towards an unworthy object. The whole force of Texas will be requisite to ward off the blow; and Texas and freedom demand that "every man do his duty."

An organization of the militia has been ordered, and we most fervently hope the people will attend to it. We would advise every company to commence preparing themselves with every thing necessary for the campaign. Let them mould bullets, procure powder, make cartridges, put their guns in order, and in short, do every thing which can be done within themselves. Nothing can save Texas, but prompt and united action. Without it all is lost; but with it, victory will attend our arms; and freedom will rule triumphantly over its enemies. A great responsibility rests with every man; and surely no man can be indifferent to the call of his country, at a time like the present.

We understand that some are not willing, under the present provisional government, to do any duty. But shall we fold up our arms, when the enemy is upon us? That our government is bad, all must acknowledge, and some will deny. But, considering all things, what country ever had a better, under the same circumstances? Had not our thirteen British colonies been for many years previous to their revolution, in strict subordination under a well organized government? And what was their condition after the commencement of hostilities with the mother country? The public credit was not so good as ours. Texas has been many years without any government; and ought we to expect a perfect model at once? We trust that the little jarings and discord, which are natural consequences arising more from our infant state, than from intention on the part of individuals or the government, will not be attributed to us as a proof that Texas does not possess virtue, honesty and talents sufficient to govern herself. We earnestly look to the meeting of the convention, which will, we hope, employ itself in putting our country in a state of preparation and defence. Let us, in the mean time, prepare ourselves to obey the first order which may emanate from our chosen representatives. One day in March, with the loss of a drop of blood, may be worth a month in May, with the loss of hundreds of lives. Will our farmers longer talk of heavy crops of cotton, when they ought to bestow what time they can spare to the raising of corn! Should the merchants think of advantages in trade, when in less than six months, perhaps, they may be stripped of all, and deprived of their rights, by the Mexicans and a foe still more formidable! Indeed we would recommend the cessation of all business, the operation of which would, in any way, retard our citizens from the prosecution of the war, and the establishing of a government of our choice. Bread must be had; and we are glad to learn that many of the farmers in the upper country have abandoned the idea of raising cotton this year, although so profitable. We pray God to bless their labors in raising subsistence for our children and our army.

—*Telegraph and Texas Register*,
February 27, 1836

Six days before he would lead his vanguard brigade into San Antonio, Santa Anna issued the following proclamation to his troops, an explicitly patriotic statement of purpose for the campaign.

The General-in-Chief to the Army of
Operations under his command:
COMPANIONS IN ARMS!—Our most sacred duties have conducted us to these plains, and urged us forward to combat with that mob of ungrateful adventurers, on whom our authorities have incautiously lavished favors which they have failed to bestow on Mexicans. They have appropriated to themselves our territories, and have raised the standard of rebellion in order that this fertile and expanded department may be detached from our republic—persuading themselves that our unfortunate dissensions have incapacitated us for the defence of our native land. Wretches! they will soon see their folly.

Soldiers!—Your comrades have been treacherously sacrificed at Anahuac, Goliad and Bejar; and you are the men chosen to chastise the assassins.

My Friends!—We will march to the spot whither we are called by the interests of the nation in whose services we are engaged. The candidates for "acres" of land in Texas will learn to their sorrow, that their auxiliaries from New Orleans, Mobile, Boston, New York and other northern ports, from whence no aid ought to proceed, are insignificant, and that Mexicans, though naturally generous, will not suffer outrages with impunity—injurious and dishonorable to their country—let the perpetrators be whom they may.

Camp on the River Nueces, Feb. 17, 1836.
ANTONIO LOPEZ DE SANTA ANNA.
—*Richmond Enquirer*, April 5, 1836

7

The Alamo Encircled

The following preamble to one of the most important contemporary Mexican military documents of Antonio López de Santa Anna's Texas campaign was printed in a June issue of the *New York Herald*.

SINGULAR DISCLOSURE.

JOURNAL OF THE MEXICAN CAMPAIGN—BY ALMONTE, AID TO SANTA ANNA. PICKED UP ON THE BATTLE GROUND OF SAN JACINTO BY ANSON JONES.

Annexed will be found a translation of the first portion of the remarkable "Secret Journal" of the recent Mexican Campaign, written by Col. Almonte, *aid de camp* to General Santa Anna.[1] The original, in the Spanish language, is now in our possession. It was picked up on the battle ground of San Jacinto by Dr. ANSON JONES, and was sent to us *via* Galveston Island, on the 12th of May last. The journal was seen and examined by Mr. Childress, the diplomatic representative from Texas, who left this city a few days ago for Washington.

—*New York Herald* of June 22, 1836

The journal's length required that it be published in five installments. The part appearing in the June 22 *Herald* is a daily tracing of the Mexican army's march north from Saltillo, then across the Rio Grande and eastward to the banks of the Rio Frio, about sixty-five miles west of San Antonio. The June 23 issue contained entries relating to the army's arrival at Béxar, and the beginning of the siege of the Alamo, including the following three.

Feb.—Sunday, 21st—At 7 ½ A.M. left Arroyo Hondo—weather cloudy—slight showers—not cold—wind south east. To Francisco Perez 4 leagues, (a stream of water very distant, but not on the road). To Arroyo del Chacon, good water, 3 leagues. To the river Medina 2 leagues; all good road, but broken by large hills. At ¼ before 2 o'clock the President arrived. The day completely overcast; The whole division at 5 o'clock when it commenced raining heavily—all wet but baggage dry, at 12 o'clock at night it cleared some.

Monday, 22d—Commenced cloudy, but cleared at 10 o'clock. The troops cleared their arms and dried their clothes; no desertions whatever or sickness. We passed the day at Medina to rest the troops. Two men from the Ranchos near Bexar arrived, one menchaca[a] and another; killed a beef; various other persons came in, reviewed the troops. Sr. Ramirez y Sermer,[b] marched to cut off the retreat of the enemy with — dragoons. It was believed the enemy discovered our movements.

Tuesday, 23—At 7 ½ A. M. the army was put in march—To the Potranca 1 ½ leagues—to the Creek of Leon, or Del Media, 3 ½ leagues—To Bexar 3 leagues, in all 8 leagues. At half a league from Bexar the division halted on the hills of Alazan at 12 ½ o'clock. General Sesma arrived at 7 A. M. and did not advance to reconnoitre because he expected an advance of the enemy which was about to be made according to accounts given by a spy of

---

[a] Antonio Menchaca of San Antonio.
[b] General Joaquín Ramírez y Sesma

David Crockett Fires the Eighteen-Pounder

In an 1881 newspaper summary of one of the last interviews she ever gave—and one that has long been overlooked by historians—Alamo survivor Susanna Dickinson, then Mrs. Joseph Hannig, provided details of the siege and battle not found in her other published interviews. For instance, when telling of the quarters she and her late husband, Capt. Almeron Dickinson, had shared inside the church building:

> Crockett occupied an adjoining room. Here, when not engaged in loading and firing a sort of "long Tom," a primitive eighteen-pounder, he was accustomed to saw his fiddle and abhor confinement within stone walls.[1]

A "long Tom" was a contemporary term that generally referred to a seagoing "pivot gun" of considerable length and most often to an eighteen-pounder pivot gun. For instance, in Caribbean waters in 1824, a pirate vessel approached a US brig, and in the words of the latter's captain:

> At 10 P. M. he gave us his pivot gun, or long tom, (eighteen pounder) loaded with round, grape and langrage, which shot away much of our running and standing rigging.[2]

Twelve years later, during the Texas Revolution, a Texian naval vessel fired three rounds from a "Long Tom (eighteen pounder pivot gun)," in the words of Judge R. S. Calder, as a signal to another Texian ship near Galveston Island.[3]

Why would the Alamo's famed eighteen-pounder gun be remembered as a long Tom by Mrs. Dickinson? In fact, when the cannon's origin is traced back a few months, it becomes clear that it *was* a long Tom pivot gun, and that there *is* an 1835 reference to it as such. And just how the eighteen-pounder arrived at San Antonio de Béxar is something of an epic in itself.

Captain Robert C. Morris's Second Company of volunteer New Orleans Greys began its journey to join the fighting in Texas by boarding the schooner *Columbus* at New Orleans on October 17, 1835. Among the military supplies accompanying the Greys were several cannon, including an iron eighteen-pounder. Three days of sailing

(Continued)

brought the *Columbus* to the Texas port of Velasco, at the mouth of the Brazos, where the Greys switched to the steamboat *Laura* for the voyage up the river to Brazoria.[4] They took two of the cannon with them, but the long Tom was left behind, on or near the Velasco shore, and a letter written at Brazoria on November 14 explained why:

> The long eighteen-pounder which came from New Orleans unfortunately, was not accompanied by any shot, fitting its caliber, and this oversight will cost the country a delay and expense greater than the cost of 50 guns.[5]

Of course it could still fire custom-made bags of grape, tins of canister, and sacks of scrap shot (langrage), and even smaller round shot combined with scrap or grape, so its value to Stephen F. Austin's army remained, even if it could not serve, for the time being, as a gun capable of battering down strong walls.

On the night of October 27, the Mexican armed schooner, *Montezuma*, appeared off Velasco and fired at the town. An extract of a letter in the *Arkansas Gazette* briefly reported what happened:

> There has [been] an armed vessel made its appearance on our coast, attempted to land at Velasco, fired one shot at the town, it was manfully returned by the citizens of the place from an eighteen pounder, and after firing four shots at her, she stood off, and has been more shy; so says an express from that place.[6]

The noise of the exchange brought the *Laura*, having dropped the Greys off at Brazoria, back down the river, while Velasco militiamen rushed "to arm the *San Felipe*," a merchant schooner. An unidentified Texian aboard the *San Felipe* wrote that eventually "we had two 12 pounders and one 6 pounder, on each side of the schooner, and a long beautiful 18 pounder on a pivot amidships."[7] The latter was, of course, the gun from New Orleans. But by this time the *Montezuma* had sailed away.

The *San Felipe* now began its hunt. Towed by the *Laura,* it first investigated the waters of the Gulf eastward as far as Galveston Bay. Then it separated from the steamboat and turned west again, cruising past Velasco and on toward Matagorda, at the mouth of the Colorado River. But strong seas, "running mountains high," drove the schooner aground onto Bird Island, near the Matagorda Peninsula. Three days later, while the crew was still unloading the *San Felipe*'s cargo onto the beach, the *Montezuma* reappeared, and in the words of the unnamed Texian, an engagement took place at long shots, the M fired broadsides and her brass 18 pounder. We fired 12 pounders and *our* 18. We put an 18 pound ball directly into her hull, and she soon put off. Not a ball from the M. reached the shore.[8]

Thus, the eighteen-pounder of later Alamo fame had, over four months earlier, engaged in two firefights with a Mexican foe and had seemingly prevailed in both.

The big gun was eventually salvaged and transported across Matagorda Bay to Dimmitt's Landing in Lavaca Bay. Sometime later in November, a small detachment from San Antonio arrived with orders to cart the cannon overland, in dismantled sections (i.e., tube and carriage) to Béxar.[9] Its arrival was eagerly anticipated by Austin's army, which was still besieging General Martín Perfecto de Cos's forces then occupying both the town and the fort (Alamo). A writer in Natchez noted:

> The eighteen pounder, purchased at New Orleans, was on the way, together with a five horse wagon load of balls. With the aid of the eighteen pounder, the work will be soon accomplished.[10]

By the time the nearly nine-foot-long gun tube arrived in Béxar, however, Cos and his army had already surrendered. Eventually reunited with its truck-wheeled carriage (trucks being small metal wheels that allowed the carriage to rotate in any direction), the eighteen-pounder was emplaced by Major Green B. Jameson in mid-January in a rooftop barbette position on the Alamo's southwest corner.[11]

Francis W. Johnson and James Grant's Matamoros expedition had taken away a number of field pieces, but a few pivot guns probably remained on the Alamo's walls, along with cannon mounted on field carriages. During the siege of Béxar by Austin's army, as remembered by William T. Austin in his 1844 memoir, the Mexicans

> had cannon mounted on pivots at the church [San Fernando Church on Main Plaza] and upon other commanding house-tops. . . . The Alamo was a fort situated on the opposite bank of the river, and was occupied by the enemy's cavalry. At this fort they had upwards of thirty pieces of cannon, mounted upon the walls behind facades, many of which were pivot guns and commanded the whole surrounding country.[12]

(Continued)

This last point is what made a pivot gun so desirable both for naval as well as garrison use: in some cases its wheels could turn the piece in a 360-degree circumference. Unlike smaller swivel guns—and during the Alamo's 1836 siege all three of the fort's *esmeriles,* or swivel guns, were unused, stored away in the armory along with a number of small arms and bayonets[13]—pivot guns came in calibers equal to any field piece. A pivot cannon had also defended the Mexican fort at Velasco during the Texian attack in 1832.[14] In late 1835, anticipating a largely defensive war against Mexican troops, the Texas General Council penned a list of "Munitions of War, Arms, &c." it needed to purchase, and on that list the number of guns "mounted for fort service" far outnumbered those "mounted for field service."[15]

Surprisingly, in addition to Mrs. Dickinson's terse remembrance, there are other wisps of tradition associating David Crockett with the cannon of the Alamo. On February 23, according to John Sutherland's eyewitness account, Col. William Barret Travis assigned Crockett and his "twelve boys" to defend "the picket wall extending from the end of the barracks, on the south side, to the corner of the church."[16] At least one gun had been positioned at this palisade; whether Crockett and his men helped to load and fire it is not known. But a published 1877 newspaper version of the recollections of Mexican sergeant Francisco Bercerra noted that, during the battle inside the Alamo compound on March 6:

> In the long room used as a hospital the sick and wounded fired pistols and rifles from their pallets. A piece of artillery, supposed to be that which Crockett had used during the siege, was shotted with grape and canister and turned upon the desperate occupants of this apartment.[17]

Could this be referring to the gun at the palisade? Who can say? Yet other evidence points to Crockett either firing or supervising cannon fire. In a 1907 interview, Alamo survivor Enrique Esparza recalled how Travis had spent much of his time directing artillery fire

> from the roof of the church. . . . Crockett and he both, however, looked after the cannonading from the convent as well, both making repeated visits to that locality and at frequent intervals.[18]

The "convent" seems to have been Esparza's term for the rest of the Alamo beyond the church complex, within the latter of which the Bexareño youth and his mother had spent most of the siege. (In one account he states that their "quarters" were in the low barracks.)

Crockett was not unfamiliar with cannon, having been billeted during the Creek War of 1813–1814 in a number of army forts and camps and having fought the Indians in at least one engagement where cannon were utilized. His later careers as a colonel of Tennessee militia and nationally recognized politician also brought him into the vicinity of saluting guns. But none of these experiences would have qualified Crockett to serve as an artilleryman at the Alamo, especially when it came to the fort's biggest gun, the eighteen-pounder. Additionally, the evidence tells us that this gun was put permanently out of commission by a Mexican battery early in the siege. According to Col. Juan Nepomuceno Almonte's journal entry for February 24:

> Very early this morning a new battery was commenced on the bank of the river, about 350 yards from the Alamo. It was finished in the afternoon, and a brisk fire was kept up from it until the 18 pounder and another piece was dismounted.[19]

That the eighteen-pounder quickly became a prime target for Mexican guns is explained both by its lethality and the fact that it had fired the first defiant shot at Antonio López de Santa Anna's troops as they marched into Béxar on February 23. And what that shot was composed of is revealed in the following Mexican military journal extract (although the gun here is called a sixteen-pounder, the Mexican gauge for an American eighteen-pounder):

> At the entrance of the column at the front, a shot of grapeshot was fire[d] at them from the 16-pounder piece.[20]

What the this quote suggests is that the eighteen-pounder was probably still not equipped with solid round shot "fitting its caliber." After the Mexican hit put it out of commission, it seems to have remained in a "dismounted" state because we no longer hear about it, other than obliquely, when Travis in his March 3 letter to the Convention urged that "two hundred rounds of six, nine, twelve, and eighteen pound balls . . . should be sent to this place without delay."[21] (Obviously Travis anticipated that the big gun would eventually be remounted.) When General Pedro de Ampudia made a postbattle inventory of the Alamo's "Mounted Artillery," the only such guns on the list were twenty-one pieces "of Brass and iron, from calibers of 12 down to 2."[22] The eighteen-pounder was not mentioned anywhere. Three carriageless tubes sat on the

(Continued)

ground of Alamo plaza, and were described by Lt. Col. José Juan Sánchez Navarro as "three cannon of iron, dismounted." This is a major military distinction: "dismounted" as opposed to simply "unmounted." It can be easily surmised that one of these tubes was the iron long Tom.

Now the question arises: after it was dismounted, just *how* was the eighteen-pounder fired every day—for fired it certainly was, as Travis had promised—as a signal gun declaring that the fort still held out?[23] One solution was to prop the large gun on a stone or low wall, as the Texians had done with their dismounted twelve-pound gunnade during the 1835 battle for San Antonio.[24] Loading it only with a powder charge would have sufficed for a signal round.

Was Colonel Crockett accorded the honor of firing this signal gun, as Mrs. Dickinson's comment almost seems to be saying? Had he also been given the nod by Colonel Travis to fire the big gun for the first time on February 23? Certainly having this celebrated American make such a symbolic statement would have been very powerfully felt by the garrison.

The illustration depicts the "long beautiful 18 pounder" still mounted on its pivot carriage, and Crockett about to apply linstock to touchhole, on either February 23 or 24. (The 1881 newspaper article calls the gun "primitive," but this simply meant that it was loaded through the muzzle and not via the breech like artillery pieces of the last half of the nineteenth century.) Described as a barbette battery—one in which cannon fired *over* a parapet rather than through embrasures—it was a position typically vulnerable to besieging artillery. For example, when a US naval officer observed the Mexican defenses at Veracruz on August 23, 1846, he commented:

> 'Tis a grim, formidable looking position, but very much overrated, and, in my own judgment, could soon be taken with the force now on the station, for many if most of the heaviest cannon are mounted in barbette, and therefore exposed to grape and canister.[25]

Protection for barbette gunners was often made by erecting "bonnets" on the parapets. Like traverses, these could be constructed of revetted earth, gabions, sandbags, or combinations thereof, and placed where the artillerymen would be most exposed to enfilade fire, or simply utilized as shields behind which they could duck during a bombardment or assault. Being improvised appendages and not part of the original walls, bonnets were not usually shown on fort plans drawn by military engineers.

1. *Galveston News*, February 3, 1881. An "adjoining room" for Crockett meant any one of the three rooms connected to the western wall of the sacristy (where it is thought the Dickinsons had been quartered): the split chamber of the "Monk's Burying Ground" or the much smaller *lavatorio*. For Crockett, the extroverted outdoorsman, the sense of claustrophobia, and "confinement within stone walls." would have been understandably acute.

2. "Extract of a letter from Captain Thomas Boyle, of the brig Panopen, of Baltimore," *National Gazette* (Baltimore), July 17, 1824.

3. "Judge R. S. Calder and B. C. Franklin report the victory at San Jacinto to Presdient Burnet at Galveston." Available at Sons of DeWitt Colony website, www.tamu.edu/ccbn/dewitt/dewitt.htm.

4. Gary Brown, *Volunteers in the Texas Revolution: The New Orleans Greys* (Plano, Tex.: Republic of Texas Press, 1999), 11, 27–28, 34.

5. *New Hampshire Statesman and State Journal* (Concord), January 2, 1836. See also extract from T. F. McKinney's letter to the Texas General Council, November 11, 1835, *The Laws of Texas* (Austin, 1898), 1:8.

6. *Arkansas Gazette*, December 12, 1835.

7. *Manufacturers' and Farmers' Journal* (Rhode Island), December 28, 1835. Written specifically to a recipient in Rhode Island, this letter was not reprinted in any other newspaper that I could locate.

8. Ibid., December 28, 1835. This reference to an eighteen-pound ball may indicate that it came from a stock unrelated to the original shipment from New Orleans. Or it might have been an improvised cannonball like the ones used in the Texian assault of Fort Velasco in 1832 and described by Henry Smith as balls " made of drawing chains wound up to suit the caliber." "Reminiscences of Henry Smith," *Southwestern Historical Quarterly* 14, no. 1 (1911).

9. Thomas Ricks Lindley, "Alamo Artillery: Number, Type, Caliber and Concussion," *Alamo Journal*, July 1992, 7; Brown, *New Orleans Greys*, 36.

10. *Nashville Banner & Nashville Whig*, January 1, 1836. What caliber the balls were is unknown.

11. Jameson to Houston, Béxar, January 18, 1836, in Todd Hansen, ed., *The Alamo Reader: A Study In History* (Mechanicsburg, Penn.: Stackpole Books, 2003), 570. Jameson noted this position as the "N.W." corner of the fort, yet on the copies of his plan that survive the position is clearly marked at the southwest corner.

12. William T. Austin, "Account of the Siege & Battle of Bexar" (1844), in *A Comprehensive History of Texas*, ed. Guy M. Bryan. Available at Sons of DeWitt Colony website, www.tamu.edu/ccbn/dewitt.htm. "Of the armament of the Alamo" at this time, Francis Johnson later wrote, "it is sufficient to say that it was well supplied with artillery, but of small calibre—four and six pounders." Francis Johnson, *A History of Texas and Texans* (Chicago: American Historical Society, 1914), 353.

13. General Pedro de Ampudia's military report, March 6, 1836, "Armory," in Hansen, *Alamo Reader*, 376.

14. Rev. Chester Newall, *History of the Revolution in Texas, Particularly of the War of 1835 and '36* (New York: Wiley and Putnam, 1838), 27; "Reminiscences of Henry Smith."; Johnson, *History of Texas and Texans*, 78.

15. *Telegraph and Texas Register*, January 2, 1836.

16. Sutherland narrative in Hansen, *Alamo Reader*, 145.

17. "The Massacre of the Alamo: One of Santa Anna's Soldiers Tells the Story of that Bloody Day," *San Franciso Bulletin*, March 23, 1877.

18. Enrique Esparza 1907 interview in Timothy M. Matovina, *The Alamo Remembered: Tejano Accounts and Perspectives* (Austin: University of Texas Press, 1995), 85.

19. Almonte's journal, in *New York Herald,* June 23, 1836. During the US army's siege of the Mexican fortifications at Matamoros in 1846, a US gun "dismounted one of their 18 pounders, and threw it fifty feet in the air," *Boston Daily Courier*, May 21, 1846.

20. Journal of the Active Battalion of San Luis Potosi, entry of February 23, 1836, in Hansen, *Alamo Reader*, 440.

21. *Telegraph and Texas Register*, March 12, 1836.

22. Ampudia military report in Hansen, *Alamo Reader*, 376.

23. Until the morning of March 6, the daily boom of the eighteen-pounder could be heard as far as "200 miles off." Samuel Houston 1844 interview in Hansen, *Alamo Reader*, 621.

24. "Veteran Jno. Ingram," *Dallas Morning News*, April 14, 1895. (See extracted account in chapter 4.)

25. *New Hampshire Gazette*, September 22, 1846.

the enemy who was caught. There was water, though little, in the stream of Las Lomas del Alazan. At 2 the army took up their march, the President and his staff in the van. The enemy, as soon as the march of the division was seen, hoisted the tri-colored flag with two stars, designed to represent Coahuila and Texas. The President with all his staff advanced to Campo Santo (burying ground.) The enemy lowered the flag and fled, and possession was taken of Bexar without firing a shot. At 3 P. M. the enemy filed off to the fort of the Alamo, where there was — pieces of artillery; among them one 18 pounder. It appeared they had 130 men; during the afternoon 4 grenades were fired at them. The firing was suspended in order to receive a messenger, who brought a dispatch the contents of which appears in No. 1, and the answer which was given will be found in No. 2. I conversed with the bearer who was Jameson (G. B.) And he informed me of the bad state they were in at the Alamo, and manifested a wish that some honorable conditions should be proposed for a surrender. Another messenger afterwards came, (Martin) late a clerk in a house in New Orleans.[c] He stated to me what Mr. Travis said, "that if I wished to speak with him, he would receive me with much pleasure." I answered that it did not become the Mexican Government to make any propositions through me, and that I had only permission to hear such as might be made on the part of the rebels. After these contestations night came on, and there was no more firing. In the night another small battery was made up the river near the house of Veramenda. I lodged in the house of Nixon, (Major) with Urriza and Marcil Aguirre. An inventory of the effects taken was made; many curious papers were found. One Smith, carpenter and cabinet maker, they say was the owner of the effects. I did not sleep all night, having to attend to the enemy and the property, the charge of which of which [sic] was entrusted to me; its value was about $3000.

—*New York Herald,* June 23, 1836

[c] Captain Albert Martin, veteran of the skirmish at Gonzales and of the battle for San Antonio in 1835.

The first message from the Alamo (Almonte's "No. 1") was written by Col. James Bowie and was published almost a month later in a Mexican newspaper.

Commander of the Army of Texas:

Because a shot was fired from a cannon of this fort at the time that a red flag was raised over the tower, and a little afterward they told me that a part of your army had sounded a parley, which, however, was not heard before the firing of the said shot. I wish, Sir, to ascertain if it be true that a parley was called, for which reason I send my second aid, Benito Jameson, under guarantee of a white flag which I believe will be respected by you and your forces. God and Texas!

Fortress of the Alamo, February 23, 1836
James Bowie
Commander of the volunteers of Bexar to the Commander of the invading forces below Bejar.

—*El Mosquito Mexicano,* March 22, 1836

The Mexican reply to Bowie's message (Almonte's "No. 2"), written by Santa Anna's aide-de-camp José Batres, was also published in the same paper.

As the Aid-de-Camp of his Excellency, the President of the Republic, I reply to you, according to the order of his Excellency, that the Mexican army cannot come to terms under any conditions with rebellious foreigners to whom there is no other recourse left, if they wish to save their lives, than to place themselves immediately at the disposal of the Supreme Government from whom alone they may expect clemency after some considerations are taken up. God and Liberty!

Jose Batres to James Bowie
—*El Mosquito Mexicano,* March 22, 1836

It was William Barret Travis who had ordered an Alamo cannon fired when the red flag of no quarter was planted on the tower of San Fernando Church. Impulsively defiant as ever, he probably still berated himself for having dismissed the Mexican army's chances of reaching San Antonio before mid-March, as well as his failure to send scouting parties far enough afield just in case that army did push forward a quick-marching division.[2] The garrison, about half of whom were barracked in the town, had been caught completely by surprise by Santa Anna's vanguard units the afternoon of February 23. The Texians had had barely enough time to grab their arms and a few pieces of personal property before rushing into the safety of the Alamo.

Ridiculously undermanned, on the first day of the siege Travis quickly ordered couriers to ride out with urgent pleas for reinforcements—one to Col. James Fannin at Goliad and another to the citizens of Gonzales and "any of the inhabitants of Texas."[3] Travis took on additional stresses and burdens when Bowie soon became so ill that he was forced into the fort's hospital, unable to share command anymore in a physically active fashion.

The following day—February 24—the Mexican artillerymen, as noted in Almonte's journal, focused on knocking out those Alamo guns that were particularly vulnerable.

Wednesday, 24th—Very early this morning a new battery was commenced on the bank of the river, about 350 yards from the Alamo. It was finished in the afternoon, and a brisk fire was kept up from it until the 18 pounder and another piece was dismounted. The President reconnoitered on horseback, passing within musket shot of the fort. According to a spy, four of the enemy were killed. At evening the music struck up, and went to entertain the enemy with *it* and some *grenades.* In the night, according to the statement of a spy, 30 men arrived at the fort from Gonzales.[4]

—*New York Herald,* June 23, 1836

That same day Travis penned the letter that became the most famous document of the Texas Revolution. It was another appeal for help, and carrying it eastward, on horseback, was Capt. Albert Martin. First published in a slightly edited form in the *Texas Republican* of Brazoria on March 2, it appeared three days later in this somewhat more faithful—if still far from verbatim—version in the *Telegraph and Texas Register.*[5]

TO THE PEOPLE IN TEXAS, AND ALL AMERICANS IN THE WORLD. COMMANDANCY OF THE ALAMO, BEJAR, FEB. 24, 1836. Fellow-citizens and compatriots,

I am besieged by a thousand or more of the Mexicans, under Santa Ana. I have sustained a continual bombardment and cannonade, for twenty-four hours, and have not lost a man. The enemy have demanded a surrender at discretion, otherwise the garrison is to be put to the sword, if the fort is taken. I have answered the summon with a cannon shot, and our flag still waves proudly from the walls. *I shall never surrender or retreat;* then I call on you, in the name of liberty, and of every thing dear to the American character, to come to our aid, with all despatch. The enemy are receiving reinforcements daily, and will no doubt increase to three or four thousand, in four or five days. Though this call may be neglected, I am determined to sustain myself as long as possible, and die like a soldier, who never forgets what is due to his honor and that of his country. VICTORY OR DEATH. W. BARRET TRAVIS, *Lieut.-Col. Command.* *P.S.* The Lord is on our side. When the enemy appeared in sight, we had not three bushels of corn. We have since found, in deserted houses, eighty or ninety bushels, and got into the walls twenty or thirty head of beeves. T.

—*Telegraph and Texas Register,* March 5, 1836

Governor Henry Smith's reaction to Travis's letter appeared in the *Texas Republican,* and it underscored the point that this was not the time for Texians to be faltering or passive. It also did not help Travis's immediate needs when it suggested that the Alamo defenders could hold the fort for thirty days.

Executive Department of Texas. Fellow-Citizens of Texas:—

The enemy are upon us, a strong force surrounds the walls of San Antonio, and threatens that garrison with the sword. Our country imperiously demands the service of every patriotic arm, and longer to continue in a state of apathy will be criminal. Citizens of Texas, descendants of Washington, awake, arouse yourselves. The question is now to be decided are we to continue as freemen, or bow beneath the rod of military despotism. Shall we, without a struggle, sacrifice our fortune, our lives, and our liberties, or shall we imitate the example of our forefathers, and hurl destruction on the heads of our oppressors? The eyes of the world are upon us, all friends of liberty and of the rights of man are anxious spectators of our conflict; or duly enlisted in our cause. Shall we disappoint their hopes and expectations? No! let us at once fly to our arms, march to the battle-field, meet the foe, and give renewed evidence to the world that the arms of freemen uplifted in defence of their rights and liberties are irresistible. "Now is the day, and now is the hour," that Texas expects every man to do his duty. Let us show ourselves worthy to be free, and we shall be free. Our brethren of the United States have, with a generosity and a devotion to liberty unparalleled in the annals of men, offered us every assistance. We have arms, ammunition, clothing, and provisions; all we have to do, is to sustain ourselves for the present. Rest assured that succors will not permit the chains of slavery to be riveted upon us.

Fellow-Citizens,—Your garrison at San Antonio is surrounded by more than twenty times their number. Will you see them perish by the hands of a mercenary soldiery, without an effort for their relief? They cannot sustain the siege more than thirty days; for the sake of humanity, before that time give them succor. Citizens of the east, your brethren of the Brazos and Colorado, expect your assistance, afford it, and check the march of the enemy and not suffer your own land to become the seat of war; without your immediate aid we cannot sustain the war.

Fellow-Citizens, I call upon you, as your executive officer, to "turn out:" it is your country that demands your help. He who longer slumbers on the volcano must be a mad-

man, he who refuses to aid his country in this her hour of peril and danger is a traitor. All persons able to bear arms in Texas are called on to rendezvous at the town of Gonzales, with the least possible delay, armed and equipped for battle. Our rights and our liberties must be protected; to the battle field march, and save the country. An approving world smiles upon us, the God of battles is on our side, and victory awaits us.

Confidently believing that your energies will be sufficient for the occasion, and that your efforts will be ultimately successful,

I subscribe myself your fellow-citizen,

HENRY SMITH, Gov'r.

—*Texas Republican*, March 2, 1836

Travis's letter was reprinted in various edited versions in papers throughout the United States. Sometimes, as in the following article from Little Rock's *Arkansas Gazette*, by way of the *Natchitoches Herald*, it was considerably—and blandly—rewritten, even adding a second postscript by extracting a sentence from the main text of the original:

Important from Texas.
SAN ANTONIO BESIEGED BY
SANTA ANNA.

We copy the following from the Natchitoches (La.) Herald of 9th inst., received by last Tuesday evening's mail, after our paper had been put to press. It was published the next morning in an extra, and sent to our subscribers by such of the mails as were then depending:

LATE FROM TEXAS.

Through politeness of a gentleman at San Augustine, we have received a copy of an express from San Antonio de Bexar, which was received at that place, on the 4th inst. bearing despatches containing the important intelligence, that Santa Anna had arrived in person before that place, with an advanced guard of about one thousand men.

A meeting of the inhabitants of San Augustine, was to take place on the 5th inst. for the purpose of raising volunteers to proceed to the seat of war.

The annexed is a letter from Col. Travis, the commander of the Alamo.

Commandancy of the Alamo, (Texas)
February 24, 1836.
TO FELLOW-CITIZENS AND COMPATRIOTS, AND ALL AMERICANS IN THE WORLD.

I am besieged by a thousand Mexicans, with Santa Anna at their head. On their arrival, they sent and demanded an unconditional surrender of the garrison under my command, or we would all be put to the sword indiscriminately. I answered their demand with a cannon shot. I have sustained a bombardment and heavy cannonade, for the last twenty-four hours. I have not lost a man. Fellow-citizens, assist me now, for the good of all, for if they are flushed with one victory, they will be much harder to conquer. I shall defend myself to the last extremity, and die as becomes a soldier. I never intend to retreat or surrender. Victory or death.

M. B. TRAVIS, *Col. Commanding.*
P.S. The Lord is on our side. When the enemy came in sight, we had but three bushels of corn in the garrison. We have since found 80 bushels in a deserted house—and have thirty beeves within the walls.   TRAVIS.

P.S. The enemy is receiving reinforcements daily, and in four or five days, will increase their numbers to three or four thousand men.
TRAVIS.

POSTSCRIPT.

The committee of vigilance and safety for the municipality of San Augustine, have, in pursuance of their duties, to inform their fellow-citizens of this and the adjoining municipalities of this section of Texas, that they have received intelligence, by express, that our land is again invaded by the tyrant foe, with his lawless mercenaries. We have now either to do our duties to ourselves, to our country, and to our God, or, at once, to doff our caps, and kneel to the merciless tyrant.

We are happy to inform you, that our citizens, in this place, are, as expeditiously as possible, organizing themselves for the purpose, and will in a few days march to the field of battle, where we have so far, always been victorious—gloriously so. Our cause, fellow-citizens, is a great one. One in which all mankind are interested; and while a drop of American blood shall warm the hearts, it will not want friends to defend it. And we are confident, that our brothers in the United States will not suffer us to be enslaved. No, fellow-citizens, they only want to be informed, that their services are here needed, and they will not hesitate a moment to fly to our relief.

We have not yet heard from the convention, but there is no doubt of their having declared independence, ere this. And will of course take the necessary steps to sustain the country in her unequal but just and glorious struggle.

A. HOTCHKISS, *Chairman.*
San Augustine, Texas, March 6, 1836.
—*Arkansas Gazette*, March 29, 1836

Aside from a few scattered companies of mounted rangers, Texas had no Minute Man-style reaction force prepared to deal with immediate military crises. Thus, Travis's letter, despite its earnest supplication for aid "with all despatch," could not shatter the Texians' modus operandi—as exemplified in both the preceding and the following report—of consuming precious time by first forming committees, and in some cases making speeches and writing up resolves and laws—most of them undeniably critical—before taking any direct martial action.

When the above letter [Travis's communiqué of February 23] had been received in San Felipe the citizens met on the 27 of February, to deliberate on the communication. Joseph Baker was unanimously called to the chair, and B. P. Cage appointed secretary. The letter from Wm. B. Travis having been read, and the objects of the meeting explained, on motion of Mosely Baker Esq.

Resolved, That the chairman appoint a committee of twelve to prepare an address and draft resolutions for the adoption of this meeting:

Whereupon, The chairman appointed Mosely Baker, J. A. Wharton, F. J. Starr, J. R. Jones, W. R. Hensley, A. Ewing, P. B. Dexter, A. Somerville, J. Fletcher, J. H. Money, James

Cochrane, and Thos. Gay, then on motion, the meeting adjourned until 11 o'clock.

The meeting, accordingly, reconvened at 11 o'clock, when the following address and resolutions were reported and unanimously adopted.

TO OUR FELLOW-CITIZENS.

The undersigned a committee appointed by a meeting held in the town of San Felipe, on this day, present you with the accompanying letter from the commandant of Bejar. You must read and act in the same moment, or Texas is lost. You must rise from your lethargy, and march without a moment's delay to the field of war, or the next western breeze that sweeps over your habitations, will bring with it the shrieks and wailings of the women and children of Guadaloupe and Colorado, and the last agonized shriek of liberty will follow. Citizens of the Colorado and Brazos, your country is invaded—your homes are about to be pillaged, your families destroyed, yourselves to be enslaved; and you must, one and all, repair to the field of war, or prepare to abandon your country. Ere this information shall be generally circulated, the blood of many of our citizens will have crimsoned the soil; and the soul of many a devoted patriot flown to Heaven.

Inhabitants of the east, your fellow citizens of the west are in danger. Of themselves, they cannot resist the foe; we appeal to your magnanimity; we implore you for succor; and we earnestly entreat that your succor may be speedy. Unless it is, Texas, and her citizens, and her liberties, and her hopes, are forever gone.

For ourselves, we will abandon the contest only with our lives, and then earnestly appeal to all, every one to do his duty to his country, and leave the consequences to God.

MOSELY BAKER,   F. J. STARR,
J. A. WHARTON,   J. R. JONES,
W. R. HENSLEY,   ALEX. EWING,
P. B. DEXTER,   A. SOMERVILLE,
J. FLETCHER,   J. H. MONEY,
J. COCHRANE,   THOS. GAY;

The committee also reports the following resolutions:

Resolved, That a committee of three persons be appointed a standing committee, whose duty it shall be to solicit individual subscriptions, for the purpose of procuring provisions, ammunitions, &c., for the use of the country.

Resolved, That said committee forward as soon as possible, provisions of every kind, to Gonzales, also ammunitions, arms, &c.

Resolved, That they procure boats of all kinds, on the Brazos river, for the purpose of crossing as expeditively as possible.

Resolved, That said committee be appointed the general guardians of our interests at home; and that they be intreated to spare no pains in raising the means for our subsistence, and that they forward on men, as fast as possible.

Resolved, That they provide expresses, to communicate with the country, so far as practicable.

Resolved, That they do all and every thing necessary for the public good; and their receipts shall be sufficient vouchers to the persons from whom they may receive.

Resolved, That we recommend the establishment of depots, on the road to Gonzales, for provisions, arms, &c.; and that the committee call on the citizens generally for supplies.

Resolved, That two hundred copies of the proceedings of this meeting, together with colonel Travis's letter, be published as soon as possible.

In accordance with the first resolution, Wm. Pettus Jr., John R. Jones, and Thos. Gay, were appointed the committee.

On motion, the meeting adjourned *sine die.*
—*Telegraph and Texas Register,*
March 5, 1836

The slowness in communicating developments in Texas to the outside world meant that New Orleans papers did not report the arrival of the Mexican army in Béxar until nine days after the Alamo itself had fallen. Included in the following report was criticism of the previous "deplorable apathy" some had observed in the Texian army, along with the implication that many "were solicitous to leave it [San Antonio, and thus the Alamo] to its present fate."

TEXAS.—It was currently reported yesterday that the town of San Antonio had fallen into the hands of Santa Anna and his army—about 4000 in number. By forced marches, Santa Anna took the citizens by surprise; and they were obliged to surrender or fly into the garrison. There were about 200 in the fort, well prepared and furnished with provisions. When Santa Anna sent them orders for an immediate and unconditional surrender, they replied that he should first attest their strength; and that they were capable of holding out against any force of his, even if it contained 5000 men.

There were 700 Texians encamped some miles distant. These immediately hastened to the town, resolved to cut off the retreat and supplies of the invading army. San Antonio may therefore be the grave of Santa Anna; and not only the triumph of Texas independence, but of Mexican liberty.

A deplorable apathy had previously manifested itself in the Texian army; all were anxious not to be garrisoned in San Antonio; and hence perhaps the capture. The journals of San Felipe greatly complain of this spirit and say that those who were determined to capture the town formerly, were solicitous to leave it to its present fate.

The Texian commissioners are beating up for recruits and loans in Kentucky and Tennessee. Cols. Archer and Wharton, arrived in Louisville on the 3d inst., and Col. Wm. H. Wharton lately wrote ourselves an encouraging letter from Nashville.

***Since writing the above, we have been informed on creditable authority, that our statement is correct in general. Colonel Travers is in command of the garrison at San Antonio; and is determined to act with vigor. But our informant states that the force gone to the relief of the town amounts to 1200 men, well equipt, prepared and provided. He also believes that General Cos and not Santa Anna has surprized the town, and that the number of the besiegers is not greater than 1000—who advanced stealthily by forced marches through unfrequented ways. The main body of the Mexican army—either

from fear of the Texian rifles, or from disaffection to the cause of Santa Anna—did not and will not enter Texas. Cos had advanced to retrieve his character—but also to ruin it, as he passed his *parole d'honneur* not to fight against the Texians. He will now receive condign punishment; and find his grave where he lost his fame.

—*New Orleans Bee,* March 15, 1836

In San Antonio on February 25, Santa Anna had launched a limited attack with his light infantry against the Alamo's southern defenses, utilizing the cover of the Tejano *jacales* in the eastern suburb of Pueblo de Valero, or La Villita. Here we have the Mexican point of view of that day's action from Almonte's journal.

Thursday, 25th.—The firing from our batteries was commenced early. The General in Chief, with the battalion de Cazadores, crossed the river and posted themselves in the Alamo—that is to say, in the houses near the fort. A new fortification was commenced by us near the house of McMullen. In the random firing the enemy wounded 4 of the Cazadores de Matamoros battalion, and 2 of the battalion of Jimenes, and killed one corporal and a soldier of the battalion of Matamoros. Our fire ceased in the afternoon. In the night two batteries were erected by us on the other side of the river in the Alameda of the Alamo—the battalion of Matamoros was also posted there, and the cavalry was posted on the hills to the east of the enemy, and in the road from Gonzales at the Casa Mata Antigua. At half past eleven at night we retired. The enemy, in the night, burnt the straw and wooden houses in their vicinity, but did not attempt to set fire with their guns to those in our rear. A strong north wind commenced at nine at night.

—*New York Herald,* June 23, 1836

The action of that day was also described by Colonel Travis in a letter to General Sam Houston, which was carried out of the fort on the night of February 25 by the captain of the Tejano volunteers, Juan Nepomuceno Seguín. Before it saw print, however, New Orleans

The Texians Capture Cos's Horse

Captain Juan Seguín left the Alamo on the night of February 25, 1836, carrying Col. William Barret Travis's latest appeal for reinforcements, which also included an account of the day's battle. That morning Antonio López de Santa Anna had launched a limited attack against the fort's southern defenses—a multipurpose strike designed to test the Alamo's firepower, establish a battery in La Villita, and obtain ready-cut timbers for the construction of a bridge across the river. Texian rifle and musket balls, and artillery rounds of grape and canister, inflicted at least eight casualties on those Mexicans who exposed themselves from behind the cover of the little village's *jacales*, while only "two or three" of the defenders were "slightly scratched by pieces of rock," according to Travis.

Most of the defenders had also kept behind cover as Mexican howitzer shells rained down upon the fort. They fired through windows and through loopholes cut through the wall of the low barracks. They also fired through two palisades: the roughly U-shaped one of the tambour that covered the main gate, and the oblique one that connected the low barracks with the church. Others crouched in exterior ditches, mainly those that surrounded the tambour.

During the action a number of men bravely sallied out to set fire to nearby jacales in order to prevent the advancing enemy from using them as cover. "The Honorable David Crockett was seen at all points, animating the men to do their duty," wrote Travis, and this might indeed mean that Crockett was among those who sallied out. Support for this is found in Dr. Joseph Field's 1836 book, *Three Years in Texas, Including a View of the Texan Revolution*, in which he mentions the loop made by the San Antonio River southwest of the fort, adding, "it was here that Crockett and Dickinson burned some houses that stood in the way of their artillery."[1]

Eventually Santa Anna's men "retreated in confusion, dragging many of their dead and wounded," read Travis's report. Most of the Mexican accounts were far terser than his and offer even fewer details. Additional information of unnamed origin, perhaps from the lips of courier Seguín, who had participated in the engagement, made their way into the papers. One of them first appeared in the *New Orleans True American* and was later reprinted in a Virginia paper:

(Continued)

By the arrival of the schooner Wm. A. Turner, from Matagorda, we learn that Gen. Cos, with 1000 to 1200 picked men attacked Capt. Travis at the Fort San Antonio, and that Cos was defeated, and fled, leaving his horse in possession of the Texians. 500 Mexicans were killed and left.[2]

If the source of this information had been Seguín, did he deliberately exaggerate the number of enemy dead, or were the figures the usually enlarged ones that resulted from news being transmitted by many mouths? Or were they just the characteristic embellishment of an editor?

In fact, General Martín Perfecto de Cos did not arrive in San Antonio until March 3, seven days after the action. But confusion over the Mexican leadership in Béxar had reigned among Travis and his men since the beginning of the siege; one unidentified "informant" told the *New Orleans Bee* that he "believes that General Cos and not Santa Anna has surprized the town."[3] So if the expensively bedecked horse of a high-ranking Mexican officer had fallen into the hands of Travis's men, it would have been a natural thing to assume it was Cos's own. It could have been the horse of any officer, perhaps tied to a post behind a jacale during the engagement and abandoned as the Mexicans retreated.

---

1. Dr. Joseph Field, *Three Years in Texas, Including a View of the Texan Revolution, and an Account of the Principal Battles* (Greenfield, Mass., 1836), 11. Field was a survivor of the Goliad massacre.
2. *Richmond Enquirer*, April 1, 1836
3. *New Orleans Bee*, March 15, 1836.

---

papers were reporting wildly exaggerated details of the action itself (misdating it to February 28), as word of mouth had transmitted them.

IMPORTANT FROM TEXAS.—The schooner W. A. Turner arrived yesterday in 7 days from Matagorda. Thru the politeness of Captain Brookfield, we have obtained the particulars of the late siege by the Mexicans of San Antonio de Bexar, as ascertained at Matagorda when he left.

The besieging Mexican army was commanded by Generals Sesma and Coss. It consisted of 40 companies of infantry, numbering at an average of 60 or 70 men each; and of about 1,500 cavalry under Folisalos—with 500 mules and baggage of all kinds. These were seen, and numbered by Captain Dermit[d] of the Texian army, previous to the engagement. The Texians in the fort were infantry and some cavalry for foraging expeditions under the commands of Colonels Bowie and Travers—numbering about 200. The assault on the fort of Alamo in the town of San Antonio commenced about 3 p.m. on the 28th of February, the Mexican army hoisting a black flag aloft as indicating no quarters. The garrison being well supplied with 18 pounders planted on the fort, made them play with dreadful effect,

---

d Captain Philip Dimitt, who claimed he had left the Alamo on the first day of the siege to raise reinforcements for its relief.

sweeping companies of the assailants before the shot. The Mexicans surrounded the fort on all sides; but on all sides were they saluted with its artillery. This continued till 7 pm when the Mexicans thought proper to evacuate the town; and retire to an encampment within two miles— after leaving 500 of their comrades slain before the fort.

The provisional government of Texas being informed of the contest, an immediate draft of one third of all Texians capable of bearing arms was ordered by the acting governor. But so eager were the Texians in general for their prompt and certain triumph, that when the order reached Matagorda, not one third only, but all able bodied citizens volunteered. Numerous companies were immediately on the march to San Antonio, to drive the Mexicans beyond the Rio Grande, or brave them on the field of battle. They will act on the offensive in their future operations.

—*New Orleans Bee*, March 17, 1836

The *Nashville Banner & Nashville Whig* reprinted the preceding article in its March 30 issue, and its April 1 edition became one of the earliest papers to publish Travis's February 25 letter describing the fighting of that day. It is also the first printed account that places David Crockett among the Alamo garrison.

The following is the official account of the engagement which took place in the town of Bejar; a short account of which we published a few days since.

Fort of the Alamo, Bejar, Texas, Feb. 25

To Major General Samuel Houston,

Commander in Chief of the Army of Texas,

Sir—On the 23d February the enemy in large force entered the city of Bejar, which could not be prevented, as I had not sufficient force to occupy both positions. Col. Batres, the Adjutant Major of President General Santa Anna, demanded a surrender at discretion, calling us foreign rebels. I answered them with a cannon shot: upon which the enemy commenced a bombardment with a five-inch howitzer, which, together with a heavy cannonade, has been kept up incessantly ever since. I instantly sent expresses to Col. Fanning, at Goliad, and to the people of Gonzales and San Felipe. To-day at 10 o'clock a.m. some two or three hundred crossed the river below, and came up under cover of the houses, until they arrived within point blank shot, when we opened a heavy discharge of grape and canister on them, together with a well directed fire from small arms, which forced them to halt and take shelter in the houses about 80 or 100 yards from our batteries.[e] The action continued to rage for about two hours, when the enemy retreated in confusion, dragging off some of their dead or wounded.—During the action the enemy kept up a constant bombardment and discharge of balls, grape and canister. We know, from actual observation, that many of the enemy were killed and wounded—while we, on our part, have not lost a man. Two or three of our men have been slightly scratched by pieces of rock, but not disabled. I take great pleasure in stating, that both officers and men conducted themselves with firmness and bravery.—Lieut. Simmons of cavalry acting as infantry, and Capts. Carey, Dickenson & Blair of the artillery, rendered essential services, and Charles Despallier and Robert Brown gallantly sallied out and set fire to the houses which afforded the enemy shelter, in the face of the enemy's fire. Indeed the whole of the men, who were brought into action, conducted themselves with such undaunted heroism, that it would be injustice to discriminate. The Hon. David Crockett was seen at all points, animating the men to do their duty. Our numbers are few, and the enemy still continues to approximate his works to ours. I have every reason to apprehend an attack from his whole force very soon; but I shall hold out to the last extremity, hoping to receive reinforcements in a day or two. Do hasten on aid to me as rapidly as possible; as from the superior numbers of the enemy, it will be impossible for us to keep them out much longer. If they overpower us, we fall a sacrifice at the shrine

---

[e] When this letter appeared in the *Arkansas Gazette* of April 19, eighteen days after it was published in the *Nashville Banner*, the "80 or 100 yards" became "90 or 100 yards."

"The Unerring Rifle of Crockett"

Despite his forty-nine years, and occasional bouts of chest pain,[1] David Crockett was one of the most physically active members of the Alamo garrison. Although John Sutherland would later recall that Crockett, upon his arrival in San Antonio, declared that he desired only the rank of "a high private,"[2] subsequent events saw him playing a major role in the fort's defense. During the Mexican attack of February 25, for instance, Crockett "was seen at all points," in the words of William Barret Travis, "animating the men to do their duty."[3] The *Arkansas Gazette* of April 12, 1836, received an account from Jesse Badgett, who had interviewed Travis's slave, Joe, that seemed to indicate that there had been an agreed-upon chain of command during the siege. According to Badgett, in the event of Travis's death, command of the Alamo would fall to Adjutant Major J. J. Baugh, and in the event of Baugh's death it "devolved on Col. David Crockett." (James Bowie, of course, was too sick to lead the men.)

Tejano survivor Enrique Esparza sometimes remembered Crockett in a leadership role. In a 1902 interview, he claimed that Crockett called the garrison together to tell them of surrender terms Antonio López de Santa Anna had supposedly sent to the fort.[4] "Crockett seemed to be the leading spirit," Esparza recalled in 1907:

> He was everywhere. He went to every exposed point and personally directed the fighting. Travis was chief in command, but he depended more upon the judgment of Crockett and that brave man's intrepidity than his own.[5]

The "brave man's intrepidity" was also displayed in Crockett's superb sharpshooting ability. In late 1836, a memoir of the Texas revolution was published, and some Alamo-related Crockett anecdotes were included:

> The village of San Antonio stands on the west bank of the river of the same name, at a place where the stream by a sudden turn leaves a point of land in shape resembling a horse shoe. Upon this peninsula it is said that David Crockett killed the first Mexican soldier, at the distance of two hundred yards. . . . It is said and generally believed in Texas of Col. Crockett, that when Gen. Santa Anna was surveying the Alamo for the purpose of informing himself of the best method of

(Continued)

arranging an attack, he made so good a shot at him as to come near taking his life, which so much enraged the General, that he resolved to storm the fort the next day and he kept his resolution.[6]

Mexican accounts virtually confirm the anecdote of Santa Anna being targeted by Alamo rifles. Col. Juan Nepomuceno Almonte matter-of-factly noted Santa Anna's brazen disregard for the Texian marksmen. On February 24 he wrote, "the President reconnoitered on horseback, passing within musket shot of the fort." On February 27: "In the afternoon the President was observed by the enemy and fired at."[7] Lt. Col. José Juan Sánchez Navarro was aghast at this behavior, writing on March 3 that Sana Anna had an "eagerness . . . of presenting himself to danger without necessity." And on March 4 he noted, "His excellency continued to expose himself to risk dying without necessity."[8]

Another account appeared in the *Xenia Gazette* (Ohio), and it was subsequently reprinted in papers across the nation, just three months after the Alamo's fall.

> During the siege of the Alamo, the Mexicans planted a piece of ordnance within gun shot of the Fort, with the intention of commencing a brisk cannonade. Five men successfully stepped forth to fire the gun, and were soon marked down by the unerring rifle of Crockett. The consequence was that the gun was abandoned.
>
> —*New York Times*, June 29, 1836

If this report is based on an actual event, *what* Mexican cannon was it referring to? Prior to the March 6 assault, the greatest number of Mexican casualties occurred on February 25, when Santa Anna launched his attack from the south while his engineers built a new battery and a new trench, both within closer range of the fort. This was the same action during which Crockett had been "seen at all points, animating the men to do their duty." The latter observation could refer to any number of activities, including the shooting down of enemy soldiers. (Santa Anna, by most accounts, lost two *soldados* killed and six wounded.)

One cannon position that the Mexicans *did* eventually plant within musket shot of the fort was the north battery. It had been advanced to that threatening location—within two hundred yards of the north wall—via the *Acequia de Alamo* on March 3, and was equipped with four cannon and one howitzer. No known account, however, indicates that any Mexicans were killed or wounded by Texian fire at that particular site.

The illustration, then, is a hypothetical one, if it reflects real conditions: a north wall in a crumbling state, buttressed on the outside by a palisade-and-earth breastwork and on the inside by more earth shoveled against it. Sandbags—and in many cases loose adobe bricks—had been placed on parapets throughout the fort to add protection for riflemen and artillerymen.

In the distance, the north Mexican battery remains unfinished as *cazadores* exchange fire with Crockett, who wears hunting coat made of India rubber. This had been presented to him while he visited Massachusetts in 1834, and because it was rainproof, he avowed he "would risk my powder under it for forty days and nights."[9] Civilian-style hunting coats of the period often had multiple pockets in their fronts, for cartridges, bullets, and small tools. It is not really known if Crockett had actually brought this garment with him into Texas; if he had, he would not have been the only revolutionary soldier wearing one; Colonel James W. Fannin was wearing an Indian-rubber coat when he was executed at Goliad on March 27.[10]

This coat of Crockett's may, in fact, have more resembled a frontiersman's hunting shirt, if the following newspaper extract regarding his 1834 New England tour is to be believed.

COL. CROCKETT. The Boston Gazette of Tuesday says: "This distinguished Congressional orator is now on a visit to this city. He has rooms at the Tremont House, where many of our citizens have called upon him. We held a conversation with him yesterday morning, and found him an intelligent, well-meaning gentleman. He has a good face and person, and although there are certain peculiarities in his speech, which are calculated to induce laughter, yet he is by no means so rough and uncultivated as we had been led to suppose. Col. C. yesterday visited the India Rubber factory, Roxbury, where the honorary degree of LL D. was conferred upon him. A number of patriotic citizens, it is said, intend to present him with a pair of leggings and a hunting shirt, made of the cloth prepared at that establishment. These will enable the Colonel to "go ahead" in the big prairies of the West.
—*Norfolk Advertiser*, May 10, 1834

In the illustration the defender in the center wears a blanketcoat, a common item in 1830s Texas, and the man to his right wears a buffalo coat, another garment known to have been worn by some Texas settlers.[11]

(Continued)

1. William C. Davis, *Three Roads to the Alamo: The Lives and Fortunes of David Crockett, James Bowie, and William Barret Travis* (New York: Harper Collins, 1998), 389.

2. John Sutherland narrative in Todd Hansen, ed., *The Alamo Reader: A Study in History* (Mechanicsburg, Penn.: Stackpole Books, 2003), 140.

3. Travis to Houston, February 25, 1836, in Hansen, *The Alamo Reader*, 34.

4. "The Story of Enrique Esparza: (1902)," in Timothy M. Matovina, *The Alamo Remembered: Tejano Accounts and Perspectives* (Austin: University of Texas Press, 1995), 70.

5. Ibid., 81.

6. Joseph Field, *Three Years in Texas, Including a View of the Texas Revolution, and an Account of the Principal Battles* (Greenfield, Mass.: n.p. 1836), 11–12.

7. Almonte's journal, *New York Herald*, June 23, 1836.

8. C. D. Huneycutt, *At the Alamo: The Memoirs of Captain Navarro* (New London, NC: Gold Star Press, 1989), 63.

9. *An Account of Colonel Crockett's Tour to the North and Down East, in Davy Crockett's Own Story, As Written by Himself* (New York: Citadel Press, 1955), 189.

10. "Death of Col. Fannin and His Men," *New Hampshire Patriot*, August 8, 1836.

11. Among the property stolen in a Gonzales house on November 4, 1835, by raiding volunteers from the notorious Red Lands district: "1 buffalo coat" and "2 fur coats." Bob Boyd, *The Texas Revolution: A Day-by-Day Account* (San Angelo: San Angelo Standard, Inc., 1986), 25.

of our country, and we hope posterity and our country will do our memory justice. Give me help. Oh my country! Victory or death!

W. BARNET [sic] TRAVIS, Lt. Col. Com.
—*Nashville Banner & Nashville Whig*,
April 1, 1836

As was the case with the transmission of most news of the day, Little Rock's *Arkansas Gazette* received word of this fight in a roundabout way and reported it thirty-three days after it occurred.

LATE FROM TEXAS—SAN ANTONIO SAFE.—*Gen. Cos again defeated.*—By a gentleman who arrived here yesterday morning, direct from New Orleans, which place he left on the 17th inst., we learn, that the Louisiana Advertiser, of that morning, contained news, derived from the Captain of a vessel from a Texian port, which he left on the 6th inst., that Gen. Cos had again been defeated at San Antonio—that he had attacked that post with 1000 men, and after a sharp contest, had been compelled to retire with the loss of 500 men killed. He then retreated across the river, with the remnant of his troops, and was pursued by 800 Texian troops. Col. Travis' force in the

garrison, it was said, amounted to 150 men—their loss is not ascertained.

If this intelligence be true, as we hope it is, it will inspire the Texian troops with fresh vigor; and the Mexican troops, having received so signal a defeat in the commencement of the campaign, will be proportionally disheartened, and will probably fall an easy prey to the victorious arms of the revolutionists.

—*Arkansas Gazette*, March 29, 1836

With some justification, an editorial in the *New Orleans Bee* put a hopeful face on recent developments in Texas.

TEXAS. Through the politeness of Captain Kimball of the steamboat Caspian from Natchitoches, we have received the newspapers of that city containing the latest intelligence from Texas—and particularly the declaration of independence. This is a well written document in many respects the plain (like the American declaration of our revolution) assertive of causitory facts of wrong and outrage leading to independence. The letter of Forbes and the address of Houston are not devoid of interest to our citizens. The intelligence of the repulse of the army of Santa Anna under Sesma and Cos by the garrison at San Antonio, has been confirmed. Colonel Travis has acted nobly and spiritedly; and there is no doubt of his example being followed throughout Texas—in expelling the invaders. We have ourselves little hesitation in asserting that the continuance of the Mexican army in Texas will be very shortlived; and we are aware that the blockade of the Texian ports is a mere gasconade. Captain Hawkins and the other officers of the Texian navy will soon sweep the gulf of all Mexican ships that dare to pass Matagorda.

—New Orleans Bee, March 21, 1836

News of the February 25 engagement and of other related events in Texas—including the adoption of the Declaration of Independence at Washington-on-the-Brazos on March 2—reached Virginia by the end of March via newspapers from New Orleans. Contained in the following selection of extracts appearing in the April 1 *Richmond Enquirer* is a rare, if all too brief, contemporary description of both the Alamo and San Antonio.

TEXAS.
Copied from the Bulletin Board of the
True American.
By the arrival of the schooner Wm. A. Turner, from Matagorda, we learn that Gen. Cos, with 1000 to 1200 picked men attacked Capt. Travis at the Fort San Antonio, and that Cos was defeated, and fled, leaving his horse in possession of the Texians—500 Mexicans were killed and left.—Capt. Travis had about 200 men. The news is confirmed by an arrival from Matagorda. The remainder of the Mexicans fled in disorder over the Prairies.

[16th March, 12 o'clock.]
(From the New Orleans Bee of March 19.)
TEXAS.—On the 2d of this month, the general convention assembled at Washington in Texas, declared the Texians to be a free, sovereign and independent people. The declaration of independence will be published in our next number. Speculation in Texian lands would now be available. It is earnestly to be hoped that our government will not precipitately act on the

rumored embassage of Gorostisa from Mexico. Let the independence of Texas be recognized by the United States; but let not that country be bought, and let it become a member of our Federal Government. Let its boundaries be extended to the Rio Grande, and to California and the Pacific ocean—and we shall have an easy access to Asia.

We have before us a very interesting letter from "Washington, *Texas*, March 2d"—for which we have no room to-day. The writer states the meeting of the Convention [was held] on the 1st—and the interest is derived from the agitating accounts which had just been received from San Antonio.—Richard Ellis, from Red River, was appointed President of the convention. The first step was to appoint a Committee to report a *Declaration of Independence.* It was reported the next day (the 2d March) and unanimously adopted by the Convention. Copies of it in MS. were making out to be dispatched to the U. States, &c. A Constitution is preparing; and the intelligent writer of the letter has no doubt the Texians will ultimately succeed, after a sharp contest.

He subjoins the following P.S. on the evening of the 2d March:

An express has just arrived from Bexar, bringing information that an attack had been made on the Alamo, on the 25th Feb., by a party of 300 men, who advanced under cover of some old wooden houses to within 80 yards of the walls of the Alamo, while an incessant bombardment was kept up on it from the city. The fire from the Alamo killed many of the enemy, who were repulsed, and the houses burnt by the Texians. The Texians lost none, and had only 3 slightly wounded. A force of 350 men, under Fanning, were advancing to the relief of Travis, from La Bahia; which, with others known to be on the march, will make the Garrison, before this time 6 or 700 strong, and that will be added to every day. The Alamo may be considered safe; and in a little while the Mexican soldiers will be driven from Bexar.

The city of Bexar is on the *West* side of the river San Antonia, where the Mexican soldiers now are. The Alamo, or *Elm Tree*

Fort, which is occupied by the Texian forces, is on the *East* side. The river is there very narrow, and was crossed by slight wooden bridges made of logs. All the country on the east side is open to the advance of Troops; but their approach can be seen, and they may be assailed by the cannon from the city.—This, however, would not prevent their entry, as the Alamo would be between them and the city. The Alamo is built of stone—is very strong—about 18 or 20 feet elevation, and covers about 1 ½ or 2 acres.
—*Richmond Enquirer*, April 1, 1836

Many newspapers took special, laudatory note of Crockett's participation in the February 25 fighting; after all, the widespread report that he had died shortly after arriving in Texas had only recently been declared false.[f] In reprinting the news from New Orleans, a New Hampshire paper related the following.

The famous Col. CROCKETT is said to have "performed wonders of Chivalry" in the defence of San Antonio de Bexar.
—*New Hampshire Sentinel*, April 4, 1836

One Virginia paper exulted:

Huzza for Col. Crockett!—The Texian official account of the entrance of the Mexican forces into the city of Bejar, and their gallant repulse by the garrison in the fort, mentions a number of officers who distinguished themselves in that affair, among whom "The Hon. David Crockett was seen at all points, animating the men to do their duty."
—*Richmond Enquirer*, April 12, 1836

Noted the *New York Times*:

Davy Crockett is fighting like a wildcat in the cause of the Texians.
—*New York Times*, April 17, 1836

The *New York Mercury* made this sober assessment:

---

[f] See chapter 5.

It appears that Davy Crockett is among the heroes who volunteered to defend the castle [the Alamo], well knowing that in case of capture, which is by no means improbable, they will all be massacred.
—*New York Mercury*, April 7, 1836

Seventeen years after the Alamo fell, a writer, identified only as "V," sent a letter dated Brownsville, April 28, 1854, to a Texas paper, in which he noted how Santa Anna—briefly back in power in Mexico in the mid-1850s—had ordered that one General Avalos be "reduced to the ranks as a common soldier for the crime of bigamy." The writer went on to recall an episode that took place during the siege of the Alamo.

It is strange that the present head of the Mexican nation should with such exemplary severity, in 1854, punish his subordinates for an offense he has been guilty of himself. In February, 1836, Don Antonio Lopez de Santa Anna arrived at San Antonio de Bexar, as President of Mexico, and commander in chief of the army of operations against Texas. Then, as now, he had in his mind's eye, almost in his grasp, a crown, a monarch's bauble. The rebellion of Texas at that time prevented the consummation of his daring scheme, as it is now prevented by the rebellion of the patriot Alvarez with his *Pintos*, in the South of Mexico. At that time, there lived in *La Villita*, close by the Alamo, on the banks of the San Antonio, a young, frail, fair daughter of Eve, whose only wealth was her fair fame and fine appearance. In my youthful days, I knew her well. The chief of the minion host failed to corrupt her, and only succeeded in doing so by dressing one of his officers in the garb of a priest, who performed the marriage ceremony. Years after this, and when he had returned to Mexico, crowned with the laurels he had gathered on the field of San Jacinto, he married his poor victim to a Colonel in the Mexican army.
—*Texas State Gazette*, May 20, 1854

On the fourth day of the siege of the Alamo, Santa Anna's army resumed its careful, methodical envelopment. General Sesma's cavalry and *caza-dore*[g] units watched the roads that led to the Anglo American settlements in the east, and Travis's garrison continued to make sorties for wood, water, and perhaps to exploit gaps in the Mexican encirclement. As noted in Almonte's journal, the weather grew blustery and colder, too.

Friday, 26th.—The northern wind continued very strong; the thermometer fell to 39°, and during the rest of the day remained at 60°. At daylight there was a slight skirmish between the enemy and a small party of the division of the east, under command of General Sesma. During the day the firing from our cannon was continued. The enemy did not reply, except now and then. At night the enemy burnt the small houses near the parapet of the battalion of San Luis, on the other side of the river. Some sentinels were advanced. In the course of the day the enemy sallied out for wood and water, and were opposed by our marksmen. The northern wind continues.

—*New York Herald*, June 23, 1836

The next day, Almonte wrote that exchanges of fire between besieged and besiegers were infrequent, although Santa Anna himself became a target of the Texian rifles—perhaps one fired by Crockett himself.

Saturday 27th.—The northern wind was strong at day break, and continued all the night. Thermometer at 39°. Lieutenant Manuel Menchacho was sent with a party of men for the corn, cattle, and hogs at the Ranchos (small farms) of Seguin and Flores. It was determined to cut off the water from the enemy on the side next to the old mill. There was little firing from either side during the day. The enemy worked hard to repair some entrenchments. In the afternoon the President was observed by the enemy and fired at. In the night a courier extraordinary was dispatched to the city of Mexico, informing the Government of the taking of Bexar, [1]

and also to Gen'ls Urrea, Filisola, Cos & Vital Fernandez. No private letters were sent.
[1-*Note by editor of the* Herald]: "Taking of Bexar"—this was the first signal victory gained by Santa Anna himself over the Texians. It appears to have cheered up their spirits wonderfully. So overjoyed were they that no private letters were written—no time—all was "pomp and circumstance of glorious war."

—*New York Herald*, June 25, 1836

The aforementioned report sent by Santa Anna to the Mexican government and his generals was eventually published in at least two newspapers, *El Mosquito Mexicano* (March 18, 1836) and *La Lima de Vulcano* (March 17, 1836).[6] The following translation of it is mostly from Richard Santos's *Santa Anna's Campaign against Texas, 1835–1836* and is based on the copy the commander in chief sent to Gen. Vicente Filisola. A few corrections have been made after studying Santa Anna's original letter book copy—also in Santos—mainly as regards certain military terminology.[7]

Most Excellent Sir,
  I have on this date written the following to the Most Excellent Minister of War and Marine:
  "Most Excellent Sir;
  On the 23rd of the current month at three in the afternoon, I occupied this City after some forced marches from Rio Grande with the Division of Sr. General Ramirez y Sesma composed of the permanent battalions of Matamoros and Jiménez, the Activos[h] of San Luis Potosi, the regiment of Dolores, and eight pieces of artillery.
  The speed with which this meritorious Division executed its march over eighty leagues of road was possible because the rebellious colonists were unaware of our proximity until we were within a musket-shot of them, leaving them no choice but to hurriedly entrench themselves in Fort of the Alamo, which they had well fortified beforehand, and in which they had sufficient supplies. It had been my intention to surprise

---

[g] The *cazadores* were the army's elite light troops, many trained as marksmen and some equipped with British Baker Rifles.

[h] The *Activos* were reserve militia troops, not regular troops.

Bombarding the Alamo

"Very early this morning a new battery was commenced on the bank of the river, about 350 yards from the Alamo," wrote Col. Juan Nepomuceno Almonte in his journal on February 24, 1836. "It was finished in the afternoon, and a brisk fire was kept up from it until the 18 pounder and another piece was dismounted."[1] The Mexican guns at this position were a five-inch brass howitzer and two 8-pounders. Their essential purpose was to act as a counterbattery against the cannon defending the Alamo's southwestern walls. Additional Mexican batteries would soon be raised to deal with Texian artillery pieces emplaced elsewhere. As Col. William Barret Travis himself wrote in his letter of February 25, "the enemy still continues to approximate his works to ours."

Although Almonte noted that Mexican guns had "dismounted" two Alamo pieces on the second day of the siege, in none of his letters did Travis acknowledge any damage done to the fort except to write that, by March 3, "at least two hundred shells have fallen inside our works without having injured a single man." Nor did he attempt to enumerate the number of enemy solid round shots that had struck his walls, saying only that those walls were "generally proof against cannon-balls."

Travis was being more than a little deceptive, of course, for even he admitted that his men were kept busy entrenching "on the inside, and strengthen[ing] the walls by throwing up dirt," thus indicating that here and there the fort *was* being shattered by Mexican round shot. Confirming that the Texians were working tirelessly to repair and reinforce the walls was the March 4 diary entry of Lt. Col. José Juan Sánchez Navarro, who noted that, aside from the Alamo's own "cannons and rifle . . . nothing else is heard except the blows of hammers and various curses."[2]

To dismount a gun positioned behind the wall of an enemy fort, besieging artillerymen generally fired ricochet shot or shell at it. Such a round would be discharged from a howitzer angled to a degree that enabled it to descend from its arced flight to within the targeted fort battery. By hitting opposing interior walls, it would either shatter, rebound, or roll, invariably wrecking the gun carriage and hurting or killing personnel.[3] The traditional position of the Alamo's eighteen-pounder was on the compound's southwestern corner platform. Just where the second piece dismounted by Mexican guns on February 24 was located is not known.

(Continued)

Hard evidence describing the composition of the main Mexican battery west of the Alamo has not been found. However, there are clues that suggest its possible appearance. In the diagram he drew of the Alamo that included the attack movements of General Martín Perfecto de Cos's division on March 6, Sánchez Navarro shows this battery as a three-embrasured one, the embrasures cut through its southern half. (The third cannon was added on March 4.) The northern half of the parapet remained without embrasures, typical of a battery wall shielding a howitzer or mortar whose purpose was to lob a round *over* the enemy's wall.

During the 1835 battle for San Antonio, one of General Cos's artillery positions outside the Alamo and on the east side of the river was described as a "sand bag battery."[4] In 1836, the Mexican army marched north also carrying a great abundance of "fortification sack," (i.e., canvas sandbags). On February 16, Antonio López de Santa Anna wrote to Gen. Vicente Filisola, who was gathering foodstuffs for the expedition: "You can make use of the fortification sacks that may be required for the transportation of the meal and grain."[5] Filisola himself marveled at the many "empty sandbags and an endless number of useless items carried by the troops," as opposed to truly useful items such as clothing, shoes, etc.[6]

Certainly sandbags would have been useful in erecting a revetment—the interior retaining wall—of an earthen battery. Other materials used to erect such revetments included "fascines, hurdles, sods, planks, casks, [and] gabions." The benefit of using sandbags was that they demanded much less construction time than did most of the other materials.[7] The Mexican battery inside the loop of the San Antonio River was begun "very early" on the morning of February 24 and "was finished in the afternoon"— approximately half a day's work.[8] (Batteries being *advanced* towards a fortress through trench lines generally employed ready-made gabions, filled with earth as the sappers dug, and fascines, for their walls.) Between the guns of many such batteries traverses would have been built: walls extending perpendicularly from the main one, acting primarily to defend against flank fire.

In the right foreground of the illustration, a frock-coated officer is ordering an artilleryman to hurry up with the next round. In left foreground, a man picks up, via a long fork, a ball of red-hot round shot from a furnace. Many artillery furnaces were like ovens, with chimneys, but a simple one could be made very quickly in the field by first digging a hole from one to four feet in depth, and then building a fire within it. Over this was fixed a grating of iron bars, upon which the round shot was placed for heating.[9]

Such heated rounds could set fire to the enemy's wooden or thatched roofs, explode his exposed powder supplies, and create diverse other havoc. It was a favorite weapon at sea, especially against an opponent's sails. No account mentions the firing of red-hot shot at the Alamo; however, just four months earlier General Cos's much smaller Mexican army had established "a furnace for heating shot" behind the breastwork built at the northeastern angle of Military Plaza.[10] Thus, it is not unlikely that Santa Anna's artillerymen in 1836 also carried a kind of furnace among their supply wagons. Even the Texians realized the importance of hot shot. Among a list of "Munitions of War" the Texas General Council wanted to purchase in November 1835 were "2 pair of shovels and pokers for hot shot."[11]

One piece of evidence that implies that the Alamo was perceived as being capable of firing hot shot at Santa Anna's positions—perhaps suggesting that Travis's artillerymen possessed Cos's "furnace for heating shot"—lies in Colonel Almonte's journal entry of Thursday, February 25:

> The enemy, in the night, burnt the straw and wooden houses in their vicinity, but did not attempt to set fire with their guns to those in our rear.[12]

1. Almonte's journal, *New York Herald*, June 23, 1836. In the key to his "Plano" of the Alamo, Sánchez Navarro noted that lying on the ground in the southwestern section of the compound's parade ground were "Three pieces [that is, cannon barrels] that had been dismounted before the attack." Evidently one of them was the still unremounted eighteen-pounder.

2 C. D. Huneycutt, *At the Alamo: The Memoirs of Captain Navarro* (New London, N.C.: Gold Star Press, 1989), 64.

3. William Duane, *A Military Dictionary* (Philadelphia, 1810), 603; *The Penny Cyclopaedia of the Society for the Diffusion of Useful Knowledge* (London, 1841), 20:7–8.

4. Charles Mason to Col. Frank W. Johnson, February 4, 1876, in Francis Johnson, *A History of Texas and Texans* (Chicago: American Historical Society, 1914), 268.

5. Santa Anna to D. Vincente Filisola, February 16, 1836, in Wallace O. Chariton, *100 Days in Texas: The Alamo Letters* (Plano, Tex.: Wordware Publishing Inc., 1990), 242.

6. Gen. Vicente Filisola, *Memoirs for the History of the War in Texas*, ed. and trans. by Wallace Woolsey (Austin: Eakin Press, 1985–1987), 2:152–153. When the Mexican army retreated from Texas following the battle of San Jacinto, its tattered soldiers were given "canvas bags" with which to "mend their pants and jackets . . . and to make knapsacks." George J. Dimmick, *General Vincente Filisola's Analysis of José Urrea's Military Diary* (Austin: Texas State Historical Association, 2007),159.

7. J. S. Macaulay, *A Treatise on Field Fortification, and Other Subjects Connected with the Duties of the Field Engineer* (London, 1834), 55.

8. Almonte's journal, *New York Herald*, February 24, 1836.

9. Nineteenth-century artillery manuals describe a variety of such field furnaces as well as more sophisticated, sometimes wheeled, ones. They had also been employed in the 1700s; see, for example, a Swedish artillery engraving, *The Eighteenth Century: Europe in the Age of Enlightenment* (New York: McGraw Hill Book Company, 1969), 189.

10. Johnson, *History of Texas and Texans*: 353–354.

11. *Telegraph and Texas Register*, January 2, 1836.

12. Almonte journal, February 25, 1836, *New York Herald*; Almonte journal, June 23, 1836, *New York Herald*.

them on the previous morning but a heavy rain prevented it.

Notwithstanding the artillery fire, which they immediately began from the aforementioned fort, the national troops with the greatest order occupied this place which will never again be occupied by the traitors. Our losses were one corporal and a cazador killed, and eight wounded.[i] As I was assigning quarters to the troops of the Division, a parliamentary[j] presented himself with the original paper which I am forwarding to Your Excellency. Indignant over its contents, I ordered the nearest adjutant to answer it as shown in the copy which I am also including. Fifty muskets and several effects from the North which belonged to the rebels have fallen into our possession which I will deliver to the Commissary General of the Army as soon as he arrives to equip these troops and sell the remainder and invest the proceeds in the regular expenditure of the same Army. From the moment of my arrival, I have so successfully occupied myself with the harassment of the enemy at their position, that they have not even shown their heads above the walls while I prepare everything for the assault which will occur at least with the arrival of the First Brigade which is presently seventy leagues distant from here.

To date, they [the Texians] have manifested their stubbornness while availing themselves of the strong position which they hold awaiting large assistance from their colonies and the United States of the North, but they will soon receive their final reproach.

After taking the Fort of the Alamo, I will continue my operations on Goliad, Brazoria and the other fortified points so that the campaign to the Sabine River which forms the boundary between this republic and that of the North may be terminated before the rainy season.

Your Excellency will please transmit everything to His Excellency the President ad-interim for his knowledge and satisfaction so that he may give me whatever orders he may see fit.

I am forwarding the above to Your Excellency for your knowledge and for that of the troops of the Army under your immediate command. God and Liberty. Headquarters at Bejar; February 27, 1836.

Antonio Lopez de Santa Anna
Most Excellent Major General
Don Vicente Filisola
Second Commander-in-Chief of
The Army of Operations

On the day Santa Anna wrote his report, a cavalry column of Gen. José Urrea's division of the Texas invasion (a division assigned to conquer Goliad) destroyed a sixty-man party of Texians under Col. Frank Johnson at San Patricio more than one hundred miles southeast of San Antonio. These Texians composed a remnant of the old Matamoros expedition, many of the members of which had left to join Fannin at Goliad. A few, including Johnson, managed to escape the attack. Another contingent under Dr. James Grant was out looking for wild mustangs and had thus far eluded Urrea. Seventeen days later, the *New Orleans Bee* published Urrea's report of the action.

Yesterday we reported the capture of San Antonio, as rumored; but we have not yet received any corroboration of that statement, altho we believe it correct. To-day were are enabled to present an official account of the first skirmish between the Mexicans and Texians, published in the Mercurio of Matamoras, of the 7th inst. It was transmitted for publication to General F. V. Fernandez, by the writer General Urrea, as sent to Santa Anna; and furnishes a ludicrous specimen of the Bombastes Furioso style:

ARMY OF OPERATIONS—*division of Goliad.* Sir: According to information received after leaving Matamoras, I learnt that the insurgent forces stationed here had sent their cavalry towards Goliad, for the purpose of making incursions. I therefore made an effort, and vanquishing all difficulties, and forcing a march during three days and nights I arrived here at the dawn of day—not having with me more than 100 cavalry men. I attacked the enemy, who

[i] These losses reflected those suffered by the Mexican army during the action of February 25, not February 23.
[j] *Parliamentario* is an envoy for a parley.

defended himself with firmness in the houses that served for barracks. But even there he left 15 dead, and 21 taken prisoners or wounded—among whom were some officers. There are 5 Mexicans among the prisoners.

I have the pleasure to inform you of this triumph obtained by the Mexican arms; and however feeble it may be, it will suffice to prove to our proud and scornful enemy what the valor and courage of Mexican soldiers can effect: for in short those with me rushed into the midst of the affray like lions; and in a moment they hewed the rebels in pieces, none of whom escaped from this city.

I have however to lament the death of a brave dragoon, who was slain; and also three other dragoons and a sergeant wounded.

I am now in search of Doctor Grant, who according to the information that I received, is now in the neighborhood of me with 50 riflemen; and I know not what number of Mexicans.

I shall hereafter give you a more detailed account of the affair; and conclude in assuring you that all the soldiers composing this division are fraught with enthusiasm, and burn to distinguish themselves in defence of the sacred rights of the nation.

I am, &c.

JOSE URREA.
God and liberty! San Patricio, 27th Feb. 1836
To His Excellency the President,
D. Antonio Lopez de Santa Anna,
General in chief of the army of operations.
—*New Orleans Bee*, March 16, 1836

Additional details of this engagement appeared a couple of weeks later.

Col. Johnson, with a party of 70 men while reconnoitering the westward of San Patricio, was surrounded in the night by a large body of Mexican troops, in the morning the demand of a surrender was made by the Mexican commander unconditionally, which was refused, but an offer of surrender was made as prisoners of war which was acceded to by the Mexicans—but no sooner had the Texians marched out of their quarters and stacked their

arms, a general fire was opened upon them by the whole Mexican force. The Texians attempted to escape but only three of them succeeded, one of whom was Col. Johnson.
—*New Orleans Bee*, March 28, 1836

On the sixth day of the Alamo siege, Almonte noted in his journal that word had been received in San Antonio that a detachment from Goliad was approaching to reinforce Travis.

Sunday, 28th.—the weather abated somewhat. Thermometer at 40° at 7 A. M. News was received that a reinforcement to the enemy was coming by the road from La Bahia, in number 200. [2] It was not true. The canonading was continued.
[2-*Note by the editor of the* Herald]: La Bahia or Goliad was situated on the west side of the river San Antonio, on the banks of one of whose tributaries is Bexar or the Alamo. Col. Fannin's command was stationed at Golaid—the main Texian army under Gen'l Houston had retreated at that time to the east of the Colorado.
—*New York Herald*, June 25, 1836

Leap year day, according to Almonte, saw the Mexican army positioning more troops between the Alamo and its avenues of communication to the east.

Monday 29th.—The weather changed—thermometer at 55°; in the night it commenced blowing hard from the west. In the afternoon the battalion of Allende took post at the east of the Alamo. The President reconnoitered. One of our soldiers was killed in the night. The wind changed to the north at mid-night, about that time Gen. Sesma left the camp with the cavalry of Dolores and the infantry of Allende to meet the enemy coming from La Bahia or Goliad, to the aid of the Alamo. Gen'l Castrillon on guard.
—*New York Herald*, June 25, 1836

Fannin had, in fact, started his column of Alamo-bound reinforcements from Goliad on February 26 in the morning: 320 men, four artillery pieces, and a number of wagons. By nightfall several wagons had broken down, and at sunup it was discovered that many of the oxen had wandered off into the chaparral. An officers' council also suddenly determined that the column lacked sufficient ammunition and provisions to be of any real help to Travis. Finally, a courier arrived with word of an enemy column having reached San Patricio, sixty miles to the south; this was Urrea's vanguard. It was decided to turn around and march back to Fort Defiance at La Bahía.

Reinforcements did, however, enter the Alamo in the early morning darkness of March 1: thirty-two men of the Gonzales Ranging Company of Mounted Volunteers, responding Travis's letter of February 24 as delivered by Captain Martin. Among them was John W. Smith, himself a previous Alamo courier. The fact that Santa Anna had, on February 29, shifted many of his soldiers from east of the Alamo to positions south of it allowed the Gonzales contingent an uncontested entry into the besieged compound.

Small as the band of reinforcements was, it nevertheless raised the defenders' morale, and, as if to underscore this, an Alamo cannon managed to make a direct hit on Santa Anna's headquarters, the Yturri house, in Béxar's Main Plaza, as related in Almonte's journal.

March 1st.—The wind subsided, but the weather continued cold—thermometer at 36° in the morning—day clear. Early in the morning Gen. Sesma wrote from the Mission de la Espador that there was no such enemy, and that he reconnoitered as far as the Tinaja, without finding any traces of them. The cavalry returned to camp, and the infantry to this city. At 12 o'clock the President went out to reconnoitre the mill site to the north west of the Alamo. Lieut. Col. Ampudia was commissioned to construct more trenches.—In the afternoon the enemy fired two 12 pound shots at the house of the President, one of which struck the house, and the other passed it. [3] Nothing more of consequence occurred. Night cold—thermometer 34° Fahrenheit, and 1° Reaumar.

[3-*Note by the editor of the* Herald]: These twelve pounders came very near levelling San Anna in the dust. Travis in this showed them good gunnery.

—*New York Herald*, June 25, 1836

While men were engaged in a merciless war in Texas, adults in New Orleans had spectacular fun at a "Fancy Ball" in Davis's Saloon on the night of February 29. A correspondent of the *New Orleans Bee* described the event in great detail, reveling in the rainbow colors of guests dressed as Henry VIII, Catherine Howard, Pizarro, Rob Roy, Tyrolean girls, English jockeys, Turkish women, monks, and many other characters.

And last though not least through that various crowd strode the strange and sturdy form of that lion of the New World, David Crockett. With his heavy rifle, hunting shirt and awful cap, over which hung in graceful stoop the shaggy tail of the Panther, he stalked wildly through the hall, looked into the faces of kings with immovable rigidity of muscle, and gazed alike with evident and equal delight upon Queens, noble women and peasantesses. I saw him in close converse with his Royal Highness Charles II, who seemed attracted by his strange appearance; and anxious to know what could be the subject of conversation I drew near—I had just time to hear him say that he had drank the "Mississippi dry and would be glad to find a Bayou somewhere about to quench his thirst," when the music struck up and he moved off in search of a pretty Indian squaw as a partner in a war dance.

—*New Orleans Bee*, March 24, 1836

Another Alamo-related curiosity is the following report from a French-language newspaper published in New York, *Le Courrier Des Etats-Unis*. Although it contains no information not found in the English-language papers, it is presented here in its original text for the unique document that it is.

TEXAS.—Le *Red-River Herald*, du 16 mars, contient l'acte de la convention, document d'une rédaction remarquable, qui déclare cet état *libre, souverain et indépendant*.

Le recit de la vaillante défense d'Antonio par le lieutenant-colonel Travis, daté du Fort de l'Alamo à Bejar, Texas, 28 fevrier, et addessé au major-géneral Samuel Houston, commandant en chef de l'armée du Texas, constate que l'ennemi entra dans la ville de Bejar, en nombre supérieur, le 23 fevrier. Le colonel Batres, adjutant major de Santa-Anna, lui fit sommation de se rendre. On lui répondit par une décharge de canon. Sur quoi l'ennemi commence un bombardment qui durait encore au moment ou ces dépêches ont été écrites. Le colonel Travis, dès le commencement de l'attaque, dépêcha des exprès au colonel Fanning, à Goliad, et aux habitans de Gonzalez et du San Felipe. L'ennemi soutint un feu nourri de boulets et de mitraille. Sa perte fut considérable et les Texiens ne perdirent pas un homme. Officers et soldats se sont conduits avec le plus grand héroisme. L'honorable David Crockett fut vu sur tous les points, animant par son exemple et ses paroles les soldats à faire leur devoir. Les assiégeans s'approchaient graduellemen de la citadelle, et le colonel s'attendait à une attaque générale. Il réclame des secours imediats, mais il est déterminé à s'enterrer sous les ruines des remparts plutôt que de se rendre.

Nouvelles plus récentes.—Un exprès arrivé le 2 mars d'Antonio, apporte la nouvelle que le colonel Travis, avec 150 hommes seulement, avait continué avec une bravoure sans égale, à défendre la forteresse contre toute l'armée Mexicaine; que le colonel Crockett était avec lui et s'était particulierement distingué, l'ennemi avait été repoussé avec une perte immense, et le colonel Fannin, de Goliad, avec 325 hommes, deux pièces des campagne et un grand nombre de citoyens voluntaires qui s'étaient rangés sous son drapeau, était à deux journess d'Antonio. Le general Houston était sur le point de partir pour l'armée.

—*Le Courrier Des Etats*-Unis (New York), April 6, 1836

Around the Alamo on day nine of the siege, according to Almonte, all was relatively quiet.

Wednesday, 2d.—Commenced clear and pleasant—thermometer 34°—no wind. An Aid of Col. Duque arrived with despatches

from Arroyo Hondo, dated 1st inst.; in reply, he was ordered to leave the river Medina, and arrive the next day at 12 or 1 o'clock. Gen. J. Ramirez came to breakfast with the President. Information was received that there was corn at the farm of Sequin, and Lieut. Menchaca was sent with a partry for it. The President discovered, in the afternoon, a covered road within pistol shot of the Alamo, and posted the battalion of Jimenes there. At 5 A. M. Bringas went out to meet Gaona.

—*New York Herald*, June 25, 1836

March 2, 1836, was a banner day in the life of Texas, for, as already mentioned in a number of reports, the Texas Declaration of Independence was approved by fifty-eight delegates convening at Washington-on-the-Brazos. Ironically on that day, too, Travis's letter describing the fighting on the 25 of February arrived there while one of the delegates was penning the news of the Declaration to a Pennsylvania newspaper editor.

Extract to the Editor, of the Philadelphia Inquirer, dated,
WASHINGTON, (Texas,) March 2, 1836.
DEAR SIR: I have much pleasure in being able to communicate to you the intelligence of the birth of a new Republic. Texas has assumed a stand among the nations of the earth, and is now free, sovereign, and Independent!

The Convention invested by the people with plenary powers, assembled yesterday morning, 1st inst. when Judge Ellis, from Red river, was elected Chairman, and a committee of five appointed to draft a Declaration of Independence. George C. Childers, Edward Conrad, John Hardeman, Collin McKinney, and James Gaines were appointed said committee; and this morning presented a Declaration, which was unanimously adopted and signed. But little discussion was elicited by the question of Independence, as there was not one voice raised in opposition to the measure. Gen. Childers and gen. Houston made a few spirited and eloquent remarks.

This is an important act in the history of the world,—it is the founding of a republic that will, from its extensive territory and unrivalled natural advantages, fill an important space in future history.

This important step was taken even in the midst of the armies of the tyrant Santa Anna. We have thrown it in defiance into his very teeth. Many may fall under wrath, but we started an avalanche that must eventually, in the common decrees of a just God, bury the usurper and his minions under its ruins. We look to the citizens of the United States, in this great crisis, for countenance and support. We have ventured our "lives upon the cast," and whatever may be our fate, we feel confident that, eventually Texas will be redeemed from Mexican thralldom.

Respectfully, Yours, &c.

P.S. An express has this moment arrived from St. Antonio, bringing us intelligence that 150 men at that garrison have still held out against the thousand of Mexicans that are opposing them.—The enemy made a desperate charge to scale the walls, but were driven by this Spartan band with great slaughter. Col. Travis, who is the commander, has refused all terms of capitulation, and answered the demand of the enemy to surrender, by the roar of his cannon. Crockett, so far famed in the United States, is said to have performed wonders of chivalry.

We learn by the same Courier that Colonel Fannin has left the Garrison of Goliad with 320 men and 12 pieces of artillery—that he was within two days march of St. Antonio, and that the citizens in considerable numbers were joining him. Before this time it is probable the battle is "lost or won."

Gen. Houston is a member of the Convention, at this place. He will leave shortly for the Army.

—*Farmer's Cabinet*, April 4, 1836

A similar, yet more detailed letter was written that same day by another unnamed correspondent to an unnamed recipient in Virginia.

FROM TEXAS.
Extract of a letter to a citizen of Richmond.
WASHINGTON, Texas, March 2d.
The Convention recently elected by the people of Texas, with plenary powers, met yesterday in this place. The attendance was remarkably full. The country had for the last two months been thrown into a state of anarchy by the discreditable schism between the Governor and Council of the provincial Government. Their personal abuse of each other, and wretched mismanagement or neglect of public affairs had lost them the confidence of the people; and all were looking with the most intense anxiety to the meeting of this Convention, to put a stop to their brief and abused authority, and to remedy as far as practicable, the mischief they had done. The meeting was made, too, more interesting by the reports received express from Bexar, of the approach of Santa Anna with a large army, and the known diminutive force which defended that place. The enclosed despatch from Colonel Travis, who commands the Texian force at Bexar, was received here the day before the meeting. All perceived the necessity of despatch, and it was feared the members would break up, and move off for the seat of war before discharging even the most pressing of the duties for which they were appointed. But not so. They met under a deep impression of the momentous crisis, and the solemn duties they had to perform. Nearly 50 members were in attendance—three of them were Mexicans. One the celebrated Lorenzo de Zavalla, favorably known to the political and literary world, by the high offices he has filled, his Republican integrity, and the beautiful productions of his pen. The other two are Col. Ruis and Antonio Navarro, Deputies from the city of Bexar, where their property and families now are. The meeting was organized by the appointment of Richard Ellis, from Red River, President, and H. S. Kimble, Secretary. The first step was to appoint a committee to report a Declaration of Independence. The minds of all were so well made up to the propriety of the measure and the necessity for despatch, that it was deemed waste of precious time to go through the usual formalities of enquiry, &c. This morning the Committee reported by their Chairman, Mr. Geo. C. Childers, who read the document in his place. It was received by the house, referred to a Committee of the Whole, reported without amendment, and adopted

unanimously in less than one hour. It was read but once; but from the single hearing I should pronounce it a succinct and fair enumeration of the grounds upon which Texas has taken her stand among the nations of the earth. By those familiar with the declaration of '76, it may be thought an imitation of that illustrious document, which the writer had probably in his eye; and may not bear a critical comparison with it as a literary production. But no effort was made to amend it, altho there were those present who were capable of doing so, had it been deemed fit. They thought the substance of more importance than phraseology. It met a hearty concurrence from all present; and from none more cordially than the three Mexican deputies, who said they were no longer Mexicans, but Texians.

The next step will be to adopt a Constitution, which they will do with more haste, I fear, than work demands, for they are impatient to adjourn and go to meet the enemy. All their energies will be put forth to drive him back. And I think there is no doubt they will succeed, though perhaps at the cost of some hard fighting. Unfortunately they have no printing press here, and copies of the Declaration are now making with the pen to despatch to the U. S. and to different parts of the country. I shall endeavor to avail myself of the express to send you this. The Declaration itself you will receive in a short time through the papers.—Should further opportunities offer, I will advise you of their proceedings.

P.S. Some predatory Indians of the Northwest, are committing depredations on the frontier settlements; several murders have been committed by them within the last week—one of two men, who were out on a surveying party about 50 miles from this place. The people here dread them more than they do the Mexicans. The Indians residing North of Nacogdoches, between that and Red River, on the head waters of the Sabine, Trinity, &c. have been conciliated, and a Treaty was concluded with 13 Tribes of them within the last 10 days. It was negotiated by Gen. Houston and Judge Forbes of Nacogdoches.

—*Richmond Enquirer*, April 5, 1836

The following letter written by the aforementioned Judge John Forbes—who in January had sworn in Crockett as a citizen soldier of Texas—also indicated that, by March 2, it was thought that the Alamo would soon be reinforced.

WASHINGTON Texas March 2:
To Col. Millard—

Dear Sir—The Convention was organized yesterday, and during the first day, matters looked equally, and disagreeable. That body was intent on making a Declaration of Independence to hurl into the teeth of Santa Anna, and his myrmidons. They accordingly appointed a Committee to report a Declaration of Independence. And this morning after the Convention assembled, the committee reported a very able one—Its adoption was moved by Gen. Houston, and seconded by Col. Palmer, of the Bayou—and after a splendid speech from the General, it was unanimously adopted. Not one dissenting voice.

But the citizens will have to maintain it, by their bravery, as the Mexicans are in large forces on the frontiers; and are already in the towns of San Antonio; but the Alamo is bravely defended by Cols. James Bowie and Travis, and numbers are marching to their relief.

The condition of the army is yet undecided. The Convention will I think, act upon it tomorrow. And I will transmit to you the earliest intelligence. Gen. Houston will not leave here until the Constitution is adopted—and a recognization of the army made. The matters relating to the Governor and Council is yet undisturbed.

I hope for the best, and I know that the independence of Texas will be sustained by the energies of her citizens and friends—as the struggle will be a severe one. And all will have to buckle on their armor in its defence.

JOHN FORBES.
—*New Orleans Bee,* March 21, 1836

On that same day, Sam Houston wrote an urgent appeal to all Texian soldiers, and it was printed in newspapers as well as distributed in broadside form.

ARMY ORDERS.

Convention Hall, Washington,
March 2, 1836.

War is raging on the frontiers. Bejar is besieged by two thousand of the enemy, under the command of general Siezma. Reinforcements are on their march, to unite with the besieging army. By the last report, our force in Bejar was only one hundred and fifty men strong. The citizens of Texas must rally to the aid of our army, or it will perish. Let the citizens of the East march to the combat. The enemy must be driven from our soil, or desolation will accompany their march upon us. *Independence is declared,* it must be maintained. Immediate action, united with valor, alone can achieve great work. The services of all are forthwith required in the field.

SAM. HOUSTON,
Commander-in-Chief of the Army.

P.S. It is rumored that the enemy are on their march to Gonzales, and that they have entered the colonies. The fate of Bejar is unknown. The country must and shall be defended. The patriots of Texas are *appealed to in behalf of their bleeding country.*

S. H.
—Telegraph and Texas Register,
March 12, 1836

On the tenth day of the siege of the Alamo, as recorded in Almonte's journal, some 850 troops of the brigade under General Antonio Gaona arrived in San Antonio, to the cheers of the rest of the army and many of the townspeople. One of the Mexican batteries was forwarded and entrenched to within three hundred yards of the fort's north wall.

Thursday, 3rd.—Commenced clear, at 40°, without wind. The enemy fired a few cannon and musket shots at the city. I wrote to Mexico and to my sister, directed them to send their letters to Bexar, and that before 3 months the campaign would be ended. [4] The General-in-Chief went out to reconnoitre. A battery was erected on the north of the Alamo, within musket shot. Official despatches were received from Gen. Urrea, announcing that he had

routed the colonists at San Patricio—killing 16 and taking 21 prisoners. [5] The bells were rung. The battalions of Zapadores, Aldama, and Toluca arrived. The enemy attempted a sally in the night at the Sugar Mill, but were repulsed by our advance.

[4-*Note by the editor of the* Herald]: "Wrote to my sister"—"before three months the campaign will be ended." What a flood of reflections these recorded sentiments of poor Almonte create! At the last accounts he was a close prisoner of war at Valasco on the mouth of the Brassos. When his sister hears of his sad fate what a burst of grief and sisterly affection! Even in the midst of war these sentiments cannot be controuled. "Wrote to my sister!" This simple passage has raised Almonte higher in our estimation than all his talents—his brief—energetic mind. He was the sole cause and occasion of the war in Texas. He stimulated Santa Anna to that expedition. Standing before the Alamo—measuring over his various fortunes—he exultingly predicts that Texas will be reduced in three months—and that he will return in triumph to Mexico, where he can embrace with the affection of a brother his beloved sister. With all his errors, Almonte's heart breaks out in the right spot—honorable to himself and to human nature. [5]: This was their second victory and their ringing the bells is highly characteristic. San Patricio is a small place on the eastern bank of the Rio de las Nueces near the bay of that name. It formed the extreme right of the base of Santa Anna's operations.

—New York Herald, June 25, 1836

The third of March also saw Travis write two important letters. One of them, addressed to the president of the Convention at Washington-on-the-Brazos, was first published in the *Telegraph and Texas Register* and afterward in many other papers, sometimes in edited form, across the nation. It frankly expressed the conflicting emotions that swirled within him: impatience to receive substantial, long-anticipated reinforcements; chagrin over the destructive political disunion of the Texian government; and a lingering heroic defiance toward the increasing numbers of the enemy that boxed him in, although it was a defiance now tinged with fatalism.

LETTER
FROM COL. TRAVIS TO THE PRESIDENT OF THE CONVENTION.
COMMANDANCY OF THE ALAMO, BEJAR, March 3, 1836.

SIR.—In the present confusion of the provincial authorities of the country, and in the absence of the commander-in-chief, I beg leave to communicate to you the situation of this garrison. You have doubtless already seen my official report of the action of the 25th ult., made on that day to Gen. Sam. Houston, together with the various communications heretofore sent by express. I shall therefore confine myself to what has transpired since that date.

From the 25th to the present date, the enemy have kept up a bombardment from two howitzers, (one a five and a half inch, and the other an eight inch,) and a heavy cannonade from two long nine pounders, mounted on a battery on the opposite side of the river, at the distance of four hundred yards from our walls. During this period the enemy have been busily employed in encircling us with intrenched encampments on all sides, at the following distances, to wit,—in Bejar, four hundred yards west; in Lavilleta, three hundred yards south; at the powder house, one thousand yards east by south; on the ditch, eight hundred yards north-east, and at the old mill, eight hundred yards north. Notwithstanding all this, a company of thirty-two men, from Gonzales, made their way into us on the morning of the 1st inst. at 3 o'clock, and Col. J. B. Bonham (a courier from Gonzales) got in this morning at 11 o'clock, without molestation. I have so fortified this place, that the walls are generally proof against cannon balls and I still continue to intrench on the inside, and strengthen the walls by throwing up the dirt. At least two hundred shells have fallen inside of our works without having injured a single man: indeed, we have been so fortunate as not to lose a man from any cause, and we have killed many of the enemy. The spirits of my men are still high, although they have had much to depress them. We have contended for ten days against an enemy whose numbers are variously estimated at from fifteen hundred to six thousand men, with Gen. Ramirez Siezma and Col. Batres, the aid de camp of Santa Ana, at their head. A report was circulated that Santa Ana himself was with the enemy, but I think it was false. A reinforcement of about one thousand men is now entering Bejar from the west, and I think it more than probable that Santa Ana is now in town, from the rejoicing we hear. Col. Fannin is said to be on the march to this place with reinforcements; but I fear it is not true, as I have repeatedly sent to him for aid without receiving any. Colonel Bonham, my special messenger, arrived at La Bahia fourteen days ago, with a request for aid; and on the arrival of the enemy in Bejar ten days ago, I sent an express to Col. F., which arrived at Goliad on the next day, urging him to send us reinforcements—none have yet arrived. I look to the colonies alone for aid: unless it arrives soon, I shall have to fight the enemy on his own terms. I will, however, do the best I can under the circumstances; and I feel confident that the determined valor, and desperate courage, heretofore evinced by my men, will not fail them in the last struggle; and although they may be sacrificed to the vengeance of a gothic enemy, the victory will cost the enemy so dear, that it will be worse for him than a defeat. I hope your honorable body will hasten on reinforcements, ammunition and provisions to our aid, as soon as possible. We have provisions for twenty days for the men we have: our supply of ammunition is limited. At least five hundred pounds of cannon powder, and two hundred rounds of six, nine, twelve, and eighteen pound balls—ten kegs of rifle powder, and a supply of lead, should be sent to this place without delay, under a sufficient guard.

If these things are promptly sent and large reinforcements are hastened to this frontier, this neighborhood will be the great and decisive battle ground. The power of Santa Ana is to be met here, or in the colonies; we had better meet them here, than to suffer a war of desolation to rage in our settlements. A blood-red banner waves from the church of Bejar, and in the camp above us, in token that the war is one of vengeance against rebels; they have declared us as such, and demanded that we should surrender at discretion, or that this garrison should be put to the sword. Their threats have had no influence on me, or my men, but to make all fight with desperation, and that high souled courage which characterizes the patriot, who is willing to die in defence of his country's liberty and his own honor.

The citizens of this municipality are all our enemies except those who have joined us heretofore; we have but three Mexicans now in the fort: those who have not joined us in this extremity, should be declared public enemies, and their property should aid in paying the expenses of the war.

The bearer of this will give your honorable body, a statement more in detail should he escape through the enemies lines.

God and Texas—Victory or Death!

Your obedient ser't.

W. BARRETT TRAVIS.

Lieut. Col. Comm.

P. S. The enemies troops are still arriving and the reinforcements will probably amount to two or three thousand.   T.

Convention Hall, Sunday morning.

10 o'clock, March 6, 1836.

On the arrival of the express with the letter, of which the above is a copy, the Convention was called together, and being called to order, on motion it was read; whereupon Mr. Parmer moved the house that one thousand copies be printed for circulation, by the Editors, Messrs. Baker and Bordens of San Felipe, which was agreed to.

H. S. KIMBLE, *Secretary.*

—Telegraph and Texas Register,

March 12, 1836

Printed in the March 24 issue of the *Telegraph* was another Travis letter dated March 3, addressed to his friend Jesse Grimes, one of the delegates at Washington.

COPY

Of a letter written by Col. Travis to a friend, dated from the Alamo, March 3d.

Dear Sir—do me the favor to send the enclosed to its proper destination instantly. I am still here, in fine spirits, and well to do. With 140 men I have held this place 10 days against a force variously estimated from 1500 to 6000, and I shall continue to hold it till I get relief from my countrymen, or I will perish in its defence. We have had a shower of bombs and cannon balls continually falling among us the whole time, yet none of us have fallen. We have been miraculously preserved. You have no doubt seen my official report of the action of the 25th ult. in which we repulsed the enemy with considerable loss: on the night of the 25th they made another attempt to charge us in the rear of the fort; but we received them gallantly, by a discharge of grape shot and musquetry, and they took to their scrapers immediately. They are now encamped under entrenchments, on all sides of us.

All our couriers have gotten out without being caught, and a company of 32 men from Gonzales got in two nights ago, and Col. Bonham got in to-day by coming between the powder house and the enemy's upper encampment.

Let the Convention go on and make a declaration of independence; and we will then understand, and the world will understand what we are fighting for. If independence is not declared, I shall lay down my arms and so will the men under my command. But under the flag of independence, we are ready to peril our lives a hundred times a day, and to dare the monster who is fighting us under a blood-red flag, threatening to murder all prisoners and to make Texas a waste desert. I shall have to fight the enemy on his own terms; yet I am ready to do it, and if my countrymen do not rally to my relief, I am determined to perish in the defence of this place, and my bones shall reproach my country for her neglect. With 500 men more, I will drive Sesma beyond the Rio Grande, and I will visit vengeance on the enemies of Texas, whether invaders or resident Mexican enemies. All the citizens that have not joined us, are with the enemy fighting against us. Let the government declare them public enemies, otherwise she is acting a suicidal part. I shall treat them as such, unless I have superior orders to the contrary. My respects to all friends, and confusion to all enemies. God bless you.

Your friend,
W. BARRET TRAVIS.
—*Telegraph and Texas Register*,
March 24, 1836

The ever-vigorous John W. Smith, who had guided in the small Gonzales relief force on March 1, rode out again with the two latest letters of Travis, as well as with a bundle of missives written by other members of the garrison.

Although resigned to the fact that his own death was probably near, Travis had received an encouraging letter from Major Robert McAlpin Williamson, a close friend from Anahuac days, carried in by James Butler Bonham on March 3. After the fall of the Alamo, the letter was found in Travis's room and was published in Spanish in at least two Mexican newspapers, *El Nacional* and *Diario del Gobierno*.

Translation of a letter from R. M. Williamson to the leader Barnet Travis.—Gonzalez, March 1, 1836.—Sr. Colonel Travis.—You cannot conceive my anxiety: today makes four complete days that we have not received the slightest report relative to your dangerous situation, and therefore we are given over to a thousand conjectures about it. From this municipality 60 men have departed, who in all human probability are with you by this date. Colonel Fannin with 300 men and four pieces of artillery has been on the march to Bejar for three days. Tonight we await reinforcements from Washington, Bastros, Brasoria and S. Felipe, to the number of 300, and we will lose not a moment in getting this help to you. Regarding *the other letter of the same date, let it pass*; today you will know what it means. If the multitude get hold of it, let them figure it out.—I am your true friend *R. M. Williamson*. P.S.—For God's sake, hold out until we can help you. I am sending to

you with major Bonham a message from the interior government. A thousand greetings to all of your people, and tell them to hold firm "for Willis" until I get there. *Williamson.*—Write us as soon as you can.

—*Supplemento al Diario del Gobierno*, March 21, 1836

Santa Anna also knew that it was just a matter of time before the Alamo would be reinforced. Should he wait for his heavy artillery to arrive, which could easily punch a breach through the fort's walls and thus ensure its fall, or should he attack now, before either the big guns or Texian help showed up? In fact he had already made up his mind, and the next day, as Almonte recorded, he held a perfunctory council of war in his Béxar headquarters.

Friday, 4th.—The day commenced windy, but not cold—thermometer 48°. Commenced firing very early, which the enemy did not return. In the afternoon one or two shots were fired by them. A meeting of Generals and Colonels was held, at which Generals Cos, Sesma, and Castrillon were present; (Generals Amador and Ventura Mora did not attend—the former having been suspended, and the latter being in active commission). Also present, Colonels Francisco Duque, battalion of Toluca—Orisñuela, battalion of Aldama—Romero, battalion of Matamoros—Arnat, battalion of Zapadores, and the Major of battalion of San Luis.—The Colonels of battalions of Jimenes and San Luis did not attend, being engaged in actual commission. I was also called. After a long conference, [6] Cos, Castrillon, Orisñuela, and Romero were of opinion that the Alamo should be assaulted—first opening a breach with the two cannon of—and the two mortars, and that they should await the arrival of the two 12 pounders expected on Monday, the 7th. The President, Gen. Ramirez, and I were of opinion that the 12 pounders should not be waited for, but the assault made.—Colonels Duque and Arnat, and the Major of the San Luis battalion did not give any definite opinion about either of the two modes of assault proposed. In this state things remained—the General not making any definite resolation [sic]. In the night the north parapet was advanced

"David Crockett . . .
Had Fortified Himself with Sixteen Guns"

If the Alamo was by March 3—according to William Barret Travis's letter of that date—desperately in need of "ten kegs of rifle powder, and a supply of lead," it was not lacking in a surplus of long arms: at least "816 rifles, muskets and pistols" were found by the victorious Mexican troops after the March 6 battle.[1] Because a significant portion of the Alamo garrison was in hospital, reports that each of the able-bodied defenders was armed "with at least a brace of pistols and four or five rifles and muskets, all loaded, besides knives," may be no exaggeration.[2]

A report from the *Natchitoches Herald* reprinted in the May 3 issue of the *Arkansas Gazette* offered "a summary of facts" regarding the battle, gleaned from unspecified sources, that included this sentence: "David Crockett, (now rendered immortal in story), had fortified himself with sixteen guns well charged, and a monument of slain foes encompassed his lifeless body." Doubtless Crockett had been similarly armed all throughout the siege when moments of critical enemy challenge arose. One such moment is found in the newspaper account that claimed he shot down in quick succession five Mexican artillerymen who attempted to fire a cannon placed "within gun shot of the Fort."[3] It is no mystery why Crockett, whose extraordinary marksmanship had helped make him a living legend, had been entrusted with so many rifles to operate on the wall.

A dozen years after the battle Mexican captain Rafael Soldana recalled one of the defenders as

> a tall man with flowing hair . . . seen firing from the same place on the parapet during the entire siege. He wore a buckskin suit and a cap all of a pattern entirely different from those worn by his comrades . . . we all learned to keep at a good distance when he was seen ready to shoot. He rarely missed his mark. . . . This man I later learned was known as "Kwockey."[4]

For the Texian garrison, however, much of the siege was a jittery watching-and-waiting game—when Mexican shells and round shot were not peppering the compound. They had to watch for enemy scouts and light troops venturing close to the walls; Sappers who dug advanced trenches for new batteries and camps; and enemy sorties at

(Continued)

all times of the day and night, devised both to harass the defenders as well as to seize such resources as timbers from the little Tejano village not far from the south gate. The resulting sleeplessness, tension, and exhaustion plagued Travis's men and, when coupled with the frequent cold, wind, and rain, made this state of eternal vigilance an uncomfortable, unhealthy, and tedious task.

---

1. "Statement and manifest of the Army, arms, munitions and other effects taken from the Enemy" (March 6, 1836), Mexican document quoted in William C. Davis, *Three Roads to the Alamo: The Lives and Fortunes of David Crockett, James Bowie, and William Barret Travis* (New York: Harper Collins, 1998), 731, n. 96. Since General Pedro de Ampudia reported that 216 muskets were found in the fort's armory after the battle, simple arithmetic tells us that six hundred "rifles, muskets and pistols" were actually used by the defenders in the March 6 engagement.
2. Report of the Alamo's fall by Jesse B. Badgett, *Arkansas Gazette*, April 12, 1836.
3. Report from the *Xenia Gazette* (Ohio) reprinted in the *New York Times* of June 29, 1836.
4. Interview with Captain Don Rafael Soldana by Captain Creed Taylor circa 1848, in Todd Hansen, ed., *The Alamo Reader: A Study in History* (Mechanicsburg, Penn: Stackpole Books, 2003), 470.

towards the enemy through the water course. A Lieutenant of Engineers conducted the entrenchment. A messenger was despatched to Urrea. [6-*Note by the editor of the* Herald]: "After a long conference, &c." Here is a remarkable disclosure. Cos who had been released by the Texians *on parole*, is the first to advise an assault upon the handful of brave men in the Alamo. Almonte also is for immediate assault. This disclosure ought to decide the question of life and death as affecting Gen. Cos. He has justly forfeited his life according to the rules of war.
—*New York Herald*, June 25, 1836

On that same day, at Washington-on-the-Brazos, after receiving word that Fannin's reinforcement column had turned back to Goliad, the delegates began to realize that the Alamo might not be saved in time.

TEXAS.
Extract of a letter from Washington, (Texas,) March 4.
"I wrote you yesterday, advising you that the *Convention* of the people of Texas now sitting

in this place, had unanimously agreed to the Declaration of Independence. They are following up the work with great zeal, and with all appearance of confidence. Besides preparing a *Constitution*, to be submitted to the people, they are going on to do such legislation as the emergencies of the occasion requires. Committees have been raised on Finance, on the Land Offices, on the organization of the army, &c. The Convention is clothed with plenary powers, and of necessity must legislate. It is in fact the only government existing here; the Governor and Council of the Provisional Government being *functi officio*, on the meeting of the Convention. To-day, Major-General Samuel Houston, formerly Governor of Tennessee, was, by resolution, created commander-in-chief of all the land forces of Texas, regulars, volunteers, and militia, and clothed with all the powers exercised by the commander-in-chief of the armies of the U. S. He is a member of the Convention from Refugio, but will immediately leave his seat and repair to the army. The Convention has adjourned until Monday the 7th, to give time for the committees to mature their business, or rather to act on it—for, as to *maturing any thing* in the present state of affairs, and with such poor conveniences for study or deliberation, in this unfurnished place, it is not to be expected. They have, however, taken the attitude of an independent nation, and they must devise a frame work for a government. Imperfect of course it will be, but it will serve for something to unite the people upon, and amendments must be made at more leisure, as experience shall point out their expediency.—The model of the United States will be followed in most things.

"An express has just arrived from Col. Fanning at Goliad. He had commenced his march to Bexar, but met with difficulties from insufficient teams, wagons, &c., and receiving information of the advance of a division of the enemy in the direction of Goliad, he had retrograded, believing the protection of the munitions and provisions at that place and Copano, to be of more importance than the relief of Bexar. This has again left the fate of Bexar in doubt, and renewed the anxious feelings of the People here. Men are flocking thither in all directions; but whether they will reach there in time, or not, is doubtful."

—*Richmond Enquirer*, April 8, 1836

The next day, at San Felipe, which sat on the Brazos about forty miles south of Washington, two editorialists in the *Telegraph and Texas Register* had a number of comments to make about the current state of the revolution—at least as far as it was known—from the volunteers now moving westward to help Travis's garrison, to the continuing "backwardness" of other Texians for failing to join such relief parties. They also offered advice regarding portable breastworks that should be adopted by all soldiers in future confrontations with the Mexican army.

We would respectfully notify the present convention, that procured a sufficiency of hands, we are prepared to execute any order, either at night or day.

The jurisdiction of Minn, first at her post during last year, against the encroachment either of Indians or Mexicans, several days since departed a company of men to the relief of our friends in Bejar. May others, less exposed than Minn, follow this generous example.

We regret to hear of the backwardness of some of our fellow citizens, in turning out in defense of their wives and children. It is with pleasure and satisfaction, that not only the men, but even the women are nobly contributing all the service in their power in defense of our country. A few days since, when despatches were to be sent to every part of the country, an elderly lady, well known to many in this colony, on hearing of the present alarming invasion, carried, with the least possible delay, the intelligence into a settlement on the Brazos below. Many other ladies are doing every thing in their power in providing clothing, and articles of equipment for those going to the field.

We hear some complain, saying, they have already served longer, or contributed more, than some of their richer neighbors: others, that they have got no credit for what they have already done; and not unfrequently do we hear men say, they are ready to fight, but are not willing to turn out, while men possessed of lands and other property are staying at home to care of their substance, the former not having a foot of land, or little else to fight for. We acknowledge that the burden of the present war has, thus far, fallen very unequally upon our citizens. We know men, whose names are not yet mentioned, who have generously devoted all their time, and much of their substance, in defense of our country, while others have done but very little. But it is hoped that none at the present time, when Texas is threatened to be thrown back again into a wilderness state, will count on the profit of former occupations, or will consider the cost of a few months service, when expulsion or death is at hand!

We have just learned that a treaty has been effected with the north eastern Indians; favorable, we trust to them, and beneficial to all parties.

The committee of San Felipe would suggest to commandants of companies fitting out, the great utility of taking with them a quantity of bags, say two for each man. In case of an attack each man could fill up his bags with sand or dirt, and in less than twenty minutes a sufficient

From the Phil Collins Collection

Flattened Cannonball from the Alamo

This rare flattened bronze 6-pound cannonball was unearthed during The History Shop dig, northeast of the Alamo's cow pen, and there was considerable excitement amongst those involved when it was found.

This ball, in addition to the other artefacts uncovered in that same small area, gives further proof that there was probably a considerable amount of activity here during both the siege and final battle, as well as during the postbattle "cleanup" by Col. José Juan Andrade, acting under orders from Antonio López de Santa Anna.

Not long after the battle, there were many reports of balls, flattened like this one, being found in or around the Plaza. Aiming a cannon in those days was not yet a science; the armed forces relied on nothing but the human eye to estimate a cannonball's destination.

However, as the strategy of siege warfare was primarily about slowly wearing the enemy down and gradually weakening a garrison's walls by consistent bombardment, it's not surprising that there were many cannonballs seemingly fired at random.

Also the continuous cannonade day and night would wear down the enemy, lessening their concentration by lack of sleep.

This in fact was the case during the 13-day Alamo siege when the only time there was any real period of silence was on the eve of March 5 when the Mexican forces deliberately halted their bombardment, resulting in the exhausted Texians falling asleep and being caught by surprise a few hours later in the predawn darkness.

Though probably not the first military force to do so, it was sometimes the practise for the Mexican artillery to "heat" the cannonballs before firing, and that may well account for these balls ending up with a clean, flattened side, as being hot when fired, they would be slightly "soft" . . . although even then, it would still be advisable to avoid being hit by one!

There were fragments of stone found on the flattened side of this ball, showing that it might have bounced off one of the Alamo compound walls during the siege. It's pictured here with the blackened earth that encased the ball when found. –PC breast work could be raised to serve for their greater security; and in a prairie country, this method of fortifying appears to the committee a good one. Common domestic for the bags would be all sufficient, and in less than twelve hours the ladies of each neighborhood could supply all the men which might turn out. The committee will furnish the San Felipe company with its quota of bags thus proposed.

John R. Jones
Thomas Gay
—*Telegraph and Texas Register*,
March 5, 1836

March 5 was also the day before Santa Anna launched his big attack on the Alamo. The generalissimo assigned command leadership to each of the four "columns of attack," as noted in Almonte's journal.

Saturday, March 5th.—The day commenced very moderate—thermometer 50°—weather clear. A brisk fire was commenced from our north battery against the enemy, which was not answered, except now and then. At mid-day the thermometer rose to 68°.—The President determined to make the assault; and it was agreed that the four columns of attack were to be commanded by Generals Cos, Duque, Romero, and Morales, and second in command, Generals Castrillon, Amador, and Miñon. For this purpose the points of attack were examined by the commanding officers, and they came to the conclusion that they should muster at 12 o'clock to-night, and at 4 o'clock tomorrow morning (Sunday, 6th,) the attack should be made.

—*New York Herald,* June 27, 1836

The attack orders issued by Santa Anna were published in at least one Mexican newspaper more than two weeks later. This new translation, done with a particular eye regarding military terminology as well as maintaining the original punctuation, corrects a few misinterpretations found in previous ones made by both English and Spanish translators.

Army of operations.—General orders of the 5th of March 1836. 2 o'clock in the afternoon.

—Reserved for the generals, chiefs of sections and corps commanders.

Being necessary to act decisively upon the enemy defending the fortress of the Alamo, His Excellency Señor general in chief has ordered that tomorrow at four o'clock the attacking columns will be situated within musket-shot of their first entrenchments,[k] in order to undertake the assault which will be verified by a signal given by His Excellency with a bugle from the North battery.

The first column will be commanded by general D. Martin Perfecto Cos, and in his absence by myself.

The permanent battalion of Aldama, excepting the company of grenadiers, will compose this first column, along with the first three companies of the active of S. Luis.[l] The second will be commanded by Señor colonel D. Francisco Duque, and in his absence by general D. Manuel Fernandez Castrillon.

The active battalion of Toluca, excepting the company of grenadiers, will compose the second column, along with the three other fusilier companies of the active of S. Luis.[m]

The third will be commanded by Señor colonel D. Jose Maria Romero, and in his absence by Señor colonel D. Mariano Salas.

The companies of fusiliers, in all their force, of the permanent battalions of Matamoros and Jimenez, will compose this column.

The fourth will be commanded by Señor colonel D. Juan Morales and in his absence by Señor colonel D. Jose Miñon.

It will be composed of the companies of cazadores[n] of the permanent battalions of Matamoros and Jimenez, and the active of S. Luis.

---

[k] Meaning the "first entrenchments" of the Alamo defenders.

[l] That is, the "Activo," or activated militia battalion of San Luis.

[m] *Fusilier* referred to the type of soldier who made up the bulk of early nineteenth-century armies, namely, a musket man essentially trained in mass maneuvers and volley firing, as opposed to executing the more specialized duties of the grenadiers and light infantry. In some translations of these orders, "fusilier companies" has been misinterpreted as "rifle companies."

[n] Light infantry.

The points these columns are to attack, will be designated by the general in chief at the opportune time, and then the leaders will receive their instructions.

The reserves will be composed of the battalion of Zapadores° and the five companies of grenadiers of the permanent battalions of Matamoros, Jimenez and Aldama, and the actives of Toluca and S. Luis.

This reserve will be personally ordered by the general in chief at the moment of attack: but the reunion of this force will be carried out by Señor colonel D. Augustin Amat, under whose orders they will remain from this afternoon, until they are led to the designated positions.

The first column will carry ten scaling ladders, two crowbars and two axes, an equal number for the second, six for the third, and two for the fourth.

The individuals who carry the ladders will place their muskets on their backs, so that they can place them wherever they may be needed.

The companies of grenadiers and cazadores will be given ammunition at six stops per square,[8] and at four for the fusiliers, with two reserve flints. These men shall not carry overcoats, blankets or anything to hinder their rapid maneuvering, and during the day all shako chin-straps will be correctly worn, which the commanders of the corps will check care-

fully, and see that they wear shoes or sandals. The troops composing the column of attack will turn in after the night's prayer, since they will have to move out at midnight. The recruits who are not yet well trained are to remain in their quarters. The arms shall be in the best condition, particularly the bayonets.

As soon as the moon rises, the fusiliers of the active of S. Luis, shall return to their quarters, leaving the points on the line so that they may have time to get their things ready. The cavalry under the orders of general D. Joaquin Ramirez y Sesma, will occupy the Alameda, and at three o'clock in the morning will saddle up. Their object will be to watch over the field and not permit the escape of anyone attempting it.

Being a matter of concern, for the honor of the nation and the army is at stake, his Excellency the general in chief expects that each individual shall do his duty and exert himself to help bring a day of glory and satisfaction to his homeland and the supreme government, which will know how to reward the distinguished actions of the courageous men who composed the army of operations.

Juan Valentin Amador. A certified copy. Bejar 6 of March, 1836.

Ramon Martinez Caro, secretary.

—*Supplemento al Diario del Gobierno,*
March 21, 1836

° Sappers, or engineers.

8

Assault

Six days after the fall of the Alamo, news of the disaster had still not reached San Felipe de Austin. In the issue of the *Telegraph and Texas Register* published there on that day, it was reported that John W. Smith was again preparing to hurry back to the Alamo with a fresh band of reinforcements, and that John Sutherland, Smith's riding companion from the Alamo on February 23, was also keeping active in providing supplies for the Texas army.

We learn, by letters from Gonzales, that a courier had been despatched to Goliad, but was driven back, the Mexican spies being within 30 miles of that place. An express had just arrived from Col. Fannin, stating that he was besieged at Goliad, and could render no assistance to the troops in the Alamo till he could obtain a victory over the force then investing him.

We also learn by letter, that John W. Smith, who had previously conducted 30 men into the Alamo, would be entrusted with the hazardous enterprise of conducting 50 more.

We again express the hope that the planters and farmers will turn their attention to the raising of bread instead of cotton, if they have an opportunity to cultivate the earth at all. Many persons who have no servants will not be able to plant any thing. We, as well as some of our neighbors, can not even cultivate our garden. Some say, we can procure provisions from the United States; but this we are not too certain of, for we are now experiencing the difficulty of procuring the necessaries of life, from scarcity of teams and the badness of roads. Flour,

at this place, scarce at twenty dollars per barrel; corn not to be had at two dollars per bushel; and had it not been for the arrival of the steamboat, San Felipe again would have been straitened for something to eat. This may appear discouraging to volunteers from the United States; but we feel bound to let them know our poverty, believing the munificence of our friends there will not be withheld from a suffering people.

We are informed, however, that provisions for the army have, some time since, been landed at Cox's Point and at Copano; and that the most prompt and energetic means are employed in forwarding them on to the seat of war. Will not the planters and farmers in the lower country turn out their teams for the transportation of provisions to the army? We greatly fear it will be in want, unless the greatest exertions are used. Major Sutherland, we understand, has again put his shoulder to the wheel, in forwarding supplies; and for his industry and perseverance in this important department, at the siege of Bejar, last fall, major Sutherland is deserving our warmest gratitude.

Arrived at this place, on Saturday, Feb. 27, the steamboat Yellow Stone, captain Ross, with full freight of merchandize, &c. The Yellow Stone, we understand, is one hundred and forty-five tons burthen. If so large a boat can reach this place, at this stage of water, what advantage to the country might we expect from one of less burthen, made suitable for the Brazos river? The Yellow Stone, on Tuesday, proceeded up the river, after a freight of cotton.

We are happy to state that the steamboat Laura, sunk twenty miles below this place, was little injured, and will, in a few days, be repaired and ready for service.

—*Telegraph and Texas Register*, March 12, 1836

This extract contains almost no sense of the life-and-death struggle that was then engulfing west Texas. Instead it suggests that Col. James Fannin intended to "obtain a victory" over the Mexicans in his vicinity, that more help was on its way to relieve the brave defenders of the Alamo, and that although the price of commodities had skyrocketed in San Felipe at least the cotton trade flowed uninterrupted along the Brazos. It was typical, in fact, of the attitude of many Texians at the time; somehow the military situation would iron itself out, and William Barret Travis, with Fannin's help—and, ultimately, Sam Houston's—would eventually destroy Antonio López de Santa Anna's army and drive its remnants back into Mexico. There was certainly an emergency situation to contend with, but it was hardly bordering on the grave. Another example of this somewhat rose-colored viewpoint is contained in a letter dated March 8, written at Washington-on-the-Brazos and published in New York City over a month later.

Texas.—The following letter, although written previously to the fall of *Bexar* and the cold-blooded massacre of its garrison by that fiend in human shape, *Santa Ana,* and that dishonored and perjured soldier, *Cos,* is not without interest. It clearly shows the spirit with which the *Texians* have entered into the contest, and the certainty of its resulting favorably to the cause of freedom. We hope soon to see the Independence of *Texas* acknowledged by our Government; and we doubt not but thousands of gallant spirits have ere this marched to the relief of the struggling Patriots from our western States. Can nothing be done for *Texas* and her holy cause, in this city?

Correspondence of the Courier and Enquirer
WASHINGTON ON THE BRASOS, TEXAS.
Tuesday 8th March 1836.

Sir—This place is at present the seat of the present Convention for Texas. You will have seen before this reaches you, that *Independence* has been declared by the Delegates of the People in convention assembled.—Yes, without debate and without a dissenting voice! Members from some of the municipalities were opposed to a declaration of independence at this time, but there was such an overwhelming majority in favor of it, not one word nor one voice was raised against it. The Constitution will be reported to the House to-day. I will endeavor to get a copy of it as practicable and forward it to you.

You have doubtless heard that *Bexar* is besieged by *St. Anna's* invading army; Col. Travis had 150 men only when the Mexican army made its appearance. He has sustained himself nobly in several attacks made upon him in the *Alamo,* (a bomb proof fort). Once he made considerable slaughter among the Mexicans. Thirty men (Americans) made their way in to him a few nights since, unmolested, and he has sent out several expresses, one of which arrived yesterday, informing us that he had provisions and ammunition to last him 30 days, requesting the Convention to send him on aid as speedily as possible, saying he was determined not to surrender only with life.[a] *Travis* thinks St. Anna is with his troops and that they now have some 6 or 7000 men, and more arriving daily. The Mexicans have thrown up entrenchments nearly around the town and have a blood red banner flying on every one of their entrenchments. It is to be a war of extermination with St. Anna. A small party with Capt. *Johnson,* were surprised

[a] Thus far, this paragraph contains some egregious errors. In his letter of March 3 to the Convention, Travis actually wrote, "We have provisions for twenty days [not thirty] for the men we have: our supply of ammunition is limited," and he went on to list specific, and urgent, ammunition requests. The *Courier and Enquirer's* correspondent also mistakenly called the Alamo "a bomb proof fort," misconstruing Travis when he wrote, "the walls are generally proof against cannon balls." Such wishful misreading of Travis's communiqués may, in fact, have led many Texians to believe he could hold out until reinforcements reached him, even if that meant enduring the siege for another two or three weeks.

a short time since and every prisoner taken put to the sword, two of them while crying for quarter! The Americans knowing this, will sell their lives dearly,—none, no not one, will ever surrender! They are hurrying and marching to the scene of battle—some of the best riflemen and hardy backwoodsmen that the world can produce. At least 500 riflemen have passed along within the last three or four days and we shall soon have 2000 men there. Gen. Houston has been appointed Commander-in-chief, and has assumed the command of the army. He left for Bexar a few days ago. The Indians on the frontier have been excited against the whites and are committing depredations weekly, particularly in *Robertson's* colony. Several murders have been committed lately in that region, which will prevent many of the inhabitants in that quarter from turning out and marching to Bexar. The Mexicans have, likewise, been endeavouring to force out the Cherokees and some other tribes in the neighborhood of Nacogdoches, against the Americans, but so far they have been still. It is supposed that, in case the Mexicans should prove victorious in the onset, the Indians will join them.

We hear that a corvette for the Mexican service is being fitted out at New Orleans, probably to invade Galveston. I have urged the necessity of throwing up a fortification on Galveston Island immediately, which will be done. We likewise expect a steamboat from the United States for the Texas service. Let volunteers join us; they will be amply rewarded. We have plenty of fine lands; and as the war will now be carried into the enemy's country, where gold and silver are plenty, there will be fine pickings in the interior. There never was, since the days of the Revolution, such an opportunity for enterprising young men to distinguish themselves. The war has fairly and fully commenced, and will never end until Mexico is completely our own and conquered. Santa Ana is obstinate and determined; has united with him many of the liberals of late, report says; and we may expect a protracted war, unless we receive foreign aid. Volunteers are arriving from the United States daily, and several influential men from there

now in Texas, are about returning back to enlist more aid. Galveston Bay will be an important rendezvous for vessels coming in with troops; a ship can enter drawing 13 feet water. We want some heavy artillery and howitzers, with shot and shells.

A. K.

—*Morning Courier and New York Enquirer*, April 12, 1836

Among those angrier, more impatient Texians who understood that only immediate and massive reinforcements would now save the Alamo—and all Texas—was Capt. Moseley Baker. A veteran of the fighting at Gonzales and San Antonio in late 1835, he had joined the regular army on February 3.[1] On March 6, the day the Alamo fell, he and his company had marched into Gonzales, where other Texian troops were rendezvousing. His impassioned letter, written two days later to his fellow committee members back in San Felipe in the hope of scaring his indifferent countrymen into prompt action, was published in the *Telegraph and Texas Register*.

LETTER
From Gonzales.

Gonzales, 8th March, 1836.
GENTLEMEN,

ON day before yesterday I arrived here, accompanied by the companies of Captains M'Nutt and Rabb. I found about one hundred and sixty men here, which, with our force, made about two hundred and seventy, fifty of which started on yesterday for the Alamo. Our force now at this place is about two hundred and twenty men, with an enemy seventy-five miles in our front, five thousand strong. Our own situation is critical—too weak to advance, and insufficient to protect this place—and daily expecting two thousand cavalry to attack us. To retreat, however, would be the ruin of Texas; and we have all resolved to abide an attack, and to conquer or die. We are now busily engaged fortifying ourselves, with the hope that the people of Texas, *en masse*, are on the march to our assistance. Unless they are, the Alamo and our post must fall, and *all*, *every* man be destroyed. Not one of us will return to tell the dreadful tale—or to reproach those that remain for their supineness, or their cowardice. We have come here to repel the enemy, and my company will die beneath their standard sooner than the enemy shall advance, or they retreat. Will the people of Texas longer remain at home? Will any man, under these circumstances, longer refuse to turn out, because his *interest* requires his attention? Will any one dare to have the effrontery to say, that his interest must be attended to, when Texas is in danger of being overrun, and the women and children in cold blood massacred, when a portion of its fellow citizens are closely besieged, and another portion daily expecting to be attacked by ten times their number. The truth is not to be disguised, unless Texas turns out to a man—unless in two weeks from this day, three thousand men are concentrated here, Texas is gone, and one universal destruction and conflagration will be the result. In the name of God, send us assistance—send out the men; and let all who remain, without satisfactory reasons, be henceforward branded as a coward and a traitor, and an enemy to Texas, and let him be so treated. Their doctrine appears to be, that we must fight the battles of Texas, endure all privation, and all toil, and spill our blood and our lives, that they may enjoy the privilege of staying at home. Such a man is a traitor, and as a traitor treat him. Send, as fast as possible, arms and ammunition. Some of my company are without guns, and no possible means of procuring them here. Not a pound of lead, except what I brought, which I have distributed. Send these things, and speedily: and be assured, that unless Texas is victorious, I shall never return.

Yours, truly,

MOSELEY BAKER,

Captain.

JOHN R. JONES,

THOMAS GAY,

WM. PETTUS,

Committee.

Published by an order of the Committee, February 10, 1836.

—*Telegraph and Texas Register,*
March 12, 1836

Houston would not arrive at Gonzales until March 11. On March 6, the day the general had left Washington-on-the-Brazos to take charge of the Texian soldiers gathering in the west, convention delegate Martin Parmer (referred to as Palmer in the following) wrote a letter to his wife that simmered with the same dire warnings and expectations expressed by Baker.

Natchitoches, 15th March, 1836.
Editor of the True American.

SIR—I send the copy of a letter received this morning by express from Texas.

COMMITTEE ROOM, WASHINGTON,
March 6th, 1836.

DEAR WIFE—I am well and we are getting along very well. We have three or four committees who are preparing a constitution and we will soon have it ready. I shall be at home in ten or fifteen days. We have alarming news continually from the west; Frank Johnson's division is all killed, but five it is supposed. We saw two shot begging for quarters. Dr. Grant with a company of men is supposed to be all slain. Travis' last express states San Antonio was strongly besieged; it is much feared that Travis and company is all massacred, as despatches have been due from that place three days and none have arrived yet. The frontiers are breaking up, Gonzales must be sacked, and its inhabitants murdered and defiled without they get immediate aid. The last accounts, the Mexicans were to a considerable number between Gonzales and San Antonio. Fanning is at La Bahia with about 500 men, and is in daily expectation of a visit from Santa Anna. Texas has been declared free and independent, but unless we have a general turn out, and every man lay his helping hand too, we are lost. Santa Anna and his vassals are now on our borders, and the declaration of our freedom, unless it is sealed with blood, is of no force. I say again that nothing will save Texas but a general turn out. You all know my views with regard to our condition; I have given you facts, judge for yourselves. I wish a copy of this letter sent immediately to Capt. Baily Anderson and Col. A. S. Sublett, and publicly read in San

Augustine. Travis closes his last express with these words, "Help! O my country."

MARTIN PALMER.

To the Committee of vigilance and safety, San Augustine, Texas.

—*Arkansas Gazette*, April 5, 1836

Another, less pessimistic letter also written at Washington-on-the-Brazos that same day (March 6) was published in the *Richmond Enquirer*, and following it was a variety of news and rumors relating to the overall military situation in Texas.

Extract of a letter from Washington, Texas,) March 6th.

A despatch has this moment been received from Col. Travis, who commands the devoted little band in the Alamo, dated March 3d. The enemy are receiving large reinforcements, and are making an investment of the fort by regular advances. One ditch was run within 400 yards of it, while a heavy bombardment was kept up from the town, without injury. Santa Anna himself is believed to be now in Bexar; and the red flag, the signal for extermination, is flying. Yet 39 men from Gonzales had got into the fort to the aid of their brethren.—Hundreds more are pouring thitherward, on every road, and if not in the fort, will be on the outskirts of the enemy. The spirit of the country is now up. It is believed the great battle is to be fought on the San Antonio, and a general rush will be made. They want munitions, they want provisions, and suitable arms—but they will fight like tigers, and must conquer. Travis and his men are in high spirits, and will hold out, as long as a man is left to resist. Santa Anna's career is nearly run. Unless he succeeds here, he will never return to Mexico. And he *cannot succeed.* If he drive this people even across the Sabine, they will roll back upon him like the reflux of the sea, and overwhelm him.

Since the above Extracts were in type, we [the *Richmond Enquirer*] have met with the following, more recent, accounts:

(From the N. O. Commercial Bulletin.)

Rumors from Texas say Santa Anna has left the army, and is hastening back to the city of Mexico, in consequence of the death of Barragan,—the acting President—by poison.[b]

The whole Mexican force now in Texas is estimated at 5500 men. The right wing, composed of 700 men, under the Mexican General Urrea, advancing by the Matamoras road upon Goliad, which was occupied by Colonel Fannin with 500 Texians. The left wing of the Mexicans under Generals Cos and Sesma, which advanced upon the Laredo road, was besieging the Alamo of Bexar, and would probably soon obtain possession of the place, although it had been reinforced by 30 men from Gonzales. The whole number of Texians in the field to oppose Generals Cos and Sesma, including volunteers and militia, is estimated at 1500. It is conjectured that the Texians will retire before the Mexican forces and concentrate their whole strength so as to make battle in the woodland upon the banks of the Colorado; and this conjecture is founded upon the information received of a party of volunteers which were advancing to join Colonel Fannin, having been ordered to halt at the Guadaloupe, 25 miles in the rear of Colonel Fannin's position. Colonel Fannin, in whom is united science, and a thorough knowledge of military tactics—with unquestioned bravery—will be more than a match for Urrea—should the plan of the campaign render it necessary for him to give the latter battle. The great strength of the Texian forces consists in their riflemen; and these placed in the thickets upon the banks of the streams, will be more dangerous enemies than the Mexicans have ever yet met. It is these which will render the country unconquerable. Even if the Mexicans were to advance into the heart of the country they must consider themselves as conquerors only of the country upon which their encampments are formed.— They may here and there burn the humble

---

[b] The *Boston Courier* of April 1836 noted the supposed return to Mexico by Santa Anna and added: "The New-Orleans Bulletin of March 23, states that information has been received, to the effect that General Cos had advanced toward Austin's colony with 4000 men, leaving a sufficient force to blockade Colonel Travis in the Alamo, or fort, of San Antonio."

Rockets over the Alamo

"At a signal given by throwing up rockets from the town," noted the *Arkansas Gazette* of April 12, 1836, the attack on the Alamo "was simultaneously made on all sides of the garrison." The *Gazette* had received this information from Jesse B. Badgett, one of the convention delegates at Washington-on-the-Brazos, who in turn had heard it "from a Mexican deserter." In 1876, Susanna Hannig, formerly Mrs. Dickinson, was interviewed by the Texas Adjutant Office about the Alamo and the men who fell there. She gave a brief summary of the final day of the siege and began by stating, "On the morning of 6th Mch. about daylight [the] enemy threw up signal rocket & advanced."[1]

Another corroboration of the use of rockets that morning is found in the words of Col. Juan Nepomuceno Almonte's black body servant—and Antonio López de Santa Anna's cook—Benjamin Harris, better known as just "Ben," who was later interrogated by a Texian officer. "I saw rockets ascending in different directions," he said, "and shortly after I heard muskets and cannon, and by the flashes I could distinguish large bodies of Mexican troops under the walls of the Alamo."[2]

Such rockets generally served a dual purpose: to order an advance, as had been the case at New Orleans in 1815, and also to briefly illumine for the attacking troops the object of their assault.[3] Signal rockets in the Mexican artillery arm were not new: Gen. Martín Perfecto de Cos had utilized them during the fight for San Antonio the previous fall. On the evening of November 8, 1835, according to Samuel Maverick, who was a prisoner of the Mexican army in town, "the Gen'l fired off some signal rockets which threw things into a little helter skelter and turned out a false alarm."[4]

When Ben Milam's volunteer force began to move into Béxar in the predawn of December 5, a Mexican guide with one of the columns suddenly "broke his long silence and said, pointing to the Alamo where several rockets were just rising: 'The way is clear; we are safe. Those sparkling, artificial stars are calling a part of the troops out of the town to help the Alamo.'"[5]

During a failed previous night attack, Texian soldiers had also realized that their movements were discovered when "up went the rockets from the walls of the Church and Alamo, illuminating everything around," in the words of veteran Richard H. Chisholm. "Occasionally a rocket would alight near us, but was scarcely on the ground

(Continued)

before some of the men had bound upon it and extinguished it. . . . The rockets were very brilliant, and sometimes they would fall very near us."[6]

General Stephen F. Austin appreciated the value of rockets, and on October 31 he had written to colonels James Bowie and James W. Fannin, then encamped on the edge of town: "I wish you to send to Seguin's ranch for some rockets, that are there—two or three dozen. In Spanish they are called quetes, pronounced quates—we may want them."[7]

The Mexican army continued to use rockets during the war with the United States in 1846–1848,[8] although by then it also possessed a variety of rockets tipped with lethal rounds: cannonballs, grape, and canister. At Contreras, Mexico, in August 1847, advancing US troops were blasted by Mexican cannon fire as well as rocket barrages. One Wisconsin soldier noted "the sublime flight of the rockets as they marked their course with a fiery curve along the clouds."[9]

---

1. Susanna Hannig (Dickinson) interview, September 23, 1876, in Todd Hansen, ed., *The Alamo Reader: A Study in History* (Mechanicsburg, Penn: Stackpole Books, 2003), 47.

2. Testimony of Ben in Rev. Chester Newall, *History of the Revolution in Texas, Particularly of the War of 1835 and '36* (New York: Wiley and Putnam, 1838), 88–89; "Jan. 15, 1852: Communications, Nicaragua No. II," *Alamo Journal*, September 2006, 10.

3. Depending on the diameter of the paper-cylindered rocket and the angle of firing, it could rise from its tripod tube anywhere from 450 to 1,200 yards before exploding. Auguste Frederic Lendy, *Treatise on Fortification: Or, Lectures Delivered to Officers Reading for the Staff* (London, 1862), 14.

4. "Account of the Siege & Battle of Bexar from Within Bexar, from the Diary of Samuel Maverick, 1835." Available at www/tamu.edu/ccbn/dewitt/bexarmaverick.htm.

5. Natalie Ornish, *Ehrenberg, Goliad Survivor, Old West Explorer*, trans. by Peter Mollenhauer (Dallas: Texas Heritage Press, 1997), 147–148.

6. "An Incident in the Siege of San Antonio" (reminiscence of Richard H. Chisholm), *Texian Advocate*, February 20, 1851.

7. Austin to Bowie and Fannin, October 31, 1835, in Frank W. Johnson, *A History of Texas and Texans* (Chicago: American Historical Society, 1914), 1:283. According to *Neuman and Baretti's Dictionary of the Spanish and English Languages* (Boston, 1839), 192, the Spanish word for rocket is *cohete*. Signal rockets were *cohetes para senales*.

8. At Monterey, for instance, "10 Dozen Signal Rockets" were found among the Mexican stores after that city surrendered to US troops in 1846. *Albany Evening Journal*, November 13, 1846.

9. Letter from Mexico, Tacubaya, near Mexico City, September 9, 1847, *Wisconsin Democrat*, December 11, 1847.

---

logcabin, and destroy the cornfield of a poor settler, who has fled with his wife and children to the dense forest—where, if they pursue, they will find enemies who will deal them death from every tree.

F. Grayson, Esq., has arrived from Washington, Texas; left on the 7th inst., and brings the cheering news of the successful defence of San Antonio. That Gen. Houston had been elected Commander-in-Chief of the Texian

Army, by the new Convention, and had left on the 6th, to join the army on the frontier, with sufficient reinforcements to relieve Col. Travis, the brave defender of San Antonio. A friend of mine has shown us two letters from Gen. H. of the 9th; all is harmony, and the friends of liberty in Texas no longer fear the power of Santa Anna.

—*Richmond Enquirer*, April 8, 1836

The "harmony" supposedly conveyed in Houston's letters had already been pulverized by sunrise of March 6, when the bloody conquest of the Alamo by the Mexican army had become an historical fact. The assault was described by Col. Juan Nepomuceno Almonte in a frustratingly scanty journal entry, almost as if the event was one he little cared to remember.

Sunday, 6th.—At 5 A. M. the columns were posted at their respective stations, and at half past 5 the attack or assault was made, and continued until 6 A. M. when the enemy attempted in vain to fly, but they were overtaken and *put to the sword, and only five women, one Mexican soldier (prisoner,) and a black slave escaped from instant death.* On the part of the enemy the result was, 250 killed, and 17 pieces of artillery—a flag; muskets and fire-arms taken. Our loss was 60 soldiers and 5 officers killed, and 198 soldiers and 25 officers wounded—2 of the latter General officers. The battalion of Toluca lost 98 men between the wounded and killed. *I was robbed by our soldiers.*

—*New York Herald,*
June 27, 1836

It was left to other, more eloquent Mexican officers to voice their great pride in the victory. First among them, of course, was Santa Anna in his battle report, written that very morning and published in Mexican newspapers just fifteen days later.

OFFICE OF THE SECRETARY OF WAR
AND MARINE
CENTRAL SECTION — DESK 1.
Army of operations—Excellent Sir.—
Victory accompanies the army, and at this moment, being eight o'clock in the morning,

we have had a most complete and glorious one that will live in perpetual memory.

As announced to you on the 27th of the past month, on communicating the capture of this city, I awaited the arrival of the first brigade of infantry in order to operate effectively upon the fortress of the Alamo: but all the divisions of which the brigade is composed not being able to come up, by doubling their marches three battalions succeeded in getting here, the Zapadores, Aldama and Toluca. With this force, and that of the Matamoros, Jimenez and S. Luis Potosi, I was enabled to select, leaving out the recruits, 1400 infantry. These being divided into four columns and a reserve, as indicated in the general orders of yesterday, a copy of which accompanies this dispatch, the assault was undertaken at five in the morning, and met with the most obstinate resistance, so that during the struggle of an hour and a half it was necessary to employ even the reserves.

The picture presented by this battle was extraordinary: the men fighting individually, each one disputing for the most heroic action. 21 pieces of artillery were played by the enemy with great dexterity, the quick fire of the muskets which seemed to illuminate the interior of the fortifications, and the ditches and surrounding walls, could not keep out our fearless Mexicans: they performed like valiants, and deserve the consideration of the supreme government and the gratitude of their compatriots.

The fortress is now in own power, with its artillery, ammunition, &c., and wedged among its fosses and entrenchments are more than 600 bodies, all foreigners, and in the immediate vicinity an additional number not yet accurately known; these, endeavoring to escape the bayonets of the infantry, fell beneath the sabers of our cavalry, whom I had placed in opportune situations. I feel assured that few, if any, have escaped to inform their companions of the outcome.

Among the dead were found the first and second chiefs of the enemy, Bowie and Travis, colonels as they entitled themselves, and the equally ranked Croket, and all the rest of their other officers, and carrying official dispatches from their *convention*. On our side, we lost about 70 men dead and 300 wounded, amongst whom are two chiefs and 23 officers, the loss made less regrettable by the just cause we have sustained, it being the duty of every Mexican subject to die in defense of his nation. To this cherished object all are disposed to make every sacrifice, determined to permit no foreigners, wherever they come from, to insult the nation and occupy its territory.

In due course I will send a detailed account of this important triumph, for the present, I extend my congratulations to the nation and His Excellency the interim president, to whom I request you submit this report.

The courier is carrying one of the flags of the enemy's battalions captured this day,[c] for by looking at it yourselves you will know better the true intentions of the traitorous colonists, and their cooperators of the ports of the United States of the North.

God and liberty. General headquarters of Bejar, March 6, 1836.

> *Antonio Lopez de Santa Anna.*

The attached documents were found in the bag of the commandant of the Alamo fort, which I direct also to be put to the attention of His Excellency the interim president, and appropriate use made of them.[d]

> *Antonio Lopez de Santa Anna.*

To His Excellency the Secretary of War and Marine, General D. Jose Maria Tornel.

> —*Supplemento al Diario del Gobierno,*
> March 21, 1836

Preceding Santa Anna's report in the same issue of the *Supplemento al Diario del Gobierno* was an editorial pointing out that the Mexican troops, although superior in numbers to the Alamo garrison,

had defeated the best soldiers the Texians could throw at them, and that their enemy had also enjoyed the benefit of a strong fortification.

The victories obtained by the dauntless general and his intrepid soldiers, chiefs, and officers of the valiant Mexican army in Texas, will resound with the most impressive productive and prosperous results, as they are the first sustained actions against the most select of the so-called regular army of the colonies and of the preference companies of volunteers from Orleans. The reports and documents set forth below have again restored the national honor and the earned concept of the valiant Mexican, which is spoken, in spite of being slightly tarnished by the capture of Bejar and in spite of the haughty threats of the perfidious colonists. The lesson they have received in the assault on the fortress of the Alamo, despite the fact that the force was greatly superior in numbers but infinitely unequal considering the advantageous position and resources of a fortified place, cannot fail to encourage the Mexican army, discouraging those who believe they have the capacity to attack the capital of Mexico. Congratulations to the always victorious general Santa Anna, to his gallant army that has added this day of glory to the many others which belong to the entire nation, so justified by the event: although we are sensitive to the disastrous effects of war and the loss of so many brave Mexican victims of the caprice and perfidy of the ingrates who dared to insult the nation of which they had come to be a part, and tried to attack its territorial integrity. To the brave conquerors of the Alamo, a laurel and eternal gratitude, and the tears of the widows and families of those killed in action, must be generously wiped by a compassionate nation.

> —*Supplemento al Diario del Gobierno,*
> March 21, 1836

If the *Supplemento al Diario del Gobierno* had printed several primary documents concerning military developments in Texas, the main *Diario* edition of March 21 included a capsule report of that campaign, in which the color of the New Orleans

---

[c] This was the blue silk battalion flag of the New Orleans Greys, now preserved in a glass case in the Chapultepec Castle museum.

[d] One of these documents was Major Robert McAlpin Williamson's letter to Travis (see chapter 7). The nature and content of the other "documents" found in Travis's "bag" are not known, nor is it known if they still survive in Mexican archives.

Greys' flag is noted, as is José Urrea's destruction of Dr. James Grant's "division" on March 2, although Grant was leading but twenty-six men when ambushed by Mexican dragoons.

LONG LIVE THE MEXICAN REPUBLIC!
Long live general SANTA ANNA and the valiant army, conqueror of the fort of the Alamo in Texas!
    Have just received from the supreme government, however extraordinary, the apparently valid news of the taking by assault of the fort of the Alamo on the 5th day of the current month.[c] Even though the brigade he was waiting for was not at full strength when it arrived, His Excellency the president general resolved to make an assault on the aforementioned fort. The brave general Cos commanded the division, and the worthy general Santa Anna the reserve, having obtained the most complete success. Six hundred of the enemy were left dead inside the plaza, and the rest in the retreat, including nearly all their chiefs and officers, among them the celebrated James Bowie, and Travis, leaving in the power of the victor twenty-one cannons, a multitude of guns, ammunition, provisions, and equipment. For our part, we regrettably lost twenty-odd officers and seventy soldiers. The enthusiasm was admirable, and one could without difficulty compare this action with the most brilliant ones sustained by the Mexican army. Moreover, general Urrea has made another attack that completely destroyed the division of Dr. Grand, leaving the latter dead.
    Inserted in the supplement are the official dispatches, and our congratulations for the brilliant victories of the fatherland. The Most Excellent general Santa Anna has sent a blue flag, taken in the action, of a company of volunteers from Orleans, which was presented today to the general congress. Solemnizing such fortunate news was done with a salvo of artillery and ringing of bells, and appearing at the national palace was a crowd of people, inspired to hear the account given by the

Minister of War to the congress, and their faces showed the joy that everyone possessed.
    —*Diario del Gobierno de la Republica Mexicana*, March 21, 1836

An account by an unidentified officer who had actually taken part in the assault was published in the April 5 edition of *El Mosquito Mexicano*. Because in several places it contains virtually the same wording found in his diary, this account can be attributed to the pen of brevet Lt. Col. José Juan Sánchez Navarro.

Leona Vicario March 16, 1836
    By extraordinary arrival from the Alamo today, at four in the morning, the following letter has been received.
        Bejar, March 7 1836
DEAR BROTHERS OF MY HEART: thanks be given to Our Lord God, because the triumphs of our arms have multiplied. The ungrateful and proud colonists, who made us suffer so many days of disgust in the previous campaign, have now succumbed to the fate their foolish temerity has allotted them. After thirteen days of continuous cannon fire, it was ordered by his Excellency the president, the night before last at two in the morning, that the fortification of the Alamo be attacked: to effect this four columns were readied, commanded by Sr. general COS, and by the Sres. colonels D. Juan Morales, D. N. Duque de Estrada and Romero. I marched under the immediate orders of Sr. COS, and therefore will tell you only what I saw close at hand. After a long, roundabout movement we situated ourselves, at three in the morning, on the North side, about three hundred paces from the enemy fort, and there a rest was given to the column, composed of the Aldama battalion and part of S. Luis Potosi: we stayed there chest on ground until five thirty (the morning left us feeling quite cool), when the call to march was sounded, ordered to be given by His Excellency the Sr. president from a battery where he was located, in a direction between North and East: immediately Sr. COS shouted "Up!" and placed himself at the head of the force, we ran to the assault, for which purpose we carried ladders,

---

[c] A misreading of Santa Anna's battle report.

beams, bars, pickaxes, &c.: although the distance was short, in order to overcome it we suffered two cannon blasts of case shot that felled more than forty men:[f] the tenacious resistance of our enemies was to be admired as was the fearless constancy of all the generals, chiefs, officers and troops: it seemed as though the balls and case shot from the cannons, muskets and rifles of the enemy, were blunted on the chests of our soldiers, who ceaselessly shouted LONG LIVE THE MEXICAN REPUBLIC! LONG LIVE GENERAL SANTA ANNA! I assure you that all ideas of fright or terror were removed at the sight of so many valiant men who by ladders, over batteries, through embrasures and even upon one another, clambered over the entrenchments.[g2] The four columns and the reserve corps, as if by magic, climbed the enemy's walls at the same time and rushed themselves into the enclosure after about three quarters of an hour of a horrible fire, which when silent, was followed by a frightful struggle with cold steel[h]; and soon afterwards, a pitiful, but deserved butchery of those ungrateful colonists, who flung away their arms, thinking to find safety in flight or in hiding places.[i] Wretches! They exist no longer: they all died, all, and up to now I have seen burned (to free us from their putrefaction) 257 corpses, not counting those which had been made previously, during the thirteen days, nor those which were gathered of those who in vain sought safety in flight. Their chief called Trawis [sic] died like a brave man with his carbine in his hand, on the shoulder of a cannon; but the perverse braggart Santiago Bowie, died like a woman, almost hidden under a mattress. For our part we have had enough officers and troops killed, and about two hundred wounded, a loss causing grief, but small, if one considers the strong position occupied by the enemy and the class of the latter. Now this avenges the insult we had formerly received. His Excellency the Sr. president gave a beautiful speech to the entire division inside the Alamo, within view of the enemy's corpses, and was pleased with the conduct of everyone.

In San Patricio died Yompson,[j] and with him sixteen, and twenty-three made prisoners by the gallant sr. general Urrea, and this same on the 2nd day of the present month killed 42 of the enemy, among whom were recognized Morris[k] and the never well considered D. Diego Grant.

This event has been solemnized by this town with the greatest enthusiasm, because in it is seen more than just a glorious triumph, which proves the courage and determination of the MEXICAN ARMY, producing hope for a pleasant future. The death of the foreigners Trawis, Morris, Grant and Bowie, principal promoters of the revolt of the colonies of Texas and of the disorders suffered by this department, should greatly dishearten their adherents. Eternal praise to the immortal SANTA-ANNA and to the chiefs, officers and troops who so heroically have avenged the outrages inflicted upon our

---

[f] The Spanish term for "case shot" used in this letter is *metralla*, a word that encompassed several forms of cannon ammunition other than a single round shot, including canister, grapeshot, and langrage (a bag or case containing scrap iron, nails, and possibly bullets). Because the Alamo defenders had stocks of grapeshot, canister, and langrage, it is clear that Sánchez Navarro was speaking in general terms about the scattershot effect such ammunition achieved. The exact nature of the Alamo's canister, however, is not precisely known. At the battle of Coleto Creek, Fannin's cannon fired at the surrounding Mexicans with "canisters of musket balls," whereas his howitzer was loaded with "grist," or unground corn (*New Bedford Gazette*, June 13, 1836); so it may be that part of the Alamo's metralla was also largely improvised.

[g] The word Sánchez Navarro uses here is *trincheras*, which essentially referred to entrenchments, an umbrella military term often used to describe fortifications in general. Trincheras was also used when specifically referring to ditches and their defensible banks of earth.

[h] Sánchez Navarro uses the term *arma blanca* here, signifying "white arms," or bladed weapons, similar to the English term, *cold steel*, which more often than not meant the bayonet. But on that cold morning of March 6, 1836, it would have also applied to swords, machetes, knives, and the lances of the cavalry outside the fort.

[i] If many of the Texians who jumped over the walls attempted to break through the curtain of Mexican cavalry without their guns, as Sánchez Navarro claims here, it helps explain why Santa Anna's horse soldiers suffered incredibly few casualties in running them down with lance and saber.

[j] Col. Frank Johnson.

[k] Maj. Robert C. Morris of the New Orleans Greys.

great nation! Eternal praise to the brave general COS, who at the head of the column that made the assault, has vindicated himself so gallantly of the gratuitous and insulting accusations of his unjust enemies.

—*El Mosquito Mexicano*, April 5, 1836

Pro-Centralist Mexican newspapers basked in the victory, and sometimes made use of it to excoriate the "anarchists"—those who wanted to replace Santa Anna with a more liberal leader.

LONG LIVE MEXICO! LONG LIVE ITS INVINCIBLE LIBERATOR!

What innocent and pure rejoicing! What enthusiastic exultation and happiness was to be seen yesterday on the face of every good Mexican when he learned the splendid news, details of which are contained in the official section of today's paper. The rebel standard lies prostrate before our national flag; they have bitten the earth they profaned; their impure blood has flowed in atonement of their great insults; and between the fire and steel of our valiant men, their black souls have expired, nourished in immorality and profligacy. Mexico has been vindicated. Mexico has received a proper satisfaction. Renown, honor, and glory to the brave army of the fatherland. A thousand hymns and a thousand feelings of admiration and gratitude to the Hercules of Zempoal.

Whine, anarchists, for there is no other consolation in your mortal despair. Deceive yourselves, if you can, by denying it or extolling it as rightfully belonging to you. If deception can nourish you, then well and good, deceive yourselves, but let us pity you in your delirium.

So much for the star of the North . . . Poor James Bowie. How quickly your stupid, inane arrogance is dissipated. These fools do not know Mexicans.

—*La Lima de Vulcano*, March 22, 1836

Riding into Gonzales on the afternoon of March 11, General Houston found three artillery pieces and 374 Texian soldiers, much fewer troops than he had expected. There had been no news from the Alamo for days, and the fort's eighteen-pounder, which Travis said he would fire as a daily signal gun to indicate that he was still holding out, had not been heard since Saturday, March 5. Not long after Houston's arrival, two Tejano rancheros met with him to report that the Alamo had indeed fallen on Sunday and that every man of its garrison was slaughtered. Although he secretly believed them, Houston ordered their arrest, hoping to prevent a panic among the townspeople or his troops. He also immediately wrote a letter to Colonel Fannin, who was still in command of Fort Defiance at Goliad, and a transcript of it would soon be published in the newspapers. But a week before the letter was printed in any Arkansas paper, the first unconfirmed report of the Alamo's fall received in Little Rock arrived via another source, the latter's information obtained in a very strange, roundabout way. As printed in the *Arkansas Gazette* on March 29, it followed the news of the first Mexican attack on the Alamo on February 25.

> LATER—*San Antonio re-taken, and the Garrison massacreed.*—Just as our paper was ready for press, a gentleman who arrived this morning, from Red river, informs us that, on Thursday night last, he spent the night, on the Little Missouri, with a man and his family, who had fled from the vicinity of San Antonio after that post was besieged by the Mexicans. This man, he says, informed him, that, on his arrival at Nacogdoches, he was overtaken by two men (one of them badly wounded), who informed him that San Antonio was re-taken by the Mexicans, and the garrison put to the sword—that if any others escaped the general massacre, beside themselves, they were not aware of it.
>
> We give the above report, precisely as it was communicated to us by our informant, who was recently a citizen of this county, and is a man of veracity. We hope it may be unfounded—but fear that our next accounts from that quarter will confirm it.
>
> —*Arkansas Gazette*, March 29, 1836

The next issue of the *Arkansas Gazette* contained the following commentary on developments in Texas, and the fate of the Alamo, as well as Houston's letter to Fannin.

"Arriba!"

"The morning left us feeling quite cool," recalled one Mexican officer in the attacking column under General Martín Perfecto de Cos, as the soldiers waited at a distance of "300 paces" from the Alamo's north wall, for the signal to advance.[1] According to this officer, the signal "was ordered to be given by his Excellency the Sr. president from a battery where he was located, in a direction between North and East: immediately Sr. COS shouted 'Up!' and placed himself at head of the force."[2]

Cos had about three hundred men: six companies of the Aldama *Permanente* fusiliers, three companies of the San Luis *Activo* fusiliers, and the Aldama *cazadore* company, some of the latter possibly armed with sword-bayoneted Baker Rifles. This "light" company acted as a vanguard unit, screening the main body as much as possible by moving and acting wherever necessary, especially as sharpshooters or skirmishers. One cazadore holds a pioneer or Sappers' axe, one of several types probably carried by Antonio López de Santa Anna's troops that morning to facilitate their ingress into the Texian fort.

Its original object of assault being the western half of the north wall, Cos's column would receive such a battering from Texian cannon and long arms positioned there, as well as from friendly fire from Colonel Duque's northeastern column, that it was forced to make a sharp oblique movement and refocus its attack against the northern half of the west wall. There it finally beat its way over and through the wall and into the compound.

In this action, General Cos proved himself courageous by leading his men directly into the sheets of fire and succeeded in erasing some of the shame attached to his name following his surrender of San Antonio three months earlier.

---

1. Decades later, Mexican sergeant Manuel Loranca recalled that the troops "were lying down at musket-shot distance." *San Antonio Express*, June 28, 1878.
2. *El Mosquito Mexicano*, April 5, 1836. This officer was probably Capt. José Juan Sánchez Navarro, judging by similarities in the wording of this newspaper account with that of his diary entries. In his letter he uses the word "Arriba!" to denote what General Cos yelled. Some historians have translated this as "On your feet!" But the Spanish meaning is simply *up*!

LATEST FROM TEXAS—RECAPTURE OF SAN ANTONIO, AND THE MASSACRE OF THE GARRISON, CONFIRMED—We are indebted to the politeness of two gentlemen, who arrived here yesterday morning, on the s. by Mount Pleasant, for duplicate copies of the following letter from Gen. SAMUEL HOUSTON, which may be considered as confirmatory of the distressing news contained in our last paper, of the recapture of San Antonio and the massacre of its garrison. This letter was brought from beyond Nacogdoches, by an intelligent and highly respectable gentleman by the name of Bedford, who had just returned from an exploring tour in Texas, and who came passenger with one of our informants from Natchez. It will be seen, that Gen. Houston does not state that the news is *positively* correct, but expressed his belief that it is; and Mr. Bedford stated to one of our informants that it was fully credited in those parts of Texas through which he traveled after its receipt. He also stated that the cause of the Americans in Texas was considered as hopeless—that great distress prevails among them—and that the roads were crowded with men, women and children, with such of their effects as they could hastily collect, who were fleeing to the borders of the United States, for safety. Their situation, he said, was really deplorable.

One of the gentlemen referred to above, brings a rumor, that three or four of the young men who left this place, last fall, for Texas, are among the slain—one in the general massacre in the garrison, and the others in a skirmish in the vicinity of San Antonio—but, as it is not well authenticated, we suppress their names, and hope the rumor may prove unfounded.

Copy of a letter from Gen. SAMUEL HOUSTON, to Col. J. W. FANNING, jun., commanding at Goliad, dated

HEAD QUARTERS,
Gonzales, March 11th, 1836.

SIR.—Upon my arrival here, this afternoon, the following intelligence was received through a Mexican, supposed to be friendly, which, however, was contradicted, in some parts, by another, who arrived with him. It is,

therefore, only given to you as a rumor, though I fear a melancholy portion of it will be found too true. He states that he left Fort San Antonio on Sunday, the 6th inst.[1]; that the Alamo (citadel) was attacked on that morning at the dawn of day, by about 2,500 men, and was carried a short time before sunrise, with a loss of 520 men, Mexicans, killed, and as many wounded. Col. TRAVIS had only 150 effective men, out of his whole force of 187. After the fort was carried, seven men surrendered, and called for Gen. Santa Anna and for quarters. They were murdered by his order. Col. BOWIE was sick in his bed, and was also murdered.

The enemy expect reinforcements of 1500 men under Gen. Cordiles, and 1500 reserves, to follow them. He also informs that Ugartechea has arrived with two millions of dollars, for the payment of the troops, &c. The bodies of the Americans were burned, after the massacre, in alternate layers of wood and bodies. Lieut. DICKINSON, who had a wife and child in the fort, after having fought with desperate courage, tied his child to his back, and leaped from the top of a two-story building, and both were killed by the fall. I have but little doubt that the Alamo has fallen. Whether the above particulars are all true, may be questionable. I am, sir, your obed't serv't,

SAM. HOUSTON.

P.S.—The wife of Lieut. Dickinson is now in the possession of the officers of Santa Anna. The men, as you will perceive, fought gallantly; and, in corroboration of the truth of the fall of the Alamo, I have ascertained that Col. Travis intended firing signal guns at three different periods of each day, until succor should arrive. The signal guns have not been fired since Sunday; and a scouting party have just returned, who approached within twelve miles of the fort, and remained for forty-eight hours.

S.H.
—*Arkansas Gazette*, April 5, 1836

[1] This line was evidently reworded by the *Arkansas Gazette* because in other papers, such as the *Kentucky Gazette* of April 16 and the *Connecticut Courant* of April 18, it reads: "Ansilma Burgura states that he left the Alamo on Sunday the 6th inst., and is now three days from Arochos Rancho."

More details concerning the two "Mexicans" who imparted the first word of the Alamo's fall are found in this report, originally published in a Mississippi newspaper.

From Texas.—The following letter, which we find in the Natchez Courier, contains the only additional information furnished us by the late mails of the state of affairs in the young republic.

WASHINGTON, (TEXAS)
March 16, 1836.

Dear Sir: An opportunity offering, I write you, not with many pleasant feelings. The Alamo has fallen, and every unfortunate creature murdered and burnt, some even before they were dead. A Mexican, whose daughters live at Beason's, and another, came into Houston's camp at Gonzales, and reported, on the 10th, that on the 6th, at day light, the cavalry surrounded the fort, and the infantry, with scaling ladders, entered the four angles of the fort and were supported until all but seven of the Americans were killed: these called for Santa Anna and quarter, and were by *his* order immediately sacrificed. In the stories of the two Mexicans, there is no material difference. Mr. McNeal (our Natches friend) said that from La Bahia, whence he has just arrived, the country from La Bahia to Bexar is alive with Mexicans; that Fannin is probably surrounded, having attempted to march to the relief of Bexar, and was beat back. Our condition is very bad. To-day we finish the Constitution, hurry through the rest of the business, and prepare for desperate efforts.

James Collingsworth, Col. Carson, of North Carolina, and D. Burnet, are in nomination for President (provisional;) Rusk, Baily, Hardiman, Potter and one of the first named will form the cabinet.—Next Congress will regulate land business. Yours, most truly.

C. B. STEWART.

Ira R. Lewis, Esq. Natchez.

From a letter dated Fort Defiance, Goliad, Texas, March 9th, we extract the following:

We have had no bread for several days. I am nearly naked, without shoes and without money; we suffer much; and as soon as Bexar falls, we will be surrounded by 6000 infuriated Mexicans. But we are resolved to die under the walls rather than surrender.

The express is anxious to start, and I am compelled to close the letter unfinished. Independence has probably been declared. We are in a critical situation. I will die like a soldier.

—*Philadelphia Public Ledger,*
April 19, 1836

On the night of March 13, Houston's chief scout, Erastus "Deaf" Smith, whom he had sent westward earlier in the day to investigate the situation around the Alamo, returned to Gonzales with three survivors of the battle he encountered on the road: Susanna Dickinson, her infant daughter Angelina, and Travis's slave, Joe. Santa Anna had released Mrs. Dickinson, who was escorted by Benjamin Harris, better known as "Ben," black body servant of Colonel Almonte, who carried a flag of truce as well as printed proclamations that communicated the general's intentions, and the reasons for his fierce retribution, to all inhabitants of Texas, both Tejano and American. They were published six months later in the *Telegraph and Texas Register.*

Shortly after the taking of the Alamo, Santa Anna sent with Mrs. Dickinson several proclamations, calculated to intimidate as well as to allure the unwary to acquiescence in his measures respecting what were then termed colonies.

ARMY OF OPERATIONS.

The General-in-Chief of the Army of Operations of the Mexican Republic, to the inhabitants of Texas:

CITIZENS! The causes which have conducted to this frontier a part of the Mexican army are not unknown to you: a parcel of audacious adventurers, maliciously protected by some inhabitants of a neighboring republic, dared to invade our territory, with an intention of dividing amongst themselves the fertile lands that are contained in the spacious department of Texas; and even had the boldness to entertain the idea of reaching the capital of the Republic. It became necessary to check and chastise such enormous daring; and in consequence, some exemplary punishments have already taken place in Saint Patrick, Lipantitlan, and this city. I am pained to find amongst those adventurers the names of some colonists, to whom had been granted repeated benefits, and who had no just motive of complaint against the government of their adopted country.—These ungrateful men must also necessarily suffer the just punishment that the laws and the public vengeance demand. But if we are bound to punish the criminal, we are not the less compelled to protect the innocent. It is thus that the inhabitants of this country, let their origin be whatever it may, who should not appear to have been implicated in such iniquitous rebellion, shall be respected in their persons and property, provided they come forward and report themselves to the commander of the troops within eight days after they should have arrived in their respective settlements, in order to justify their conduct and to receive a document guaranteeing to them the right of enjoying that which lawfully belongs to them.

Bexarians! Return to your homes and dedicate yourselves to your domestic duties. Your city and the fortress of the Alamo are already in possession of the Mexican army, composed of your own fellow citizens; and rest assured that no mass of foreigners will ever interrupt your repose, and much less, attack your lives and plunder your property. The supreme government has taken you under its protection, and will seek for your good.

Inhabitants of Texas! I have related to you the orders that the army of operations I have the honor to command comes to execute; and therefore, the *good* will have nothing to fear. Fulfil always your duties as Mexican citizens, and you may expect the protection and benefit of the laws; and rest assured that you will never have reason to repent yourselves of having observed such conduct, for I pledge you in the name of the supreme authorities of the nation, and as your fellow-citizen and friend, that what has been promised you will be faithfully performed.

ANTONIO LOPEZ DE SANTA ANNA.
Head Quarters, Bexar, March 7, 1836.
—*Telegraph and Texas Register*,
October 11, 1836

From Mrs. Dickinson and Joe, both in their early twenties, was drawn much of the information about the siege and battle of the Alamo that soon appeared in newspapers across the United States. An early, and full, attempt to tell the story was made by the *Telegraph and Texas Register*, and it did not stint on glorifying the defenders' stand in the most heroic terms. It also included the first printed list of the known garrison members, which thus far added up to only 115 (in many cases their first names not known).

MORE PARTICULARS RESPECTING THE FALL OF THE ALAMO.

That event, so lamentable, and yet so glorious to Texas, is of such deep interest and excites so much our feelings that we shall never cease to celebrate it, and regret that we are not acquainted with the names of all those who fell in that Fort, that we might publish them, and thus consecrate to future ages the memory of our heroes who perished in the Thermopylae of Texas. Such examples are bright ones, and should be held up as mirrors, that by reflection, we may catch the spirit and learn to fashion our own behaviour. The list of names inserted below, was furnished by Mr. Jno. W. Smith, and Mr. Navon, and as we obtain more we will publish them. To Mr. Smith, who has rendered good service to Texas, and to Judge Ponton we are indebted for the particulars, as communicated to them by Mrs. Dickinson, who was in the "Alamo" during the siege and assault.

At day-break of the 6th inst. the enemy surrounded the fort with their infantry, with the cavalry forming a circle outside to prevent escape on the part of the garrison; the number consisted of at least 4000 against 140! General Santa Ana commanded in person, assisted by four generals and a formidable train of artillery. Our men had been previously much fatigued and harrassed by nightwatching and incessant toils, having experienced for some days past, a heavy bombardment and several real and feigned attacks. But, American valor and American love of liberty displayed themselves to the last; they were never more conspicuous: twice did the enemy apply to the walls their scaling ladders, and twice did they receive a check; for our men were determined to verify the words of the immortal Travis, "to make the victory worse to the enemy than a defeat." A pause ensued after the second attack, which was renewed on the third time, owing to the exertions of Santa Ana and his officers; they then poured in over the walls, "like sheep;" the struggle, however, did not even there cease—unable from the crowd and for want of time to load their guns and rifles, our men made use of the but-ends of the latter and continued to fight and to resist, until life ebbed out through their numberless wounds and the enemy had conquered the fort, but not its brave, its matchless defenders: they perished, but they yielded not: only one (Warner) remained to ask for quarter, which was denied by the unrelenting enemy—total extermination succeeded, and the darkness of death occupied the memorable Alamo, but recently so teeming with gallant spirits and filled with deeds of never-failing remembrance. We envy not the feelings of the victors, for they must have been bitter and galling; not proud ones. Who would not be rather one of the Alamo heroes, than of the living of its merciless victors? Spirits of the mighty, though fallen! honour and rest are with ye: the spark of immortality which animated your forms, shall brighten into a flame, and Texas, the whole world, shall hail ye like demigods of old, as founders of new actions, and as patterns for imitation!

From the commencement to its close, the storming lasted less than an hour. Major Evans, master of ordnance, was killed when in the act of setting fire to the powder magazine, agreeably to the previous orders from Travis. The end of David Crockett of Tennessee, the great hunter of the west, was as glorious as his career through life had been useful. He and his companions were found surrounded by piles of assailants, whom they had immolated on the altar of Texas liberties. The countenance of Crocket, was unchanged: he had in death that freshness of hue, which his exercise of pursuing the beasts of the forest and the prairie had imparted to him. Texas places him, exultingly, amongst the martyrs in her cause. Col. Travis stood on the walls cheering his men, exclaiming, "Hurra, my boys!" till he received a second shot, and fell; it is stated that a Mexican general, (Mora) then rushed upon him, and lifted his sword to destroy his victim, who, collecting all his last expiring energies, directed a thrust at the former, which changed their relative positions; for the victim became the victor, and the remains of both descended to eternal sleep; but not alike to everlasting fame.

Travis's negro was spared, because, as the enemy said, "his master had behaved like a brave man;" words which of themselves form an epitaph: they are already engraved on the hearts of Texians, and should be inscribed on his tomb. Col. James Bowie, who had for several days been sick, was murdered in his bed; his remains were mutilated. Humanity shudders at describing these scenes; and the pen, as if a living thing, stops to gain fresh force, that sensibility may give way to duty.

Suspended animation has returned to the instrument of our narration, and we continue. Mrs. Dickinson and her child, and a negro of Bowie's, and as before said, Travis's were spared.

Our dead were denied the right of Christian burial; being stripped and thrown into a pile, and burned. Would that we could gather up their ashes and place them in urns!

It is stated that about fifteen hundred of the enemy were killed and wounded in the last and previous attacks.

Colonels.
  W. B. Travis, Commandant
  James Bowie
  David Crocket, of Tenn.
Captains.
  Forsyth, of the regular army
  Harrison, of Tenn.
  Wm. Blazeby, N. O. Grays
  Baker, Miss. Volunteers
  Evans
  Carey, militia of Texas
  S. C. Blair, volunteer militia
Lieut's.
  John Jones, N. O. Grays
  J. G. Baugh, N. O.

Rob't. Evans, mast. ord. Ireland
Williamson, serg't major
Dr. Michison
" Pollard, surgeon
" Thompson, Tenn.
Chas. Despallier
Eliel Melton, quarter master
Anderson, assist't qr. mast.
Burnell, " "
Privates.
  Nelson
  Nelson (cl'k. of Austin, mer.)
  William Smith, Nacogdoches
  Lewis Johnson, Trinity
  E. P. Mitchell, Georgia
  F. Desanque, of Philadelphia
  John (cl'k. in Desanque's store)
  Thurstor
  Moore
  Christopher Parker, Natchez
  Heiskill
  Rose, of Nacogdoches
  Blair, "
  David Wilson "
  John M. Hays, Tenn.
  Stuart
  Simpson
  W. D. Sutherland, Navidad, Tex.
  Doctor Howell, N. O.
  Butler "
  Charles Smith
  McGregor, Scotland
  Rusk
  Hawkins, Ireland
  Holloway
  Browne
  Smith
  Browne, Philadelphia
  Kedeson
  Wm. Wells, Tenn.
  Wm. Cummings, Penn.
  Voluntine, "
  Cockran
  R. W. Valentine
  S. Holloway
  Isaac White
  Day
  Robt. Muselman, N. O.

Robt. Crossman, "
Richard Starr, England
J. G. Ganett, N. O.
James Dinkin, England
Robt. B. Moore, N. O.
Wm. Linn, Boston
Hutchinson
Wm. Johnson, Philadelphia
Nelson, Charleston, S. C.
George Tumlinson
Wm. Deardorf
Dan'l. Bourne, England
Ingram, England
Lewis, Wales
Chas. Zanco, Denmark
James Ewing
Robert Cunningham
Burns, Ireland
George Neggin
Maj. G. B. Jamieson
Col. J. B. Bonham, Ala.
Capt. White
Robinson, Scotland
Sewell, shoemaker
Harris, of Ky.
Devault, of Mo. plasterer
Jonathan Lindley, of Illinois
Tapley Holland
Dewell, blacksmith, N. Y.
James Kinney
Cane
Warner
John Garvin, Mo.
Wornel
Robbins, Ky.
Jno. Flanders
Isaac Ryan, Opelousas
Jackson, Ireland
Capt. A. Dickinson, Gonzales
Geo. C. Kimball "
James George "
Dolphin Floyd "
Thomas Jackson "
Jacob Durst "
George W. Cottle "
Andrew Kent "
Thos. R. Miller "
Isaac Baker "

Wm. King "
Jesse McCoy "
Claiborn Wright "
William Fishback "
Millsap "
Galby Fugua "
John Davis "
Albert Martin "
                    —*Telegraph and Texas Register*,
                              March 24, 1836

A few additional names of possible Alamo victims were included in an *Arkansas Gazette* piece almost three weeks later, as was an episode of no clear origin that had David Crockett bringing in a fifty-man relief force during the siege.

The papers received by us contain nothing farther from Texas. But several gentlemen who came up on the Arkansaw, inform us, that the fall of San Antonio, and the massacre of the garrison, is fully confirmed. Only three lives were spared: those of the lady of Lieut. DICKINSON, a black servant woman, and a child. Among those who were massacred were, we are informed, Col. TRAVIS, (the commanding officer of the post), Col. DAVID CROCKETT, Col. JAMES BOWIE, Col. JESSE BENTON, (a brother of one of the Senators from Missouri), &c. It is also said, (though we believe it is not certain), that Messers. *Charles E. Rice, Nathaniel Dennis,* and *Wm. Badgett,* of this place,[m] are among the slain. Col. Crockett, with about 50 resolute volunteers, had cut their way into the garrison, through the Mexican troops, only a few days before the fall of San Antonio.
                    —*Arkansas Gazette*, April 12, 1836

Rumors that the surviving Alamo defenders had been burnt while still alive began to make their way into a few papers.

Extract of a letter, dated
            MATAGORDA, April 1, 1836.
Some spies taken by Houston, here, reported that the prisoners taken alive at the Alamo, were

_____
[m] Little Rock.

dragged through hot embers, and their flesh cut off previous to being burnt in a pile.
                    —*Richmond Enquirer*, May 17, 1836

The *Memphis Enquirer* gave a paragraph-long summary of the now confirmed news of the Alamo's fall and also indicated that the survivors were "BURNT TO DEATH."

> MELANCHOLY NEWS FROM TEXAS.
> SAN ANTONIO TAKEN BY THE
> MEXICANS—150 TEXIANS SLAIN.
> Such is the report that has had current circulation here for the past three days; and we regret to add our painful fears that all is true. The disastrous news has come by different gentlemen, and from different parts, all stating the fall of San Antonio and its 150 gallant soldiers. The fort it is said was besieged by Santa Anna with several thousand troops, (some say by Cos who is mortally wounded,) and the Texians fought until but six were left alive; that the Mexicans scaled the walls, and BURNT TO DEATH THE GALLANT SIX that remained. Col. Bowie it is said was sick in his hammock, and was one among the burnt. For humanity's sake we wish not to believe this cruel and horrorful report, but our fears confirm it. It is said the Texians slayed 500 of the enemy. A letter is in town dated at Nacogdoches from Gen. Houston, who gives the amount of what we have stated. He received it from a friendly Mexican who saw the storming of San Antonio. San Antonio has undoubtedly fallen. Col. D. Crockett is among the killed.
>   —*Memphis Enquirer*, April 5, 1836

A week later, the same paper published a lengthy account of the battle of the Alamo, buttressed to no small degree by the testimony of Travis's slave Joe as told to George C. Childress, chairman of the recent committee to draft the Texas Declaration of Independence, and in fact, the man largely responsible for writing it. The account also included more names of slain defenders, mostly Tennesseans.

"Capt. Jamison . . . Discharged the Artillery under His Command, Thirty Times'"

As his *soldados* tore their way through sheets of lead, round shot, and scrap iron, Antonio López de Santa Anna on the cold, dark morning of March 6, 1836, marveled at the way "21 pieces of artillery were played by the enemy with great dexterity."[1] Twenty-four years later, San Antonio's 1836 *alcalde*, Francisco Antonio Ruíz, remembered "the deadly fire of Travis's artillery, which resembled a constant thunder."[2] Witnessing the attack from a house in town, Col. Juan Neopmuceno Almonte's black servant, Benjamin Harris, would afterward remark how "the report of the cannon, rifles, and musketry, was tremendous."[3] According to a "summary of facts" about the Alamo battle as they were then known to the citizens of Nacogdoches on March 26, "On the 6th, Capt. Jamison is said to have discharged the artillery under his command, thirty times."[4]

What this last statement probably means is that the Alamo's cannon did not fire much more than thirty times in total during the assault, not that each individual piece shot off thirty rounds. Considering that only about seventeen to twenty-one guns were mounted for use that morning and that many Mexican troops seem to have already reached the base of the walls before the gunners had time to fire, the "thirty times" seems about right. Either Mrs. Susanna Dickinson or Travis's slave Joe might have provided this figure in one of their untranscribed interviews.[5]

Three of the Alamo's guns sat on the fifteen-foot-high platform Gen. Martín Perfecto de Cos's engineers had built in the chancel section of the church in the fall of 1835. (Cos had erected this platform as high as the interior cornices—the horizontal molded ledges where the arches began their upward curve—which stood approximately fifteen feet above the 1836 level of the church floor.) This platform, or tereplain, extended partway into the transept area that formed the "cross" of the building, and was ascended by a scaffold-like "flat ladder," as Gen. Vicente Filisola described it, rising from a spot very close to the front door of the church.[6] The caliber of the guns placed here is not known; three decades later, Sgt. Francisco Becerra of the Mexican army remembered them as "small pieces . . . firing on the cavalry and on those engaged in making the escalade."[7]

Judging by the plat of the fort drawn by Mexican engineer officer Ignacio La Bastida—as well as by the dimensions of the chancel/transept area as it still exists—the size of the tereplain was not large: about twenty-five feet long east-west and twenty-

(Continued)

four feet wide north-south. Filisola noted that upon this "high cavalier or barbette . . . could be placed up to three pieces with some inconvenience."[8] In his 1878 *The Fall of the Alamo*, Reuben Marmaduke Potter claimed that the eastern-pointing cannon was a twelve-pounder but gives no calibers for the other two guns.[9] According to Lt. Col. José Juan Sánchez Navarro, this "high battery of three cannons, called Fortin de Cos [was of] little use because they could only make plunging fire towards the East, with a short and incommodious declination towards the North." The latter observation is nebulous, perhaps indicating that the platform itself had a northward slant to it, or that the wall on the north, hacked down from its original height by Cos's men to create a rough parapet for the battery, was still too high and irregularly slanted to allow "plunging fire" in that direction. With the exception of scattering grape, canister, and scrap shot, the rounds from this particular gun would be most effective against long-range targets in the north.

If all three pieces had been field guns with long split trail carriages, it would have been a particularly crowded platform for any number of gunners to operate upon. But if just one of the cannons had been a pivot gun, mounted on a compact, garrison-type wooden platform with small iron "truck" wheels—which allowed the tube to be pointed in any direction with little effort—the gunners' maneuvering process would have been less challenging. Because pivot guns were known to have defended the Alamo in the fall of 1835, and some of Stephen F. Austin's guns were also pivots, it is a logical assumption that one of them might have been subsequently placed here. According to Lt. Col. Enrique de la Peña, Colonel Romero's column was to

> attack the east front, which was the strongest, perhaps because of its height or perhaps because of the number of cannon that were defending it, three of them situated in a battery over the church ruins, which appeared as a sort of high fortress.[10]

Because Romero's column "had been sorely punished on its left flank by a battery of three cannon on a barbette that cut a serious breach in its ranks," it was forced to shift toward the fort's northeastern corner.[11] To General Cos's engineers, and afterward Major Green B. Jameson—not to mention Lt. Almeron Dickinson and the other men manning these guns—must go the credit for the effectiveness of this position. Responsible for refortifying the Alamo as well as positioning its artillery, Jameson was an amateur engineer but had proved smart and enthusiastic in the task.

At the time of the battle the height of the stone parapet here was between seventeen and eighteen feet. More than two months later, when Gen. Juan José Andrade was ordered to demolish the defensible works of the Alamo, his men hacked down these walls to a point about even with the height of the tereplain: fifteen feet. In just a few years the height of the latter mound was reduced to about twelve feet by erosion, local residents seeking strong stones to build with, souvenir hunters, or simply children rolling the rubble down into the interior of the church.

The strange story that Lieutenant Dickinson had jumped from a high wall of the church with a baby in his arms, only to meet his death below, sprang up quickly after the battle. Sam Houston mentioned it in one of his early letters concerning the Alamo's fall, and now and then others would recall the same event, if the man was not always identified.[12]

Potter also repeated it in his two versions of *The Fall of the Alamo* (1860 and 1878), but his most interesting take on it is found in his handwritten commentary on his own copy of the 1860 monograph.

> The reality of Dickinson's leap has been questioned. . . . I heard it related with some doubt in the earliest verbal accounts which I listened to; but it was afterwards [told] many times by my servant, ex-Sergeant Becero, who said he witnessed it. His reference to it was not suggested by any inquiry or allusion of mine; and though he may have heard it spoken of before by others, it seemed to come up spontaneously among his recollections when he first narrated the actions to me. I therefore consider it authentic. The leap is generally spoken of as being from the terrace roof of the chapple; but Becero, according to my present recollection, said it was from an upper window of the south side. When I first saw the building, there was at the point referred to, not a window, but a small breach or notch in the upper part of the wall, which may have been knocked out to serve as a cannon port. I then supposed that opening to be the right spot for locating that incident.[13]

1. Santa Anna's battle report, March 6, 1836, in *Supplemento al Diario del Gobierno*, March 21, 1836.
2. Account of Francisco Ruíz in Frank W. Johnson, *A History of Texas and Texans* (Chicago: American Historical Society, 1914), 409.
3. Interview with Ben in Rev. Chester Newall, *History of the Revolution in Texas, Particularly of the War of 1835 and '36* (New York: Wiley and Putnam, 1838), 87–89.
4. *Arkansas Gazette*, May 3, 1836.
5. Forty-two years after the battle, Mexican veteran Manuel Loranca claimed that the attack "was so sudden that the fort had only time to discharge four of the eighteen cannon which it had." *San Antonio Express*, June 28, 1878.

(Continued)

6. Gen. Vicente Filisola, *Memorias para la Guerra de Tejas* (Mexico, 1849), 2:184.

7. Recollections of Sgt. Becerra in Todd Hansen, ed., *The Alamo Reader: A Study in History* (Mechanicsburg, Penn.: Stackpole Books, 2003), 457.

8. Filisola in Hansen, *Alamo Reader*, 184.

9. Potter, "The Fall of the Alamo," as reprinted in Johnson, *A History of Texas and Texans*, 411–412.

10. José Enrique de la Peña, *With Santa Anna in Texas: A Personal Narrative of the Revolution*, ed. Carmen Perry (College Station, Texas A&M University Press, 1975), 45–46.

11. Ibid., 48.

12. See, for example, Ibid., 52.

13. Potter's handwritten notes, *Fall of the Alamo* (1860), copy in possession of Phil Collins.

FALL OF SAN ANTONIO AND ITS ONE HUNDRED AND EIGHTY SEVEN GALLANT DEFENDERS.

This melancholy intelligence is confirmed. Geo. C. Childress, Esq., late editor of the Nashville Banner, is now by our side, having left Washington, on the Brassos, on the 19th March. Mr. Childress in conjunction with Mr. Hamilton from Texas is on a mission to Washington, D. C. authorized and accredited by the new government to open a negotiation with the Government of the United States, for the purpose of obtaining a recognition of the Independence of Texas.

The subjoined statement of the fall of San Antonio we have from the lips of Mr. Childress, who received it personally from the servant of the gallant Travis who fell fighting from the ramparts of the Alamo. This servant was the only being left to tell the mournful fate of the Spartan band. He arrived at Washington, and gave the sad intelligence to the governor and council in presence of Mr. Childress. The negro is intelligent, and known to be faithful and honest.

San Antonio fell on Sunday morning the 6th of March, after 8 days siege, by night and day. SIXTEEN HUNDRED of the Mexicans killed in the siege, is the imperishable monument left to their memory by the ONE HUNDRED AND EIGHTY-SEVEN Texians—we may say AMERICANS. History affords no parallel. Since the defence of Thermopylae by the brave Leonidas, the world has witnessed no instance of valor so intrepid, as displayed by the heroes of the Alamo. Not one was taken alive! After eight days and night's constant fighting, besieged by four thousand effective troops commanded by daring officers, the last one of the noble band poured out his blood with sword in hand upon the rampart defended with such desperation.

The servant of the lamented Travis, says his master fell near the close of the siege. That the Texians had picket guards stationed some hundred yards around the Alamo, (as the fort of San Antonio is called,) and upon its walls; that on Sunday morning at about 3 o'clock the guard upon the wall cried out, "Col. Travis the Mexicans are coming!" Whether the picket guards were asleep or killed is not known; they were not heard, if they sounded any alarm. The Mexicans were encamped around the Alamo, out of the reach of its cannon. Col. Travis sprang from his blanket with his sword and gun, mounted the rampart, and seeing the enemy under the mouths of the cannon with scaling ladders, discharged his double-barreled gun down upon them; he was immediately shot, his gun falling upon the enemy and himself within the fort.—The Mexican General *leading* the charge mounted the wall by means of a ladder, and seeing the bleeding Travis, attempted to behead him; the dying Colonel raised his sword and *killed him!* The negro then hid in one of the apartments of the fort, until the spirit of bravery was entirely quenched, when he heard a voice inquiring if there "were no negroes here." The negro replied, "yes here's one," and came out; a Mexican discharged a gun at him, but did him no injury; another ran his bayonet at him, injuring him slightly, when the Mexican officer speaking English interposed and saved him. This officer conversed freely with the negro as also did Santa Anna; this general was there, and made the negro point out Col. Travis; by which conversation he knew his master had killed the general leading the siege, as their blood then congealed together. The body of Col. Travis and his little yet great band were burnt by order of Santa Anna. The lady of Lieut. Dickinson was within the fort and begged to share the honorable fate of her husband; Santa Anna, honor to his name,—thrice honor to his name, here proved himself a soldier, and protected her; he replied "I am not warring against women." He sent her away with the servant who carried this news, and who left her safely near Washington. He has raised the blood red flag of extermination and no quarters, and swears he will not stop until he has planted his banner upon the capitol of our Washington, if he understands our government in the least abets the Texians. If his bones bleach upon any other field than that of Texas, our prophesy fails. Instead of marching against the colonies in the interior, he is now storming Laberdee, (Goliad) defended by a strong fortress with a garrison of about 700 brave Texians, commanded by Col. Fanning, a daring and intrepid officer, who it is tho't will give Santa Anna a *"fanning"* that he little anticipates. Mr. Childress says there are now at least 5000 Texian soldiers in the field. And we are also happy to state on his assertion, that the government is amply supplied with provisions and ammunition, and money. A negotiation has been effected in N. Orleans by the government for $250,000: he also says that many other loans have been offered the government. Santa Anna has threatened the destruction of New Orleans as a "nest of pirates."

Below we give all the information we can obtain upon this exciting subject. The letter from Gen. Houston will be read with great interest.[n] We have been opposed to this Texas

War from first to last; Gen. Santa Anna is now defending his own country; but he should defend it as a soldier,—not as a tyrant; we say we *have been* against the war; but our feelings we cannot suppress—some of our own bosom friends have fallen in the Alamo—were refused quarters and life—young men with whom we have associated—endeared to us by the power of goodness and greatness. We would avenge their death, and spill the last drop of our blood upon the altar of Liberty. "Down with the Tyrant!"

There are feelings now agitating all here, worthy the noblest and the bravest. The spirits of the brave are crying, "revenge!"—the blood of their gallant brothers *will be* avenged. Mississippi and Louisiana are rushing with one heart and voice to the rescue!!! Now's the *hour!*

Jesse Benton, Esq. Mr. C. left at Washington; D. Durham, Esq. at Natchitoches; his son Thomas at Washington.

Mr. C. said he heard a list read of the killed: the following only he recollects.

Charles Haskell, son of Judge Haskell, of Jackson this State, a brave young man, and Maj. Autry of the same place.

John M. Hays of Nashville.

Young Washington of Robertson county.

Young Thomas of do

Cloud, of Kentucky, a most intrepid soldier.

Lieut. Dickinson.

Col. Bowie was sick in his hammock; the negro saw him murdered.

Col. David Crockett is also among the fallen! it is said he fought with heroic desperation to the last, and was one of the last that perished, almost burying himself with his slain.

We fear our young friend from Randolph, David Murfree, as noble and daring a spirit as ever marched to the field of battle, poured out his youthful blood on the walls of the Alamo. Capt. Peacock was there, sick, and young Murfree, at last account, was attending him; the Capt. died, and the brave young hero we are pained to think, has fallen. We have given every minutiae of information within our reach.

A gentleman from Texas a day or two since says he saw Charles Haskell Esq. two days after the battle; but we fear not.

---

[n] Houston's letter to Fannin of March 11.

Before we conclude we would plea for the blood of our brothers. But we make no appeal, lest it offer insult to the chivalry and heroism of Tennessee! The appeal is already made. It rises from the smoking blood that crimsons the Alamo. Its voice crieth from the ground! The scene of the Alamo; the mangled bodies of our brothers and friends, gloriously fallen; the refusal of life; the threats of a tyrant; would any of them, be a sufficient appeal to draw forth our best and bravest blood to avenge its oppressed and fallen kindred. The chivalry of Tennessee can never sleep undisturbed over the blood that is now enriching and already made sacred, the ground of San Antonio; poured from the breasts of her young heroes. The feelings of the brave throughout Mississippi and Louisiana, have burst forth in a volume that nothing but blood, liberty or death can appease. To Tennesseans we make no appeal.

We have a $20 bill for the cause, for any committee raising funds for Texas; and if volunteers are few, our quill shall be placed in the hand of some one of "the fair," and with trusty firelock and bristling bayonet, ourself shall be a host against tyranny—and for Liberty.

—*Memphis Enquirer*, April 12, 1836

The same issue of the *Memphis Enquirer* reprinted a report from the *Natchez Courier* of April 1 about a meeting "on behalf of Texas" in Natchez on March 31 that had also been attended by George C. Childress, during which he had again told the story of the Alamo. Because it contains some additional details, establishing among other things that it was General Martín Perfecto de Cos's brother, Col. Dionicio Cos, not the general himself, who had stabbed at Travis's corpse after the battle, it is included here.

[After several speeches by other attendees of the meeting] Mr. Childress who had just arrived from Texas followed, and though unexpectedly called upon gave a lucid and eloquent exposition of the state of affairs, and recounted the heroism and valor, the suffering and unshrinking firmness of the gallant *one hundred and eighty-seven* patriots, who, before they fell,

overpowered by numbers, slew *sixteen hundred* of their foes. The gallant Col. Crockett, to the last, said Mr. C., continued to "go ahead"—when he fell the corpses of the enemy were literally piled up around him. The brave, young and accomplished Col. Travis, fell from the rampart mortally wounded into the fort. His musket fell forward among the foe who were scaling the wall. After a few minutes he recovered sufficiently to sit up when the Mexican officer that led that party, attempted to cut off Col. T's head. The dying Hero, with a death grasp drew his sword and plunged it into the body of his antagonist, and both together sank into the arms of death. When the conflict was over, and all the gallant band had ceased to breathe, Santa Anna walked among the slain, and ordered Col. T's servant (whom we mentioned yesterday) to point out the corpse of his master. He looked at it in silence, and then turned away. Cos, the brother of the Mexican general that surrendered San Antonio with 1200 men to the Texian force of 320, then came up, and insultingly waved his sword over the lifeless remains of him, whom when alive, he would no more have had the courage to face, than to "beard the lion in his den"—Before the close of the meeting, Gen. Felix Houston addressed his fellow citizens in his usual happy style. He also announced that the next week would find him in the company with the Chairman on his way to Texas, with as many of the lovers of Liberty as chose to accompany them. In alluding to the vain threat of Santa Anna, "to extirpate that den of Pirates at the mouth of the Mississippi, called New Orleans, and to unfurl the banner of Mexico from the walls of the Capitol of the U. States," Gen. H. remarked that this despot would find in Texas, against which he had waged a "war of extermination," American hearts, that would teach this "Second Napoleon," as he has been vauntingly called, that sooner would the Stars and stripes of America wave freely and gloriously from the ancient domes of Mexico.

We have heard it stated as an argument against the Texians, that they are land speculators! Suppose they were land *pirates*, is that any reason why they should be BUTCHERED by a blood thirsty USURPER? Others talk about the "Law of Nations." What is the Law of Nations but the Law of NATURE? Let our government pause upon questions of national law; for it is *their duty*. Let the frigid speculators of the North—the "philanthropists," who may take part with their own and Santa Anna's "brothers," as they severally have styled the slaves of the United States, and of Texas,—let them, we say, cavil about qualms of National law;—but never, *never, while the spirits of Marion and Sumpter* look down upon us from high, will the people of the South—the generous, the high-souled South—as individuals, suffer that fiend, Santa Anna, to hew down *their* brethren when they sue to him for *quarter!*

—*Memphis Enquirer*, April 12, 1836

Another summary of Childress's address to the citizens of Natchez appeared in the *New York Mercury*.

NATCHES, March 31.—*Texas.*—Col. Geo. C. Childers arrived last evening from Texas, and gives us the following authentic particulars of the late disastrous affair of the Alamo. The only individual that escaped, was a negro servant of Col. Travis, who concealed himself, but being discovered and wounded by the Mexican soldiers, was saved by the interference of an officer. He states that all the Texans fell fighting valiantly to the last, with the exception of Col. Bowie, who being sick, was butchered in his bed, and a soldier who during the final massacre, concealed himself, but on coming out and claiming the protection of Santa Anna, was shot down by that savage fiend's orders. Col. Crocket, and Capt. Dickerson, fought with a desperation worthy of a better fate. We are glad to contradict the report that some of the Texians laid violent hands on themselves. They sold their lives dearly, and that barbarian Santa Anna, and his savage hordes, will long remember the terrible fight of Bexar, and the voice of fame, when she proclaims in future time, the names of the illustrious who died in glory's arms, will not omit the horrors of the Alamo.

Col. Fannin with 800 men, was at La Bahia, and felt confident, that in case of an attack,

he could make a successful resistance. Gen. Houston was on the Colorado, with a force of 2500 men. We should have stated above, that Mrs. Dickerson fell into the hands of the Mexicans, and in company with the servant above mentioned, was sent to Gen. Houston's camp. After the slaughter, Santa Anna in person, ordered the bodies of the slain to be thrown in a pile and burned, as stated in the former account.

—*New York Mercury,* April 21, 1836

By far the most complete and detailed account gleaned in large part from statements given by Travis's slave Joe appeared in the *Commonwealth* (Frankfort, Kentucky) of May 25, 1836. The writer appears to be traveling Virginian and diarist William Fairfax Gray. What follows is an intact, unedited transcription of the entire article.

LETTER FROM TEXAS.
Correspondence of the Fredricksburg Arena.
GROCE'S RETREAT, March 20th, 1836.

I sent you an uninteresting scrawl under yesterday's date, not expecting to have an opportunity of writing to you again so soon. But persons are continually coming and going here. Some are every day starting to the United States to raise men, and money, or provisions for the aid of Texas. May success attend their efforts! The members of the Government are diligent in their new duties, and they are likely to have enough to do.

I have this day had an interesting treat. It was the examination of JOE, the black servant of the lamented TRAVIS, who was in the ALAMO when it was taken. He is about 21 or 22 years of age. He is the only male of all who were in the Alamo, when attacked, that escaped death, and he, according to his own account escaped narrowly. I heard him interrogated in the presence of the Cabinet. He related the affair, as far as known to him, with much modesty, apparent candour, and remarkable distinctness for one of his class. The following is, as nearly as I can recollect, the substance of his statement. You will find it in part a repetition of what has already been told—but it corrects the previous statements in some points.

The Garrison was much exhausted by hard labour and incessant watching and fighting for thirteen days. The day and night previous to the attack, the Mexican bombardment had been suspended. On Saturday night, March 5, the little Garrison had worked hard, in repairing and strengthening their position, until a late hour. And when the attack was made, which was just before daybreak, sentinels and all were asleep, except the officer of the day who was just starting on his round. There were three piquet guards without the Fort; but they too, it is supposed, were asleep, and were run upon and bayonetted, for they gave no alarm that was heard. The first that Joe knew of it was the entrance of Adjutant Baugh, the officer of the day, into Travis' quarters, who roused him with the cry—"the Mexicans are coming." They were running at full speed with their scaling ladders, towards the Fort, and were under the guns, and had their ladders against the wall before the Garrison were aroused to resistance.[o] Travis sprung up, and seizing his rifle and sword, called to Joe to take his gun and follow. He mounted the wall, and called out to his men—*"Come on Boys, the Mexicans are upon us, and we'll give them Hell."* He immediately fired his rifle—Joe followed his example. The fire was returned by several shots, and Travis fell, wounded, within the wall, on the sloping ground that had recently been thrown up to strengthen the wall. There he sat, unable to rise. Joe, seeing his master fall, and the Mexicans coming near the wall, and thinking with Falstaff that the better part of valor is discretion, ran, and ensconced himself in a house, from the loop holes of which, he says, he fired on them several times after they had come in.

Here Joe's narrative becomes somewhat interrupted; but Mrs. Dickenson, the wife of Lt. D., who was in the Fort at the time, and is now at San Felipe, has supplied some particulars, which Joe's state of retirement prevented him from knowing with perfect accuracy. The

enemy three times applied their scaling ladders to the wall; twice they were beaten back. But numbers and discipline prevailed over valor and desperation. On the third attempt they succeeded, and then they came over *"like sheep."* As Travis sat wounded, but cheering his men, where he first fell, General MORA, in passing, aimed a blow with his sword to despatch him—Travis rallied his failing strength, struck up the descending weapon, and ran his assailant through the body. This was poor Travis' last effort. Both fell and expired on the spot. The battle now became a complete *melee*. Every man fought "for his own hand," with gun-butts, swords, pistols and knives, as best he could. The handful of Americans, not 150 effective men, retreated to such cover as they had, and continued the battle, until *only one man*, a little weakly body, named Warner, was left alive. He, and he only, asked for quarter. He was spared by the soldiery; but on being conducted to Santa Anna, he ordered him to be shot, which was promptly done. So that not *one white man*, of that devoted band, was left to tell the tale.

Crockett, the kind hearted, brave DAVID CROCKETT, and a few of the devoted friends who entered the Fort with him, were found lying together, with 21 of the slain enemy around them. Bowie is said to have fired through the door of his room, from his sick bed. He was found dead and mutilated where he had lain. The body of Travis, too, was pierced with many bayonet stabs. The despicable Col. Cos, fleshed his dastard sword in the dead body. Indeed, Joe says, the soldiers continued to stab the fallen Americans, until all possibility of life was extinct. Capt. Barragan was the only Mexican officer who showed any disposition to spare the Americans. He saved Joe, and interceded for poor Warner, but in vain. There were several Negroes and some Mexican women in the Fort. They were all spared. One only of the Negroes was killed—a woman—who was found lying dead between two guns. Joe supposes she ran out in her fright, and was killed by a chance shot. Lieut. Dickenson's child was not killed, as was first reported. The mother and child were both spared and sent

---

[o] This significant, but rarely considered, detail—that one or more sections of Mexican troops had planted its ladders against the walls even before the Alamo defenders were out of their sleeping quarters—is mentioned in a few other newspaper accounts attributed to information obtained from Joe.

home. The wife of Dr. Aldridge and her sister, Miss Navaro, were also spared and restored to their father, who lives in Bejar.

After the fight, when they were searching the houses, an officer called out in English, "are there any negroes here?" Joe then emerged from his concealment, and said, "Yes, here's one." Immediately two soldiers attempted to despatch him—one by discharging his piece at him, and the other by a thrust of the bayonet. He escaped with a scratch only from the steel, and one buck shot in his side, which, however, did little damage. He was saved by the intervention of Captain Baragan, who beat off the soldier with his sword.

The work of death being completed, the Mexicans were formed in hollow square, and Santa Anna addressed them in a very animated manner. They responded to it with loud *vivas.* Joe describes him as a light built, slender man, rather tall—sharp, but handsome and animated features; dressed very plainly, somewhat *"like a Methodist preacher,"* to use the negro's own words. Joe was taken into Bejar, and detained several days. He was shown a grand review of the army after the battle, and was told there were 8,000 troops under arms. He supposes there were that many. But those acquainted with the ground on which he says they formed, think that not half of that number could be formed there. Santa Anna took much notice of him, and questioned him about Texas and the state of the army.—Among other things, he asked if there were many soldiers from the United States in the army, and if more were expected? On being answered in the affirmative, he sneeringly said he had men enough to *march to the city of Washington if he chose.*

The slain were collected in a pile and burnt.

Thus perished this gallant and devoted band of men, sacrificed by the cold neglect—the culpable, shameful neglect—of their country-men. Who can read the stirring appeals and calls for help from the despairing Travis, and the bitter reproaches that burst from him but a day or two before the massacre, without feel-ing the blood rush to his face with shame for Texas—shame for the hundreds and thousands

that might have gone up to the rescue—but they would not. Texas will take honor to herself for the defence of the Alamo, and will call it a second Thermopylae, but it will be an ever-lasting monument of national disgrace. "If my countrymen," says he, on the 3d March, "do not rally to my relief, I am determined to perish in the defence of this place, and my bones shall reproach my country for her neglect." Poor fellows—the immolation of a thousand lives cannot restore your gallant spirits, or remove the stigma that your sacrifice has left on the National escutcheon.

—*Frankfort Commonwealth*, May 25, 1836

A shorter version of Joe's experiences as he related them, yet containing some details not found in the preceding two accounts, originally appeared in the *New Orleans Commercial Bulletin*; the letter writer is unidentified. Its most shocking, if historically unsubstantiated, allegation is that Mrs. Dickinson suffered a brutal sexual molestation at the hands of Mexican officers.

From the New Orleans Bulletin, April 11.
Extract of a letter from a friend to the Editor.
AT WHARTON'S PLANTATION, 31st March 1836.
The garrison of the Alamo of Bexar have immortalized themselves. Colonel Travis, who commanded, was a man of transcendent talents. He has a little son 6 or 7 years of age, who will live, I hope, to revenge the death of his sire. The Honourable Davy Crockett died like a hero, sur-rounded by heaps of the enemy slain. Colonel James Bowie was sick and unable to rise. He was slain in his bed: the enemy allowed him a grave—probably in consideration of his having been married to a Mexican lady, the daughter of the late Governor Berrimundi. The enemy had made daily and nightly attacks upon the place for 10 days. The garrison was exhausted by incessant watching; at last the enemy made a final assault with 4000 men, half an hour before daylight, on the morning of the 6th instant. It was dark, and the enemy were undiscovered until they were close to the walls, and before the sentinels had aroused the garrison, the

The Last Moments of William Barret Travis

The earliest known published mention of the death of Lt. Col. William Barret Travis occurred just fifteen days after the battle, when Antonio López de Santa Anna's March 6 battle report appeared in Mexico City's *Supplemento al Diario del Gobierno* on March 21. But no details of just *how* Travis died saw print until the *Telegraph and Texas Register*, its office located at San Felipe de Austin on the west bank of the Brazos, published a lengthy account of the fall of the Alamo in its March 24 edition. The pertinent extract from this account follows:

> Col. Travis stood on the walls cheering his men, exclaiming, "Hurra, my boys!" till he received a second shot, and fell[1]; it is stated that a Mexican general, (Mora) then rushed upon him, and lifted his sword to destroy his victim, who, collecting all his last expiring energies, directed a thrust at the former, which changed their relative positions; for the victim became the victor, and the remains of both descended to eternal sleep; but not alike to eternal fame.

According to this article, the "particulars" of the battle had been related to John W. Smith and Andrew Ponton by Mrs. Dickinson, whose presence in San Felipe is documented at least as early as March 20.[2] Whether Travis's slave Joe had also been in San Felipe is unknown; this particular account only mentions him in passing as "Travis's negro," and does not credit him as a source of any eyewitness testimony.

What *is* known is that on March 20—four days before the *Register* account was printed, and while the widow Dickinson was still in San Felipe—Joe was at Groce's Retreat, fifteen miles north of San Felipe, relating his own account of the battle. By March 20 most of the Convention delegates from Washington-on-the-Brazos had also removed themselves south to Groce's Retreat, fearing that Santa Anna's rapidly advancing columns might cut them off. William Fairfax Gray was among their number, and in his diary entry of the March 20 he writes, "the servant of the late lamented Travis, Joe, a black boy of about twenty-one or twenty-two years of age, is now here. . . . I heard him interrogated in presence of the cabinet and others." Without any input from Mrs. Dickinson, who was still in San Felipe, Joe communicated much the same account of

(Continued)

his master's death as would be published in the *Telegraph and Texas Register* four days later. The relevant quote from Gray's diary follows:

> Travis ran across the Alamo and mounted the wall, and called out to his men, "Come on, boys, the Mexicans are upon us, and we'll give them *Hell*." He discharged his gun; so did Joe. In an instant Travis was shot down. He fell within the wall, on the sloping ground, and sat up. The enemy twice applied their scaling ladders to the walls, and were twice beaten back. But this Joe did not well understand, for when his master fell he ran and ensconced himself in a house, from which he says he fired on them several times, after they got in. On the third attempt they succeeded in mounting the walls, and then poured over like sheep. The battle then became a *melee*. Every man fought for his own hand, as he best might, with *butts of guns,* pistols, knives, etc. As Travis sat wounded on the ground General Mora, who was passing him, made a blow at him with his sword, which Travis struck up, and ran his assailant through the body, and both died on the same spot. This was poor Travis' last effort.[3]

That same day Gray also wrote a letter to the editor of Virginia's *Fredericksburg Arena*, which was reprinted in the May 25 edition of the *Frankfort Commonwealth*. He reiterated that Joe underwent an "examination" on March 20, which means that Gray had to weave together all of Joe's answers into a narrative form. The Travis-related extract follows, which in most respects echoes the above journal quote:

> [Travis] mounted the wall, and called out to his men—*"Come on Boys, the Mexicans are upon us, and we'll give them Hell."* He immediately fired his rifle— Joe followed his example. The fire was returned by several shots, and Travis fell, wounded, within the wall, on the sloping ground that had recently been thrown up to strengthen the wall. There he sat, unable to rise. Joe, seeing his master fall, and the Mexicans coming near the wall, and thinking with Falstaff that the better part of valor is discretion, ran, and ensconced himself in a house, from the loop holes of which, he says, he fired on them several times after they had come in.
>
> Here Joe's narrative becomes somewhat interrupted; but Mrs. Dickinson, the wife of Lt. D., who was in the Fort at the time, and is now at San Felippe, has supplied some particulars, which Joe's state of retirement prevented him from knowing with perfect accuracy. The enemy three times applied their scaling

ladders to the wall; twice they were beaten back. But numbers and discipline prevailed over valor and desperation. On the third attempt they succeeded, and then they came over *"like sheep."* As Travis sat wounded, but cheering his men, where he first fell, General MORA, in passing, aimed a blow with his sword to despatch him—Travis rallied his failing strength, struck up the descending weapon, and ran his assailant through the body. This was poor Travis' last effort. Both fell and expired on the spot.[4]

If Mrs. Dickinson was the source for Travis's killing of the Mexican officer, as well as some other "particulars" of the battle, as stated previously, how was it that she knew such details, considering that during the fighting she and a number of other noncombatants remained sheltered in one of the rooms of the Alamo church, far from the north wall battery where Travis fell? One possibility is that she learned these things from Mexican officers after the battle. According to John Sutherland, the testimony of both Mrs. Dickinson and Joe could be relied upon, even if they related events they had not witnessed, for they would have "received their information from the [Mexican] Army, whilst prisononers [as they] understood the Mexican language and and [sic] it is presumable would give as correct an account" as any given by other eyewitnesses of the battle.[5]

This explanation would make perfect sense were it not for the fact that convention delegates other than Gray who had also heard Joe's testimony at Groce's Retreat did not mention Mrs. Dickinson as having been the source for the details of Travis's death. One of them was George C. Childress, who provided an account of the battle for the *Memphis Enquirer*. According to this, as published in the paper's April 12 edition, Joe had first arrived in Washington-on-the-Brazos.

> The subjoined statement of the fall of San Antonio we have from the lips of Mr. Childress, who received it personally from the servant of the gallant Travis [who] says his master fell near the close of the siege. . . . Col. Travis sprang from his blanket with his sword and gun, mounted the rampart, and seeing the enemy under the mouths of the cannon with scaling ladders, discharged his double-barreled gun down upon them; he was immediately shot, his gun falling upon the enemy and himself within the fort.—The Mexican General *leading* the charge mounted the wall by means of a ladder, and seeing the bleeding Travis, attempted to behead him; the dying Colonel raised his sword and *killed him!* The negro then hid in one of the apartments of the fort.[6]

(Continued)

Childress, then, makes Joe a *witness* to his master's death, Joe fleeing the scene only *after* seeing Travis kill the officer.[7] Another convention delegate, Jesse B. Badgett, provided the editor of the *Arkansas Gazette* with the latest intelligence concerning the Alamo's fall, and mentions "a Mexican deserter" as his source for many of the details of his account. But clearly someone else—either Joe or Mrs. Dickinson, or both—had also provided him with information. On Travis's death, Badgett noted:

> Col. Travis was killed within the first hour of the storming of the garrison, having first killed, with his own hand, Gen. Moro, who led the storming party, by running him through with his sword. On his fall, the command devolved on Adj't Maj. J. J. Baugh, who fell in the course of an hour or two, when the command devolved on Col. David Crockett, who likewise soon fell.[8]

Only someone who had been within the Alamo during the siege would have known about this chain of command arrangement.

Sword in hand, taking down the enemy even as he lay dying—this then became the generally accepted early version of Travis's final moments. It was repeated for many decades in books, articles, artwork, even motion pictures. But during the last half of the twentieth century most Alamo historians began to dismiss this concept as excessively romantic, as too Byronic, or reminiscent of Sir Walter Scott, to be embraced by the sophisticated and cynical modern mind. Some suggested it was simply the dramatic invention of Mrs. Dickinson.[9]

In fact such encounters were hardly uncommon during the age of black powder warfare. A few examples will suffice here. On November 16, 1776, Pennsylvania Col. William Baxter, while "bravely encouraging his men" as British troops overran his redoubt on upper Manhattan island, was killed by a sword thrust from a redcoat officer.[10] At Connecticut's Fort Griswold in 1781, a British officer, stabbing an American colonel with his sword, was in turn stabbed by another American officer.[11] During the early Napoleonic Wars, French general François Argod was killed on the parapet of his fort on the Adda River, sword in hand, while trying to beat back an assault of Austrian troops.[12] At the battle of Buena Vista in 1847, Lt. Col. Henry Clay Jr., badly wounded in both legs, told his retreating men to "place me on my back, face to the foe, place my sword in my grasp, and take this pistol to my loved father, and tell him I died in honor, with my last thought on him and my country." Clay was last seen "lying on his back, fighting with his sword the enemy who were stabbing him with their bayonets."[13]

Again, melodramatic as such moments and attitudes may seem to us now, the military history of two and three centuries ago is rife with them. Travis employing his sword in one last act of resistance is not something found only in a Waverly romance: it was illustrative of the ugly, bloody reality of close personal combat in his day.

Another question asked by the skeptics is, how could a man with a head wound, presumably made by a .75-caliber Brown Bess musket ball, survive long enough, and with enough energy and mental focus, to sword-kill a similarly armed but healthy opponent? The *only* source for Travis having a head wound, however, is the account of the battle written by Francisco Ruíz in 1860 for the *Texas Almanac*. The acting *alcalde* (mayor) of Béxar in 1836, Ruíz wrote that Santa Anna had directed him to help identify the corpses of Travis, James Bowie, and David Crockett. Noted Ruíz: "On the north battery of the fortress lay the lifeless body of Col. Travis, shot *only* [Ruíz's emphasis] in the forehead."[14]

Assuming that Ruíz, twenty-four years after the battle, was correct about Travis's head wound, how indeed could Travis have survived it as long as the accounts claim he did? To begin, we know neither the caliber of the ball that hit him nor the nature of the wound. Santa Anna's troops carried not only .75-caliber bullets but balls of other sizes; in 1985, unfired lead balls from bullet molds of .44, .49, and .69 calibers were unearthed at the site of an L-shaped Mexican trench near the corner of today's East Nueva and Alamo streets, about sixteen hundred feet south of the Alamo.[15] (These may have been bullets for pistols and carbines as well as muskets.) An excavation of part of the Alamo's south gate tambour in 1988 yielded balls of .41, .49, .59, .69, .70, and .72 calibers, probably representing a mix of Texian and Mexican bullets.[16] Santa Anna's *cazadores* were likely equipped with a few British Baker Rifles, which fired a .61-caliber ball. There were also light arms of other manufacture.

Pea-sized buckshot was another favorite of the Mexican infantry; Joe himself was wounded by "one buck shot in his side," after the Mexicans had infiltrated the compound.[17] Buckshot was nothing new in Mexico; at the battle of Peotillos in 1817, the anti-Royalist infantry under General Francisco Javier Mina "had been supplied with buck shot, and many of the men loaded with eighteen in addition to the ball. They committed havoc among the enemy."[18]

It must also be kept in mind that at least two contemporary reports have Travis wounded more than once. And many years after the battle, Travis's brother James visited the battlefield in company with Joe, who told him that his master "was struck by

(Continued)

a rifle ball, but continued to fight."[19] Something else to consider: according to young survivor Enrique Esparza, at the end of the battle Santa Anna's troops "kept firing on the men who had defended the Alamo. For fully a quarter of an hour they kept firing upon them after all the defenders had been slain and their corpses were lying still."[20] At Goliad three weeks later, three Mexican soldiers were assigned to shoot each wounded Texian soldier as he was brought out of the church hospital of the La Bahía presidio "so that if after the discharge of two muskets death should not have been dealt forth, the third soldier placed the muzzle of the musket near their head or breast, and so ended them."[21] Was Travis's head shot really a coup de grace, or simply a bullet fired into an already-dead *Americano* by an enraged *soldado*?

If, however, we allow that this head wound *was* the mortal one, it is not impossible that he might have survived long enough to wield his sword in a final defensive act. A musket bullet to the head was not always immediately lethal; at the battle of Coleto Creek, less than two weeks after the fall of the Alamo, one of James W. Fannin's men named Cash "received a ball in the corner of his head . . . the ball cut the size of it out of his head but did not kill him."[22] Lieutenant Juan Alzucaray, one of the *Zapadore* officers attacking the north wall, was "gravely wounded in the head by grape-shot" but survived the battle.[23] (Grapeshot was essentially a scattering array of lead bullets or even larger iron or copper balls.) In 1933, outlaw Clyde Barrow's brother Buck, after two shootouts with lawmen, suffered three bullets to the head—one of them a .45-caliber slug plowing entirely through his forehead—not to mention getting shot in the hip, shoulder, and back. He was reloading his gun just before being captured, even though brain tissue was oozing from one of his head wounds. While being driven to a doctor's office for treatment, Buck freely conversed with the officers about his life of crime. He managed to live for another six days.[24]

Another controversy stemming from the early reports of Travis's death is his supposed killing of a Mexican general named Mora. In fact there *was* a Gen. Ventura Mora present at the Alamo battle, but he commanded the Dolores cavalry regiment well beyond the walls and was neither personally involved in the assault nor killed that day. Another Mora, Lt. Col. Esteban Mora, *did* participate in the storming of the north wall, yet he, too, survived the battle.[25] On the other hand, a number of Mexican officers of lesser ranks *had* been killed either during the assault or as a result of their wounds—eleven, according to Sánchez Navarro—so it is not inconceivable that a captain or a lieutenant had been felled by Travis's sword.[26]

The widespread misconception that General Mora had led the attack apparently stemmed from information "obtained from a Mexican deserter," as Badgett explained to the editors of the *Arkansas Gazette* in early April. Precisely where and when this soldado was interrogated is uncertain; it might have been at Gonzales, or perhaps Washington-on-the-Brazos. According to the deserter, "on the night of the 5th ult., the Mexicans formed, to the number of 3100 infantry, led by Gen. Moro [sic], in four columns, supported by 2000 cavalry, led by Santa Anna, in person." Those who listened to the deserter evidently assumed that "Moro" also personally led the infantry columns against the Alamo walls; thus, when Badgett described Travis's death, he related how the lieutenant colonel had "killed, with his own hand, Gen. Moro, who led the storming party."[27]

It is an understandable mistake and seems to eliminate both Joe and Mrs. Dickinson as the source for "General Mora" being the slain officer. But that an officer *was* slain by Travis does apparently derive from Joe or Mrs. Dickinson—or both. If Joe did not actually witness the event, either of the two survivors might have overheard Santa Anna's officers conversing about it. One of these conversations might have occurred when Joe was conducted around the smoking fort to assist in the identification of the dead garrison leaders. According to one of the Childress accounts derived from the testimony of Joe and published in the *Memphis Enquirer*, Santa Anna "made the negro point out Col. Travis; by which conversation he knew his master had killed the general leading the siege, as their blood then congealed together." Joe also noted that Santa Anna

> looked at it [Travis's body] in silence, and then turned away. [Lt. Col. Dionicio] Cos, the brother of the Mexican general that surrendered San Antonio with 1200 men to the Texian force of 320, then came up, and insultingly waved his sword over the lifeless remains of him, whom when alive, he would no more have had the courage to face, than to "beard the lion in his den."[28]

Gray's letter from Groce's Retreat, also taken from Joe's deposition, noted that

> the body of Travis, too, was pierced with many bayonet stabs. The despicable Col. Cos fleshed his dastard sword in the dead body. Indeed, Joe says, the soldiers continued to stab the fallen Americans, until all possibility of life was extinct.[29]

Another variant on this episode was first published in the March 28 *Louisiana Advertiser*.

(Continued)

Gen. Cos on entering the fort ordered Col. Travis's servant to point out to him the body of his master; he did so, when Cos drew his sword and mangled his face and limbs with the malignant feeling of a savage.[30]

Thus, we have confirmation in 1836 of what Esparza would recall decades later: that the corpses of the defenders had been mutilated even after death. Joe's honesty—a trait noted by both Gray and Childress—is therefore corroborated. So it must be wondered how, with so many bayonet and sword thrusts making a gruesome perforated wreck of Travis's body, Ruíz could truly say that he had been shot only once, in the forehead. Although the latter wound would certainly be consistent with a situation in which a defender had leaned over the parapet, exposing only his head, shoulders, and arms to fire his weapon, this is simply not what Travis had done.

All the evidence points to Travis actually standing *atop* the parapet of the north wall battery—called *Fortin de Teran* by the Mexicans—not behind it. "Col. Travis stood on the walls"—"Travis . . . mounted the wall"; "Travis . . . mounted the rampart"—as the contemporary testimony from Joe tells us. This is confirmed in Gen. Vicente Filisola's account of the battle: lacking a firestep behind the wall, "it was necessary in order for them [the Texians] to take the offensive to mount the parapet, where as it is easily understood they could not remain for a single second without being killed."[31]

The nature of the battery works there virtually forced Travis to take such a reckless defensive position. According to Filisola, when Cos occupied the Alamo in 1835, the north wall was in such a ruinous condition that, in order to create a battery in its central area, "it was necessary to repair it with timbers of five or six inches in thickness placed horizontally and supported on the outside part with some straight legs, also of timber." The horizontal timbers—the interior basketwork revetting creating the "embrasures and head-guards" of the battery—were further reinforced in front by an earthen parapet and embankment that sloped into the space between the "straight legs" (palisade) and ruined adobe wall.[32]

Sánchez Navarro noted that the height of the battery—that is, the height of its earthen terraced floor, or esplanade—was "eleven feet Mexican yard," which translates into 10.175 feet by US standards.[33] Adding approximately 6 to 6½ feet of cannon embrasure and "head-guards" (cover for the gunners) above the terrace made the total height of the defense work around 16 feet. In his plans of the Alamo, Sánchez Navarro clearly shows these embrasures, and the dirt fill between the ruined wall and outer palisade. It made for a very thick wall, and a somewhat uneven "parapet." No defender could have simply leaned over it and fired into Mexicans massing directly beneath the wall.

Accessing the top of the parapet would have been easy for Travis and his men. Such batteries were often reinforced with defilade traverses—walls of earth, sandbags, gabions, or combinations of same—placed between each gun position perpendicularly to the main wall to protect the cannon and their crews against flanking fire. In the case of the *Fortin de Teran*, these traverses would have also served to buttress the wall as the Mexican battery in the north advanced ever closer. According to Gray's newspaper-published letter, "Travis fell, wounded, within the wall, on the sloping ground that had recently been thrown up to strengthen the wall."[34] And Gray repeated this in his diary: Travis "fell within the wall, on the sloping ground."[35]

This explains how Travis's body ended up "on the north battery of the fortress . . . on the gun carriage," as Ruíz remembered it.[36] Sánchez-Navarro agrees, noting in his 1836 letter, "Their chief called Travis died like a brave man with his carbine in his hand, on the shoulder of a cannon."[37] Reuben Marmaduke Potter, in his early "Attack and Defence of the Alamo," published in the *San Luis Advocate* of November 18, 1840,[38] wrote this about Travis's death:

I have heard different statements as to where and when Travis was killed; but that most to be relied on is, that he was found dead at the breech of a gun, near where the right column entered.

Some early printed versions of Travis's death claimed he had committed suicide: "The brave and gallant Travis, to prevent his falling into the hands of the enemy, shot himself," read the *Louisiana Advertiser* of March 28. Another reported, "Col. Travis stabbed himself to escape the cruelties of the enemy."[39] But quickly the press repudiated these rumors as false. "We are glad to contradict the report that some of the Texians laid violent hands on themselves," wrote the *New York Mercury* of April 21. "They sold their lives dearly."

Lt. Col. Enrique de la Peña misidentified Travis as one of the garrison who did not retreat into the barracks and other buildings after the Mexicans began pouring over the walls. Nevertheless the man he described could easily have been Travis:

Not all of them took refuge, for some remained in the open, looking at us before firing, as if dumbfounded at our daring. Travis was seen to hesitate, but not about the death that he would choose. He would take a few steps and stop, turning his proud face toward us to discharge his shots; he fought like a true soldier. Finally he died, but he died after having traded his life very dearly. None of his men died with greater heroism, and they all died.[40]

(Continued)

1. This is a rare contemporary reference to Travis being wounded more than once. Another account, originating in the *Natchitoches Herald* and reprinted in the May 3 *Arkansas Gazette*, indicated that "Travis fell in the breach . . . prostrate with wounds," before killing the enemy officer.
2. Letter from Groce's Retreat, March 20, 1836, *Frankfort Commonwealth*, May 25, 1836. Susanna Dickinson soon afterward became absorbed into the crowds of fugitives fleeing eastward in the Runaway Scrape.
3. William Fairfax Gray, journal entry, March 20, 1836, in Todd Hansen, ed., *The Alamo Reader: A Study in History* (Mechanicsburg, Penn.: Stackpole Books, 2003), 77.
4. *Frankfort Commonwealth*, May 25, 1836.
5. John Sutherland, draft account of the siege and battle of the Alamo, in Hansen, *Alamo Reader*: 177.
6. *Memphis Enquirer*, April 12, 1836.
7. Childress was the source for another account of the battle, printed in the *Natchez Courier* of April 1, in which he similarly described Travis's heroic death, although without mentioning Joe.
8. *Arkansas Gazette*, April 12, 1836.
9. For example, see William C. Davis, *Three Roads to the Alamo: The Lives and Fortunes of David Crockett, James Bowie, and William Barrett Travis* (New York: Harper Collins, 1998), 733, n. 102.
10. Baxter's redoubt was one of many outerworks of the doomed Fort Washington, which fell that day to General Howe's army. Richard M. Ketchum, *The Winter Soldiers* (Garden City, NY: Doubleday & Company Inc., 1973), 141; account by Alexander Graydon, in Henry Steele Commager and Richard B. Morris, eds., *The Spirit of 'Seventy-Six: The Story of the American Revolution as Told by Participants* (New York: Bonanza Books, 1983), 493–494.
11. Commager and Morris, *The Spirit of 'Seventy-Six*, 730–731.
12. "Field-Marshal Suwaroff and the Campaign of 1799," in *Monthly Chronicle* 3 (January–June 1839): 334.
13. Samuel E. Chamberlain, *My Confession* (New York: Harper & Brothers Publishers, 1956), 131; *A Sketch of the Life and Character of General Taylor by the One-Legged Sergeant* (New York, 1847), 36.
14. Francisco Antonio Ruíz, "Fall of the Alamo" (1860), in Hansen, *Alamo Reader*, 501.
15. *La Villita Earthworks: A Preliminary Report of Investigation of Mexican Siege Works at the Battle of the Alamo*, Archaeological Series Report No. 159 (University of Texas San Antonio: Center for Archaeological Research, 1986), 65, 76.
16. Anne A. Fox, *Archaeological Investigations in Alamo Plaza*, Archaeological Survey Report No. 205 (University of Texas San Antonio: Center for Archaeological Research, 1992), 57–58.
17. *Frankfort Commonwealth*, May 25, 1836.
18. "Events from Robinson's Memoirs of the Mexican Revolution," *Daily National Intelligencer*, January 29, 1821.
19. Davis, *Three Roads to the Alamo*, 732–733, n. 102.
20. Narrative by Enrique Esparza, *San Antonio Express*, May 19, 1907.
21. Account of survivor Joseph H. Spohn, *New Hampshire Patriot*, August 8, 1836.
22. Reminiscence of Abel Morgan, quoted in Jeff Long, *Duel of Eagles: The Mexican and U.S. Fight for the Alamo* (New York: William Morrow and Company, Inc., 1990), 276–277.
23. "The Dead and Wounded of the Zapadores Battalion, Alamo, March 6, 1836," in Hansen, *Alamo Reader*, 439–440.
24. John Neal Phillips, *Running with Bonnie and Clyde* (Norman: University of Oklahoma Press, 1996), 143–156; Miriam Allen deFord, *The Real Bonnie and Clyde* (New York: Ace Books, 1968), 89, 93.
25. Account of Ramón Martínez Caro, 1837, in Hansen, *Alamo Reader*, 384. Esteban Mora would meet his death at San Jacinto.
26. C. D. Huneycutt, *At the Alamo: The Memoirs of Captain Navarro* (New London, NC: Gold Star Press, 1989), March 6, 1836, entry, p. 66.
27. *Arkansas Gazette,* April 12, 1836.
28. *Memphis Enquirer*, April 12, 1836.
29. *Frankfort Commonwealth*, May 25, 1836. Such mutilation of the body of a despised enemy was not unusual as far as the Mexican army was concerned. R. R. Brown, a survivor of the ambush of Col. James Grant's detachment at Agua Dulce, noted: "After Grant fell I saw some ten or a dozen officers go up and run their

swords through his body. He was well known to them, having lived a long time in Mexico. They had a bit of a grudge against him." Frank W. Johnson, *A History of Texas and Texans* (Chicago: American Historical Society, 1914), 423.

30. *New York Evening Post*, April 11, 1836.

31. Filisola's notes in the second edition of his *Memorias* of the war in Texas in Hansen, *Alamo Reader*, 392–393.

32. General Vincente Filisola, *Memorias para la Historia de la Guerra de Tejas* (Mexico, 1849), 2:184–185.

33. A Mexican *vara,* or yard, was 33.3 inches.

34. *Frankfort Commonwealth*, May 25, 1836.

35. William Fairfax Gray journal, March 20, 1836, in Hansen, *Alamo Reader*, 77.

36. Ruíz in Hansen, *Alamo Reader*: 501.

37. *El Mosquito Mexicano*, April 5, 1836. That Travis might have been armed with a carbine when he died, after his other gun had fallen over the wall, should be no surprise: the defenders were said to have been equipped with multiple arms that day, and the nearby artillerymen would have had small arms such as carbines, light muskets, and swords at the ready in case they were overrun by the enemy.

38. Reprinted in other papers, as in the *Madisonian* of December 8, 1840.

39. *New Orleans Commercial Bulletin*, March 28, 1836.

40. José Enrique de la Peña, *With Santa Anna in Texas: A Personal Narrative of the Revolution*, ed. Carmen Perry (College Station: Texas A&M University Press, 1975), 50.

enemy had gained possession of a part of the ramparts. The garrison fought like men who knew there was but a brief space left them in which to avenge the wrongs of their country's possession. When driven from the walls by overwhelming numbers, they retired to the barracks, and fought hand to hand and man to man until the last man was slain—no, there was a man yet left; a little man named Warner had secreted himself among the dead bodies, and was found when the battle was over, and the dead men being removed without the walls of the fort. He asked for quarters; the soldiers took him to Santa Anna, who ordered him to be shot. The order was executed, and the body taken out and burnt with the heroes who deserve as bright a remembrance as those who died on the pass of Thermopylae.

I learnt these facts from a negro boy, the servant of Colonel Travis, whose life was spared—probably in consideration of his kindred blood. There was a woman in the fort—a wife of a Lieut. of artillery. She was taken, and suffered from the Mexican officers the most odious pollution that ever disgraced humanity. She barely escaped with life—but is diseased, and in a situation exciting pity and horror. There are no tidings from Colonel Fannin. Alas, that science and talents and bravery should fall before brute numbers! His wife is here with three infant daughters.
—*Portland Advertiser* (Maine), May 3, 1836

The supposed abuses committed upon Mrs. Dickinson were given "confirmation"—without actually characterizing what they were—in a Philadelphia paper following the report's first publication in New York.

Confirmation of the horrid outrages on the person of Mrs. Dickinson—It is with the deepest pain and with feelings of utter shame and mortification, for the honor of our species, that we state from *undoubted authority,* that the rumored outrages of Santa Anna's officers and soldiers on the person of Mrs. Dickinson, after the death of her husband, Lieut. D. at the fall of Alamo, are not only true, but of a still more infamous character than has yet been published. It would be shocking to humanity and offensive to all the decencies of society to state in print the particulars of this transaction, which is of itself sufficient to bring down not only the scorn of every civilized people, but the wrath of an avenging heaven on the heads of the perpetrators.

—*N.Y. Star.*
—*Philadelphia Public Ledger,* May 21, 1836

Additional details of Mrs. Dickinson's ordeal were included in a letter written in Natchez by William Parker to the editor of the *Mississippi Free Trader and Natchez Gazette*. Parker had received these details firsthand from Major Ira Ingram, who had spoken with Mrs. Dickinson in Gonzales. The pertinent extracts follow.

To the Editor of the Free Trader:
Sir,—Having just returned from a trip to Nacogdoches, made for the purpose of obtaining information concerning the fate of my son,[p] who fell in defending the Alamo, I take this method to correct the erroneous news in circulation among my fellow citizens, concerning the position of the belligerents of Texas, and concerning the part which the Indian tribes, near the frontiers, are likely to act in this momentous and exterminating crusade against civil and religious liberty.... Concerning the position of the belligerent armies, up to the 13th inst. inclusive, my information is drawn from the written dispatches of the Commander-in-Chief of the Texian army, and from very full verbal communications, made by Mjr. Ingram direct from Gen. Houston's Head Quarters and now at my house in this city.... My informant above quoted states, that on his way in, he saw and conversed with Mrs. Dickerson, the widow of one of the gunners at the fall of the Alamo, and the only white person in the fortress at the time of the final catastrophe of this post, who was spared by the enemy, and permitted to return into the American settlements. He says that Mrs. D. informed him, that of the five who, for a moment survived their companions, and threw themselves on the victor's clemency, two

were pursued into her room, and subjected in her presence to the most torturing death. They were even raised on the points of the enemy's lances, let down and raised again and again, whilst invoking as a favor, instantaneous death to terminate their anguish, till they were at last too weak to speak, and then expired in convulsion.

William Parker.
Natchez, April 29th, 1836.
—*Mississippi Free Trader and Natchez Gazette,*
April 29, 1836

Another account of the battle that first appeared in the *New Orleans Commercial Bulletin* was reprinted in a New York City paper about a month later.

The following communication from the New Orleans Commercial Bulletin, gives some interesting particulars of the assault at San Antonio:—
BRAZORIA, TEXAS, March 17, 1836
To the Editor of the Commercial Bulletin:
Our force in the Alamo at the time of its being stormed, amounted to one hundred and eighty-seven, every soul of whom was put to death—extending mercy only to a female, the wife of one who nobly lost his life in the engagement—to tell the melancholy news. The Mexican force was six thousand; having bombarded the Alamo for two days without doing any execution, a tremendous effort was made to take it by storm, which they succeeded in doing after a most sanguinary engagement, lasting near an hour. History, neither ancient nor modern, can give evidence of such bravery and heroism as was evinced on the occasion. No quarters were called for until every soul had perished save seven, who on asking quarters, and being told none could be given, again commenced the work of death and the last died as did the first, without yielding an inch of ground.
The Alamo was attacked at four different points; the walls being only about breast high, the enemy was enabled to scale them by means of scaling ladders, our force not being sufficient to protect it at all points.
The loss of the enemy was great; 533 killed, 600 mortally wounded, and many slightly.

---

[p] Christopher Adams Parker.

Thus the fort which cost us so much hard fighting, has been retaken at great cost to Texas, but much greater to the enemy. It is much to be regretted that our force in the garrison was not greater, though it was always supposed to have been sufficient to maintain the post.[q] Texas has to mourn the loss of Wm. B. Travis in command. The celebrated Col. David Crockett, of Tennessee, was among the slain. His conduct on the occasion was most heroic; having used his rifle as long as possible by loading and discharging, and the enemy crowding upon the walls, he turned the breech of his gun, and demolished more than twenty of the enemy before he fell.

The declaration of independence I presume you have received ere this.

—Mercantile Advertiser and New York Advocate, April 26, 1836

In the second week of April, Little Rock received a fresh account of the battle and of its ripple effect throughout Texas from Jesse B. Badgett. A member of the Alamo garrison in early February, Badgett, along with Samuel Maverick, had been elected by its soldiers to represent them at the convention at Washington-on-the-Brazos, and he was one of the signers of the Declaration of Independence. Much of what follows was drawn by Badgett from the testimony of a "Mexican deserter," and obviously from additional information supplied by Joe or Mrs. Dickinson.

LATEST FROM TEXAS—DIRECT.

Mr. JESSE B. BADGETT, who was one of a small party who left Little Rock, for Texas, last fall, and who was a member of the late Convention at Washington, the Seat of Government of Texas, returned to this place, on Sunday evening last, direct from that country, and has communicated to us the following highly interesting news from the theatre of war.

San Antonio, as heretofore stated, was taken by storm, by an overwhelming force, commanded by Gen. Santa Anna, in person, early on the morning of the 6th ult. The whole force of Col. Travis, at its capture, was only 183 men (14 of whom were on the sick list, and unable to take part in the battle). They were ALL SLAIN. The siege lasted 14 days and nights, and, from the best information that could be obtained from a Mexican deserter, the Mexican loss during the siege amounted to 881 killed, and about 700 wounded. The deserter reported that, at 11 o'clock on the night of the 5th ult., the Mexicans formed, to the number of 3100 infantry, led by Gen. Moro, in four columns, supported by 2000 cavalry, led by Santa Anna, in person, and, at between 3 and 4 o'clock, on the next morning, at a signal given by throwing up rockets from the town, the attack was simultaneously made on all sides of the garrison. The besieged, considering their small number, were well prepared for the assault—every man being provided with at least a brace of pistols and four or five rifles and muskets, all loaded, besides knives—and poured in a most deadly fire on the assailants, with cannon and small arms. The struggle, for a short period, was most desperate, but the garrison could not long sustain the attack of so overwhelming a force. By half an hour before sun-rise, on the morning of the 6th, the gallant spirits who had so bravely defended the post, and killed and wounded more than five times their own number, were numbered with the dead—and Santa Anna, surrounded by his life-guards, made his triumphant entry into the fort. In this assault, the Mexican loss was said to be 521 killed, and nearly the same number wounded.

Col. Travis was killed within the first hour of the storming of the garrison, having first killed, with his own hand, Gen. Moro, who led the storming party, by running him through with his sword. On his fall, the command of the Texians devolved on Adj't Maj. J. J. Baugh, who fell in the course of an hour

---

[q] This incredible supposition, despite the letters from colonels Neill and Travis begging for reinforcements, may help explain why much of Texas was slow in sending help to the Alamo. Even Governor Henry Smith, in his open letter to "Fellow-Citizens of Texas" in the March 2 issue of the *Texas Republican* (see chapter 7), allowed that the Alamo could sustain the Mexican siege for at least thirty days.

or two, when the command devolved on Col. David Crockett, who likewise soon fell.[r]

The following are the names of such of the officers who fell in defending San Antonio, as are recollected by Mr. Badgett:

Col. W. B. Travis, commandant; Col. James Bowie, Col. David Crockett, Maj. Green B. Jameson, (formerly of Ky.), Capts. Baugh, of Va., Blair, formerly of Conway county, A. T. Cary of La., Baker of Mississippi, Blasby of the New Orleans Grays, J. G. Washington of Tenn., Harrison of Tenn., Forsyth of N. York, Jones do, J. Kemble of Gonzales; Lieuts. Dickinson and Evans; Sergt. Maj. Williamson from Philadelphia; Dr. Mitcherson of Va, Surgeon Pollard.

The previous report of the death of Col. JESSE BENTON, is incorrect. Mr. Badgett saw him near Nacogdoches, about the 25th, on his way to Jonesborough, Miller county, in this Territory, where a volunteer company was organizing, and with whom he intended marching for the seat of war.

On the 11th March, Santa Anna marched from San Antonio, with 3000 men, for Laborde (Goliad), which post was defended by Col. Fanning, with about 800 men, with plenty of provisions and ammunition, and who said he could defend his position against any force the Mexicans could bring against him.

On the 12th, Gen. Almonte and Col. Ball (an American) left San Antonio for Gonzales, with 2000 men, but, after marching 27 miles, to the Sea willow river,[s] changed their direction, and bent their course toward Laborde, to assist Santa Anna in reducing that post. From the Sea willow, they sent Mrs. Dickinson, the widow of Lieut. Dickinson, who was killed in the storming of San Antonio, with her child (who was not killed, as previously reported) and servant,

to Gen. Houston's camp at Goliad; and at the same time Gen. Almonte sent his servant to Gen. Houston, with Santa Anna's proclamation, offering amnesty to the inhabitants and Texian troops, provided they would yield submission, and give up their arms, to the Mexican authorities. Gen. Houston detained the servant, and sent to the Mexican commander, by a Spaniard, a copy of the Declaration of Independence recently agreed on at Washington.

Mr. Badgett left Washington (Seat of Gov't) on 18th March, and, on the next day, arrived at General Houston's camp, at Beason's Crossing of the Colorado, 90 miles this side of San Antonio, to which point Gen. H. had fallen back from Gonzales, which he burnt before abandoning it. Gen. H. was fortifying his camp, had about 2000 men, and reinforcements were arriving daily. Mr. B. thinks there is no doubt he had a force of at least 4000 men, in a few days after he left his camp.

On the 20th, Mr. Badgett left Gen. Houston's camp, on the Colorado, and on the next day, reached Washington, where the Convention were still in session, but adjourned on the following day, 22d, after forming a Constitution for the Republic of Texas.

An express returned to Gen. Houston's camp, on the 19th, from the vicinity of Col. Fanning's post, which was besieged by Santa Anna, and the express waited part of a day and a night without being able to gain admission—during which period a heavy cannonade was kept up by both parties. The result had not transpired when Mr. B. left.

On his return from Gen. Houston's camp, Mr. Badgett says the road was literally crowded with volunteers, and thinks he passed at least 1000 men before he reached the Sabine—all hurrying to join their brethren in arms on the frontier.

Mr. B. left Natchitoches on the 30th, at which time no information had been received there of a second battle having been fought, and the Mexicans defeated with the loss of 800 or 1000 men, as mentioned in our summary of Texian news on our first page. He thinks there is no foundation in the report, which reached us via Natchez.

---

[r] This battle command structure—not mentioning the sick James Bowie of course—may have been decided upon while Badgett was still in San Antonio because he was not discharged until February 14, and by that time Travis, Bowie, and Crockett were all present. Or it might have been arranged after Badgett left, the information coming from Travis's Joe
[s] Cibolo River or Creek.

The report of the death of his brother, *Mr. William Badgett*, it gives us pleasure to state is incorrect. He left him with the forces of Sam Houston, on the Colorado. He, however, we regret to state, confirms the report of the death of Mr. *Charles B. Rice* and Mr. *Nathaniel Dennis*. They were of the party of Col. Johnson, who were all cut off (except J. and one other) at San Patricio, by a large party of Mexican troops, who promised to spare their lives on condition of their surrendering, and, on their giving up their arms, commenced an indiscriminate massacre of them. This occurred a short time previous to the fall of San Antonio.

—*Arkansas Gazette*, April 12, 1836

The following accounts of the siege and battle originally appeared in the *Louisiana Advertiser* of March 28, although slightly edited versions were also printed in the *New Orleans Bee* and the *New Orleans Post and Union* of the same date. The *Advertiser*'s full text was republished in the *New York Evening Post* the following month.

From the Louisiana Advertiser, March 28.
THE FALL OF BEXAR—THE ENTIRE OF THE TROOPS IN GARRISON PUT TO DEATH—COLONELS CROCKETT AND BOWIE KILLED!

We are indebted to a gentleman, passenger on board the steamer Levant, from Natchitoches, for the annexed letter, giving the particulars of the fall of Bexar—it is a copy of one addressed to the editor of the Red River Herald:

"Sir:—Bexar has fallen! Its garrison was only 187 strong, commanded by Lieut. Col. W. Travis. After standing repeated attacks for two weeks, and an almost constant cannonade and bombarding during that time, the last attack was made on the morning of the 6th inst. by upwards of 2000 men, under the command of Santa Anna in person; they carried the place about sunrise, with the loss of 520 men killed, and about the same number wounded. After about an hour's fighting the whole garrison was put to death, save the sick and wounded and seven men who asked for quarter. All fought desperately, until entirely cut down; the rest

were cooly murdered. The brave and gallant Travers, to prevent his falling into the hands of the enemy, shot himself. Not an individual escaped, and the news is only known to us by a citizen of Bexar, who came to our army at Gonzales—but from the cessation of Travis' signal guns, there is no doubt of its truth. The declaration of independence you have no doubt received, and you will, in a few days, receive the constitution proposed by the republic.

Cols. James Bowie and David Crockett are among the slain—the first was murdered in his bed, to which he had been confined by illness—the latter fell fighting like a tiger. The Mexican army is estimated at 8000 men; it may be more or less."

A. BRISCOE.

FURTHER PARTICULARS.—We learn by the passengers of schooner Camanche, 8 days from the Brazos River, that the war at Texas has at length assumed a serious character. Many of those who left this city, determined to lay down their lives in the cause of Texas, have bravely yielded them up at Bexar. Three young men from our office, we learn, are among the slain; the names of Wm. Blazeby and Robert Moore have been mentioned to us; that of the other we could not ascertain.

On the 25th February the Texian garrison in Bexar of 150 men only, commanded by Lieutenant Colonel W. B. Travis, was attacked by the advanced division of Santa Anna's army of about 2000 men, when the enemy were repulsed with the loss of many killed and wounded, variously estimated from 450 to 600, without the loss of a man of the garrison.

This great slaughter was ascribed to the fact, that every man of the garrison had about eight guns loaded by his side. About the same time Colonel Johnson, while reconnoitring to the westward of San Patricio, with a party of 70 men, were surrounded in the night by a large body of Mexican troops. In the morning the commander sent in a summons to surrender at discretion, which was refused, and an offer to surrender as prisoners of war made. This was acceded to by the Mexican officer, but no sooner had the Texians marched out of their encampment and stacked their arms, than a general fire was opened upon them by the whole Mexican force, when the prisoners endeavoured to escape—three only of whom effected it, among them Colonel Johnson and one man who had been wounded.

Between the 25th of Feb. and 2d March the Mexicans were employed in forming entrenchments around the Alamo and bombarding the place. On the 2d of March Col. Travis wrote that 300 shells had been thrown into the Alamo, without injuring a man.

On the 1st of March, 32 men from Gonzales made their entry through the enemy's lines, and reached the Alamo—making the whole number in the garrison 182.

On the 6th March, about midnight, the Alamo was assaulted by the entire force of the Mexican army, commanded by Santa Anna in person. The Texians fought desperately until daylight, when seven only of the garrison were found alive. We regret to say, that Col. David Crockett and his companion Mr. Benton, also the gallant Col. Benham, of South Carolina, were of the number who cried for quarter, but were told there was no mercy for them. They then continued fighting until the whole were butchered. One woman (Mrs. Dickinson) and a wounded negro servant of Col. Travis's were the persons in the Alamo whose lives were spared. Gen. Bowie was murdered in his bed, sick and helpless. Gen. Cos on entering the fort ordered Col. Travis's servant to point out to him the body of his master; he did so, when Cos drew his sword and mangled his face and limbs with the malignant feeling of a savage.

The bodies of the slain were thrown into a heap in the centre of the Alamo and burned. On Gen. Bowie's body being brought out, Gen. Cos said that he was too brave a man to be burned like a dog; then added, *pero no es cosa, echadlo*—never mind, throw him in. The loss of the Mexicans in storming the place was estimated at not less than 1000 killed and mortally wounded, and as many more disabled—making their loss in the first assault, between 2000 and 3000 killed and wounded. It is worthy of remark that the flag of Santa Anna's army at Bexar was a *blood red one*, in place of the old constitutional tri-colored flag. Immediately after the capture of the place, Gen. Santa Anna sent Mrs. Dickinson and Col. Travis' servant to Gen. Houston's camp, accompanied by a Mexican with a flag, who was bearer of a note from Santa Anna, offering the Texians peace and a general amnesty, if they would lay down their arms and submit to his government. Gen. Houston's reply was, "True, sir, you have succeeded in killing some of our brave men, but the Texians are not yet whipped." The effect of the fall of Bexar throughout Texas was electric. Every man who could use a rifle, and was in a condition to take the field, marched forthwith to the scene of war. It was believed that not less than 4000 riflemen were on their [way] to the army when the Camanche sailed, to wreak their vengeance on the Mexicans, and determined to grant no quarter.

Gen. Houston had burnt Gonzales, and fallen back on the Colorado with about 1000 men.

Col. Fannin was in the fort at Goliad, a very strong position, well equipped with munitions and provisions, and from 400 to 500 men.

The general determination of the people of Texas seemed to be to abandon all the occupations and pursuits of peace, and continue in arms until every Mexican east of Rio del Norte should be exterminated.

—*New York Evening Post*, April 11, 1836

In Rhode Island, the editor of the *Providence Journal* received a letter from a Texas correspondent summing up the Alamo battle and other events as they stood near the end of March. It was full of the writer's own gloomy prognostications.

FROM TEXAS.

The following letter, although it contains little that has not before been published relative to the war in Texas, will be read with deep interest for the details with which it fills up the general outline of the struggle.

Correspondence of the Providence Journal.

BRAZORIA, (Texas) March 26, 1836.

With this document please accept my assurance of continued friendship. I send it to you under the presumption that some little item of our political proceedings will be interesting.— Texas is now in a state of complete chaos— divided into a thousand conflicting parties and clashing interests. Santa Anna is between the Guadaloupe and Colorado rivers, with an army of 8000 Mexicans. Gen. Samuel Houston is at the head of our army on the Colorado, consisting as far as is known, of 2000 brave Texians.—There is much alarm, however, throughout Texas, for the success of our *now* foolish struggle for *Independence*. While fighting for the Constitution I was with them; but I never was, and never can be for Independence, in our poor and penniless state and with so sparse a population. All of the families west of the Colorado are on the removal towards the Brazos, and even towards the Sabine. They are leaving the results of many years' labor to a brutal foe, and flying for life alone, for the war which Santa Anna brings, is not honorable, but a war of extermination. Early in March, the Alamo (castle) at San Antonio, garrisoned by 190 of our best and bravest, was taken by 2000 Mexicans, and every one put to the sword.—Albert Martin, Esq., our townsman, was there, and died fighting like a man and a hero. Davy Crockett, the high-minded, generous Crockett, suffered with the rest. Twenty-four Mexicans, however, fell to his unerring shots from the rifle presented him by the young men of Philadelphia. He died, while using it as a club, in the thickest of the fight. I have lost many intimate associates, whom I regret; there is one consolation, however: they will be nobly, gallantly avenged, and Santa Anna may rue the "Conquest of the Alamo!" Every patriot, however, I find, fears more from Texas herself, than from an invading foe.

There is so much difference of opinion—so much contrariety of habit, interest and manner, that years must roll over this beautiful but unfortunate land, ere the people can assimilate, and find a capability of governing themselves. Our Army is much increased by volunteers, who came for the aid of our cause—after fighting our battles will they return with guns in their hands and become quiet citizens? Will they look on the large land holders with complacency? Will they not rather go for Agrarian laws and sap the civil foundations of the Republic? Texas has much to fear—the cloud which impends is dark and dreadful, and though war with its lightning, may successfully pierce its folds, yet the time is distant, I imagine, when the sunlight of peace and prosperity will illume its shadowy grandeur.
—*Providence Journal*, April 26, 1836

In another Texas town, Nacogdoches, Travis's "Victory or Death" became the motto of its leading citizens, who were determined to make good the Alamo's sacrifice. The following article also provides a number of intriguing details about the battle not found in any other account.

From the *Natchitoches Herald.*

At a meeting of the citizens of Nacogdoches, on the 26th March, the following preamble and resolutions were unanimously adopted, and ordered to be published:

The citizens of the municipality, in common with all Texas, feeling the profoundest grief for the loss of their gallant countrymen in the storming of Fort Alamo, at St. Antonio de Bexar, on the 6th of the present month, and entertaining the highest admiration for their heroism, cannot refrain from a public expression of these sentiments.

Brave men, struggling for liberty in distant lands, receive the sympathy of generous and liberal minds of all nations; but when their achievements are in our own immediate defence, they arouse the strongest sensations of the heart. The reflection comes home to our bosoms, that valuable lives have been offered up a willing sacrifice, for our safety and precaution. We embalm it with our tears, and give utterances to our gratitude and praise. The tongue of eulogy shall bestow its tribute, and the record of history emblazon their fame.

It is due to the occasion, that we give a summary of facts. Cols. Travis and Bowie, with one hundred and eighty-seven volunteers, and only one hundred and fifty effective, for fourteen days maintained an extensive fortress against a

Mexican army of eight thousand strong, commanded by the FAMOUS Gen. Santa Anna. During this period, they repulsed the enemy in repeated assaults by day and night, repaired successive breaches in the fortification, made a terrible slaughter of the assailants, and remained almost unhurt. On the morning of the 6th, worn out by incessant toil, exhausted nature could endure no longer, and during a temporary suspension of the bombardment, they sought repose. The enemy became apprised of their situation, by the supposed treachery of a Mexican, in the fort, and surrounded it with their whole force of infantry and cavalry. They were roused from their sleep by the cry, "The enemy on the wall"—and as giants, they arose to the fight, and thrice drove them back. Before undaunted courage, the whole host cowered, and were forced again to the charge at the point of the lance.[1] They came in thousands, and as a herd of cattle, overrun a handful of men. But the gallant band remained undaunted to the last. The conflict was terrible, and almost superhuman. Five hundred and twenty one of the enemy were slain, and as many wounded. In previous encounters, they had sustained an equal loss. This statement is credible from the fact, that the fort contained cannon and muskets, to a very large amount, captured by the gallant Milam, at the surrender of Gen. Coss, and that each man was armed with five to ten loaded pieces, for every assault. On the 6th, Capt. Jamison is said to have discharged the artillery under his command, thirty times. The generous Bonham, who, with thirty brave fellows, had entered the fort during the siege, was forced from his comrades, and eighteen Mexicans laid around him. David Crockett, (now rendered immortal in story), had fortified himself with sixteen guns, well charged, and a monument of slain foes encompassed his lifeless body. Their few details are evidence of the facts of all. They

were determined to conquer or die. From a merciless enemy, they had no quarter to expect, and resolved to ask none. Every man fought to his last breath, and NOT ONE SURVIVES. The chivalric Travis fell in the breach, and prostrate with wounds, grasped his sword, and with the last ebb of life, felled to the earth the officer who first entered the fort, and they were both extended lifeless corpses.

The tongue of every noble spirit of whom we speak is silent in death, and we anticipate in a succinct and perfect narrative, the future story of their fame. They died martyrs to liberty; and on the altar of their sacrifice will be made many a vow that shall break the shackles of tyranny. Thermopylae is no longer without a parallel; and when time shall consecrate the deeds of the Alamo—Travis and his companions will be named in rivalry with Leonidas and his Spartan band.

The impotent revenge of the Mexicans, in mutilating the dead bodies of these brave men, and in denying them the rites of sepulchre by burning them in heaps, we cannot forbear to mention, as deserving the execration of all mankind, as an evidence of their deep-rooted ferocity. It was indeed an appalling sight to the usurper Santa Anna to behold such havock of his myrmidons by a handful of intrepid volunteers, and we are told he stood aghast at the spectacle! He might truly have exclaimed—"a few more such victories, and I am destroyed." And that he will be destroyed, the whole country has every confidence.

Resolved, 1st. That we entertain the highest admiration for the sublime and noble defence of Fort Alamo, by our lamented countrymen; and that we will ever venerate their memory.

2d. That we call upon the government of Texas to obtain a correct list of the names of these patriots, and preserve it in the archives for the future award of appropriate honors.

3d. That we offer our deepest sympathy to the relatives of these distinguished worthies.

4th. That animated by their spirit, we will continue to maintain the good cause in which we have embarked, and adopt the motto of the Alamo, "Victory or Death."

HENRY RAGUET, Chairman.
—*Arkansas Gazette*, May 3, 1836

---

[1] Santa Anna's cavalry had been positioned in key locations to prevent the escape of both garrison members and fleeing Mexican soldiers, but this passage maintains that their lances also pushed entire sections of troops back into the attack.

A strange rumor about the attacking Mexican soldiers having been inebriated on the morning of March 6 was mentioned in the following extract.

Correspondence of the Journal of Commerce, Matagorda (Texas), March 28.

Santa Anna has taken possession of San Antonio, putting to the sword all who remained alive in the Fort, about a dozen in number—all the others, say 150, have been killed during the bombardment. About 1000 Mexicans were killed. The famous *Davy Crockett* was in the Fort, and when the Mexicans entered, was sick in bed.—He however called for his arms, with which he killed 14 Mexicans, and then throwing them down resigned himself to his fate. The retaking of the Fort, it is said, would not have been effected but for the influence of liquor, which had been used to excess. I do not, however, vouch for this. In any case the Mexicans have not much to brag of, for the Fort was much exposed, and they ought to be ashamed that they had not taken it sooner.
—*Albany Evening Journal* (New York),
April 26, 1836

A Massachusetts paper summed up Crockett's demise in matter-of-fact terms.

A writer from Texas says, that when fort Bexar was taken, Col. Davy Crockett was sick in bed, but he just got up, took his rifle and killed fourteen Mexicans, and then agreed to be shot.
—*Gloucester Democrat*, April 29, 1836

Back in Arkansas, more details of the battle itself—as well as of Crockett's heroic role in it—continued to arrive.

The following letter from a friend in Miller County, contains all that is *certainly* known with regard to matters in Texas.—Flying reports are abundant, but nothing certain. Of this much, however, we are sure. *Unless the number of American volunteers in Texas is doubled, Santana will inevitably conquer.*

SULPHUR FORK, April 7, 1836
Bejar has fallen into the hands of the Mexicans, and the garrison indiscriminately put to the sword. Only one woman and a negro were left living. They report that the Mexicans kept up a continual fire on the fort for ten days and nights, without intermission, and then retired; and as soon as the firing ceased every man in the fort fell to sleep, and the Mexicans were on the walls before they were discovered. The work of death then commenced in earnest. Five hundred and twenty of the Mexicans are said to have fallen inside of the walls, and something over four hundred in the twelve or fourteen days fighting previous. The Hon. David Crockett is no more. He was one of the heroes who were in the fort when it fell. Twenty-three of the colored hireling slaves of Santa Ana were seen to fall before the muzzle of his rifle, and after the massacre he was found with the breech of his gun broke off, and it grasped by the muzzle in his left hand, and his butcher knife in his right. Both told a tale of death—for they were bathed in the blood of his enemies.

Thirty-seven men who were in their beds sick, were inhumanly butchered, and the whole number, amounting to 187 men, were thrown together in one heap, and burned.

General Houston is on the Colorado, with fifteen hundred troops, and between four and five hundred are on their march to join him. Two hundred and forty more from New York are at Brazoria, and ready to march. Both have joined him before this. Col. Fanning is at La Bahia, with eight hundred men.

The whole of the Mexican forces were reported to be about eight thousand men, when they first arrived in Texas, and it is thought that they have lost two thousand of that number in killed and wounded, since their arrival.
—*Arkansas Advocate*, April 22, 1836

The slow dispersal of news in 1836 meant that by the fourth week in April Kentuckians had still not read a complete list of the known Alamo dead. The following was reprinted from the *Louisville Journal.*

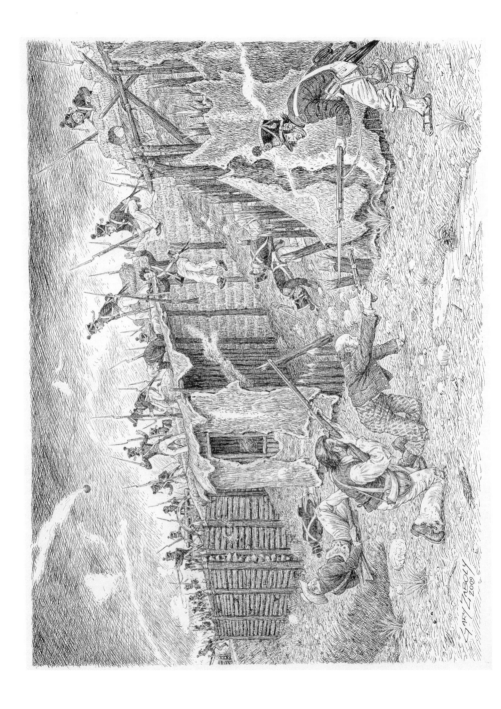

They Came over 'Like Sheep'"

The combined testimony of Travis's slave Joe and Mrs. Susanna Dickinson provided the telling detail that, once Texian resistance on the walls collapsed, the Mexican soldiers "came over 'like sheep.'" But the *Frankfort Commonwealth* of May 25, 1836, suggests that this particular quote may have come from Mrs. Dickinson, not Joe. During the battle several men, including her husband, had rushed into the Alamo church room where she and her daughter were sheltered, telling her that the enemy were over the walls and that all was essentially lost. One of them may have used the "sheep" analogy to underscore how impossible the situation had become.

The scene depicted here is the moment when the grenadier companies of the reserve column began jumping over the eastern section of the north wall. Combined with the *Zapadore* battalion, this column totaled some four hundred men, and was led by Colonel Augustín Amat. The previous attempts by the columns of Duque and Romero to climb up the palisade bulwark protecting the fragile north and northeast walls had been stymied by a fierce Texian defense, and by the attackers' own crowded disorder below. But when Antonio López de Santa Anna sent in the reserves, the sheer momentum of their numbers helped drive them up and over the walls.

At far left is the earthen ramp ascending to the north wall's central three-gun battery, the *Fortin de Teran,* as the Mexicans called it (on its platform William Barret Travis met his death). To its right is the blasted ruin of a *chamacuero,* a *jacale* built of upright posts and covered with hides instead of plaster.[1] This "hide house" had been the property of Carmel de los Reyes, the son of one of the presidial troopers who had been barracked in the Alamo in pre–Texas Revolution days.[2] Such chamacueros had been fairly ubiquitous in San Antonio in earlier decades.[3]

The Mexican battery to the north had been pounding this wall for seven days, and the defenders had to transform themselves into amateur engineers, working around the clock, to keep enough dirt shored up against it as a buttressing. Here and there they reinforced the dirt slopes with rough log revetments. Much of the north wall had been built of adobe brick, which poorly resisted solid round shot. The two howitzers of Santa Anna's north battery had also lobbed powder-filled shells *over* the wall to explode inside the compound, and perhaps even hot shot, which would have incinerated combustible parts of the fort's structures. Thus, chances are that the post-and-hide chamacuero, by the morning of March 6, was in a shredded, splintered condition.

(Continued)

1. Mardith K. Schuetz-Miller, *The History and Archaeology of Mission San Juan Capistrano, San Antonio, Texas* (Austin: State Building Commission, Archaeological Program, 1968), 194.
2. James E. Ivey, *Mission to Fortress: The Defenses of the Alamo*, unpublished typewritten manuscript in the collection of the UTSA Center for Archaeological Research, 14.
3. Paul A. Ramos, *Beyond the Alamo: Forging Mexican Ethnicity in San Antonio, 1821–1861* (Chapel Hill: University of North Carolina Press, 2008), 44.

TEXAS.

The last mails from the South furnish us with some additional information on the subject of the late transactions in Texas. We expect to receive, in a day or two, a list of the names of the brave spirits, who were massacred at San Antonio. As yet, we have seen but eight or ten names, among which is that of a Mr. Cloud, of Kentucky, who is said to have been "a most intrepid soldier" to have died "fighting like a wounded tiger." John M. Hays, of Nashville, is also among the fallen.

Calvin Henderson, Esq. writes from Washington, the capital of Texas, that he was in the Convention Hall when the mournful intelligence of the massacre arrived. One of the members instantly rose and made a most stirring and inflammatory appeal, and the whole assembly clenched their teeth and stamped the floor with rage. The first measure of the Convention was to order a draft of two-thirds of the population, confiscating the property of all, who should refuse to serve. Mr. Henderson says, "Poor David Crockett was one of the Garrison. His bravery was more than gallant—his example animated every body; his death was worthy of himself—he certainly killed 25 of the enemy during the siege! Tell his friends to *come and avenge his death.*" Mr. Childress, one of the gentlemen, departed from the Texian Convention to the U. S. Government to obtain the recognition of the independence of his country, says, that there are now at least 5000 Texians in the field, and that the Government is amply supplied with provisions, ammunition, and money. From his statement it appears, that the Government has effected a negotiation in New Orleans for $250,000 and received offers of many other loans.
      —*Kentucky Gazette*, April 23, 1836

In New York City, the *Herald*'s editorialist—perhaps James Gordon Bennett himself—pulled out all the stops in elevating the fallen garrison to the pantheon of war heroes, and in condemning "the inhuman monster" Santa Anna and his "race of miscreants."

TEXAS.

About four hundred and eighty years before the Christian era, a man, palsied with fear crossed the Eurotas, and entered breathless in the ancient city of Sparta. He soon collected around him a group of old men, women, and children. Spartan taciturnity was unbroken—their looks of surprise put the question. "I am from Thermopylae, your king Leonidas is slain—I am the only survivor—three hundred Spartans held at bay the whole Persian army, for ten days—they fell to a man, covered with wounds, defending the liberty of Greece—I only am left to tell—look at that wound—rouse Spartans, rouse." The news of that disastrous day, flew like lightning from Mount Athos to the remotest shores of Peloponnesia. Thebes, Athens, Corinth, all were in consternation. But what of it? Did they despair? Did they despond? The barbarous massacre of Leonidas only roused to deeper vengeance and higher daring the whole people of Greece, Athenians, Thebans, Corinthians, Spartans, Achaians, and all forgot their local feuds—cast to the wind their private quarrels, and united to a man in resisting the military tyranny of Persia, the countless hosts of Xerxes—the myriads of ignorant barbarians who dared to invade the classic soil of Hellas. They assembled at Platea—they fought—they conquered—they drove the invader back to his jungles and his forests. Greece was triumphant—liberty secure—and civilization unscathed.

Such is a brief view of the crisis through which Greece—beautiful enchanting Greece passed and for the first time established the principle that courage guarantees freedom—and the blood of the devoted patriot only waters more freely the tree of liberty.

What Thermopylae was to ancient Greece—what Bunker Hill has been to the United States—so will Bexar be to Texas.

The bloody, brutal massacre of the gallant little garrison of Bexar or San Antonio, will rouse a spirit of noble vengeance throughout the United States, only to be paralleled by the sensation produced in ancient Greece, on the fall of Leonidas being known throughout her smiling land. Alas! poor Davie Crockett! where be thy sarcasms now! thy shrewd remarks! thy pointed absurdities! thy cunning stories whose very vanity made them a delightful study to the philosopher!—all gone—all chopfallen—all lost but in the recollection of those who knew thee!

It is utterly impossible at this distance from the scene of action, to realize the horrors of the bloody massacre perpetrated by the Mexicans at San Antonio, against bone of our bone and flesh of our flesh.

The sensation realized at New Orleans, at Mobile, at every town on our western and south western frontier, is without a parallel in the history of human excitement, since the fatal day of Bunker Hill, when the blood of freemen flowed freely for a similar cause. It is idle—utterly so—futile—completely so, to enter into an examination of miserable technical points, in the affairs between Mexico and Texas. Under the form of a legitimate war, Santa Anna has perpetrated deeds more atrocious than those of the pirate on the high seas—of the wandering, houseless Arab of the desert. Not content

with overwhelming the gallant little band of 187 patriots commanded by Col. Travis, by forty times their number, their very remains are mutilated—their hallowed ashes are scattered to the four winds—by those fiends actuated by the spirit of demons, and spirited on by the vengeance of hell itself.

Is it possible to hold terms at all with such a race of miscreants as these Mexicans have proved themselves to be? No—never. The period of vengeance has arrived—the cup of wickedness is turning over. Let the people of the United States rouse as one man—let them demand of their government the instant recognition of the independence of Texas—let the Mexican embassy be drummed out of the country. They only represent a band of savages worse than the Seminoles. Not a moment is to be lost. The blood of our murdered brethren in the Alamo, cries to high heaven for instant and immediate vengeance. The inhuman monster, Santa Anna, has thrown his last cast. The government in Mexico is toppling to its foundation. He cannot conquer Texas—he may retard its peace—its prosperity—its independence—but he never can reduce that beautiful land of the brave and free, if the people of the United States still retain the slightest throb resembling that which animated the hearts of their glorious ancestors.

Let a meeting be instantly called in the largest hall in New York. The Commissioners of Texas are now among us. Let us hear what they have to say—let us sympathize—let us act.

—*New York Herald,* April 14, 1836

On the same day, an editorial in the *New York Sun* concerning Texas took a less acclamatory, and sometimes cynical, view of developments there, and attempted to put the Mexicans' slaughter of the Alamo garrison into historical perspective.

From Texas.—The Star of last evening has new intelligence from New Orleans about Texas, which it heads "Glorious News from Texas," but which appears to us to be mere glorification:

Extract of a letter, dated New Orleans, March 29, 1836—"In my next, I shall have the pleasure to advise you of the extermination of Santa Anna's army. The rumor of the day is, that he has offered to capitulate, and let us alone in future, if safe conduct of himself and army, to the west of the Rio Grande be conceded to him. *Not granted.*"

The Texians are, no doubt, as determined as they are brave; but the above rumor appears, at least, to be premature, and looks very much like a gasconade. The Star says the above rumor "is no doubt correct," but what is the news upon which it forms so sanguine an opinion? Why merely the following:

"Col. Fanning with 500 men at the fort at Goliad, and a detachment of about 1000 men, of Santa Anna's army, has besieged him there. The volunteers from Matagorda, would march directly on that point, and by a simultaneous sortie from the fort, and attack from the volunteers in the rear of the detachment, it was expected the enemy would be routed, and Col. Fanning could then march with an increased force, and fall upon the rear of Santa Anna's main army, near San Antonio."

Now we wish well to our Texian countrymen, and hope that these intended plans and simultaneous sorties may be successfully executed; but it is evident that at present they exist only in the visions of hope, and we see no use in tantalizing the public's mind with "glorious news" created by the imaginative. We strongly suspect that the "Galveston Bay, and Texas Land Company" would supply us with such "glorious news" for six months to come, if they could keep back stubborn facts.

Our expectations, or rather sincere hopes, of the success of our Texian brethren are founded on their bravery and perseverance, and upon the strong excitement which is created in their behalf throughout the country by the cold-blooded massacre at Bexar—a massacre, which though *not* a violation of the strict laws of arms, under the circumstances of the case, was nevertheless a revolting outrage upon the superior claims of civilized humanity. If a garrison persists in defiance after it has been summoned to surrender, and is at length carried by assault, the laws of war place the lives of the prisoners

at the mercy of the captors, who have a right to put them to death; and although civilization generally spares their lives by an act of grace, there are many melancholy instances in modern warfare in which this has not been done. The *Commercial Advertiser,* in an article upon this point, says that our own General Wayne ordered all the Garrison of Stony Point to be put to death, in revenge for the massacre of Paoli; but being wounded he was preceded in command by an officer who countermanded the order. During the last Peninsular War in Europe, an indiscriminate massacre of the captured defenders of fortresses was not an infrequent occurrence. The Mexicans at Bexar, were doubtless doubly exasperated by the great loss of life which their ranks had suffered from the Texian garrison after its defence was hopeless, and we cannot but think that there was much more of chivalrous bravery than of military prudence in the obstinate defence of that fort against besiegers whose numbers ensured them victory, and from whose character no mercy could then be expected. Our brave countrymen, however, did not sell their lives cheaply, for the last accounts from New Orleans assert that more than 1000 Mexicans were either killed or wounded before the fort was captured.

The enthusiasm in New Orleans in behalf of the Texians, is said to be so great that the city resembles a military barracks; and although the number of Texians actually in the field is not represented as being more than 1500, crowds of volunteers were every day marching to their aid.

—*New York Sun,* April 14, 1836

A totally unsympathetic view of the Alamo's fall was published, not surprisingly, in an abolitionist newspaper, the *Republican Monitor* of the upstate New York town of Cazenovia. To make its point, it included an extract from a New York City paper.

The Texian War.—It is by such appeals as the following, from the N. Y. Evening Star and the Journal of Commerce, that the sympathies of the people of this country are sought to be enlisted in behalf of as scurvy a set of ingrates and straggling political adventurers as ever disgraced

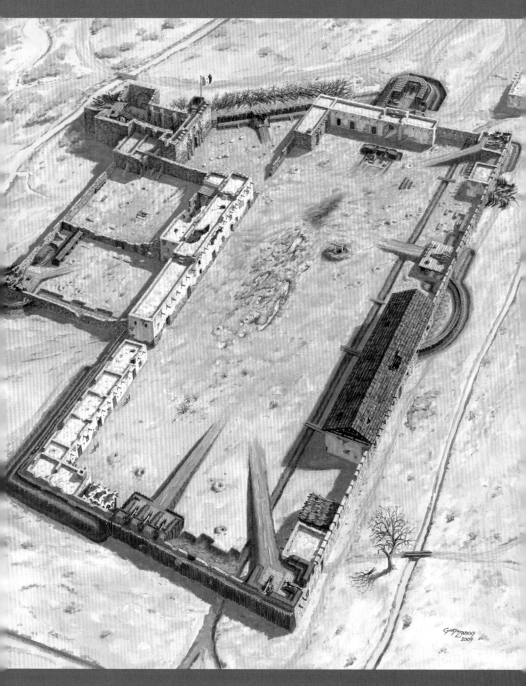

The Alamo as seen from the northwest, 1836

The Alamo during the 1836 Siege

What did the Alamo look like during the storied siege of February 23 to March 6, 1836?

In attempting to answer this, modern writers and artists (myself included) have generally placed a too-heavy reliance on postbattle drawings and paintings—primarily those made between 1837 and 1849—that depicted what remained of the Alamo long after the Mexican army had destroyed and abandoned it in late May 1836. What these on-the-spot pictures actually show us, then, is a rubbly Alamo, a fort deliberately stripped of its main defensible elements, including all of its curtain walls as well as some entire houses and parts of other buildings, in order to guarantee that the Texians, barring a monumental construction effort, would never again use it as a stronghold.

As these pictures do not give us an accurate image of the Alamo during its siege, neither can a clear understanding of its defense works be drawn from any of the written descriptions of the ruins made during that same period by travelers, military men, and even a handful of historians. Based on what they saw and what little they learned of the actual history, a few of them drew speculative plans of the 1836 compound. These plans also continue to mislead.

In order to reconstruct the Alamo's appearance during Gen. Antonio López de Santa Anna's siege, we must first appreciate how truly extensive its subsequent dismantlement was. Entrusted with an unambiguous task—"to demolish the Alamo's fortifications, render them useless for all times and under any circumstances, and to spike the guns captured from the enemy"[1]—General Juan José Andrade carried out his orders with swift and thorough efficiency. Observing the Mexican troops in Béxar as they began the job of destruction on May 22, 1836, captive Texas surgeon Joseph H. Barnard wrote in his diary, "they are now as busy as bees tearing down the walls, etc." Two days later he recorded how they had also set on fire the wooden ramp leading up to the high cavalier battery platform at the eastern end of the church. Then he added:

> The Alamo was completely dismantled, all the single walls were leveled, the fosse filled up, and the pickets torn up and burnt. All the artillery and ammunition that could not be carried off were thrown in the river.[2]

The doctor's account closely echoes the instructions found in *A Treatise on Field Fortification, and Other Subjects Connected with the Duties of the Field Engineer* (1834), by Captain J. S. MaCaulay of the Corps of Royal Engineers. That is, if a post "is to be abandoned, destroy the fortifications, fill in the ditches, set fire to the abatis, break down the palisades, fraises, and dams, &c.; which done, commence your retreat."[3]

US newspapers offered only sketchy reports of the Mexican army's evacuation of San Antonio; one such mention was found in "a letter from a citizen of Texas."

> The enemy spiked all the cannon, threw them into the river, blew up the Alamo, left San Antonio, and joined the main army at La Bahia.[4]

When Santa Anna complained to ad interim Texas Republic president David G. Burnet about the treatment he was receiving as a prisoner of war, supposedly in violation of the treaty he had signed, Burnet replied, in part:

> I am induced to advert to another fact, in relation to which it would be diffi-cult to extend the same charitable exculpations to the officers of the Mexican army. It has been reported that the walls of the *Alamo*, at Bexar, have been prostrated, and that the valuable brass artillery attached to that fortress, have been melted down and destroyed. There were many painful, and pleasing, and glorious reminiscences connected with that Alamo, which renders its wanton dilapidation odious to every Texan spirit; and your excellency need not be informed that the destruction of it was an infraction of the armistice, and a violation of the treaty.[5]

In its immediate postrevolution existence, the mutilated Alamo was not without new residents (aside from numerous bats, snakes, owls, and swallows who were "for-ever passing in and out like bees around a hive").[6] Parties of Texas army regulars or militia would occasionally be billeted inside the remaining barrack buildings, and pris-oners were sometimes held in the church. Eventually local Tejano citizens reclaimed and repaired some of the rooms that also survived along the line of what had been the west wall, and moved into them.

Tourists began visiting the remains of the Alamo as early as 1837. Two years later, one of them noted that the fort was "a heap of ruins, having been destroyed by the

Mexicans at the last storming of the Alamo, three years ago. The church and fortress are now as desolate as the dwellings of Monia."[7]

In 1842, *New Orleans Picayune* editor George W. Kendall observed, "The Almo [sic] is now in ruins, only two or three houses of the inner square being inhabited."[8] Englishman William Bollaert visited the site the following year and heard "an old Mexican woman" sadly remark, "I never look into the ruins of the Church without shedding a tear; not half the walls are now to be seen."[9]

Traveler William A. McClintock noted the overall appearance of the fort in 1846.

> The Castle [church building] is an irregular parallelogram built of large blocks of soft limestone finely cemented together. A wall formerly enclosed the fortress, court-yard, offices etc. containing an area of about one acre of ground, this wall has the appearance of having been in a state of utter ruin for a long time past; and is only discernible from the heap of rubbish elevated a few feet above the surrounding plain.[10]

Many years after his own first visit to the Alamo in 1845, one old Texan recalled:

> it looked as it did at the time of the memorable siege. Not a stone had seemingly been disturbed. The blood stains were visible on the walls. It was a veritable ruin, partly from the destruction caused by the battle, but mostly from its long abandonment as the abode of man.[11]

Of course this was not an Alamo looking "as it did at the time of the memorable siege," when it had fairly brimmed with such military appurtenances as batteries, ramps, tambours, palisades, traverses, bonnets, battlements, embrasures, ditches, banquettes, and so on. But as the years went by, many of these engineered defense works slipped from the local memory and were rarely if ever mentioned again. They became lost to time, even as many people began to assume that the Alamo church, alone, had been the *entire* fort in 1836, and the sole target of the Mexican assault.

The first serious English-speaking Alamo historian, Reuben Marmaduke Potter, attempted to do early justice to the history as well as to the military architecture of the fort. Long before his initial visit to what was left of the compound in 1841, Potter, a resident of Matamoros, had become fascinated with the subject, interviewing *soldado* veterans of the battle as they returned to Mexico following their failed 1836 campaign. From these and other firsthand accounts he began to weave a narrative, "Attack and Defense of the Alamo," which eventually appeared in the *San Luis Advocate* of November 18, 1840. What follows is his summation of the composition of the fort during the siege.

> The Alamo, as I have heard it described, was an enclosure nearly of a quadrangular shape, and surrounded by a wall varying in height from five to ten feet; the area being traversed by inner walls, which partitioned into three subdivisions. In one angle was a chapel; and in the different subdivisions of the area, apartments of different sizes were built against the walls. Several of these had been prepared for defence, and the largest, a saloon extending along one of the partition walls, had a parapet of hides and earth within, to cover the lower parts of the windows. The chapel and its environs, with the aid of some raised works, forming the most commanding positions in the fort, and was mounted with one or more guns. About twenty pieces were planted in different parts of the fortress, but, from its extent and situation, only a few could be brought to bear at once upon a storming party, if judiciously brought up. A part of the wall was dilapidated and some of the cannon ports, which had been hastily and rudely broken out, were so large as to serve as breaches for the enemy's entrance. One side of the Alamo was covered by the river San Antonio, which divided it from the town of Bexar. The whole area was so extensive that a thousand soldiers would have been barely competent to have manned its circuit.[12]

There are particular military and architectural minutia in the above paragraph that could only have sprung from sources familiar with the Alamo compound, and Potter was correct when he wrote that he had "gathered more clear and explicit details than I think have yet been published." Twenty years later he would publish the first of two additional studies that expanded on his initial article: the paperbound 1860 monograph *The Fall of the Alamo: A Reminiscence of the Revolution in Texas* and, eighteen years after that, "The Fall of the Alamo," for *Magazine of American History* (January 1878). In both works he included simple outline maps of the fort, largely based on the measurements and observations he had made

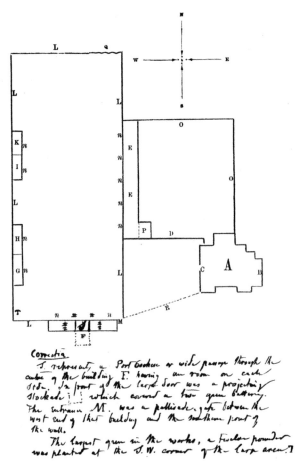

Correction
S. rehouseout, a PortCookee or wide passage through the
centre of the building. E. having an room on each
side. In front of the large door was a projecting
stockade ! ' which covered a two gun battery.
The entrance M. was a pallisade, gate between the
west end of that building and the southern point of
the wall.
The largest gun in the works, a Pedro pounder
was planted at the S. W. corner of the large area.?

Reuben Marmaduke Potter's plan of the fort from his
Fall of the Alamo *(1860),* with his own handwritten notes added
after publication.

at the site in 1841, with keynoted descriptions of salient points. He came closer than any other nineteenth-century North American historian to getting the Alamo's fortifications right, although his interpretation was still an error-laden, vastly incomplete picture.

Other plats of the Alamo were also drawn in the decades immediately following the battle, but the majority of these were either surveys for establishing old or new ownership claims in the compound grounds, or maps of the ruins and vicinity (sometimes delineating new structures built within them) made by the US Army during its occupation beginning in the late 1840s.[13] None of them attempted to re-create the fort's 1836 military makeup.

A plan of the compound printed in Henderson Yoakum's 1855 book, *History of Texas, from Its First Settlement in 1685 to Its Annexation to the United States in 1846,* was obviously based on one of these surveyed plats, and also failed to show any of the fort's 1836 defense works.

It was not until 1917, with the publication of Adina De Zavala's *History and Legends of the Alamo and Other Missions in and around San Antonio,* that a hand-copied version of one of Capt. Green B. Jameson's original plans of the Alamo saw print. It proved a goldmine of military and architectural information because it was accompanied by Jameson's key delineating specific rooms and quarters, redoubts, breastworks, batteries, portholes, powder magazine, and so on, as well as "contemplated" additions to the fort. In mid-January and mid-February 1836, respectively, Jameson had sent out at least two copies: one to Governor Henry Smith and one to General Sam Houston.[14]

By the middle decades of the twentieth century three important contemporary plans of the Alamo, drawn by two Mexican officers with Santa Anna's division in San Antonio—Lt. Col. José Juan Sánchez Navarro y Estrada and Col. Ignacio de Labastida—had been reproduced in publications both north and south of the border. Also accompanied by keys, they added immensely to our knowledge—and frequent confusion—concerning the Alamo as a military position. They showed not only the extensive fortifications erected by General Martín Perfecto de Cos within and without the perimeter of the old mission in 1835, but also the sometimes makeshift ones added by the occupying Texians between December 1835 and March 6, 1836.

The combination of the new and the old evidence allowed for a reinterpretation by a fresh crop of historians and illustrators, and for the first time, Col. William Barrett Travis's fort took dimensional shape on the printed page in persuasively graphic fashion. Yet even as books, articles, drawings, and paintings—not to mention motion pictures—strove to get it right, the Alamo that invariably emerged resembled a kind of broken-down, armed hacienda with its defenders leisurely walking the flat roofs or banquettes, sometimes leaning against stone parapets to scrutinize the terrain for enemy movements or the help that never came. It was an all too casual picture; and in fact, it was not supported by the historical documentation.

One of the frequently overlooked aspects of the Mexican siege was that, aside from sorties made by the defenders, or an occasional skirmish, the besiegers rarely saw the besieged. Santa Anna explained it this way in his report to Mexico City dated February 27, 1836.

> I have so successfully occupied myself with the harassment of the enemy at their position, that they have not even shown their heads above the walls.[15]

If the general was often guilty of hyperbole, in this case his statement is not without support. Wrote Lieutenant-Colonel Sánchez Navarro in his diary entry of March 2, "The enemy did not show themselves behind their parapets." Two days later he noted:

> The tactics of the enemy are unchanged. It is only known that there are men in the Alamo by the cannons and rifles that they fire. Nothing else is heard except the blows of hammers and various curses.[16]

Exposing themselves to Mexican cannon fire without good reason—and in consequence, those parts of the walls they stood behind—would of course have been reckless, especially as the bombardment only grew more lethal as Santa Anna's batteries eventually covered all four sides of the fort. General Pedro de Ampudia's "Report on the consumption of munitions . . . in its batteries during the siege" recorded that 334 rounds of solid shot, 112 grenades (each fired with double cartridges of powder), and 86 rounds of cannister had been fired at the Alamo over twelve days of siege. That adds up to 532 projectiles either hurtling into the compound or striking its walls (averaging just under 45 rounds per day).[17]

In his March 3 letter to the president of the Convention at Washington-on-the-Brazos, Travis noted, "I have so fortified this place that the walls are generally proof against cannon balls." He added that his men had been shoring up the walls with dirt, obviously an attempt to keep Mexican solid shot from piercing or collapsing them, or to prevent existing fractures from developing into breaches. In Fort Defiance, Goliad, on March 9, Captain John Sowers Brooks wrote, "We have again heard from Bexar . . . Santa Anna . . . has erected a battery within 400 yards of the Alamo and every shot goes through it as the walls are weak."[18] The source of this information is unknown; a few sections of the fort *were* in undeniably bad condition—a condition that had existed even before the fall of 1835, when General Cos first occupied the place. Most often mentioned was the adobe-built north wall, which was in such eroded shape that Cos's engineers had to construct an outer palisade-and-earth breastwork to redefine its entire length. But most of the perimeter walls, and the largest of the buildings, had been built of mortared limestone, and their resistance level during the 1836 siege proved high.

Santa Anna had failed to bring with his vanguard division a siege train of heavy battering pieces; his biggest guns were eight-pounders, and it was not until the night of March 4 that a Mexican battery was moved close enough to the north wall—well within musket shot—to be in a position to possibly generate a breach.[a] Strangely enough, according to Sánchez Navarro, once in position, "it was ordered not to fire."[19] This officer had arrived fairly late in San Antonio, on the night of March 2, and the following day, after having a good look at the Alamo, he penned the frank observation, "There was no sign that the batteries had caused serious damage."[20] In his 1878 version of "The Fall of the Alamo," Reuben M. Potter remarked that when he first visited the remaining structures of the Alamo in 1841 "they seemed less battered than might have been expected," although it must be kept in mind that these still standing walls and buildings were mostly of strong limestone, not softer adobe.[21] In 1889, while workmen were digging in "central Alamo plaza . . . within fifty yards of the famous structure," they excavated "several copper cannon balls . . . some of the balls are flattened from having been fired against the stone wall."[22] So Travis's March 3 comment about the general strength of the walls was, for the most part, true.

Herman Ehrenberg of the New Orleans Greys, however, told of the supposed effects on the Alamo walls of two "small" Texian cannon placed behind a dirt embankment about three hundred yards northwest of the fort in 1835.[b] (From that position, close by the San Antonio River, he noted that "the Alamo . . . offered an imposing view.") During their cannonading, according to Eherenberg, "we could in fact see pieces of the old walls roll down from time to time." One well-aimed shot fired by scout Deaf Smith allegedly knocked out a sizable section of the long barracks, taking away "the third and fourth windows" of the second floor.[23] Known to stretch the truth at times in his memoirs, Ehrenberg may have been wildly exaggerating the effects of the latter shot because it was not corroborated in any other account. According to Dr. Joseph Field, another veteran of the 1835 campaign, in its two days of operation this battery "had accomplished nothing but the tumbling of a few rocks from the walls of the Alamo."[24]

Most descriptions of the Alamo compound prior to the March 6 battle declared it to be a formidable place. In 1835, as the Texian army laid siege to Cos's force, one of Stephen Austin's spies in San Antonio warned the general, "the Alamo is very strongly arranged."[25] A letter written by a volunteer in Gonzales on October 25, 1835, relayed information describing the Alamo as "a strong fortress commanding most of the town."[26] Colonel Francis Johnson, one of the officers present at the 1835 siege, wrote:

---

[a] The heavier Mexican twelve-pounders did not arrive until March 7, the day after the battle.
[b] At this time, Stephen F. Austin's army had nothing bigger than six-pound guns.

> The Alamo is on the east bank [of the San Antonio River] enclosed by a high and strong wall. Though built for a mission, it was a place of considerable strength, and of capacity to quarter at least one thousand troops, and was occupied as a fortress.[27]

On November 18, 1835, Johnson composed a "personal situation report" to Robert McAlpin Williamson, stating that "The Town and Garrison [the Alamo] is strongly fortified, much stronger than you could imagine and they are hourly engaged in fortifying and strengthening the place[;] we can do nothing without battering Cannon ball &c."[28]

After the surrender of Cos, the Alamo was considered a position well worth holding by its new occupants. Major Green B. Jameson, the Alamo's chief engineer, contemplated making a few important exterior additions to the fort, as he wrote to Houston on January 18, 1836: "it is a strong place and better it should remain as it is after completing the half moon batteries than to rebuild it." He further assured Houston, "we will all move into the Alamo and whip 10 to 1 with our artillery."[29]

A terse description of the Alamo appearing in the *New Orleans Bee* of March 19, 1836, noted: "The Alamo is built of stone—is very strong about 18 or 20 foot elevation, and covers about 1 ½ or 2 acres." Years later Santa Anna himself would call the Alamo "a solid fortress erected by the Spaniards."[30]

The conclusion to be drawn from the preceding accounts is that the Alamo was, at the beginning of the 1836 siege, a "strong," "imposing," "solid" fortress, in both an actual and a discernible sense. It was not a blighted, rubble-strewn compound as often later described and depicted by observers of its postdemolition state, even though here and there crumbled sections *had* been heavily repaired or buttressed, and other parts—such as the church itself—deliberately gutted or cannibalized for building material. No Texian or Mexican participant in the 1835–1836 campaigns ever described the fort as a shabby, flimsy place. The fact is, considering the time frame and available materials with which they had to work, General Cos's engineers had renovated the rambling old mission compound into fairly formidable, if not altogether complete, fighting shape.

After its cavalry arm, the Mexican military's most effective departments were its artillery and engineer corps. A US observer outside Mexico City in late 1847, during Winfield Scott's final push, wrote of the fortifications surrounding that capitol.

Our own engineers were forcibly struck with the admirable style in which all the batteries of the enemy were constructed. . . . The science of engineering is probably as well understood by the Mexicans as by any of the European nations, as an examination of their works will at once prove, while their artillery practice is most effective. . . . Works complete in every part sprang up, as if by magic; the morning light would dawn upon some well barricaded approach which the night before was apparently open to the advance of armed men.[31]

When General Cos led his army into San Antonio de Béxar on October 9, 1835, his strategic thinking was to attack and annihilate the divided corps of Austin's approaching forces. But after his soldados were defeated at Concepción on October 28, Cos realized that he would have to wage a defensive war until reinforcements arrived. This meant strongly entrenching his troops within both the town and the Alamo, and in fact he had already begun fortifying these positions.[32] The diary of captive Texian Samuel Maverick noted the daily activities of the Mexican soldiers as they raised batteries, breastworks, palisades, and other positions in the streets of Béxar as well as in the fort east of the river.

OCT. 12th. Great flurry and excitement by arrival of Mex. Spies reporting that great crowds of Americans were on the road coming. This moment commence to mount cannon, pressing into service Smith and other citizens (3 cannon already mounted; 2 now being mounted.)

OCT. 17th. Timbers &c. taken to El Alamo to fortify the quartel, & begin, on 13th, to blockade the streets, which is finished by the 17th.

OCT. 18th. On 17th, finished mounting one cannon (had before only 3). All the powder &c. taken to the Church 3 or 4 days ago. Forces are divided here; part in the quartel (of the infantry) in Presidio on W. side of the rio, and the whole troop on E. side in their quartel in Alamo 300 cavalry and 2 [200] Infantry. (The actual number, officers, soldiers, guards etc. of Effectives is 647)

OCT. 26th. An 18 pounder just mounted Was carried by to the Alamo, and raised to the top of the church; besides this, they have 10 (smaller) cannons mounted—5 in Presidio, of which 4 are in the Plaza and 1 in front of the church and 7 [in] the Alamo, of which one, the 18 pounder, is on the top of the old church of San Antonio [de Valero].

OCT. 31st. Some more cannons mounted here and great activity to secure the place.

NOV. 3rd. The Mexicans have gone on with their work of defense briskly.— Cannons now mounted. The place could much easier have been taken with 200 men after the affair of Gonzales than it can now with 1500 men. The quartel in the Alamo is very strongly fortified, and the streets to the plaza here well guarded; and all trees, grass, fences and other lurking places and barricade removed and being removed in order to see the Americans when they come up.

NOV. 4th. Redoubled exertions today in fortifying and clearing away hereabouts and mounting cannons.[33]

The unnamed spy of Austin's in town confirmed this activity.

All are busy in preparing to do their duty, they are clearing away fences, cutting down fruit-trees, etc. Three more cannons are to be mounted to day. . . . Every day they are adding to the fortifications, as well as arming guns.[34]

In 1844, William T. Austin, another veteran of the 1835 campaign, recalled that Cos's Alamo "had upwards of thirty pieces of cannon, mounted on the walls behind facades, many of which were pivot guns and commanded the whole surrounding country."[35]

It was not the first time that the Mission San Antonio de Valero had undergone military alterations. The surrounding walls themselves had been added by the Franciscan monks some seventy-five years earlier in order to enclose the rows of houses occupied by their Indian converts, thus protecting them from Apache raiders. They had also given the south wall a large gateway, with embrasures for three cannon.[c] In 1803, ten years after the secularization of the mission, a presidial cavalry company from the Mexican town of Alamo de Parras was quartered in the compound. During their long occupation they repaired the buildings, turned the top floor of the *convento* into a hospital, built barracks on either side of the main gate, and converted the old cloister and workshop enclosures into corrals for livestock and the troopers' mounts. (The sacristy of the never-completed church was their place of worship.) Around 1810,

---

[c] Although Green B. Jameson considered the Alamo "a strong place" in 1836, he also unfairly criticized the "Mexicans" who had built it as showing "imbecility and want of skill," mainly because it lacked corner "redoubts" (bastions) and was nothing more than a "plain wall." He apparently forgot that the wall's original purpose was to keep out Indians, not a European-style army equipped with artillery.

Outline drawing based on Sánchez Navarro's original as sketched from the roof of the Veramendi house during the first week of March 1836.

some twenty-five hundred feet of "battlements" were added to certain parapets of the enclosure, and these might very well be those seen in Lieutenant Colonel Sánchez Navarro's drawing of the Alamo as it looked during the first week of March 1836—the only known eyewitness image of its kind made during the siege.[36]

Although often dismissed as a gross distortion of what the fort really looked like (and thus unworthy of meticulous scrutiny), Sánchez Navarro's depiction merits repeated, more analytical study. The drawing, along with one of his two keyed plans of the Alamo, exists on a circa 1839 Mexican manuscript map showing part of southern Coahuila.[37] Above the drawing is written, "View of the fort of San Antonio de Valero, commonly called the Alamo, made from the roof of the Veramendi house in the city of Bexar." Obviously the drawing in its final form on the map was refined from a rougher sketch done atop the Veramendi house, although the original sketch has yet to be found.

Even when compared to the drawings and paintings made of the fort's postbattle ruins by various other untrained artists, Sánchez Navarro's lightly washed sketch appears almost ludicrous in its seemingly streamlined, exaggerated forms. The church building is a massive square block, its west-facing rooftop lined with castle-like battlements. The convent building to its left still has its *entire* second floor (unlike all postbattle depictions). The west wall, its carefully drawn brick pattern showing that it lacked plastering, appears quite strong, and is lined with evenly distributed crenelations. All of the walls display a crack or two, and brickwork where plaster has fallen off. The cast shadows of *canales*—wooden gutter pipes draining the flat roofs—can be seen on a number of buildings.

Cannon embrasures are visible on the west and north walls. At far right is the U-shaped tambour, its lower part apparently made of stone or adobe and its upper half an obvious stockade. What appear to be loopholes run the course of most of the west wall. Two doors also pierce this wall, as does a strangely large round opening, and a long shingled roof overhangs much of its northern half.

Immediately to the left of the tambour can be seen the "low barracks," along with a building connecting to it at a right angle. There are other features of note: the large pecan tree, a semicircular log work outside the west wall, a ditch that follows the contours of the outer perimeter, and a flagpost rising from what appears to be a stockaded watchtower.

Could most of these features have been the calculated inventions of Sánchez Navarro, perhaps his attempt to deliberately magnify El Alamo's fortifications in order to elevate the glory of the Mexican victory?

Or were these elements actually *seen* by him and drawn by him to the best of his frustratingly amateurish ability? Had he simply put onto paper his flawed but honest impression of a "strong," "imposing" fortress?

Answering these and many other questions relating to the appearance of the Alamo in early 1836 requires a reexamination of much of the already carefully explored evidences. It also necessitates a retranslation of certain Mexican documents, with an eye particularly attuned to specific military references of the period. And along this line, it means that we must acquire a reasonable grasp of the science of fortification in the early nineteenth century, not to mention of the weapons and tactics of the day.

We must also weigh the evidence found in a myriad of less conventional sources—from the small, stray anecdotes printed in newspapers decades after the battle, to the vague wisps of local traditions that tend to nag and haunt the mind of even the most cynical historian.

Thus forearmed, we can proceed to launch a point-by-point reassessment of the entire Fort Alamo, as it was sometimes called in 1836, and by so doing arrive at some new conclusions, and in other places, provide food for further thought and investigation.

The Church

Gauging the actual appearance of the Alamo church in 1835–1836 has often leaned heavily on the visual evidence of postcampaign sketches by such on-the-spot artists as George W. Fulton (1837), Mary Maverick (ca. 1838), Thomas Falconer (1841), William Bollaert (1843), Lt. Edward Blake (1845), Edward Everett (1847), Capt. Seth Eastman (1848), and others. These invariably show the skyline of the west-facing church front to be battered and very uneven, with significant gouges near the northern and southern ends of that roof line. Because these images were created in the immediate postbattle years, they have been accepted as faithful representations of the building as it had also looked in early 1836. Yet the evidence that exists in the *only* sketch of the church drawn during the siege itself—the artist in this case being Lieutenant Colonel Sánchez Navarro—indicates a completely different roof line: instead of two large gouges, we see crenelations, also known as battlements.

When construction of the Church of San Antonio de Valero was prematurely halted in the late eighteenth century, it was still unroofed, and had been "built only as high as the cornices," in the words of a visiting padre. "In the front, its beautiful facade of wrought stone had been completed to the same height as the walls."[38] There is no evidence that any ragged dips in the top of the facade remained to mar this beauty: it had been finished to a straight and even skyline.

Another reason to doubt the existence of the gouges at the time of the 1836 battle is found, again, in Sánchez Navarro's sketch. He shows a stockaded booth-like structure, with the garrison flagpole rising from its center, atop the church's southwest corner (where one of two bell towers would have stood had the church been completed).[d] Thus it would have made little sense for Cos's engineers in the fall of 1835 to have hacked out a large gouge near this same corner, for it would have served no purpose. As the sketch confirms, it remained a straight skyline, except for the battlements. The latter, as already mentioned, may have been plastered on as early as 1809–1810 as part of an effort to convert the old mission walls into something more martial, and conceivably the front roof of the church would have been included in this revamping.[39] (It was probably no overstatement when General José Manuel Mier y Terán described the Alamo in 1828 as "an enormous battlement."[40]) Another possibility is that the church crenelations were added by Cos's soldiers, much as they had arranged "unburnt bricks, with portholes" along many of the rooftop parapets in the town prior to Austin's assault.[41] William T. Austin also described this arrangement: "The tops of the houses were flat, with rock breastworks around the edges of the roofs, intended to be occupied by their infantry."[42]

Some four decades later, veteran Mexican sergeant Francisco Becerra remembered:

> The doors of the Alamo building were barricaded by bags of sand as high as the neck of a man, the windows also. On the top of the roofs of the different apartments were rows of sandbags to cover the besieged.[43]

So the fort probably supported a mix of battlements, both cemented and improvised, made of stone, loose adobe bricks, or sandbags—also called "fortification sacks"—which seem to have been commonly available in both the Texian and Mexican armies.

---

[d] A somewhat similar structure had been built in the center of the Mexican fort at Velasco, although instead of holding a flagpole it served as a parapet covering a pivot gun.

Mission San José in the late 1800s. Note decorative porthole battlements in upper left.

It should be remembered that Sánchez Navarro also drew crenelations, cannon embrasures, windows, doors, and even loopholes for small arms elsewhere in his sketch. His faults as an artist can be forgiven, for his drawing was not intended as an exact architectural rendering; rather, as one officer's impression of the compound's military features that could be ascertained from his particular vantage point in town. And he specifically places crenelations, not gouges, at the top of the church.[44]

If the idea of constructing "battlements" on the front of a Catholic mission church may seem sacrilegious, it was not unprecedented in early San Antonio. The Mission San José y San Miguel de Aguayo, two-and-a-half miles south of the Alamo, had only one bell tower, but on the opposite side three embrasures pierced the facade's parapet, each benignly topped with an arch. These were decorative but also utilitarian, and would allow armed defenders on the roof to engage any enemy on the plain beyond. Three of the gates to San José's compound also had similar "loopholes" above them, with scaffolded platforms behind them.[45]

So just *when* were the two large gouges in the Alamo church skyline made, and the crenelations removed? The best answer is in late May 1836, more than a month after Santa Anna's defeat at San Jacinto and as the remaining Mexican troops in San Antonio, under General Andrade, prepared to abandon the town and return to Mexico. These soldiers were given orders to demolish all of the Alamo's defensible positions, and knocking the crenelations from the front roof of the Alamo church, as well as further invalidating its defensive nature by hacking deep gouges below the same roofline, would of course have been part of this assignment. It was obviously a selective, deliberate destruction because the central window and its flanking statue niches were left untouched. What the two gouges essentially achieved, then, was to deprive the front wall of the church of a usable military parapet.

Everett's 1847 watercolor of the front of the church shows a considerable scattering of loose stones lying directly in front of it, almost as if they had been thrown down. Curiously, too, the loose-appearing stones that do remain on the roof line are of a darker color than the limestone of the rest of the facade—could this mean that they were once part of the battlement add-ons? (The battlements atop the west wall in Sánchez Navarro's drawing are also darker than the rest of the wall.) When the US Army added the famous "hump" design to the roof in 1850, the color of the new stones was markedly darker than the old ones.

Naturally for such battlements on the church roof to have been useful to soldiers, a banquette had to be raised to an appropriate height behind them. The tops of the two rooms immediately to the left and right of the main door—the confessional and the baptistry—offered ready-made foundations upon which two separated banquettes could be built.[e] At some point in time these small floor areas had been connected with the central choir loft to form one continuous gallery. But was this the case in 1836?

Some scraps of evidence suggest that such a gallery might have indeed existed in 1836. Everett's watercolor of the *interior* of the Alamo church (like his exterior view also painted in 1847) shows a dark curving streak between the main door and the central window. This streak presumably marked where the arch holding up the choir loft had once butted against the inside of the church's west wall.[f] That it might have been General Andrade in 1836, and not General Cos in 1835, who demolished the choir loft is hinted at in the memoirs of Herman Ehrenberg. When describing the Alamo church

---

[e] These two matching rooftops also marked the locations of the planned, but never constructed, mission bell towers. Theodore Gentilz's painting, *Battle of the Alamo*, shows Texian riflemen manning these two positions.
[f] The reconstruction of the similar mission church of Concepción provides a vivid example of what such a choir loft probably looked like.

as he saw it in 1835, he wrote in his melodramatic way, "there were several large arches at the front entrance, under which it appeared dangerous to tarry long."[46] Did he assume that because all the other arches were gone (torn down by Cos to construct the high cavalier battery in the east end of the church), that the remaining frontal ones were also bound to collapse sooner or later?

An even fuzzier clue is found in Potter's 1878 "The Fall of the Alamo." At the time of the battle, he wrote, "the chapel, except the west end and north projection, had been unroofed."[47] Did he mean that the *entire* west end, including the choir loft, remained intact?

Hypothetical arrangement for scaffolding and banquettes on church choir loft.

The tradition that some kind of upper floor had stood behind the front of the church was echoed in 1884 when an Alamo guide made the claim to visitors that the garrison had placed a cannon in a second-story window, which "mowed swaths through the Mexican ranks."[48] No Mexican account or plan of the captured fort indicated a gun at the church facade window, although Potter was told by John Davis Bradburn, an expatriate Kentuckian who had allied himself with the Mexican army, that "'a small piece on a high platform' . . . was wheeled by those who manned it against the large area after the enemy had entered it." Potter theorized in 1878 that this might have been the "twelve-pound carronade which fired over the centre of the west wall from a high commanding position."[49] Yet in his first published account of the battle, thirty-eight years before, he had concluded that this "small gun [was] mounted on the upper works" of the "chapel."[50] In his 1860 *Fall of the Alamo*, Potter was less certain: "A small piece on the roof of the chapel or one of the other buildings was turned against the area while the rooms were being stormed."[51] (Wherever this "small" gun was located, it was not a swivel; the inventory written by Mexican general Ampudia explicitly showed that all three of the Alamo's swivel pieces, or *esmeriles*, were stored harmlessly away in the fort's armory during the battle, along with unused longarms and bayonets.)[52]

William S. Oury, whose presence at the Alamo has never been verified, nevertheless observed many years later, in the words of a descendant, that "in the chapel, a scaffold was erected to serve as a catwalk for riflemen."[53] In 1878, Potter agreed, noting that "high scaffolds of wood enabled marksmen to use the top of the roofless wall as a parapet."[54] The timbered watchtower/flag booth seen in Sánchez Navarro's drawing is evidence enough that *some* woodworking had been raised by the Mexicans immediately behind the front of the church (whether or not the choir loft existed). Logic tells us that this booth would have been used as a rifleman's platform as well, and was probably cut with loopholes. According to the testimonials of Mexican battle participants gathered by Potter, when Santa Anna thought the fort had at last been conquered, he "moved up towards the Alamo, escorted by his aides and bands of music, but turned back on being greeted by a few shots from the upper part of the chapel."[55]

The flag of the Alamo as depicted by Sánchez Navarro is corroborated in Col. Juan Nepomuceno Almonte's journal entry of February 23, 1836, which described the Mexican army's approach to San Antonio.

> The enemy, as soon as the march of the division was seen, hoisted the tricolored flag with two stars, designed to represent Coahuila and Texas. The President with all his staff advanced to Campo Santo (burying ground.) The enemy lowered the flag and fled, and possession was taken of Bexar without firing a shot.[56]

In later years, local Tejanos also recalled seeing a tricolor flag flying over Travis's fort.[57] Despite such evidence, it has been suggested that the mostly independence-minded garrison would never have fought under anything resembling the Mexican tricolor. But documentation placing a Texas independence flag either in or over the Alamo has not been found. The fort evidently flew its biggest "colors," as verified by Sánchez Navarro and Almonte. (Being strictly a unit flag, the small [4' × 6'] blue silk banner of the New Orleans Greys was not flown over the Alamo.) As it was, the two-starred tricolor was enough of a symbolic slap in Santa Anna's face, reminding him of his Centralist usurpation of rights that had been guaranteed to each Mexican state, including that of Coahuila y Tejas, by the Constitution of 1824.[58]

Since the fall of 1835, the Texian revolutionists had generally striven to maintain good relations with those native Tejanos who were either allied with them or still undecided (not to mention their efforts to cultivate the assistance of the "liberals" throughout the rest of Mexico). In early January Col. James C. Neill had estimated that three-fourths of the *Bexarenos* would join the push for independence as long as the town could be successfully held against an attacking Centralist army.[59] So the two-starred tricolor served the additional purpose of declaring that the armed resistance against Santa Anna was not solely an Anglo American one.

Comprising the largest military works within the church were the high three-gun battery in the chancel area, and the long, ramp-like structure that provided access to it. The exact makeup of both of these works has long remained in dispute because the available documentation is often confusing or contradictory. In order to partially resolve these issues, the author has made new translations of two key Mexican descriptions, and the results do, in part, offer some fresh clues.

Although he did not arrive in San Antonio until three days after the battle,[60] Gen. Vicente Filisola collected much firsthand information about both the siege and the Alamo's fortifications, which he included in his *Memorias para la historia de la Guerra de Tejas*, published in two volumes in Mexico in 1848 and 1849. Among his observations concerning the fort was this:

> The church was never finished, it was roofless, but its walls of hewn stone and lime[g] are kept in the best state; and remain joined to the buildings that must have been destined for the sacristy and the habitation of the chaplain or missionary. In the inner part of the wall and attached to it several rooms were made to serve for the officers, corps of guards, &c., but these houses

---

[g] Lime was an essential ingredient of both the mortar and of the plaster that covered mission walls.

hardly had 25 square varas.[h] General Cos tereplained the head of the church up to the cornice and formed of her a high cavalier or barbette in which could be placed up to three pieces with some inconvenience. They ascended it by means of one flat ladder that began from the very door of the church.[61]

In noting that Cos had "tereplained the head of the church up to the cornice," that is, raised a horizontal platform for mounting artillery pieces, Filisola actually gives us its height. The cornice was the narrow ledge that ran just beneath the point where the interior arches began their curving ascent, and in terms of the 1836 ground level the cornice stood approximately 15 feet above the floor of the church.[i] Because the surviving wall of the east end of church, after the battle, itself measured about 15 feet, it is apparent that here, too, General Andrade's demolition crews had been at work, knocking down at least 2 ½ to 3 feet of parapet cover. Thus, the 18-foot wall was reduced to a height about even with Cos's tereplain—15 feet—leaving the position a completely exposed one. Andrade had certainly carried out his orders to "render [the fortifications] useless for all times."

Dr. Joseph Barnard, who entered the Alamo church the day Andrade's troops began marching out of Béxar (May 24), seems to have confirmed the fifteen-foot height of both tereplain and wall when he noted in his journal that the platform reached "the *top of the wall* on the back side" (italics mine).[62]

By the time Potter first visited the fort, five years later, the height of this battery's platform had been degraded both by the elements and by people, who had either carried away pieces of the arches Cos had incorporated into its construction, or had playfully tumbled them down its slope into the nave of the church. (Everett's 1847 painting of the church's interior indeed shows a few broken arch pieces many feet distant from the high tereplain.) Thus, when Potter measured it, this platform stood "12 feet high, with a slope for ascension to the west."[63] By 1846, the mound had diminished another two feet, being "ten feet deep in rubbish and ruins," according to William A. McClintock.[64]

Lt. Col. José Enrique de la Peña had noted the impressive height of this battery during the siege, when he recorded how Col. José María Romero's column was assigned, on the morning of March 6,

---

[h] A *vara* is a Mexican yard or about thirty-three inches.
[i] Previous estimations that this platform stood twelve feet high neglected to consider what Filisola was actually saying. The height of the lower cornice of the front of the church was also fifteen feet high in 1836 ground terms.

[t]o attack the east front, which was the strongest, perhaps because of its height or perhaps because of the number of cannon that were situated in a battery over the church ruins, which appeared as a sort of high fortress.[65]

Called *Fortin de Cos* by the Mexican army, it was a typical cavalier battery, a work raised higher than any other artillery position in the Alamo. Theoretically a cavalier battery should command not only a fort's interior positions but all the country surrounding it. However, the much taller transept, nave, and west walls of the Alamo church blocked the gunners' sights to most of the rest of the compound. The muzzles of their three cannon were about even with the lower part of the church window to the west (which lower part stood some nineteen feet above the 1836 ground level), and perhaps a well-aimed round of grape or canister *might* have shot through the window and done damage to a massed enemy well beyond it, but not to any troops immediately below it. A mortar would have been better suited for such a task at this position, but there is no evidence that a mortar was emplaced in the Alamo during the battle.

Just how this high platform was constructed was not made clear. No contemporary Mexican account specifically states that the church's main arches had been pulled down by Cos for its erection. Sánchez Navarro, in his "Plano" key, simply noted that part of the church's "fabric was destroyed in order to use the material for the defenses of the fort." In the key to his plan of the Alamo that included the assault movements of Cos's column, he wrote "the rooms or habitations that are observed on the side of the same church were useful and strong, serving to raise the park."[j]

In an 1847 letter to a US officer in San Antonio, Samuel Maverick recalled:

> I was myself in San Antonio during the month of November '35 [when] with great labor, Cos for the first time turned the Alamo into a fort. He threw down the arches of the Church which now lie embedded with the earth in order to make an inclined plane to haul cannon on top of the church.[66]

By this account the impression is conveyed that the stone arches were combined with earth to make a ramp so that cannon could be rolled up to the cavalier platform. But in truth no 1836 document described it as a ramp made of stone and earth. We

---

[j] Author's translation of original handwritten Spanish versions of Sánchez Navarro's keys; photocopy in author's possession.

must refer again to the on-the-spot commentary by Dr. Barnard, who, in company with several acquaintances, approached the abandoned fort after Andrade demolished it, observing that

> a large fire streamed up from the Alamo. . . . We found the fire proceeding from a church, where a platform had been built extending from the great door to the top of the wall on the back side for the purpose of taking up the artillery to the top of the church. *This was made of wood* [italics added], and was too far consumed for any attempt to be made to extinguish it.[67]

Filisola described the inclined plane as "*de una escala plana.*" *Escala* means staircase or ladder, and *plana* or *plano* means level or smooth. In English terms, a "flat ladder." (Had he meant a ramp, he would have used the simple Spanish word, *rampa*.) Filisola's distinct wording is purposeful: flat ladders were commonly used in shipbuilding, among other industries; they were sturdy inclined wooden walkways, resembling gangways, for carrying or rolling up heavy components. Their construction was relatively simple in design: long, strong logs were laid lengthwise on a scaffold-like support, and over them straight sticks were laid horizontally, at intervals, which acted like cleats to prevent slippage while ascending.[68]

Remarkably, the account by Mexican veteran Felix Nuñez seems to be describing this very arrangement when he noted how, in the church, "the Americans had constructed a curious kind of ladder, or gangway, of long poles tied together with ropes and filled up on top with sticks and dirt."[69] The "sticks and dirt" may refer to the terreplain at the "top," or else to a layer of dirt that had been laid over the flat ladder for extra traction. The "ropes" were probably strips of rawhide. In 1809, when the Alamo's hospital was slated for repair work, among the items needed were "12 beef hides to make leather straps for tying the scaffolds."[70] The tops of Cos's palisaded breastworks in San Antonio had also been tied with "raw hide ropes."[71]

It would appear, then, that the collapsed arches had not been used in the construction of the "inclined plane," as Maverick called it, but solely in the raising of the 15-foot gun platform to which the wooden flat ladder connected. Just how this gun platform was built is not known; one possible way would have been to pile up the sundered pieces of curved limestone into opposing revetments, some against the chancel walls, and at least one placed

about halfway into the transept area (according to La
Bastida's plan of the Alamo).
The arches were about 3½
feet thick, and if each revetment was composed of four
stacked rows of the detached
arch pieces it would have
achieved a height of approximately 14 feet. The area
between the revetments
would then be filled with
dirt and stone rubble, and
rammed level on top. Over
this would typically be laid
a number of "sleepers" of
six-inch scantlings, and
then a final layer composed
of planks, forming the battery floor.[72]

Around 1876, Susanna
Dickinson related a description of the cavalier battery
to Captain John E. Elgin
that nearly approaches the
preceding concept of its
construction.

*Hypothetical evolution of the construction of the
church cavalier battery.*

Her husband, Lieutenant Dickinson, was in charge of one of the cannon
placed on top of the rocks at the rear of the church, and which were fired over
the roofless wall to the east. The body of the roofless Church was filled with
stones and debris on which large trees were growing. Mrs. Dickinson said
that she came out of her room several times during the siege and climbed over
the rocks up to her husband's position at the top of the east wall of the Church

for a visit with him. She remembered distinctly, she said, seeing the enemy's cavalry moving about in every direction. . . . She also told of Lieutenant Dickinson jumping down off the rocks in the Church and rushing into the room [to say goodbye]."[73]

Additional evidence that only the battery mound and not the "inclined plane" was built of stone (Mrs. Dickinson's climbable "rocks") and earth is found in Potter's 1878 "Plan of the Alamo." The eroded mound he drew in the chancel area—as he had "viewed it in 1841"—has an abrupt, compact slope to the west, barely reaching beyond the cross of the transept.[74] This is also reflected in both the exterior and interior views of the church painted by Everett in 1847, which confirm that there was no great dirt embankment stretching all the way to the door. All we see on the flat floor of Everett's church, as previously mentioned, are a few dispersed blocks of tumbled arches or other stones, and small clumps of debris that had been washed or pushed down from the eastern battery platform. (Eastman's 1848 views of the church front also reveal no remains of a long "inclined plane" of earth.)

Military manuals of the period specified that for every foot in height of a gun position, its ramp should be allowed six feet in base length; this gave a gradual slope up which a cannon could be rolled fairly easily to its platform. The east-west length of the Alamo's cavalier tereplain measured about twenty-four feet, thus leaving some seventy-four feet of church floor upon which to raise its ramp. But because the battery floor stood fifteen feet high, according to Filisola's cornice measurement, the six-feet-to-one rule would have required that the ramp—or flat ladder in the Alamo's case—be some ninety feet in length, stretching twenty-four feet beyond the front door of the building. Clearly a moderately steeper slope had to be built, and in fact military manuals did allow for exceptions as steep as four-feet-to-one if necessary.[75] But with seventy-four feet available, the flat ladder's slant up to the cavalier battery did not have to be *that* steep, so its construction would have been closer to a five-feet-to-one ratio.

The flat ladder seems to have had a cousin of sorts at San Fernando Church, situated in the heart of San Antonio midway between the two big plazas. This information comes from John Sutherland, when he later described in considerable detail the pivotal events of February 23, 1836, the day Santa Anna's army arrived. He told how he had been made "Officer of the day," and how Colonel Travis ordered him to keep a centinall constantly on the top of the Old church, (the ascent of which, made by a scaffle way, leading from the ground to the top of the church, which had been erected by the Mexicans, during the Siege [of 1835]).[76]

General Cos had, in fact, not only sent his marksmen to the cupola of San Fernando Church in 1835, but he had also raised at least one artillery piece to its flat roof as well. Thus, it can be inferred that the "scaffle way" might have resembled the Alamo church's flat ladder and would have similarly provided ramped access to San Fernando's roof for both infantry and cannon (although it might have been set *against* the wall and not perpendicularly to it).[k]

Another military conversion made to the interior of the church by General Cos had been turning the confessional room, which stood immediately to the left upon entering the main door of the building, into a gunpowder magazine. It was "plastered perfectly tight," remembered Sutherland, and thus ideal for the purpose.[77] The key to one of the copies of the Jameson Alamo plans denotes both it and the opposing room, the baptistry, as magazines.[l] He describes them as "two very efficient and appropriate rooms, each 10 feet square; walls around and above are 4-feet thick." Sánchez Navarro's "Plano" of the Alamo also designates the confessional as a "powder storeroom." Several contemporary accounts tell us that artillery major Robert Evans had been assigned by Travis to blow up this magazine in the event the fort was captured, but it was no suicide mission, since he was to set fire to "a train of powder." He was in the process of running to the powder line when shot by the Mexicans.[78]

Despite the church's martial transformation, those who beheld its facade invariably marveled at its splendor, as did one tourist of 1839.

[It is] a church of great architectural strength and beauty, with a chime of three bells, and several statues of saints of exquisite chiseling, and worthy of Athens in her best days.[79]

A US officer stationed in Béxar less than ten years later, during the Mexican War, had a similar reaction. He noted the

---

[k] The plan of the Alamo and San Antonio by Col. Ignacio La Bastida shows a U-shaped black formation atop San Fernando Church: Does it indicate the gun position established by Cos, and perhaps also part of the "scaffle way" noted by Sutherland? There is no evidence of a great dirt ramp having been built to the top of this church.
[l] A number of noncombatants were herded into the baptistry during the Mexicans' mopping-up operation.

large ornamented door fronting the west, on either side of which, between two deeply fluted stone columns, stands a figure of some holy saint, executed and finished with taste that would do credit to some of the best European sculptors.[80]

The Palisade, Abatis, and Inner Courtyard

Closing the wide gap between the southwestern corner of the church and the southeastern corner of the low barracks was a palisade of undetermined height. Sánchez Navarro called it "short," but by what yardstick? Macaulay's 1834 *Treatise on Field Fortification* recommended that palisades be ten feet in length before being placed in a narrow trench three or four feet deep, thus leaving standing posts of six to seven feet in height.[81] Stockades protecting gorges of forts were often one to two feet higher, and D. H. Mahan recommended that they "be at least eight feet above the ground."[82] So we can assume that the palisade closing the gap in the Alamo, if it was considered "short," was closer to six or seven feet in height. A palisaded breastwork Cos had constructed immediately outside Béxar's San Fernando Church was only six feet high.[83]

Filisola noted that to plug the gap in the Alamo's southern defenses, General Cos in 1835 had "opened a ditch and raised in a diagonal line a parapet with one porthole in the middle."[84] Unlike the breastworks Cos had raised around Béxar's two plazas, this palisade—according to the 1836 plans drawn by Sánchez Navarro and La Bastida—was just a single line of posts. Clues to the nature and makeup of the "porthole," where a single cannon was positioned, can be found by again referring to an eyewitness description of the 1835 Mexican fortifications around San Antonio's "public square,"

> where Gen. Cos had entrenched himself with the greatest possible care, by making a strong breast-work in each opening; by cutting a fosse or trench about eight feet deep; by sinking two rows of piles about six feet apart, filling the interstices with earth taken from the trench; and by tying the tops of the piles with raw hide ropes. At each of the places so fortified, there was a piece of artillery stationed, and completely masqued, having a roof over it, and a small opening for the muzzle of the gun left in the breastwork.[85]

The "masqued" roof over the gun was essentially meant to protect it and its gunners from descending howitzer shells and rooftop snipers. The top of such a shed-like covering,

supported by posts, was often layered with earth or sandbags to further cushion the impact of a grenade. This arrangement can be seen in the 1851 lithograph based on Carl Nebel's illustration, "Storming of Chapultepec—Pillow's Attack," depicting a party of US infantry assaulting two angles of the Mexican fortress in 1847. A Mexican artillery position on the wall is seen "completely masqued" by a forward slanting "pentice" roof covered with sandbags. US batteries protected by overhead earth-and-rubble-covered timbers can be seen in at least two Mexican War paintings by James Walker.

There is no direct evidence that the Alamo's southeastern palisade had such a "masqued" gun position, but considering the structural design of Cos's artillery breastworks in town, each possessing this feature, it must be assumed that a similar concern for the ground-level palisaded battery at the Alamo would have likely required one to be erected there as well.[m]

---

[m] None of the 1836 Alamo plans show such a covering over this gun either, but plans of forts did not always show every supplemental defense feature that may have existed.

Despite the evidence seen in the Sánchez Navarro and La Bastida plans, scholars continue to debate the overall physical structure of this position, often referred to in studies as "Crockett's palisade." Archaeologists even disagree about how to interpret the results of excavations made at the location. One report noted the discovery of three separate trenches in the gap; it was assumed that the two inner ones had held rows of posts, while the southernmost, wider one was apparently a defensive ditch.[86] This double-walled breastwork somewhat concurs with Sutherland's own description of the palisade. Sutherland, in fact, had been at the Alamo on February 23 and had witnessed Colonel Travis assign David Crockett the defense of "the picket wall extending from the end of the barracks, on the south side, to the corner of the church."[87] After Sutherland read Potter's description of this position, in the latter's 1860 *Fall of the Alamo*, as simply "an entrenchment running from the south-west angle of the chapel to the gate,"[88] he penned his own description as a corrective, in an unpublished manuscript.

> Now this work or space was stopped by a double row of Picket, with a pitt its whole length eight feet wide & eight feet deep ever kept full of water from the ditch, running by the chappell—this ditch was made by the Mexicans during the siege, when Coss surrendered.[89]

Sutherland may have sent this description to Potter because when the latter's revised version of "The Fall of the Alamo" was published in 1878, along with a new keyed plan of the compound, the position was thus delineated:

> The intrenchment (R) consisted of a ditch and breastwork, the latter of earth packed between two rows of palisades, the outer row being higher than the earthwork. Behind it and near the gate was a battery of four guns (4 5 6 7), all 4-pounders, pointing south.[90]

It must be noted, however, that Sutherland wrote nothing about earth filling the space between the "double row of Picket," assuming that there had been any space to fill. According to James Ivey's analysis of this problem, based on Mahan's rules for a palisade, the Mexican engineers who had built it would have left occasional gaps in the single row of trench-planted posts. On the exterior of these gaps shorter posts would have been fixed, resulting in slit-style loopholes above for infantrymen. Ivey also explained that a rear trench would have provided earth for the banquette or firing step, while dirt from an outer ditch (only a third of which was ever completed for the Alamo's palisade) would have been shoveled against the wooden wall as a banked glacis to absorb cannonballs.[91] In a way, then, this *might* explain what Sutherland meant by a "double row of Picket," but obviously more extensive archaeology needs to be done.

What was the source for Potter's four guns at the palisade? Sánchez Navarro and La Bastida show only one piece there, and Filisola describes but one porthole. One of the two hand-copied Jameson plans indicates four guns there,[92] but the suspicion is that they were added by the copyist after referring to Potter's second plan. Potter himself might have been influenced by the testimony of Mexican veterans or Bexareños who were actually describing the renovations General Andrade made to the fort after the March 6 assault. Andrade, in his own words, "did what I could to improve it. I wanted to insure a victory," in the event a Texian army returned to attempt a recapture.[93] Obviously planting four guns at the palisade was a vast improvement over the one piece that had defended it from February 23 to March 6.

Because the ditch in front of the palisade—at least at the time of the 1836 siege—had not been completed, an auxiliary defense work had to be built as a substitute. In his plan drawn mainly to show the assault made by General Cos's column on the morning of March 6, Sánchez Navarro noted, for the area of the stockade (marked "D" on the plan):

> This was the thinnest part of the fort, only defended by a short palisade and one bad cutting of trees; on this point a few colonists tried in vain to escape when they saw all was lost.

The "bad cutting of trees" was an *abatis*, throughout military history a not uncommon (and cheaply and quickly made) barrier to cover the exterior of earthworks and other positions. Trees would be felled, their limbs and branches sharpened to points, and then dragged trunk-wise to the outside of the position being defended, where they presented a tangled obstacle almost as effective as barbed wire in terms of slowing down an assaulting enemy. Abatis had been instrumental in the winning of such battles as Assieta in 1748 and Fort Carillon in 1758, and in each case the number of casualties inflicted on the attackers was enormous. Even though Sánchez Navarro described the Alamo's abatis as "bad," there is no evidence that the palisade was ever attacked frontally by Santa Anna's troops.[n]

The *camposanto* (cemetery) of the Mission de Valero was located, like so many southwestern mission cemeteries, in front of the church. Sánchez Navarro's battle plan of the Alamo shows another mission tradition: a cross atop a prominent stone foundation a little distance beyond the door of the church, and he makes the notation for this area on his key, "Ruined church, with cemetery."

Most graves in the early Spanish settlements went unmarked, especially those of deceased Indian converts, but around 1820 that began to change, and tombstones and wooden crosses became more common.[94] Early Texas settler and Béxar citizen John Duff Brown related how, following the deaths from smallpox of three family members in 1833, "all were buried in the grounds of the Alamo. The graves were afterward shown to my son, Dr. J. Duff Brown, Jr., in a little grass plot near the old ruin."[95] Colonel Sánchez Navarro had himself hoped that "the brave officers and soldiers who died in the assault [of March 6, 1836] be buried in the chapel cemetery" of the Alamo, but "my suggestion was not approved."[96]

Any grave markers still in evidence by March 1836 would surely have exhibited the destructive effects of the elements, neglect, and recent warfare.

Forming the western boundary of the inner courtyard was a wall that Potter in 1878 had described as "being only four feet in height."[97] However, Mary Maverick's circa 1838 drawing of the ruins (among those made by other artists) proves that the wall was about as high as the doors of the adjoining *convento*. Her drawing also shows a gap in the wall, which is confirmed in the two Sánchez Navarro plans (one of them showing a cannon covering the gap) and the La Bastida map. It does not appear that this wall survived long after 1840. Until a US Army detachment stationed itself at the Alamo in the late 1840s, all unoccupied parts of the postbattle fort continued to experience despoilment by locals scrounging for building materials, by souvenir hunters, and even by itinerant sculptors.

---

[n] The concept of an *abatis* in front of the Alamo's palisade had long remained unknown or misinterpreted, mainly because Sánchez Navarro's scraggly cross-hatching of it in both of his compound plans was assumed to indicate ditches. When I studied this position in 1993 while planning my compound illustration for Stephen L. Hardin's *Texian Iliad*, my previous researches into the French and Indian War, including the 1758 battle of Fort Carillon at Ticonderoga, eventually provided the answer because it was apparent that what Sánchez Navarro had drawn precisely resembled the abatis depicted on maps of the 1758 French fort. Abatis would continue to be effectively employed in many subsequent conflicts, from the Mexican and Civil wars well into the twentieth century.

The Low Barracks, Tambour, and Sallyport Traverse

The low barracks building, which was bisected by the Alamo's main gate, was another strong stone edifice that stood up well against Santa Anna's artillery. In mission days it had been topped by two towers or watch boxes and between them embrasures or portholes for three small guns, but by 1836 all this was mostly gone.[98] The parapets of the rest of the rooftop were too short to defend, only inches high, and even had they been lined with sandbags or adobe battlements the roof was still badly exposed to shot and shell, being in a direct line of enfilade fire from the Mexican battery in the loop of the San Antonio River. This was just one more reason why the besiegers saw so little of the Texian garrison during the first twelve days of siege.

The room west of the gate was described as a "Guardhouse" by Jameson, the "Guard Corps" room by La Bastida, and "Room of the Officer of the Guard" by Sánchez Navarro. East of the gate the rooms were dubbed "Soldiers quarters" by Jameson, "Officers quarters" by La Bastida, and "Hospital" by Sánchez Navarro, who also noted that James Bowie was killed in "the front of the large room that is against the gate." Sutherland merely gave the word *barrack* to these rooms.

In his 1860 *Fall of the Alamo*, Potter unwittingly hints that Crockett might have positioned himself in Bowie's room after the compound was overrun.

> Crockett had taken refuge in a room of the low barrack near the gate. He either garrisoned it alone, or was left alone by the fall of his companions, when he sallied to meet his fate in the face of the foe, and was shot down.[99]

No particular source is given by Potter for this, but of his sources for much of his information he offered the following:

> Of the foregoing details which do not refer to documentary authority I obtained many from Gen. Bradburn, who arrived at San Antonio a few days after the action, and gathered them from officers who were in it. A few I had through a friend from Gen. Amador. Others again I received from three intelligent Sergeants, who were men of fair education and I think truthful. One of them Serg. Becero, of the battalion of Matamoros, who was captured at San Jacinto, was for several years my servant in Texas. From men of their class I could generally get more candid statements as to loss and other matters than from commissioned officers. I have also gathered some minor particulars from local tradition preserved among the residents of the town.[100]

Was one of his "local" sources Madam Candelaria, who gave a somewhat similar account of Crockett's fall in the general vicinity to William Corner in 1888? According to Corner, Candelaria said that Crockett

> was one of the first to fall; that he advanced from the Church building towards the wall or rampart running from the end of the stockade, slowly and with great deliberation, without arms, when suddenly a volley was fired by the Mexicans causing him to fall forward on his face, dead.[101]

A northern extension attached to the low barracks was composed of a hospital room in its southern part and a kitchen in its northern room, according to Sánchez Navarro. The latter's "Vista" drawing shows this wing as flat-roofed, as tall as the low barracks, and somewhat darker than the latter building, indicating that it was probably of unplastered adobe. The fact that it was apparently torn down by Andrade in May 1836 also points to its easily dismantled mud brick construction.

Protecting the exterior of the main gate was a work erroneously called a "lunette" by Potter in 1878, and more accurately described by Filisola in 1849 as "a tambour in which they could position two pieces leaving the entrance by the right hand."[102] Potter never saw the original work of course, nor were there sufficient remains left in 1841 by which he could gauge its true 1836 appearance. At first glance, the three compound plans by Sánchez Navarro and La Bastida also seem to show a standard, U-shaped lunette built of earthen walls. It must be remembered, however, that these are essentially *aerial* views, giving us only the dimensions of length and width, not height.

Lunettes were essentially detached bastions, "frequently open at the gorge" (that is, its rear part), although this was "sometimes closed with a stoccade, or palisade."[103] They could be semicircular as well as bastion-shaped. Like redans, they were mainly advanced works, if sometimes connected to a perimeter line.

A tambour's specific function was to protect gates or other openings by covering them frontally. It could be formed as a simple V-shape, but, in the words of a British military textbook:

> The best figure for a tambour is that of two faces and flanks, returned also to the gorge if necessary. Generally, the faces should be at least 30 feet long, and the flanks 20 to 25 feet.[104]

Remarkably the latter measurements coincide closely with those revealed during the 1988–1989 excavations of sections of the "lunette" and its outer ditch.[105]

The feature that most distinguished a tambour, however, was its stockade, the timbers generally rising two to three feet higher than the doorway to keep enemy fire from penetrating it.[106] These timbers were given loopholes and, behind them, banquettes for musket men. But because the Alamo's tambour contained at least two artillery pieces, it was obviously intended as a combined cannon-and-small arms emplacement. (Potter, at least, had described it as a "lunette of stockades and earth, mounted with two guns.")[107]

Sánchez Navarro's drawing ("Vista") of the fort from the west *does* show a stockaded wall at the location of the tambour, and indeed it does stand at a height just a few feet below the low barracks parapet, well covering the main gate. But this particular stockade rises from behind a shorter wall composed of stone or adobe. If this arrangement appears odd, it nevertheless helps explain why archaeology has failed to detect any trace of a palisade trench there.

To arrive at this explanation, parallels must be drawn from similar military structures that may offer clues. The main disadvantage in this quest is that, like the rest of the fortifications Cos's engineers had constructed at the Alamo in 1835, the tambour's design was partly improvisational and dictated to no small degree by the peculiarities of the adjacent architecture.

The stonework seen in Sánchez Navarro's drawing evidently indicated that Cos had had every intention not only of defeating the Texians but also of ensuring that the Alamo would long remain a strong fortress garrisoned by Mexican troops. A clue to this is found in the following extract from 1862's *Aide-Memoire to the Military Sciences*.

> Although tambours are usually made of timber, it may be advantageous in some cases to adopt more permanent construction for this description of a small defensive post; and then a crenelled wall of brickwork, with a groined corridor, having a ridge or batardeau-like top, will be preferable to a temporary construction.[108]

The Mexican plans of the Alamo's tambour indicate that it had ramparts approximately six to eight feet thick. Obviously these would not have been made of laborintensive *solid* banks of stone or adobe, but probably more like the walls of the following 1867 battery built on a bridge near Queretaro, Mexico, during Benito Juárez's revolt against Maximilian.

> This side the bridge, leaving only a narrow passage for one man abreast, was raised a battery of adobes, which are bricks made of sun-dried clay, of a foot square and four inches thick. Between two walls made by them earth was filled in, and this wall contained embrasures for three twelve-pounders, one of which raked the bridge.[109]

What a formation like this would have given the Alamo's tambour was a readymade box-rampart at least six feet high filled with earth and rubble stones into which palisade posts could be sturdily embedded without leaving any trace of their presence for later archaeologists. The concept was nothing new: the Roman army had created entire walls and forts made of log or turf box-ramparts also filled with earth and stones and studded with palisades.[110]

On the colonial American frontier, the same building method was sometimes used in erecting log forts, as witness this description of one constructed in Augusta County, Virginia, in 1756.

> The Walls or Sides are about 9 Feet high, and between 4 and 5 feet thick; they consist of 2 Tier of large Logs, laid at some Distance from each other, and well tied together, the Space between them is fill'd in with Earth, Stones, &c. On the Top between the two Tier of Logs, are fixed strong palisadoes, which reach about 7 Foot higher than the Wall.[111]

Another defensive feature recommended for tambours hearkens back to the "masque" roof built over the Mexican gun positions in Béxar's plazas in 1835. As these extracts from nineteenth-century military manuals reveal, such appendages on tambours were common—and crucial—to enable them to effectively withstand plummeting howitzer and mortar shells.

> Strong joists or beams, supported by pillars of wood, and covered with boards, should be raised above the tambour. This roof must be covered with soil 2 feet thick,[o] that has been taken out of the ditch in front of the tambour. Where gates and doors are defended by a tambour work, such a roof is necessary to protect the men against the *grenades* which might be thrown by the enemy.[112]

> It is desirable that the interior line of tambour should be covered by a blindage sufficiently strong to resist the effect of grenades, thus forming a gallery about 6 feet wide, the roof being supported on a row of inner columns.[113]

> The summit of the tambour is furnished inside with a small pentice 20 decimetres (6 $^2/_3$ feet) wide, to defend it from grenades: this pentice in the salient place of arms causes the grenades to roll into the ditch.[114]

---

[o] Or as in the case of the battery roofs at Chapultepec, with sandbags.

Hypothetical arrangement for main gate tambour.

It is hardly surprising, then, that during the 1988–1989 excavations of sections of the tambour a number of bronze howitzer shell fragments, as well as a howitzer shell's lead plug, were unearthed from its outer ditch, seemingly confirming the effectiveness of the blindage.[115]

The western side of the tambour had an entrance; as drawn by Sánchez Navarro, it resembles an embrasure. Perhaps it served both purposes. Sixty-five years later Enrique Esparza recalled that a drawbridge spanned the tambour's ditch, the ditch itself "as deep as two men."[116] No contemporary evidence points to the existence of such a drawbridge, although Jameson, in early February 1836, had outlined planned additions to the fort that included "a trap door across [a more extensive ditch], which is contemplated to be raised by a tackle from inside the half moon battery."[117]

La Bastida's plan of the tambour shows a triangular-shaped section abutting its southeastern angle, possibly a storage space under the blindage roof, perhaps even a sunken magazine (covered further by timbers, or banks of earth or gabions).[118] The existence of the posts that held up the blindage may have been proven by the 1988 dig, which uncovered some nine postholes four inches in diameter, each roughly located where they would have been placed within the tambour to support overhead pentices.[119]

La Bastida's plan also shows a raised work of some kind, resembling an embankment, closing off about two-thirds of the gate entrance. This is probably what Mexican sergeant Manuel Loranca was referring to forty years later, in his account of the campaign.

> The Fort Alamo had only one entrance, which was on the south; and the approach was made winding to impede the entrance of the cavalry.[120]

This feature was called a traverse, which was usually made of earth and often revetted with sandbags, gabions, stones, or other material. Like the high palisade posts, it helped protect the interior of the compound from enemy projectiles.[121] (Intriguingly, Theodore Gentilz's *Battle of the Alamo* shows the *entire* south gate filled with stones of various sizes.)

Pointing directly at the open, inner part of the gate was a "Breastwork made by the colonists for the defense of the gate," according to Sánchez Navarro. Jameson described it as one of the Alamo's "temporary redoubts of stakes on end and rocks and dirt between."[122] Technically this was known as a sallyport traverse, or a "parapetted traverse," devised to guard the main entrance of a fort or redoubt, or smaller points of egress and ingress.[123] Its length was gauged by the width of the entrance because it had to intercept angles of incoming fire. Two guns had been positioned there at the time of the battle. Based on the way Sánchez Navarro drew batteries in his plans, this work had conventional embrasures with *genouillères,* or *soles,* of about 3½ feet high, beneath the open parts, or merlons.[124] Such a position was not meant to be suddenly abandoned in the event of an enemy breakthrough, but held as long as possible.[125]

Southwest Corner Gun Position

A stone wall about eight feet high connected the west end of the low barracks with an adobe house at the southwest corner of the compound.[126] This house had originally been the quarters of Indian converts, and most recently the carpenter shop of a French settler, Pierre Charlis. The Charlis family lived in the stone house immediately beyond the southwest corner outside the compound, and this dwelling played an important part in the March 6 assault.[127] According to Potter, the Mexican troops attacking the south side of the fort "fell back in disorder behind the old stone stable and huts that stood south of the southwest angle."[128] Filisola confirmed this in his *Memoirs of the History of the War in Texas,* noting that these troops, "skillfully taking advantage of the shelter they were

offered by some small huts with walls of stone and mud, which were in the neighborhood of the angle that corresponded to the West," made a "daring move" to seize the
cannon at that angle.[129]

This cannon was posted on the platform of another improvised battery built over the roof of the carpenter shop. Here was where the Texians had placed the iron eighteen-pounder, and where the latter was dismounted by a well-aimed Mexican artillery round on February 24.[130] As a barbette position, according to La Bastida's map and Filisola's *Memoirs*,[131] it was more exposed than an embrasured one, as this dismounting had proved. Its vulnerability remained even if the garrison raised a bonnet (or bonnette) made of earth, gabions, or sandbags, or a combination of these, along the corner parapets.[132] The arc flight of a grenade, or a lucky ricochet shot, often got around such obstacles. (The caliber of the piece that replaced the eighteen-pounder can only be guessed at, and it is not known if the replacement was mounted on wooden wheels or pivot trucks.)

A ramp approximately sixty feet long provided access to this battery, which stood about ten feet high. The composition of the ramp is not known; it might have been a flat ladder, similar to the one in the church. But if made of earth it would not have required a revetment of palisades (as is often depicted in Alamo art and motion pictures). Noted the 1822 *Course of Elementary Fortification:*

> The sides of ramps are very seldom reveted, and therefore it becomes necessary to give them a slope.[133]

That is, both the inclined ramp and its gradually sloping sides are made entirely of earth. The soil on the Alamo grounds, according to Jameson, was fairly stable in terms of its ability to stay molded, as he wrote in a letter to Houston while conveying his ideas for a revamping of the south gate defenses.

> In excavating our ditches we can with perfect safety rely on a fall from the two ditches or acqueducts of at least 20 feet, consequently we can make our ditches deep enough with perfect safety, and the earth here is of such a nature that it will not wash, and we can ditch very near the half moon batteries with perfect safety.[134]

West Wall to the Gunnade Battery

Just north of the southwest gun position was an empty space where another dwelling had formerly neighbored Charlis's carpenter shop. North of this space was the third, and intact, house of the original southwestern block. (In mission days the west wall connected a line

of five such blocks of flat-topped stone and adobe buildings, each being one story high and containing three houses, their fronts shaded by arched patios.)[135] This third house marked the quarters of the "Commandant of the Artillery," according to La Bastida, whereas Sánchez Navarro calls it a "Depository of iron tools and wood, or weapons workshop."

Nearby, and across the blocked-off remains of the mission's interior *acequia* and upon the Alamo's main parade ground, sat "three cannon of iron, dismounted"—that is, dismounted by Mexican artillery fire—and one of the pieces was the nine-foot tube of the eighteen-pounder.

The west wall stretched some forty feet from the "Depository" to the site of the next block of houses, but none of these dwellings still stood in 1836. Almost all of their walls had long since been torn away by the presidial troopers of the *Compania Volante* and, after the latter abandoned the fort in the late 1820s, by local citizens. In the early 1900s, Enrique Esparza recalled his early, prebattle boyhood.

> The Alamo was old and gray and tumbling when I first remember. It was very large. Near the west walls the good Padres had built houses for the tame Indians. Many years passed after they were gone. From the tumbling stones of these buildings we built our jacalita. The old wall of the Alamo made one side of it. Our roof was of tula that grew along the river bank, and sometimes of short grass.[136]

(During the siege, the garrison, attempting to clear their field of fire, made several sallies to either torch the *jacales* that were close to the wall or to yank down their mesquite posts for firewood.)

According to Sánchez Navarro's drawing of the fort, the west wall, including the parapets of some of the surviving houses, was crenelated as well as loopholed. In his compound plan featuring Cos's attack movements of March 6, he marked "Y" for those rooms along the west wall that "had loopholes for rifles toward both the inside and the outside" of the fort. Decades later Esparza remembered: "Senor Crockett seemed everywhere. He would shoot from the wall or through the portholes."[137]

Where the northernmost room of this mostly expunged second block of buildings had stood, Major Jameson had established another battery. This piece supposedly was a stubby iron twelve-pound gunnade, a type of weapon frequently used in naval service.[138] In late 1835, the gunnade had been shipped from New Orleans to Velasco by the schooner *Columbus*; from there, along with Capt. Robert Morris's company of New Orleans Greys, it was transported up the Brazos on the steamboat *Laura*. The last leg of its journey was overland to San Antonio. Austin's army had eagerly awaited its arrival, for the expectation was that it would "be sufficient to knock down the enemy's defenses." Unfortunately, during the assault on Béxar, it was dismounted by a Mexican round.[139]

Sánchez Navarro shows that the piece placed here—if indeed it was the twelve-pound gunnade[140]—was perched on a platform firing through an embrasure. The Jameson and Potter plats also show a gun in the general vicinity on a platform (Potter claiming that it was a "high commanding position").[141] Jameson's key significantly distinguishes it from those "cannon mounted on the ground with ports in the main wall."[142] La Bastida, however, draws no platform for it, and Filisola calls the opening, simply, a *tronera*—which could mean either embrasure or loophole.[143] The *tronera* may in fact have been one of the windows that lined the west wall. The inconsistencies of the documentation have yet to be resolved. Because the overall height of this wall did not exceed nine feet—and if a true embrasure had been cut, which required at least six feet of battery wall to shield the gunners—the platform probably stood no more than two to three feet high. The latter's base may have been the stone- and earth-filled remains of the house's foundation walls.

West Wall Tambour

Approximately forty feet north of the so-called "gunnade position" the next block of houses began. But roughly stretching this entire distance *outside* the wall, and a little beyond stood an unusual defense position: a semicircular row of palisades fronted by a ditch, with an earthen banquette behind it. On his "battle" plan Sánchez Navarro describes this as one of two "circular saps with ditch and stockade for the defense of the exterior of the enclosure." In his 1837 account of the Texas campaign, Ramon Caro, Santa Anna's secretary, noted: "Around the fortress there were ditches which were used by the enemy to fire upon our troops," during the Mexican attack through LaVillita on February 25.[144] This is not really confirmation that such a semicircular position existed, but the latter would have been perfectly placed for riflemen to add their fire to the general defense of the fort that day. As Macaulay noted:

Every part of the exterior of a fortification should be flanked by some other part—that the assailants may be seen by the defenders in every step of their attack.[145]

Now covered by city buildings, the site is out of reach of the archaeologist's shovel and trowel. But its existence may in fact have been confirmed by the discovery in the 1970s of a similar semicircular entrenchment on the other side of the fort, at the northeast corner of the cattle pen. (This other "sap" can be seen on La Bastida's map, and to some degree on both of Sánchez Navarro's plans, if the latter's imprecise draftsmanship has it almost entirely fronting the main north wall.) The excavation determined that this work had a radius of about twenty feet, and the ditch itself six feet wide and four feet deep.[146] There was no mention of traces of a stockade post, but then only a fraction of the position was unearthed.

Had additional digging been done, a discovery similar to that noted in the following 1914 newspaper report, apparently in the same general area (probably on East Houston Street), might have been made.

WORKMEN UNCOVER PALLISADE OF ALAMO
Rows of Cypress and Cedar Posts Found at San Antonio in Excavating.

SAN ANTONIO, Feb. 21.—Workmen excavating for a telephone company this week discovered the ancient palisades of the famous Alamo missions.

A row of cypress and cedar posts, closely united, was located and investigation showed the spot to be where the breastworks had been built.

The line of posts formed part of a circle, giving additional proof of the discovery.

—*Fort Worth Star-Telegram*, February 22, 1914

Lieutenant Colonel de la Peña noted that "cedar is found in the vicinity of Bejar [it is] of the pine family [and] is as high or higher than the elm."[147] As for cypress trees, they were also common there: legend has it that a Mexican sniper was positioned in one when he killed Ben Milam in December 1835.

In calling this west wall outwork a "sap," Sánchez Navarro simply meant that it was essentially an advanced, parapetted trench linked to the garrison wall itself. Technically speaking, it was also a kind of tambour, differently designed and on a smaller scale than the one defending the south gate, but nevertheless of the same breed of fortification, as Macaulay's 1834 *Treatise on Field Fortification* indicates.

> When a loop-holed wall is of great extent, and in a right line, it would be desirable to flank it: for this purpose, tambours may be constructed, and the wall be broken through, to obtain an entrance into the tambour. . . . The interior of the tambour may be defended from loop-holes pierced in that part of the wall it covers. . . . Tambours serve also, in certain circumstances, to cover the gates of communication with the exterior; then openings are left between the tambour and the wall, and these passages are closed by barriers, chevaux-de-frise, or loop-holed doors.[148]

Sánchez Navarro's drawing of the fort as seen from Béxar does indeed show a large round hole in the west wall, located about centrally behind the "sap" he depicted—the "entrance into the tambour" mentioned above. (The hole apparently is in the southern-most room of the Trevino block.) The irony is, however, that such a rough opening only expedited the Mexican infiltration of the fort on the morning of March 6. Sánchez Navarro marked on his "battle" plan where the soldados had "entered the plaza through the postern [door] as well as over the walls and by the various points" (all indicated by an asterisk). These points correspond with the doors, windows, and holes in the west wall of his drawing.

Verification of this exists elsewhere. In his 1840 article, "Attack and Defense of the Alamo," Potter wrote:

> A part of the wall was dilapidated and some of the cannon ports, which had been hastily and rudely broken out, were so large as to serve as breaches for the enemy's entrance.[149]

In his own published letter of the March 6 attack in a Mexican newspaper, Sánchez Navarro noted how "the many valient men" of Santa Anna's army entered the fort "by ladders, over bastions, through embrasures and even upon one another."[150]

A report in the *Memphis Enquirer* of April 12, 1836, claimed:

> It is said that San Antonio was betrayed into the hands of the foe by a Mexican wretch who deserted the Alamo on the evening previous to the

fall, and that the enemy found their way into the fortress through the wall, and not by scaling it.

In 1913, one old Texan, J. W. Darlington, recalled having seen the Alamo when just a boy, and noted how its walls "had been breached some eight or ten times by Mexican cannon. They were sufficiently large to admit several men abreast."[151]

Not until the day of the final attack, in fact, was the west wall ever threatened by a direct enemy approach because its field of fire was unobstructed. The side "fronting the San Antonio River," wrote Peña, had "clear and open fields."[152] (In the years immediately following the battle, these fields became covered by a "dense mesquite thicket.")[153]

Shingled Roof Complex

According to Sánchez Navarro's drawing, a large shingled roof entirely covered the third and fourth blocks of houses along the west wall, as well as the approximately forty-foot gap between them. This gap is all but verified in both his drawing and his "Plano," which show a door in the west wall located midway of the two roof-combined blocks, probably indicating the corridor to this postern.

The southernmost block was the property of Capt. Alexandro Trevino of the Presidial Company of Béxar. It was described as a "ruined building" when he petitioned to buy it in 1828. At the time of the purchase all three rooms were roofless. The northernmost block of houses under this roof had also been purchased by an officer, Lt. Francisco Castañeda of the Compania Volante. The rooftop condition of this grant is not known. A few of the original patio arches attached to these two blocks still stood when the Texas Revolution broke out.[154]

The conclusion to be drawn from the preceding is that the long shingled roof appeared to be an agreed-upon solution by both property owners to the poor or non-existent roofs of these two old blocks of houses. (Long after the 1836 battle, the ruins of the buildings were reoccupied and repaired, and at least one of the single houses was reroofed with shingles.)[155] That Sánchez Navarro shows no thatch roofing on any visible building of the compound is also telling, for during a siege hotshot would have targeted it: "If the houses are thatched," notes Macaulay's 1834 *Treatise*, "the thatch should be taken off, because the enemy would otherwise easily set fire to them."[156]

La Bastida places a more or less ground-floor cannon (probably on a requisite platform) about where the northernmost room of the Castañeda house would have been.

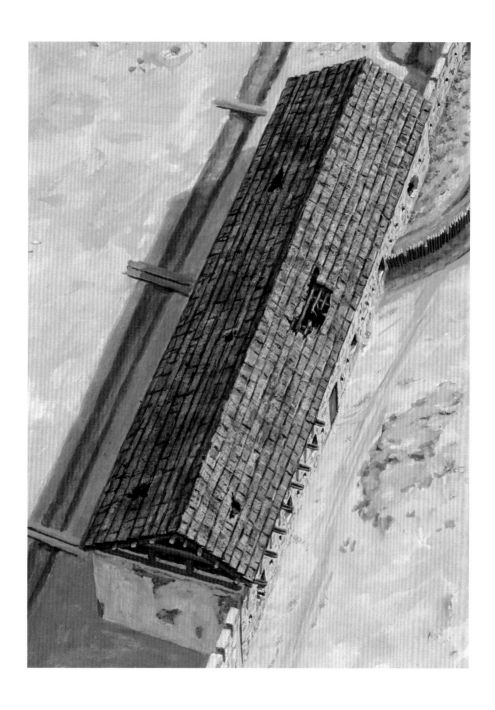

The two copies of the Jameson plan show at least four "ports in the main wall" in the northern quarter of the west wall, cut for cannon "mounted on the ground," by January 1836.[157] Sánchez Navarro's drawing confirms the presence of these ports as well as others that had been cut (by early March) through the entire west wall. Jameson's plats also show these four cannon *inside* a building block, but they are a little farther north than the gun on La Bastida's map. It can thus be concluded that by the time of the battle only one gun occupied any of the ground-level gunports in the northern part of the west wall and that it was probably inside the northernmost Castañeda room, or what was left of it. The shingled roof was a ready-made pentice for deflecting grenades, although there is no evidence of an earth or sandbag cover for it, so it would have been somewhat vulnerable to such impacts.

These two blocks of houses, along with the two surviving ones in the fifth and final block along the west wall, were indicated by Sánchez Navarro as the houses of "the families of the officers and troops of the Compañia del Alamo de Parras." During the Alamo siege they became Texian officers' quarters. Jameson's key merely refers to them as "soldiers' quarters built of stone" but specifically marks the southernmost Trevino house as "Head-quarters of the Alamo." La Bastida somewhat agrees with this ("Officers' Quarters"), but he drew a rather condensed and isolated house, not the block that was known to exist.

John S. Ford, in a newspaper article published in the early 1890s, wrote:

> These quarters were also occupied by Col. Bowie, Col. Travis, Col. Crockett and other officers, principally for the small period time allowed them for sleep. Col. Bowie became sick of typhoid fever, and was removed to other quarters.[158]

Sutherland later insisted that Bowie had remained in one of these rooms, and was not moved to the low barracks or anywhere else in the fort. He also claimed to have seen Bowie's splattered brains still staining the wall of the room Bowie was occupying the day Sutherland left the Alamo (February 23).[159]

Mrs. Juana Alsbury, who had also been quartered in one of the rooms under the shingled roof, later noted that she and her sister "were in a building not far from where the residence of Col. Sam Maverick was afterwards erected. It was considered a safe locality."[160] Ford noted that her quarters were thought to be "bomb proof."[161] This was possibly one of the rooms in the northern half, the Castañeda block.

While the Mexican troops were overrunning the fort on the morning of March 6, Mrs. Alsbury was "excitedly" ordered out of her room by a Mexican officer, and she had to "pass out of the room over a cannon standing nearby the door"—that is, positioned just outside the door, muzzle toward it. Other Alamo guns had also been wheeled around by the soldados to fire into the quarters lining the perimeter. "Don't you see they are about to fire that cannon?" yelled the officer. "Leave!"[162]

Northwest Corner Battery

Forty feet or so north of the shingle-roofed blocks was another, final group of houses, also belonging to Lieutenant Castañeda. According to James Ivey—from whose work much of our knowledge about the Alamo's early architecture, as well as its shifting shapes due to erosion or changing ownership, has been drawn—the southernmost room of this block was gone.[163] (A crude jacale is shown in its place in the illustration and is meant to convey the *possibility* only of such a makeshift dwelling within the fort.) The middle room was intact, and Sánchez Navarro gives it a postern door for access outside the west wall. (On his courier mission to James Fannin, according to his own later testimony, Juan Seguín left the fort by "sallying from the postern on the northern side, and took the high road to the east.")[164] The northernmost room, however, like that of the southwest corner, had had its roof converted into a battery by General Cos.[165] Called *Fortin de Condelle*, it was drawn by La Bastida as an embrasured position for two guns, one facing west, the other north, while Filisola called it "barbette."[166]

According to Sánchez Navarro, this battery had been the focal point of General Cos's initial assault, but due to the "sustained fire of the battery and because the [friendly] fire of the Toluca battalion hurt them, he ordered an oblique movement toward the right." This movement forced Cos's column around to the west wall, where it finally broke through along much of its length. Like the southwest corner gun and some other batteries in the compound, the salient angle here may have been covered with bonnets, especially as the northern Mexican battery kept pushing closer almost daily.

The existence of the "Large Pecan Tree," as it was described in both Jameson plans, is also confirmed on the La Bastida map as well as in Sánchez Navarro's drawing, which suggests that a limb or two might have been knocked off during the Mexican bombardment or perhaps even during the Texians' own two-gun cannonading from the northwest in 1835. The acequia west of the Alamo had apparently been dug by the Mexican army in 1835.[167]

North Wall

In his *Memoirs* General Filisola wrote of the north wall east of the northwest battery:

> a little more than halfway down this front in a direction facing to the East he [Cos] constructed another esplanade with embrasures and head-guards[p]; but since this curtain was ruined it was necessary to repair it with timbers of five or six inches in thickness placed horizontally and supported on the outside part with some straight legs, also of timber.[168]

Filisola is saying that the part of the ruined adobe wall against which this battery was erected was first reinforced and straightened, on the interior, with horizontal timbers. As for how the battery itself was raised—that is, the foundation upon which the battery's "esplanade" stood—its construction makeup is not really known. It has been generally thought that some of the Alamo's batteries were essentially mounds of earth revetted by standing palisade posts. Yet there exists no contemporary evidence for this. In an 1847 letter, Samuel Maverick wrote only that Cos had "erected mounds at different distances on the sides for cannon."[169] Thirty-one years later, Potter contended that "all the guns of this area were mounted on high platforms of stockades and earth, and fired over the walls."[170] But this is somewhat nebulous in its description, not quite telling us how or where the timbers were really used. It is curious that Sánchez Navarro shows definite standing palisade posts covering the fort's inner courtyard as well as the entirety of the north wall's outer side, not to mention the semicircular tambours, yet he never draws them around any of the gun platforms. Neither did La Bastida or Jameson. (The boxlike, horizontal timber construction seen in the painting for this essay is theoretical, but it is in keeping with Filisola's description of the repairs done to this interior part of the north wall.)[q]

It is likely that the battery *parapet* itself was also constructed of a basketwork of earth-filled horizontal timbers, which was standard for many field forts. Sánchez Navarro's "Plano" reveals that the "head-guards" between each embrasure were about twice as wide as the adobe wall, suggesting such a thick, earth-filled cribbing structure. Perpendicular

---

[p] Head-guards were the parts of the rampart between the embrasures, high enough to cover the gunners' heads.

[q] It is not impossible that the battery foundations were, like the ramps, constructed entirely of earth; the platforms alone made of wood. This would essentially be the case in battery construction during the Civil War, as the photographic history of that conflict reveals.

traverses of earth, possibly braced with gabions, would have been logically raised between each cannon, buttressing against the cribbing, to check enfilade fire (for further discussion of this see *The Last Moments of William Barrett Travis*, in chapter 8).

In the key to his "Plano," Sánchez Navarro wrote of this position:

> Battery of two cannon called by the Mexicans fortin de Teran, placed upon the wall to the height of eleven feet Mexican yard [10.175 feet by American measurement]: the wall was two feet thick [1.85 feet thick], and reinforced on the outside with a palisade with earth in between with a thickness of five feet [4.625 feet].

Clearly what he is describing is a standing palisade (the "straight legs" Filisola mentions) "on the outside" of the north wall, and his "Plano" shows that it covered the *entire* wall. Peña's narrative of the campaign noted that "the wall reinforcement on this front was of lumber"[171] (observe that he doesn't say only *part* of it was of lumber). In a testimonial written on June 22, 1836, to recommend Peña for his courage, General Ampudia, declared:

> This young Man [de la Peña] with bravery, climbed, in my sight, the palisade that formed part of the enclosure, and in the interior of the fort (the Alamo), he fulfill[ed] his duty like a good officer.[172]

Peña himself described the height of the palisade "reinforcement" as "eight or nine feet."[173] If the battery platform stood at just over ten feet as Sánchez Navarro wrote, then adding about six feet of battery parapet ("head-guards") gave the latter a total height of some sixteen feet. From the genouillères of the embrasures, an earthen glacis may have sloped into the packed earth between the palisade and the main wall.

During the attack on the morning of March 6, three Mexican columns (Duque's, Cos's, and Romero's) momentarily converged at the base of the north wall in a "confused mass," as Peña described it. "The few poor ladders that we were bringing had not arrived, because their bearers had either perished on the way or escaped. Only one was seen of all those that were planned."[174] (A total of twenty-six ladders accompanied these three columns).[175] Macaulay's 1834 *Treatise* recommended that a storming party be equipped with "ladders to scale the stoccades."[176] Over three months earlier, during Austin's siege of Béxar and the Alamo, Mexican soldiers reported a false alarm of "Americans coming in with a great many ladders to scale the walls" of the Alamo. But to captive Maverick, this was absurd. "Poh! No need of ladders," he scoffed.[177] As far as the north wall was concerned, the Mexicans proved Maverick right for, in the words of Peña, the palisade "could be climbed, though with some difficulty."[178] And so it was.

In the latter stages of the siege the garrison worked hard to further shore up the fort's walls, and although some well-constructed trenches and banquettes were indicated on La Bastida and Sánchez Navarro's plans, just how much rough excavation was really done, and where, may never be known.

Potter marked a breach near the northeastern end of the north wall, and although it would have been an understandable result as the northern Mexican battery advanced ever closer, no solid evidence for it has been found.

Ehrenberg described the landscape north of the Alamo, as he remembered it during the 1835 campaign, as partly composed of "large corn fields and partly by prairies, which were overgrown in places by mesquite brush and by enormous groups of gigantic cactus."[179]

Northeast Sector

Not far to the east of the north wall's central battery stood a *chamacuero*,[180] a type of hut once common in San Antonio de Béxar, but instead of being constructed of mesquite posts and plaster, and a thatched roof, its timber frame was entirely covered with hides.[181] Marching into the south Texas borderland in 1836, Peña wrote of Mexican ranchers "who sheltered me in their hut of hides and branches."[182] In an 1892 interview, Madam Candelaria spoke of her childhood at Laredo: "There were only a few houses there at that time and they were mere jacales covered with hides."[183]

A few feet east of the chamacuero stood an adobe kitchen, followed by an adobe residence. All three structures were the property of a son of Silvestre Reyes, one of the soldiers of the Compania Volante.[184]

From the northeastern corner house a row of connected adobe houses stretched southward for approximately 150 feet. La Bastida calls these "Artillery Quarters." Sánchez Navarro's "Plano" of the fort places "ditches" inside these rooms (as he did elsewhere in the compound), dug by the garrison "in order to protect themselves from injury by the grenades and shot of the artillery." Peña confirms this: "They had bolted and reinforced the doors, but in order to form trenches they had excavated some places inside that were now a hindrance to them."[185] Macaulay's 1834 *Treatise* suggested a similar defense resort, along with one for houses with upper floors:

> Behind the barricaded doors interior intrenchments of wood-work or furniture, &c., are to be made, and openings must be cut in the floors, through which the soldiers may fire down on, or bayonet the assailants.[186]

Sánchez Navarro's "Vista" drawing gives this block a straight-parapet roofline, higher than the compound's surrounding walls (it is not known if this height was artistic embellishment).[187] That these houses were made of adobe is documented in Jameson's letter to Governor Henry Smith of February 16, 1836, in which he refers to this entire northeastern angle of buildings ("H") in his plan of the fort and its accompanying key.

> I would recommend that the doby houses, letter H, to be torn down and stone houses erected in their stead. The stone can be obtained out of the old Church San Antonio, which is now a wreck or ruin of a once splendid Church.[188]

One can assume that he suggested they be rebuilt for one or all of the follow-ing reasons: because the adobe was beginning to naturally decay; because the walls and roofs had been perforated by the brief Texian bombardment the year before; or because he simply wanted to create a sturdier, more permanent fort.

In addition, Jameson's key denotes these northeastern structures as "Soldiers quar-ters built up of doby houses and picketted all round as letter B." This helps us solve a mystery related to this sector, for letter "B" refers to the sallyport traverse he drew—the two-gun barrier defending the inside of the main gate. He described the latter as one of the fort's "temporary redoubts of stakes on end and rocks and dirt between." Thus, he is telling us that the outer sides of the northeastern sector walls were also "picketted" in this manner. (In contrast he uses the letter "I" elsewhere in the fort to indicate "strong stone walls *without* [italics added] pickets all around.")

This conforms to the Mexican descriptions of the palisade-and-earth "front" Cos's men had raised against the north wall. Evidently a ditch was also planned to eventually cover both the north and northeastern walls, but as indicated in La Bastida's map ("Exterior Ditch"), it was far from complete, draping around the angle for only about one hundred feet on each side. Yet the inference is clear: although he does not show palisades anywhere on the north wall or its eastern angle, La Bastida is also informing us that both the north and northeast walls were connected on their outside by the same defense work.

When in May 1836, General Andrade's demolition crews tore down much of the Alamo, they seemed to focus on both the military improvements and the easily dis-mantled adobe structures. This explains why the Alamo's postcampaign ruins were virtually devoid of any adobe houses or walls, such as the entire north wall and the entire northeastern row of dwellings.

Between the southern end of this block and the northern end of the granary build-ing was a gap of about 5½ feet wide.[189] This may have been originally a passageway for grain wagons or carts.

Long Barracks Complex

The granary building (in mission days both a granary and a workshop)[190] has been traditionally included as part of the "long barracks" section of the fort. Over eighty-two feet long and just under twenty high, it was an almost entirely windowless stone structure (Sánchez Navarro shows a pair of small windows high up on its northern end, typical of granaries). An adobe floor had been laid within it in 1793.[191]

La Bastida simply labels this building, *Quarteles*, or "lodging for soldiers." Jameson refers to it as "soldiers' quarters built of stone." Sánchez Navarro's "Plano" indicates that it also contained a *calabozo*, or jail.

Joined to the granary's southern end was the two-storied convento building, running a length of approximately one hundred feet. Sánchez Navarro's drawing of the Alamo reveals that, unlike all the postbattle sketches of the ruins that show only the southern half of the second floor surviving, during the siege the entire second story was still very much in evidence. He does draw a number of cracks and large gaps in its plaster coating, but clearly the second floor is there. (That he is indeed showing us the *entire* convent building can be seen when comparing the drawing to its related schematic in his "Plano.") In the key to the latter he describes the convento as a "two-story barracks with its hallway and corral." Nevertheless it is not known if the second floor *remained* in this condition during the last days of the siege.

Did Sánchez Navarro execute his drawing *before* Santa Anna's cannon actually inflicted prodigious damage to the upper floor of the convento? The lieutenant colonel had arrived in Béxar on the night of March 2, and the brigade he came with brought more guns. Did the addition of a fourth gun in the river loop battery to the west, and the north battery's advancement to within musket range of the fort at about the same time, start a more destructive process? If he drew his "Vista" on March 3, the day after his arrival, that still left two more days of heavy cannonading and bombardment against the Alamo. According to Esparza, the Mexican

> shot and shell tore great holes in the walls. They also sawed out great jagged segments of the walls of both the Convent and the church. The roof of the Convent was knocked in, the greater part of it falling . . . nearly one-half of the Convent walls were knocked off.[192]

Was this the muddled memory of a survivor, uttered seventy-one years after the event, or did it contain some kernels of truth? On the other hand, the already compromised second floor of the convent's northern half may have been simply dismantled by Andrade's men two months later.

The southern half of the convent was thus described by Jameson:

> The hospital upstairs in a two-story building of stone; the lower story being represented by K and now occupied as an armory for small arms.[193]

He labels the northern half as another section of "Soldiers quarters built up of stone houses."[194] As stated previously, La Bastida refers to the convent as Quarteles, but because he drew the entire long barracks complex as three exploded sections, his plan is problematic and misleading.[195] One of these sections sits east of the granary, and at first glance appears to be a completely unrelated structure.[r] On closer examination, however, it is revealed to be his attempt to depict the northernmost section of the surviving arcaded patio wing, that is to say, in the southern courtyard, or horse pen, and not an isolated building in the northern courtyard (cattle pen). La Bastida's

---

[r] It has been theorized that this was a remaining workshop building from mission days, but no such little building appears on any other contemporary or postbattle plan of the Alamo compound and is not mentioned in any account. Because La Bastida labels *every* building in his fort plan with the exception of this one, clearly his intent was that it was part of the neighboring "F" complex of buildings—the long barracks—which he calls *Quarteles*.

error is further compounded by the fact that he meshes the two courtyards into a single, much reduced one.

As mentioned, only a few of the arched patios that had surrounded the monks' cloistered yard—used in 1836 as a horse corral—still survived, and all of them along the east side of the convento. The center portion of the roof that had covered these was also gone. From the horse corral a stone stairway led to a second-floor landing.

Potter noted that the defenders retreated into the compound buildings after the outer walls were seized, "but mainly in the long barracks"—no doubt because of their strength, and the defenses prepared within them.[196] Peña observed that as the Mexicans climbed to the top of the north wall, "a lively rifle fire coming from the roof of the barracks and other points caused painful havoc, increasing the confusion of our disorderly mass."[197] Of the long convent building as a fortified position Sánchez Navarro remarked:

> This building was serviceable; because of its construction and because it was united to the Church, it formed a "high cavalier," and the strongest position of the fort. If the enemy had made a second line of defense of this [meaning, had artillery been placed within it], it would have been very difficult to drive them out or take it from them.

In the Alamo's main plaza close to the long barracks, ponds or small morasses would often form after a rain, and sometimes remain boggy for weeks.[198] Carl G. Von Iwonski may have drawn one in his circa 1849 view of the Alamo.[199] Others may be seen in circa 1880s photos of Alamo Plaza.[200] In 1877, the Plaza was called, after it rained, "a mere bog, a convention for frogs."[201] Almonte recorded that it "commenced raining heavily" on the night of February 21, two days before the siege began;[202] so it is possible that small morasses existed during the siege.

Not far from the west wall the garrison had begun digging for water on February 23, rightly fearing that Santa Anna's men would eventually cut off their supply of acequia water. According to Potter, they "struck a fine vein of water" that day.[203] (Esparza would say, in 1907, "I do not recollect the inmates having suffered for either food or water during the entire period of the siege.")[204] This well was probably a very makeshift affair, without a curbstone or wall, perhaps resembling the crude one seen in a drawing of the outskirts of San Francisco in the 1850s.[205] All around it, and elsewhere in the grounds of the fort, small craters had been dug by the spinning and exploding Mexican shells.

The Courtyards

The northern courtyard, located east of the granary building, had a tambour work defending its northeastern corner, similar in structure to the west wall tambour except that this one was equipped with a cannon on a platform. The latter has been adjudged by archaeology to have stood about three feet high. The circular ditch was also estimated to have had a radius of about twenty feet.[206] The walls of this courtyard probably averaged six feet in height, and against the north wall an earthen banquette had been raised with a ditch behind it. What has sometimes been misinterpreted as an earthen glacis in front of this wall, as supposedly observed in La Bastida's plan, is shown on closer scrutiny to be the wall itself, merely drawn a little thicker than its connecting sides.

Nearby was a long row of the garrison's latrines—*comunes* on Sánchez Navarro's "Plano." In basic structure these may have resembled the two-door outhouse seen in Eastman's 1848 sketch of the northern side of the Alamo church.[207] Frequented in earlier decades by the presidial troopers and their families, as well as by General Cos's soldiers and *their* camp-following noncombatants in 1835, it is assumed that these latrines would have been kept in reasonably good condition in 1836 also, enclosed and roofed for privacy's sake and for protection against the elements.

Sánchez Navarro merely calls this courtyard a "Corral." Potter describes it as a cattle pen, although instead of a stone wall he inexplicably encloses it with a picket fence, that is, palisades. Sutherland later wrote that it was "the Slaughter pen or [was] used as Such on this occasion [when he was there, February 23], into which cattle were driven."[208] He may be telling us that all the cattle were slaughtered on the first day of the siege.

Sergeant Becerra claimed that General Manuel Fernández Castrillon's column gained first entrance into the fort via "the upper part of the Alamo, in a sort of outwork, now a court-yard."[209] Sánchez Navarro's key to his "battle" map notes that Colonel Romero had led the Jimenez and Matamoros battalions through the corral. Whichever had been the case, clearly the corrals were not held for long by the defenders.

According to Adina de Zavala, "tradition says that the first funeral pyre was lighted in the courtyard but that orders were given later to burn the rest of the bodies elsewhere, and that three pyres were made beyond the walls."[210]

The southern courtyard was labeled as a horse corral in the Sánchez Navarro and Jameson maps. This was the space formerly enclosed by two tiers of arcaded patios that had shaded

the monks' cells, most of which had long since been knocked down and carried away for a myriad of construction purposes, civilian and military. In the center were the remains of the padres' garden well, although there is no evidence that it was useable in 1836.

Susanna Dickinson later said that one of the garrison's horses was killed during the siege.[211] Sutherland drew a rough map of the compound and indicated a "back shed" under the surviving arches in the "horse pen." The map also marked where, he claimed, Colonel Travis had been killed on the eastern wall of this corral.[212]

The wall enclosing this corral was about the same height as that of the cattle pen, six feet more or less: fairly low, yet still too high to fire over without a banquette.[213] F. S. Rountree, a retired Texas ranger and acquaintance of the widow Dickinson, later repeated an anecdote of the siege she had related.

> The daring David Crockett during the Alamo siege was recalled by Mrs. Dickinson, Rountree said. He said she told him that because the wall

surrounding the Alamo was too high for a man to shoot over, Crockett had his men lie down and that he stood on them to shoot Mexicans attempting to fire cannon into the fortress.[214]

The following interesting recollection of the courtyards as they stood in 1848, when the Alamo was a US Army station, was written by one A. C. Gray in 1907.

> Back of them [ground-floor convento rooms] was a room used as a stable for the horses in use, and back of the building was an open inclosure where condemned horses were kept until they were sold at auction. I bought one there myself. I do not remember seeing any staircase leading to the second story, and do not know whether it was in use. Captain Smith told me the place was used very much in the same way by Travis. In the front provisions and forage were stored. In the division used as a stable the cattle were kept, and such horses as were not tethered in an inclosure on the other side of the church were allowed to run loose in the open lot, around which was a stone wall.[215]

From this courtyard entry into the church proper was obtained through a door into the latter's *lavatorio*. Nearby another door had formerly allowed access into the inner courtyard before the front of the church, through the high wall that connected the latter with the convent, but it had apparently been blocked off in mission days. In the 1840s, it was reopened by the US Army.[216]

East of the Alamo ran an irrigation ditch called the *Acequia Madre*, and sometimes it would flood and form its own ponds or grassy bogs, as seen in La Bastida's map. The eastern horizon was dominated by a range of hills that stood between fifty and seventy-five feet high.[217] On one of these heights stood the old *Garita*, or powder house, and near it Santa Anna's cavalry had made their main camp.[218] Past it ran the road to Gonzales and the other Texian colonies.

humanity. If the "heroes" who are fighting for liberty (i.e., the *liberty* to hold men in *slavery*) in Texas, had remained in the United States, they would not have been "murdered" nor molested by Santa Anna; and they could here, under our *republican* government, have enjoyed this high privilege, secure from any other let or hindrance except such as arises from the secret goadings of a guilty conscience, and the paper bullets hurled at them by the northern abolitionists. But this did not satisfy them. The field of slavery must be enlarged, and a new market opened for the *sale* of human beings, among a people, who, "fiend-ish" as they may be, had solemnly inhibited slav-ery by their constitution. To this end, (and hav-ing neither fame nor fortune to lose,) they crept into the bosom of a friendly and too confiding community, whose laws it should have been their purpose to obey and not to subvert; or, if they could not do this, the door by which they entered stood wide open, through which they would have been permitted to depart in peace. That the native population of Texas is favorable to the views of these interlopers, we have seen no evidence to convince us. There is, on the contrary, much evi-dence of an opposite character. What says col. Travis—the "brave," the "heroic" col. Travis, in his *last letter,* written just before the capture of Bexar, where he lost his life?

"The citizens of this municipality," says col. Travis, "are all our *enemies,* except those who have joined us heretofore; *we have but* THREE *Mexicans now in the Fort.*"

He then goes on to say what ought to be done to those who refused to take up arms against the government of their choice.—"Those who have not joined us in this extremity," says he, *"should be declared public enemies, and their property should aid in paying the expenses of the war."* Is there anything like mildness in this? Away with the sickly sensibility that would involve our nation in a quarrel with another, to sustain such a cause as this!

From the New-York Evening Star.
TEXAS.
The Journal of Commerce, this morning, in referring to the horrible butchery at Bexar by the Mexicans, says:

"The tragedy of San Antonio, cannot fail to beget a deep sympathy for the Texians in their heroic struggle, and of indignation against the murderous fiends, who, disregarding the rules of honorable warfare, imbrue their hands in the blood of prisoners."

The whole country is indignant at this atro-cious act of Santa Anna. It will be remembered that Col. Johnson, with a scouting party of 70 left Goliad, and arrived at Patricio, a few months ago, and was there surrounded by a large body of Mexicans, and called upon to sur-render. This they refused, but offered to capitu-late, and be received as prisoners of war; and the conditions were accepted. Col. Johnson and his men stacked their arms, and *were all mur-dered forthwith,* but three, who escaped. It is now a question with our government, whether, if such are to be the principles and practices of the Mexicans, we can safely, or consistently with our national honor, hold further inter-course with them.
—*Republican Monitor*, April 26, 1836

A more guarded criticism of the Texas revolutionists appeared in an editorial in the District of Columbia's *Daily National Intelligencer.*

We have published, in another part of this day's paper, a communication on the subject of the pending contest in TEXAS, from a known source, and a respectable one. The views which it presents of the contest in Texas, however, we think it indispensable to say, differ widely from those which have impressed themselves on our minds, from a survey of all the circumstances of the case. We grieve for the loss of life in this struggle. We abhor unnecessary and wanton war, under whatever pretence waged. We sin-cerely sympathize with the relatives and friends of those citizens of the United States who have fallen in the conflict. We mourn over the fate of Col. CROCKETT and of all those of his degree of merit who have become victims to their own daring, in defending, at a distance from their own firesides, what they considered the cause of freedom. But we cannot shut our eyes to the fact that the citizens of the United States who have entered the Mexican territory (of which TEXAS was as much an integral part as the city of MEXICO itself) in hostile array, with arms in their hands, have done so at their own peril, and have themselves only to blame for the consequences. From these consequences we wish that the Government of the United States could rescue them, but not by making war upon Mexico, the People and Government of which have committed no offence (that we know of) against the People or Government of the United States. We should approve almost any thing else that our Government could do for the relief of the survivors of the emigrants to Texas.

—*Daily National Intelligencer*, April 27, 1836

The *Memphis Enquirer* was among the newspapers that had once "been opposed to this Texas War from first to last," but with the deaths of so many Americans, not to mention fellow Tennesseans, at the Alamo, its policy had completely changed.

TEXAS.

We have received no intelligence from the theatre of war later than published in our extra. We are anxious to hear from Goliad, as victory or death has doubtless ere this time been achieved, or met, by Col. Fanning. It is said that San Antonio was betrayed into the hands of the foe by a Mexican wretch who deserted the Alamo on the evening previous to its fall, and that the enemy found their way into the fortress through the wall, and not by scaling it. The traitor is taken. Five hundred of the Mexicans were slaughtered in the Alamo, before the spirit of bravery was extinguished; and all within the space of two hours; overpowered by infuriated numbers, and worn out in the labor of killing the enemy, the barbarians triumphed in the death of the heroic band.

The excitement in favor of Texas throughout Mississippi and Louisiana is almost incredible; money is given to the cause in the spirit of southern liberality. *Three thousand* volunteers at least will immediately be on their way to Texas from these States, headed and accompanied by the best and bravest men of the land. The Western District of Tennessee will doubtless send out hundreds of her "sharp shooters"—their prowess and rifles are needed. Their friends and brothers have been denied life—and its denial taught tyrants how nobly patriots can die upon the altar of liberty—drowning themselves in the blood their own swords wrought from the breasts of tyrants. In Louisville and Cincinnati also, volunteers are rallying round the flag of freedom and Texas. The most eloquent men in both places are haranguing in public and exciting the emigrating spirit; there is no secrecy manifested at all. The swelling tide of public sympathy, unable to restrain itself, has burst forth in a tremendous volume.

Col. Robert I. Chester is now in the District from Texas, and wishes to raise ten companies of fifty each. Five hundred Tennessee riflemen could conquer Mexico. Let our brave young men marshal immediately at Memphis and Randolph and emigrate to Texas. The blood poured out on the ramparts of the Alamo has sealed the freedom of Texas. It has inspired a spirit of patriotism and sympathy that will secure its liberty. We will emigrate with any gallant company, at as early a day as they may wish, the sooner the more desirable. Bounties of land and pay are offered, and the credit of the government now ensures its responsibility for its obligations. It is a noble field for young men—its fine lands will be a fortune to every emigrant or soldier. In another column will be found the rates of pay for emigrants. But let not *pay* be the price of Tennesseans—it will not be—'tis an insult to them. *Liberty* is sufficient recompense for them—the protection of its sacred principles drew forth the blood of their sires; and the matrons of America would blush with shame for their sons that inherited not the spirit of their fathers. The blood they poured out upon the field of Lexington and Concord sealed the freedom of our country; and the blood that moistens and crimsons the Alamo, will prove to be as rich a legacy for struggling and oppressed Texas.

In another column will be found the last relic from the hand and heart of the brave Travis:[u]

---

[u] Travis's letter of March 3 to "the President of the Convention."

and a most glorious one truly: well might he have exclaimed when he left his friends, in the language of Montgomery, as he parted from his young bride to fall at the storming of Quebec—*"you shall never blush for your TRAVIS."* There was not a soldier in the Alamo that might not have truly declared the same patriotic sentiments.

In Memphis we are proud to see many friends of bleeding Texas. Purses are opened with great liberality, and were our own firesides invaded, a greater sympathy could scarcely manifest itself.

Charles Haskell, Esq. of Jackson, who was said to be killed at the siege of San Antonio, we are happy to learn is well and was not there.

Jesse Benton Esq. has been commissioned a Colonel of a corps of rangers and is now in active service against the plundering Indians, who are said to compose nine tenths of the population of Texas. They are the wretched and cowardly refuse of several tribes, and live by pillage.

On the morning of the 4th of March at day-light a company of 10 surveyors on the Brushy, a tributary of the Brassos, while encamped, were fired upon by a party of one hundred renegade Indians, killing two of the party and wounding two others. Mr. Holsclau, late of Jackson, escaped with a bullet through his pan-taloons. The rest escaped through the grass and arrived at the nearest settlement, 30 miles dis-tant, naked and torn by the briers. The wounded were also protected and conveyed there by one of the brave surveyors, who jumped up with his rifle, after the volley from the savages, exclaim-ing, "Indians, boys let's give it to them," but finding their number so superior, was advised to postpone the actions of bravery. The Indians dragged the tent into a fire supposing all its for-mer inmates to be there; but who had crawled out the backway through the high grass.

—*Memphis Enquirer,* April 12, 1836

The passage of time brought out more details of the Alamo siege and battle, but the precise origins of many of these details are not, and may never be, known. For instance, there is the following, origi-nally from a newspaper in Augusta, Georgia, that

tells of Crockett's sharpshooting skill and of "a plan and description of the Alamo" on exhibit in the paper's "Reading Room." Unfortunately, the where-abouts of said plan and description are unknown, if indeed they survive at all.

Texas.

From a friend at Washington on the Brazos, in Texas, we have lately received a letter mailed at Natchitoches, with sundry documents, and information relative to the state of affairs in that country. At the date of this letter, March 11th, he had not yet heard of the fate of San Antonio, and its brave defenders under Col. Travis. The Alamo, the fortification of that city, was stormed on the night of the 6th. At the close of this letter, the writer had heard of only seven days of unsuccessful cannonade of the Alamo. It was stormed on the night of the tenth day. Col. Crockett's activity on the occasion is noticed, and he is said to have killed with his rifle, at the distance of 150 yards, the first two Mexicans who fell. Accompanying the letter, is a plan and description of the Alamo, which any person can see in the Reading Room, who may be curious in such matters.

Geor. Cour. [Georgia Courier]
—*Edgefield Advertiser* (South Carolina),
April 21, 1836

A letter originally published in an Ohio newspaper, also dealing with Crockett's marksmanship as well as James Bowie's final moments, was printed in the *New York Times* in late June.

Colonels Crockett and Bowie—The following facts, characteristic of these brave and lamented men, which are well authenticated, are extracted from a letter recently received from a friend residing in Natchitoches, Louisiana:

During the siege of the Alamo, the Mexicans planted a piece of ordnance within gun shot of the Fort, with the intention of commenc-ing a brisk cannonade. Five men success-fully stepped forth to fire the gun, and were soon marked down by the unerring rifle of Crockett. The consequence was that the gun was abandoned.

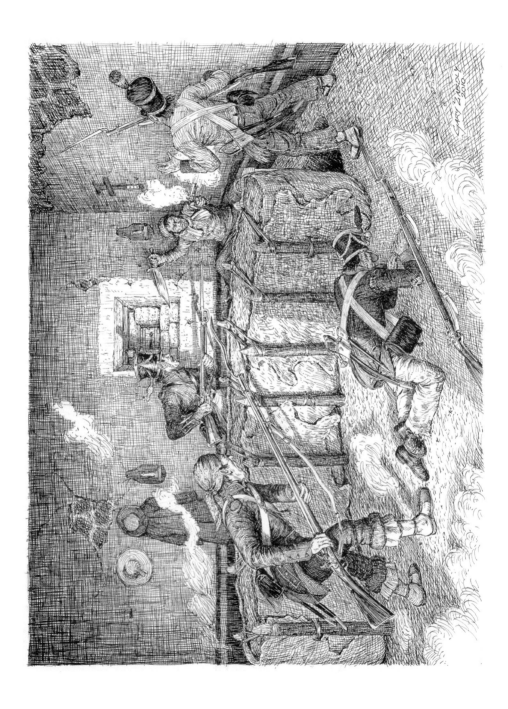

The Fighting Death of James Bowie

"Poor James Bowie. How quickly your stupid, inane arrogance is dissipated. These fools do not know Mexicans." So read an exultant editorial in Mexico's *La Lima de Vulcano* of March 22, 1836. One of Antonio López de Santa Anna's officers, most likely Lt. Col. José Juan Sánchez Navarro, afterward noted in a letter describing the assault: "the perverse braggart Santiago Bowie, died like a woman, almost hidden under a mattress."[1]

The first reports of the Alamo's fall, brought to General Sam Houston by Tejano observers, claimed that "Col. BOWIE was sick in his bed, and was also murdered."[2] And this is what Houston relayed to Col. James W. Fannin at Goliad in a letter dated March 11, but two days later Houston wrote to Henry Raguet, "Our friend Bowie, as is now understood, unable to get out of bed, shot himself, as the soldiers approached it."[3] The first printed report in English, in the *Telegraph and Texas Register* of March 24, simply stated, "Col. James Bowie, who had for several days been sick, was murdered in his bed; his remains were mutilated."

Other contemporary accounts differed. From a long narrative testimony by Travis's slave Joe, penned by William Fairfax Gray, "Bowie is said to have fired through the door of his room, from his sick bed. He was found dead and mutilated where he had lain."[4]

By the summer of 1836, reports of Bowie fighting to the end had become the standard version of his death. One of these, "well authenticated [and] extracted from a letter recently received from a friend residing in Natchitoches, Louisiana," read:

> A characteristic fact is also related of Colonel Bowie, who formed one of that ill-fated garrison. When the fort was carried he was sick in bed. He had also one of the murderous butcher knives which bears his name. Lying in bed he discharged his pistols and with each discharge brought down an enemy. So intimidated were the Mexicans by this act of desperate and cool bravery, that they dared not approach him, but shot him through the door, and as the cowards approached his bed over the dead bodies of their companions, the dying Bowie, nerving himself for a last blow, plunged his knife into the heart of his nearest foe at the same instant that he expired. Such are a few of the facts I have learned connected with the fall of San Antonio.
>
> —*New York Times*, June 29, 1836[5]

(Continued)

Another less than heroic version of Bowie's death originating from Sánchez Navarro is found in the key to his plan of the Alamo, included on an 1840 map of the state of Coahuila. He indicated Bowie's location ("L") as being in a large room of the low barracks, on the south side of the compound:

> L: Hospital; in the front of the large room[6] that is against the gate, without making resistance died the braggart and assassin Santiago Wuy [Bowie].

Sánchez Navarro is the only Mexican participant in the battle to claim, contemporaneously, that Bowie "died like a woman, almost hidden under a mattress." But how did he know this? He does not state that he *saw* Bowie killed, so one must assume that he was either told by fellow soldiers, or made his own conclusion by a personal observation of Bowie's bullet- and bayonet-riddled corpse. On the other hand, how did *Joe* know that Bowie "fired through the door of his room, from his sick bed," unless also told by Mexican soldiers, or via his own postbattle eyewitness conclusion?

In his 1860 account of the battle, Francisco Antonio Ruíz, *alcalde* of San Antonio in 1836, verified Sánchez Navarro at least in terms of location, when he recalled inspecting the body-littered fort with Santa Anna: "Col. Bowie was found dead in his bed, in one of the rooms of the south side."[7] Reuben Marmaduke Potter also concurred regarding this location in his 1860 and 1878 versions of *The Fall of the Alamo.*

Many decades after the battle, the aging Madame Candelaria maintained she had been nursing the sick Bowie when the Mexican soldiers burst into his room. Her claims have been dismissed by most historians as false, yet in at least one detail she verified Sánchez Navarro; most of her accounts state that Bowie was in such an ailing condition that he made no resistance; in one statement she said he was already dead.

A curious entry in an 1839 magazine article on Texas offered the following:

> The fate of Bowie is ascertained with greater clarity, from a female servant, who was so fortunate as to escape the general destruction. On the night of the attack, he was confined to his room by sickness, and was scarcely able to leave his bed. When the Mexicans broke over the walls, some rushed to his apartment. He was up in time to take his stand in the door; and with the knife which bears his name, he for some time kept the enemy at bay. When his mighty arm was at last tired with the work of death, he fell upon the heaps of the slain which he had thrown around him.[8]

If this "female servant" was not the young Madame Candelaria, who was she, and had she actually witnessed Bowie's death? The only female servant of Bowie's known to be in the fort, according to scattered bits of evidence, was a black woman named Betty. The early report of the Alamo's fall in the March 24 *Telegraph and Texas Register* noted that, along with "Travis's negro" and Mrs. Dickinson, "a negro of Bowie's [was] spared." William Neale, who was living in the state of Tamaulipas, near the mouth of the Rio Grande, when Santa Anna's army marched out of Texas in 1836, recalled that "a colored woman came with the Mexican troops, called Bettie, who represented herself as the former cook of Col. James Bowie." Her account claimed that during the assault of March 6 she was in the Alamo's kitchen with Charlie, a black man, whose life was also spared after a brief struggle.[9] The journal of Dr. Joseph Barnard also mentions "a negro of Bowie's" as surviving the battle.[10]

Other locations for Bowie's death, culled from the testimonies of survivors made decades later, included the church baptistry, the second-floor hospital of the convent building, and the Trevino house in the center of the west wall, site of Travis's headquarters.[11] One account even had Bowie being thrown onto one of the funeral pyres while still alive, after his tongue had been cut out!

So just how did James Bowie die—fighting, suicide, or without making resistance? In none of these cases is the evidence rock solid and irrefutable. There is no substantiated eyewitness testimony, just an assortment of conflicting hearsay and conjecture.

Common to many of the fort's rooms throughout the siege, including those of the low barracks in which Bowie was said to have died, were "ditches made [by the colonists] inside the houses in order to protect themselves from injury by the grenades and artillery shot," according to Sánchez Navarro's key and plan. Lt. Col. Enrique de la Peña confirmed this when he wrote, "They had bolted and reinforced the doors, but in order to form trenches they had excavated some places inside that were now a hindrance to them."[12] Potter, from accounts he had gathered on his own beginning in 1836, described these interior defenses: "most of those doors [of the soldiers' quarters] had within a semicircular parapet for the use of marksmen, composed of a double curtain of hides, upheld by stakes and filled in with rammed earth."[13]

---

1. *El Mosquito Mexicano*, April 5, 1836.

2. *Arkansas Gazette*, April 5, 1836.

3. Houston to Fannin, March 11, 1836, Houston to Raguet, March 13, 1836, Todd Hansen, ed., *The Alamo Reader: A Study In History* (Mechanicsburg, Penn.: Stackpole Books, 2003), 513, 517.

(Continued)

4. *Frankfort Commonwealth*, May 25, 1836.

5. This article originally appeared in Ohio's *Xenia Gazette*, no date given.

6. "Large room" is translated from Sánchez Navarro's word, *sala*, which means first large room in a house, parlor, or hall.

7. Ruíz account of 1860, in Frank W. Johnson, *A History of Texas and Texans* (Chicago: American Historical Society, 1914), 409.

8. "Notes on Texas," *The Hesperian: A Monthly Miscellany of General Literature* 2, no. 1, (November 1839): 197.

9. Article on Sergeant Francisco Becerra, 1882, in Hansen, *Alamo Reader*, 462–463.

10. Dr. Barnard's journal, entry of May 17, 1836, in Hansen, *Alamo Reader*, 613.

11. John Sutherland, who had been in the Alamo on February 23, 1836, asserted that Bowie shared these quarters with Travis and that he was also killed there. Sutherland returned to the fort about two years after the battle, with Travis's slave Joe as he claimed, and was shown the spot in this house where, supposedly, Bowie's brains had been splattered against the wall from three Mexican balls to the head. He said that Mrs. Dickinson verified this location. Sutherland narrative in Hansen, *Alamo Reader*, 154, 160.

12. José Enrique de la Peña, *With Santa Anna in Texas: A Personal Narrative of the Revolution*, ed. Carmen Perry (College Station: Texas A&M University Press, 1975), 50.

13. Reuben M. Potter in Johnson, *History of Texas and Texans*, 411.

A characteristic fact is also related of Colonel Bowie, who formed one of that ill-fated garrison. When the fort was carried he was sick in bed. He had also one of the murderous butcher knives which bears his name. Lying in bed he discharged his pistols and with each discharge brought down an enemy. So intimidated were the Mexicans by this act of desperate and cool bravery, that they dared not approach him, but shot him through the door, and as the cowards approached his bed over the dead bodies of their companions, the dying Bowie, nerving himself for a last blow, plunged his knife into the heart of his nearest foe at the same instant that he expired. Such are a few of the facts I have learned connected with the fall of San Antonio

—*Xenia Gaz.* (Ohio)
—*New York Times,* June 29, 1836

For many Americans, the violent death of Crockett provided the greatest shock, and it was a loss that was almost universally mourned by the press, no matter the political stance of the writer.

DAVY CROCKETT is dead! He has often said "he wished he might be shot," and he has been.

Unquestionably, he was a brave and daring man, rich in those qualifications which fit one to be a pioneer in a new country, and to head hardy spirits in the paths of enterprise. He was out of his element in Congress;—but he was an *honest* man; which is more than could be said of many who used to ridicule his homely good sense. He fell bravely, and he will be long remembered, as a patriot and a soldier, when the recollection of his coarse eccentricities will have faded from every mind.

—*New York Gazette and General Advertiser*,
April 13, 1836

The *Memphis Enquirer* offered a similar appraisal.

COL. CROCKETT.—A general expression of deep sympathy pervades the press, over the lamentable fall of Col. Crockett. Though not a great, he was an honest, noble, generous, brave and good man. No stranger left him in hunger or naked, if he had an ear of corn or a sixpence to divide with his suffering brother. His political life rendered him obnoxious to his opposition, whose weapons of detraction were sped at him even while pouring out his blood in the cause of oppressed humanity, upon the walls

of the Alamo. Peace to the manes of the generous and brave!
— *Memphis Enquirer,* April 27, 1836

Crockett's earlier status as a living American folk hero was only magnified many times over by his death.

> *Eloge Funebre on Col. Crockett.*—The Coatesville (Chester co., Tenn.) General Advertiser contains the following obituary *a la Ossian*, dedicated to the memory of the celebrated Crockett:
> *Col. Crockett.*—"All flesh is grass," saith the preacher, "and as the flower of the field it passeth away!" It is even so. He that came off victorious from a hundred contests with the stern chieftains of the forest—at whose approach the bear and the panther shook with affright—and the deer and the buffalo fled as from the messenger of death—the redoubtable Crockett, is no more! Fallen is Alamo! Fallen is the hero of Tennessee! The places which have known him, shall see him no more—the halls which have re-echoed with the thunders of his eloquence are silent, and the bear, the wild cat, and the alligator, no longer tremble at the sound of his carabine. The victor is overthrown—the champion is dead. He has "gone ahead" of his competitors to that land "from whose bourne no traveller returns." May he rest in peace.
> — *New York Evening Star*, April 22, 1836

In the quiet early hours of Sunday, May 1, New Yorkers who went out and bought the *Morning News* would have read a fairly lengthy eulogy, including a psychological analysis, of Crockett the frontiersman, politician, celebrity, and soldier.

> *David Crockett is dead.*—He was indeed a character—one that no other country but our own ever did or ever will produce. The whole man, physical and mental, was of frontier growth. The pioneers of civilization in the west were, most of them, born in more thickly settled portions of our country; but, pushing westward, took possession of the wilderness, and made it bow beneath their exertions. Labour and exposure gave hardihood and independence to their character; and they felt and acted like lords of the soil. The axe and the rifle were familiar to their offspring from their infancy. In this society was David Crocket educated, and became distinguished, in his youth, for feats of strength and skill; few were stronger, and none had a more unerring aim than Crocket. He soon, in the flash language of the country, became a *steamboat*. In the war of 1812 he turned a soldier, and was a brave one; a man to be led, not driven; one who had more courage than discipline. There was a romance in his character not uncommon among his countrymen, but in him it was full and exalted. The light of nature's sagacity, which the white man on our frontiers possess in greater degree than the Indian, makes education less necessary than in thickly settled countries. After the war was over, Crocket was a successful hunter, and a prosperous planter, and every way a busy man. His hospitality was unbounded; his doors were open to the wayfaring man, and he could not pass without breaking bread with him, and washing it down with a glass of Monongahela.

Among the evils of a new country is the rage for political life; and Crocket was infected by this mania, and placed himself before the publick as a candidate for congress. His struggle for this honour was a long one, but he at length succeeded. He had good lungs, fine health, and persevered in his electioneering with untiring assiduity. His voice was loud, and well suited to stump oratory. He sometimes softened his accents to coax his friends, but met his antagonists with the growl of a bear, and the spring of a panther. No disasters ever broke him down; if one campaign failed, he was soon in the field for another. If his vocabulary was scanty, he was master of the slang of his vernacular, and was happy in his coarse figures. He spurned the idle rules of the grammarians, and had a rhetorick of his own. When he came to congress he imagined that he should awe many of the dandy members by his corporeal prowess, and that his skill in shooting and strength in wrestling, would serve as well in Washington as at an electioneering assembly. He had promised to reform many abuses, and that in a direct, short way. The first thing, he said, that *bothered* him, was the rules and orders; what those rascally things were made for he could not reckon, for they did not do any good. If he happened to violate the rules and orders and get on a fair track, he found that his tongue did not wag so glibly as it used to on the stump; and he frequently found his respiration difficult and his knees weak, when he attempted to harangue in the house. He could not understand this, but still he found it was so day after day. He often looked around to see if there was any one bigger or stronger than himself, that caused this fear; until then he had never known any other cause of fear than that of a stronger man than himself. His great visions of reform, one after another, vanished, for he could not make the members listen to his reasonings. And after a while he began to suspect that there was not so much honesty among men as he had believed there was. If he got a fair shot at a political wildcat, he found that he had more lives than ever was fabled of grimalkin—and even if he knocked his brains out the creature would not die. As he picked up a few more words of English, and softened some of his bold sayings, in fact the more he lost of the man of the woods the less interesting he became as a curiosity. The last time we saw him he reminded us of the savage who had lost the energy and pantomime grace of the war dance, in taking lessons from a French master to figure in a cotillion. Such were the fascinations of Washington, and of a life in the capital, that he was anxious to be continued in congress, but he must have his own way; he, like an honest man, would not be trammelled, and they at length refused to send him. Excitement he must have; and just as he lost his election the troubles at Texas began, and here was a field for him. He could not live without being before the publick. He had been half inebriated with distinction for eight or ten years, and inglorious seclusion would not answer for David Crocket, and he found it hard work to gain and support a literary reputation. His court phrases did not look as they sounded from his tongue.

He was brave, and had the ardent soul of a warriour.—He knew that military renown was more rapidly acquired, if acquired at all, than any other. One bold adventure has fixed the soldier's fate—either sent him to sleep in the bed of honour or raised him to fame and power. Reasoning thus, he went "ahead". Nor was his destiny long doubtful; he met the enemy and boldly died. Thousands of his countrymen will arise to avenge his death—God speed them. The ashes of Crocket were not given to the winds in vain. A hotter flame than that which consumed his mortal remains, will burn in the hearts of indignant freemen, until the murderer leaves the clench of his dagger, and the bigot, with his fagot and his torch, are stamped to dust.

—*New York Sunday Morning News*,
May 1, 1836

The very next day, the *New York Sun* reprinted an article from the *Philadelphia Gazette* that offered hope that perhaps Crockett was not dead after all.

Crockett Redivivus.—We have astounding news to tell. The coon-killer yet lives: bearing a charmed life, he was scotched, not killed, and is still enumerated among the quick—capable of still going ahead, and giving pleasure to those who feared, with one of our contemporaries, when the news arrived of the fall of San Antonio, that he had "shot ahead so far, that there was no redemption thence." It is devoutly to be wished that the following statement (which we copy from the Cincinnati Whig) may be true; but take it altogether, and it leaves an unpleasant dubiousness in the mind, betwixt a hope and fear. However, we hope for the best. Time will decide.—*et douc nous verrons.*

Col. Crockett not dead yet.—We are much gratified in being able to inform our readers that Col. Crockett, the hero and patriot, it is said is not yet dead. This cheering news is brought by a gentleman now in this city, directly from Texas, and who left the Colonel, as he states, three weeks ago, at the house of his brother-in-law in Texas, where the Colonel was lying quite ill, but gradually though slowly recovering from his wounds.

The gentleman who brings this news is known to a number of our citizens, who believe him to be a man of veracity. He states that Crockett was left upon the battle ground at St. Antonio covered with wounds, and as the Mexicans supposed, dead. That after the Mexicans had abandoned the place, Crockett was discovered by some of his acquaintances to be lying among the slain, still exhibiting signs of life. He was immediately taken care of, and conveyed to comfortable lodgings, (as before stated) where his wounds were dressed, and every attention necessary to his recovery paid him. He had received a severe gash with a tomahawk on the upper part of the forehead, a ball in his left arm, and another through one of his thighs, besides several other minor wounds. When the gentleman who brings this intelligence left his brother-in-law's house, Crockett was doing well.

In relation to the death of Col. Crockett, the Natchez Courier relates the following:—While Col. Childers was questioning Col. Travis's servant (who escaped the general massacre) about the battle, he asked, "How did Col. Crockett behave?" The negro simply replied, "It was thought Col. Crockett killed the most, as he had the biggest pile around him."

—*New York Sun*, May 2, 1836

The *Morning Courier and New York Enquirer* also published the preceding article by way of the *Cincinnati Whig* and added a commentary on its questionable veracity.

The editor of the Whig is compelled to doubt the story, and still, he says, the respectability of the gentleman, who saw the Colonel with his own eyes, induces him to give it credit. We, too, are compelled to doubt the statement, glad as we certainly should be, to have it true. We do not understand how any of the Colonel's "acquaintances" could have got into the fort, in full possession as it was, of the Mexican troops; much less, how the wounded man could have been carried into comfortable lodgings, in a part of the country where every foot of ground was occupied by the enemy: and it must be remembered, too that the survivors of that sanguinary massacre, state that the bodies of all the victims

were burned on the spot. The account of the Colonel's resurrection, we fear, cannot be true.

—*Morning Courier and New York Enquirer*, May 7, 1836

Two weeks later, the same New York paper published a brief description of Crockett's death that seemingly settled the question—for now.

The following letter lately received from Louisiana, by a member of Congress, leaves no doubt of the actual death of Col. Crockett; as indeed, there was no reasonable doubt before. The Cincinnati Whig says not a word of its "respectable gentleman's" account of the Colonel's recovery of his wounds, since the first statement, and we notice that the Gazette of that city said nothing of it at all—a circumstance among others that led us from the first to have no confidence in the story. The poor creature who put it afloat ought himself to be delivered over to Santa Ana.

"CROCKETT was found—within the Alamo—in an angle made by two houses, lying on his back, a frown on his brow, a smile of scorn on his lips—his knife in his hand, a dead Mexican lying across his body, and twenty-two more lying pell-mell before him in the angle."

A Whig of a later date, seems to give up its information, and his story to the buffelings of Satan.

—*Morning Courier and New York Enquirer*, May 21, 1836

"Humbug," noted a Virginia paper when it came to all the wild rumors about how the famous colonel died.

There is no reason to doubt the destruction of Col. Crockett and all who were with him, at the fall of the Alamo, except Mrs. Dickinson and the negro, who were spared and sent to the Texan camp by Santa Anna. The bodies, we have been told, were all burned; and of course Crockett was consumed among the rest. The story of his being lately found with 30 dead Mexicans lying around him, must be a humbug. The victorious Mexicans would not be likely to leave their own dead unburied.

There are persons in Texas who seem to be deeply interested in getting up terrible tales of Mexican outrages, for the purpose of exciting the sympathies of our people in behalf of the Texans. We don't believe more than half of the horrible which reaches us from that quarter—and we intend to publish only such reports as appear to be well authenticated.

—*Norfolk Advertiser*, May 14, 1836

In early June, Tennessee's *National Banner and Nashville Whig* reprinted a passionate Crockett eulogy originally published in a Mississippi newspaper, with a slight edit made for its own state's citizens.

COLONEL CROCKETT.

The Natchez Courier sighs the following lament over the premature demise of the brave and honest Crockett:—

We ourselves on learning the melancholy intelligence of the fall of San Antonio, felt an extra pang of grief when we found that Davy Crockett was among those gallant patriots, and foremost among them too, who nobly perished in its defence. We had hoped to see Davy coming out of war, at its termination, with new honors bound thickly round his brow. But alas, he has passed from among us, and been gathered to his fathers in the full meridian of his glory. We never expect to look upon his like again. He was indeed one out of a thousand—ay, of a million. Poor Davy Crockett—we lament the fate of the sick Bowie—we feel sad and angry by turns when we think of the butchery of the gallant Travis; but there is something in the untimely end of the poor Tennessean, that almost wrings a tear from us. It is too bad—by all that is good, it is too bad. The quaint, the laughter moving, but the fearless and upright Crockett, to be butchered by such a wretch as Santa Anna—it is not to be borne! can we bear it? ought we to bear it? Will TENNESSEE bear it? If we mistake not, she will not? A hundred, perhaps a thousand of her rifles will avenge his death. Alas poor Davy! thine was a horrid fate, but like a man and an American, you met it. By the speech of Mr. Childress we learned (what

we could have ventured to assert before) that he sold his life at a most precious price—that he hewed down the myrmidons of the usurper on all sides of him at a most fearful rate—or, in the happy phraseology of the speaker, "nobly did he, go ahead, to the last." Alas poor Davy! thou art gone forever from the earth, but thy blood cries aloud from it for vengeance. It will be repaid, terribly, awfully, or we know not the nature of his countrymen.

—*National Banner and Nashville Whig*, May 30, 1836

Some other, lesser known members of the garrison were not being ignored by the newspapers.

Col. James Bowie, who was killed by the Mexicans in the fortress of San Antonio, was a sort of gentlemanly desperado, well known in Mississippi and Louisiana for his numerous quarrels. He was the inventor of a sort of knife, longer than a butcher knife, made to be carried under the coat, and called by the gentlemen stabbers the "Bowie Knife."

—*The Liberator* (Massachusetts), June 11, 1836

Another article purported to tell how the Bowie Knife earned its name.

THE BOWIE KNIFE.—This weapon, which has been several times named in our columns, is longer and heavier than a butcher's knife, intended to cut or thrust, and was invented by Col. James Bowie, who was killed by the Mexicans at the capture of the Alamo, in Texas. The circumstance which gave rise to its name, was about as creditable, as the purposes which it has since subserved. Some 12 or 18 months ago—the particulars of which we published at the time[v]—three brothers by the name of Bowie, in one of the southern states, had a deadly conflict with several other persons, armed with every species of weapon, and among the rest, the large knife of which we are now speaking. This was handled by the brothers with such

[v] This particular report has not yet been located.

dexterity as to decide the conflict in their favor, although numbers were against them—and it has ever since been called by their name, the Bowie knife. It is made to carry under the coat, and is now always worn by "gentlemen stabbers" in the South and West.

We understand that an order has been received at the Sheffield cutlery establishment, at this place, for several thousand of these knives, intended for the southern and western markets.

—*Germantown Tel.*
—*Baltimore Gazette and Daily Advertiser*, July 11, 1836

More on the origin of the Bowie Knife appeared in a July issue of the *New York Herald*. The article mentioned a portrait of Rezin Bowie and made a vague allusion to the fact that he had recently joined the Texian army, "breathing vengeance on his brother's slayers."

BOWIE KNIFE: —Who invented the Bowie Knife? Who wrote the Orphic poetry? Who are the Eikon Basileike? Who the letters of Junius, or War in Disguise? Who wore the iron mask? Not James Bowie—nor any more did he conceive the knife which bears his name. That kind of knife was the production of Reson Bowie, a brother of James—one of a desperate daredevil family, who have been the terror and the proverb of the whole south-west. Do you wish to see his likeness and the formidable, terrible weapon—which his bloodthirsty ingenuity contrived? Go to Bishop's barroom in New Orleans—there hangs his portrait. A brown and swarthy creature with hard face, stern cold eye and firm lip, open bosom, and the blood chilling knife in his clenched hand. If you wish to see the original, there he is at Donaldsonville, on the Mississippi, half blind and yet a terror, breathing vengeance on his brother's slayers, and ready to fight them from the corner of a handkerchief, at a moment's warning. In a duel some years ago, Reson holding a corner of his handkerchief and his antagonist another, cut up a Spaniard most terrifically.

—*New York Herald*, July 12, 1836

Mrs. Dickinson's husband, Almeron, received a brief notice in a few papers, including Massachusetts's *Sun*.

Lt. Dickinson, who was mentioned as having his wife and child with him at the massacre of the garrison of Bexar, was a son of the late Gen. Lemuel Dickinson, of Hatfield, in this State. He went to Texas some years since and married his wife there. She is the only survivor except one, of the slaughtered.

—*The Sun*, May 5, 1836

Another defender claimed by New England was Robert Cochran.

We notice that Mr. Robert Cochran, formerly of Portsmouth, was among the 180, who were killed at the retaking of the Alamo, by the Mexicans, Feb. 6.[w] He volunteered in defense of his adopted country about the first of September last, and continued in the front ranks of soldiers up to the time of his death.

—*The Portsmouth Journal* (New Hampshire), May 21, 1836

South Carolina's *Edgefield Advertiser* provided some sketchy biographical material on Travis and James Butler Bonham and attempted to link them together in boyhood days.

The Edgefield Advertiser takes the following notice of two youthful patriots from that district: Col. James B. Bonham, emigrated to Alabama two or three years ago, and thence to Texas. He was a liberally educated gentleman, a lawyer by profession, and one of the Aids of Gov. Hamilton during the most eventful period of our history. He was in the Alamo when it was besieged by the Mexicans. Col. Travis, with a force of only 150, was contending against eight or ten thousand of the enemy. At what period of the siege, Bonham joined him, we cannot say with certainty. Col. Travis, in the last appeal which he makes to the President of the Convention, and which was written but three

---

[w] This article has the Alamo's fall occurring a month before it actually did.

days before the Alamo fell, speaks of him more than once by name. We think it *almost certain* that he was with him *throughout*. Travis speaks of him as his special messenger, and as having despatched him to the surrounding country for aid. He speaks particularly of a mission to the town of La Bahia 8 or 10 days before. He was also a messenger to the town of Gonzales. During this time, it is known that the Alamo was besieged by about 10,000 of the enemy, who were firing upon it from five different points. Who will not admire that daring spirit which led him alone to make his way through the almost countless numbers of the enemy on the noble errand of obtaining succor for the perishing— and alone to have made his way back again? This he did repeatedly when the enemy were firing from all quarters upon this devoted little band. His last mission was to the town of Gonzales. Here he succeeded in obtaining a reinforcement of thirty-two, whom he dispatched to the Fort and who reached it in safety at 3 o'clock on the morning of the 1st March. Col. Bonham remained behind, engaged in the noble objects of his mission; but reached the Fort alone on the same day at 11 o'clock. In two days the Fort fell, and all were massacred.

Col. W. Barrett Travis, the commandant of the Alamo, was also a native of this District. His family removed to Alabama about sixteen years ago. He was also a lawyer by profession, and a gentleman of fine character. His various appeals from the Alamo, are couched in the strong and lofty language of a soldier and a patriot; and we know that the history of military achievement does not furnish an instance of more desperate defence.

It is not an uninteresting fact, that Bonham and Travis were about the same age (30 years;) that they were born within two miles of each other; that their professions were similar, and that after a separation of 16 years, they again met in a foreign land, and fell together in a noble struggle against a tyrant.

—*Baltimore Gazette and Daily Advertiser*,
July 27, 1836

Texas's Judge Advocate General William Harris Wharton had traveled east with Stephen Austin as a commissioner to explain why the Texians had revolted against Mexico, and to enlist whatever assistance they could. In a long, fervent address delivered at the Masonic Hall in New York City on April 26, Wharton gave an account of the see-saw history of Texian relations with Mexico, of the beginning of hostilities in 1835, and in the following extract, of the character of the leaders who fell at the Alamo.

Of the other unconquerable spirits who perished in the late massacre at San Antonio, it would seem invidious not to speak. The gallant Travis was cut off in the flower of his life. He was accomplished and dignified in his deportment, and collegiately and legally educated. Bowie is a name that was synonymous with all that was manly and indomitable in the character of man. Colonel Bonham was a native of South Carolina; he lately acted as aide to Governor Hamilton, and has not left a more chivalrous gentleman behind him. Of Colonel David Crockett it is unnecessary here to speak; he was known, at least by character, to all of us. Suffice it to say, that although the world has been often amused with his innocent eccentricities, no one has ever denied him the character of a firm and honest man—qualities which would cancel ten thousand faults if he had them. Gallant, departed, lamented, martyred, and mangled heroes,

"How many age hence
    Will these your lofty deeds be acted o'er,
In states unborn, and accents yet unknown."

My feelings will not permit me, gentlemen, to dwell upon the brutal atrocities and cold blooded massacres of the Mexican army. It is too evident to require argument, that in the refusal of quarter and in hoisting the red flag, the inhuman despot, Santa Anna, has denationized himself. That he now stands before the world as a pirate—the common enemy of mankind. That he has offered an insult to every civilized nation, and has made it their imperious duty to check his blood-stained career. But those martyred patriots have not fallen in vain. Although their blood has been swallowed by the sands of that field of death, and their ashes have been scattered by the whirlwinds of heaven, yet the light of their funeral pyre will gather together the sons of liberty, who will teach these *Mexican murderers* that the Anglo-American race in a cause so sacred can never die unhonored and unavenged.

—*United States Telegraph* (Washington, D.C.), May 19, 1836

Defender Daniel Cloud was lovingly remembered in a Kentucky newspaper, and the article was reprinted in a Mississippi paper.

From the Russellville Advertiser.

At a meeting of the young men of Russellville, on Tuesday April 18th, for the purpose of paying a tribute of respect to the memory of DANIEL W. CLOUD, Esq., formerly of this place, who was killed on 6th March, at San Antonia De Bexar, in an engagement with the Mexicans, Dr. Joel C. Rice was called to the chair, and George W. Norton appointed secretary. Whereupon the following preamble and resolutions were offered by T. P. Ware, esq. and unanimously adopted:

WHEREAS, we the young men of Russellville, are informed by late intelligence from Texas, that our very esteemed young friend, Daniel W. [C]loud, late of this place, was slain among the chivalrous little band who fell while bravely defending the Alamo in San Antonio, on the 6th day of March. And whereas the relations which he sustained among us as a member of the bar—as a friend—a companion, and a citizen, have been thus untimely severed, as we feel deeply afflicted for his loss—it is therefore

Resolved, That the many ties of friendship which he twined about our hearts—the high respect we cherished for his talents and enterprise, and our admiration of his amiable deportment, and his virtues, shall embalm his memory in our recollections.

Resolved, That we deeply condole with those who are bound to him by the endearing ties of relationship.

Resolved, That the early fate which closed his mortal career, has stricken from his profession a scion among the most cultivated and flourishing our country has reared.

Resolved, That if any reflection can lighten the gloom that is spread in our hearts, it is the conviction that he has nobly bared his bosom as a patriot, and received the fatal shaft in the defence of liberty and humanity.

After a few preliminary remarks by T. P. Ware, a letter written by Mr. Cloud, from Natchitoches to a young friend in this place, was read.[3]

—*The Missippian* (Jackson), May 6, 1836

Most Mexican newspapers continued to applaud Santa Anna. "Our pen is inadequate to praise your heroism; we can only admire you," read the editorial in the March 24 issue of *La Lima de Vulcano.* But Toluca's *La Luna* wondered if too many Mexican lives had already been lost in Texas, and *El Cosmopolita* underscored the fact that General Cos had broken his oath not to take up arms against the Texians again.

This discredit allied to the other damage we have already mentioned persuades thoughtful men that the victory at the Alamo has not been a real gain, a true triumph of the nation. The invaders' pride was humbled, the valor of Mexican soldiers proved, and although these are reasons for some joy, the advantage they bring is neither of such size nor of such importance in the light of what we have indicated should be celebrated as a real triumph of the nation.

—*El Cosmopolita* (Mexico City), April 2, 1836

Mexican newspapers, a few of them including Santa Anna's own report of the March 6 assault, began to arrive in the United States via merchant vessels.

From Mexico.—By an arrival from Mexico, the official account by Santa Anna, of his movements in Texas, have been received.

In conformity with the reckless course of this unprincipled and blood-thirsty tyrant, we perceive he wishes to give a coloring of chivalry and heroism to this atrocious conduct, asserting that after storming Alamo, he found within the walls the dead bodies of 600 Texians, and that Gen. Sesma was sent in pursuit of the fugitives. We have no doubt the obstinate and gallant resistance of the brave Travis, Bowie and Crockett, made the fortress seem to Santa Anna's eye peopled with innumerable hosts. And it is quite probable also, that there may have been 600 dead bodies within the walls, but if so, all except the immortal band of 182, who so gallantly and fearlessly met their death, must have been the minions of Santa Anna himself, who paid with their lives in three fold numbers the price of storming a citadel, defended by such men as were there.

Te Deums have been ordered in every part of Mexico. Coro, the President of Mexico ad interim, has been succeeded by General Parez. Santa Anna admits a loss of 60 killed and 300 wounded. He calls for 5000 more troops and more money. This last request proves the falsehood of the previous assertion.

—*New York Evening Star*, May 5, 1836

Also arriving north were rumors that many of the Mexican soldiers who had attacked the Alamo were convicts.

A very intelligent gentleman, just arrived from Texas, has given us an interesting account of the manner in which Santa Anna stormed the fortress of San Antonio. The Tyrant brought with him 1508 convicts from the Mexican prisons. On arriving at San Antonio, he placed the whole body of them as a forlorn hope in advance of the rest of the army, half encompassing them in the rear with 3,300 infantry, and placing still further in the rear 2,200 cavalry, with orders that each convict, who attempted to retreat, should be instantly shot or cut down. He then ordered the convicts to storm the fortress, setting before them liberty and promotion if they succeeded, and immediate death in the event of their failure.

They rushed forward with the fury of devils, and, in less than an hour, every man in the garrison was massacred. The carnage among the convicts was dreadful. Out of the fifteen hundred, all but three or four hundred were either killed or mortally wounded.

—*Louisville Journal.*

—*Memphis Enquirer*, May 18, 1836

Crockett was not out of the news for long. Following the battle of San Jacinto, members of the Mexican army imprisoned on Galveston Island were interviewed concerning events at the Alamo. One of them, unidentified in the following extract, offered up details about Crockett's death that had been hinted at in a few earlier reports. Among the information offered by the prisoner: a total of nine defenders, including Crockett, had survived the battle, only to be ordered executed by Santa Anna.

TEXAS.
Correspondence of the Courier & Enquirer.
GALVESTON BAY, 9th June, 1836.

Dear Sir—You have been furnished with such full details of past and passing events, by the numerous scribblers in this country, that nothing is left for my pen in a general way. Yet, there are certain little events which have occasionally transpired, and are transpiring daily, that few others than myself have had an opportunity of knowing; some of which may not be uninteresting. Therefore, I have concluded when I have a leisure moment from more important duties, to scribble a little myself. There may be hundreds besides yourself, who are willing—possibly anxious to hear of every event of interest connected in any way with the struggle for liberty and independence in Texas.

Well then, I will begin with the fall of the *Alamo*. Its fall and the massacre, must be fresh in the memory of every American. But I will relate one circumstance, detailed by an eye-witness, not before known, that will at once establish (if not before established) the blood thirsty cruelty of the tyrant, Santa Anna. After the Mexicans had got possession of the Alamo, the fighting had ceased, and it was clear day light, *six* Americans were discovered near the wall yet unconquered, and who were instantly surrounded and ordered by Gen. CASTRILLON to surrender, and who did so under a promise of his protection, finding resistance any longer in vain—indeed, perfect madness. Castrillon was brave and not cruel, and disposed to save them. He marched them up to that part of the fort where stood "his Excellency", surrounded by his murderous crew, his sycophantic officers. DAVID CROCKETT was one of the six. The steady, fearless step, and undaunted tread, together with the bold demeanor of this hardy veteran—"his firmness and noble bearing" to give the words of the narrator, had a most powerful effect on himself and Castrillon. Nothing daunted, he marched up boldly in front of Santa Anna, looked him steadfastly in the face, while Castrillon addressed "his Excellency," "Sir, here are *six* prisoners I have taken alive; how shall I dispose of them?" Santa Anna looked at Castrillon fiercely, flew into a most violent rage, and replied, "Have I not told you before how to dispose of them? Why do you bring them to me?" At the same time his brave officers drew and plunged their swords into the bosoms of their defenceless prisoners!! So anxious and intent were these blood thirsty cowards to gratify the malignity of this inveterate tyrant, that CASTRILLON barely escaped being run through in the scuffle, himself. Castrillon rushed from the scene apparently horror-struck—sought his quarters, and did not leave them for some days, and hardly ever spoke to Santa Anna after. This was the fate of poor Crockett, and in which there can be no mistake. Who the *five* others were, I have not been able to learn. Three other wounded prisoners were discovered and brought before "his Excellency", and were ordered to be instantly shot. There are certain reasons why the name of the narrator of these events should not be made known. I will only repeat that he was an *eye witness.*

I may tell you more about the Alamo yet, that Travis' boy, Joe, and Mrs. D. had not an opportunity of seeing or knowing.

—*Morning Courier and New York Enquirer*, July 9, 1836

A very similar account of Crockett's death also originated from Galveston Island in a letter written forty days after the date of the preceding one by an orderly sergeant in an Ohio volunteer company. Also based on the testimony of an unidentified Mexican, it was printed in a Detroit newspaper in early September, and the relevant extract follows.

TEXAS.

Extract from a letter written by Mr. George M. Dolson, an officer in the Texian Army, to his brother in this city; dated Glaveston [sic] Island, Camp Trevos[x] July 19, 1836.

"I am employed a considerable part of the time in interpreting Spanish for Colonel James Morgan, commander of this station. He sent for me yesterday and told me there was a communication of importance from one of Santa Anna's officers, which he wished me to interpret; accordingly the officer of the day was despatched for the Mexican officer, who came in in a few minutes, and the Colonel's quarters were vacated of all, save us three. The Mexican was then requested to proceed with his statement according to promise; and he said he would give a true and correct account of the proceedings of Santa Anna towards the prisoners who remained alive at the taking of the Alamo. This shows the fate of Colonel Crockett and his five brave companions—there have been many tales told, and many suggestions made, as to the fate of these patriotic men; but the following may be relied on, being from an individual who was an eye witness to the whole proceedings. The Colonel has taken the whole in writing, with the officer's name attached to it, which he observed to him, if he had the least delicacy, he might omit but he said he had not and was willing to be qualified to it in the presence of his God, and General Santa Anna, too, if necessary. He states that on the morning the Alamo was captured, between the hours of five and six o'clock, General Castillion, who fell at the battle of St. Jacinto, entered the back room of the Alamo, and there found Crockett and five other Americans, who had defended it until defence was useless; they appeared very much agitated when

---

[x] Camp Travis, or Fort Travis, an entrenched work.

The Capture of David Crockett

The most enduring mystery connected to the Alamo story remains the manner and moment of the death of David Crockett. The question has been explored and debated in numerous books, articles, and panels, not only of recent decades, but at least as far back as 1884, when Reuben Marmaduke Potter took to task another historian who had had the temerity to suggest that Crockett was one of six garrison members to have surrendered in the closing minutes of the battle. "This assertion is all wrong," wrote Potter in his rebuttal:

> Not a man of that garrison surrendered, but each one, Crockett among the rest, fell fighting at his post, except the few skulkers referred to. Even they did not surrender; but were dragged from their hiding-place and executed. . . . Crockett's body was found, not in an angle of the fort, but in a one-gun battery which overtopped the center of the west wall, where his remains were identified by Mr. Ruiz a citizen of San Antonio, whom Santa Anna, immediately after the action, sent for and ordered to point out the slain leaders of the garrison.[1]

Potter's surety, however, flies in the face of a compelling array of other Mexican sources—namely, officers of Antonio López de Santa Anna's army—that tell us that Crockett met a much different demise. In 1975, a small media stir was created with the publication of *With Santa Anna in Texas: A Personal Narrative of the Revolution* by José Enrique de la Peña. This campaign memoir attracted popular attention mainly because Peña states that Crockett "had survived the general carnage" and, with six other survivors, "under the protection of General Castrillon . . . were brought before Santa Anna." The Mexican commander "answered Castrillon's intervention in Crockett's behalf with a gesture of indignation," and, addressing himself to the Sappers, the troops closest to him, ordered his execution." The *Zapadores* refused, but "several officers . . . thrust themselves forward" and killed all seven prisoners with their swords.[2]

The reason this episode sparked such media ballyhoo was easy to understand: that Crockett did not die fighting proved something of a cultural shock to the Baby Boom generation, nurtured as it had been on the Disney *Davy Crockett* television miniseries in the mid-1950s (along with the merchandising craze it spawned). Yet the execution

(Continued)

concept was nothing new: it had been related in many previous studies, even textbooks. But because *With Santa Anna in Texas* was the lengthy, self-assured memoir that it was, there was an air of legitimacy, of finality about it.

A smaller book, Dan Kilgore's *How Did Davy Die?* was published three years later, and although it remained overshadowed by the Peña chronicle, it nevertheless created its own flutter of controversy among Alamo buffs and scholars. Kilgore discussed the Peña extract but added evidence confirming that Crockett had been executed from five other Mexican sources: Colonel Fernando Urissa, Sergeant Francisco Becerra, General Martín Perfect de Cos, Lt. Col. José Juan Sánchez Navarro, and an unidentified officer captured at San Jacinto. (The latter's account had been penned by Texian sergeant George M. Dolson for an article published in the *Detroit Democratic Free Press* on September 7, 1836.)

In the more than three decades since *With Santa Anna in Texas* and *How Did Davy Die?* appeared, all the "evidences" in these two books have been microanalyzed, often repetitiously, in many scores of printed works and online forums, by both scholars and amateur historians. (The debates have sometimes even severed friendships.) Yet for all this, the historical question has never been settled either way. Some have even declared a few of the Mexican sources—especially Peña's—as modern hoaxes, and the verifiably authentic ones as post–San Jacinto fabrications by captured Mexican soldiers who were bitter about what they perceived to be Santa Anna's betrayal to their country. What better way for them to ensure his punishment, so goes this line of thinking, than to say he had ordered the barbaric stabbing death of the beloved American celebrity Davy Crockett?[3] Others claim that the Texians themselves made up the story in order to guarantee the *generalissimo*'s execution.

On the other hand, the contemporary reports of Crockett fighting until he was killed are too numerous to be blithely dismissed (see the many newspaper examples of this in chapter 8). Most of them place his death inside the church, although another, insistent one says he fell "in an angle made by two houses."[4] At least two later accounts agree that he had ensconced himself in a small room or "niche" of the church, standing to one side of the opening and with his rifle braining every Mexican who dared enter, or else dispatching them with his knife or sword.

Crockett's ghost may be doomed to roam forever through the thick fog of these unanswered questions.

There is a curious anecdote provided by the captive Dr. Joseph H. Barnard, who had been sent by General José de Urrea to care for the Mexican wounded in San Antonio. From a number of *Bexareños* he was told that the Alamo garrison,

> with the full prospect of death before them, were always lively and cheerful, particularly Crockett, who kept up their spirits by his wit and humor. The night before the storming, he called for his clothes that had been washed, stating that he expected to be killed the next day, and wished to die in clean clothes, that they might give him a decent burial. (Alas, he was stript and burnt with the rest!)[5]

1. Reuben M. Potter, rebuttal, *Magazine of American History with Notes and Queries*, 11 (January–June 1884): 177–178.
2. José Enrique de la Peña, *With Santa Anna in Texas: A Personal Narrative of the Revolution*, ed. Carmen Perry (College Station: Texas A&M University Press, 1975), 53.
3. Many Mexican soldiers provided information about the battle and its aftermath, most of it obviously never recorded. There was the case of Captain William Scurlock, saved from execution at Goliad because of his medical abilities. Noted the *Red River Gazette* of July 16, 1836:
   > Captain Scurlock remained with the Mexican army for two months after the massacre attending to the sick and wounded, having to perform the most menial acts of drudgery and toil, during which time, he gathered many particulars, relative to the fall and slaughter of the Alamo, from a number of Mexicans, who were present at that action.—They informed him, that their loss amounted to 1525, ten of whom fell by the hand of Colonel Bowie, and seventeen by the hand of Colonel David Crockett.
   It is not mentioned if they confirmed that Crockett had been executed.
4. *Morning Courier and New York Enquirer*, May 21, 1836, quoting a "letter from Louisiana, by a member of Congress."
5. *Missouri Argus* (St. Louis), August 26, 1836.

the Mexican soldiers undertook to rush in after their General, but the humane General ordered his men to keep out, and, placing his hand on his breast, said "here is a hand and a heart to protect you; come with me to the General-in-Chief, and you shall be saved." Such redeeming traits, while they ennoble in our estimation this worthy officer, yet serve to show in a more hedious [sic] light the damning atrocities of the chief. The brave but unfortunate men were marched to the tent of Santa Anna.[4] Colonel Crockett was in the rear, had his arms folded, and appeared bold as the lion as he passed my informant (Almonte.) Santa Anna's interpreter knew Colonel Crockett,[5] and said to my informant, the one behind is the famous Crockett.[6] When brought in the presence of Santa Anna, Castrillon said to him, "Santa Anna, the august, I deliver up to you six brave prisoners of war." Santa Anna replied, "who has given you the orders to take prisoners, I do not want to see those men living—shoot them." As the monster uttered these words each officer turned his face the other way, and the hell-hounds of the tyrant despatched the six in his presence, and within six feet of his person. Such an act I consider murder of the blackest kind. Do you think that he can be released? No—exhaust all the mines of Mexico, but it will not release him. The one half, nor two thirds, nor even the whole of the republic, would not begin to ransom him. The combined powers of Europe cannot release him, for before they can come to his release, Texas will have released him of his existence; but I coincide with the secretary of war, as to the disposal to be made of him, that is, to try him as a felon. Strict justice demands it and reason sanctions it.

—*Democratic Free Press* (Detroit),
September 7, 1836

Eight years after the battle, a Maryland newspaper published the following segment from a pamphlet that professed to tell the authentic manner of Crockett's death, supposedly based on information gathered in San Antonio.[7]

The fall of the Alamo, or the last days of Crockett.

A pamphlet with this title has been issued in St. Louis, it is by John Henry Brown, a gentleman who has resided many years in La Vanca, Texas, and written from observation and correct information derived by enquiry on the spot. It gives an account of Fannin's Massacre, as well as the battles of Concepcion, Goliad, San Antonia, and in fact the whole history of the war. We copy a part of the narrative of

THE DEATH OF CROCKETT.

Colonel Crockett, wounded and closely pursued by a number of the enemy, retreated into the church, felling them as they approached. He stationed himself in a niche, in the corner, determined to face the foe to the last, and sell his life dearly; with his favorite rifle and a superabundance of side arms, he hewed and shot them down with the same awful certainty which was wont to characterize his indomitable spirit. His position rendered access to him impossible, except by a direct and exposed approach in front; and after some eight or ten of them were laid dead before him, a feeling of awe seemed to seize hold of the assailants— One of them, who could speak a little broken English, probably preferring to have the signal honor of capturing so noble a specimen of American valor, to present to his dread master, said to Crockett, "Surrender, senor." A flash

of the most sovereign scorn darted from the fiery eye, and as it pierced that of the enemy, he seemed to be transfixed. In a voice of thunder, Crockett answered—"Surrender! No!—I am an American!" and as he spoke he sent a ball through the heart of the paralized foe. He appeared for the moment like a wounded tiger, strengthened and buoyed by each additional wound; now hewing them down with his well tried sword—next dealing death with his fire arms. His person was literally drenched with his own blood; his strength must soon yield to its loss—yet such physical power, wrought to the highest degree of excitement, can perform incredible prodigies. This was the last concentrated energy of a powerful man, aroused, animated and guided by one of the noblest attributes of man—love of liberty. He knew for what his life was about to be sacrificed; that devastation and butchery would follow the footsteps of his heartless foes; that helpless woman would be sacrificed to satiate the cruel desires of the conqueror; and feeling the holy inspiration of a dying patriot, he fought manfully till the loss of blood and approach of death stayed his upraised arm; his rifle was broken to pieces, his pistols fell to the floor, and nothing but his faithful sword was left. In the agony of death with a terrible grasp, he brought this last weapon upon the head of the nearest assailant, and fell victoriously across his body, into the arms of death.—In this corner of the church there were TWENTY SIX dead Mexicans, and no other American having fought or fallen at that point, it is considered beyond all reasonable doubt that all of them fell by the hands of Tennessee's favorite son! All were now dead. Not a man left to relate the wonderful deeds of this illustrious band of heroes! Not a compatriot left to rear a monument to their memory! But, ah! no monument is required to perpetuate their fame. So long as freedom has an abiding place in America, will their heroic deeds and proud names be sacred!

—*Easton Gazette*, January 27, 1844

One of the earliest—yet little known—attempts to fully describe the siege and battle of the

Alamo, as well as the fort's physical makeup, first appeared less than five years after the event in the November 18, 1840, issue of Texas's *San Luis Advocate* and was subsequently reprinted in a number of newspapers in the United States. Attributed to one "MARMADUKE," it is clearly the work of Reuben Marmaduke Potter, whose 1860 monograph, "Fall of the Alamo," and expanded version of same in the January 1878 *Magazine of American History*, have long been recognized as pioneer works in Alamo scholarship. Why this incipient effort of Potter has never been referred to may be due simply to its unavailability to later historians, and Potter's own failure to mention it.

Born in Woodbridge, New Jersey, in 1802, Potter was living in Mexico by 1827, where he sought his fortune in the mercantile business. During the Texas Revolution he helped save the lives of twenty-one Texian prisoners held at Matamoros, where he resided, by aggressively appealing against their executions. In July 1837, he moved to Texas, where he worked as deputy collector and later collector of customs at Velasco from 1838 to 1844.[8]

In his "Fall of the Alamo," Potter noted that while living in Matamoros he "had opportunities for obtaining the kind of information" necessary for his study from Mexican soldiers as they retreated southward from their failed campaign. (In the following, he remarks that he had also observed a part of Santa Anna's army as it had marched toward Texas.) In addition he mentions that he had visited the Alamo grounds in 1841, taking measurements of the compound walls and buildings, one year after this article appeared in the *San Luis Advocate*. In the following he alludes to the fact that his description of the Alamo as it stood in 1836 is based on "as I have heard it described."

INCIDENTS OF THE TEXIAN WAR.
From the San Luis Advocate, Nov. 18.
ATTACK AND DEFENSE OF THE ALAMO
    "He who against two valiant foes
    Contendeth till he die,
    Doth mightier seem than he whose shout
    Makes twenty craven fly."
    —OLD BALLAD.

A departure from historical truth may be somewhat palliated when intended to cover disgrace; but even then the policy is bad; for such deviations, if touching matters of importance, are in general eventually exposed. There is, however, no excuse for such misrepresentations when the truth would reflect sufficient honor on those interested, and leave no trait of improbability in the events narrated.

The defence of the Alamo by Travis and his band, told without a touch of extra coloring, exhibits an instance of heroism almost unequalled; and any attempt to heighten its effect by embellishment would be injurious to the memory of those martyrs; since the truth is liable to be doubted if it appears linked with fiction.

The assault of the Alamo, too, by Santa Anna was executed with far more bravery than any fete of arms which the Mexicans have performed in Texas, or perhaps elsewhere; and to deny it would not only be a lack of candor towards them, but injustice towards the defenders, whom it required not only a superior but a determined force to crush. Hence there is little need, on either side, of the puerile exaggeration so lavishly used by both, as I will endeavor to show.

In Santa Anna's official report, made immediately after the action, he states that the garrison consisted of over 600 men; that he made the assault with 1,400 troops; and that after a desperate conflict, in which he owns the rebels fought with great determination, the fortress was carried and the Texians killed to a man; all which he accomplished with a loss of only 60 killed and 300 wounded.

As this statement was not believed in his own country, there is little need of making a formal refutation of it here; but it would be well to examine certain accounts of the same affair which are current in Texas, and have appeared in print.

A sample of these was lately published in the Texas Sentinel, under the head of "Reminiscences of the Alamo." The writer seems to have taken the most extravagant form of rumor for sufficient authority, without examining its credibility or seeking corroborative information; a method which may answer for filling up a gazette, but will not serve in gathering the materials of history. He asserts that the force which took the Alamo amounted to 10,000 men; that, after repeated assaults had been repelled with great slaughter, the final attack was made simultaneously against the four sides of the fortress by as many divisions, each of which had another in its rear to prevent its flight; that this attack lasted incessantly for three days, when the fortress was carried at the point of the bayonet with the loss of 1,600 men, just ten times the number of the defenders.

In all this the only assertion which does not show glaring exaggeration to any one acquainted with the details of the action and campaign is the strength of the garrison, whose effective force is acknowledged by both sides to have been 150 or 160. As the other statements can be refuted by the enemy, and perhaps some day will be, if recorded by us as historical facts, it would be wise as well as just to refute them ourselves.

From the best information which I have obtained, the whole force with which Santa Anna invaded Texas amounted to about 7,500 men.—Of these all but about 1,000 moved by the upper route upon Bexar; but not quite half of that portion had arrived there when the Alamo was taken. There are probably authentic proofs existing in Texas of the total of the invading force, of the number employed in that assault, and of the loss there incurred; for the archives of the chief command and several regiments were probably taken at San Jacinto; and it is to be hoped that they have been preserved. The reports therein contained might be depended on, as they were made for the commander's use, and correctness was indispensable. There are other facts known, however, from which something near the truth on those subjects may be inferred. The whole of the upper division halted a week at Saltillo; and several intelligent Americans then there, who had opportunities of observing, estimated its force to be about 6,500: which does not disagree with the reports of some of the military made both before and after the campaign. The lower division moved from

Matamoras upon Goliad; and at the former place I was able to ascertain about the amount of it, which did not exceed 1,000 men. This would make the whole number to be 7,500.

To calculate from other data, the number of troops who retreated from Texas was, according to Filizoli's report, about 4,100; which may be relied on, for, had the statement been too low, it would have been contradicted by Urrea and others, who denied the necessity of the retreat. The number agrees, too, with observations made after the arrival of the same force at Matamoras. Add to this 4,400 killed and taken at San Jacinto, and 2,000, an ample allowance for their losses at the Alamo, the Coleta and elsewhere, as also by desertion and sickness, and it will give the same estimated number of the whole, 7,500.

An estimate with similar result may be made from the number of regiments. I have never known these corps in Mexico, taking several together, to average over 500 men; for though their nominal complement is 1,000, they are seldom full. Some of those which I saw belonging to Santa Anna's "Army of Operations," before the invasion, numbered less than 400, and such as returned without being exposed to much loss were of nearly the same force; as several others, however, had been larger at the outset, I believe 500 to have been a fair average of their strength. The corps which composed that army were the cavalry regiments of Cuautla, Dolores, and Tampico, and the infantry of Yucatan, San Luis, Matamoras, Jimenez, Los Zapadores, Toluca, Guadalaxara, Queretara, Tres Villas, Morelos, Guerrero, and La Primera Activa, in all fifteen. Counting these at 500 each, will give the same total as the other estimates, 7,500.

I have been thus particular to show the true probable force of the invader, not only from a regard for the verity of historical statements, but in opposition to the propensity so common in Texas to overrate an enemy's strength, which has caused credence to be given many a false alarm.

The first-named regiment of cavalry and the first-named of infantry moved from Matamoras upon Goliad, under Urrea; and the rest, composing the upper division, marched from Loredo and its vicinity upon Bexar. Between those places is a broad tract of dry and sterile country over which they could not pass in one body; and they proceeded in four successive brigades.—Santa Anna arrived at Bexar on or about the 22d of February with the first brigade, consisting of the regiment of Dolores, San Luis, Matamoras, and Jimenez, and immediately commenced the siege of the Alamo. He sent orders to the next brigade to advance by rapid marches, and, till its arrival, confined his operations to besieging. I never learned that he made any regular attempt at storming till the final assault, though he kept up the investment of the Alamo with skirmishing, petty attacks, and feints, especially in the night, with the view of harassing the garrison. In these preparatory arrangements he no doubt lost a number of men, but I see no reason to believe that any extensive slaughter occurred.

Gen. Cos, with the regiments of Toluca and Los Zapadores, arrived about the beginning of March; and on the 5th, orders were issued for storming the fortress on the following morning. The rest of the upper division was still on the road. The time and manner of the movement above stated are too well known to be disputed, and it will thus appear that only one regiment of cavalry and five of infantry had then arrived.

The order of the day, issued on the 5th, and published soon after the action, is explicit as to the dispositions and the corps employed, but does not state the numbers; and I can only infer them from the premises before referred to.—Of the devoted tenants of the Alamo, none save a woman and a negro survived; and it cannot be expected that they would be able to give other than confused accounts of the vicissitudes of the action, or of the numbers or the loss of the enemy. What is related by different individuals of the enemy there engaged, men of various ranks, some from among those who returned to Mexico, and others who were afterwards prisoners, and are now domesticated among us, so far as their separate accounts are in accordance with each other and with probability, may, I think, be received as authentic. From these sources, mostly, I have gathered more clear and explicit details than I think have yet been published.

The Alamo, as I have heard it described, was an enclosure nearly of a quadrangular shape, and surrounded by a wall varying in height from five to ten feet; the area being traversed by inner walls, which partitioned into three subdivisions. In one angle was a chapel; and in the different subdivisions of the area, apartments of different sizes were built against the walls. Several of these had been prepared for defence, and the largest, a saloon extending along one of the partition walls, had a parapet of hides and earth within, to cover the lower parts of the windows. The chapel and its environs, with the aid of some raised works, forming the most commanding position in the fort, and was mounted with one or more guns. About twenty pieces were planted in different parts of the fortress, but, from its extent and situation, only a few could be brought to bear at once upon a storming party, if judiciously brought up. A part of the wall was dilapidated and some of the cannon ports, which had been hastily and rudely broken out, were so large as to serve as breaches for the enemy's entrance. One side of the Alamo was covered by the river San Antonio, which divided it from the town of Bexar. The whole area was so extensive that a thousand soldiers would have been barely competent to have manned its circuit. A hundred and fifty or sixty harrassed and exhausted men were, of course, far from sufficient; but, had the works been concentrated in proportion to the size of the garrison, the assault could not have succeeded, though made by the whole army. This was admitted by a general officer of the army.

Before day, on the sixth, all the troops in and about Bexar, except a few of the rawest recruits, were drawn out. The five regiments of infantry were formed, outside of the lines of circumvallation, into four columns of attack and a reserve, which were respectively commanded by Generals Cos and Castrillon and three colonels. These had their points of assault designated, which were on the three sides not covered by the river; and each column was provided with a certain number of ladders, axes

The Funeral Pyres

"The bodies of the slain were thrown into a heap in the centre of the Alamo and burned," reported the *New Orleans Bee* of March 28, 1836. In fact at least two big funeral pyres were built by Antonio López de Santa Anna's men and conscripted local labor on either side of the cottonwood-lined Alameda.[1] Constructed of alternate layers of bodies and mesquite wood with "kindling wood distributed through" the piles,[2] the larger pyre, about eighty feet long, ten feet wide, and ten feet high, sat diagonally south of the road; the smaller one, sixty feet long, sat north of the road.[3] However, a year later, burial-party leader Col. Juan Seguín reported that "the ashes were found in three heaps," indicating the possibility of a third pyre. In a speech, also in 1837, he added that the corpses of the defenders had been "bound by their feet" and dragged to the pyres.[4] Mexican soldier Felix Nuñez confirmed this in his account, adding that the infantry first tied the ropes to the bodies.[5] Pablo Díaz recalled that *carrettas* had brought many bodies to the pyres.[6]

"Grease of different kinds, principally tallow," recalled Bexareño Díaz, "was melted and poured over the two pyres."[7] Around five o'clock in the afternoon, as shown in the illustration, the pyres were lit.[8] The fire of each pyre, according to Díaz, created an "immense pillar of flame . . . the dense smoke from it rose high into the clouds," and burned for two days and two nights.[9] Many Tejanos would never forget the horrible stench that ensued. The flames and sparks of the southern pyre's fire skipped to a nearby orchard, destroying a number of fruit trees.[10] "Thousands of vultures" waited for the flames to subside.[11] For months afterward the two sites were littered with charred heads and other body parts.

Because the pyres were lit in the late afternoon of the very day the Alamo fell, it tells us that their construction had been very swift. It may be that the already felled trees of the *abatis*—most likely mesquite—that protected the outside of the Alamo's southeastern palisade had been drawn away to accelerate that construction. Other local traditions, according to an 1886 article about San Antonio, tell of a somewhat different construction for the pyres:

> After the Alamo had fallen and the massacre complete, Santa Anna ordered the Texan dead to be burned; accordingly they were stripped, and after being subject to indignities, in which Santa Anna joined, were taken to a point on

(Continued)

Alameda Street, near the present location of St. Joseph's (German) Catholic Church, where the funeral pyre was erected, there first being a layer of fence rails, then bodies, then rails over, and so on until all the bodies were in place. Brush was then piled on and around the pyre and the torch applied.[12]

The following contemporary newspaper report suggests that some of the Texians were still alive during these "indignities."

Extract of a letter, dated MATAGORDA, April 1, 1836.

Some spies taken by Houston here, reported that the prisoners taken alive at the Alamo, were dragged through hot embers, and their flesh cut off previous to being burnt in a pile.

—*Richmond Enquirer*, May 17, 1836

Mexican veteran Nuñez claimed that this was one of the darker resolutions of Santa Anna, who had "made the fatal promise, that he would burn the last one of them [Alamo garrison] when taken whether dead or alive."[13]

One of the eeriest related accounts dealing with the pyres and the garrison, in this case with James Bowie in particular, appeared in the newspapers in 1883. It is offered here in its entirety.

THE LAST MOMENTS OF COL. BOWIE

A sensational article in the Houston *Daily Post,* written by W. P. Zuber, of Grimes county, professes to give the first full account of the massacre of the Texan garrison in the celebrated Church of the Alamo, at San Antonio, March 6, 1836. Zuber says he got the account from a Mexican fifer known in Texas as Polin, who was with the Mexican army at the time of the capture of the Alamo. Polin says that after the Mexicans had taken the fort, scaled the walls, and put the garrison to the bayonet or sword, Santa Anna, accompanied by members of his staff, entered the fort and viewed the Texans slain. Polin, being a fifer and a privileged character, entered with Santa Anna, and immediately behind the Mexican dictator.[14] Santa Anna ordered the citizens of San Antonio to pick up the corpse of Col. Travis, the Texan commander, which he ran his sword through. After Santa Anna had retired from the fortress, two Mexican officers, with a number of soldiers, entered and proceeded to pile up the bodies of the dead Texans in order to burn them. In the search for corpses they discovered the celebrated Texan patriot, Col. Bowie, in a secluded department of the fortress, lying sick upon stretchers. One of the officers looked at the sick officer and asked the other if he knew him. The latter said he thought he did, and that it was the infamous Bowie. The officers then berated Bowie for fighting against the Mexican Government, after having married a respectable Mexican lady. He denounced them for fighting under a tyrant like Santa Anna. They ordered him to shut his mouth. Bowie said, "Never, for your sort." "Then," said the senior officer, "we will relieve you of your tongue." They then had soldiers take knives and split open his mouth, cut out his tongue, and throw his body, still writhing, upon a pile of corpses. The latter was saturated with camphene, and while Col. Bowie's body, still bleeding, but speechless, lay alive upon the funeral heap, a match was stuck into the combustible fluid, and a tall pillar of flame immediately shot up, and one of the Mexican officers, pale and trembling, said to his companions, "That fire takes Bowie's soul up to God."

This is the first account of the last moments of Col. Bowie ever published.—*San Francisco Call.*

—*Grand Forks Herald,* July 7, 1883

By 1846, according to William A. McClintock, the site of one of the pyres was "marked by a heap of black and mouldering earth, covered with a rank and noxious growth of weeds."[15]

---

1. Pablo Díaz was one of the Tejanos "impressed and forced to go out and cut bush." Captain John Elgin, "Reminiscences of the Story of the Alamo," in Todd Hansen, ed., *The Alamo Reader: A Study in History* (Mechanicsburg, Penn: Stackpole Books, 2003), 61. Sergeant Francisco Becerra also later noted that Colonel Mora was ordered to "make prisoners of all the inhabitants they might meet to gather wood." Hansen, *Alamo Reader*, 458.
2. 1906 account of Pablo Díaz, in Timothy M. Matovina, *The Alamo Remembered: Tejano Accounts and Perspectives* (Austin: University of Texas Press, 1995), 76; account of José Francisco Ruíz in Matovina, *The Alamo Remembered*, 44.
3. *San Antonio Express*, March 26, 1911, article on pyres and eyewitness accounts, in Matovina, *The Alamo Remembered*, 102, 105; account of Juan Antonio Chavez, *San Antonio Express*, April 19, 1914, in Matovina, *The Alamo Remembered*, 116. Tejano J. M. Rodríguez said that the smaller pyre stood "in the rear of where the Menger Hotel now stands," meaning, near the intersection of Bonham and Blum streets; *Daily Express* (Texas), May 28, 2009.
4. Juan N. Seguín to General Albert Sidney Johnston, March 13, 1837, and speech by Seguín, April 4, 1837, Matovina, *The Alamo Remembered*, 19, 21.
5. Account extract of Felix Nuñez, in Alan C. Huffines, *Blood of Noble Men: The Alamo Siege and Battle: An Illustrated Chronicle* (Austin: Eakin Press, 1999), 190.

(Continued)

6. Díaz account in Matovina, *The Alamo Remembered*, 105.

7. Ibid., 105.

8. Ibid., 44.

9. Ibid., 75, 103.

10. Ibid., 105.

11. Ibid., 75.

12. G. Norton Galloway, "Sketch of San Antonio," *Magazine of American History with Notes and Queries* 15 (January–June 1886): 534.

13. Felix Nuñez account in Hansen, *Alamo Reader*, 480.

14. Confirmation of a sort can be found in the testimonials of Mexican battle participants gathered by Reuben M. Potter, who related that when Santa Anna thought the fort had at last been conquered, he "moved up towards the Alamo, escorted by his aides and bands of music, but turned back on being greeted by a few shots from the upper part of the chapel," Frank W. Johnson, *A History of Texas and Texans* (Chicago: American Historical Society, 1914), 415. In an interview in the *San Antonio Express* of June 28, 1878, Mexican veteran Manuel Loranca said that Santa Anna was with "the music of the regiment of Dolores and his staff" while the battle was in progress.

15. "Journal of a Trip through Texas & Northern Mexico in 1846–1847," *Southwestern Historical Quarterly* 34, no. (1930): 146.

and other implements which might be serviceable in effecting an entrance. The cavalry were stationed in the rear of the columns, at convenient points, for cutting off any of the garrison who might attempt to escape.

Santa Anna, with his staff and escort and the regimental bands of music, posted himself at one of the batteries situated westerly from the Alamo.[9] At half past five, it not yet being fully light, he ordered the signal of charge to be sounded with a bugle from his position and the four columns moved at a rapid pace upon the fortress. The wearied garrison, it is supposed, had scarcely time to muster, when the enemy were within sixty paces of their walls. Their columns were raked by a discharge of cannon and rifles, which checked their advance, and one of them, contrary to orders, opened its fire: for they had been commanded to reserve it up to the wall.—General Amador, then acting as Santa Anna's second, brought up the reserve, and gave a new impulse to the assault. The Texians were too widely scattered on the works to concentrate a sufficient defence at each point of attack. The right column of the enemy arrived first at the wall; and, for a short time, their attempts to cross a low part of it, were repelled with severe loss; but while most of the resistance was drawn to this quarter, the left column effected an entrance on the opposite side, which was followed by the successive escalades of the others, the right entering last. It is generally considered that once a fortress is scaled, resistance is nearly at an end; but in this instance it had scarcely begun. Such of the garrison as could, took refuge in the different defensible quarters before described; others, cut off from such refuge, fought and fell in their exposed positions. Storming parties immediately assaulted the rallying positions, but the assailants fell at every step—

"For, still, all deadly aim'd and hot,
From every crevice comes the shot;
From every shatter'd window pour
The volleys of the sulphurous shower."

In spite of this destructive resistance, the smaller rooms were soon forced, and the scanty defenders, after the pistol and Bowie knife had done their utmost, sank under the bayonets of numbers. One of the rooms thus swept of its inmates was serving as a hospital, and contained the sick and wounded of the garrison, who were all massacred. The long saloon and the angle at the chapel were now the only positions that held out. The former, being built against a partition wall, looked out upon two

From the Phil Collins Collection

Mexican Sappers' Axe

Of all the artefacts in my collection, I find this the most chilling. It's a Sappers' Great Axe and is thought to have initially seen service during the Napoleonic Wars. It measures 39 inches long and is 15 inches wide at the blade and extremely heavy! The haft is of black japanned wood. The term *japanning* was given when referring to the black lacquer that was applied to the wood to make it waterproof, quite a common practise in the 18th and 19th centuries.

Sappers (*Zapadores*) were an invaluable asset to their army because they were responsible for digging the trenches that gave their infantry and artillery units more cover from enemy fire, thus enabling them to advance on the enemy while remaining hard to hit. Of course, the axe was also used as a weapon as these were well-trained soldiers as well as engineers.

As seems generally the case regarding the Mexican army's weaponry, much of it came from Europe. After the Napoleonic Wars, in the 1820s many of the captured French weapons found their way into the hands of the newly formed and grateful Republic of Mexico Army. Axes like the one pictured here could likely have been used by the Mexican Zapadores at the Alamo and certainly during the campaign in Texas in general.

In the final assault on the Alamo on March 6, the Zapadores were in the reserves and were called in to join the second and third columns in the attack on the weakening North Wall. Despite the incredibly high numbers of casualties, the Zapadores helped breach the North Wall and in doing so, sealed the fate of those inside.

(Continued)

They would then have been called into action to break down the barricaded doors and barred windows of the Long Barracks where the last Texian resistance remained. This would lead to the bloodiest part of that morning's battle. Fighting in the darkness as the sun slowly rose, the Texian defenders and Mexican soldiers fought hand to hand, face to face, in what would become a bloodbath. It's said that such was the frenzy of those moments that many Mexican soldiers lost their humanity and went on a killing and maiming spree that involved the repetitive bayoneting and even decapitation of those left lying in the dirt breathing their last.

If you add to that the Mexicans turning the Texian cannons around and firing inwards, hitting anything in the random path of the balls or canister fired, it was a human's worst nightmare. Carnage of the worst kind, *in the dark*!

In the 2004 Alamo movie, one of the scenes that still haunts me is that of the large Zapadores marching with their large axes, intent on doing as much damage as possible.

And although it's "only a movie" and to be taken with a pinch of salt, when lifting the axe shown here as I have done, it's unnerving to think of the damage it could, and probably did, inflict. –PC

subdivisions of the area. From each side incessant volleys of musketry were directed against its doors and windows; but at each attempt to storm it with the bayonet, the assailants fell in heaps at the entrance, and recoiled from the charge. A heavy gun, planted in an adjoining angle, was now turned, and poured its discharges into the building. The fire from within slackened. At the next charge the saloon was carried, and its remaining occupants perished like the rest in the fierce resistance of despair. The chapel and its environs still resisted, and a small gun mounted on the upper works, which had been wheeled against the assailants within, was still playing; but the whole force of the enemy being now turned against the position, it was speedily stormed.[10] In a few moments its defenders were added to the mass of carnage, and Santa Anna found himself in possession of the Alamo.

It might almost be literally asserted that only when the garrison had ceased to breathe the din of battle was hushed. Some three or four of the defendants, after the fort was entered, leaped from the walls to escape, but were cut down by the cavalry. One of them, who was pursued by two dragoons, shot one of them with a pistol and was lanced by the other. Mr. Dickinson, of Gonzales, an officer of artillery, who had his family in the fort, leaped from the wall, near the church, with his child in his arms, and was shot in the act. The child also was killed, but whether by the fall or inadvertently by the same bullet, or intentionally, does not appear.

Santa Anna, soon after he fortress was scaled, had come up, with his attendants and the music, with a view of entering, as he supposed the place was taken; but on being fired at from the chapel, he retired to his former station. He returned towards the conclusion of the action, reiterated his orders to stay, and directed some of the concluding operations.

I have heard different statements as to where and when Travis was killed; but that most to be relied on is, that he was found dead at the breech of a gun,[y] near where the right column entered.

About half an hour after the fire had ceased, three men of the garrison were found in one of the rooms concealed under some mattresses. They were spared by the soldiers who found them; and the officer to whom the discovery was reported supplicated Santa Anna for their lives; but the miscreant immediately ordered them to be butchered. The command was fulfilled; but in doing it a struggle ensued, in which a Mexican was also shot inadvertently by the executioners. This concluded the tragedy of the Alamo.

---

[y] That is, at the rear part of the cannon.

The two surviving individuals of all the inmates of the fortress, before alluded to, were Mrs. Dickinson, the wife of the officer whose death, and that of his child, have just been related; and a slave of Col. Travis. They were spared, and were soon after liberated to be the bearers of a proclamation.

The number of troops employed in the assault, if estimated from the average force of their regiments, before stated, omitting the cavalry, would be 2,500; and I am convinced it could not have greatly varied from that amount. There is much diversity and vagueness in the confession of the Mexicans respecting their loss; and till better proof can be obtained, we can only infer its probable amount from various circumstances. Judging from the diminution which certain regiments are known to have suffered in the campaign, only a small part of which can be accounted for elsewhere than at the Alamo, and from other data which it would be tedious to detail, I think they probably had about three hundred killed, and four or five hundred wounded. This number is excessive, considering the size of their force and the time it was engaged, which was but half an hour; for by this computation one assailant must have been slain or stricken, on an average, every two seconds. If, notwithstanding this rapid slaughter, they carried the fortress without giving way to more than brief and partial checks, as they must to succeed in that brief space, it is a sufficient proof that in this assault there was none of that lack of determination which they showed on other occasions. The supposition of there having been a thousand or more Mexicans killed, on the ground, is absurd; and it is not the less so from its having been admitted by some sycophantish captive; though I have never heard such admission even from that source. Most accounts agree in making the number of wounded larger than that of the killed; but if a moderate proportion be added to that extravagant estimate of the slain, it would amount to a loss which would have rendered the capture of the fortress impossible.

The conduct of the garrison, as I have observed, appears sufficiently heroic when related without any violation of known truth or real probability. A handful of exhausted men had to maintain a weak fortress of scattered, untenable positions, against an active and determined assault made by fifteen times their number, of well-drilled and well-appointed troops, and in this charge well commanded. (Troops who were led in a charge by such officers as Castrillon were well-commanded, as any one must admit who witnessed his gallant efforts to retrieve the fortunes of the day at San Jacinto, and the fearless manner in which he courted death on finding all was lost. The manner in which the same troops behaved on that field, so different from their previous conduct, may in some measure be attributed to the disparity which always appears in the energy of men when they attack and when they are attacked; an inequality which exists among the Mexicans in an unusual degree. But it is probable that their lack of firmness at San Jacinto is still more to be attributed to a recollection of the havoc which a few Texians had made among them at the Alamo). Under these circumstances, they must inevitably be crushed; but, if they resisted till the last was felled, and destroyed or disabled four or five times their number, it was a defeat whose renown most victors might envy; and, had they repelled a more cowardly horde of ten thousand, it would have redounded less to their honor.

They sealed the charter of our liberties with their blood; for though their stern resistance failed to repel the foe in the career of his first and fiercest onset, the memory of it chilled his energies in the succeeding combat, where the name of *"Alamo"* became the battle cry of the most fatal field that invader ever entered.

However long our poverty may leave unmarked the spot where rest the ashes of that self-devoted band, I trust that at some future day a monument will there arise, whose inscription, like that on the Mausoleum of Thermopylae, will say to the passer-by: "Go, stranger, and declare to the Texians that we died in defence of their sacred rights."

MARMADUKE.
—*The Madisonian*, December 8, 1840

9

Retreat and Massacre

The day after Antonio López de Santa Anna captured the Alamo, a courier arrived in San Antonio with word of another, albeit much smaller, Mexican victory, as noted in Col. Juan Almonte's journal.

> *Monday, 7th.*—Commenced with a north wind. A special despatch was received from General Urrea, dated 3d March, from San Patricio, in which he communicated that the preceding day, at a place called Los Cohates, he attacked Dr. Grant and his party, and killed Dr. Grant and 41 of his men, and afterwards 2 out of 5 who fled. There was no loss on our side. By the 14th General Urrea would be in Goliad. The greater part of the 1st brigade arrived under the command of Gen. Gaona. The mail arrived from Matamoras and Mexico—dates to the 2d and 3d February.
>
> —*New York Herald*, June 27, 1836

Over the next few days, Almonte's journal turned an official blind eye to the agonies of the hundreds of Mexican soldiers whose wounds went largely unattended because Santa Anna had neglected to bring a competent medical staff with him into Béxar, and focused instead on the weather and the arrival and departure of various officers and dispatches.

> *Tuesday,* 8th.—Fine clear day, but cold. Letters were written to Mexico under date of 6th inst. Commenced blowing hard. I wrote to ********. Official reports were forwarded to-day.
>
> *Wednesday,* 9th. Commenced with a violent north wind, weather not very cold. Generals

Filisola, Arago, &c. &c. arrived. Orders to march were given to Gen'l Sesma and Colonel Gonzales. Two persons arrived from the interior to see the President. The wind continued all night.

> *Thursday,* 10th. Day broke mild, but soon the cold north wind commenced blowing, though with clear weather. The cavalry under command of General Andrade came in. They were quartered in the Alamo. The Commissary and the Treasury of the Army arrived.
>
> —*New York Herald*, June 27, 1836

By March 9, news had still not reached Sam Houston of the annihilation of the Alamo garrison, nor had it yet reached Col. James Fannin at Goliad, where one unnamed officer penned his impressions of one corner of the La Bahía presidio and of campaign developments in general.

> *Extract of a letter from an officer in the Texas army, to a gentleman in Tallahassee.*
>
> GOLIAD, March 9th 1836.
> "I write to you by a gentleman, who leaves here today for the United States, but I have my doubts, if he gets fifty miles from this post, as we are surrounded by the Mexican troops.—By the last express yesterday, from San Antonio, we learned that our little band of 200, still maintained their situation on the Alamo; the fort out-side of the town. They have been fighting desperately for ten or fifteen days, against four or five thousand Mexicans—SANTA ANNA is said to be there himself, and has there and in this vicinity, at least six thousand troops. The greater portion of the Mexican troops,

are mounted, and of course have greatly the advantage over us. We now muster 400 strong, and from the preparations we have made, shall be enabled to give any number a desperate fight: San Antonio, I fear has fallen before this. From its situation and construction, I cannot believe it possible so small a band could maintain it, against such fearful odds. David Crockett is one of the number in the fort.[1] We are expecting an attack hourly. An express yesterday was chased in by 200 cavalry, 18 miles from this. Sixty miles north of us, is another party of 650, who have been quartered at San Patricio for some days, waiting reinforcements; several of our parties of 20 and 30, have been cut off by them.

I have been offered a higher command than I now hold; for the present, I desire none but my own command. The men are devoted to me, and they cannot be surpassed for boldness of chivalry, with such a corps as I command, I will gain the laurels I may wear, or die without any. I am situated at present with my command, in a strong stone house, immediately across the street, and opposite the bastions of the fort. From the bastion I have built a bridge to the top of the house, on which I have a brass six pounder. It is the best, and most commanding situation we have.[a] Before I am driven from it, hundreds must perish.

This is decidedly a richer country than I expected to find, and much more healthy than any other southern country. This part is generally high and dry, though generally level. The San Antonio descends with the velocity of a mountain stream.

We have just learned from Washington, our seat of government, that the convention has declared independence, if such is the fact, and I do not doubt it, we must beat the Mexicans.— Our young men who wish to acquire distinction and fortune, should now flock to Texas.—Now is the time, for fame and fortune, or a glorious death, in the defense of their brothers, and the dearest rights of freemen.—Let all who are

friendly to the cause of Freedom, lend a ready and quick helping hand.—The little band of volunteers now in the field, must breast the storm and keep a powerful army in check, until relief comes or all is lost—we want provisions, arms and men. I have never seen such men as compose our little army here; no man ever thinks to retreat or surrender. They can be conquered only by extermination—nothing can depress their ardour, we are frequently for days without anything but Bull beef to eat, and after working hard all day, could you but see these men, who have made up their minds to die—laughing, joking, and singing, you would think them the happiest and best fed men in the world."

Since the above letter was written, this devoted band of daring patriots have had much desperate fighting with the overwhelming force of the Mexican army—the last official accounts received in this city, was from an officer of standing in the Texian army, who was a few days since in New-Orleans. Colonel Fanning had cut his way through the enemy, and was united with General Houston, having only saved 150 men out of 400 under his command.

We have not yet the report of the killed or the particulars of the action—which is said to have taken place on the 19th of March, the last ten days after the date of the preceding letter.
—*Floridian and Advocate*, April 30, 1836

The following day another Goliad garrison member, named Wood, wrote to the editor of the *New Orleans Bee*, updating the current situation and also providing a capsule summary of the events, and seesaw fortunes, thus far transpiring in the Texas Revolution.

Correspondence of the Bee.
Fort Defiance, (La Bahia) Texas.
March 10th, 1836.

MY DEAR SIR.—Since I last wrote you from Bejar, the affairs of Texas have assumed an aspect which must not only awaken the bravest sympathies of the friends of constitutional liberty, in every clime, but act well for the prompt and efficient efforts of our devoted patriots now in the field, or all will be lost. We

---

[a] This was the detached prison house, standing just east of the fort's southeast bastion. On a plan of the fort drawn by Joseph M. Chadwick, this is labeled as "Madam Garcia's house, new & strongly built."

left Bejar, you may remember, with the flush of victory yet glowing upon our cheeks, and the laurel yet unfaded upon our brows to seek new conquests at Matamoras; but scarcely had we reached this place on our way thither, ere the apple of discord was raised among us, by several ambitious aspirants for the command of the army; and the dissentions arising from this cause have hitherto paralized all our efforts, and proved the ruin of one portion of our little army.

To put our present attitude in its true light, it is necessary to recur to past transactions. When we arrived in the camp before Bejar, General Austin had just retired, and the command had devolved upon General Edward Burleson, an honest, unassuming gentleman,

"Who never set a squadron in the field
Nor the division of an army knew, more than a spinster,"

And who possessed scarcely a single requisite qualification to constitute him a good military commander. Confusion and dissatisfaction soon became the order of the day; and a retreat upon this place and Gonzales was ordered on the 3d of December last; but the two companies of N. O. Greys, with one from Mississippi (Peacock's) resolved not only to maintain their ground, but, unaided by the Texians, to make an attempt upon the town. The drum was accordingly beat for volunteers; and only 216 daring spirits from an army of upwards 700 men enrolled themselves for the enterprise to be undertaken next morning. It is needless to say that the two N. O. companies amounting to about 113, turned out to a man; and when the Mississippi company is taken into account, it will be seen how very small a share the Texians had in the reduction of Bejar. This little band of volunteers was determined not to be led by Gen. Burleson; they therefore elected Col. Benjamin R. Milam to command the attack, and he called to his aid F. W. Johnson and James Grant; the two aids of Burleson, Robert C. Morris of N. Orleans being previously elected major of the regiment before Bejar, led on one of the attacking divisions. During the conflict Milam fell, and Johnson his aid, thereupon usurped the command, as Col.

of the regiment. After the surrender of Bejar, the troops demanded a new election to supply the place of the lamented Milam, but, Johnson, conscious of his own unpopularity, and ambitious of power, contrived to put them off, upon one pretext or another, until the expedition to Matamoras was got up, which, he vainly hoped would hush up all discontent and confirm him and Grant in power.

The expedition started under these auspices, on the 1st of January; but before our arrival at this place, five days afterwards, it being discovered that the expedition was not authorized by the provisional government, the troops refused to proceed until they were satisfied on this point. While lying here in this state of suspense, the arrival of Gen. Saml. Houston, commander-in-chief of the forces of Texas was hailed as the harbinger of union, and the forerunner of victory. After several days of deliberation, the troops were finally mustered under Houston; and took up the line of march for the Mission Refugio, near to Copano, to await the arrival of Col. Fanning with a reinforcement of about 200 troops, and further orders. Johnson and Grant manifested much dissatisfaction at this order; and endeavoured to raise a force which should proceed upon their own responsibility upon Matamoras. They easily succeeded in inducing two companies, in all about 60 men, under the command [of] Major Morris and Captains Thos. Llewellen and T. Pearson (formerly of the American Theatre N. O.) to join their enterprize. The balance of the regiment obeyed the orders of Houston, and remained at the mission of Refugio; but this little division took up the line for San Patricio, on the river Nueces, the frontier of Texas where they halted to recruit horses, and to concentrate with some Mexican troops, which had promised to join them from the state of Tamaulipas, upon a junction with which mainly depended the success of their expedition against Matamoras. While lying thus in a state of fancied security, they became suddenly apprized of the perfidy of their Mexican allies, by a hostile midnight attack upon a small division of their party, while every soul was asleep in two houses at San Patricio.

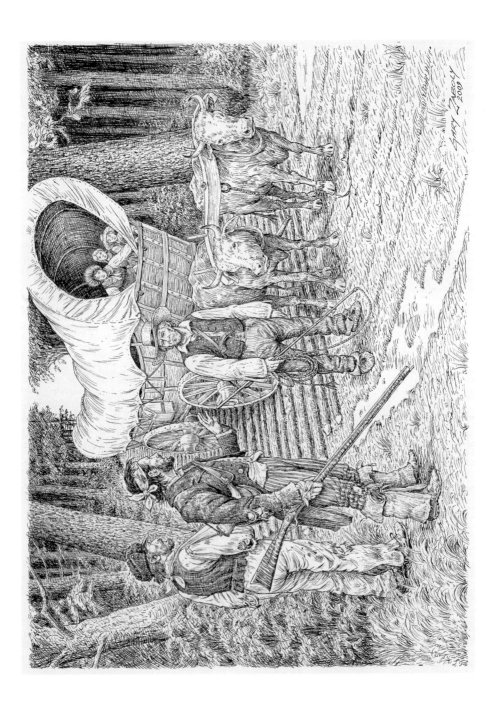

Alamo Survivors on the Road to Nacogdoches

One of the most mystifying 1836 newspaper reports concerning the Alamo battle was one that appeared in the *Arkansas Gazette* of March 29. The first confirmed account of the Alamo's fall was printed in the March 24 issue of the *Telegraph and Texas Register*, and Little Rock's papers would not publish such confirmation until April 5, after General Sam Houston's letter from Gonzales, written on March 11, finally arrived there.[1] Thus, the following report in the March 29 *Arkansas Gazette* presents many scholarly challenges.

> *San Antonio re-taken, and the Garrison massacreed.*—Just as our paper was ready for press, a gentleman who arrived this morning, from Red river, informs us that, on Thursday night last, he spent the night, on the Little Missouri, with a man and his family, who had fled from the vicinity of San Antonio after that post was besieged by the Mexicans. This man, he says, informed him, that, on his arrival at Nacogdoches, he was overtaken by two men (one of them badly wounded), who informed him that San Antonio was re-taken by the Mexicans, and the garrison put to the sword—that if any others escaped the general massacre, besides themselves, they were not aware of it.
>
> We give the above report, precisely as it was communicated to us by our informant, who was recently a citizen of this county, and is a man of veracity. We hope it may be unfounded—but fear that our next accounts from that quarter will confirm it.

"Thursday night last" would have been March 24. The Little Missouri River in southwest Arkansas, where the refugee family was camping, lies over four hundred miles from San Antonio. Could such a family have traveled so far in a month's time, as the account indicates, estimating that they had left "the vicinity" of Béxar soon after the arrival of Antonio López de Santa Anna's army—meaning, around February 23 or 24?[2] That would have required them to have covered about fourteen miles per day. (A good travel day for a wagon train, on the plains leg of the Oregon Trail, was about twenty miles.)[3] Did they carry their possessions in a wagon, or in a horse- or ox-drawn sleigh? Or did they travel light, on horseback? According to John Sutherland, the mass exodus

(Continued)

of many Bexareños began on February 20, although John W. Smith had "engaged wagons to remove his family into the colonies" as early as mid-January, so it is possible that this particular family encountered on the Little Missouri may have actually been traveling for well over a month.[4]

According to the *Gazette* account, upon the family's approach to, or entry into, Nacogdoches, it was "overtaken by two men (one of them badly wounded)," who told them that the Alamo had fallen, its garrison massacred, and that they had been lucky to escape with their lives. How long would it have taken two survivors of the March 6 battle, one of them wounded, to walk to Nacogdoches, about 270 miles east of San Antonio? If the family they had met thereafter needed about ten days to travel the approximately 150 miles from Nacogdoches to the Little Missouri River, that would have put the family's arrival at Nacogdoches on or around March 14. Thus, the two "survivors" of the Alamo battle would have had only about eight days to trek the 270 miles, an average of over 33 miles a day. This seems an almost impossible feat of walking, considering that one of the men was "badly wounded." On the other hand, it took Smith and an injured Sutherland only a day to cover the 70 miles between San Antonio and Gonzales, on horseback, on February 23–24, so had these two unidentified "survivors" ridden part of the way, their arrival at Nacogdoches on or about March 14 *would* have been possible.

That a number of Alamo defenders may have survived the battle is well known and has often been the subject of historical speculation and debate.[5] General Joaquín Ramírez y Sesma's report of the assault describes at least three groups of Texians who attempted breakouts when the battle appeared lost, and although Sesma claimed that his lancers and dragoons killed all of them, it might have been a case of wishful thinking on Sesma's part that dusky, smoke-filled morning.[6]

One document that may partly, and perhaps only suggestively, confirm the story in the *Arkansas Gazette* is William P. Zuber's letter to General William Steele of September 14, 1877. Zuber's account of Louis (Moses) Rose's March 3 escape from the Alamo, published in the 1873 *Texas Almanac*, is well known and need not be rehashed here, except to point out that Rose's tale had him leaving the fort immediately after he refused to cross William Barret Travis's line in the dirt, not during the assault itself. Supposedly drawing from Rose's own testimony as related to Zuber's parents in 1836, Zuber informed Steele that, while making his way homeward to Nacogdoches, Rose had first spent two nights in the house of one Mr. Leaky, in Washington County, the western edge of which begins about seventy miles east of San Antonio. He told his story to the

Leaky family, but two other men who arrived there deemed him a liar and afterward spread the word that there was an imposter named Rose who claimed to have escaped the Alamo siege. Other men—many of them deserters from the Texian army—carried the warning east to Nacogdoches, even telling it to Rose himself, whom they passed en route, although he did not reveal his identity. Zuber asserted that for this reason Rose forever after told his story only to a handful of people, Zuber's parents among them, who housed him for over two weeks while nursing his cactus-gored legs.[7]

Could two of the many men traveling east on the road to Nacogdoches have disguised the fact that they were deserters by claiming to have escaped annihilation at the Alamo, even to the point of displaying a mock wound or two? Did they simply borrow and expand Rose's story of leaving the Alamo during the siege into one of retreating from it during the fighting? Or did they capitalize on the information that Travis's daily signal gun, the booming eighteen-pounder, was no longer heard after March 6 and employed *that* as a handy alibi with which to back up their story that the Alamo had fallen? We simply do not know.

There is also the final possibility that two legitimate, if unnamed, survivors of the March 6 carnage did indeed arrive at Nacogdoches over a week after the battle, and thereafter blended themselves into the mists of history.

1. *Arkansas Gazette*, April 5, 1836.
2. The "vicinity of San Antonio" is a somewhat nebulous phrase, one that could encompass any number of square miles in south central Texas.
3. Huston Horn, *The Pioneers* (New York: Time-Life Books, 1974), 91.
4. Sutherland account in Todd Hansen, ed., *The Alamo Reader: A Study in History* (Mechanicsburg, Penn.: Stackpole Books, 2003), 142; J. C. Neill letter, Béxar, January 14, 1836, in *Telegraph and Texas Register*, January 23, 1836.
5. See for example, Walter Lord, *A Time to Stand* (New York: Harper Brothers, 1961), 207–209; Wallace O. Chariton, *Exploring the Alamo Legends* (Plano, Tex.: Wordware Publishing Inc., 1990), 19–35; Hansen, *Alamo Reader*, 305–328.
6. Sesma's military report, March 11, 1836, in Hansen, *Alamo Reader*, 369–371.
7. William P. Zuber to Gen. William Steele, September 14, 1877, in Hansen, *Alamo Reader*, 252–253.

Johnson, with four others, succeeded in escaping by flight; but Pearson was shot while calling for "quarters," and his men, amounting to about 25, either shared his fate, or have fallen into the hands of the Mexicans as prisoners of war;—a fate scarcely more enviable. Grant, Morris & Llewellen, who, with the company of the latter, amounting to 24 men, were out at the time of the attack upon their comrades, in search of horses, but were suddenly fallen upon by a company of mounted lancers, while on their return to San Patricio, were completely put to the rout. Grant, Morris and Llewellen fell on the spot, and only eight escaped to tell their fate. We learn from our spies that there are only eight American prisoners at San Patricio; 40 out of 60 men must, consequently have lost their lives in this rash enterprize. The conduct of Johnson, Grant and Morris is severely censured on all hands; and the former will, no doubt be put upon his trial for disobedience to orders &c. Among those who fell in this latter rencontre was Samuel McNally, a native of West Feliciana, La., a youth of about 20 years of age, who in the battle of Bejar and throughout the campaign has displayed the qualities of a brave and gallant soldier.

While these things were going on at San Patricio, Fanning arrived at Copano with the expected reinforcement; the army was concentrated, and ordered to garrison this post, and to put it in complete order for defence, it being by this time satisfactorily ascertained that Santa Anna was on his march with 7 to 8000 men, destined to act against this place and San Antonio. We have here upwards of 500 men for duty, with a good position, a strong fort, a tolerably good supply of provisions and ammunitions, abundance of artillery, and stout hearts to stand out a protracted siege. Since the rout of Johnson, the enemy have taken possession of San Patricio with 650 men—(250 cavalry and 400 infantry) and it is supposed are only awaiting a reinforcement of 1000, when they will either attack or invest us. Meanwhile the Lafayette Batallion in which are the Greys are beseeching Colonel Fanning, who is in command here, to send them on to San Patricio to annihilate the force already there, before the expected reinforcement arrives. We are momentarily expecting a favorable answer to our request, and eager for the unequal encounter of two to one.

We have certain intelligence that Santa Anna is in person before Bejar, with five to six thousand men. There are upwards to 200 men in the garrison there, with provisions for 40 days. The enemy have made three several charges upon the fort, and been as often repelled with severe losses. They have thrown upwards of three hundred bombs into the fort, without doing it any damage or killing any men, and were (at the last dates) throwing up entrenchments around the fort, in all directions, for the purpose of preventing the introduction of provisions or reinforcements. Colonel Neil, with about 400 troops consisting of militia and volunteers from the U. S. and a supply of provisions was at Gonzales, 65 miles distant, about to march upon Bejar, determined to force the lines of the enemy and relieve our fellow countrymen in the garrison. Since the fall of Bejar, the colonists have remained supinely at home,—the provisional government has been squabbling about offices—and the volunteers are unprovided for and unpaid. They however hope much from the new convention, now in session; but, if the presence of a formidable enemy in the field, does not call forth the yeomanry of the country, in defiance of their homes and their firesides, in numbers sufficient to overwhelm the invaders, all will be lost.

Such is a rapid outline of the progress of events in this interesting country, since the date of my last. Should my life be spared, I will write you more in detail by an opportunity which will occur in a few days. It must be observed from what I have written that the volunteer army now in the field, amounting in all to about 1700, is unable, alone, to cope with the enemy. If it can maintain its present positions in Bejar, La Bahia and Gonzalez until the colonists shall have rallied, they will have done all that can be expected of them; and this they are determined to do, or perish in the attempt. The fate of Texas, therefore, is entirely in the hand of the colonists; if they to a man rally around the standard of the country, in its present extremity, a force more numerous than that of the enemy will soon be concentrated, the footsteps of invasion turned backwards of Rio Grande, and Texas will soon be free and independent.

It was a capital mistake on the part of the authorities and colonists of Texas to imagine that hostilities would cease upon the downfall of Bejar; yet upon such an hypothesis, they seem to have acted, else would the victorious army of Bejar instead of being dissipated by one after another returning home in disgust, been hurried upon the heels of Cos, Loredo and Mier, Matamoras and all the towns upon the Rio Grande would have been ours, and our little army, augmented by the numerous federalists of Tamaulipas, Coahuila, Neueva, Leon, Chiahuahau and Zacatecas, would have presented a front so formidable to the dictator that terms would ere now have been granted to us, the ball of revolution would have acquired an irresistable impetus in other parts of the republic, and the fair soil of Texas would not have been the theatre of strife. We might thus have retrieved, in some measure the advantages which were barely surrendered by Johnson, through cowardice or a worse principle, when we had Cos and his army completely in power. But it is not even now too late. The volunteers are sanguine of ultimate success against the enemy now in the field; and many appearances indicate that the march of revolution in the rear of Santa Anna will speedily induce him to retrace his footsteps and withdraw his troops or devolve the command upon some other leader who is far less formidable than the general president. This event, by no means improbable, would raise our spirits in proportion as would depress those of the enemy, and a single advantage will be but the prelude to a general route of the enemy, which may be followed up by the occupation of the towns I have above enumerated, which are necessary to round off the boundaries of the new republic, give it a respectable port of entry, and produce a permanent revenue. The declaration of independence will doubtless bring us more recruits from the "father land," so that whatever else you may do, never despair our success in the general engagement which is about to take place, and upon which the issue is suspended.

The New Orleans volunteers are here and in excellent spirits, they still maintain their pre-eminent reputation. The bugle calls, a two days march is ordered—doubtless to relieve the prisoners at San Patricio, of which you shall here of in *future*, should my life be spared. God prosper the right.
Yours truly.   W. P. M. W.
—*New Orleans Bee*, April 20, 1836

The next day another letter was written at Goliad by Henry Ripley, son of War of 1812 general Eleazar W. Ripley, addressed to his father. It expressed

pessimism regarding the leadership qualities of Colonel Fannin, and two and a half months, later an extract was published in a New York newspaper.

Gen. Ripley had received a letter from his son, dated at Goliad, March 11, 1836. This letter, containing news of the investment of the Alamo, the fight at San Patricio, and other encounters in that quarter, was kindly furnished to us by Gen. Ripley. In this letter, the writer but too truly foretells his own fate. Speaking of the repeated expresses sent for succor to Fanning, from those besieged in the Alamo, he says:

"Fanning does not know what to do. He has from 500 to 600 men at this place. The men are all anxious to march. We did so once, but after marching a mile, the order was countermanded. He (Fannin) states as a reason, that this place will soon be attacked, and he will not have men enough to defend it, should he spare men to march to Bowie. He is very unpopular, and I think will resign. Times look squally and dangerous in Texas. In all probability the men now in the field will die at their posts. For myself, I have that opinion. It would be dishonorable for me to leave Texas now."
—*Mercantile Advertiser &
New York Advocate*, June 29, 1836

Meanwhile, over the next six days in San Antonio, news of the movements of Mexican army divisions elsewhere, as well as of troops dispatched from Béxar itself, was recorded in Almonte's journal.

Friday, 11th. Day pleasant, but somewhat windy. Gen'l Tolsa came in with the 3d brigade, but the divisions of Sesma and Gonzales had already marched with four six pounders and one howitzer. Marches detailed being 9 days to Goliad, 5 to Gonzales and 14 to San Felipe.

Saturday, 12th. Day broke mild—became windy—but clear and temperate. We consumed many fish. Sesma wrote from El Salado, giving the details—Romero likewise. The troops were reviewed in the afternoon in the Square.

Sunday, 13th. Day clear but windy. *Heard mass in the Square.* Very warm in the afternoon. Thermometer 85°. Nothing particular.

Susanna Dickinson, Ben, and Cavalry Escort Leaving Béxar

The two funeral pyres were still smoldering when the newly widowed Susanna Dickinson left San Antonio two or three days after the fall of the Alamo. Accompanying her, aside from her infant Angelina, were Benjamin Harris, black body servant of Col. Juan Nepomuceno Almonte and cook for both his master and Antonio López de Santa Anna, and an escort of Mexican cavalry, probably presidial troopers who would have been well familiar with the country east of San Antonio. In one newspaper account Ben was referred to as a "Mexican with a flag," obviously due to his dress and affiliation, for he also carried Santa Anna's printed proclamations assuring all peaceful Texians that *they* would obtain the general's mercy, and that all "audacious adventurers" would be punished, as had those at "Saint Patrick, Lipantitlan, and this city."[1] In 1852, Ben was described as "some five feet in height and thirty-two or so around the chest—quite a dapper little colored gentleman."[2] After he delivered the proclamations to Sam Houston, Ben was permanently "detained," and in fact became Houston's own cook.[3]

Although Mrs. Dickinson had been given "a bag of provisions," some money, and what was variously described as a "mustang," "pony," or simply, "horse," and was sent on her way by a polite Santa Anna, the journey became one of great physical and emotional distress. The wound she had received in her right calf from a Mexican bullet during the chaotic aftermath of the battle had been "carefully dressed and tended" in the *generalissimo*'s headquarters, but it remained "very . . . painful" as she rode.[4] Shocking allegations that she had been sexually abused by "Santa Anna's officers and soldiers" also appeared in a number of newspapers. What this meant, and whether they were reports based on even a particle of truth, may never be known.[5]

Travis's slave Joe had not been allowed to leave with Mrs. Dickinson's party but was "taken into Bejar, and detained several days."[6] By the time he did leave and manage to catch up with her, according to an 1878 interview she gave, "the cowardly Mexican cavalry [had] deserted her, probably fearing the vengeance of Deaf Smith and his scouts."[7] Joe made his appearance by suddenly popping up from the high grass alongside the road to Gonzales and frightening Mrs. Dickinson. In later decades, the then Mrs. Hannig began to confuse the two ex-servants, sometimes referring to Joe as Ben, and vice versa, further complicating things for future historians.[8]

(Continued)

In one of her final interviews, she told

of her flight, accompanied by the negro Ben, of the intervention of Deaf Smith, who saved her when almost dying of thirst, fatigue and of pain caused by her wound. Hear her tell of her interview with Houston, and how the hero of Texan independence used the hideous story to exasperate his followers. She told him that when she was leaving San Antonio the town and country were perfumed with odors arising from the holocaust made of the bodies of those who fell within the Alamo. She beheld the flames that consumed the body of her husband and of Crockett and Travis, and was instructed by Santa Anna to describe the horrible scene to Houston and his followers. She executed the order with painstaking care. The effect was little dreamed of by the bloody Mexican leader.

—*Galveston News*, February 3, 1881

---

1. *New Orleans Bee*, March 28, 1836; *Arkansas Gazette*, April 12, 1836; interview with Susanna Hannig, *San Antonio Express*, March 14, 1878; interview with Susanna Hannig, *Telegraph and Texas Register*, October 11, 1836.

2. From a review written by Dr. James McCune Smith of E. G. Squier's book, *Nicaragua*, January 15, 1852, in *Alamo Journal,* September 2006, 10.

3. Interview with Ben in Todd Hansen, ed., *The Alamo Reader: A Study in History* (Mechanicsburg, Penn.: Stackpole Books, 2003), 474. Even before he became Almonte's servant in 1835, Ben had "been a steward on board several American vessels." Rev. Chester Newall, *History of the Revolution in Texas, Particularly of the War of 1835 and '36* (New York: Wiley and Putnam, 1838), 87.

4. Interviews with Mrs. Dickinson in Hansen, *Alamo Reader*, 50, 55, 59.

5. For example, see *New Orleans Bulletin*, April 11, 1836, and *Philadelphia Public Ledger*, May 21, 1836.

6. *Frankfort Commonwealth*, May 25, 1836.

7. Interview with Mrs. Hannig, *San Antonio Express*, March 14, 1878. Jesse Badgett's letter in the *Arkansas Gazette* of April 12 suggests that the troopers may have gone with her only as far as the "Sea willow river" (Cibolo), about twenty-five miles east of San Antonio.

8. *San Antonio Express*, March 14, 1878; *Galveston News*, February 3, 1881.

Monday, 14th. Cloudy and windy, and warm.—Weather cleared and the wind abated a little. The correspondence from Mexico, Monterey and Matamoras was received, and a despatch from Gen'l Urrea stating that he would be at Goliad the 14th, that is to-day.— Orders to march were issued to the battalion of Tres Villas.

Tuesday, 15th. Windy and warm. The battalion of Queretaro was ordered to march to Goliad, with one 12 pounder and the corresponding munition. Tomorrow the two battalions of Queretaro and Tres Villas will march. In the afternoon the courier was despatched to Gen'l Urrea. Accounts came from Gonzales by a Mexican that the *Americans, in number 500, fled as soon as they heard of the taking of the Alamo* and the approach of our troops, leaving their stores and many goods, and throwing two cannon in the water, &c. &c. This was Sunday in the afternoon. The same man said that the Convention had met at Washington and

declared the independence of Texas. The battalions of Guerrero and Mexico were ordered
to get ready to march to Gonzales to-morrow
with about 200 horses selected from Dolores
and Tampico. A courier extraordinary arrived
with accounts of the sickness of Gen'l Barragar
and the election of Mr. Corro as President, ad
interim by 27 votes. For Bravo 18 votes, and
Parres 8. *This election did not please Gen'l
Santa Anna; he preferred Gen'l Bravo.* It is said
that Gen'l Michilena voted for Bravo.

Wednesday, 16th. Accounts were received
from Gen'l Ramirez—it was determined that
Gen'l Tolsa should march with two battalions
to Goliad, and he started at 3 o'clock P.M. It
was also determined that I should join Sesma.
Monoga left with two battalions for Goliad, to
reach there in seven days. Wind continues.

—New York Herald, June 27, 1836

On March 12, Fannin sent a hundred men under Col.
William Ward to the relief of Capt. Amon King's
small detachment at Refugio Mission, which had
been assisting in the evacuation of the settlers there
and was now battling a vanguard of General José
Urrea's cavalry. Two days later, Gen. Sam Houston,
after speaking with Mrs. Susanna Dickinson,
Travis's slave Joe, and Colonel Almonte's released
servant, Ben, ordered the citizens of Gonzales to
abandon their homes and retreat with his army to
the east bank of the Colorado River. At the end of
March, these and other developments, including the
fate of King and Ward and their men, were transmitted in a letter from east Texas first published in a
Pennsylvania paper.

FROM TEXAS—We have been favored with
the following letter to a gentleman of this city
from a Pennsylvanian, who settled in Texas as a
merchant several years ago.—*Phil. Gazette.*

NACOGDOCHES, TEXAS,
March 31, 1836.

DEAR SIR:—I write you whilst our country
is in a state of extreme excitement. Five weeks
ago we were surprized by the arrival of eight
thousand Mexican soldiers (2000 cavalry and
6000 infantry,) at San Antonio de Bejar. Judge
of the panic of the settlers, who, by a feint of

Santa Anna, after the massacre of the Alamo,
believed this whole army was marching into
the Colonies. Almost the entire settlers west
of the Brazos moved over, and were on their
way here: women driving the teams and stock,
the men being in the field with the army; their
retreat being subject to being annoyed by the
Indians here. It was reported that the Mexican
cavalry had come through above the settlements
and joined the Indians in our immediate neighborhood, and were bringing them down upon us.—In
this alarming situation we have been constantly
kept sleeping on our arms; keeping one fourth
of us on our guard every night expecting nightly
attacks. In this situation I got my family off a
week ago. They left here, and I had the satisfaction of hearing of their reaching the Sabine. It is
hard to imagine the relief that I felt at their leaving here. The idea was horrible, that when they
laid down at night, they might be waked by the
Indian whoop only to feel their tomahawks and
to meet in the Mexican soldier a more inhuman
and savage enemy than even the North American
Indian, as the dread tale of the massacre of the
Alamo must inform you. Before my family got
off every Mexican family left the place the two
preceding days, and in three days hence we
shall have no female in the place. All the female
part of the families are seeking safety beyond
the Sabine; but the men remain to fight, to die,
or drive from the country the Tyrant's minions.
Already two thousand of the enemy are killed
and disabled. Goliad, (La Bahia) is occupied
by 520 of our men, principally Volunteers from
the United States, commanded by Col. Fannin.
It is a very strong fortress and the troops in it
feel confident that they cannot be taken by the
whole Mexican force. The Mexican army have
now surrounded it with four thousand men, and
it is supposed their intention is to try and take
it by siege, they having suffered so much in the
assault of the Alamo. Our men have in the Fort
6 months provisions and plenty of ammunition and arms. Col. Fannin had a scouting
party of 25 men out who were routed by the
enemy, but safely reached our main camp.
He then sent out 60 men to burn the town
of Mission del Refugio. They were attacked

by four hundred of the enemy's cavalry. He then sent out 150 men to their relief, when they fought a whole day. Our men lost 16 and killed a great many of the enemy, and then retreated to our main army, which is on the Colorado, commanded by Gen. Houston; where he has at this moment two thousand men, and will soon be increased, as companies are leaving every settlement every few days for the main army. On the 5th of April we shall have 250 men here on their march from the neighborhood of San Augustine. Eighty left our town some time since, and 100 passed through from the Sabine, and another company will go to-morrow. Was it not for the dread of the Indians here, we would soon destroy Santa Anna and his army. We know we have a bloody war to go through, but the more difficulty they meet, the more resolution do the people of Texas display. We are by no means appalled by the overwhelming numbers of the enemy, who have six Generals in the field.

—*Richmond Enquirer*, May 3, 1836

General Joaquín Ramírez y Sesma's official report concerning the Texians' abandonment of Gonzales was published in a Mexican newspaper and later translated for a Washington, D.C., paper.

To His Excellency the President, General-in-Chief of the Army, Don ANTONIO LOPEZ DE SANTA ANNA:

FIRST DIVISION OF THE ARMY OF OPERATIONS,
The ruins of the town of Gonzales, March 15, 1836.

MOST EXCELLENT SIR: On leaving Sibolo for Carrizo, we found first some baskets containing bacon and meat, hanging on a pole, then some handkerchiefs, and, next, a saddle with the name of Richard Storr on it. These things, and the fresh tracks which were discovered, convinced me that some one—whose object it was to observe the movements of the army—on seeing this division, had returned in great haste to Gonzales, and that his horse giving out, he had disencumbered himself of every thing, and had fled bareback. As it was

evident that this notice would alarm the place, I immediately sent to the inhabitants one of the proclamations in English, which your Excellency addressed to the People of Texas; notwithstanding which, they have so consummated their barbarous conduct, by burning down entirely three houses which stood on the road to the river, and the whole town, with the grain, furniture, and all that it contained; after they had set fire to everything, without exception, they fled. The craft and boats on the river are all burnt, and although I have found a ford for the infantry, a day's work is necessary to enable me to transport the artillery, baggage, and horses, across, as impediments have been placed on each side.

The cavalry, at the slow pace we have come, has twenty-eight jaded horses, for which reason I did not send it forward to catch any of the fugitives, and have only pushed on 150 *cazadores* for that purpose, with directions not to go further than four or five leagues, and then to return.

The example of barbarism and insolence set by these men, induce me to believe that they will resist the passage of the Colorado river, and that after overcoming that obstacle, I shall find at Austin nothing but a desert covered with ruins like this place, which, from the remains left, appears to have been a town of some importance.

If this should be the case on my arrival at Austin, I shall ask your Excellency to have the goodness to inform me where I am to direct my operations.

I have the honor to renew to your Excellency the assurances of my attachment and respect.

God and Liberty.

JOAQUIM RAMIREZ Y SESMA.
—*Daily National Intelligencer*, May 9, 1836

As far as most newspapers in the East were concerned, Fannin's fort at Goliad was undergoing a siege by Santa Anna, while Houston continued his eastward retreat. Rumors of the Mexicans' policy of genocide had also sent nearly all Texians hustling to stay ahead of the enemy.

TEXAS.—We have this morning seen and conversed with GEO. C. CHILDRESS, Esq. late a member of the Texas Convention, and now on his way to Washington city, in connection with Mr. Hamilton, also a member of the Convention, to lay before the Government of the United States the Texian Declaration of Independence, and if practicable to procure a recognition from our Government.

Mr. Childress left Washington, Texas, on the 19th ult. The most recent intelligence received, prior to his departure, in reference to the position and movements of the contending armies is as follows:

After the capture of San Antonio, Santa Anna had made a feint on Gonzales, where General Houston was, with a very inferior force, which induced the latter to fall back on the Colorado, under the belief that the whole Mexican army was marching to attack him. A similar feint was also made by the Mexican General on Bastrop, a town on the Colorado north-east of San Antonio. Gonzales lies east of that place. Having in both instances effected his object, Santa Anna concentrated his forces, and marched directly for La Bahia, or Goliad, which is situated about ninety miles south-east of San Antonio and forty-five or fifty from Houston's position on the Colorado. The fort at Goliad is of great strength, and defended by Col. Fanning with eight hundred men, who have abundance of ammunitions and provisions. It was confidently believed to be impregnable. Heavy firing was heard in that direction on the 14th, and no doubt was entertained that a desperate attack was then being made on the fort. Fanning and his men continued up to the latest date to be in high spirits—even after the fall of San Antonio.

The plan of the campaign on the part of the Texans appears to be, to oppose continued resistance to the progress of the Mexican army at all available points—falling back in case they should be too far outnumbered to risk a general and decisive battle.

Much depends upon the result of Santa Anna's attack on Goliad. If repulsed there, it will be necessarily with great slaughter to his troops—in which event it is possible his march may be immediately arrested.

Among the slain at St. Antonio, we regret to record the names of John M. Hays, of this place; Mr. Washington and Mr. Thomas, of Robertson county; Mr. Haskell, of Jackson; and Mr. Autry, formerly of this county, but late of Jackson. Col. Crockett's death has been heretofore announced. Mr. Cloud of Kentucky, and Mr. Bonham of South Carolina, young gentlemen, it is said, of great promise, were also among the dead.

POSTSCRIPT.

Since the above was in type, we have received the following letter from a person who went out in the Matawankeag, under Col. Stanley. It will be seen that Matagorda had not then been taken possession of by the Mexicans, but they were supposed to be near, and as the Texians had been ordered away, the former would of course enter without opposition.

Correspondence of the Journal of Commerce.

MATAGORDA, (Texas) March 28th.

I embrace the present opportunity, although not a very convenient one, of dropping you a few lines. I write in much haste, for the Mexicans are close upon our heels, and we are to march this evening for the head quarters of the Texian army, which are at San Felippe. You will see we are obliged to "take time by the foretop," in order to keep clear of a large body of Mexican cavalry, who are now supposed to be on the march for and within a few miles of this village. The women and children have all left the town, as they are also leaving all parts of Texas.— Every thing appears to be quite deserted, and nothing is to be heard but the din of war in every quarter. I did not come out to Texas as a soldier,—but who can view this beautiful country in its present wretched condition, and reflect what it might be, but for the hellish ambition of a military despot, and not gird on his sword, and say: "As far as my frail *influence* can go, Texas shall be free!"

Santa Anna is now in Texas, with 8000 cavalry, with which he is scouring the country, committing the most horrid cruelties, putting to death every one he meets, without regard to age, sex, or condition. The females are usually given up to the brutal passions of the soldiers, and afterwards butchered.

Yet, notwithstanding the great force of the Mexicans, the Texians are sanguine of success. They are men who feel the charms of liberty, and who, under present circumstances, are fighting not only for that, but for their own lives, and those of their wives and little ones. Will not Texians fight when all these are at stake? The most decisive answer I can give is, Texians are not only Texians, but *Americans.*

—*Nashville Banner & Nashville Whig,*
April 11, 1836

Events swiftly overtook Fannin at Goliad. Despite all the reports, he was not being besieged by the Mexican army. Ordered by Houston to abandon Fort Defiance (the name the Americans had given the La Bahía presidio), Fannin hesitated, and it was not until March 18 when he finally issued orders for an evacuation. Word of the disaster that followed reached New Orleans on April 10.

FROM TEXAS.

The most distressing intelligence was received yesterday from this delightful (but at present unfortunate) country, by the arrival of the General De Kalb from Brazoria, whence she sailed on the 3d instant.

On the 23d ult. Col. Fanning had sent out a scouting party of about 50 men; they were massacred. On the 24th, he sent out a skirmishing party of 150; they were also cut off. He then resolved to destroy the fort of Goliad; burn the town; and cut his way thro' the enemy encamped in his neighborhood, as his provisions failed, and his garrison had diminished to 300. But in attempting this, he was surrounded by the Mexicans, and compelled to capitulate and lay down his arms—after which with characteristic treachery he and all were shot.

The detachment of volunteers from Georgia under Major Ward, has been also cut off, with the exception of three persons, one of whom had arrived in Brazoria before the De Kalb sailed.

On the 26th ult. General Houston found it necessary or convenient to retreat 20 miles rearward from the Colorado river, as one wing

of the Mexican army had arrived on the opposite bank.

The Mexicans were advancing in two columns—one upon General Houston, the other towards the mouth of the Brazos.

The army under Houston was posted near the Brazos river on the 29th ult; and contained about 2000 men; that column of the Mexicans opposed to him had then crossed the Colorado, and numbered about 3000. The Texicans think and Houston has determined that the enemy shall never recross the Colorado; and we think and trust that they shall not pass the Brazos.

The Texicans have actually become desperate from the massacre, and situation of their affairs. They have burned San Felippe de Austin; and destroyed all the country in their retreat. They have sent hither their women and children, with whom the De Kalb and other vessels are crowded. They have resolved in case of necessity to burn Brazoria and Bell's landing on the approach of the Mexicans; and are transporting most of their effects to Galveston, for which place the sch'rs, Columbus and Flash, were ready to sail. The Pennsylvania and Shenandoah were bound for this port; the Santiano was at the mouth of the river; and the Julius Cesar within.

—*New Orleans Bee,* April 11, 1836

General Urrea's reports to Santa Anna of the defeat and surrender of Fannin's and other Texian detachments was first published in Matamoros's *Mercurio* on April 3 and afterward reprinted in a Washington, D.C., paper.

GUADALOUPE VICTORIA,
MARCH 21, 1836.
General-in-chief of the Army of Operations:

Most Excellent Sir: The fortress of Goliad was abandoned by the enemy on the 19th instant, after a sally made in the hope of beating this division; the fortress, therefore, remains at the disposition of the Supreme Government. So are likewise their leader, Fannin, his co-adjutors, and more than three hundred soldiers, (as they call themselves,) who formed the garrison of the abovementioned fort. They carried out of their trenches with them nine pieces of artillery, and almost one thousand muskets, with abundant munitions. With about three hundred men, infantry and cavalry, I came up with and attacked them in the Perdido plain; I drove them out of a beautiful wood, which they contended the possession of with me by repeated discharges of artillery, attacking them, notwithstanding their superior force, and the advantages of their armament and artillery, my own not being come up. The action was very severe, but the valor of our soldiers was distinguished upon the occasion. At the close of daylight I collected my forces, and took a position in columns, in front of the enemy, at less than 200 yards distance. Thus we passed the night; and the following day (yesterday) as soon as 2 six pounders reached me, which I had sent for to Goliad, I planted my battery at 160 yards from the enemy.

I was preparing a second attack, but the enemy, disheartened by the intrepidity of our soldiers, although they had fortified themselves in the night time with a square trench they had dug, surrendered at discretion, as soon as we opened our fire, as is confirmed by the accompanying document and petition which the enemy's leader made to me, and by my answer, which they agreed to; they, all of them, with their arms and ammunition, fell into my power. Notwithstanding the fatigues and foot sore state of the troops, I immediately marched with two pieces of artillery to occupy this place, before the enemy could be reinforced in sufficient numbers to hinder the passage of the river; this was a very opportune step, for at the moment of taking possession of the town I fell in with a party of about 80 of the enemy, who fled as soon as I charged them, and, entering a thick wood on the bank of the river, escaped; another party, however, of 20 that were endeavoring to gain the same point, fell into my hands; seven of them remained prisoners, and the rest were killed, including their leader and another officer.

It now only remains for me to recommend generally the conduct and intrepidity of the valiant chiefs, officers, and soldiers, who with so much honor and determination displayed, in the action of the 19th, the valor which characterizes the Mexican army, their courage giving place to the most admirable indulgence on seeing their enemy had surrendered. This generous feeling, after so fierce an engagement, is worthy of especial recommendation.

JOSE URREA.

Articles of Capitulation proposed by Fannin.

ARTICLE 1. The Mexican force having established their battery at the distance of 160 paces, and opened their fire, we hoisted a white flag, upon which Col. Don Juan Morales, Col. Don Mariano Salas, and Lt. Col. of Engineers, Don Juan Jose Holsinger, came to us, when we proposed to surrender at discretion, to which they assented.

ART. 2. That the commandant, Fannin, and the wounded, be treated with all possible consideration, proposing to them also to deliver up all our arms.

ART. 3. The whole detachment to be treated as prisoners of war, and placed at the disposition of the Supreme Government.

JAMES W. FANNIN,
B. C. WALLACE,
J. M. CHANDEVILLE.
Camp near Goleto, between Guadaloupe and La Bahia, March 20, 1836.

When the white flag was hoisted by the enemy, I sent to inform them that they must surrender at discretion, without any other condition; the other articles proposed by those who sign the above are not assented to, which they were informed of and which they agreed to, as I neither would or could assent to anything else. &c. &c. &c.

JOSE URREA.

GUADALOUPE VICTORIA, March 23, 1836.
General DON FRANCISCO VITAL FERNANDEZ:

Comrade and Friend: I am so fatigued that I have only time to enclose to you copies of my despatches to our General-in-Chief, referring to my last operations. I have in my power more

than 600 prisoners, who I intend shall rebuild the houses they burnt at Goliad.
&c. &c. &c.

JOSE URREA.
DIVISION OF OPERATIONS
Guadaloupe Victoria, March 23, 1836.
Most Excellent Sir: Yesterday I marched from this place, as I informed your Excellency on the 21st. I directed my march to the house of Lim, which is situated upon the Lagoon of La Baca and the river Guadaloupe. Two motives took me there: one was to collect some supplies I knew were about there; the other to cut off a party of about 100 Americans, who got away from me on the 21st, into the woods on the banks of the river. At two P. M. I reached the mouth of the stream Zorillo, and captured four Americans, whom I compelled to inform me of the retreat of their companions. As soon as they made me acquainted with it, which was in a remarkably thick piece of wood, I surrounded, and sought the enemy in its centre; having found him, I summoned him to surrender at discretion.

Five minutes of parley sufficed, and Col. Ward, as he entitled himself, ten officers, and ninety men, delivered up their arms, surrendering at discretion; and they now remain at the disposition of your Excellency and of the Supreme Government. I shall send the prisoners to Goliad, where the rest are. &c. &c. &c.

JOSE URREA.
To His Excellency the President and General-in-Chief of the Army of Operations,
Don ANTONIO LOPEZ DE SANTA ANNA.
—*Daily National Intelligencer*, May 9, 1836

More details of the slaughter of Fannin and his men continued to trickle out of Texas.

TEXAS.—The following letter published in the Columbus Herald, confirms the news of the destruction of Fannin's forces and other disasters of the Texians:—
ON BOARD SCHOONER DE KALB,
Mississippi River, April 7, 1836.
Dear Sir—You are no doubt somewhat surprised at the heading of this page; but a few words will explain all. I am on board one of a number of vessels that are laden with the unfortunate, who are flying from the terrors of war. You have perhaps heard of the storming of St. Antonio, and the massacre of the Texian garrison. All without an exception perished, save a woman and two negroes. Davy Crockett, was among the number. He had fully sustained his great character for intrepidity, during an unsuccessful attempt of the enemy to storm the Alamo, just one week before the massacre. A short time previous to this, a party of sixty or seventy under Col. Johnson, were cut off, save four.—John Love was among the number who escaped. Reuben Brown fell here, and young Mitchell of Harris county, fell in the Alamo. The taking of the Alamo was followed by the retreat of the main army from Gonzales, and by the extermination of Fannin's regiment, 500 strong. Major Ward, and the Georgia Battalion (Capt. Wardsworth's company included,) had been detached by Fannin, then at Bahia, to protect some families who were flying from the enemy; when they were attacked, and after fighting and retreating for nearly two days, were at length overpowered by numbers, and all put to the sword, but five who escaped, and only two of them Georgians; one was Richard Rutledge, formerly of Columbus, and the other David I. Holt.

In the mean time, Fannin had received orders to abandon the fortress of La Bahia, which he immediately executed, and returned towards the main army with the balance of the troops, 360 men, and 7 pieces of artillery, where they were attacked in an open prairie by a large Mexican force, mostly cavalry. A small advance guard having been separated from the main body, saw the fight but could not tell the result. The termination of this unhappy affair, was explained by three men who escaped about the time of the catastrophe. Fannin sustained a great many charges in quick succession, sustaining some damage and doing much execution, and kept retreating during the fight, which lasted the greater part of a day, until he gained some post oak woods, when the Mexicans ceased their charges, but closely invested the place on all sides. Here Fannin received propositions from the enemy, and capitulated upon the promise of the Mexicans that they should be treated as prisoners of war. Their arms were immediately secured, and the next morning they were all shot, save the three who escaped. Mrs. Fannin had just arrived in Texas, but not in time to see her husband.

Many other barbarities have been committed. The army of Texas after making a stand for a short time on the Colorado, has retreated to the east side of the Brassos. San Phillippe is burnt (by the citizens) and there is a probability that Brazoria and Washington have shared the same fate. I do not expect that there are half a dozen families west of the Brassos. The enemy is known to be marching into the country in two divisions, of 2000 men each; one thro' the interior upon San Phillippe and the other along the coast towards Velasco. They were constantly expected at the latter place when I left it, and the advance of the other division had already reached San Phillippe. The Indians had begun to be troublesome, and many negroes have runaway—in some instances whole plantations of them had gone off in a body, but had done no further mischief. Very many families and negroes were going eastward, some for the United States by land and water—others are making a stand in the east, covered by the army.

—*Baltimore Gazette and Daily Advertiser,*
April 30, 1836

One of the most important eyewitness accounts of the events at Goliad and the battle of Coleto Creek was written by artillery captain Benjamin H. Holland. Originally published in a New Orleans newspaper, it was reprinted in several other US papers.

From the N. Orleans Bulletin.
MASSACRE OF COL. FANNIN.
FORT TRAVIS, GALVESTON ISLAND,
April 26, 1836.
Edward Hall, Esq.

Dear Sir—The enclosed statement of the awful massacre of Colonel Fanning's division of the Texian Army, has this moment reached me. I transmit it to you for publication.

Some few others of that unfortunate detachment effected their escape and have got in. I presume the statement of the tragic scene made in the enclosed is substantially correct. The unprecedented perfidy—the shameless cruelties of our enemies must and will be chastised.

In great haste, your obedient servant,
Signed, DAVID G. BURNET.

Mr. Editor:—Dear Sir—Should the annexed account of the battle of the Colette on La Bahia, be deemed of sufficient interest to be worthy of publication, it is at your service.
Yours, &c. BENJ. H. HOLLAND
Captain of Artillery.

On or about the 12th of March, orders were issued by general Houston, to destroy the town and Fort of La Bahia, and the forces to fall back to Gonzales to unite with him and concentrate all the Texian forces.

Prior to the receipt of these orders captain King's company was ordered to the Mission, a distance of about 25 miles, in order to relieve some families who were in danger of falling into the enemy's hands. Upon their arrival at the Mission they were met and attacked by a large body of the enemy, and after a gallant and well sustained fight, retreated in an orderly and judicious manner to the Church, where they sustained themselves against a very superior number of Mexicans and Indians with but small loss to themselves, but a severe loss to the enemy, until relieved by the Georgia battalion under Colonel Ward, who had been sent to their aid. The separation of our forces, caused us to delay our retreat. An express was sent to Colonel Ward at the Mission, to fall back and join the forces at Goliad with all possible despatch, or should he be cut off by the enemy, (of whose advance from San Patricio we had intelligence,) to make good his retreat through the Guadaloupe bottom and join the army at Victoria.

On the 10th or thereabouts brought intelligence that a body of the army,[b] 1500 strong, were on the San Antonio road. Many of the cannon having been dismounted preparatory to a retreat, we immediately remounted them,

---
[b] That is, the enemy.

Texian Settler Attacked and Eaten by a Giant Alligator during the Runaway Scrape

A few days before the battle of San Jacinto, refugee Texian families continued to stream eastward, with the Mexican army, as reports had it, not far behind them. One grisly episode of this exodus was described in a letter written on June 9, 1836, on Galveston Island, by the correspondent of the *Morning Courier and New York Enquirer* who also reported the supposed surrender and execution of David Crockett in that same letter. The name of the unfortunate victim of the alligator attack was Grey B. King.[1]

> After the fall of the Alamo, and the retreat of Gen. Houston from the Colorado, the people became panic-struck, and began to fly in every direction. St. Felipe was evacuated and burnt. All that could get with their families towards the Trinity and Sabine, did so. Some sought one place of refuge—some another. Some took to the bottoms and swamps; but all who could well get off in the direction of the United States, did so. Some sought the sea-shore; some Galveston Island. Some few families believed there would be safety at *Anahuac.* In fact, they could get no farther. Horses and cattle had given out; some were lost in the road; some could not cross the Trinity on account of the overflow. Indeed, the confusion and distress occasioned by the panic created by this blood thirsty monster, Santa Anna, is totally indescribable. The families who sought safety at Anahuac, finding the Mexicans close upon their heels, on the opposite side of the Bay, and expecting them every moment, left that place for the next place of safety, keeping on the Bay side towards Redfish bar, where boats might possibly be found to take them to the sea shore. Among the families that took this route was a Mr. King, his wife, and three small children. At Double Bayou about twelve miles below Anahuac, Mr. King attempted to ford it, and ascertain if a team could cross to safety. When about twenty or thirty feet from the shore, he was seized by an alligator. He struggled and cried for help; but alas! there was no help at hand; none but females and helpless children were at that moment near him. His wife and little children were sad and distracted spectators of this distressing scene. He was taken under water by the alligator after a short struggle, and never seen afterwards! Thus in a moment was Mrs. King left a widow, with three helpless children, on the Bay shore—the enemy close in her rear—had lost nearly everything at the burning of

(Continued)

St. Felipe—but finally was taken off by a passing boat, and landed at Galveston Island, in a most destitute condition. She was, however, made as comfortable at Galveston Island as circumstances would admit, and provided for when she left. I will here add that Mrs. King was from Salmon Creek, Birtie County N.C., and is the sister of the editor of a respectable paper.

—*Morning Courier and New York Enquirer*, July 9, 1836

Among the children taking part in the Runaway Scrape was Dilue Rose (later Harris), who in her adult years penned her "Reminiscences," based on her recollections, interviews she made, and her father's diary. Regarding the fate of poor Mr. King, she adds some details not found in the newspaper account.

It had been raining two days and nights. There was a bayou to cross over which there was no bridge, and the only way to pass was to go three miles through the bay to get around the mouth of the bayou. There were guide-posts to point the way but it was very dangerous. If we got near the mouth of the bayou there was quicksand. If the wind rose the waves rolled high. The bayou was infested with alligators. A few days before our family arrived at the bay a Mr. King was caught by one and carried under water. He was going east with his family. He swam his horses across the mouth of the bayou, and then swam back to the west side and drove the cart into the bay. His wife and children became frightened, and he turned back and said he would go up the river and wait for the water to subside. He got his family back on land, and swam the bayou to bring back the horses. He had gotten nearly across with them, when a large alligator appeared. Mrs. King first saw it above water and screamed. The alligator struck her husband with its tail and he went under water. There were several men present, and they fired their guns at the animal, but it did no good. It was not in their power to rescue Mr. King. The men waited several days and then killed a beef, put a quarter on the bank, fastened it with a chain, and then watched it until the alligator came out, when they shot and killed it. This happened several days before the battle. We passed the bayou without any trouble or accident, except the loss of my sunbonnet. It blew off as we reached the shore. The current was very swift at the mouth of the bayou. Father wanted to swim in and get it for me, but mother begged him not to go in the water, so I had the pleasure of seeing it float away. I don't remember the name of the bayou, but a little town called Wallace was opposite across the bay. We saw the big dead alligator, and we were glad to leave the Trinity.[2]

1. J. Frank Dobie, "Texans Who Have Associated Intimately with Alligators," *Dallas Morning News,* April 11, 1943.
2. "Reminiscences of Dilue Rose Harris." Available at www.tamu.edu/ccbn/dewitt/roseharrishtm.

as we anticipated an attack that night. About 12 o'clock the picket guard gave the alarm, and retreated into the fort; it however proved to be only the enemy's spies reconnoitering. On the 12th the enemy forded the San Antonio river and showed themselves at the old Mission, a distance from our fort of about 4 miles. This day we destroyed the whole town of La Bahia by fire, battering down all ruined walls so as to secure us a full sweep of the enemy, should they attack the fort. March 18. The enemy still hovering around the old Mission, a council of war was called, when it was decided, that inasmuch as our ammunition was not sufficient to sustain a siege, and as our provisions were short, and as we were well aware of the overwhelming force of the enemy, it was advisable to fall back to Victoria. This night we made every preparation for an early retreat in the morning, and by daylight every one was in marching order; before day a scouting party was despatched to ascertain the position of the enemy, who returned shortly after daylight and reported the lower road being clear. Col. Horton was then ordered by Col. Fannin to post all advance, rear, right and left guard.

March 19th, at about 6 1-2 A. M. took the line of retreat towards the lower Ford, and about 9 A. M. got our luggage and cannon across, we had nine pieces of brass artillery, consisting of one six inch howitzer, three short sixes, two long and two short fours, with several small pieces for throwing musket balls; we then commenced our advance towards Victoria, we had advanced several miles without receiving any intelligence of the enemy by our videttes, and at about 10 A. M. halted to graze our cattle and take some refreshment on the outskirts of some timber we had just passed; we tarried about

three-fourths an hour when we again took up the line of march; we had advanced about four miles into the prairie when we had intelligence of the enemy's approach; Col. Horton's cavalry, who were ordered in the rear, had neglected to remain in that position, and in consequence the enemy had advanced within the distance of from one to two miles ere they were descried upon both flanks, evidently with the design of surrounding us; captains Hurst and Holland of the artillery, were ordered to the rear to keep up a retreating fire, under cover of which the army advanced about a mile and a half in the face of the enemy; it now became necessary for us to take a position as we were entirely surrounded, our cavalry cut off from us and escaped, leaving us now two hundred and fifty effective men, consisting of the following companies:
New Orleans Greys—Capt. Pellis.
Red Rovers—Capt. Jack Shackleford, from Alabama.
Mustangs—Capt Duval.
Mobile Greys—Capt. McManaman.
Regulars—Capt. Westover.
1st Company Artillery—Capt. Hurst.
2d   do   do —Capt. Holland.
3d   do   do   —Capt   Schrusnecki, (a Polish Engineer)
We were about 300 yards to the left of the road, in a valley of about six feet below the mean base, of about one-fourth of a mile; we were unfortunately obliged to take that very disadvantageous position in consequence of our having pursued our advance so far in order to gain the woods. We drew our wagons into a cluster, formed ourselves into an oblong circle around them, and posted our artillery into position to defend it; the circle was about 40 feet of shortest central diameter, and about 60 feet

of longest diameter. It was now one o'clock, P. M., at which time we were attacked on all sides by the enemy, with a brisk fire of musketry; we were ordered not to fire until the word of command was given, in order to draw the enemy within rifle shot—we reserved our fire for about ten minutes, and several were wounded in our ranks previous to our firing; at the request of the officers, the artillery was permitted to open fire; the wind was blowing slightly from NE, and the smoke of our cannon covered the enemy, under which they made a desperate charge but were repulsed with a very severe loss; our cannon was loaded with canisters of musket balls, and the howitzer with grist[c]—in this manner the action was kept up with great fury by the enemy: charge after charge being made by cavalry and infantry, and always repelled with heavy loss on their part. Our men behaved nobly, and although surrounded by overwhelming numbers, not a change of countenance could be seen.

Thus was the battle kept up, and upon the repulse of each charge, column upon column of the enemy were seen to fall like bees before smoke. Here would be seen horses flying in every direction without riders, and there dismounted cavalry making their escape on foot, while the field was literally crowded with dead bodies;—it was a sorry sight to see our small circle; it had become muddy with blood, Col. Fannin had been so badly wounded at the first or second fire as to disable him; the wounded shrieking for water, which we had not to give them. The fight continued until dusk, when the enemy retreated, leaving us masters of the field, with ten men killed and wounded, and while the enemy lay around heap upon heap. We possessed a great advantage over the Mexicans, they having no artillery, and we having nine brass pieces with which we kept up an incessant fire of musket balls.

It now became prudent to take measures as to our next procedure: accordingly the officers were all summoned to Col. Fannin, where he lay wounded, and the question was whether we should maintain our present position or retreat;

it was carried, that we should sustain ourselves as long as possible. Consequently, we commenced heaving up a redoubt some three feet above the mean level of the prairie, exclusive of the dyke.

The night was now very dark and cloudy, drizzling with rain and misty fog, the enemy encompassed us, and kept up a continual sound to charge, so that we appeared to be surrounded with bugles.[2] We had with us about 1000 spare muskets, which we loaded and each man took an equal share, our cannon ammunition being nearly exhausted. Day light broke in upon us in this situation, and some of our men went out about a hundred yards and brought into camp two Mexican prisoners, both badly wounded; from these we ascertained that the number opposed to us was 1900 men, and that a reinforcement of two brigades of artillery would be there that morning if they had not already arrived; we had no sooner received this intelligence than this very artillery opened their cannon upon us; they had placed them behind a small hillock and were entirely under cover; we could neither touch them with our cannon or charge as they had so placed their cavalry that the moment we should quit our artillery they would cut us to pieces. We accordingly met in council to devise means and measures; it was accordingly decided that we should send a flag of truce to the enemy, and if possible obtain a treaty, upon fair and honorable terms. Accordingly Capt. F. J. Desanque, (the bearer of the express from Gen. Houston,) Capt. B. H. Holland of the artillery, and an ensign, were despatched with a flag of truce; the flags met midway between the two armies, and it was decided that the two commanders should meet and decide the matter—in pursuance of which Col. Fannin was conveyed out and met Gen. Urea, Governor of Durango, commander of the Mexican forces; and the following treaty was agreed upon, and solemnly ratified; a copy of it in Spanish was retained by Gen. Urea and one in English by Col. Fannin.

Seeing the Texian army entirely overpowered by a far superior force, and to avoid the effusion of blood, we surrendered ourselves prisoners of war, under the following terms:

---

[c] Unground corn.

Art. 1st. That we should be received and treated as prisoners of war, according to the usages of civilized nations.

Art. 2d. That the officers shall be paroled immediately upon their arrival at La Bahia, and the other prisoners should be sent to Copano within eight days, there to await shipping to convey them to the United States, so soon as it was practicable to procure it: no more to take up arms against Mexico until exchanged.

Art 3d. That all private property shall be respected, and officers' swords should be returned, on parole or release.

Art. 4th. That our men should receive every comfort, and be fed as well as their own men.
(Signed)

> Gen. UREA,
> Col. MORATEAS,
> Col. HOBZINGER,

On the part of the enemy; and on our part signed by

> Col. FANNIN, and
> Maj. WALLACE

The officers were then called upon to deliver their arms, which were boxed up, with their names placed by a ticket upon each, and a label upon the box stating that they should soon have the honor of returning them, and it was their principle to meet us now as friends, not as enemies.

Col. Fannin and the men were that afternoon marched back to La Bahia; the wounded together with the captain of each company, and the surgeons were left on the field to dress the wounded, which was completed on the 21st when we were all conveyed back to the fort, where we found the men in a most miserable state. They were brutally treated—they were allowed but very little water to drink, in consequence of its having to be brought from the river, and but a small piece of meat, without salt, bread or vegetables—On the 23d, Major Miller and 90 men, were brought into the fort prisoners; they had just landed at Copano from the United States.

On the 25th, the Georgia battalion was also brought in; it had been surprised and captured between Victoria and Demill's Point, and marched back and confined with us.—Here we were now nearly 500 strong guarded by 1000 Mexicans, without being allowed the slightest liberty in any respect.

The Mexicans had always said that Santa Anna would be at La Bahia, on the 27th, to release us. Accordingly on that day, we were ordered to form all the prisoners; we were told that we were going to bring wood and water, and that Santa Anna would be there that day; we were ordered to march all the officers at the head of the file, except Col. Fannin, who lay wounded in the hospital. As we marched out of the sally port, we saw hollow squares formed ready to receive us; we were ordered to file left, and marched into a hollow square of double filed cavalry, on foot armed with carbines, commonly called scopets and broad swords.

This square was filled and closed, and the head of the remaining files wheeled off into the other squares, and so on until all were strongly guarded in squares; the company of which the writer of this was one, was ordered to go forward, and no more was seen of our unfortunate comrades; we marched out on the Bexar road, near the burying ground, and as we were ordered to halt, we heard our companions shrieking in the most agonizing tones, "Oh, God! Oh, God! Save us" and nearly simultaneously a report of musketry. It was then we knew what was to be our fate. The writer of this then observed to Major Wallace, who was to be file leader, that it would be best to make a desperate rush—he said no—we are too strongly guarded; he then appealed to several others, but none would follow; he then sprung and struck the soldier on his right a severe blow with his fist, they being at open files, the soldier then turned his gun and struck the writer a severe blow upon the left hand. I then seized hold of the gun and wrenched it from his hand, and instantly started and ran towards the river.

A platoon of men (I have since been informed, by two others who made their escape by falling when fired upon among the dead bodies of their comrades) wheeled and fired upon me, but all missed. I then had a chain of sentinels to pass at about 300 yards distance;

they were about 30 yards apart, three of them closed to intercept my retreat; the central one raised his gun to fire—I still ran towards him in a serpentine manner in order to prevent his taking aim—I suddenly stopped—dropped my piece, fired, and shot the soldier through the head and he fell instantly dead. I ran over his dead body, the other two firing at me but missing, and immediately ran and leaped into the river, and while swimming across, was shot at by three horse men, but reached the opposite bank in safety; and after wandering six days without food in the wilderness, succeeded on the 10th of April in joining General Houston's army, after having been retaken by the enemy once, but succeeded in making my escape in company with a wounded man who had got off from La Bahia, by falling among the dead as before stated. I am happy to state, six more succeeded in saving their lives and regaining their liberty by the same stratagem. The number of the enemy, according to their own account, killed at the battle of Coletto, was from 9 to 1100.

—*New Bedford Gazette*, June 13, 1836

Another massacre survivor was Joseph H. Spohn, who had originally come to Texas in Captain Thomas H. Breece's company of New Orleans Greys. He included in his account a poignant, highly detailed description of the execution of Colonel Fannin.

DEATH OF COL. FANNIN AND HIS MEN.

Mr. Joseph H. Spohn, one of the survivors of Fannin's command, has arrived in New York in the ship Mexican from Vera Cruz. He owes his escape to being able to speak the Spanish language, which made his services necessary as an interpreter to the savage Mexicans. Spohn was one of the Red Rover volunteers, and went to Goliad with Col. Grant, Col. Johnson, and Maj. Morris, uniting there with Fannin's party, the Georgia Battalion and Alabama Greys. He has furnished the N. York Evening Star with many interesting particulars, given editorially in that paper, which begin with the battle and unfortunate surrender at Colleto, and come down to his escape from Vera Cruz. We make the following extract, detailing the circumstances of the murder of his unfortunate friends.

"On Palm Sunday, being 27th, March, the prisoners were formed into line, and Mr. Spohn, who was then sleeping in the church, (the hospital) being about 6 o'clock in the morning, was called out and told to form into line, being the last he fell at the end. They were then marched out of the fort and ranged before the gate, when an officer stepped up and asked Spohn what he was doing there, and ordered him to go back to the hospital where he was wanted, and when on his way was stopped by another officer, who told him to order the assistants to have the wounded of the Texians brought into the yard; such as could not walk were to be carried out. Being astonished at these preparations, he asked why, when the officer said, 'Carts were coming to convey them to Copano,' the nearest seaport. The orders of the officers were obeyed, and the wounded brought into the yard, and they were all full of the hope that they were to be shipped to the United States, which had been promised, but their hopes were cruelly blasted when they heard a sudden continued roar of musketry on the outside of the fort, and observed the soldier's wives leap upon the walls and look towards the spot where the report came from. The wounded were then conscious of what was passing, and one of them asked Spohn if he did not think that their time was come; and when they became convinced from the movements about the fort that they were to be shot, greater part of them sat down calmly on their blankets, resolutely awaiting their miserable fate; some turned pale, but not one displayed the least fear or quivering. Spohn, who was employed in helping them out, was accosted by a wounded Mexican soldier, on whom he attended, and told to go ask the commandant for his life, as he might save him, as they were all to be shot. About this time, Colonel Fannin, who had a room in the church for his use, came out of the church for a particular purpose, when a Mexican captain of the battalion called Tres Villas, with six soldiers, came up to Spohn, and told him to call Col. Fannin, at the same time pointing to a certain part of the yard, where he wished him to be taken. Spohn asked him if he was going to shoot him, and he cooly replied, 'Yes.'—When Spohn approached Fannin the Colonel asked him what was that firing, and when he told him the facts he made no observation, but appeared resolute and firm, and told him he also was to be shot, which made no visible impression on Col. Fannin, who firmly walked to the place pointed out by the Mexican captain, placing his arm upon the shoulder of Spohn for support, being wounded in the right thigh, from which he was very lame. All this while the soldiers were taking the wounded, two at a time, near the gate and setting them down on the ground and bandaging their eyes, would shoot them off, with the same indifference they would a wild animal. There were three soldiers to each two, so that if after the discharge of two muskets, death should not have been dealt forth, the third soldier placed the muzzle of the musket near their head or breast, and so ended them.

When Col. Fannin reached the spot required, the N. W. corner of the fort, Spohn was ordered to interpret the following sentence:—'That for having come with an armed band to commit depredations and revolutionize Texas, the Mexican government were about to chastise him.' As soon as the sentence was interpreted to Fannin, he asked if he he could not see the commandant. The officer said he could not, and asked why he wished it. Colonel Fannin then pulled forth a valuable gold watch, which he said belonged to his wife, and he wished to present it to the commandant. The Captain then said he could not see the commandant, but if he would give him the watch he would thank him—and he repeated in broken English, *'tank you—me tank you,'* Col. Fannin told him he might have the watch if he would have him buried after he was shot, which the captain said should be done—'con ted as las formalidades necessarias'—at the same time smiling and bowing. Colonel Fannin then handed him the watch, and pulled out of his right pocket a small bead purse containing doubloons, the clasp of which was bent, he gave this to the officer, at the same time saying that it had saved his life, as the ball that wounded him had lost part of its

force by striking the clasp, which it bent and carried with it into the wound a part of a silk handkerchief which he had in his pocket, and which on drawing out drew forth with it the ball. Out of the left pocket of his overcoat, (being cold weather he had on one of India Rubber) a piece of canvass containing a double handful of dollars, which he also gave to the officer. Spohn was then ordered to bandage his eyes, and Col. Fannin handed him his pocket handkerchief. He proceeded to fold it, but being agitated he done it clumsily, when the officer snatched it from his hand and folded it himself, and told Col. Fannin to sit down on a chair which was near, and stepping behind him bandaged his eyes, saying to Col. Fannin in English, "good, good"—meaning if his eyes were properly bound—to which Fannin replied, "yes, yes." The captain then came in front and ordered his men to unfix their bayonets and approach Col. Fannin, he hearing them nearing him, told Spohn to tell them not to place their muskets so near as to scorch his face with the powder.

The officer standing behind them, after seeing their muskets were brought within two feet of his body, drew forth his handkerchief as a signal, when they fired, and poor Fannin fell dead on his right side on the chair, and from thence rolled into a dry ditch about three feet deep, close by the wall. They then led Spohn near the gate, from which another officer took him and placed him in the room of Colonel Portia, with a sentinel over him. He asked the officer if he was going to shoot him, he replied, "no hijo," grinning maliciously as the same time. In the room he found a Frenchman of the Copano company, who told him the rest of his corps had early in the morning been placed in a garden outside the fort under guard. After he had been there a short time a soldier with his gun, came to the door, telling him he was wanted at the gate. When he came to the gate he found Commandant Portia surrounded by his officers, who, on seeing Spohn, seeing him before, begged Portia to save him, but he said he could not, as his orders were positive, but they persisting, he rather impatiently said, "Well, take him away." At the same time he saw them lead young Ripley, who was second sergeant of the Mobile Greys, who was badly wounded in the left arm, to the place of execution. Spohn was then taken to the house of an officer, where he was left, where every moment he could hear the muskets roar, the death knell of his companions. Spohn had been in the house but a little time when a young Mexican soldier with a bloody sword, entered the room and asked him what he was doing there, and would have run him through had not the servants told him he was placed there by the officers. Dr. Field came in with a sergeant—the Doctor told Spohn that all were shot, and they had roughly dragged Captain Brooks, of West Point, who laid with his thigh broken, from a house outside the fort and despatched him brutally on the street. In an hour more, Spohn re-entered the fort, where he found the Mexican soldiers placing the bodies of the dead on a large wagon and carrying them off. Two or three days after Spohn was taken by a Captain Corono to the place outside the fort where his countrymen had been murdered and piled one on top the other, and partially burnt or roasted, presenting a most frightful, horrible and disgusting spectacle, by which he found that they had been divided into four parties before they were shot, as they were four piles, surrounded by torn pieces of bloody clothing, shoes, caps, pocket books and papers. Among the rest was the bloody cap of Fannin, which leads us to expect he was burnt or roasted with the others.

Five men were saved from the general massacre to attend upon the Mexican sick; Skerlock, Smith, Bills, Vose, and Peter Griffin: the latter, who happened to be in the hospital at the time, was saved by a wounded Mexican soldier, who hid him beneath his blankets, Griffin having always attended him and dressed his wounds. Bills died afterwards, from a sickness of 24 hours.

Spohn was retained a prisoner with the Copano detachment under Major Miller, Captain Israel, and Mr. Burton, who had been sent with their companies to Goliad. They told him that like their own, in the end, his case was desperate; and that to escape, any means he might employ were justifiable.

Urrea treated him kindly, taking him as a coachman to Matamoras, where, by his permission, he entered the Mexican sea service in the Correo, under Thompson, for the purpose of getting away, and effected his escape at Vera Cruz. He speaks with the warmest gratitude of the kindness and humanity of Captain Kimball of the Mexican.

—*New Hampshire Patriot*, August 8, 1836

The Texas coastal town of Matagorda saw the arrival of one of the Goliad survivors.

Extract of a letter, dated,
"MATAGORDA, April 1, 1836.

"At a late hour last evening, a gentleman arrived and informed us, that he was one who luckily made his escape from the general massacre of Fannin's party, and that there were 6 or 7 made their escape also.—Their names are Simpson, Cooper, Brooks, Leddington, and Hadden—the others not recollected. Col. Fannin was wounded and carried off by the Mexicans, which was the last our informant heard of him."

This cold-blooded cruelty has not had the effect which the Mexicans expected. Instead of intimidating the Texians, it has roused them, and nerved their arm. It has excited every feeling heart against Santa Anna—and whatever may betide him, his fate will scarcely meet with any sympathy from a civilized world. The spirit of the age declares against him.

—*Richmond Enquirer*, May 17, 1836

The following letter, originally published in the *New Orleans Bee*, was written by an unnamed Mexican general and shows that Santa Anna's directive for taking no prisoners was a dictate not universally relished by his officers.

Col. Fanning's Command.—The following horrid picture of the Massacre of Fannin's command, is from a Mexican General to his wife. Dreadful as the alternative is, it cannot be read without coming to the conclusion that justice, humanity, and a warning voice to all tyrants, demand equal retribution on Santa Anna and his officers—the blood wantonly, cruelly shed, calls aloud for justice. Santa Anna can make no treaty with Houston, that Mexico will sanction.—*N. Y. Star.*

GOLIAD, March 25, 1836.

Immediately after leaving Metamoras, I began to witness disorders of considerable magnitude committed by M—— and his soldiers, and a captain from Guanajato, named Dr. R. P.——; and, becoming completely disgusted, I obtained permission to proceed in advance of that body, and incorporate myself with Gen. Urrea's division. I did so, and joined the latter in San Patricio. Before I reached Agua Dulce, the dead foreigners, already mangled by wild beasts, appeared by the way and in San Patricio I saw the graves of the fallen, both of Americans and Mexicans. On marching to the ruins of the Mission del Refugio, we found the enemy in possession of the church. We commenced the assault at six in the same morning and the action continued until midnight when they fled. They fought with an enthusiastic valor equal to that of our own men. Several of our troops were shot within four paces of the wall, the enemy being invincible,[d] and their station only known by the voluminous flashes which issued from the building. Our loss that day, in killed and wounded, amounted to 40; and of the enemy 25 out of 30 who fell in our hands, as also some others whom we found in the church. But what an awful scene did the field present when these prisoners were executed, and fell dead in heaps; and what spectator could view it without horror! They were all young, the eldest not more than 30, and of fine florid complexion. When these unfortunate youths were brought to the place of death, their lamentations and the appeals which they uttered to Heaven, in their own language, with extended arms, kneeling, or prostrate on the earth, were such as might have caused the very stones to cry out with compassion.

We passed through this town, where, except for fortifications and cannons, we found nothing but ashes, rubbish, and wounded men. The number of the latter amounts to 116 Mexicans and 40 foreigners, so badly attended that it sickened me to view what suffering had been caused by the ambition of that ungrateful Austin. Previously to this, 82 prisoners had been taken at Copano, without firing a gun, as I have already informed you: these are all at full liberty.

There are now in this place 250 prisoners[*] awaiting their death as pirates and incendiaries, there being only two who did not participate in the latter crime. The images and saints in the church served them for fuel. There are in Guadaloupe 100 other prisoners who were taken at La Vaca. There is, as yet, no intelligence from the Divisions which marched for the towns of Austin and Nacogdoches; but I will send you the first news that may come from that quarter.

You will perceive that neither the rifles nor the double barrelled guns with which the enemy were armed; nor the pistols they carried about them in such numbers; nor the sure aim with which they strike a dollar at so great a distance, nor yet their artillery, have been of any avail against the intrepid Mexicans. Such they certainly are. Horse and foot have vied with each other and all have fought with order and enthusiasm. It is said that in Bejar 700 of the enemy were killed. Of this I cannot speak with certainty, but it is known that in every place they have occupied, numbers of their brave have fallen.

P. S.—This day, Palm Sunday, March 27, has been to me a season of heartfelt sorrow. At 6 in the morning the execution of 412 *American* prisoners was commenced and continued till 8 when the last of the number was *shot*. At 11 began the operation of burning the bodies. Who can tell when they will be consumed! I assure you that the number of foreigners who have fallen in Texas during the campaign must exceed 1,000. We have still 80 of them living.

*They were taken one league from the town, and then *shot*. [Private letter.]

—*Rhode Island Republican*, June 1, 1836

Then there was the strange case of Dr. Benjamin Harrison, the twenty-nine-year-old son of General William Henry Harrison. The young doctor had

[d] The intended word was probably *invisible*.

arrived in Texas earlier in 1836 to arrange a loan for the infant Texas government. But initial reports from New Orleans related that he had suffered a ghastly demise.

Dr. Benjamin Harrison, son of Gen. Harrison, of North Bend, Ohio, was, while travelling with three American gentlemen, taken by the Mexicans, horribly mutilated, his body cut down, and his bowels torn out, and left in that situation before life was extinct! The wife of Dr. Harrison came passenger in the Invincible.
—*New York Sun*, May 10, 1836

Weeks later there was more confusion about his fate, and the claim was made that he had escaped the slaughter of the Alamo garrison.

Dr. Benjamin Harrison, son of General Harrison, whom it was reported had been cruelly butchered by the Mexicans, it appears, is still alive. He was one of the few who escaped from the massacre of the Alamo. He was, however, captured by another party, and the commanding officer allowed his departure and furnished him with means to aid his arrival in the United States. He was, on his arrival in Texas, through the treachery of a servant, apprehended as a spy and was conveyed on board a Texan vessel of war, and placed in confinement. These particulars are gained from a letter from him to his friends.
—*New York Times,* June 2, 1836

Not until midsummer, when a letter from Texas was published in a New York paper, would the mystery of Dr. Harrison's oft-discussed peregrinations and fate, as well as of the accusations against him of siding with the enemy, be cleared up.

From the Charleston Mercury.
To Col. James Watson Webb, Editor of the N. Y. Courier & Enquirer:
SIR—Your Correspondent from Galveston, Texas, has stated things in his communication to you, which are false and unfounded, and as he has calumniated the character of a friend, I demand, as a matter of right, that you will allow

me to respond to such parts of his article as relates to Dr. Benjamin Harrison, (son of the Hon. E. H. Harrison.)

He says that Dr. Harrison "boasted that he was the Surgeon General of the Mexican Army, and that he distributed Santa Anna's Proclamations." I deny it unequivocally. Dr. H. never boasted of being in the Mexican service; on the contrary, he always spoke in the most contemptible terms of those blood thirsty hell hounds, those worse than brutal hirelings, the Mexican Legions.

I became acquainted with Dr. H. at Matagorda, on my way to join the brave but unfortunate Fanning. I met the Doctor at Victoria, a small town on the Guadaloupe River, distant 25 miles from the Army,—it was his intention to have joined our troops and proceeded with me, but the afternoon previous to our starting, a Capt. Desauque, of Philadelphia, arrived and gave us the news that the Alamo had fallen. He was then bound on to Fanning, and a man by the name of Duffield, who belonged to the Infantry, borrowed the Doctor's horse to accompany Captain Desauque to Goliad, with a promise to return him next day; the Doctor assented, and as the individual did not return we were compelled to leave him. Immediately after our vacating the town, the inhabitants became extremely insulting to the few Americans who remained, and as soon as they ascertained Fanning's defeat, they, headed by the second Alcalde, bound Dr. Harrison's hands behind him, in conjunction with two other Americans, and commenced butchering them; they began on the others first, and by the time they had finished their damned work, Dr. H. had succeeded in separating his hands, and immediately ran into the Guadaloupe timber, (which is uncommonly thick) and secreted himself. He was, however, after many days, taken by the troops of Gen. Urrea and brought into his presence. As soon as he found out he was a physician he spared his life, and requested him to attend on the sick. Dare Dr. Harrison refuse? He was a prisoner, and even were he not, common humanity would revolt at the villain who would not strain every nerve to alleviate the sufferings of the distressed. Dr. H's practice met with success, and Gen. Urrea, like a brave man, granted him his life and gave him his own horse, and sent him to his afflicted wife. He gave the Doctor Santa Anna's Proclamations, and requested him to distribute them among the people—the Doctor declined; then, said Gen. Urrea, give them to some of your leading men. I will do this General, but recollect if we meet in the field I will hold you the enemy of Texas, and consider me your political foe. The instant he arrived in the American settlements he presented the papers (not to the populace,) but to one of the leading men. He was instantly charged with high treason and arrested. He was carried before David G. Burnet and honorably acquitted and discharged. On his way to join his family, who had fled to the United States, he was again arrested by orders from President Burnet, and sent to Galveston Island, from thence he was conveyed on board the prize brig Packet as a prisoner and traitor. And the orders that accompanied him said, "keep a watchful eye upon him, for he is the most dangerous man in Texas." I was detailed to guard him, and so satisfied was I of his innocence that I treated him as he deserved—like a gentleman. Capt. Wheelwright, of the Texian Navy, who was then in command, did likewise.

Dr. H. engaged me as Counsel. I wrote to President Burnet, stating that my client was extremely anxious to have his trial. The next day I went on shore, had an interview with his Excellency, who told me as soon as the Cabinet met he would gratify the Doctor. In a few days the Cabinet met, but Dr. Harrison "the traitor," was not called upon to appear before the August tribunal, although I demanded either a trial or an honorable acquittal, as suspense to the prisoner was worse than condemnation. Without a trial, it at last pleased David G. Burnet, President of the Republic of Texas, to discharge Dr. Benjamin Harrison, the "dangerous traitor." These are facts, Sir, and I ask you whether the reputation of an honest man has not been basely trampled upon? Whether the feelings of his honored father have not been awfully lacerated? But lastly mark, aye well mark the

President's conduct; he takes the responsibility upon himself in time of War, to discharge a "traitor" without a trial. This single isolated act, proclaims Dr. Harrison an injured and an innocent man.[3]

HENRY REILLY, Prisoner's Counsel
—*Morning Courier and New York Enquirer*,
July 28, 1836

A constant flow of rumors added to the general confusion of the Texians, both soldiers and fugitive settlers, as they strove to stay several steps ahead of the advancing Mexicans. And of course newspaper readers across the United States were often no less puzzled about the course of the conflict. Meanwhile, opinion about the causes of the Texas Revolution remained, in some places, very divided. But in Washington, D.C., one supposed boast of Santa Anna's generated great laughter.

The story of the massacre of 60 American traders by the Camanche Indians, on Red river, turns out to be *not true*. The story that Col. Crockett was yet alive is probably not true. The story that the Indians had taken possession of Nacogdoches, is not true, though the inhabitants were sadly frightened. The story that Col. Fannin and his 300 followers were deliberately shot, after surrendering as prisoners of war, is probably too true, notwithstanding the Spanish official accounts. They surrendered at discretion. The story that the Americans in Texas are fighting on their own hook, *is* true. If they can defend Texas and establish Independence, we have no particular objection—but with the quarrel the United States have no interest whatever. We have land enough at $1.25 per acre; these emigrants want it cheaper; for 12 ½ cents, with the right to fill it with slaves. Santa Anna says no, and we see not why he has not a very good right to say no; but this gives him no right to murder his prisoners, and act the part which would disgrace Tecumseh or Black Hawk. Had they remained good subjects, and conformed to the government of Mexico, they would have enjoyed all the privileges they were promised.

Should the account be fully confirmed, (and there seems to be little or no doubt of

Proposed Regiments of Mounted Riflemen Volunteers

Perhaps the oddest of the occasional oddball who found his way to Revolutionary-era Texas was a man named James Dickson, of whose origins little is known. Possibly English, he had spent some time in Mexico and would later dub himself "Montezuma II" because it became his stated goal to free all of the Indians of Mexico and the southwest and coalesce them into one great kingdom, with himself at its head.[1] He appeared in Washington, D.C., in early 1836, at a time when Antonio López de Santa Anna's threat to march his troops across Texas to the banks of the Sabine River was being taken seriously by the US government. Thus, Dickson's timing could not have been better, in terms of submitting a petition for raising an army of volunteers, ostensibly for "the defence of our Frontier," but no doubt to also serve his long range scheme of empire.

In the April 29, 1836, issue of the *United States Telegraph*, a Washington-based newspaper, Dickson spelled out in remarkable detail—detail that certainly proved he had indeed known of soldiering and field conditions in the Southwest—his idea for a four thousand-man force.

SECOND ADDRESS TO THE
BRAVE AMERICANS
OF THE SOUTH AND WEST.

To all brave Americans who are under the influence of those noble feelings which have animated the patriot in every age and clime—to all whom ties of dearest kindred, imperative duty, and indissoluble engagements do not enchain to their present homes—to all to whom philanthropy and the love of true glory have been a guiding star in life—to all those do I now address myself!

Brave Americans! Four thousand mounted Riflemen Volunteers are wanted to rendezvous on the Western Frontier, on the 1st day of August, 1836, there to be ready to offer themselves as volunteers, for the defence of our Frontier, to the United States Government; to which class of defence allusion has been made in Congress, and a law offered for the appropriation of money, &c.

Let each individual who wishes to volunteer and join me, furnish himself as follows:

(Continued)

1 rifle.

1 lance, 13 ½ feet long, steel blade inclusive, being 18 inches, and sharp edged; haft of lance of lancewood or hickory, with one pound of lead at the butt end.

1 pair of cavalry pistols, with holsters not of fur.

1 long double edged sharp knife to cut lassos, *or any thing else.*

1 haversack or knapsack to fit to the horse's saddle.

The knapsack to contain and be provided with 25 sea biscuits—5 pounds of ham—1 pound of salt—2 pounds of rifle powder—and one hundred rounds of rifle and pistol balls; as also a tin canteen to hold 4 pints of water.

To be provided with money to purchase two horses—horses being cheaper on the frontier prairies than elsewhere.

Each ten volunteers to subscribe and purchase two baggage mules to carry additional provision and munitions of war.

Each volunteer to furnish his uniform as follows: The uniform of each regiment, till regulated otherwise by the United States government, to be a pair of cavalry boots, made large for the feet; for when swollen with exercise, or wet by rain and the crossing of rivers, they will become cramped, and the feet will be injured; buck-skin leather pantaloons; 2 leather shirts, do.; 1 leather jacket do.; 1 large slouched Spanish hat; a blanket, and *those who wish sheets* to provide themselves with buck-skin leather sheets, as used in Norway and Sweden. It would be preferable if each State of the South and West formed its own regiment, each regiment to consist of 400 men inclusive of officers.

All officers, commissioned and non-commissioned, to be chosen by the ballot of each regiment, save the Colonel, Lt. Colonel, 1st Major, 1st Captain, and 1st Lieutenant, who may be selected by the U. S. government, should the government be pleased to accept our services; or filled otherwise by officers of the regiment already balloted for by the whole regiment.

One corps of men to be drafted to make a horse artillery corps for six brass 6-pound field pieces.

One regiment to be filled with picked men from the other regiments, to consist of three hundred men inclusive of officers, to be named the "Immortal Guard of Lancer Cuirassiers"—each private and officer to be balloted for by the first fifty selected, which fifty are to be first selected by ballot of the whole of the regiments; ten black balls to exclude. Each Lancer Cuirassier shall furnish himself with a cuirass and helmet made of *prepared buffalo hides.*

This "Guard" to be pledged on solemn oath never to leave the battle field save victorious or covered with wounds, and to bind themselves on their scared honor to provide honorably for the orphan and widow of their fallen comrades. And may God save us all!

I hereby engage and bind myself, my heirs and executors, and pledge my honor, that to each regiment, ten days after their arrival at a certain designated point on the western frontier, they shall be furnished with army rations at my individual expense, until their services be accepted by the United States Government, or are disbanded: and I do further bind myself, my heirs, and executors, to pay or cause to be paid to each individual when they shall disband themselves with my consent, the sum of $30 each toward defraying their expenses homeward.

JAMES DICKSON.
Washington, 29th April, 1836

Dickson's plan apparently met with little luck in Washington, for by late July he was three hundred miles to the northwest, in Buffalo, New York, having gathered some sixty recruits, many of them Montreal-area residents and the offspring of Canadian trappers and Indian women. His new idea was to travel west across the Great Lakes and raise an army of Indians and Metis; with these followers he would march south, attack Santa Fe, and then California. Mexico itself would afterward also fall under his conquering legions.

Martin McLeod was one of these volunteers, and while he was en route to meet with Dickson, he was met by an interested correspondent of the *Morning Courier and New York Enquirer*, which printed a brief report in its August 5, 1836, issue.

The Texas Fever has crossed the line 45 deg. We met on Saturday last a young gentleman on board the steamer Henry Broughan, which plies between Lackin and the Cascades, dressed in a blue undress military frock, with white buttons, scarlet facing to the collar; trowsers similar to those worn by our Engineers, and a sash round his waist. On enquiry, we learned that his name was McLeod, a resident at Lachine, who had lately been promised, or had received a Captain's commission in the Texian army, and was going to Buffalo, from which place other volunteers were about to proceed to Texas. It was the Texian uniform which he wore. He appeared to be in high spirits. Other young men in this Province we understand have taken "the fever" also.[2]

(Continued)

This second attempt accomplished little more than a fifteen-hundred-mile journey west to Fort Garry, in Winnipeg, Manitoba, but by the time Dickson's party arrived there, it had been whittled down to twelve men, thanks to the hazards of crossing the lakes and the trek over a snowbound Minnesota. The following spring a revived Dickson pushed south along the Missouri River as far as Fort Clark (in today's North Dakota), but eventually he grew either too sick or too discouraged to carry on, for one day he wandered off by himself "to die," as he said. Nothing more was ever heard of him.[3]

Six years later, English traveler William Bollaert would echo Dickson's description of his intended mounted riflemen's "uniform" when writing of the "rancheros, or herdsmen," of San Antonio, who wore, as Bollaert wrote in his diary, "a slouched hat, leather hunting shirt, leggings and Indian moccasins, armed with a large knife, musket or rifle, and sometimes pistols."[4]

---

1. Bernard DeVoto, *Across the Wide Missouri* (Boston: Houghton Mifflin, 1947), 272–274.
2. Lachine is a suburb of Montreal in Quebec Province, and "the Cascades" probably refers to the head of the St. Lawrence River rapids, beyond the limits of the canal that had been dug in the 1820s, west of Lachine.
3. DeVoto, *Across the Wide Missouri*, 272–278; "Dickson, James," *Dictionary of Canadian Biography Online*. Available at www.biographi.ca/009004-119.01-e.php?BioId=37477.
4. W. Eugene Hollon, ed., *William Bollaert's Texas* (Norman: University of Oklahoma Press, 1989), 217.

the fact) that 400 prisoners have been deliberately shot, Santa Anna is a cold-blooded MURDERER, deserving the execration of the civilized world. He had some excuse, at the Alamo, as that fortress was taken by storm, the commander refusing to surrender. The Southern country may yet rise to avenge their brethren—and it may be even difficult to restrain an outbreaking within the walls of Congress.

Mr. Preston, on presenting a memorial from Philadelphia, praying Congress to take steps to stop the effusion of blood in Texas, indulged in severe remarks, as did others upon Santa Anna, and referred to a letter in the possession of Mr. Walker of Mississippi. Mr. W. read the letter, and believed every word of it, while Mr. Porter of Louisiana, classed it with the stories of the celebrated baron *Munchausen*. The writer had it from an English gentleman, who had it from Lord somebody, that Santa Anna, before leaving Mexico, declared he would cross the Sabine, liberate the negroes, march to Washington, burn the city, plant his standard upon the walls of the capitol, and pluck the laurels from Gen. Jackson's brow!!!! The Senate was convulsed with laughter.

—*New Hampshire Sentinel*, May 19, 1836

≋10≋

San Jacinto and the First Year of the Texas Republic

Antonio López de Santa Anna's columns continued knifing through Texas, and Sam Houston's army kept retreating. But something had changed in Texian hearts: impatience, anger, and vengeance had replaced dread, terror, and mourning, despite the vast incongruity in the numbers of the opposing forces.

(From the Mobile Chronicle.)

We have been politely favored with the perusal of a letter from Col. Samuel M. Williams, who recently left our city for Texas, which states that he had received a letter from Brazoria of the 1st April, which informed him of the retreat of General Houston to the East side of the Brazos—it seems against the advice of his officers. General Houston has command of the principal forces, and doubtless feels the responsibility of his position. His officers and men are brave and gallant soldiers, with feelings of indignation justly excited against a ruthless tyrant: and their impetuosity, whilst it bespeaks firmness and resolution, ought to be restrained within the bounds of prudence. The brave are not always victorious. The Texians are few in numbers, and the troops of Santa Anna are well trained and disciplined. It is, therefore, the more necessary to await a favorable moment, when the Texians are well prepared to meet and conquer their enemy. Such was the policy of Washington, and it may be prudent to follow it in this instance.

The policy of Gen. Houston is to draw the enemy into the heart of the country, where the difficulties of receiving provisions and ammunition are increased, and will allow time for the volunteers to join the standard of the Texian army.

We hope that the noble and generous friends of Texas will not permit any intelligence of disaster to damp their efforts in behalf of a brave and suffering people. It should only serve to awaken their sympathies the more, and to confirm them in the determination to afford the most prompt and efficient assistance.

A letter has just been received in this place from Col. J. Dorington, dated March 25, which states that the inhabitants on the Brassos above San Felipe, had secured their families by placing them on the east of the Trinity—that the panic was over; every man able to bear arms, was rushing to join Houston: That Santa Anna had let the important hour slip, and that the people had become confident that they would be able shortly to expel the invader from Texas. For several days previous to the date of the letter, nothing has been heard of the Mexican army; that Santa Anna had either retreated, or was endeavoring to make a flank movement on Houston.

—*Richmond Enquirer*, May 3, 1836

What happened next is perhaps best summarized in a letter by a soldier in Houston's army that was first published in a Tennessee paper and later reprinted in the *New York Herald*.

Annexed is a letter taken from the Nashville Banner, written by R. Stevenson to his brother in Shelbyville, Tennessee:—

LYNCH'S FERRY, (Texas,) 23 April.

Santa Anna, not meeting with any opposition in his march through the country, pushed on from the Brasos river with about six hundred of his best soldiers, to take possession of Galveston Bay, the only port in Texas which he had not in his possession. Houston, aware of his intention, and who was then on the Brasos river, sixty miles above the position of the enemy, determined to pursue Santa Anna, expecting to come up with him about Harrisburg by forced marches. We arrived at that place on the evening of the 18th inst., but the enemy had left for Galveston Bay. General Houston, to facilitate our movements, left all baggage, wagons, and the sick at Harrisburg, under the charge of about three hundred men, and by marching all night of the 19th, on the morning of the 20th came within sight of the enemy. We immediately took possession of a strong position on the bank of Buffalo bayou, and the enemy came on to attack us, but were repulsed by the discharge of two four pounder cannon loaded with grape and canister shot. They then returned into a heavy body of timber about a mile on our front, and remained there until the next morning, the 21st inst., when they were reinforced by about five hundred and fifty men under Gen. Cos. We were then certain of being attacked in the course of the day, but towards evening, Gen. Houston seeing that they did not intend bringing on the attack, and fearing they would receive further reinforcements, determined to attack them on their own ground. With this intention, he formed his little army into three divisions,

with our artillery in front, and marched on to the attack. The left wing commanded by Col. Sherman, were first attacked by a heavy fire of musketry from the timber, when the centre and right wing commanded by Col. Burleson and Gen. Houston, marched forward under a discharge of grape and canister from the enemy's artillery in front, which we at last were obliged to charge, and the battle became general along the lines, we rushed forward with great impetuosity, jumped the enemy's breast-works, the ALAMO being our war cry, took possession of their artillery, and drove them from their position. Our rifles then committed dreadful havoc among them, and they gave way in every direction, we kept up the pursuit until night, scarcely one escaped, about five hundred is said to have been killed, among them many officers of distinction and among the others Gen. Cos. Santa Anna was taken yesterday morning about seven miles from this place, his Adjutant General and Secretary, with Col. Almonte, and many officers were taken the evening after the battle was over. Our force was about seven hundred and fifty men engaged in the battle, and our loss was seven killed, and about twenty wounded.— Never was there a greater victory according to the number of men engaged, and the results are glorious to the army and prospects of Texas.

I forgot to say that we had to march through the open prairie to come to their position, which was on the edge of the timber. Gen. Houston had two horses killed under him, and was shot through the leg. I commanded in the centre division, a company who behaved with a great deal of bravery. Tell old Mr. Greer, of Sugar Creek, that his son Thomas was in the action, and behaved with much bravery.

Gen. Houston is about to treat with Santa Anna, and the war is probably at an end; and our independence will be acknowledged by the Mexican Government. Hurrah for Texas!

Yours respectfully,
R. STEVENSON.
—*New York Herald*, June 14, 1836

In the manner typical of the period, news of the victory was recycled by paper after paper; in the following case, the report had already appeared in three newspapers before finding print in the *Jackson Mississippian*.

GLORIOUS NEWS
FROM TEXAS.

The following from the Louisiana Journal Extra, published at St. Francisville, May 2, 1836.

By the politeness of a gentleman who arrived this morning from Alexandria, in the Steamer Levant, we are put in possession of the following highly important and gratifying intelligence from Texas. It will be seen the account is official.

From the Red River Herald.
Head-Quarters of the Army,
April 23, 1836.

TO THE PEOPLE TOWARDS
NACOGDOCHES.

We met Santa Anna on the 21st. We attacked him with six hundred men. He had eleven hundred men and two howitzers. We entirely routed his whole force, killed half of his men, and made the rest prisoners. SANTA ANNA himself, and all his principal officers, are our prisoners.

The history of war does not furnish a parallel to the battle. We had six killed and twenty wounded. I have not time, or I would send a full report. I will do that in the course of to-morrow.

I again call on my friends to come to the field. Let us fall on and conquer the remaining troops, and our country is free. Turn out at once—there is no excuse now—and let us finish the work.

THOS. J. RUSK.
Secretary of War.

P.S. We have just received per the steamboat Missourian, another Extra to the same effect, published at Alexandria on the 1st instant.

Natchez Courier.
—*Jackson Mississippian,* May 6, 1836

The *New Orleans Bee* published an early outline of the battle, and details of the capture of Santa Anna in its May 11 issue.

Yesterday we received more minute and confirmatory accounts of the late Texian battle near Harrisburg. One letter states that Santa Anna and his seconds narrowly escaped being taken prisoners while at New Washington, on the 18th ult, after leaving San Felippe. It appears that on the 20th, Houston made a forced march from Harrisburg, and an unexpected attack on the enemy in the evening; but without much effect, except that of leading Santa Anna into the wood that night. Next day at 4 p.m., the attack of the Texian army commenced simultaneously by a preconcerted signal from their general, who had disposed them previously in proper places without the view or cognizance of the enemy. Houston sounded aloud the word CHARGE; and every Texian promptly responded by shouting ALAMO! ALAMO!! in voices that resembled the Indian warwhoop; and struck the terror of vengeance into the souls of the butchering enemy. The Texians opened with the canons, which had been presented to them by the ladies of Nashville[1]; and with their grape shot did great execution. The brass howitzer of the enemy was silenced after the first fire; and all Mexican gunners picked out by the Texian rifles. Humanity and exhaustion alone terminated the deeds of death that followed: for the Mexicans were terrified into inaction; they laid down their arms, were killed, taken prisoners and fled. The cavalry sought to retreat by the bridge, but it had been cut down in the morning; and they were compelled to fly thro' the woods, where most of them perished or were captured.

That was the resort and fate of Santa Anna. He escaped on horseback immediately after the action for the bridge, but fell back into the wood that night, where he reposed with the mosquitoes up in a tree. But the Texians being on the alert, caught him next morning disguised in common clothes. Two of them seized him without knowing him. He instantly took out 200 doubloons from his belt, which he offered them to permit his flight; but without avail. He then offered also a costly diamond brooch—the two Texians instead of being tempted, suspected him to be an "hidalgo;" and immediately brought him into Houston's tent.

Being still unrecognized, the Mexican gene-rallisimo exclaimed *"Viva los Texianas! Viva el General Houston!"* But young Zavala who was lately in this city, coming in recognized the president in the captive hypocrite.

This is one of the most singular contests recorded in history. The enemy had about 1100 men in the action, scarcely more than a score of whom escaped being killed or taken prisoners: not one officer of name or note. The Texians had only 580 in the contest, as a *corps de reserve* was left to guard the baggage; yet out of that number only 7 were killed and 20 wounded.

Most of the privates taken prisoners are employed in constructing a fort at Galveston bay. The officers are reserved for further requisition.

About 300 horses and mules, with large quan-tities of plate, clothing, etc that the enemy had plundered in his march, became booty to the Texians—with about $14,000 in specie, which was divided as prize money amongst the victors.
—*New Orleans Bee*, May 11, 1836

Houston's detailed report of the battle saw print in a mid-May edition of the *New Orleans Bee*, and was afterward reprinted in many papers across the nation, such as the *Richmond Enquirer* the follow-ing month.

(From the New Orleans Bee of May 24.)
"HEAD QUARTERS OF THE ARMY,
San Jacinto, 25th April, 1836.
"To his Excellency D. G. Burnett,
President of the Republic of Texas.
"SIR: I regret extremely that my situation since the battle of the 21st, has been such as to pre-vent my sending you my official report of the same previous to this time.

"I have the honor to inform you that on the evening of the 18th inst., after a forced march of fifty-five miles, which was effected in two days and a half, the army arrived opposite Harrisburg: that evening a courier was taken, from which I learned that General Santa Anna, with one division of his choice troops, had marched in the direction of Lynch's ferry, on the San Jacinto, burning Harrisburg as they passed down. The army was ordered to be in readiness

to march early on the next morning. The main body effected a passing over Buffalo Bayou below Harrisburg, on the morning of the 19th, having left the baggage, sick, and a sufficient camp guard in the rear. We continued the march throughout the night, making but one halt in the prairie for a short time, and without refreshment. At daylight we resumed the line of march, and in a short distance our scouts encountered those of the enemy, and we received information that General Santa Anna was at New Washington, and would that day take up his line of march for Anahuac, crossing at Lynch's. The Texian army halted within half a mile of the ferry in some timber, and were engaged in slaughtering beeves when the army of General Santa Anna was discovered to be approaching in battle array, having been encamped at Clopper's Point eight miles below.

"Disposition was immediately made of our forces, in preparation for his reception. He took a position with his infantry and artillery in the centre, occupying an island of timber, his cav-alry covering the left flank. The artillery then opened upon our encampment, consisting of one double fortified medium brass twelve pounder. The infantry in column advanced with the design of charging our lines, but were repulsed by a discharge of grape and canister from our artillery consisting of two six pounders. The enemy had occupied a piece of timber within rifle shot of the left wing of our army, from which an occasional interchange of small arms took place between the troops, until the enemy withdrew to a position on the bank of the San Jacinto, about three quarters of a mile from our encampment, and commenced a fortification. A short time before sunset our mounted men, about eighty-five in number, under the special command of Colonel Sherman, marched out for the purpose of reconnoitering the enemy. Whilst advancing they received a volley from the left of the enemy's infantry, and after a sharp recontre with their cavalry, in which ours acted extremely well, and performed some feats of daring chivalry, they retired in good order, hav-ing had two men wounded severely, and several horses killed; in the meantime the infantry under the command of Lieutenant Colonel Millard, and Colonel Burleson's regiment, with the artillery, had marched out for the purpose of covering the retreat of the cavalry if necessary: all then fell back to our encampment in good order about sunset, and remained without any ostensible action until the 21st, at half past three o'clock, taking the first refreshments which they had enjoyed for two days. The enemy in the meantime having extended the right flank of their infantry so as to occupy the extreme point of a skirt of timber on the bank of the San Jacinto, and securing their left by a fortification about five feet high, constructed of packs and baggage leaving an opening in the centre of the breastwork in which their artillery was placed, their cavalry upon their left wing. About 9 o'clock on the morning of the 21st, the enemy were reinforced by 500 choice troops under the command of General Cos, increasing their effective force to upwards of 1500 men, while our aggregate force for the field numbered 783. At half past 3 o'clock in the evening, I ordered the officers of the Texian army to parade their respective commands, having in the mean time ordered the bridge, on the only road communicating with the Brassos, distant 8 miles from our encampment, to be destroyed, thus cutting off all possibility of escape. Our troops paraded with alacrity and spirit, and were anxious for the contest. The conscious disparity in number, only seemed to increase their enthusiasm and confidence, and heightened their anxiety for the conflict. Our situation afforded me an opportunity of making an arrangement preparatory to the attack, without exposing our designs to the enemy. The first regiment commanded by Col. Burleson, was assigned the centre. The second regiment, under the command of Col. Sherman, formed the left wing of the army. The artillery, under the special command of Col. George W. Hackley, Inspector General, was placed on the right of the first regiment, and four companies of infantry, under the command of Lieutenant-Colonel Henry Millard, sustained the artillery upon their right, and our cavalry, sixty-one in number, commanded by Colonel Mirabeau B. Lamar, (whose gallant and daring conduct on

the previous day had attracted the admiration of his comrades, and called him to that station,) placed on our extreme right, completed our line. Our cavalry was first dispatched to the front of the enemy, left for the purpose of attracting their notice, whilst an extensive island of timber afforded us an opportunity of concentrating our forces and deploying from that point agreeably to the previous design of the troops. Every evolution was performed with alacrity, the whole advancing rapidly in line and through an open prairie, without any protection what ever for our men; the artillery advanced and took station within two hundred yards of the enemy's breastwork, and commenced an effective fire with grape and canister. Colonel Sherman with his regiment having commenced the action upon our left wing, the whole line at the centre and on the right advancing in double quick time, rung the war cry *"Remember the Alamo!"* received the enemy's fire and advancing within point blank shot before a piece was discharged from our lines. Our lines advanced without a halt until they were in possession of the woodlands and the enemy's breastwork. The right wing of Burleson's, and the left of Millard's taking possession of the breastwork; our artillery having gallantly charged up within 70 yards of the enemy's cannon, when it was taken by our troops. The conflict lasted about 18 minutes from the time of close action until we were in possession of the enemy's encampment, taking one piece of cannon, loaded, four stand of colors, all their camp equipage, stores and baggage. Our cavalry had charged and routed that of the enemy upon the right, and given pursuit to the fugitives, which did not cease until they arrived at the bridge which I have mentioned. Capt. Karnes, always amongst the foremost in danger, commanded the pursuers. The conflict in the breastwork lasted but a few moments, many of the troops encountered hand to hand and not having the advantage of bayonets on our side, our riflemen used their pieces as war-clubs, breaking many of them off at the breach.—The route commenced at half-past 4 o'clock, and the pursuit of the main army continued until twilight. A guard was then left in charge of the enemy's encampment, and our army returned with four killed and wounded. In the battle our loss was 2 killed and 23 wounded, six of which proved mortal. The enemy's loss was 630 killed, among which was one general officer, 4 colonels, 2 lieutenant colonels, 5 captains, 12 lieutenants, wounded 208, of which 5 were colonels, 3 lieutenant colonels, 2 second lieutenant colonels, 7 captains, 1 cadet. Prisoners 730—Gen. Santa Anna, Gen. Cos, 4 colonels, aids to Gen. Santa Anna, and the Colonel of the Guerrero battalion, are included in the number. Gen. Santa Anna was not taken until the 22d, and Gen. Cos, on yesterday, having escaped. About 600 muskets, 300 sabres, and 200 pistols, have been collected since the battle. Several hundred mules and horses were taken, and near $12,000 in specie. For several days previous to the action our troops were engaged in forced marches, exposed to excessive rains, and the additional inconvenience of extremely bad roads, illy supplied with rations and clothing, yet amid every difficulty they bore up with cheerfulness and fortitude, and performed their marches with spirit and alacrity—there was no murmuring.

"Previous to and during the action my staff evinced every disposition to be useful, and were actively engaged in their duties. In the conflict, I am assured that they demeaned themselves in such manner as proved them worthy members of the army of San Jacinto. Col. T. J. Rusk, Secretary of War, was on the field. For weeks his services have been highly beneficial to the army; in battle he was on the left wing, where Colonel Sherman's command first encountered and drove the enemy: he bore himself gallantly, and continued his efforts and activity, remaining with the pursuers until resistance ceased.

"I have the honor of transmitting herewith, a list of all the officers and men who were engaged in the action, which I respectfully request may be published, as an act of justice to the individuals. For the Commanding general to attempt discrimination as to the conduct of those who commanded in the action, or those who were commanded, would be impossible. Our success in the action is conclusive proof of their daring intrepidity and courage; every officer and man proved himself worthy of the cause in which he battled, while the triumph received a lustre from the humanity which characterized their conduct after victory, and richly entitles them to the admiration and gratitude of their General. Nor should we withhold the tribute of our grateful thanks from that Being who rules the destinies of nations, and has in the time of greatest need enabled us to arrest a powerful invader whilst devastating our country.

I have the honor to be,
With high consideration,
Your obedient servant,
SAML. HOUSTON,
Commander-in-Chief.

"Return of the killed and wounded in the actions of the 20th and 21st April, 1836.

Major General Houston, wounded severely.

First Regiment Texas Volunteers.

Company A—George Waters, private, slightly wounded, 21st.

Company B—James Chuly, private, wounded, Wm. S. Wake, do.

Company C—Capt. James Bellingly, Lemuel Blakely, killed, Logan Vandeveer, wounded, Washington Anderson, do., Martin Walker, do.

Company D—Capt. Moseley Baker, wounded, C. D. Anderson, private, wounded, Allen Ingram, do.

Company F—Levy Williamson, private, wounded, James Nelson, do., Michael Putnam, do.

Company H—A. R. Stevens, private, wounded, J. Tom, do.

Total—Killed 3; wounded 15.

Second Regiment Texas Volunteers.

Company D—2d Lieutenant Lamb, killed 21st; G. W. Robinson, private, severely wounded, 21st; Wm. Winters, private, do.; 1st serg't, Albert Gallatin, private, slightly wounded, 21st.

Company E—Washington Lewis, private, severely wounded, 21st; E. G. Rector, do., slightly do.

Company F—Alphonso Steele, private, severely wounded.

Company K—1st Lieut., J. C. Hale, private killed, 21st.

Company J—Capt. Smith, private, wounded slightly, 21st; 1st Serg't, Thomas P. Fowl, private, killed do.; Wm. F. James, private, wounded severely;—Trask, private, wounded severely.

Total killed, 3; severely wounded, 5; slightly, 3; total 11.

Dr. Wm. Mosely, and A. R. Stevens, wounded severely, died since.

Lieut. Col. J. C. Neil, of the artillery, wounded severely on the 20th.

Wm. A. Park, of the artillery, wounded slightly on the 20th.

Devereaux J. Woodliff, of the cavalry, wounded severely on the 20th."

—*Richmond Enquirer,* June 10, 1836

More details about the battle and the capture of Santa Anna appeared in a Maine newspaper, which essentially reprinted an account from an Alabama paper.

TEXAN VICTORY. The Mobile Mercantile Advertiser publishes particulars of the battle, furnished by Joseph Andrews a respectable Georgian, who was in the battle. He states that the action commenced about four o'clock, and that in 15 minutes, many of the Mexicans called for quarters. The Mexican troops broke and fled in about twenty minutes; the pursuit of the fugitives, and the firing lasted for about two hours.

Upwards of 650 Mexicans were killed, and 600 taken prisoners. There were 6 or 7 Texans killed and about 10 wounded. Generals Cos and Almonte were among the prisoners first taken.— The former was pale and greatly agitated, but the latter displayed, as he had done during the engagement, great coolness and courage.

SANTA ANNA fled among the earliest who retreated. He was seen by two boys, one about 15, and the other about 17 years of age, to go into a thicket of wood. They kept watch of the place during the night, and the next morning a man came out dressed like a common Mexican soldier. Not suspecting him to be Santa Anna, they took him prisoner. He offered no resistance, but wished to be taken to General Houston. He was conducted to that officer, when he made himself known as Santa Anna, asked the respect due officers of rank, and made the offers for his liberty, which have been published. Santa Anna, Mr. Andrews says, is about 45 years of age, of rather small stature, dark complexion, black hair, black bright eyes, and altogether a good looking man.

When questioned respecting the fight near the Mission, between the Mexicans and Col. Ward's company, he stated that about 400 of the Mexicans were killed, but that Col. Ward and his men were protected by the walls of the church in which they had stationed themselves.

The following named persons under the command of Colonels Fanning and Ward, made their escape: Joseph Andrews, (our informant) David Holt, Lewis Washington,

——Dickinson, Horace Bullock, Samuel Hardway, and Benjamin Mordecai, all Georgians. Dr. Shackleford, of Alabama, had his life spared, and is now in attendance upon the wounded Mexicans.

The Mexicans and the Texans who made their escape, agree in stating that when Col. Ward was about to be shot, he was ordered to kneel, but could not be made to do so either by threats or promises. His gallant spirit nothing could subdue. He proudly bid them defiance and died like an American soldier!

In the battle between Houston and Santa Anna, Col. Mirabeau Lamar, of Georgia, greatly distinguished himself for his valor and intrepidity, and gained the applause of all. It is said there were not fifty Texans in the battle; that the Texan army was composed almost entirely of volunteers.

Santa Anna is a prisoner on board of an armed vessel, near Galveston Island, while the Mexican prisoners, who are able to labor, are engaged in building breastworks on the Island.[a]

Accounts from N. Orleans, by schr. Flash, from Galveston Bay, corroborate Mr. A's. account, and state that Gen. Houston had great difficulty in restraining his troops from preceeding summarily with Santa Anna, as the Texans made their attack under the watchwords of *"Alamo and Fanning."*

---

[a] These works were called Fort Travis.

Seguín's Tejanos at San Jacinto

"I am pleased to say," read a letter from Texas to the *New Orleans Bee* in the aftermath of the battle of San Jacinto, "that Captain (now Col.) Juan Nepemucene Seguin, a native of Bexar, and whom I have known from a boy, commanded 25 men, all natives of the same place, and performed wonders."[1] Although known for their equestrian skills in such pursuits as cattle herding and buffalo hunting, nearly all of Juan Seguín's Tejano volunteers in the April 21 charge at San Jacinto served as foot soldiers, not cavalry. Attached to Col. Sidney Sherman's division on the far left of the Texian line, they joined the attack on the three *"preferencia"* companies positioned at the far right of Antonio López de Santa Anna's line.[2]

The letter-writer in the *Bee* went on to describe the actions of Seguín's small company:

Every man signalized himself in the most distinguished manner. One of them, with a Bowie knife, killed 25 of his countrymen, and one of them Col. Batres, whom I knew well. Dionicio Cos, brother of the General, the same who mutilated the body of the lamented Travis, was killed. Twenty-three field officers were among the slain.

The ferocity of the Tejanos at San Jacinto is confirmed in the following extract from a New York newspaper, culled from several other papers.

There was a company of friendly Mexicans, from Nacogdoches, among the Texian troops. Who behaved very bravely and dealt death and destruction to the wounded Mexicans as they went![3]

Typical *Bexareño* frontier or campaign wear of the period included such garb as a slouched hat, leather hunting shirt or jacket, leggings, a white or calico shirt, a sash, and moccasins or brogans. Captain Seguín had only recently, in fact, purchased twenty-two pairs of brogans for his men in San Felipe.[4] During the battle the Tejanos also wore, in the words of one of them, "large pieces of white paste board on their hats and breasts, least they should be mistaken for Santa Anna's men and killed."[5]

(Continued)

Sherman's men drove out the Mexicans posted in the woods and went on to attack those behind the breastwork and in the camp itself. Those "preference" companies—*cazadores*—in the woods were the cream of the crop, but Sam Houston's charge had been so sudden and unexpected that they, along with most of Santa Anna's men, were unprepared to resist it to any significant degree. For instance, that morning Gen. Martín Perfecto de Cos had arrived with five hundred reinforcements, but because "these men had not slept the night before," wrote Colonel Pedro Delgado, Cos had "instructed them to stack their arms, to remove their accouterments, and to go to sleep quickly in the adjoining grove." When Houston assaulted the camp at 4:30 that afternoon, most of the other Mexican troops were also in siesta, the remainder "eating, others were scattered in search of boughs to prepare shelters."[6] Many were in their fatigue clothing and had to quickly grab whatever arms and accouterments they could, if any, with which to meet the oncoming tide of Texians.

The improvised breastwork Santa Anna had ordered erected that morning was made of whatever was available: baggage, pack saddles, barrels, sacks, boxes, logs, etc., built to a height of from four to five feet. "A trifling barricade of branches [*abatis*] ran along its front and right," noted Colonel Delgado, who also recorded the furious attitude of one of Seguin's men.

> [O]ne of our own countrymen, who had joined the enemy's cause, assailed us, in our own language, with such a volley of threats, insults and abuse, that the tongue of that vile and recreant Mexican seemed to have been wrought in the very caves of hell, and set in motion by Lucifer himself. "Now you shall see," he said, "contemptible and faithless assassins, if you do not pay with your vile blood for the murders at the Alamo and La Bahia. The time has come when the just cause we defend triumphs over you; you shall pay with your heads for the arson, robberies and depredations you have committed in our country," &c. &c.[7]

1. *New Orleans Bee*, June 10, 1836, reprinted in the *Richmond Enquirer* of July 1, 1836.
2. Gerald Eugene Poyo, *Tejano Journey, 1770–1850* (Austin: University of Texas Press, 1996), 59; Santa Anna's report, March 11, 1837, in Frank W. Johnson, *A History of Texas and Texans* (Chicago: American Historical Society, 1914), 454.
3. *Morning Courier and New York Enquirer*, July 9, 1836.
4. Stephen L. Hardin, *Texian Iliad: A Military History of the Texas Revolution, 1835–36* (Austin: University of Texas Press, 1994), 197.
5. Antonio Menchaca quoted in Poyo, *Tejano Journey*, 60.
6. Colonel Pedro Delgado, "Mexican Account of the Battle of San Jacinto," in *The Texas Almanac for 1870*, 44–45.
7. Ibid., 44, 46.

The Advertiser of the 11th, gives a particular account of the interview between Houston and Santa Anna. He asked him why he had put the few survivors of the Alamo to death. He replied that his troops were so much exasperated at the number of their killed and wounded, that he could not restrain them. He was then asked why Fanning's command was slaughtered. His answer was, there were so many prisoners, it was impossible either to keep them or to feed them. He also asserted that Col. Fanning and Dr. Shackleford still remained prisoners at Victoria.

—*Eastern Argus*, May 31, 1836

A number of battle-related reports, including one that listed the names of the dead and captured Mexican officers, were culled by a Philadelphia paper.

We take from the New York papers, of Thursday, various articles respecting the affairs of Texas. The massacre which took place at the battle of the 21st of April, would seem quite sufficient to satisfy the most earnest desires of "the friends of humanity" who have been so horrified by Mexican cruelties.

(From the N. Y. Courier and
Enquirer of Thursday.)

The arrival of seven or eight mails yesterday from New Orleans placed in our possession some very important advices from Galveston Island, which we give below. It will be found they contain more details of the great battle of the 21st, than have yet been published, besides many interesting particulars of the President of Mexico and the state of things in Texas. It appears that previous to the 21st, Harrisburg and New Washington had been burned by the Mexicans.

GALVESTON ISLAND, May 6, 1836.

The particulars of the battle with Santa Anna, will probably have reached you; as however the presence of Santa Anna and his officers here have placed me in possession of particulars not generally known, and as besides every circumstance connected with this memorable event is of vivid interest, I dare say the details I am about to give you will be found worthy attention.

Santa Anna had just fired New Washington, when news reached him on the 20th, of the appearance of Texian troops. He was completely taken by surprise, and says that as he had found all the farms deserted, and could learn nothing of General Houston, he concluded all the inhabitants had left the country. A skirmish only took place on the 20th with a small detachment or scouting party. Houston keeping the main body in the woods under a hill, where none could be seen. The next day, the 21st, Santa Anna was quietly taking his *siesta*, when he was awoke by his aid with the news of our approach, which he swore was a d——d lie. General Cos had arrived after a forced march with a reinforcement, about an hour or two before, and was likewise taking his *siesta*. Some of the men were sleeping, some cooking, some washing, in short in any situation but that of preparation for battle, when they were pounced upon by us at about 4 o'clock P. M. of the 21st.

Our troops marched up in front of the enemy on the open prairie, never firing a musket or rifle until within 80 yards. The enemy were posted behind breast-works, and in the woods, and commenced with their artillery at a distance of 400 yards. Our artillery opened at 210 yards. When the charge was sounded we rushed upon them; the cry of "the Alamo and LaBahia" resounding through the lines. Their artillery (one piece only) was taken loaded, and when in the act of being primed, and every artillerist put to the sword who did not fly. The battle lasted 19 minutes, and then commenced the rout and slaughter. The poor Mexicans would hold up their hands, cross themselves, and sing out "me no Alamo," but nothing would save them: the blood of our countrymen was too fresh in the memory of our people to let one Mexican escape, until worn down with pursuit and slaughter, they commenced making prisoners. Officers and all fled; none dare attempt to stem the torrent. The Mexicans threw down their guns loaded, and sought safety in every direction, while our cavalry and infantry pursued and cut them down. Muskets and rifles were clubbed when they had not time to reload, and the brains of the Mexicans beat out as they came up with them. The Captains of one of the companies of regulars pointed out one of his men to me who fired 19 rounds, and used 3 muskets, two of them having got choaked, and he having broke their breeches off over the heads of the Mexicans.

The battle was fought just above a place marked on the map lithographed last summer, in New York, "M'Cormick's." The enemy were driven and retreated, until many were forced into the water, which you will see bounds the land there. They ran in up to their necks, but our riflemen would shoot them in the head. Santa Anna and Almonte, in flying, plunged their horses into a quagmire, were thrown off and nearly suffocated before extricated. Both continued their flight on foot. Santa Anna was furnished with a fresh horse, on which he escaped ten miles further, and was taken next day in disguise. Almonte, finding all was lost, and fearing all would be cut to pieces, placed himself at the head of 3 or 400 men, made them form in column, 4 or 8 deep, throw down their arms, and then held up a white flag and surrendered them at once to a small body of our troops who were in pursuit, and they were all marched into camp together. Santa Anna was not recognized until presented to General Houston, whom he complimented highly by saying, "The man who conquered the Napoleon of the South was born to no common destiny."

With Santa Anna all his staff were taken or killed. If any escaped, it was a captain of cavalry, and it is supposed about ten others. There never was so complete a defeat with so little loss on the one side.—Ours consists of 4 killed on the field of battle, 5 dead since of their wounds, and 15 more wounded, in all 23 killed and wounded. The Mexican dead were strewed around for ten miles, and must have amounted to at least 600; as many or more are prisoners.—Almonte says that there were 1200 Mexican troops in the engagement; the best they had. We made the attack with less than 600 men. All Santa Anna's camp equipage, baggage of every kind, in short, all the Mexicans had with them, fell into our hands; some 8 or 10,000 dollars in specie. There were supposed to have

been 50,000 in cash in the army chest. The gold part of it disappeared very soon. Some of the troops had fine pickings.

GALVESTON ISLAND, 8th May, 1836.
We have all the Mexican prisoners here, consisting of the President Santa Anna, General Cos, Almonte, and a number of Generals, Colonels, &c. &c. I enclose you a list of them, their ages, &c. as also of the officers killed in battle—the officers made it out themselves for me. These prisoners, as I expected, all came down in the first steamboat after I left the camp, and were landed last evening. Santa Anna, Almonte, and Secretaries have been placed on board an armed schooner in the harbor.

All the Mexican prisoners (soldiers) are at work here at the fortifications. They are extremely servile, and express great gratitude that their lives are spared, and that they are well treated.

The Mexican troops are running out of Texas much faster than they came in. Thirty men who went on with Santa Anna's express came up with 200 Mexicans with 9 pieces of artillery, and they immediately surrendered, saying if Santa Anna and the officers were taken, there was no use in their fighting. General Wall, a Frenchman, came in from another division of the army, and surrendered himself. He said he did not wish to fight any more if Santa Anna was taken. He has been released and sent back. I send with this a duplicate of Santa Anna's letter to Filisola. He handed it to me with a request that I would endeavour to forward it, but as there is no chance that I shall be able to do this, I send it to you as a curiosity.

The Mexican dead lie yet unburied, and the stench in the neighbourhood is intolerable.

GALVESTON ISLAND, 10th May, 1836.
I have this moment parted with Santa Anna and Almonte, whom the Cabinet take with them to Velasco, which, for a while, will be the seat of government. They are both under great apprehension for their personal safety—though I have no doubt their lives will be spared—and disliked leaving here very much. Santa Anna embraced me in the most cordial and affecting "Mexican" manner on parting. He and Almonte

were kept on board the Invincible until the moment of their departure. Notwithstanding his cruelties, I could not help pitying the President of Mexico, as I escorted him from the side of the vessel to the steamboat. His eyes were suffused with tears. The steamboat was filled to overflowing—music playing a quick American air—smiling faces all around, even among the lowest classes, who had lost their all.

GALVESTON ISLAND, 12th May.

The planters are all returning to their farms who have not left the country altogether, and some will make nearly half crops and some full ones. The ground has been seeded before they left their homes, both cotton and corn were growing finely, and has remained undisturbed in most instances. I have not heard of more than two cotton gins or farm-houses that have been destroyed by the enemy. The best farming country was entirely out of their route. But notwithstanding, this country has received a shock that will be felt for some time. Hundreds have been ruined, and hundreds have been left here that will never return.

The Cabinet are making constant changes.

Colonel Lamar is now Secretary of War.

Colonel Collensworth, Secretary of State, (Carson absent).

Grayson, Attorney General.

Charles B. Hawkins, Esq., is Commodore of the Texas Navy. We have four vessels in commission, Invincible, Independence, Liberty and Brutus. Two of which are here, and two in New Orleans.

Military Commandancy of Galveston, May 8, 1836.

LIST OF MEXICAN OFFICERS, PRISONERS.

President of the Republic of Mexico—Antonio Lopez de Santa Anna. Brigadier General—Martin P. de Cos. Colonels—J. M. Romero, Manuel Cespedes, J. Nepumucemo Almonte. Lieut. Colonels (Brevet Colonels)—Juan Bringas, Manuel Portilla, Pedro Delgado, Eulogo Gonzalez. Captains (Brevet Lieut. Colonels) Jose Mia Castillo, Ygnacio Perez Valiante, Lorenzo Arcos, Nicholas Enciso, Jose Ma Villafranca, Salvador Mogico, Cayentana Villasenor, Telespero Carion.

Captains—Vincente Avica, Nicholas Teller, Juan Bananeh, Jose Lizanla, Miguel Bachilla. Lieutenants (Brevet Captains)—Martin Estrado, Mariano Gonzalez Vega, Mariano Arias, Jose Ma Ortego, Yldefonse Vega. Lieutenants—Felipe Briones, Ygnacio Arenal, Severiano Vencas, Geronimo Calatayad, Augustin Sanches, Miguel Perroes, Manuel Cosio, Rafael Castilla, Mateo Parezo. Sub Lieutenants (Brevet Lieutenants)—Ygnacio Cananza, Toribo Caseres, Juan Nieto. Sub Lieutenants—Jose Ma Obregon, Estanislar Pino, Meriano Reyes, Nicholas Diaz, Jose Maria Castro, Raphael Arcanzid. Cadet—Joaquim Agercieno. Chaplain—Augustin Garza. 1st Agt. (Brevet Lieut. Col.)—Felipe Romero.

List of Mexican Officers killed on the 21st of April, 1836, at the Battle of San Jacinto.

General—Don Manuel Castrillon. Colonels—Don Jose Batres, Don Antonio Trevino, Don Augustin Peralto, Don Jose Arenas, Don Esteban Mora. Lieut. Colonels—Don Marcial Aguire, Dionisio Cos, Santiago Luelmo, Cirillo Larambe, Manuel Valdez, Mariano Olazaron, Francisco Agualdo, Miguel Valdsquez. Captains—Don Nestor Guzman, Benito Rodriguez, B. Ygnacio Barra, Ramon Herrera, Alonzo Gonzales, Antonio Frias, Juan Monjarra, Ramon Hocha. Lieutenants—Don Jose Ma Puellas, Luis Valejo, Trinidad Santiesteban, Juan Santa Cruz, Pedro Gonzales, Antonio Castro, Jose Souza, Ygnacio Brassail, Antonio Navarro, Francisco Molina. Sub Lieutennats—Don Joaquin Peralta, Basilio Espino, Juan Montano, Jose Maria Torrices, Victoriano Martinez, Secundino Rosos. Total, 38 officers.

The names of several Sergeants, with brevet rank of officers, are omitted, not being known.

(From the Journal of Commerce.)

TEXAS.—The following letter (says the Natchez Courier, of the 19th ult.) was received yesterday by a gentleman in this city:

"*Natchitoches, May 14.*—"I have just learned that Gen. Ball, an American of New York, has surrendered his command to Gen. Houston, amounting to 1200 men, as prisoners of war, done by order of Santa Anna. Texas is now free, and nothing but our folly can prevent this country from becoming the Garden of North America."

This is important if true, and it agrees with some previous reports of the stipulations between Santa Anna and Gen. Houston. In the letter of the former to Gen. Filisola, dated 22d of April, the day after his capture, he directs him and Gen. Gaona to countermarch to Bexar with their respective divisions, and there "await orders." He also directs Gen. Urrea, with his divisions, to retire to Guadaloupe Victoria, inasmuch 'as an armistice has been agreed on with Gen. Houston, until certain negotiations are concluded which will put an end to the war forever.' It is probable that these contemplated the surrender of the remaining divisions of the Mexican army, neither of which however was commanded by General Ball, of N.Y. nor did we ever hear of such a person. Probably it should be General Wall, a Frenchman and in this shape the news is confirmed by one of the letters, copied from the Courier and Enquirer. It is a little singular, however, that with a knowledge of this fact, and others stated in these letters, clearly indicating that the war is at an end, troops and munitions should be sent on from New Orleans and elsewhere, with the knowledge and concurrence of the gentlemen intimately acquainted with Texian affairs, to re-inforce an army already amounting to 1800 men.

—*National Gazette* (Philadelphia),
June 11, 1836

Another letter written from Galveston Island describing the engagement, the "horrible and disgusting" human litter of the battlefield, and the appearances of three of the highest-ranking Mexican prisoners, first appeared in a New Orleans paper.

GALVESTON, May 1, 1836.
Dear Sir:—On the 26th of March the Texian army under General Houston, took up its line of march from the East bank of the Colorado and retired, and a few days afterwards established an encampment on the West side of the Brazos, between a lake and the river, in a thicket almost impenetrable, near Groce's Ferry. This

position they continued to occupy two or three weeks, keeping spies out to observe the movements of the enemy, who crossed the Colorado at Tuacasite, and occupied that position several days, when not being able to learn any thing of the main Texian army, they advanced upon San Felipe, which place had been burnt, and made a feint to cross the Brazos at that place—then made a forced march to the Fort Bend, 20 or 30 miles below, and crossed a part of their forces over before they were discovered. The movement was notified to Houston by express, and he immediately crossed his army to the East side of the Brazos, by the help of a steamboat, which he had pressed and detained for that purpose. The army remained on the east bank of the river for a day and a half, when having learned that the enemy had made a movement towards Harrisburg, they made a forced march, and the fourth day crossed Buffalo Bayou, three miles below the town, which the enemy had laid in ashes. The Mexicans had continued their march and burnt New Washington, and were returning up the San Jacinto to cross the river at Lynch's Ferry, when on the 19th ult., their advance, to their surprise, fell in with small parties of the Texians. On the 20th the two armies were encamped within a mile of each other—the Texian above and the Mexican below Lynch's Ferry. On the same day there was a sharp conflict between the Texian cavalry and a body of the enemy, cavalry and infantry, six or eight times their number. When the conflict had terminated, most of the Texian infantry were literally *angry* that the General had not permitted them to take part in the engagement, feeling confident that they could have annihilated the enemy—which consisted of about 700 men, and was commanded by Santa Anna in person. Early the next morning General Cos joined Santa Anna with a strong reinforcement, by a forced march.

Never did men engage in battle with a firmer determination to conquer or die. They had nothing to hope of mercy from the perfidious and cruel enemy. They had no hope of life—but in victory.

The numbers of the Mexican army was estimated at from 1150 to 1500 men. The Texian forces are estimated at from 610 to 780 men. The sick, the lazy and the cowardly had been left behind in the forced march, and I found several of my friends with no other apparel but that which they had upon their persons, and they were without even blankets to cover them at night. On the 21st, at 4 o'clock, P. M. the Texian army marched out of their encampment to attack the enemy. They had two pieces of small iron artillery—a present from the citizens of Cincinnati—57 cavalry, 300 regulars and volunteers, armed with muskets and bayonets, and the residue were armed with rifles and belt pistols. The Mexicans were encamped on a high prairie, with their right resting in a cedar thicket upon the border of a lake connected with the San Jacinto river. The division of Cos was about 150 yards in the rear of their front line, resting in careless security after their forced march. The Texian army, taking advantage of the undulations of the ground, approached and placed themselves in line 3 or 400 yards in front of the enemy, in the open prairie, and advanced upon them. The General rode in front of the line, and gave the first order to fire upon the enemy.

The enemy fired their cannon five times only. It was loaded the sixth time and primed—the man who held the match was killed by a boy and the piece taken. It is a splendid brass nine pounder, bearing the inscriptions "El Volcan," and "Violati fulmina Regis," in Roman capital letters. The cannon was taken and the enemy put to rout nineteen minutes after the first gun was fired.—The slaughter among the enemy's ranks was tremendous. I took a deliberate look over the field three days after the battle. The sight was horrible. Here lying in clusters, there scattered singly—the ground was strewed with dead men, dead horses, guns, bayonets, swords, drums, trumpets—some shattered and broken—books, papers, shoes, sandals, caps—the chaos of a routed army, was strewed upon the ground—in a confusion which the imagination cannot conceive—the natural eye must behold, to be convinced of the reality.

The faces of most of the dead were as black as negroes—horribly swollen and distorted—the tongues protruding—the skin blistered—the limbs in many instances swollen, elevated and half extended—horrible and disgusting masses of corruption.

When the Texian army made the charge, the shouts of Alamo! Alamo!! Alamo!!! filled the air—braced the hearts of the assailants to avenge the death of their deceased friends—while the hearts of the enemy quailed with the conscious guilt of the cruel massacre of brave men, and the dread of the day of vengeance having come. The shouts of Alamo! Travis! Crockett! Fannin!! were terrible to the enemy, as the trump which may call the guilty to their final account.

Of the whole right wing of the enemy, one man only escaped death. They were slaughtered and finally driven into the water, and the rifles ceased not their cracks while an object appeared above its surface.

The left wing of the enemy fled in confused order, commanded by Col. Almonte, and laid down their arms and surrendered to a small body of cavalry, two miles from the battlefield.

The number of the enemy's killed is estimated at about 700, and the prisoners taken amount to above 500, more than 200 of them wounded. There are 42 officers prisoners, including Almonte, Cos, and Santa Anna himself.

Santa Anna was taken the next day after the battle, about 10 miles above, in the woods, in a mean citizen's dress, and did not make himself known until he was taken in the presence of General Houston, to whom he immediately offered a feast of soft corn.

You will be gratified by a description of Santa Anna's person. His forehead is high, but narrow in front, spreading as it extends back obliquely—hair moderately black—small whiskers, a little muted with grey. The skin wrinkles on the lower part of his forehead as he elevates his eyes to speak. He has large, mild, black eyes—his nose is narrow between the eyes, but is tolerably straight, and becomes fleshy towards the end. His mouth is nothing extraordinary, the upper lip rather projecting;

one of his upper front teeth is gone; his under jaw is long. His countenance is animated when speaking—His complexion is a little tawny; but he shows more of the Moorish than the Mexican tincture. He might pass for a white man, but would not pass for a native, in the United States. His height is five feet ten inches, or perhaps more, and he is tolerably well proportioned. His age is forty-one.

Gen. Cos was taken two days after the battle, and was brought back to camp, a picture of fear. When I first saw him, he was lying upon the ground, and had hid himself under a little old blanket—the only parts which could be seen of him was his hair, which is dark brown, and his hand which held the blanket over his head, was small and had *remarkably short* finger nails. I saw him afterwards, when his fright was over. He is about five feet nine inches high, built for activity—has a high forehead, but not very broad—his nose is long, straight and well formed—his eyes a brilliant black. He has large, long black whiskers, sun-burnt at the ends, and red, sandy moustaches. His complexion is sun-burnt, and he wears little gold rings in his ears. He is a cousin to Santa Anna.

The third personage, Colonel Almonte, is the reputed natural son of a Spanish priest, by a full-blooded Mexican woman. He has a good countenance—was educated in Europe, and speaks English well, and is regarded as a man of superior talents.

But all these Mexicans appear but as ordinary men in personal appearance, when compared with General Houston himself, who possesses a manly and noble countenance, rarely surpassed among men. But he now appears pale and sickly, in consequence of a wound which he received in the battle, which shattered his leg above the ankle. There was 14 other Texians wounded and 7 killed—among the latter a son of Major Brigham of Brazoria, one of the most promising youths of Texas.

Your obedient servant,   S.

—*Richmond Enquirer,* June 14, 1836

Another intimate account of the battle of San Jacinto was penned the day after the victory by a captain of a company of Kentucky volunteers, in a letter to his brother.

FROM THE LOUISVILLE JOURNAL.

We take pleasure in laying before the Public the following letter from our estimable fellow-citizen Captain Tarlton, who is commander of the company of Texian volunteers that first went from this place.—The very high estimation in which Capt. Tarlton is held in this community as a brave soldier and an honorable man, will cause his letter to be read with deep interest.

LYNCHBURG, TEXAS, April 22, 1836. My Dear Brother: My last letter to you, dated at San Felipe de Austin, was concluded in rather gloomy language. I had then a sad tale to tell you. Now, and thank my God for it, I can tell you another and a very different story. The retribution, called for by my butchered friends at Goliad, has not been invoked in vain. The arch-fiend, Santa Anna, is now in our camp, with several of his principal officers, a prisoner at our discretion, and his choice and veteran troops lie in hundreds over the prairie, in which a battle the parallel to which perhaps cannot be found in the annals of civilized warfare, was yesterday fought.

Our army, under the command of General Samuel Houston, became tired of retreating, and expressed great anxiety to be led to meet the enemy at once to decide the fate of Texas. Accordingly, on the 14th instant, General Houston took up the line of march for this place, situated at the junction of the San Jacinto river and the Bayou Buffalo. The two streams form what is called the San Jacinto Bay, on the east side of which, by looking at the map of this country, you will see Lynchburg, or rather Lynch's ferry, for in reality there is no town or village to be seen; and, on the west there is a most beautiful prairie, handsomely variegated, with small groves of timber. At about ten o'clock on the morning of the 20th, we pitched our camp in the edge of the timber on the southeast side of Buffalo Bayou, with the intention of breakfasting, having first dispersed a small party of the enemy we found in the neighborhood. Before we had breakfasted, it was announced that the enemy in force was in sight. Our little band of heroes were instantly formed in the best position the ground enabled us to take, when we anxiously awaited his arrival. At about half past 11 o'clock his near approach was confirmed by the report of his cannon and small arms, which was instantly returned by us. This skirmishing continued for some time without any injury to either side, when the Mexican troops were marched beyond the reach of our fire, and of course it ceased.

At about 3 P. M. Col. Sheerman, (with whom you are acquainted,) of the 2d Regiment of Volunteers, offered to head the cavalry for the purpose of bringing on a general engagement and at once to decide the contest. His offer was accepted, and about 63 men mounted their horses and proceeded to the neighborhood of the enemy's cavalry, which they soon found already mounted, 68 in number, backed by four companies of infantry, 160 strong, and ready to receive cavalry. The enemy had not long to wait. Col. Sheerman, with his characteristic bravery, gallantly led on his little squad of horses to the charge. The artillery and both regiments of foot, including the regulars, rushed with that ardor which the love of liberty so nobly and so naturally inspires, to the support of our brave companions on horse back, but our commander-in-chief thought it expedient to order them to return to camp. In this little affair we had none killed, and only two or three wounded; none dangerously. The enemy's loss has not been ascertained; but must have been considerable. His Adjutant General was severely wounded, and is now lying in the adjoining room, to the one in which I indite this narrative.

The next day, that is yesterday, the 21st, at length arrived, and the whole army expected, as soon as breakfast was over, to be led to the enemy's encampment, which, by this time, had become considerably strengthened by having thrown up a breastwork, and by the acquisition of a reinforcement of 500 men under the command of Gen. Cos, who to gratify his master, had violated his parole of honor solemnly pledged at San Antonio in December. At last, at 3 3/4 P. M. we were ordered to prepare for battle, which was soon done; and then commenced a conflict, the parallel of which I presume, cannot be found on record. To see a mere handful of raw, undisciplined volunteers, just taken from their ploughs, and thrown together, with rifles without bayonets, no two perhaps of the same calibre, and circled only by two pieces of artillery, six pounders, and a few musketeers some with and some without bayonets, and some forty or fifty men on horseback, to meet the trained bands of the hero of so many victories—to see them, with trailed arms, marching to within some sixty or seventy yards of such an army, at least double in number, entrenched too behind a breastwork impregnable to small arms, and protected by a long brass nine pounder—to see them, I say, do all this, fearless, and determined to save their country and their country's liberty or to die in the effort, was no ordinary occurrence. Yet such was their conduct, and so irresistible was that Spartan phalanx, that it was no more than from fifteen to twenty minutes from our first fire until a complete rout of the enemy was effected; and such slaughter on the one side, and such almost miraculous preservation on the other, have never been heard of since the invention of gunpowder.

The commencement of the attack was accompanied by the watchwords, "Remember the Alamo, Laborde, and Tampico," at the very top of our voices, and in some ten minutes, we were in the full possession of the enemy's encampment, cannon, and all things else, whilst his veterans were in the greatest possible disorder, attempting by fight to save their lives. I happened to be so placed in the regiment to which I was attached, that I was enabled to be the third man who entered the entrenchment, which I soon left in company with the balance of the regiment in pursuit of the defeated enemies of Texian liberty. I feel confident that I do not exaggerate when I state their loss in killed as nearly if not quite equal to the whole of our number engaged; whilst we had only six killed on the spot, and some twelve or fifteen wounded, two of whom have since died, one of them Doctor Motley, of Ky., a relative of Mr. Shapeley Owen, who died to-night, and since

I commenced writing this letter.—The number of prisoners have not yet been officially announced, but I should suppose it to be nearly if not quite 600, many of whom are wounded. So complete has been *our* triumph and *their defeat*, that my antipathy to them has subsided, and I can now commiserate their condition.

If the people of Texas shall act wisely, the war is ended, and its terrified inhabitants may return in peace and quietness to their homes, and yet make bread sufficient for their support. Santa Anna has agreed to send all his troops home, and to deliver to us their arms, ammunition, money and all other public property, and to acknowledge our independence and separation from Mexico. He and his principal officers will of course be held as hostages until the fulfilment of the treaty, and our army will not be disbanded until Texas is safe, which I have no doubt will be in a few weeks, when I shall return to Kentucky with the intentions of making arrangements for permanently settling in this country.

I am told that Gen. Houston has ordered the spoils of the enemy to be divided equally among the captors, and that he will use his influence in attempting to prevail on Texas to allow, for his splendid victory, a gratuity of two leagues of land, in addition to the regular bounty and pay to each member of the patriot army. Whether this be true or otherwise, I do not know. If true, and success follows, a judicious selection will, in a few years, produce to each man an affluent fortune; for I am sure that such another country as this cannot be found. We have here the climate of Italy and the fertility of the valley of the Mississippi; and, under a Government of wholesome laws, properly administered, Texas will soon become densely populated with industry, wealth, and honest talents, and be able to compete with any country in our western hemisphere. I hope the glorious news I here communicate will reach Congress officially before its adjournment, so that the United States may be the first to acknowledge our independence, and enter into a treaty with us.

Enjoying, as I do, uninterrupted good health, I do not despair of living to see a rail road communication from Natchitoches, on Red River, to the Rio Grande—the country being peculiarly adapted to this kind of improvement, and the best of all possible materials being abundant, and easily procured. In some places we have cedar so abundant that not only are all the house, even to the covering and flooring, made of this material, but whole plantations, hundreds of acres in size, are enclosed with it; and then there are millions upon millions of live oak, out of which to make the sills to receive the rails. Moreover, from Red river to Rio Grande, there probably would not be required a single inclined plane, nor so much as a deviation of half a degree from a straight line, unless indeed to avoid some house, or to run upon the dividing line of some two plantations owned by different persons.

In my last letter to you I unfortunately stated that Chas. B. Shain and Daniel Murphy were among the slain in the butchery at Goliad on the 27th ultimo. Not so, they both escaped, miraculously escaped; nor had the letter which contained my former statement left my hands one hour when I had the gratification of being disabused of the error into which I had been led by the tale told by the first four men who made their escape. The four supposed themselves to be the only survivors of that bloody and inhuman tragedy; but thanks to God, others did succeed as well as they, and I still have hopes that John Duvall, son of Gov. William Duvall, has succeeded also, as he was known to have swam the river, near which there stands a tremendous thicket, in which, if he reached it in safety, he might safely hide from those worse than blood-hounds until night, and then get out of their reach. Charley Shain was not wounded, but the poor fellow suffered immensely in his feet, having lost his shoes, and been compelled to run through prickly pears, briers, and grass stubble, until he could travel no longer; but fortunately he was out of danger, and was finally found and brought to camp by some of our spies. Murphy received a slight wound on his knee from a bullet, but it is now nearly well, and they both look much better than I have ever seen them, and Shain will, I think, soon be at home. You will please tell his parents that I am truly sorry for having been the cause, although innocently, of giving them so much unnecessary grief.

I had almost forgotten to inform you that, in our glorious and triumphant battle, General Houston was wounded in his left ankle; and I seize this occasion to state that on the field he appeared cool, collected, and fearlessly brave. I have but one fault to find with him, and that was, that he requested us to cease pursuit, and return to camp whilst the enemy was in sight, and flying before us. I have no doubt he thought he was right in so doing, but, fortunately for the country, he might as well have attempted "to still the billows of the raging deep." If we had obeyed his request (for it was not an order) Santa Anna and his right hand men, Almonte and Cos, with 400 of the prisoners, might have escaped, and hundreds, who were afterwards slain, would perhaps have enabled the despot to continue his crusade for months to come and to harrass, if not to subjugate, the country. We obeyed no order and no command but the impulse of our own feelings. We came, we saw, we conquered, and I thank God that I was one of the few who did achieve this great and glorious victory. And now for the present, fare thee well.

JAMES TARLTON.
—*Baltimore Gazette and Daily Advertiser*,
June 11, 1836

In an 1847 issue of the *Wisconsin Democrat*, the following extract from C. Edwards Lester's "Houston and His Republic," published in New York in 1846 and pronounced the only authorized biography of Houston, was printed. It offers a rare presentation of the highly dramatic exchange—"as nearly as possible the exact words used by the speakers"—between Houston and Santa Anna after the battle.

Gen. Houston and Santa Anna.
BY C. EDWARDS LESTER

The battle of Independence had been fought. Seven hundred soldiers had met nearly three times their number, and had come off victorious. Six hundred and thirty men were left dead on the field; and among them were one general

officer, four colonels, two lieutenant colonels, seven captains and twelve lieutenants. Multitudes had perished in the morass and bayous. Of the survivors, upwards of two hundred and eighty were wounded, and there were nearly eight hundred prisoners. Only seven men were known to have escaped from the field. And yet, incredible as it may seem, this bloody engagement had cost the Texians the lives of only seven men, and less than thirty had been wounded. It was incredible, and when the commander-in-chief awoke the next morning, he asked— "Are we really victorious, or is it only my dream!"

At ten o'clock the next morning, Gen. Houston sent a detachment to bury those who had fallen in the battle, but decomposition had taken place so rapidly, the troops returned and reported they could not execute the order! This extraordinary circumstance excited the greatest surprise, and the Mexican prisoners accounted for it by resolving it, like the defeat of the previous day, into a "malignant blast of destiny."

In the meantime, a large number of Texians were scouring the prairie thro'out the day bringing in prisoners. The grass was every where four or five feet high, and those who had not been taken the day before, were now crawling away on their hands and knees, hoping thus to make their escape. Santa Anna had not been taken, but the victors were scouring over the fields in search of the Dictator.

"You will find the hero of Tampico," said Houston, "if you find him at all, making his retreat *on all fours,* and he will be dressed as bad at least as a common soldier. Examine every man you find closely."

Lieut. Sylvester, a volunteer, of Cincinnati, was riding over a fine prairie on a fine horse, about three in the afternoon, when he saw a man making his way towards Vince's bridge. The moment he saw he was pursued, the fugitive fell down in the grass. Sylvester dashed on in that direction, and his horse came very near trampling him down.—The man sprang to his feet, and apparently without the slightest surprise, looked his captor straight in the face.

He was disguised in a miserable rustic dress. He wore a skin cap, a round jacket, and pants

Santa Anna's Tree Berth

Antonio López de Santa Anna "escaped on horseback immediately after the action for the bridge," read an account of the battle of San Jacinto in the *New Orleans Bee* of May 11, 1836, "but fell back into the wood that night, where he reposed with the mosquitoes up in a tree." The *generalissimo* himself would later pen a report of that disastrous day, and explained that during his flight from the battlefield he managed to elude Texian pursuers by jumping from his horse "and with much difficulty succeeded in concealing myself in a thicket of dwarf pines," as night came on.[1]

When he had fled his camp, he was wearing a fine linen shirt with diamond studs, a fine grey vest with gold buttons, white silk drawers, and red morocco slippers. Before abandoning his horse he took off the blanket attached to its saddle, a water gourd, a cotton sheet, and some chocolate; evidently he was anticipating spending some time in the open.[2]

Just how he spent most of the night in the grove is described by him in positive terms: "the hope of reaching the army [General Filisola's division] gave me strength."[3] But of course he had just witnessed the opening phase of the annihilation of most of his command at the hands of Sam Houston's angry army, so it must have been an exceedingly stressful, sleepless night for him. Perhaps he held his medal of Our Lady of Guadalupe, kissing it and praying to her in the hope that she would bring him better luck on the morrow.

The next morning he found clothing in an abandoned slave's cabin on Vince's ranch, but despite the new apparel he was shortly swept up by Texian horsemen hunting for Mexican fugitives. He had kept on his expensive shirt with the diamond studs, which naturally drew the curiosity and suspicion of his captors. What he was actually wearing, aside from the shirt, when he was brought to the main body of Mexican prisoners, has been the subject of much confusion thanks to a myriad of descriptions found in contemporaneous accounts as well as subsequent memoirs. One of these noted that he "was dressed as a common soldier with dingy white uniform." Another described his dress as primarily "a striped jacket [and] coarse white linen pants." Yet another noted that he wore a "round-jacket, and pants of blue domestic cotton." One veteran remembered him dressed in "a corporal's uniform." Another even asserted that he was "disguised as a sailor." But several of the accounts do agree on his headgear: a crude leather cap.

(Continued)

1. Santa Anna's report of the battle of San Jacinto, written the following year (March 11, 1837), in Frank W. Johnson, *A History of Texas and Texans* (Chicago: American Historical Society, 1914), 455.
2. Frank X. Tolbert, *The Day of San Jacinto* (New York: McGraw-Hill Book Company, 1959), 174.
3. Santa Anna's report in Johnson, *A History of Texas and Texans*, 455.

of blue domestic cotton, and a pair of coarse shoes. But his face and his manners, bespoke too plainly, that he belonged to a different class than his garb betokened; and underneath his coarse disguise, Sylvester saw that he wore a shirt of the finest linen cambric.

"You are an officer, I perceive, sir," said the horseman, raising his cap politely.

"No, soldier," he replied, drawing out a letter addressed to Almonte.

When he saw there was no hope of escape, he inquired for Gen. Houston—By this time, Sylvester had been joined by several of his comrades, and mounting his prisoner behind him, they rode off together on the same horse to camp, several miles distant. As he rode by the Mexican prisoners, they exclaimed with the greatest surprise, as they lifted their caps, *"El Presidente!"*

In a single moment the news spread through the camp that Gen. Santa Anna was a prisoner, and the Dictator was taken to Houston. The General who was lying on the ground in consequence of his wound, had fallen into a doze.— Santa Anna came up behind him and took his hand. Houston roused himself and turning over gazed up in the face of the Mexican when he extended his left arm, and laying his right on his heart said—

"I am Gen. Antonio Lopez de Santa Anna, President of the Mexican Republic, and I claim to be your prisoner of war."

Houston waved his hand to a box, for it was the only seat in the camp and asked his prisoner to be seated; and then sent for Almonte, who spoke English perfectly, and requested him to act as interpreter.

Almonte approached his captive general with evident respect and grief, and the following conversation took place between the two commanders, Houston in the meantime lying on the ground, resting on his elbow. Great pains have been taken to get nearly as possible the exact words used by the speakers, and those who were present at the interview have assured us that all here related they do remember, and they recollect nothing else of importance.

Santa Anna, (after embracing Almonte and recovering perfectly from his embarrassment,) rose, and advancing with the air of one born to command, said to General Houston—

"That man may consider himself born to no common destiny, who hath conquered the Napoleon of the West; and it now remains for him to be generous to the vanquished."

Houston—You should have remembered that at the Alamo.

S. A. You must be aware that I was justified in my course by the usages of war. I had summoned a surrender, and they refused. The place was then taken by storm, and the usages of war justified the slaughter of the vanquished.

H. That *was* the case once, but it is now obsolete. Such usages among civilized nations have yielded to the influence of humanity.

S. A. However this may be, I was acting under the orders of my government.

H. Why, you are the government of Mexico.

S. A. I had orders in my possession commanding me to do so.

H. A Dictator, sir, has no superior.

S. A. I have orders, Gen. Houston, from my Government, commanding me to exterminate every man found in arms in the province of Texas, and treat all such as pirates; for they have no government, and are fighting under no recognized flag. This will account for the positive orders of my government.

H. So far as the first point is concerned, the Texians flatter themselves they have a government already, and they will probably be able to make a flag. But if you feel excused for your conduct at San Antonio, you have not the same excuse for the massacre of Col. Fannin's command. They capitulated on terms proffered by your general. And yet after the capitulation, they were all perfidiously massacred, without the privilege of even dying with arms in their hands.

Those who were present say that when Houston came to speak of the Goliad tragedy, it seemed impossible for him to restrain his indignation. His eyes flashed like a wild beast's, and in his gigantic effort to curb his wrath, cold sweat ran from his brow in streams.

S. A. I declare to you General, (laying his hand on his heart,) that I was not apprised of the fact that they had capitulated. Gen. Urrea informed me that he had conquered them in battle, and under this impression, I ordered their execution.

H. I *know*, General, that the men had capitulated.

S. A. Then I was ignorant of it—And after your asseveration I should not have a shadow of a doubt, if it were not that Gen. Urrea had no authority what ever to receive *their capitulation*. And if the day ever comes that I can get Urrea into my hands, I will execute him for his duplicity in not giving me information of the facts.

Here the conversation was suspended for a while, and Santa Anna requested a small piece of opium. It was ordered by Houston, who asked if he would desire his marquee and luggage, and the attendance of his aids and servants. Santa Anna thanked him very politely, and said "it would make him very happy since they were proffered by his captor."

While the order was being given, Almonte manifested a disposition to continue the conversation with Houston. After remarking to the Texian General that fortune had indeed favored him, he asked him why he had not attacked the Mexicans the first day the armies met.

"You had reason to suppose we should be reinforced. And yet if you had risked a battle

that day, you would have another story to tell, perhaps, for our men were then ready to fight and so anxious for battle to come on that we could hardly keep them in the ranks. Why did you wait till the next morning General?"

"Well," replied Houston, "I see that I was right. I knew that you expected that I should bring on the battle that day, and were consequently prepared for it. Now if I must be questioned by an inferior officer in the presence of his General, I will say that was just the reason why I did not fight, and besides I thought there was no use having two bites at one cherry."

After some remarks of Almonte, which irritated Houston, and which, in the opinion of all who heard it, ill befitted the occasion, he said—

"You have come a great way to give us a great deal of trouble—and you have made the sacrifice of the lives of a great many brave men necessary."

"Oh, flippantry," replied Almonte, "what are six or eight hundred men!—And from all accounts, only have a dozen of your BRAVE men have fallen."

Houston replied—"We estimate the lives of our men, I perceive, somewhat higher than you do," and gave him a look which seemed to say, "taunt me again and you don't live an hour."

Almonte very politely changed his tone.

"You talk about reinforcements, sir," said Houston raising himself up. "It matters not how many reinforcements you have sir, you can never conquer freemen," and taking from his pocket an ear of dry corn which he had carried for four days, only a part of it being consumed, he held it up, and said, "Sir, do you ever expect to conquer men who fight for freedom, and whose general can march four days with one ear of corn for his rations?"

The exhibition of the ear of corn stirred up all the enthusiasms of the Texian soldiers, and they gathered around their general, and asked him to allow them to divide the corn. "We'll plant it," said they, "and call it the Houston corn." "Oh, yes, my brave fellows," said the General smiling, "take it along if you care anything about it, and divide it among you—give each one a kernel as far as it will go, and take it home to your own fields, when I hope you may long cultivate the noble arts of peace as well as you have shown yourselves masters of the art of war. You have achieved your independence—now see if you cannot make as good farmers as you have proved yourselves gallant soldiers. You may not call it Houston corn, but call it *San Jacinto* corn—for then it will remind you of your own bravery."

It is also said that in one of his despatches that day to the people of the Sabine, the General said, to those that fled from their homes, "return and plant corn." The soldiers distributed their corn, and it now waves over a thousand green fields of the Republic.

Santa Anna had become interested in the conversation, and Almonte related to him what had been said. The Mexican General seemed to be transported with rage, and he cursed Almonte for losing the battle. He was mortified beyond measure, to think that his army perfectly armed and munitioned, with officers whose camp was filled with every luxury, should have been conquered by an undisciplined band of raw troops, incompletely armed, and whose officers were destitute of most of the necessaries of life. It is worthy to remark also, that Santa Anna afterwards said—

"That this was the first moment he had understood the American character, and that what he had witnessed, convinced him that Americans COULD NEVER BE CONQUERED."

—*Wisconsin Democrat* (Madison),
May 8, 1847

Houston went to New Orleans to have his wound cared for, while Thomas Jefferson Rusk took charge of the Texian army.

(From the New Orleans Advertiser, May 21)
In the schooner Flora, arrived yesterday, came passenger, Gen. Samuel Houston, Commander-in-Chief of the Texian army, for the purpose of obtaining medical advice, being badly wounded. By him we have the official confirmation of the capture of Santa Anna, and also of the battle of April 21st.

Former accounts are substantially correct, Santa Anna was at Velasco under a strong guard. The army was left under command of Rusk, Secretary of War, who had been elected Brigadier-General.

The Texian force is said to have accumulated since the battle to 1800 men, and had advanced to and were crossing the Brazos, flushed with victory. The Mexican army under Seizma and others had concentrated and amounted to 2500; the remnant of 7000 men that entered Texas. They were crossing the Colorado by rafts and swimming, and were in the utmost confusion, those who escaped having reported that the late battle was fought by 5000 Texians; Colonel Burleson was close to the enemy, with 200 cavalry, and they were retreating before him, all was panic and confusion in the Mexican army. General Santa Anna had offered an armistice, which had been refused; he had made further offers to acknowledge the Independence of Texas, making the Rio Grande the boundary line, and remaining a hostage until the Government of the United States should consent to guarantee the treaty, and it should be approved by the Mexican Senate. Texas was considered safe and the war ended; the Mexican army would probably be totally destroyed. Gen. Houston has a cane presented him by Santa Anna, and also his saddle; he has been recognized by Gen. Zavalla, and hundreds of others had identified him. The Mexican prisoners also shouted when he was brought in, "Vivo Santa Anna."

—*Richmond Enquirer*, June 10, 1836

The above-mentioned cane of Santa Anna, judging by the following extract from a 1902 Texas newspaper article, was no ordinary cane.

RELIC OF SANTA ANNA.
A short while ago the writer was in the home of Dr. J. B. Cooksey of Corsicana. In the course of our conversation we drifted into a discussion of different topics of Texas history. Presently Dr. Cooksey remarked that he had a relic which he prized very highly, because it was once the property of Santa Anna. He walked into

an adjoining room and soon returned with an unique contrivance, which resembled in almost every respect an ordinary walking cane. "This is a complete gun," he said, "and was taken from Santa Anna by Sam Houston at the battle of San Jacinto."

The barrel is about three feet in length, and at the end where other gun barrels are attached to the stock it has a piece of wood about four inches long and one inch in diameter, deftly attached at right angles with the end of the barrel. The tube and hammer are on the under side instead of the upper side of the barrel and the hammer lies in a lateral position along side the barrel, resembling a clasp more than the hammer of an ordinary gun.

—*Dallas Morning News,* April 25, 1902

Other relics of Santa Anna taken at San Jacinto are described in the following July 1836 report.

MEMENTOS FROM THE BATTLE FIELD OF SAN JACINTO. An officer of the Texian army, U. J. Bullock, Esq., of Macon, Georgia, who was one of the aids of General Houston at the battle of San Jacinto, called at our office yesterday and left for inspection a silver fork and spoon, the latter apparently inlaid with gold, which formed a part of Santa Anna's service of plate taken on the battle field. They are enclosed in an old fashioned black box, ornamented in front with a silver crucifix, and were presented by Thomas J. Rusk, (then Texian Secretary of War, now commander in chief,) to Miss Troutman, of Knoxville, Georgia, who presented the Macon volunteers with a flag on their march through Knoxville on their way to Texas.

How interesting are these memorials of one of the most brilliant victories in modern times! It appears that Santa Anna's plate which he carried along with him, consisting of every thing necessary for the table, is of the most costly description and were valued at $1000 or $1200. His silver coffee pots were of a most beautiful construction. We further learn that the saddle which was sent by Col. Webb to the American Museum, cannot by any possibility belong to

General Cos. The Mexican Generals only rode on the most magnificent saddles—and the one in the Museum is almost too mean for a cavalry soldier. We deeply regret that our friend Col. Webb (who is recovering rapidly, thanks to God,) has been hoaxed with Gen. Cos's saddle, but it was not our fault. The real saddle was presented by Gen. Houston to Mr. Christie of New Orleans.

—*New York Herald,* July 14, 1836

Affairs in Mexico were summarized by another New York paper.

Mexico.—The arrival yesterday of the ship Congress, Captain Trask, from Vera Cruz, has placed in our possession papers of that city of the 10th, and of the city of Mexico, of the 7th ultimo. At the latest dates, there had been no publication in Mexico of the capture of *Santa Anna*, and every thing remained tranquil under the Government established by him, although private letters state that the information of his capture had been received and suppressed. The papers are still full of pompous eulogies of the invincible Mexican army in Texas; and one paragraph says, there is no doubt that army is now on the Sabine river, where it will definitely adjust the treaty of limits with the United States, adding, that Napoleon had observed, *"that treaties were always best observed that were concluded at the head of an army."*

"The celebrated National Brig of War, *Vencedor Del Alamo,* (conqueror of the Alamo, which we believe was formerly the Brig *Paragon,* of this port,) and the Schr. General Cos, it is stated in the papers before us, had sailed for the waters of *Texas,* for the purpose of protecting Mexican commerce and punishing the ungrateful colonists."

—*Morning Courier and New York Enquirer,* June 6, 1836

The *Richmond Enquirer* published a number of letters from Texas concerning post-San Jacinto events, including the situation on Galveston Island, where a nervous General Martín Perfecto de Cos and several hundred Mexican troops had been incarcerated.

TEXAS.

(From the New York Evening Star.)

Extract from a letter dated at Velasco, 25th May, and received this morning from a distinguished individual, whose situation in Texas gives him full opportunity to know every thing that passes in that country:

"We have General Santa Anna still with us as a prisoner; and I believe he will yet remain so for some time. He has, however, made a compact with the Texian Government, the basis of which is, the evacuation of the Territory to the Rio Grande; solemn pledge under oath not to take up arms against Texas; delivery of the prisoners; and the liberty of Santa Anna himself when the Government of Texas shall deem expedient. The people are much incensed against him, and the Government has with difficulty saved his life.

"I believe the war is ended, and that the fate of Texas is settled. Now we alone wait for the tranquility of Mexico. A great revolution threatens her."

(From the New Orleans Bee, June 10.)

General Houston and his staff have left for Texas, via Natchitoches.

As proof that the affairs of Texas are restored to comparative tranquility, we have been informed, by a letter dated Lynchburg, (Texas,) 21st of May, that lands which previously could scarcely realize one dollar an acre, are now selling readily for 4 to 5. Speculation produced war, and will follow peace; but it is not yet very safe to invest capital in Texas lands.

The editor of the Baltimore Patriot has been favored with the following extract of a letter from an officer to the Texian army, dated

"GALVESTON BAY, (TEXAS,)
May 27, 1836.

"I take the earliest opportunity to inform you of my arrival here after a tedious and unpleasant trip of four days from the Southwest Pass, Louisiana, through the Gulf of Mexico. On our arrival here, we found the island in possession of the Texians, who had resorted here as a place of protection and rendezvous, previous to the late successful battle of the Texians. They have an entrenchment erected on the island, which is called Fort Thomas.[b] It was in command of Col. Morgan, who, with 150 men, have under guard 301 Mexican prisoners, taken at the battle of San Jacinto. Among the number of prisoners are 47 officers of rank, all of whom I have seen and was introduced to; among them is the great, celebrated General Martin Perfecto Cos, Colonel Cesperer, and Captain Paraza, all fine-looking men, rather darker than the Americans. They received us very civilly, and Gen. Cos apologized that he could not receive us in greater style. I attributed their civilities and condescension entirely to their situation, which is rather an unpleasant one. What they intend doing with them is as yet undecided. The common order of the Mexican soldiers are the most wretched race of men I have ever seen; they are generally small in stature, and some of them very dark, approximating the negro race; they are poor miserable creatures, and I cannot but commiserate their unfortunate situation; they are at present at work round the island, facilitating the completion of the entrenchments. I shall leave this place to-morrow, with despatches to the Government, at Velasco, where the celebrated Gen. Santa Anna is prisoner. The distance from Galveston to Velasco is 45 miles. As there was some doubt in the city of New Orleans, when I took my leave from them, respecting Santa Anna being prisoner, and no doubt the same may be the case in your city, you will please to inform the editors of the papers that he is safe, and a prisoner, with all his staff, with 500 prisoners. I regret that I cannot give you some particulars of the country. Galveston is a beautiful island, surrounded by one of the best harbors in the Union. I have no news at present worth your attention; perhaps, in my next, I will be able to write something more entertaining."

The Mobile Morning Chronicle of the 11th of June publishes the subjoined extracts of Letters, the particulars of which, the Editor says, may be relied upon as strictly correct:

GALVESTON BAY, May 27, 1836.
I arrived here in safety on the 25th, in the Ocean: we left the mouth of the Mississippi on Sunday, about 11 o'clock. We were com-

[b] Other accounts call it Fort Travis.

pelled to come to anchor on Tuesday morning to cleanse our boilers; we remained at anchor 15 hours. The boat is a first rate sea boat, and performed well. Fearing we should be too deep, we did not have as much fuel as we ought, and were compelled to cut up our spars to get in with.

I am happy to inform you that the enemy did not get to Quintanas, although they remained five or six days at Brasoria, which place, and Columbia, they sacked of every thing which had been left there; but cotton they could not move, and did not touch. When they heard of Santa Anna's defeat and capture, they retreated, precipitately, and left many things behind them; therefore, with our many losses, we have saved our cotton. The enemy have crossed the Colorado on their way to the West. It is presumed they will concentrate at Bexar, if not captured by our army, which is pursuing them.—Santa Anna is at Velasco, where our Government is at present. Gen. Cos is on the island. I saw him yesterday: he looks badly, and was very much agitated when the company with which I visited him approached: he appeared to me as if he was beside himself. As I did not go to him with a view to exult over his wretched situation, I made a few observations to him, and remained but a few moments. I believe he is persuaded that he will be shot or hung. I have heard it rumored here that our Government are making some negotiations with Santa Anna; if they are, they will be defeated, for I am persuaded that the people are determined on the death of Santa Anna, and for this I shall go with all my faculties and all my strength.

The Mexicans will not make any more expeditions before winter. Many farmers have returned to their homes to clear their crops, and do what they can. The brig Durango sailed from here yesterday for Matagorda, with women and children returning home.

GALVESTON, May 28.
I went ashore on the island, and saw Gen. Cos; think him much the gentleman; fine countenance. I asked him what he thought of matters and things. He said it was Santa Anna's fault that they were taken; that he had too contemptible

an opinion of the Texians, and did not expect that they would have made headway against his army, or he would not have entered so far into Texas; that he felt very comfortable here; that the Texians generally treated him with the greatest politeness; but that several persons were allowed to come to see him who did not treat him as a gentleman, but complained of his having shot their brothers, their fathers, their sons, and their friends; that he thought this unmanly, womanly, as it was the fortunes of war. He said this was the only inconvenience he had suffered.

MAY 29.
Seven hundred and thirty bodies of the enemy are now lying on the field of battle, and are strewed for miles.—More than 200 rifles and muskets were broken to pieces, beating out the brains of the Mexicans. The riflemen rushed upon Santa Anna's artillery, and took the guns from him loaded. A desperation was evinced on the part of the Texians never equalled in the annals of fighting. The enemy had the advantage in position. The battle was fought principally on the open ground. The enemy stood the charge about fifteen minutes—the killing lasted for hours. The night before the battle, Gen. Cos reinforced Santa Anna with 500 men. There are now between 500 and 600 prisoners, between 200 and 300 wounded, and between 700 and 800 killed; and all this done with less than 700 men.

I saw Gen. Cos yesterday, he is evidently very much alarmed, and to me appeared to be almost beside himself. He attempted to excuse his conduct, and said that his enemies had made charges against him that were false. As I did not wish to exult over his fallen fortunes and wretched situation, I made few remarks, and remained with him but a few moments. He feels conscious he must die.—Santa Anna is at Velasco. I fear our Government will be duped by him; but he cannot escape—he must die.

You will have seen the official reports, that will give you more detail than time will allow me to condense. I am pleased to say, that Capt. (now Col.) Juan Nepemucene Seguin, a native of Bexar, and whom I have known from a boy, commanded 25 men, all natives of the same place, and performed wonders; every man signalized himself in the most distinguished manner. One of them, with a Bowie knife, killed 25 of his countrymen, and one of them Col. Batres, whom I knew well. Dionicio Cos, brother of the General, the same who mutilated the body of the lamented Travis, was killed. Twenty-three officers were among the slain.

—*Richmond Enquirer*, July 1, 1836

On May 14 on his own initiative, Santa Anna had signed the two treaties of Velasco, which recognized Texas as an independent republic, stipulated that Mexicans would never again invade Texas, and ordered the Mexican divisions inside Texas to return to Mexico.

One of the sections of the Mexican army still stationed in Texas was commanded by Brigadier General Juan José Andrade, who had been entrusted by Santa Anna to hold the recaptured San Antonio and improve the fortifications of the Alamo. Also put under his charge were about three hundred *soldados* wounded in the March 6 assault, nearly all of them still suffering—if they had survived that long—from lack of proper medical attention. Leaving Monclova and arriving in Béxar more than six weeks after the battle, Mexican surgeon Don José Faustino Moro was shocked at what he saw. What follows is part of a letter he wrote to an official, which was published in at least two Mexican newspapers.

I arrived at Bejar and was simply appalled to learn all that happened there. Without any resources to set up a field hospital, an assault was mounted, and the result was more than two hundred wounded, but there was no place to house them, although up to the last hour efforts were made to locate one; meanwhile the suffering patients wandered from one place to another, their sufferings made greater by reflections naturally occurring to them in their pitiable situation. Hurtado, Reyes, and the practitioners with them did not arrive at Bejar until many days after the events, and Arroyo, who was there at the time, had almost exhausted the few things I had left him during the month of December of the previous year.

He had neither bandages, nor material for making them, no gauze for the initial dressings, and nothing had been ordered or prepared for him. Lacking everything, he made repeated requests but was always answered negatively. The bandages that were finally given to him were a sort of cotton, harmful, as your Excellency knows, to the wounds. Many had been admitted, among them two superior officers and some twenty others, to whom not a single surgeon could attend. Was the medical corps of the army at fault in this, or the persons who had so ordered these things? You very well know Your Excellency that an injured person not only needs to be cured, but to be in a bed that will help alleviate their sufferings, but all these unfortunate people remained prostrate on the ground until the day, finally, that the Sr. General Andrade arranged to make beds for some of them. As provisions were very scarce, and bad, for the healthy and able, it was even worse for the sick ones.

—*El Mosquito Mexicano*,
September 30, 1836

The day after the battle of San Jacinto, the captive Santa Anna had written in a letter to his second in command, Gen. Vicente Filisola: "Your Excellency will direct General Gaona to countermarch to Bejar to await orders in like manner as your Excellency will do with the troops under your orders. You will direct General Urrea to retire with his division to Guadaloupe Victoria."[2] Although he considered the option of disobeying Santa Anna and attempting his rescue, Filisola felt that the Mexican divisions were currently too scattered and otherwise unprepared to advance. They would have to fall back and regroup. Thus, instead of marching to San Antonio, he ordered a limited withdrawal toward Goliad. On May 18 he sent instructions to General Juan José Andrade to destroy all of the renovations his troops had laboriously made upon the Alamo fortifications—and any other parts of it that the Texians might employ in its future defense—and evacuate Béxar. Andrade received these orders on May 22, and by May 24 the demolition had been completed and his troops were marching out of town.[3] Shortly afterward, to the chagrin of General José Urrea and other officers, Filisola put his signature under Santa Anna's to the Treaties of Velasco, which decreed that all Mexican forces had to withdraw south of the Rio Grande.

In trying to make sense of the swirl of these and other developments in the wake of Houston's victory, a correspondent of the *Morning Courier and New York Enquirer* penned a report that covered many aspects of the last days of the campaign, including the April 21 engagement itself.

I will trouble you with no more incidents, or reflections at present, but give you a few more facts. Six hundred and one dead Mexicans have been counted, that were killed in the battle of the 21st April, without taking into consideration those shot in the lake, perhaps 50 or 100 more. There are 630 prisoners that I know of—perhaps 650 in all. We can make out 1200 and odd dead, wounded and prisoners. *Thirteen* are supposed to have escaped; General Ball, I have understood gave that account. The Mexican account of the battle is, that we had 5000 Americans, and 2000 Indians, opposed to them in battle! It will never be possible to convince them to the contrary. The balance of Santa Anna's army fled—General Rusk was close in their rear, occasionally cutting off small detachments and harrassing them with his cavalry at every step, until he was ordered to stop; that a treaty had been made. The enemy had passed La Bahia and Bexar, blowing up the ALAMO; spiking and throwing the cannon in the river, in his retreat. The Comanche Indians commenced depredating in the rear of the Mexican army as they advanced from Bexar upon the settlements. All their horses and mules, of which they had many, as well as much baggage, were taken by the Indians. At every step they met with trouble and are hurrying with all possible despatch, towards the interior. At the battle of the 21st April Almonte's and Cos' private journals and letters fell into the hands of the Americans— among them some letters from NEW YORK.[c]

Some having slips of *newspapers* in them: some letters in English, some in Spanish, &c &c.!! As they will in all probability, find their way to New York, you will be enabled to see the effects of MEXICAN GOLD in that great city.

While the Texians were marching towards the Colorado, to meet the Mexicans, meeting hundreds who were flying from their homes; among the rest an aged lady, whose eyes were diffused with tears, and when told to be of good cheer, that the Mexicans would soon be driven out of the country, "Ah!" replied the old lady, "all the beating you can give the Mexicans now, won't restore *my son who was murdered in the Alamo.*"

You were before informed that the battle of the 21st lasted 19 minutes; some say 14 some 16—that the American loss, was 4 killed on the field and some 15 wounded. In all that were killed on the field or have died since of wounds received in the battle, I make out *eight*—The other wounded have recovered, or most of them. The last who died was a worthy young man from Gloucester, Massachusetts by the name of Trask. He died at Galveston, on the 2d inst. and was buried with all the honours of war. I do not think that the wounded exceeded 15, they have been stated at 11 only. The number of wounded Mexicans was small in proportion to the killed. It may be accounted for, in a measure by their having some of their own countrymen, as enemies to deal with, who used "the knife to the hilt." There was a company of friendly Mexicans, from Nacogdoches, among the Texian troops, who behaved very bravely and dealt death and destruction to the wounded Mexicans as they went!

Col. *Cos*[d] was seen in the early part of the engagement near the Mexican breast work, brandishing his sword and encouraging his men, with great bravery. He was pointed out by the Captain of one of the rifle corps, to one of his men, and ordered to be brought down, which was done instantly. When found after the battle, he had been shot through the *shoulder* only. His head, however, bore the marks of a rifle or musket ball. His skull was mashed in, as

---

[c] Although Almonte's journal was published in the *New York Herald*, nothing more was heard of General Cos's journal or papers. One can only speculate as to their fate and what priceless historical information they might have contained.

[d] Dionicio Cos.

Andrade Demolishes the Alamo

Lt. Col. Enrique de la Peña could empathize with General Juan José Andrade after the latter had been ordered by General Vicente Filisola to destroy the Alamo and evacuate Béxar.

> During his stay in that city, he had labored to put the Alamo in the best possible condition for defense; this had already been improved when it became necessary to raze it; and few do not know the pain such an operation causes a soldier, a pain even greater to one who knows the duties of his profession well.[1]

Andrade had led his cavalry brigade into San Antonio four days after the battle. "They were quartered in the Alamo," noted Col. Juan Nepomuceno Almonte, and one can only wonder at the living conditions they were forced to endure so soon after the bloodbath there.[2] Left in command of San Antonio after Antonio López de Santa Anna embarked on his ill-fated San Jacinto campaign, Andrade had to hold both the fort and the town with one thousand men—most of them his cavalry—including three hundred who "were either wounded or ill."[3]

After San Jacinto, renovation work on the Alamo's fortifications was escalated because there was real fear that a Texian army might soon descend upon Béxar. By May 15 the captive Dr. Joseph Barnard wrote: "Yesterday I strolled over to the Alamo with the hospital captain (Martinez). They are hard at work fortifying."[4]

When Filisola decided that the remaining Mexican troops in Texas were ill-equipped to resume an offensive, he ordered Andrade to effectively destroy the Alamo as a defensible post, spike all the cannon, and dump or bury all of the munitions. "They are now as busy as bees tearing down the walls, &c.," wrote Barnard on May 22. Two days later, their job done, Andrade's troops marched out of San Antonio, leaving in their wake a huge fire coursing out of the Alamo church as its wooden ramp burned, and "all the single walls . . . leveled, the fosse filled up, and the pickets torn up and burnt. All the artillery and ammunition that could not be carried off were thrown in the river."[5] Noted the *New York American* of July 7, 1836: "The enemy spiked all the cannon, threw them in the river [and] blew up the Alamo."

(Continued)

If Andrade had felt any pride in his reconditioning and expansion of the Alamo's defenses, his bitterness and cynicism overpowered all in a letter he afterward wrote to a Mexican official:

> Another time I will tell Your Excellency how many men I should have had in order to defend what has been mistakenly called "The Fort of the Alamo." I did what I could to improve it. I wanted to insure a victory which would have been difficult to obtain, had we been fighting against a trained and disciplined enemy. From a military standpoint, the Alamo was nothing more than a corral with a few poorly constructed buildings that at one time offered the presidial soldiers and their horses refuge from the environment, and at times protected them also from marauding Indians, common in the frontier.[6]

According to Adina de Zavala, Andrade's demolition crews would have inflicted even more damage on the fort had not the ghosts of the Alamo scared them away:

> it is said that his men were everywhere met by spirits with flaming swords who barred their progress and soon frightened them off; that almost as fast as new relays of men were sent with orders to destroy the walls, they were overcome by fright; nor could threats or punishment induce them to return. They were permitted by the ghosts for a space to disarm the batteries, but the moment the walls of the buildings were threatened, there was the flaming sword in ghostly hands. . . . These spirits ordered them to desist in hollow tones which struck terror to their hearts, "Depart, touch not these walls! He who desecrates these walls shall meet a horrible Fate! Multiplied afflictions shall seize upon him and a horrible and agonizing and avenging torture shall be his death!"[7]

Andrade, well educated, versed in French, and evidently somewhat dashing, no doubt shrugged all of this off, if in fact some of his men had been spooked. A brief description of him was written by Goliad captive Jack Shackleford, who was brought before Andrade at the Alamo when he arrived there from Fort Defiance.

> Was immediately conducted to the head-quarters of Gen. Andrada.—Found him wearing a fine fur cap, which had been the property of some of our gallant countrymen who had fallen in the Alamo; smoking a cigar held by golden tongs;

and was surrounded by some of his principal officers. . . . The General received us politely.[8]

Andrade would later remark: "Calm reigned at the evacuation of Bejar. Absolutely nothing was done in haste."[9]

1. José Enrique de la Peña, *With Santa Anna in Texas: A Personal Narrative of the Revolution*, ed. Carmen Perry (College Station: Texas A&M University Press, 1975), 188.
2. Almonte, journal entry, March 10, 1836, *New York Herald*, June 27, 1836.
3. Peña, *With Santa Anna in Texas*, 135.
4. Barnard's journal, May 15, 1836, in Todd Hansen, ed., *The Alamo Reader: A Study in History* (Mechanicsburg, Penn: Stackpole Books, 2003), 613.
5. Ibid., 614–615.
6. Andrade to unnamed official, Monterrey, 25 July 1836, "Documents Published by General Andrade about the Evacuation of the City of San Antonio de Bejar in the Department of Texas," typewritten transcript copy.
7. Adina de Zavala, *History and Legends of the Alamo and Other Missions in and around San Antonio* (San Antonio, 1917), 55.
8. Account of Jack Shackelford, in Henry Stuart Foote, *Texas and the Texans* (Philadelphia, 1841), 2:246.
9. Andrade, "Documents," 15.

were hundreds of them, with the breeches of the guns! Castrillon was equally as conspicuous in battle and fell early in the engagement pierced with many wounds. He, Castrillon, was brave and not cruel, as I have said before. His bravery cost him his life as well as Cos who fell early in the engagement, and lay not far off, near the breastwork. The skeletons of the dead yet cover the plain—their bones will long bleach in the prairie. But I must stop about Mexicans, battles, &c. &c., as my sheet is full, or nearly so.
—*Morning Courier and New York Enquirer*, July 9, 1836

The all-too-rare mention of the demolition of the Alamo and of the retreat of the Mexican divisions in the preceding letter was slightly expanded upon in the following article.

The *Philadelphia Gazette* contains the following extract of a letter from a citizen of Texas, dated Natchitoches, June 13, 1836.
By Dr.——and two other gentlemen of Virginia, who reached here from our army

yesterday, we have news up to the first of this month, when our army were near La Bahia. The enemy had passed there, which was the last place there was any apprehension of their making a stand. The Mexican division at San Antonio had been insulted by the Camanches in that place, who took from them all their mules and horses and left them no means to retreat. The enemy spiked all the cannon, threw them into the river, blew up the Alamo, left San Antonio, and joined the main army at La Bahia, as they had no means of conveying baggage, to enable them to leave by a more direct route for Mexico. The main army, on their retreat between the Colorado and St. Bernard, lost in one bog upwards of 100 mules, 14 baggage waggons, and made causeways of their muskets to get over the morasses—burnt the carriages of their cannon, and buried their guns. This is a true account of the glorious retreat of the Mexican army, consisting of between 4 and 5000, who fled thus lest they might be overtaken by our army of 6 or 700 men. The enemy have now left our country. San Antonio is entirely deserted by its citizens. They say there are not six souls in the place."

—*New York American*, July 7, 1836

Dr. J. H. Barnard, one of the Texian surgeons deliberately spared from execution at Goliad, had been sent to San Antonio by General Urrea to tend to the many wounded Mexican soldiers there. In early June, now freed, he wrote a letter to a Chicago friend and included a few Alamo-related facts as he had learned them from "several friends who were saved."

We have been favored by one of our citizens, with the following extract of a letter, from our fellow townsman, Dr. J. H. BARNARD, who was with Col. Fannin, at his capture and massacre, dated,

VELASCO, 9th June, 1836.

DEAR SIR:—

Well, Texas has been invaded and overrun by barbarians—blood and rapine have marked their way—they swept the country like the blast of the simoon—all is past, and the memory of it is more that of an airy dream, than the impression of fixed reality. Yet it is real; although the existing events—the appalling barbarities—the undaunted heroism, and the glorious success, and final triumph of Texas, are incidents which we seldom meet with, but in the over wrought tales of romance.—But more—the wonders of fiction have been surpassed in real life, and a true history of the war in Texas, will shew as much to wonder at and admire, as any thing that has yet been recorded for amusement or instruction. The enemy first appeared at Bexar: and so rapid was their approach that they were actually in the town before they were apprised of it in the fort. The Texan force here was 120 men—30 more fought their way in, after a few days; making 150 in all. The Mexican force amounting to between 2 and 3000, besieged them for a fortnight, and then took the place by storm, with a loss of 600 killed and wounded. The Americans fought to the last, and were killed to a man. There were several friends who were saved, and who informed me that the men, with the full prospect of death before them, were always lively and cheerful, particularly Crockett, who kept up their spirits by his wit and humor. The night before the storming, he called for his clothes that had been washed, stating that he expected to be killed the next day, and wished to die in clean clothes, that they might give him a decent burial. (Alas, he was stript and burnt with the rest!) Travis was stationed at one angle of the fort, where he fought till death; Bowie was confined to his room by sickness, and is supposed to have shot himself. I afterwards visited the spot where the bodies of the gallant band were buried; some of the friendly citizens set out to bury them, but Santa Anna forbid it.—I was shown the spot where the bodies of Bowie, Travis, and Crockett, were placed, side by side, and dropt a tear on their ashes.[e] Our division under Fannin on our retreat from Labahia, was surrounded on the open prairie, by 6 or 8 times our number, and under every disadvantage fought them for 3 hours, steady loading and firing and taking aim with the utmost coolness. By the by, I feel a little proud of my own behavior, in this, my first of battles; and therefore must take some other opportunity of telling you of my deeds, &c., however, 'twas all in vain, we were obliged to capitulate—the treaty was shamefully broken—our men massacred; a few of us only being saved. After this, the enemy pushed on and overrun the country. Houston with his small force, retreating before them; and destroying as he retreated. At length Santa Anna, with 700 crossed at Bayou and pushed on some distance in advance of his army; he was reinforced by Cos with 600. The Texans about 650 strong, now broke down the bridge over the Bayou, making a retreat impossible to either party—pursued the enemy and attacked him in his entrenchments where he had timber to cover his men. The attack was made in the afternoon when the Mexicans were at dinner; and so sudden and unlooked for was the assault, that the Texans were inside of their entrenchments before half their men could form; it was no longer a fight but a rout. "Labahia & El

---

[e] This is the only contemporary document stating that the bodies of the three Alamo leaders had been burned side by side.

Alamo," was the cry; above half the Mexicans were killed, and 8 Texans. Santa Anna and Cos, with many others taken. The enemy immediately commenced retreating from the country in confusion. Rain had lately fallen, and the prairie was all a quagmire—wagons, horses, mules, and men were destroyed and left. And now not a hostile Mexican is within Texas, but Santa Anna and the other prisoners.

This fiend in human shape is here. I have seen him at a distance, but have avoided an interview. I cannot take the hand of such a murderer. I should reproach him in the strongest terms, for his barbarities, but I hate to insult a fallen enemy.

Yours, &c,
J. H. BARNARD.
—*Missouri Argus* (St. Louis), August 26, 1836

Impatient to be released, Santa Anna wrote a list of protests and addressed it to ad interim Texas president David G. Burnet on June 9. Among his complaints:

For having been treated more like an ordinary criminal than as a prisoner of war. . . [For] the non-fulfillment of the exchange of prisoners . . . For the act of violence committed on my person, and abuse to which I have been exposed . . . [for] being placed in a narrow prison, surrounded with sentinels, and suffering all the privations which absolutely render life insupportable, or tend to hasten death; and finally for being uncertain with regard to my future fate, and of the other prisoners, notwithstanding a solemn treaty.

—*New York American*, November 25, 1836

Burnet's answer was published in the same paper and included the following points.

The citizens and the citizen soldiers of Texas have felt and do feel a deep, intense and righteous indignation at the many atrocities which have been perpetrated by the troops lately under your excellency's command; and especially at the barbarous massacre of the brave colonel Fannin and his gallant companions. How far your excellency participated in that

abomination and inglorious slaughter, I am not disposed to conjecture; but it is both natural and true that the people of Texas impute it to your excellency's special command. . . . It is due to your excellency to say, that the Government confidently believed that these restorations would be effected as early as a proper convenience would admit. But I am induced to advert to another fact, in relation to which it would be difficult to extend the same charitable exculpations to the officers of the Mexican army. It has been reported that the walls of the *Alamo*, at Bexar, have been prostrated, and that the valuable brass artillery attached to that fortress, have been melted down and destroyed.

There were many painful, and pleasing, and glorious reminiscences connected with that Alamo, which renders its wanton dilapidation peculiarly odious to every Texan spirit; and your excellency need not be informed that the destruction of it was an infraction of the armistice, and a violation of the treaty.

—*New York American*, November 25, 1836

Recalled to Mexico for having signed the Treaties of Velasco, which an irate government immediately annulled upon learning about it, General Filisola was replaced as commander of the Mexican forces in the north by General Urrea, who had achieved most of the victories in the campaign—over Johnson, Grant, Ward, and Fannin. As for the Texian government, it understood all too well that the war might resume at any moment.

FROM THE LOUISIANA ADVERTISER, AUG. 2.

By the arrival of the schooner Indiana, Captain Rantiford, in five days from Tampico, we learn that 1,800 men were on the eve of marching from that place for Metamoras; 4,000 more were said to be on their march from San Luis, for the same destination. It appears that the main body of the army are about to rendezvous at Metamoras, previous to marching against Texas. Gen. Fernandez is to act second in command of the Mexican army under Gen. Urrea. Captain R. contradicts the report that the

Mexicans are indifferent about the prosecution of the war in Texas; on the contrary, he states that nothing can exceed the military enthusiasm that seems to pervade all classes, almost causing a general suspension of business, and naught else was talked of but war.

We are indebted to Capt. Bridges, of the schooner Urchin, for the annexed:

GALVESTON BAY, JULY 21. SIR: I arrived here on the 17th, after a passage of four days, and was convoyed down by the Independence, Com. Hawkins, off the bar of Galveston. I saw the Texan schooner Brutus and brig Durango. I could not learn that the Mexicans had a single armed vessel at sea; the schooners Invincible, Captain Brown, and Terrible, (formerly the Union,) Captain Allen, have gone on a cruise along the coast of Mexico. The Mexican army (about 3,000) are still at San Patricio, 125 miles from Victoria, where they concentrated after the battle of San Jacinto: they have made no movements since. It is reported that 500 troops are at Metamoras; but as they apprehend an attack on that place by the Texan army, they are somewhat certain to remain there. Our army (200 infantry and 500 cavalry) are at Victoria: the cavalry made an excursion a few days ago to the immediate vicinity of the Mexican encampment, and brought off a few prisoners. The cabinet is at Velasco, but expect to remove to Matagorda. Santa Ana and Almonte are yet at Columbia, with the army; and rumor has it that Santa Ana is to be tried. Gen. Cos and other officers are at Galveston Island. It is supposed that our army will, in three weeks, amount to 3,500 men. Col. Crockett's nephew[f] has just arrived here: he left the colonel's son,[g] with 200 men, a short distance from the army. As soon as the reinforcements now on their way arrive, it is expected they, with the troops here, will march to and attack Metamoras.

—*Daily National Intelligencer*,
August 17, 1836

News of the annihilation of the Alamo and Goliad garrisons had long since spawned a fresh rush of volunteers for Texas from all across the United States, as exemplified by the following reports.

Texas.—By arrangements made between Gen. Houston[h] of Natchez, Col. Rezin Bowie of Louisiana, and Gen. Green of Texas, in conjunction with several influential men in the upper part of the State, all the volunteers from Mississippi and the upper part of Louisiana, who can get ready by the 5th of May, will unite at different points on the river, and proceed together by way of Plaquemine to Harrisburg, at the head of Galveston Bay, in Texas. It is confidently expected that from 500 to 700 men will unite—and constitute the largest force of infantry and cavalry which has ever gone to Texas from the U. S. It is not desirable that all should have arms as there is an ample supply of muskets, yagers, swords, pistols, and ammunition, provided at Harrisburg, sufficient for 5000 men.

Col. Rezin Bowie, who is well acquainted with the route by Plaquemine, through Attakapas, and has often travelled it, thinks it far preferable to any other—it is shorter, and there is abundance of corn and provisions—which is evident that the district through which the volunteers will march, annually sends to New Orleans, from 10 to 1500 head of cattle. If the waters are high they can be headed by taking the upper route by Opelusas, which is only about 30 miles farther.

(*Natchez Cour.*, April 28.)
—*Arkansas Gazette*, May 10, 1836

The ladies of Cincinnati, propose to make 75 pair pantaloons and 75 hunting shirts for the volunteer corps about leaving there for Texas.
—*New York Times,* June 9, 1836

FOR TEXAS, HO!—A company of 100 volunteers, denominated the "Buckeye Rangers," embarked at Cincinnati for Texas, on the 6th inst. They are commanded by Capt. Allen, late

---

[f] Thomas J. Crockett.
[g] Robert Patton Crockett.

[h] Felix Huston.

editor of the Cincinnati Republican. Their uniform is a blue hunting shirt and a white wool hat.

Col. Harrison, of Louisville, (Ky.) was to have set off from that city, on the 5th inst. for Texas, with a corps of emigrants, which, according to the Advertiser, would muster upwards of 200 fine fellows of the true stuff.

—*Pittsfield Sun* (Massachusetts),
June 23, 1836

The New Orleans Bulletin of the 6th says:—The steamer Heroine, arrived last evening from Louisville, brings 94 fine looking men, commanded by Captain Earl, armed and equipped like regulars—all bound for Texas.

—*New York Times*, July 23, 1836

NATCHITOCHES, JUNE 11.

The steamer Statesman arrived at this place on Monday last, bringing a company of volunteers of about fifty men, from Georgia, well provided with muskets—they are on their way to Texas.

—*Daily National Intelligencer*,
July 13, 1836

TEXAS.—We learn, that a vessel sailed from New Castle on Saturday, with between sixty and seventy volunteers for Texas. The Mexicans are making great preparations to renew the war in Texas. —*Delaware Journal.*

—*Baltimore Gazette and Daily Advertiser*,
July 21, 1836

THE PHILADELPHIA VOLUNTEERS
IN TEXAS.

It will be recollected that the vessel which sailed from this port a few months since, with volunteers for Texas, was driven by adverse winds to Bermuda. It now appears that a part of these chivalrous warriors have reached their destination, and are comfortably quartered at Galveston Island. One of them writes to a Lady in this city, with whom he had boarded, giving some account of their adventures. We have obtained permission to make a few extracts from his letter, which bears date September 12th, 1836. We shall offer no comments at present.

After mentioning his arrival at Galveston Island, he says:—

"The company have joined the service for during the war. We found it would best suit us, as we will be better taken care of, and our bounty of land is more, and are more respected. We belong to an artillery company, stationed in the fort on the island. Ramsey does not belong to us; he is trying to get to be a surgeon, but I do not think he will succeed.

"You wished me to state how I thought business was here. I would inform you that there is nothing doing in Texas at present, nor will there be until the war is over; and then I think there will be fortunes made here. At present a person with capital, here, would make money in buying soldiers' rights. (Titles to bounty land.) There are no houses on this island—nothing but soldiers' camps, or huts built of grass. This island is something like 40 miles long, and abounds in game. You need not go four miles from our camp to shoot as many deer as you want; and you can stand in the tent door and shoot as many land or water fowls as you wish; and the bay is literally alive with fish of an excellent kind. There are 300 prisoners here, they do all the drudgery, and build our huts. *They are very humble and good natured.* They look like North American Indians, with respect to color, and they say that all Santa Anna's army was composed of the same kind of people."

—*Pennsylvania Freeman*, November 5, 1836

Where shall we go and not find a Yankee?—Maj. Norton informs us that he had no idea there were so many New Englanders in Texas, until he gave notice that he would carry letters for persons having friends there. He tells us that his portmanteau was literally laden with epistles to sons, brothers and sweet hearts. Amongst them is one from an old lady to her son, whom she supposed dead, until the Major informed her that he knew him well, and that he is third officer of the Texan schr. Invincible; and there is another from a young girl who had actually gone into mourning for her lover, whose name was erroneously published amongst the list of

killed at the Alamo—but who is still living and in command of a company.   *—Boston Trans.*
—The Pittsfield Sun, June 16, 1836

Volunteers were also called up in Tennessee to help protect the western borders of the United States against a possible Mexican invasion.

> Volunteers will supply themselves with suitable clothing for a six months' tour of duty; and it is strongly recommended that each company furnish itself with one suit of uniform: such as a hunting shirt and pantaloons of the same color; or such other uniform or dress as they find it most convenient to adopt;—but it is not expected that they will allow it to occupy so much time as to prevent them from meeting at the place of general rendezvous by the appointed day.
> *—Memphis Enquirer,* May 11, 1836

Military and political flags had been numerous in Revolutionary-era Texas, but the Republic's first official flag had been adopted at the Convention at Washington-on-the-Brazos on May 11, 1836, designed by Lorenzo de Zavala.[4]

TEXIAN FLAG.
The Texian Flag is a plain red ground, with a single white star of five points, and between the points the letters TEXAS.
—New York Times, June 28, 1836

A letter designed to encourage volunteers to flock to Texas contained unambiguous sentiments and occasional distortions that disparaged the Mexican soldier's fighting ability and character and used battles from the recent war to make its point.

TEXAS.
EXTRACT *of a letter from a Citizen of the West, intimately acquainted with the situation of Texas, to his Correspondent in the City of Richmond—dated August 2d:*
Any number of volunteers can be had for Texas—Enough from Kentucky to go to Mexico, if Texas had funds to pay the expenses of transportation, and to support them until they reached camp—then but little is required, for the country abounds in beeves—and a crop has been generally made. I believe the Mexicans will be resisted at the Colorado, and there delayed until the crop is gathered. There was ample time after the battle of San Jacinto, for the inhabitants to return and put in their crops, and they generally did so. The season there is short—the growth of the crop very rapid: By the 1st of July it would be in roasting ears, and fit to gather, probably, by the 1st of September. It could be "laid by," requiring no more work, by the 15th of June; and the planters could be then spared for the army.—Therefore, I think, that, with the volunteers and citizens, a sufficient army will collect in time to make head against the Mexicans, by the time they reach the Colorado. Nine-tenths of the population lies east of the Colorado, and Gen. Houston fell back from the Colorado before, in hopes the citizens would rise in mass, and come to his standard, to defend their homes[i]—but as he fell back, the families had to decamp, and the husbands, brothers and sons, to take care of them. In lieu of increasing his army, it diminished daily. Those in it whose families had to move, left it to protect them. This lesson will be of service; and they now know that in order to keep their army strong, they must not allow the population to be driven off. Their former reencounters with the Mexicans have given them confidence. At the battle of Conception—the "Grass Fight," and the capture of San Antonio, the Mexicans were beaten successively: in the two first with four to one; in the latter with 350 to 1,300; and the 1,300 in the Alamo and in the town, with the walls of the houses as forts—yet they were stormed by 350 men, and after a fight of five days surrendered.—Then, in turn, when they (the Mexicans) attacked the Alamo—garrisoned by 180 Americans—the Mexicans several thousands—they lost 1,050 men before they captured it, and only succeeded finally, by a continued attack for many days and nights,

---

[i] A rarely considered explanation for Houston's retreat strategy after the Alamo.

wearing out the garrison; so that nature gave way under the continued fatigue; and when the Mexicans ceased the attack, no doubt to allow the garrison to fall asleep, they did so; and the Mexicans were upon the walls of the fort before they were discovered. The storming party, forced on by those behind, not inspired by enthusiastic love of country or courage, but by the fear of the bayonet behind; and here, though they massacred the garrison, they lost at least eight in killed and wounded, where they killed one. In Fannin's case, 300 or 400 men whipped five times their numbers—but the next day surrendered, because they were out of ammunition, and surrounded on all sides, a reinforcement having arrived in the night. In no instances, have the Mexicans, in fair fight, proved victors, (unless this may be called a victory,) except where they have killed every man; and the Americans know so well that they can whip them, and that their victories have not been the effect of accident, that they are doubly confident, and anxious for a contest, almost without regard to disparity of numbers. The Mexicans, very commonly when they fire, turn their heads away from the flash of the gun. They never take aim; and one shot of theirs, in one hundred, does not take effect; whereas one in ten of the Americans does. Hence the disparity in killed and wounded! But in physical strength, one American is equal to three Mexicans, hand to hand. Add to this their great superiority in courage, and you have a difference about equal to the demonstration at the battle of San Jacinto, where 680 Americans, in the open prairie, assailed 1,300—one half covered by a thick timber, and the other behind a breastwork of brush and baggage, lost 8, and killed 600, taking the remainder prisoners— And this army, the elite of the Mexicans, and commanded by their ablest Generals, not surprised either; for, on the day previous, they had a skirmish, and as a matter of course—as the two armies lay in sight of each other—a battle might be hourly looked for. It is said they have 15,000 men on their march. Not so, but suppose it to be so—3,000 Americans are a full match for them. But, suppose even this small number

should not be raised, and the Texians are driven back into the neutral ground—they will stand on tiptoe watching the first favorable moment to strike. Such an army of Mexicans cannot be long sustained by such an imbecile government as that of Mexico; for, the Texians will have the advantage at sea, and all provisions for the Mexican army must come over land from 4 to 600 miles. Each barrel of flour will cost in transportation, not less than $30 packed, as it must be, in sacks upon mules. As the Texians retreat, they will destroy the corn, and drive the cattle before them. The cost of sustaining 15,000 men, under such circumstances, will not be less than $2,000 per day, for bread alone, if it could be transported—but it could not be. It would, allowing 20 miles per day for a mule's journey, supposing the average transportation 500 miles, take 50 days to make a journey to and fro. If each mule carries a barrel of flour, there must arrive 75 mule loads per day, to suffice, or 50 to 75. 3,750 mules must be employed in the transportation, with drivers and guards. And would this line not be broken? Would there be no attack upon it? And where would be the provisions for the mules? Could they transport 200 pounds 20 miles per day, and live on grass? They could not. Let us see their ultimate condition. If they reach the borders of the neutral ground, Gen. Gaines there stops them. The Texians on the neutral ground are safe, and lie in wait for a fair opportunity to strike. Suppose none occurs, and, finally, the Mexicans, worn out as they must be, commence their retreat— then Gen. Gaines, finding no longer a necessity for regarding the neutral ground, disbands his army—how many of them will return home? Not one in three.—Two thirds will join the Texians. And now will commence a pursuit, and such a route will ensue as it sickens the heart to contemplate. The whole Mexican army will be annihilated, and the pursuers will probably sack the city of Mexico, before they stop.

In case the Texians are driven to the last extremity, the foregoing, I prophesy, is to be the winding up of the business. But, I believe the Mexicans will never cross the Brazos. View the subject in any way you please, and success to the Texians, eventually, is inevitable.—The Mexicans cannot keep a large standing army in Texas—they cannot occupy the whole country. And, as certain as fate, any small number of troops left there would be surprised and cut up in time. Let the Texians be beaten—they will not stay beaten. There is a recuperative quality in the American character, no where else to be found; and unless he is killed, his enemy is never out of danger from him. A crusade is now being preached against Mexico. Knights are buckling on their armour, in all directions, to avenge the cold-blooded butchery of Fannin and his men. Such a feverish excitement exists as cannot well be allayed. I view the days of the Government of Mexico as numbered. This campaign will not end without satisfying her own statesmen of that fact.

Few persons are aware that the Mexican Army is composed of a population at least half Indian; they seem, indeed, at first view to be all Indian but without the ferocity or spirit of the Indian—yet cruel and unforgiving, though tame in spirit, and cowardly in the extreme. They are the same race with a mixture, who were so easily overcome by Cortez; and if that mixture, aided by the use of fire-arms, makes them superior to their original subjects of Montezuma in battle—the greatly superior skill of the Americans over the troops of Cortez in the use of fire-arms, makes almost the same difference between the Americans and Mexicans now, that existed between Cortez' troops and the Mexicans formerly.

—*Richmond Enquirer*, September 2, 1836

The battle of the Alamo had already become iconic and its defenders models of inspiration to many Americans. At a festival in La Grange, Tennessee, in May, "Volunteer Toasts" were given by citizens to a number of people and institutions, including the following.

By Maj. E. T. Collins. The memory of Col. Travis. (Drank silent standing.)

By E. J. Moody. Col. Crockett—A second Samson—who piled his enemies heaps upon heaps, but with a different instrument.

By Dr. A. Goode. To the memory of David Crockett—Peace be to his ashes, for he was a patriot; and green be the turf that covers his body, for he was brave. (Drank silent and standing.)

By S. McManus. The Alamo of Texas—A modern Thermopylae—Another altar erected to civil and religious liberty, consecrated by the blood of a band of martyrs. The flames that consumed them have wafted their dying prayer to the throne of eternal justice in behalf of their suffering country.

—*Memphis Enquirer*, May 11, 1836

At a "Texian Dinner" in New York City's American Hotel, in July, attended by "distinguished individuals from different parts of the nation . . . who have evinced in their public or private capacities an interest in the success of the inhabitants of Texas in their contest with Mexico," speeches were given and toasts were made, among them the following to some heroes of the Revolution.

Col. Lewis, in a very excellent speech, in which he described the causes of the war in Texas, and her present condition, made a touching allusion to the death of the brave men, Fannin, Crockett, Milam, Bowie, and others, whose names ornamented a triumphal column, represented in a transparency which hung on one side of the room, and where the deathless record of their deeds was seen, borne by the goddess of America, of Fame, and of Liberty, encircling a laurel wreath, with the national colors of Texas and the United States, the name of Gen. Houston, the immortal avenger of those murdered heroes.

Behind the chair of the President, was the Texan standard, on a blood red field, with a large white star. On each side of it, in majestic folds, hung the American colors.

By W. J. Hanington—The memory of the fallen brave—may the massacre at the Alamo stimulate all freemen to avenge them.

(By guests) . . . The memory of David Crockett, whose life was sacrificed in the cause of Texas. To the surviving defenders of that country we say "go ahead."

—*New York Spectator*, July 21, 1836

The dramatic potential of the Alamo story was quickly recognized. It was still springtime 1836 when a play based on the battle was staged in Philadelphia.

Rather expeditious. "The "Fall of the Alamo" was brought out at the Arch Street Theatre, Thursday evening. Mr. Walton played Travis—the gallant commander not yet cold in his grave; and Hathwell personated the immortal Crockett; Mr. Darley did Santa Anna—Houston has done him better. The piece took well. (N.Y. Star.)[5]
—*Eastern Argus* (Maine), June 14, 1836

Capitalizing on the heroic death of David Crockett, Richard Penn Smith quickly wrote a spurious "memoir" of the frontier congressman's Texas experience, and it was rushed into publication that summer. Some ten thousand copies were sold in the space of a year, the public evidently assuming it was a genuine Crockett book.[6] Advertisements throughout the states trumpeted its debut, such as the following in a Baltimore newspaper.

Colonel Crockett's Exploits and Adventures in Texas, wherein is contained a full statement of his Journey from Tennessee to the Red River and Natchitoches, and thence across Texas to San Antonio, including his many Hair-Breadth Escapes together with a topographical, Historical, and Political view of Texas.
"Say, what can politicians do,
When things run riot, plague and vex us
But shoulder-flook, and strait anew
Cut stick, and *go ahead* in *Texas!!!!!!*
The Author written by himself. The narrative brought down from the Death of Col. Crockett to the Battle of San Jacinto, by an eyewitness.
For sale by   WM. & JOS. NEAL
No. 174 Market st.
—*Baltimore Gazette and Daily Advertiser,*
August 17, 1836

Not everyone was fooled, however. A writer in the *Western Monthly Magazine* commented on its authorship and on Crockett himself—man and myth—as extracted in the following from the review as reprinted in an Arkansas paper.

Goodnatured, inoffensive, humorous and playful, yet brave, spirited and full of shrewd common sense, was this same David Crockett. The cause of his remarkable celebrity is not so much that he was in himself remarkable as that he was the representative of a remarkable class of men—the Western settlers. He was completely identified with them. He loved them, and they loved him. He became their type—their reflected image—the embodiment of their peculiar characteristics. Many things are, therefore, ascribed to him which are only metaphorically true of him as such type and representative—and not actually true of him as an individual. The true David Crockett is an ideal, not an actual man. . . . The backwoodsmen have taken up our hero and adorned him with all the honors of their brief history and traditionary exploits. The wild mythological divinities of the Northmen have hardly performed more wonderful deeds than Crockett. They may have breakfasted upon whales, and bottled up the aurora borealis, and drank lakes, and eaten mountains at a meal. But David has greased the lightning and ridden it through a cane brake. He has breasted the rushing current of the fathers of waters, towing a dozen steamboats with his teeth. He has whipped his weight in cougars—grinned whole menageries into convulsions—and screamed the earthquake into silence. Nothing gives to the imagination such a romantic play as the wild life of a backwoodsman, or western boatman.

But as these thoughts would take us far beyond our limits, we will close this notice by giving some short extracts from the book. The book is probably written *for* David, and not *by* him. The tone is humorous throughout, except towards the close—the style is ingenious: but introduction of worn out anecdotes, sayings and newspaper stories, give it a *made up* and patched appearance. The best part of the volume is the description of the prairies, and Crockett's wild adventures with the bee hunter, the gambler, the politician, the herd of buffaloes, the drove of wild horses, the cougar and the party of the Comanche Indians. There is a great spirit and

Crockett's "Rifle, and Other Warlike Equipments" Brought into New York City

David Crockett was known to have brought more than one rifle with him on his journey to Texas in 1835–1836. Did he also bring more than one powder horn and bullet pouch? In the many years since the battle of the Alamo, personal relics supposedly associated with one defender or another have occasionally surfaced, if only a handful have had their historical ownership authenticated. In the case of Crockett, a few newspaper accounts in the summer of 1836 provide intriguing contemporary testimony to the fate of what apparently were his primary rifle and accouterments kit at the Alamo. We begin with a *New York Times* notice of a ship arrival listed in its July 26, 1836, edition.

> Ship News:
> Arrived, Ship Mexico, Kimball, from Vera Cruz July 3, with specie, hides, &c. to E. K. Collins.

That same day the *New York Evening-Post* detailed other things carried into port by the ship, not to mention delivering one of the few survivors of the Goliad massacre.

> LATEST FROM MEXICO.
>   By the arrival at New York, of the ship Mexican, Captain Kimball, the Editors of the New York Journal of Commerce have received Vera Cruz papers to the 1st July, and the Diario del Goberno of the City of Mexico, of the 26th June. Captain Kimball has brought on the rifle, powder horn, bullet pouch, &c., of Colonel David Crockett, given him by Captain Davis, of the Mexican navy, who obtained them from Colonel Bradburn, of the Mexican army. Came passenger in the Mexican, Mr. Joseph Henry Spohn, of New Orleans, one of the number who escaped during the massacre of Colonel Fannin's men.

On the twenty-seventh, the *New York Times* encapsulated the story as follows:

> Captain Kimball, of the ship Mexican, from Vera Cruz, has brought with him the rifle, and other warlike equipments of Colonel Crockett. He obtained them

(Continued)

from an officer in the Mexican navy, who received them from an officer in the Mexican army, who was present at the assault and capture of the Alamo—where the valorous Crockett was killed.

In fact the "officer in the Mexican army," the expatriate Kentuckian Col. John Bradburn, had *not* been present in San Antonio during the battle but instead had arrived "a few days after the action," in the words of Reuben Marmaduke Potter. Also according to Potter, Bradburn had gathered information about the engagement "from officers who were in it."[1] Presumably this is how he had also obtained Crockett's rifle, horn, and bullet pouch. (Antonio López de Santa Anna's officers had managed to salvage a few other prized pieces of Texian effects during the *soldados'* postbattle looting rampage, including William Barret Travis's saddlebags containing official documents and letters.) It had probably been no difficult identification process; the surviving noncombatants all knew the gregarious Crockett, and some were undoubtedly able to identify his "warlike" property. Or perhaps the items simply had his name on them.

As for the naval captain in the Mexican service, one Davis, the following extract from a letter written in Veracruz, dated March 8, 1836, offers slight additional detail.

> This government has resolved upon an increase of their Navy. . . . The schr. Bravo sailed on a cruise four days since, commanded by Davis, an American, for some years attached to the Mexican navy.
> —*Albany Evening Journal,* March 25, 1836

Evidently Bradburn, at least, had felt obliged to get the celebrated Crockett's property sent to a US port, although the process had taken over three months.

Just whom it was who had received these items is not made clear. Was the *New York Evening Post* saying that they had been given to the "Editors of the *New York Journal of Commerce*"? What their immediate fate was after their arrival in the city is not known. However, eight years later, the bullet pouch reappeared in Boston.

> TO ANTIQUARIANS. At the Apollo Saloon, near the National Theatre, are to be seen a ball pouch worn by Davy Crockett at the battle of the Alamo, and also a sword belonging to Capt. Miles Standish, who led the puritans against the Sipican Indians in 1639, where Mattepoisett now stands.
> —*Daily Evening Transcript* (Boston), January 11, 1844

After this, all of Crockett's "warlike equipments" seemed to vanish in the ether of time, although chances are they currently reside in private collections, their story unknown to both their latest owners, and thus to history.

And what should we make of the other accounts of Alamo-related Crockett rifles, such as the following from Alvia M. Ingram, who penned the life of her grandfather, Texas Revolution veteran John Ingram, as he related it to her? This extract concerns the aftermath of the battle of San Jacinto:

> Grandfather was also one who went with Captain Cook to escort Santa Anna's army back to LaBahia. On their way back they stopped at a ranch to rest a few days and there found a house that had locked in it all the guns of the men that were killed at the Alamo.
>
> There was but one whole gun there, that being Davy Crockett's. Grandfather knew the gun. It also had four inches of silver set in the barrel in four different places and "Davy Crockett" was engraved in the silver. Crockett had a nephew in the party who wanted the gun and grandfather gave it to him to take to the brave hero's wife, who lived in Tennessee.
>
> —*Dallas Morning News*, April 14, 1889

Finally, there is the following report from an 1889 Texas paper.

Davy Crockett.

Austin Statesman.

> Gen. King yesterday had a beautiful life size portrait of Davy Crockett, handsomely framed, placed in the hall of representatives. It is the work of Mrs. Henry M. Marchant of Texas. The hunting-shirt, coonskin cap, shot pouch, powder horn and bowie-knife were painted from the originals now preserved in the national museum. The features were taken from a portrait in the possession of David Crockett's grandson, and said to be the most perfect likeness of Crockett in existence. The picture is well executed and will rank high as a work of art. It should be placed in the portrait gallery in the new capital.
>
> —*Dallas Morning News*, March 18, 1889

---

1. Reuben M. Potter, *The Fall of the Alamo* (San Antonio, 1860), 15.

life in this part of the book, and there is also enough *vraisemblance* to make it interesting.
—*Arkansas Advocate*, December 16, 1836

On September 5, Houston received 79 percent of the vote to become the first citizen-elected president of the Republic of Texas. Meanwhile, his conquered nemesis Santa Anna—or at least a portrait of the Mexican general—was being offered to the public as a curiosity at twenty-five cents a view.

GENERALS SANTA ANNA AND COS.

THE proprietor of the St. Louis Museum has the pleasure to announce to his friends and the citizens of St. Louis and vicinity, that he has received two splendid likenesses of Gen. Don ANTONIO LOPEZ DE SANTA ANNA, President and Commander-in-Chief of the Army of the Republic of Mexico, and Gen. Cos, the brother-in-law of Santa Anna. The above mentioned likenesses have been examined by several gentlemen, who were personally acquainted Santa Anna and Cos, and pronounced them correct and excellent likenesses. They have also been examined by Mr. ISAAC FOSTER, who is direct from Texas, and was present at the battle of San Jacinto, when Santa Anna and Cos were brought in prisoners, whose certificate of their accuracy is subjoined.

———

Having just arrived in this city, from Texas, some handbills, advertising an exhibition of Generals Santa Anna and Cos, attracted my attention. Having been in most of the battles between the Texians and Mexicans, and also at the battle of San Jacinto, and present when Santa Anna and Cos were brought in prisoners, and stationed as one of the guard over them during their removal from San Jacinto to Galveston Island, I had a curiosity to call immediately at the St. Louis Museum, where I found two superb likenesses of Santa Anna and Cos, and with pleasure I recommend them to the public as very correct likenesses, both in physiognomy and stature. I have understood that an objection was made by some that Cos was represented too young. For the information of such, I will merely state that Cos is 24

years of age, and the brother in law of Santa Anna, (having married his sister.)
ISAAC FOSTER.

Doors open from 9 A. M. till 10 P. M. Admittance 25 cents; children half price.
ALBERT KOCH.
—*Daily Commercial Bulletin* (St. Louis), August 12, 1836

An unflattering description of Santa Anna's portrait, and of one made of Colonel Almonte, was published in a Natchez, Mississippi, newspaper and was later reprinted in a Detroit paper.

Portraits of Santa Anna and
Colonel Almonte.—
The portraits of these distinguished characters are now in exhibition at the Mississippi Hotel, and may be seen from nine o'clock A. M. to 9 P. M. The portraits are certified to be correct and striking likenesses not only by Santa Anna and Almonte themselves, but several distinguished citizens of Texas, who have sufficient cause to know them well.

Santa Anna is a man of medium size, dressed in a dark blue coat, light blue vest, with red trimmings upon the breast, gold buttons and a gold epaulette on each shoulder. He has an intellectual forehead and the contraction of his brows indicate a mind addicted to frequent and intense thought. The expression of his eye and the lower part of his face is that of a cold blooded assassin, smiling scornfully at the victims of his cruelty and bent upon the execution of his purpose with no other design than the gratification of a morbid ambition stimulated by the predominance of the animal propensities. The first impression of the portrait, uninfluenced by a knowledge of his deeds, is that of a man destitute of the finer feelings of the human heart, and evincing a contempt for every thing that serves not to gloat his unnatural appetite.

Colonel Almonte, is of Indian and Mexican descent, and is the son of General Morales of the Mexican Patriots, by an Indian woman of the Tlascala nation. He is of mulatto complexion, with an expression of countenance rather amiable than otherwise. His cerebral developments, however, show a predominance of the animal propensities over the intellectual faculties.

His dress is a light blue coat with a green collar, red belt and silver buttons. Those of our friends who have felt a deep interest in the affairs of Texas are now offered an opportunity to behold the object of their execration, at least in portraiture.

—*Natchez Free Trader.*
—*Democratic Free Press* (Detroit),
November 9, 1836

The identity of the artist of the aforementioned two portraits was revealed, along with additional details of the paintings, in an article first appearing in the *Texas Telegraph.*

From the Texas Telegraph, Aug. 2.

Major J. Strange, an artist from the United States, has taken bust likenesses of Gen. Santa Ana, and Col. Almonte, which, with those of the suite, are to be embodied into an historical painting, with the "Longwood" of Texas, and adjacent scenery.—Santa Ana's likeness is remarkably striking and correct; but the painter has not been so successful in delineating Almonte. Santa Ana is in his uniform, as Major General, (General de Division) the highest military grade known in the Mexican service, with the light blue sash of his rank; he bears three crosses, of three separate orders instituted by that government—to which, however, no pay is attached. Col. Almonte's portrait bears one cross, that of the epocha "Independence," with the uniform of colonel of cavalry. The artist intends to make a painting of Gen. Cos, now a prisoner on Galveston Island.

A letter signed by Santa Ana, manifesting his approval of his likeness, and that of no other of the same description has been taken to the United States, is in the possession of Major Strange.

(Major Strange arrived at New Orleans with his busts, on the 17th of August.)
—*New York Mercury,* September 15, 1836

As for the two captive subjects of the paintings, their fate was explained in the following report.

(Correspondence of the N. Y. Daily Express)
GEN. SANTA ANNA AND COL. ALMONTE
On board steamer Adriatic, Ohio river, near
LOUISVILLE, December 24, 1836.

Dear Sirs—We have among our passengers on board this steamer, Gen. Santa Anna and his secretary, Col. Almonte—also Cols. Hackley, Patton and Bee, of the Texan army. The latter persons act as protectors to Santa Anna during his journey to Washington City for the purpose of obtaining the mediation of the U. States Government, in a treaty in which he has promised to acknowledge the independence of Texas.

The Texan officers state that Santa Anna some time since, wrote to Gen. Jackson, requesting his mediation in such a treaty, and that the latter, in a written reply, stated that he could not mediate between parties, one of which was a prisoner of war. Therefore the Texan authorities have authorized his release and return to Mexico, for the purpose of securing a treaty recognizing their independence and obviating the difficulty stated by Gen. Jackson.

Now, if you will excuse this illegible communication on the ground that I write on board a steamboat in motion, I will attempt to describe to you as well as I can, the appearance of those two individuals, viz., Santa Anna and his Secretary.

Imagine to yourself a man of full ordinary stature, 40 years of age, weighing about 180 pounds, of graceful form and step, round shouldered, with black glossy hair, tolerably full white face and round forehead, a short, squarish, inferior looking nose, and a round, dark eye somewhat sunken. Suppose him dressed in a genteel trail-bodied black coat and blue pantaloons, walking about or sitting cross-legged in a pair of slip-shod pumps, tolerably pleasant of countenance and speech, (which is exclusively Spanish,) very polite, and using stately compliments.—Such is the appearance of Gen. *Antonio Lopez de Santa Anna.* He has, in my view, nothing military in his look, and nothing indicating great talents. He would readily be taken, I think, for an active, intelligent merchant or man of general business. He is very reserved, plain and modest in his conversation and manners, as far as I have observed him. I can see nothing villainous or deceitful in his countenance. Under his dark eye one can imagine (but not clearly perceive) a lurking demon.— I think that with the exception of an inferior stubby nose, he may be considered as elegant in figure and respectable in features. He confined himself to his State Room, under the pleas of indisposition, although it is well understood that his true reasons are, fear of the popular gaze, and an attack from some incensed person.

Col. Almonte, whom I will next introduce to you, has been almost constantly about the cabin cracking his jokes, as well as conversing freely and laughing heartily with all who are intimate with him or choose to seek his conversation. He is said to be 33 years of age—although a few would take him to be not over 25. He is of a copper or Indian complexion, with a thick head of straight, black glossy hair. Although he speaks the English language well, yet a glance at him convinces you that he is Mexican or Spaniard. He is a short, thick set, square built young man, with a large head and broad, open mouth and features—very muscular, active and lively. His countenance as well as conversation is very intelligent. There is a noble sincerity and frankness depicted in his countenance and manner. His dress is a frock coat and pantaloons of black cloth, with a cloth cap and genteel calf skin boots. He seems to be perfectly at home and quite happy. He is related to be very brave and of remarkable fortitude—as instances—it is related that while Santa Anna and the other Mexican officers at San Jacinto made their escape from the battle field—he continued rallying to the last 30 or 40 of his men; and when he saw that hope had fled he folded his arms and received the deliberate but erring shots of his enemies till Gen. Houston rescued him. Again, report says that when shackles were applied to him and Santa Anna, soon after their capture, that the latter complained and asked them to shoot him, while former smilingly said, *"that philosophers were sometimes obliged to submit to such things!"*

Yours, in haste.
—*Richmond Enquirer*, January 10, 1837

Captain Juan Seguín, who had been chosen by the Alamo garrison midway during the siege to carry a message to Houston, had returned to San Antonio on June 4, 1836—just eleven days after Andrade had evacuated the town and fort—with twenty-two men and took possession of Béxar "without any opposition whatsoever." Three months later, he was commissioned a lieutenant colonel in the cavalry of the Republic of Texas and was ordered by Texas secretary of war John A. Wharton to serve as commandant of Béxar and recruit men for both a regular battalion and the civic militia.[7] Seguín posted an advertisement in the *Houston Telegraph*.

NOTICE.

Having been authorized by the Government, to raise a corps of regular Cavalry for the army of Texas, in the county of San Antonio de Bexar, to serve during the present war, notice is hereby given to individuals desirous of enlisting for that time, to apply to the Lieut. Col. of Cavalry, John N. Seguin, commandant of Bexar, and they will be received on the terms prescribed by law.

JOHN N. SEGUIN.
Columbia, September 20, 1836.
—*Houston Telegraph*, October 25, 1836

News of Seguín's activities at San Antonio, and of the rumored approach of a new Mexican army, appeared in various newspapers over the next few months.

We learn from Col. SEGUIN, that a company of the enemy, some three weeks since, entered San Antonio, their object being to drive off cattle, and to annoy that portion of the Mexican citizens, favorable to our cause. Should our Mexicans friends receive harm from these predatory excursions of the enemy, they will, perhaps, in future, better appreciate the advice of and orders of our friend, Col. Seguin, who cautioned them of the danger of remaining in Bejar, and urged the necessity of their assisting him in driving off the stock, and removing eastward, which would be a proof to our government, of their attachment to the just cause in which we were engaged. But the good advice and admonition of Col. Seguin, were

From the Phil Collins Collection

Erastus "Deaf" Smith's Collection of Personal Effects

Erastus "Deaf" Smith was, without argument, an invaluable asset to the Texas Revolution and its endeavours; his heroic exploits need not be repeated here.

Pictured here are just some of the items he carried with him throughout his life. His pouch, powder horn, pistol, and knife, all believed to have once been owned by the renowned scout.

Let's consider first a general overview.

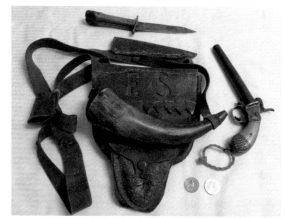

Quite clearly embossed on the "possibles" bag are the initials *E.S.* There are two major players in the Texas Revolution with the initials *E.S.* They are Erastus (Deaf) Smith and Ezekiel Smith, both important to the outcome of the events in Texas during the 1800s.

Because the pistol seen here has a percussion firing system, the mission was to discover who of those two men would be more likely to own one.

My good and learned friend and former Alamo curator Sam Nesmith, re-

membered reading reports that Capt. Edward Burleson had received three boxes of percussion caps prior to the Battle at San Jacinto *and* that Secretary of War Thomas Rusk reported "just as (Deaf) Smith fell, he drew his pistol and the percussion cap exploded without the gun going off."

(Continued)

Thus, proving that Deaf Smith did have a percussion pistol in his possession. Smith was not wounded and indeed went on to perform countless acts of bravery at San Jacinto that shaped the outcome of the bloodiest 18 minutes in Texas history.

The knife, a miniature Bowie knife, has an incredible detail, and it is difficult to see without close examination the initials *W.B.T.* on the knife guard.

William Barret Travis wrote a letter at the Alamo in February 1836, and it was delivered by Deaf Smith himself to Gov. Henry Smith, declaring that Smith was "the bravest of the brave" and should be well taken care of by the Texas authorities.

Clearly, Travis had the utmost respect and admiration for Deaf Smith. Therefore, it is possible that Travis gave this knife to Smith as a gift, someone that he knew would do all he could to gather and return with the much-needed reinforcements for the Alamo.

There is another tangible possibility that the knife was given to Deaf Smith by Travis's slave Joe, when Smith discovered him with Susanna Dickinson and her baby, Angelina, wandering aimlessly on the road out of San Antonio, shell-shocked by the awful carnage they had witnessed on their exit from the Alamo compound a few days previously.

Joe is said to have grabbed everything he could find after his master William had fallen dead. Suffering shock at what he was witnessing, he probably went to their quarters, and with the battle noise reduced to a distant rumble in his ears, he most likely rummaged around and gathered up all he could carry of both his and his Travis's possessions. These would have included personal items, weapons, papers, and things the colonel hadn't had time to pick up or organise having being awoken suddenly by the calls informing him of the dawn Mexican attack.

Whichever way it arrived in Deaf Smith's possession, one can be sure that it had once been the knife of Travis.

Another thing that suggests these articles being owned by Erastus "Deaf" Smith is that when another distinguished historian, Alex McDuffie, looked closer at the pistol, he unscrewed the pistol grip and found inside a silver *milagro* of a female wrapped in cloth.

Married to a young Tejana woman, Guadalupe Ruíz Durán, it was probably her gift of protection to Smith, and something he kept safe within the grip of his pistol.

Altogether a collection of breathtaking artefacts, once owned by a true hero of the Texas Revolution. –PC

little attended to; and we shall be truly glad, if the enemy and our pretended friends in Bejar, do not save us the trouble of securing the stock and other property west of the Guadaloupe.

Our enemy, no doubt, are doing what we should have done some time since. It is well enough to have assistance in effecting an object, and in a short time, we shall not be put to the trouble of driving stock, or taking care of Spanish cattle.

—*Houston Telegraph*, November 9, 1836

GALVESTON ISLAND, NOV. 5, 1836
The Mexican residents in the vicinity of

Bejar seem to expect a descent of the enemy soon, as they have been for some time past collecting their cattle for his subsistence. A party of the cavalry belonging to the corps of General Houston, who is now in command of the army, is detached for the purpose of preventing these movements, and has made some lucky captures.

Captain Sequin, who was stationed with a small body of men at Bejar, announced the arrival of forty mounted Mexicans at that place; he supposed them to be the advanced guard of a larger force, and made a retreat. It is not generally believed, however, that the Mexican army will return till January, or later.

—*Daily National Intelligencer* (Washington, D.C.), December 5, 1836

TEXAS—As our paper was put to press, news reached this place, that the Mexican advanced guard, 180 in number, had arrived at San Antonio, Fort Alamo, and taken possession. Red R. Gaz.

—*Richmond Enquirer,* December 13, 1836

The news of the appearance of the Mexicans at Bexar is contradicted by the same Red River Gazette which first published it. The truth is, that about 20 or 30 *Rancheros,* or Mexican farmers, brought to Bexar a great number of mules and horses for sale. At their approach the people fled, but when the real object of the visitors was known, they returned to town and bought the cattle. The Rancheros then retired to their Rancherias, or farms, and the alarm subsided.

—*Baltimore Gazette and Daily Advertiser,* December 22, 1836

By the politeness of Mr. Edward Linn, we learn that Col. Seguin, the untiring friend of Texas, has under his command at San Antonio, about eighty regular troops, Americans, and about two hundred Mexican citizen volunteers, under good subordination—that a strict police is constantly kept up, and is vigilant in keeping spies out westward. A Mexican, supposed to be a spy from his evasive answers, had been put into the calabozo a few days previous to Mr. Linn's departure.

—*Houston Telegraph*, December 17, 1836

Gen. Sam. Houston, president, has returned from the army, and reported in extraordinary health and fine spirits.—the most efficient body of men that he has ever seen to their number. He thinks that there are not twenty men in the army over forty years old. We learn that he has directed Gen. Felix Houston,[j] commanding the army, to order the collection, by Col. John N. Seguin, and interment of the ashes and bones of the immortal heroes, who fell at the Alamo, with all the honors of war. This is due to the brave, and we trust the day will come, when a monument will be erected to the memory of the first martyrs of constitutional liberty, on the spot where they perished, bearing the inscription of their names, and the deeds which valor alone can demand, or the present or future generations emulate and admire.

—*Houston Telegraph*, January 21, 1837

Our latest date from San Antonio is 26th ult., Col. Seguin had sent to head quarters five prisoners, which he had taken in that vicinity. They were direct from Laredo; little information as it regards the movement of the enemy could be obtained from these prisoners. Colonel Seguin had learned, however, that Bravo[k] was still in command of the Mexican force—was at Saltillo on the 10th Dec.; and it was thought by many the campaign would open in the spring; "that a majority of the Mexicans were opposed to the independence of Texas," but were anxious the question should be terminated in any way not derogatory to the national honor.

—*Houston Telegraph*, February 14, 1837

We have heard nothing from the west since our last to excite much interest. Col. Seguin is still at San Antonio: all quiet at that place on the 23d inst. Last year Santa Anna entered that place on the 24th of February. We hope he is

---

[j] Felix Huston.
[k] Gen. Nicholas Bravo.

now in Mexico, and we believe he is sufficiently acquainted with this country.

—*Houston Telegraph,* February 28, 1837

LATEST FROM TEXAS.
From the New Orleans Bulletin of March 6th.
Reports from San Antonio.
February 16th, 1837.
Gen. S. A. Johnson, commanding the Texian army, received communications from Col. Seguin at Bexar, that he received information that the town was to have been surprised and taken on the night of the 6th, by a party of Mexican cavalry from six to eight hundred strong, and some of the principal men of Bexar were to combine with them. Seguin instantly made prisoners of several of those personages, and took up his line of march for head quarters, where he was expected to arrive on the 18th inst. Our army is strong, and in high spirits, and anxious to encounter the foe.

—*Pennsylvania Freeman*, March 18, 1837

The most memorable assignment carried out by Seguín during his occupation of Béxar was the gathering of the ashes of the burned Alamo defenders from the grisly remnants of the funeral pyres, and the elaborate, dignified ceremony in which he had them buried.

In conformity with an order from the general commanding the army at head quarters, Col. Seguin, with his command stationed in Bexar, paid the honors of war to the remains of the heroes of the Alamo; the ashes were found in three places, the two smallest heaps were carefully collected,[8] placed in a coffin neatly covered with black, and having the names of Travis, Bowie and Crockett, engraved on the inside of the lid, and carried to Bexar and placed in the parish church, where the Texian flag, a rifle and a sword were laid upon it for the purpose of being accompanied by the procession, which was formed at 3 o'clock, on the 25th of February; the honors to be paid were announced in orders of the evening previous, and by the tolling knell from day-break to the hour of interment; at 4 o'clock the procession

moved from the church in Bexar, in the following order:

Field officers; staff officers; civil authorities; clergy; military not attached to the corps, and others.

| Pall bearers. | Coffin containing the ashes. | Pall bearers. |

Mourners and relatives; music; battalion; citizens.

The procession then passed through the principal street of the city, crossed the river, passed through the principal avenue on the other side, and halted at the place where the first ashes had been gathered; the coffin was then placed upon the spot, and three volleys of musquetry were discharged by one of the companies; the procession then moved on to the second spot, whence part of the ashes in the coffin had been taken, where the same honors were paid; the procession then proceeded to the principal spot, and place of interment, where the graves had been prepared, [and after] the coffin had been placed on the principal heap of ashes, Col. Seguin made the following address, in his native tongue, the Castillian:

(TRANSLATION.)

COMPANIONS IN ARMS!!! These hallowed relics which we have now the melancholy task of bearing onward to consign to their kindred earth, are all that remains of those heroic men who so nobly fell, valiantly defending yon towers of the Alamo! If they, my brave associates, preferred rather to die a thousand times, than basely to bow down under the vile yoke of tyranny, what a brilliant, what an illustrious example have they bequeathed to us! How worthy to illumine with unchanging splendor the ever growing pages of history! Even now the genius of liberty is looking down from her lofty seat, smiling with approbation upon our proceedings, and calling to us in the names of our departed brethren, Travis, Bowie, Crockett, and their iron-hearted band—bids us, in imitating their mighty deeds, to secure, like them, a high place upon the scroll of immortality. Since then, soldiers and fellow-citizens, undying fame is the glorious reward of those who fell in this noble contest, cheerfully will I encounter the most formidable dangers which fortune can crowd in the path of glory, in the noble attempt to achieve my country's independence, or regardless of whatever indignity the brutal ferocity of my enemies, may offer to my lifeless body, joyfully perish on the field of battle, shouting the warcry of these heroes; God and liberty, victory or death!!

Major Western then addressed the assemblage in the following words:

FELLOW SOLDIERS AND CITIZENS— Honors are due the brave! Upon us has devolved the duty of doing military honors to the immortal heroes of the Alamo, the bravest of the brave—a band of choice spirits who preferred death to slavery, and whose deeds of valor stand unparalleled on the pages of history.

Friends and compatriots—The spontaneous tear of sorrow I perceive glistens in every eye; but weep not the untimely fate of departed worth; for although in these ashes before us we behold naught but the tangible remains of a Travis, a Bowie, a Crockett, and their heroic companions, now mere dust returned to mother earth; their souls are with God in the regions of bliss, their memory is engraven on the heart of every votary of freedom throughout the universe, and their names are inscribed on the brightest shaft on the pinnacle of the temple of fame, lasting as time and imperishable as adamant.

Companions in arms!—At this moment and while we are performing this act of our sacred obligations to the valiant slain, the genius of liberty is hovering o'er this spot and with smiles of approbation at this grateful tribute of respect, beckons us onward to similar sacrifices at her shrine, and points to us the path to glory. Let us then, my brave fellows, upon this hallowed ground pledge ourselves to honor her call; let the noble acts of the illustrious dead stimulate us to vie with them in valor, and let our motto be—liberty! Texas free or death.

The coffin and all the ashes were then interred, and three volleys of musquetry were fired by the whole battalion.

JOHN N. SEGUIN, *Lieut. Col. Comm'dt.*

Thus have the last sad rites of a christian burial been performed over the remains of these brave men. In after times when peace shall have returned to smile upon our prosperous country, a towering fabric of architecture, shall be reared by their grateful countrymen above their ashes—designating Bexar as the monumental city of Texas, where long after the massive walls of the Alamo have crumbled into dust, the votaries of freedom shall yearly assemble at *this tomb of heroes,* the mighty achievements of the unreturning brave.

—*Houston Telegraph,* March 28, 1837

11

Memories, Legends, and Legacy

The Alamo and its heroes grew to near pantheon status in after years. David Crockett, William Barret Travis, James Bowie, James Butler Bonham, and Almeron Dickinson were names that commanded respect, celebration, and unending curiosity. To have been associated with them in any manner evoked great personal pride as well as inevitable public interest. Thus, when one of Crockett's sons was advised to try a run for a congressional seat, it was major news.

CROCKETT'S SON UP FOR CONGRESS.

John W. Crockett, Esq. of Trenton, Tenn. son of the late lamented Col. David Crockett, is proposed as a candidate for Congress, by a writer in the Paris West Tennessean. The writer says:

"This gentleman is truly the growth of our district—he is modest, patriotic, intelligent, and highly qualified, from his talents and information, to be a useful man to the public. He will devote himself honestly and wholly to the service of the people; and, if he will permit his name to be used, he will receive the support of MANY VOTERS."

We have heard the lamented Colonel Crockett speak of this son. He used to say, in Washington, to the Members of Congress, "They may laugh at my ignorance as much as they please—I never studied farther than *b-a-k-e-r*—but I have a son that is College-*larnt*, and he'll some of these days show them a thing or two." For the sake of the father, if for no other reason, we hope the son may reach Congress,

and fulfil the prophecy. If he should show Congress and our rulers "a thing or two," after the honest and independent manner of his sire, he will indeed "do the State some service."— North Alabamian.

—Arkansas Advocate, January 27, 1837

John Crockett quickly answered the summons to duty in this way.

From the Western Union [Trenton, Tennessee].
Mr. Editor.—In your paper of the 16th December, I discover a communication taken from the "Paris West Tennessean" over the signature of "Many Voters of Henry County," calling upon me for the use of my name as a candidate for Congress, in this District in the ensuing canvass; and in the last number I see that this call has been reiterated by "Many Voters of Dyer County." A call of this kind, coming from those among whom I resided for several years and who are intimately acquainted with me, cannot fail to inspire me with feelings of the deepest gratitude, and stimulate me to more vigorous exertions to qualify myself for usefulness. If I believe myself qualified to serve my country in a station so high and responsible, in a manner calculated to promote and advance the interests of the people, nothing would afford me more pleasure than to gratify the wishes of my friends. But I must candidly confess that "Many Voters of Dyer County" seeks to place a much higher estimate of my abilities than I do

myself. I have never, in any part of my life, had the least inclination to engage in political life, and if were so inclined at this time, the situation of my own private affairs is such as to render it absolutely impossible, without a total disregard of the obligations I owe to my family: and these I look upon as paramount to all others, except those I ow[e] to my Creator. I hope, therefore, my friends will excuse me and permit me to join them in the support of some other individual, from whose age and experience they may calculate on receiving more able and efficient service than I should be able to render them.

Respectfully,

Your ob't servant,

JOHN W. CROCKETT."

—*Arkansas Advocate,* February 3, 1837

Notwithstanding the young Crockett's protestations, he was swiftly persuaded to run for office and found himself elected by a wide margin as a Whig delegate to the Twenty-Fifth Congress, which began in March 1837.

Like Juan Seguín, Texian scout Erastus "Deaf" Smith had narrowly avoided being killed at the Alamo because Colonel Travis sent him to carry dispatches and other news to Governor Henry Smith on February 15, 1836, eight days before Santa Anna's army arrived in Béxar. Travis wrote the governor that Smith "has proven himself to be the bravest of the Brave in the cause of Texas."[1] Born about forty miles north of New York City in 1787, during his adolescence, Smith had moved with his family to Natchez, Mississippi Territory. By 1821, he had settled near San Antonio, eventually marrying a Mexican woman named Guadalupe.[2] The following article in a Houston newspaper attempted to summarize his heroic role in the Texas Revolution for those readers who knew little or nothing about him.

There is a personage familiarly called "Deaf Smith," (not Deaf Burke) of whom we know nothing further than the New Orleans American calls him the "Harvey Birch" of Texas[a]—*N. Y. paper.*

Having seen in some of the northern papers, a passing notice of this individual, who has distinguished himself here by his brave and decisive, as well as his patriotic and chivalric conduct in our revolution, it may not be amiss to know something more about him, than merely to permit his fame and actions to be wafted on their own merits, unrecorded to other climes. We will merely state what we know of him, and, contrary to all precedents, we will not begin his biography by saying that "he was born of poor, but respectable parents," for it is not intended that they should figure here.

On the morning of what was called the "grass fight" before Bexar, the writer was at the tent of Gen. Austin, when, at a distance, an elderly man came at full speed, over the rough and broken ground, on a noble horse, and gave the information that the enemy was receiving a large reinforcement by the Laredo road.

His singular costume, half Mexican and half American, together with the caparison of his horse, and the attention paid to his information, convinced me that he was *somebody.* On enquiring, I found that he was known in camp by the *sobriquet* of "Deaf Smith"—his real name, a subsequent enquiry proved to be Erastus Smith; that before the war he resided in Bexar, and married there; that on the approach of our army, he, heart and hand joined our cause, and brought his family into the American camp. To delineate his numerous feats of daring would be beyond our limits, but suffice it to say that he was in every action except that of La Bahia and the Fall of the Alamo. He particularly distinguished himself at Conception, at the grass fight, in the sundry skirmishes which happened about that time, he was always a party concerned—and he led the attack at the storming of the San Antonio. To the American army in the retreat from Gonzales to San Jacinto, he was particularly useful, and his capture of the Mexican courier was probably the cause of the battle, which sealed the independence of Texas, and, on that field, he increased the debt of gratitude the country owes him.

He has since been employed on the frontier, and he is well known, and much liked by every

---

[a] Harvey Birch is the title character of James Fenimore Cooper's *The Spy.* In 1830s Texas, the word *spy* was used to denote *scout.*

man in the army, and we have only to add that Texas cannot boast of a better citizen or a braver man than *"Deaf Smith."*

G. W. P.

—Houston Telegraph, March 28, 1837

The following report describes one of Smith's post–San Jacinto scouting excursions with a company of rangers along the still-dangerous Rio Grande frontier.

Deaf Smith, the far famed Spy of Texas, arrived at Columbia on the 5th from Loredo, on the Rio Grande, where he had been on a reconnoitering expedition with a party of 20. While in the neighborhood of Loredo on the 17th of March, he was attacked by a party of cavalry numbering near sixty, which commenced firing at the distance of one hundred and fifty yards. Smith ordered his men to reserve their fire until the Mexicans approached within gunshot. They did so, and on the first discharge of their pieces, the enemy retreated, leaving ten of their number dead on the field and carrying off ten others wounded. Smith's party obtained twenty of their horses and mules, with a quantity [of] blankets and other goods. Only 2 of the party were slightly wounded. From a prisoner whom they took Smith learned that there was a much larger force of cavalry stationed at Loredo and therefore deemed it best to return immediately to Santo Antonio, which place they reached on the 27th March.

—The Floridian, May 13, 1837

One of the best character studies and descriptions of Smith appeared in a number of newspapers during the summer of 1837.

DEAF SMITH.

There are few people who have not heard of Deaf Smith. He is one of the most daring of the many brave men who will be remembered in the history of the Texas revolution—a revolution in which reality has surpassed the fictions of romance.

As Jack, or Billy, or—Mr.—Smith, is next to no name at all, the Harvey Birch of Texas, is known by the simple *sobriquet* of *Deaf Smith—,*

his christian name (which I do not remember to have heard) being obsolete in speaking or writing of one who has rendered many signal services in the struggle for Texian independence and liberty. He is, (I suppose) about forty-five years old, of very muscular though not robust proportions, a little above the ordinary height, with a face deeply bronzed by severe exposure, a calm and not very unusual countenance, except the eye, which when "in the settlements," or in the social circle, indicates by its keen, searching glance, just enough to give warning of the intrepidity and energies of the spirit that slumbers within. He is a native of the State of New York, and went to Texas about the year 1822, in very feeble health. His constitution was soon renovated by the effects of a good climate and active exercise. He married a Mexican woman, by whom he had several children. He is a man of limited, plain education, speaks the Spanish language well, is a close observer of men and things, thoroughly acquainted with the manners and customs of the Mexicans, and with the topography of Texas and its frontiers. At the commencement of the revolution, he resided in the town of San Antonio or Bexar, on the San Antonio river, and about the period of its capture by the Mexicans, removed his family to Columbia, on the Brasos. He had been engaged, and with distinguished coolness and courage, in most of the hard fighting that has occurred in Texas, happening always to "drop in" as by chance, just on the eve of battle, though he was never regularly attached to the army. He has the entire confidence of the President and cabinet, and indeed of the citizens of Texas, with authority to detail such men and munitions as the dangerous and irregular excursions (in which he is continually engaged) require. On these excursions, he is accompanied by some twenty or thirty picked men, well equipped and mounted, who are generally commanded by a captain, who in turn is commanded by Mr.—Smith. Thus attended, he leads these scouting parties far into the interior, reconnoitering the outposts of the enemy, surprising their pickets, capturing their expresses, and bringing to head quarters the earliest and most authentic intelligence of events in Mexico. Such a man on such enterprises must have met many a perilous risk, and shed much blood. The history of what this man of the prairie and the woods has seen and suffered, would cast the fabulous heroism of romance in the shade.

Deaf Smith is a man of great modesty and propriety of deportment, and when he can be prevailed on to narrate some of his adventures, he does it as if he were not at all conscious of the thrilling interest which they are calculated to excite. Like thousands of others (who have been unjustly and ignorantly regarded as fighting for the spoil of conquest,) he has staked his life for liberty—against the oppression of a corrupt clergy, and an impotent court. Like his comrades in arms, he is nerved for the unequal (but already gloriously successful struggle) by the sacred impulses of freedom; and both he and they have learned to endure hardships, and to encounter dangers without a dollar in their pockets, or a ration in their knapsacks.

Deaf Smith bears the character of a frank, open-hearted, honest, and humane man—for humanity is a virtue not unknown in the camp—the best soldier is he who can and *does* feel for the sufferings, which duty compels him to inflict. He is very deaf, and hence his name. When asked one day, if he did not find much inconvenience from this defect, when on his campaigns, he answered—"No! I sometimes think it is an advantage—I have learned to keep a sharper look out—and am never disturbed by the whistling of a ball—I don't hear the bark, till I feel the bite."

Deaf Smith had just returned from one of his incursions on the Rio Grande, when I saw him. He brought back many horses and some valuable information as to the bungling movements of the inert Mexicans, and tarried just long enough to greet his family and refit his party, before he set out on another expedition. Several friends who had gone from the United States to see the young republic, joined him. They could not have found a better pioneer. As the party took leave of us, and moved off in fine cheer, I was struck with their appearance, and we mutually wondered if they would be recognized at *home* in their present caparison. Each was mounted on a mustang, (Deaf Smith's horse bore evident marks of superior breeding,) with a Mexican saddle, consisting of the bare tree, with a blanket or great coat girted over it, Mexican spurs (the shank about from one to two or three inches long)—bridles of ponderous and very rank bits—a Mexican *gourd** swung from the saddle bow—holsters—a pair of pistols and bowie knife in the belt, a rifle on the shoulder—a Mackinaw blanket rolled up *encroupe*—a *cabarrus* or rope of hair around the horse's neck (with which the animal is hobbled while he grazes at night)—a Sumpter mule either following or driven ahead, laden with supplies of salt, sugar, liquors, a small camp equipage, cooking implements, &c. &c. for the campaign.

---

* The Mexican gourd is a sort of natural bottle—growing in the most convenient possible shape for the traveller's purposes. It is large at each end and compressed in the middle, so as to hold a great deal, and to be easily handled or slung on the saddle.
—*Memphis Enquirer,* August 26, 1837

Deaf Smith did not survive 1837, dying in Richmond, Texas, on November 30, shortly after declining health forced him to resign from the ranging service.

For Joe, the former slave of Travis, there was no freedom to be had after the Alamo: after all, he was still the property of the Travis estate, and the executor of that estate was John Rice Jones, former postmaster general of Texas during its first year as a republic.

EXECUTOR'S NOTICE.

THE undersigned having been appointed the executor of the last will and testament of Wm. Barret Travis, deceased, requests all persons indebted to the estate to make immediate payment: and those having claims against it must present them within the time required by law, or they will be barred.

It is well known to all who had an acquaintance with colonel Travis that he was in possession of many papers of great value, either to himself or clients, of which it is believed many are missing. I would, therefore, respectfully request of all who may have any such papers, pamphlets, books, (either written or printed,) or other property, to deliver the same to me, or furnish such evidence as will enable me to procure them.

Marion, March 12, 1837.

JOHN R. JONES, Executor.

—*Houston Telegraph*, April 4, 1837

On April 21, Joe ran away from his new master, who posted another ad in the papers.

Fifty Dollars

Will be given for delivering to me on Bailey's Prairie, seven miles from Columbia, a negro man named Joe, belonging to the succession of the late Wm. Barret Travis, who took off with him a Mexican and two horses, saddles and bridles. The negro was in the Alamo with his master when it was taken; and was the only man from the colonies who was not put to death: he is about twenty-five years of age, five feet ten or eleven inches high, very black and good countenance: had on when he left, on the night of the 21st April ult. a dark mixed sattinet round jacket and new white cotton pantaloons. One of the horses taken is a bay, about 14 ½ hands high very heavy built, with a blaze in his face, a bushy mane and tail, and a sore back; also the property of said succession, the other horse is a chestnut sorrel, above 16 hands high. The saddles are of the Spanish form, but of American manufacture, and one of them covered with blue cloth. Forty dollars will be given for Joe and the small bay horse, (Shannon,) and ten dollars for the Mexican other horse and saddles and bridles.

If the runaways are taken more than one hundred miles from my residence, will pay all reasonable traveling expense, in addition to the above reward.

JOHN R. JONES, Ex'r of W. B. Travis.

Bailey's Prairie, May 21st, 1837.

—*Telegraph and Texas Register*,
August 26, 1837

Elected to the Texas Senate near the end of 1837, Juan Nepomuceno Seguín became the only Texian of Mexican blood then serving in that body.

Further Texian Items.

In the late Congress, which adjourned on the 24th ult., we perceive that the gallant young officer, Col. Seguin, Senator from San Antonio, made his speeches, which are said to have been short and pointed, in the Castilian tongue. He is the only member, of either House, that requires an interpreter. He is a noble-hearted man, and is one of the few in the Bexar neighborhood that adhered to the patriot cause in its darkest hour. When he took his seat in the Senate, one of his first official acts, was the introduction of a bill for the relief of the widows and orphans of the soldiers of his company, who fell at the storming of the Alamo.

—*Times-Picayune,* June 13, 1838

The legend of Jim Bowie began to burgeon in the immediate postbattle years; previous to this time, the knife was known more than the man. Now both became inseparable in fame—and not always in a favorable light.

CARRYING OF CONCEALED WEAPONS.

A correspondent, in this week's *National Enquirer,* justly ascribes the prevalence of this murderous custom, in America, to the influence of the cruel spirit of Slavery. It is strictly consistent with our knowledge of human nature, to suppose that men, habitually engaged in the support of the most outrageous tyranny, should look upon others, generally, as their enemies; and to sustain themselves in their wicked, reckless course, they must necessarily resort to all the acts of violence which vengeance, prompted by conscious guilt, may dictate. It is an indisputable fact, that, in no other part of the American Continent is the vileness of the human heart so conspicuously exhibited, as in our Southern and South-Western slave-holding States. In the latter, particularly, the boldest and the most daring are congregated. Trained in the school of wickedness and cruelty, they carry with them the principles thus imbibed, and the habits thus contracted, in their excursions abroad, whether they are in the pursuit of pleasure, fame, or fortune. As a proof of this, we may instance the violent occurrences at Nashville, Tennessee,—in which the Jacksons, Bentons, &c. exhibited their vindictive fury,—and the still more bloody scenes near Alexandria, in Louisiana, where the Bowies, Wrights, and others enacted their horrible deeds of murderous tragic ferocity.

Bowie, one of the last named, was the inventor of the tremendous *knife,* which is distinguished by his cognomen. In some degrees it resembles a butcher's *Cleaver!* The writer of this was acquainted with him at Monclova, in Mexico, a little more than two years since. He had the appearance of a man partially insane, —while the emblems of conscious bloodguiltiness were distinctly marked in the workings of his countenance. He finally closed his wicked career in the "Alamo," at San Antonio de Bexar, where he fell by the sword, a "martyr" in the cause of SLAVERY!

—*Pennsylvania Freeman*, March 25, 1837

The origin of the Bowie knife proved to be a favorite subject of discussion and one generally laced with speculation and inaccuracy.

The Bowie Knife.—A correspondent of the Baltimore Transcript, communicates some interesting facts respecting the origin and first use of the Bowie knife, being a sketch of Mr. Bowie the inventor. He was one of that class of men who are found only on the frontiers of civilization in the Western Sates, a second Daniel Boon—who had wandered from Kentucky into the western and wilder parts of Arkansas, where he could enjoy uninterrupted the pleasures of the chase. For some months he lived alone, supplying all his wants by his success in hunting, till his solitude was broken in upon by a wandering blacksmith. Bowie, had long wanted a weapon with which he could with greater safety attack the furious bears, which he found in the low marshy grounds thickly covered with canes, and where his rifle was useless. He soon struck a bargain with the blacksmith supplying him with provisions and skins, and he in return, under Bowie's directions, out of an *old file* fashioned the formidable and since famous Bowie knife. The instrument was twelve inches long, its point curved and hollowed at the back, cutting both ways, like a two edged sword. It was two inches broad at the hilt, and a proportional thickness.

Mr. Bowie, wearied of a life of solitude, after a time returned to the haunts of civilization, when he visited the banks of the Red River, where he learned that his brother was about to fight a duel. He hastened to the battle ground, where he found his brother and his antagonist in the act of taking aim at one another with their rifles. His brother's rifle missed fire, and his antagonist's shot passed harmless. Bowie then stepped up and offered his trusty weapon, observing that it never failed. It was accepted, and the other party provided himself with a butcher's cleaver, and the murderous conflict was renewed. Col. Bowie killed his antagonist, and ever after retained the fatal knife. Soon after he visited Philadelphia, where he engaged a mechanic to make a more perfect specimen of his brother's invention, who retained a model, which was soon sent to manufacturers at Smithfield, where thousands have since been made. Col. Bowie was killed at the taking of the Alamo, where Col. Crockett fought and died so bravely. He was murdered in his bed where he was confined by sickness at the time of the attack. "This is all of his Biography, 'He lived and he died'," and tho' his name is known in every corner of the United States, he did no act while living which should distinguish him from the common mass of men. His reputation fills every corner of the United States; but it is a reputation which is not to be desired, and was one which was not rightfully his own.

Respecting Mr. Bowie, the inventor of the knife, the correspondent before alluded to gives the following sketch of his character: "Mr. Bowie is well known in Louisiana, as an intelligent planter; kind and affable in his manners and as an enemy to violence. But he is also known as a man of courage and nice honor: never seeking a difference, and a peace maker

between others. When a real affront is given, he sees that it is righted. He has had his single combat. While in Havana, many years since, a Spanish gentleman reiterated his doubts; Mr. Bowie threw down the glove,—knives were selected;—Mr. Bowie desired that their feet might be shackled; the allusion was understood and the request acceded to—*Mr. Bowie lives*."
—*Jamestown Journal* (New York), June 27, 1838

Murders committed with Bowie knives became frequent news items in the papers of the late 1830s, and inspired this blistering "autobiography" of the weapon.

History of the First Bowie Knife.
WRITTEN BY ITSELF.
The following conceit appears in the N. York Transcript. Whether or not the sketch is faithful to the original, we leave to our readers to judge:—

I owe my existence to Resin Bowie. My first feats were among the bears. And the dying growls of many a one after a fierce contest, attest my science and courage. But I pass over, (for the present) this preface to a far more glorious career, and come to the time when, as Lord Byron says, "I awoke one morning and found myself famous." The following is the history of the part I took in the first *affair of honor* between two *gentlemen.* Col. James Bowie, the brother of Resin Bowie, had a trifling dispute with a neighbor, which they resolved to settle in an *honorable way!* They exchanged two shots without effect. Rezin, hearing of the combat, with genuine fraternal affection, hastened with me, (we had always been inseparable companions) to the assistance of his brother. We arrived just as the second shot had been exchanged. In single combat the exchange of shots twice without injury, always prove the parties *gentlemen.* According to the laws of *honor,* therefore the affair might now have been settled. But Resin Bowie, grateful for my services in destruction of the bears, wished now to give me more honorable work. And I, feeling a strong affection for the whole Bowie family, *thirsted* for the

blood of the Colonel's antagonist. Through the persuasion and kind offices of Resin, the contest was renewed. He presented me to the Colonel, whose antagonist had the assistance only of an ordinary butcher knife—my grooved two edged point soon proved my superiority. I entered the body of my friend's antagonist to the hilt, and was bathed in the sweet warm blood of his heart. When the Colonel withdrew me I knew that *Bowie Knife* would be immortal. I looked in unspeakable triumph at the agonized play of the muscles of the dying man's face, at the convulsive quivering of his lips, at the life blood fast bubbling through the passage I had made in this my first thrust for immortality. I watched till the last death sob and the glazed eye announced the work finished. But even yet my triumph was not complete. I saw the wife I had made a widow, and the children I had made fatherless and left to an unfeeling world without a protector, bewailing with frantic lamentations their bereavement. Then my triumph *was complete.* Suddenly I received the gift of second sight, and looked onward and onward; but what I saw, and what exploits I afterwards performed, I may hereafter tell.
—*Times Picayune*, July 13, 1837

Attempting to set the record straight about the origin of the Bowie knife—and threatening to "punish" anyone who denigrated the conduct of either himself or his family—Rezin Bowie submitted a letter to a Louisiana newspaper, parts of which were later extracted in a Wisconsin paper.

BOWIE KNIFE.—The Louisany Planters' Advocate contains a curious communication under the signature of Rezin P. Bowie, generally known as the father of the "Bowie knife," in reply to a writer in the Baltimore Transcript upon the history of that rather notorious weapon. He says that the Bowie Knife was made by himself in the Parish of Avoyelles, La., as a hunting knife, for which purpose it was used exclusively for many years, that it was nine and a quarter inches long, one inch and a half wide, single-edged, and blade not carved; that he loaned it to his brother James to defend himself against a man who had once shot him and who was expecting to renew the attack; that James subsequently made use of it in a rough fight or chance medley; in which it was the means of saving his life; and, that neither of the two brothers ever fought a duel with any person whatever. It appears from Mr. Bowie's closing paragraph, which we give below, that our brethren of the press must be pretty careful hereafter how they speak of Mr. B. and his family. As he is sire of the Bowie knife, that "hopeful blade" itself is of course of the family, and we must consequently abstain scrupulously from any imputation upon that:—*Lou. Jour.*

"I have born impertinent attacks for nearly ten years. During that period no opportunity has been lost to comment upon the conduct of my family; and the only grounds for this unwarantable interference are the facts which I have herein narrated. Whether they be or not be sufficient to justify such remarks, is immaterial, as I am resolved either to prevent a repetition of such mention of myself and family, or to punish those who have any agency in such publication. And I hereby state equivocally, that I shall hold an editor personally responsible for all such observations, original or communicated, found in his journal. I rely on the courtesy of all editors adverse to the invasion of the sanctity of the private reputation, to give this an insertion in their columns.

I am, sir, your obedient servant,

R. P. BOWIE.

Iberville, Aug. 34, 1838.

—*Wisconsin Enquirer*, November 15, 1838

Somewhat incongruously, while touring in the United States, the beautiful English actress Annette Nelson was given a Bowie knife as a gift, although it is not clear in the following brief reports if the knife was supposed to be the one Bowie had *actually* carried at the Alamo.

ELEGANT PRESENT FOR A LADY.
Miss Nelson, now at Cincinnati, has been presented with the Bowie knife which belonged to Col. Bowie, who was butchered at the fall of the Alamo.

—*Norfolk Advertiser,* August 4, 2010

It is stated in one of our exchange papers that Miss Nelson has been presented with the identical Bowie knife that Col. Bowie used at the Alamo.

—*Times-Picayune*, August 7, 1838

Now and then claims to the estates of deceased Alamo defenders were made, as in the following advertisements appearing in the *Houston Telegraph*.

Notice.

ELIZABETH ROWE having petitioned the judge of the probate court in and for the county of Gonzales at the June term, June 25th, 1838, for letters of administration in two cases, viz: on the estate of her former husband *James George*, late deceased in the Alamo; also in the case of her brother *William Dearduff*, who also fell in the Alamo. Now therefore it is ordered and decreed by the judge of the court of probate that when this advertisement shall have been published in a public newspaper 60 days, in compliance with the law, that if there be no objections that letters will issue to the said petitioned.

July 7   ELIZABETH ROWE.
—*Houston Telegraph,* July 7, 1838

REPUBLIC OF TEXAS,
County of Harrisburg.   Probate court,
Nov. 23, 1838.

JOHN JACOB MATTERN, of the free city of Frankfort, Germany, having this day applied, by attorney, for the succession of Peter Mattern, deceased, who was killed in the Alamo, in the month of March, 1836, claiming the inheritance as father of deceased. NOTICE is hereby given, for all persons interested to come forward, within sixty days, and make objections, if any they have, to the claim of the said John Jacob, as father and heir of Peter Mattern aforesaid.[b]

By order of the hon. Andrew Briscoe, judge of Probate.

J. A. SOUTHMAYED,
Cl'k of Probates per tem

---

[b] Peter Mattern had actually been one of the victims of the Goliad massacre, not the Alamo.

NOTICE is hereby given that letters of administration have been this day applied for in the courts of probate of Bexar, on the estate of Samuel Blair, deceased, soldier of the Texan army who fell at the Almo [sic], this notice is given to conform to an act passed the 18th day of May, 1838, all persons having any objection, can file the same within sixty days or appointment will be made.

JAMES McGLOIN, *Adm'r.*
San Antonio, Nov. 27, 1838
—Houston Telegraph, January 9, 1839

The Alamo itself quickly became a tourist destination for many travelers, domestic and international. A Maryland newspaper printed one early description of the fort, written less than three years after its fall.

THE ALAMO.—The eloquent writer of Summer Rambles in Texas, thus describes the ruins of the Alamo, in the last New Orleans Bulletin:

"The Alamo, now familiar to every one, is a military outpost to the city, established by the Spanish government in 1718, as a place of refuge and defense from the Indians. It is a quadrangular enclosure of about an acre of land, with walls of mud and freestone, about ten feet in height; and three in thickness, having barracks within the walls, and a church of great architectural strength and beauty, with a chime of three bells, and several statues of saints of exquisite chiseling, and worthy of Athens in her best days. They are now, however, a heap of ruins, having been destroyed by the Mexicans at the last storming of the Alamo, three years ago. The church and fortress are now as desolate as the dwellings of Monia. The flowers around seem to languish, and the birds sing less gaily. But the spirits of Bowie, and Travis, and Crockett, will hallow the scene forever, and render it dear to the pilgrim of liberty, and an object of interest to all ramblers, who, like myself, have been curious to learn the legends of this sunny land."

—The Sun (Maryland),
February 18, 1839

In January 1839, Mirabeau B. Lamar took office as the new president of the Texas Republic. His attitude toward most Indians was hard-hearted, and his policies sparked new hostilities between the settlers and the Cherokees and Comanches. An attempted parley with a large Comanche delegation in San Antonio's Council House on March 19, 1840, turned violent; seven Texian soldiers were killed and eight wounded. Of the Indians, thirty men and five noncombatants were killed, and thirty women, children, and old men were taken prisoner.[3] Around Béxar, tensions reached a fever pitch as Comanche vengeance raids often struck within gunshot of the town.

From the N. O. Courier of June 11.
FROM TEXAS.

North of San Antonio de Bexar, the Indians were more troublesome every day. A general movement against the savages, on the Trinity, Brassos, and Colorado rivers, was contemplated.

From the Austin (Texas) Sentinel, June 27.

On the 18th inst. James Campbell, of Gonzales, formerly of Tennessee, was killed, one mile below San Antonio, by the Indians. He had twenty six wounds.

On the same evening, a party of Indians made an attack upon four Mexican women, within one hundred yards of the Alamo, and shot one of them with an arrow in the shoulder. They were discovered by two gentlemen from the Alamo, who fired upon the Indians, and rescued the ladies. The Indians are represented as being very troublesome about San Antonio at this time.

Seven or eight of the Comanche prisoners made their escape a short time since, from San Antonio. One of them, called the rich squaw, had an infant child, which she killed—it not being convenient for her to carry it away.

—New York Spectator, July 23, 1840

The following account tells us that the aforementioned Indians, taken at the Council House affray, had been imprisoned within the ruins of the Alamo.

LATEST FROM SAN ANTONIO.

By an arrival late last evening from San Antonio we glean the following important items of news:—Capt. Pierce, commander of

Davy Crockett: Mexican Mine Slave

Like Elvis Presley, Davy Crockett would not stay dead for long. "Astounding news" came out of Texas shortly after the Alamo's fall: a badly wounded Crockett had been carried away from the battlefield "by some of his acquaintances," and was being nursed back to health in "comfortable lodgings."[1] Considering all the earlier published accounts that had verified his death at the fort, either by fighting to the end or by execution, most newspapers dismissed this latest report. "Must be a humbug," said the *Norfolk Advertiser* of May 14, 1836. And so quickly the story died.

Little over three years later, however, another newspaper account maintained again that Crockett *was*, indeed, still among the living.

> *Col. David Crocket.*—Extract of a letter from Holly Springs to a gentleman of Wheeling, dated 22d ult.
> "It is stated that Col. David Crocket, is yet alive, and in Mexico, working in the mines. There were two men, who were known to be in the battle of Alamo, passed through Memphis a few days ago, who say they escaped from the mines in Mexico, and that Crocket was certainly there—these men are known by some of the citizens of Memphis, to be men of respectability. These men went from Giles county, Tennessee. It will appear in a few days, and if it is the case, there will be at least ten thousand troops from Tennessee, volunteer in less than two weeks I am determined to go."
> —*Norwich Aurora* (Connecticut), September 18, 1839

A different, more elaborate spin on the preceding story, originally appearing in the *Austin City Gazette* in the early spring of 1840, was reprinted in many national papers.

COL. CROCKETT ALIVE
The following letter which appeared in an extra of the Austin Gazette of a late date, we copy from the New Orleans Bulletin. The story certainly partakes largely of the marvellous, and will require strong proof to give it credence, though we confess it bears the impress of truth:
COMARGO, TAMAULIPAS, Feb. 6, 1840.

(Continued)

To the Editor of the Austin City Gazette:

SIR:—I was formerly a citizen of the United States, and have been living in Mexico for 17 years. My business in this country is such, and has been, as to require me to travel from place to place. I was, not long since, at a mining district in Mexico, in the neighborhood of Guadelejera; and while there, a Mexican came to me, and said that there was a man from Texas, working in Salinas' mine, who had requested of him to ask the first American he saw, to come and see him, as he wished to send some word to a family he had left in the State of Tennessee. To enter a mine in Mexico you have to obtain permission from the worker or owner, and he sends with you the overseer, who is ordered to keep strict watch that you take out of the mines no ores or valuables.

I went to the owner, and obtaining permission, went with the overseers, and was taken to that passage of the mine where the convicts are placed to work. There were some 20 or 25 at work, and amongst them I recognised the manly form of one of my countrymen, who, the owner told me, was one of the prisoners brought on by a part of Filisola's division, when he retreated from Texas.

The American upon seeing me, stepped forward and grasping me by the hand, said "Well, stranger, you are the first American I have seen in this damned country; and I don't think I would have seen you, if I had not made a friend of one of these devils that oversee the mine."

"My unfortunate friend," I replied, "I have been made aware of the circumstances that placed you here, and they are such as to debar me from rendering you any assistance more than bearing for you any message which you may wish." "I know that," he returned, "so let us go about it: my name is David Crockett—I am from Tennessee, and have a family there—they think I am dead, and so does every one else; but they are mistaken. I should have written to them as the overseer told me I might, if I could get any body to take a letter for me; and thanks be to God, I have got one at last."

He related to me the particulars of his having been taken at Fort Alamo, at Bexar, and sent, together with two other men, to Loredo; from which place they had been removed; with a part of the army that moved to Monterrey—and when the troops marched from Monterrey to Mexico, they went to Guadelejera, and placed in the mine by the Alcalde, at which place they have been ever since.

He wrote a letter to be sent by me, to his wife and children in Tennessee, which I sent from Matamoras, with directions to mail it in New Orleans, retaining in my possession a copy thereof, for fear, by some mischance, it should miscarry.

To Lieut. Col. D. L. Wood, with whom I met in Loredo, I gave another copy, which he promised me to publish; but I have since heard he did not get in safe, which is the reason I write you by a Mexican, going from here to Bastrop and Austin. I have directed him to give it to any American he saw in either place, who would know where to send it.

In great haste, I am,

Your humble servant,

WM. C. WHITE.

—*New Hampshire Patriot*, April 20, 1840

The reaction in Texas was generally one of immediate skepticism.

We are afraid this is news much too good to be true. To say the most, it is extremely improbable, and should be received with caution. Should it prove a hoax, it is one of the most cruel kind, and its author would deserve universal censure! It would start again the dried up tear, and renew the wail of mourning. There are hearts in Tennessee that would beat quicker at the news, and the name of Crockett would be a spell to all to arm thousands of her chivalry; and no design would seem too daring or too improbable, the object of which was the restoration of Crockett. Presid't LAMAR has written to the family of Col. CROCKETT, and also to our consul in New Orleans, communicating the intelligence.

—*Brazoria Courier* (Texas), March 31, 1840

The story was still major news a few weeks later, as exemplified by the following:

CONFIRMATION OF THE COL. CROCKETT REPORT.___The St. Louis Bulletin of the 21st says, a gentleman arrived in that city the day previous, from the South, who brings news confirming the report that Crockett is a slave in the mines of Mexico. The letter spoken of in the previous account, has been received by Mrs. Crockett, and her son. The Hon. John W. Crockett has started for Mexico, with a view to regain his father. The whole South (says the Bulletin) is alive to the liberty of so noble a hearted man, and, if the present exertions of the son do not succeed, the Mexicans will have hot work of it before long. The Colonel's motto will be the motto of the South and for Texas. "Go ahead for Davy!"

—*Gloucester Telegraph* (Massachusetts), May 6, 1840

(Continued)

According to Dan Kilgore in *How Did Davy Die?*, the "William C. White" of the letter from Mexico was actually one David L. Wood, who had come to Texas in 1839 carrying a letter of recommendation from the Illinois secretary of state to President Mirabeau B. Lamar. Wood began publishing a newspaper in Texas devoted to literature and the sciences but resigned his post several weeks later due to political differences with his associate. Eventually indicted of the crime of miscegenation, he fled to Mexico, but why he invented the tale of Crockett as a Mexican mine slave remains a mystery.[2] How far Congressman John W. Crockett went in pursuit of his father is not known, but the tale itself soon died in the press. In after years it was occasionally revived by uninformed writers who stumbled upon the old reports and found them intriguing enough to republish.

1. *New York Sun*, May 2, 1836, from an article originally appearing in the *Philadelphia Gazette*. Rumors of Crockett dying even before he had reached Texas in 1835 had also circulated in the papers.
2. Dan Kilgore, *How Did Davy Die?* (College Station: Texas A & M University Press, 1978), 42–44.

the Pitkin Guards, has accidentally shot himself. Judge Campbell, of Seguin, and a Mexican woman, have been murdered by the Indians. Seven of the Comanche prisoners, together with the Queen, or principal squaw, have made their escape out of the Alamo. The Indians are becoming more and more troublesome.
    —*Austin City Gazette*, June 24, 1840

Events soon exploded into major battles with large bodies of Comanche warriors, in which the Texians eventually prevailed. As conditions on the Republic's frontiers settled down again, travelers resumed their visitations to San Antonio.

SAN ANTONIO OR BEXAR.
    Mr. George W. Kendall, the humorous Editor of the Picayune, is writing some interesting letters from Texas. The following description of San Antonio will be read with avidity by all who recollect the fate of the lamented Col. Crockett:
    "This place has been the scene of more and harder fought battles than any other city in America, and the marks left by cannonballs, and grape shot are still visible on many of the houses. The Alamo is now in ruins, but the different places where the heroes who so nobly defended it in 1836 were killed, are still standing, and the names of many of them, among others that of David Crockett as written by himself, are yet to be seen on the wall.
    "The houses here are all of one story with flat tops, are built of lime-stone of immense thickness and strength, have few or no windows, and were originally built for the double purpose of serving as habitations and forts. Indeed, one cannot stand in the centre of the public squares without imagining himself in the interior of a large fortification. Every man's house here is literally a castle in every sense of the word.
    "The population, which was formerly some fifteen thousand, has been reduced to three by the different revolutions, but it is now on the increase. Should things ever become settled and a peace with Mexico be agreed upon, the place will rapidly increase; for the climate is dry, healthy and beautiful, the situation the most

delightful in the world—the San Antonio river meanders through the centre of the city affording the best of water, and the country around is exceedingly fertile."

—*Jamestown Journal* (New York),
July 29, 1841

An editorial recommending that a monument be erected over the gravesite of the Alamo defenders appeared in an 1841 issue of the *Austin City Gazette*. It even suggested that it might do double duty as an observatory.

To-day it becomes our duty to announce the results of the election which has just terminated; the choice of the people has fallen on Houston, the Hero of San Jacinto, and Burleson, the Hero of the West. We cannot resist the temptation of embracing the present opportunity to suggest the propriety of some immediate steps being taken for the erection of some memento in testimony of a nation's gratitude, to point to future generations the spot which is consecrated by the ashes of the brave defenders of the Alamo.

We are aware that to many of our readers it will seem strange that we have chosen the present as a fit season for the advocacy of a project of this kind.—"Why," some will exclaim, "select the day on which you record the triumph of political aspirants, as a fit season to urge the erection of a monumental pile to the memory of departed heroes?" "Why," others will ask, "breach this subject now, when the people have little or no money to spare for such an undertaking; whereas, if you wait a little, business may improve and our currency, which is now depreciated, may become better, when, there can be no doubt, monuments will be erected not only at Bexar, but also at Goliad and San Jacinto." Yes, it may seem strange to some, and they may bring forward arguments like the above, but, prejudices apart, and what time could, in reality be more propitious to commence the advocacy of a monumental fame to record the deeds of heroes than the day on which we record the final results of the late election, which has resulted in the elevation, by the approving voice of their fellow-citizens, to the

highest offices in the gift of the people, of two of the heroes of that revolution which Travis, Crockett, Bowie and Milam died defending.

Unless a something be done, and done speedily, no trace will remain to mark the spot where the calcined ashes of the brave defenders of the Alamo lie scattered over the surface of the ground exposed to the action of the weather. At present there are few individuals in the city of Bexar who can point out the place, and in a few brief years they will be gathered to their fathers and all will be forgotten.

As to the cost, we hope that will never be allowed ever for an instant to enter into the conversation, for it would be comparatively a trifle; for all the materials necessary for the purpose are already collected on the ground. We allude to the ruins of the Alamo, the stone of which would be far more appropriate for the erection of a monument to its defenders than the most costly marble which Italy could furnish. And there breathes not one, we should hope, on Texian soil, so dead to every feeling for his adopted country's glory as to refuse to contribute his mite in such a cause; we know of many who, hard as the times at present are, would contribute liberally; not only so, should Texas not be able to raise the necessary sum at home, let it but be known in Tennessee that such a project was on foot and her gallant sons would not be backward in tendering their aid, for they claim, in common with Texas, an interest in the fame of Crockett and Travis. The battle field and the cause were ours—the heroes were originally hers. In like manner, Louisiana claims Bowie, South Carolina Bonham, and Kentucky Milam.* In fact, every state may be said to have its representative among those who fell defending or conquering the stone-built city of the West.

Ten thousand dollars would afford means, if not ample for the erection of a monumental pile to cope in splendor with the Bunker Hill Monument in the United States, yet fully sufficient to defray the expence of a good, substantial, plain fabric: one worthy of the occasion, and becoming a Republic. The edifice might even be so constructed as to be not only an ornament but a defence to Bexar—it might be so constructed that it would answer every purpose of a Martello Tower and an Observatory, thus combining the useful with the ornamental.

We are firmly of opinion that if subscription lists were opened in each county in the Republic, in Tennessee, Kentucky, and Louisiana, funds more than sufficient for the purpose could be obtained within the term of six months.

———

* We include Milam, although he fell not defending the Alamo he fell at the retaking of Bexar, and his bones repose in a court yard behind one of the houses there, without a stone, a block, or aught else to mark the spot.
    —*Austin City Gazette,* October 6, 1841

More stories and profiles of James and Rezin Bowie continued to see print.

(From the N. Orleans Picayune.)
PRAIRIE SKETCHES.
COL. JAMES BOWIE.—We are in possession of a little anecdote highly characteristic of those remarkable men, Col. James Bowie and his brother Rezin, which has never, we believe, yet appeared among the various printed relations of their battles, dangers, bravery, &c. that have met the public eye. The incident we are about to relate occurring among the wild prairie regions of Texas, we shall here introduce it among our prairie sketches.

Col. Bowie was undoubtedly a man of vigorous intellect as well as of firm and flintlike nerve. His character is one of bold and captivating individuality, and would form a magnificent study for some native novelist. We say "some," meaning only a few, and we will mention Simms as one; there are also "some" that we hope that will never mar so excellent a subject. From the wild forest life to which his bold and daring nature led him, and deeds and scenes in which he constantly appeared as the master-spirit, an untractable and coarse disposition is apt to be imputed to him, yet directly the opposite to this was one of Col. Bowie's most distinguished traits of character.—His manners in social intercourse were bland and gentle, so much so as to heighten materially the interest of his character. He spoke with a slow and impressive intonation, nicely *ar-tic-u-la-ting ev-e-ry* syllable he uttered, and with strict yet easy politeness observing every form of delicacy and good-breeding. In society he was stared at as a lion; but acquaintance attracted a gentler interest towards him, and it was curious as well as pleasant to find how the lord of the forest had known the embrace of the lamb. The following anecdote relates immediately to Rezin, but being here given as told by the Colonel himself, it will be found to convey a very vivid and just idea of both men's characters:

In one of the Texas wilds a brave little band of which the Colonel and Rezin, were, as usual the leading men, fell into an engagement with a vastly superior number of mounted Camanches. Upon detecting his red enemies, Col. Bowie so maneuvered his men as completely to conceal his inferiority of force, and securing a position for defence, he very coolly awaited the moment for action. A favorable chance for execution soon occurred and a few American rifles began to blaze away upon the savages in such a manner as to convince them that the party told about double its actual number. Still the Camanches were appearing in all directions, flying about in great force and the condition of the little American party became extremely critical; for, once knowing the possession of advantage, these Indians are sufficiently warlike, and daring to be of very respectable consideration as enemies, even to Americans; though, until they obtain this confidence they will seldom venture upon much hazard. Now, every moment seemed to convey information to the Camanches of the miserable weakness of Bowie's party, and the Colonel disposed his men with the coolest caution, in expectation of an overwhelming assault.

In such ticklish emergencies it is customary for a hunter to pat his good rifle affectionately, and say, "I'm sure of at least *one* man before I fall!" but it seems Rezin Bowie had made up his mind for two. Rezin possessed the best rifle in the camp—a weapon which was considered by connoisseurs a perfect prince of shooting irons, and with which its owner was as sure of his mark as of lifting food direct to his mouth. At this position of the opponents the Colonel observed his brother reclining behind a log, with his favorite rifle in rest across it, his eye to the sight, the hair trigger sprung, and his finger in place for sending out the well-directed leaden messenger.

Looking in the direction of Rezin's aim, the Col. saw two mounted Camanches (important chiefs, as appeared by the gleaming of their ornaments in the sun) dashing about, farther, than nearer apart, and seeming to be a pair of the most daring warriors, endeavoring to learn the true condition of the American party.— They were beyond the reach of any ordinary rifle, where they took care to keep; but the Col. knew that Rezin's beautiful weapon was equal to the distance, and wondered why he delayed firing.

"Brother Rezin," said the Colonel, in the smooth and deliberate manner which we have attempted to describe—"brother Rezin, do you not see those two red rascals wheeling about there, near each other? Why don't you pull one of them down from his horse?'

"Don't hurry me, brother James," returned Rezin, keeping his eye steadily upon the sight, and speaking slowly like the Colonel. "If I pull *one* of the red rascals down, brother, the other red rascal will get out of my reach; but wait till they *lap*, and then I'll pull them *both* down, brother James."

"They *did* lap, gentlemen," said Col. Bowie, and these were the brave fellow's own words, as he used to tell the story—they *"did* lap—Rezin pulled the trigger—and, as I am an honest gentleman, they *both fell from their horses!"*

The engagement with the Indians terminated with some loss for Bowie's party, but the two brothers lived to pass through many perilous adventures after that.

—*New Bedford Register,* July 14, 1841

Rezin's "perfect prince of shooting irons" was further described in the following article.

A ROARER.—Mr. Rees Fitzpatrick, gunsmith, Union street, Natchez, has the identical gun owned by the famous brothers, James and Resin Bowie, and used by them in their various border warfares. The Free Trader says it is just such a gun as many of our feather and pasteboard citizen soldiers now-a-days, could scarcely bring up to the aim. The weight of the gun is twenty-four pounds; the length of the barrel is four feet and one inch; the diameter of the bore seven-eights of an inch, carrying balls of only six to the pound. It was made in London, expressly to the order of James Bowie, and cost, at the time it was made, $96.

The Bowies used to say, that when the Indians were approaching them they were able to give them three effective shots with this gun before the yellow-skins could get near enough to make their rifles tell; and before this took place the battle was generally decided in favor of the big gun. The gun is of excellent workmanship, and if it could be seen in the northern cities would excite both admiration and astonishment. They would wonder that southern muscles were tough enough to wield such a formidable piece of border artillery, and learn better to appreciate the bones and sinews, as well as the brave and unconquerable hearts of the southerners.

—*Times Picayune*, August 18, 1841

As for the famed knife of the Bowies and its deadly reputation as well as origin, this scathing commentary appeared in a Washington, D.C., paper.

THE BOWIE KNIFE.

The far-famed, deadly instrument had its origin, we believe, in Hempstead county. The first knife of the land was made in this place by MR. JAMES H. BLACK, for a man named JAMES BOWIE, who was killed at the Alamo, in Texas, and hence it is sometimes called the Black knife sometimes the Bowie knife. The small dagger usually worn, in former times, has given place to this more formidable invention, and the Bowie knife, throughout the West is now the most common weapon of attack or defence. Could each of these knives speak for itself, what a catalogue of bloody deeds would be unfolded! One would tell of assassinations, and lawless assaults—another of murders committed in secret to gratify revenge or avarice, and another of unavoidable violence and unfortunate rencountres. What acts of infamy and moral degradations, what scenes of domestic sorrow and heart-rending distress would be exhibited! One would inform us how it was plunged, at the dead hour of night, into the bosom of its sleeping victim, and another tells us how it leaped forth to take sudden satisfaction for some fancied insult. Some would point to the Penetentiary and gallows—others to mourning and afflicted families and friends and exclaim—"We have been the instruments of men's passions—behold the fruits!"

But terrible as have been the uses of the Bowie-knife, we cannot say that if it had not been invented, the dark consequences of the passions of men would have been, in any great degree, prevented. As long as those passions are unsubdued, they will be liable to outbreaks, and would have found other instruments of vengeance if there had never been a Bowie-knife; and when we have improved our mind, and learned to govern our passions, and to confine them in their proper channels, we will have no use for Bowie-knives and pistols.

Whilst on this subject we cannot forbear mentioning the sad dispensation with which Mr. JAMES H. BLACK, the inventor of this knife has been visited. Several years since he lost his eyesight, and the green earth and shining heavens are to him alike, unchangeably dark. The events of the past must give employment to his mind, nor do we imagine that the thought of his having invented the Bowie-knife will for a moment disturb his bosom's lonely quietude for whilst the manufacture of the article afforded the means of a comfortable subsistence, its appearance did not create nor would its suppression have destroyed the stormy passions of the soul.
—*United States Telegraph,* December 8, 1841

Englishman William B. Nangle, inspired by Reuben Marmaduke Potter, set about designing and constructing a monument to the Alamo fallen, using

for his stone pieces of the dismantled fort itself. He planned to eventually place within it some of the ashes of the defenders.

RELICS OF THE ALAMO.—We have lately seen several beautiful miniature monuments, urns, candlesticks, vases, pipes, and other articles carved from the rock composing the walls of the Alamo, by Mr. Nangle. This gentleman with undefatigable industry, has devoted his whole time for the last two years to these pious labors; and with a zeal unexcelled by that of the noted "Old Mortality," whose name has been rescued from oblivion by the master spirit of Scottish story, has chiseled hundreds of monuments to perpetuate the glorious achievements of the first and bravest martyrs of Texian Freedom. Thrown by the pecuniary embarrassments of the times upon his own resources, he has by this means succeeded in procuring a scanty support.—Among other specimens of sculpture that he has completed, is a small monument about six feet high, consisting of a square column supported on a small square pedestal, and terminated by an urn neatly carved. The four faces of the column are ornamented with beautiful devices of various kinds, and appropriate inscriptions. He has also a portion of the soil containing the ashes of the heroes of the Alamo, which he intends to enclose in the monument. Under the expectation that it will be purchased by Congress, and placed in the Capitol, he has taken it to Austin, where it is now set up.—*Telegraph.*
—*Austin City Gazette,* February 2, 1842

According to the following article, the next year saw the appearance of another Alamo monument that sounds strangely like the one described above.

We find the following in the New Orleans Picayune, of the 2d inst:
THE ALAMO MONUMENT. An artist by the name of Cox is now in the city, preparing for public exhibition a beautiful monument, the production of which has cost him two years labor. It is constructed of white stone taken from the ruins of the Alamo. The design is chaste, the

work beautifully executed, and as a product of art it is worthy of comparison with any other of the kind. The names of all who fell at the Alamo are commemorated upon the stone, TRAVIS, CROCKETT, BOWIE, and BONHAM, appearing prominent upon the four sides of the obelisk. The upper panels present the following forcible sentences to the beholder:

To the God of the fearless and free is dedicated this Altar, made from the ruins of the Alamo.

Blood of heroes hath stained me; let the stones of the Alamo speak, that their immolation be not forgotten.

Be they enrolled with Leonidas in the host of the mighty dead.

Thermopylae had her messenger of defeat, but the Alamo had none.

Every Texan and every friend of Texas should visit the monument; and Texas herself should buy it and reward the artist, as we believe the Government is now aiming to do.

—*Daily Evening Transcript* (Boston), December 15, 1843

If the government was planning on buying the monument, such a purchase was never made because three months later it was put up for auction—slated for the eighth anniversary of the Alamo battle—and this advertisement placed in a New Orleans paper.

The Alamo Monument.
BY J. A. BEARD & RICHARDSON
WILL be sold at auction, on WEDNESDAY, the 6th March, at 11 o'clock, at the Auction Mart, Camp street—

The ALAMO MONUMENT which has been lately exhibited in this city. This celebrated piece of sculpture has been carved from the bloody-consecrated walls of the famed Alamo, and commemorating the immortal deeds of the gallant band of heroes whose names are carved on this splendid monument.

The sale will be positive, as the owners are compelled to sell from necessity. Terms at sale.

—*Times-Picayune,* March 1, 1844

Other artists and writers found inspiration in the ruins of the Alamo. One traveler not only described the Alamo but also its sister missions, the town of San Antonio de Béxar, and the history that had happened there just a handful of years earlier.

SAN ANTONIO.

We take the following description of the Texas city, San Antonio, from the series of articles on the Santa Fe Expedition, which George W. Kendall, Esq., recently returned from Mexico, is writing for the Picayune:—

The most pleasant place in Texas, and perhaps I might say in any part of America in possession of the Anglo-Saxon race, is San Antonio, or Bexar as it is perhaps more frequently called. The San Antonio river, which heads a short distance above, meanders through the city, and its limpid waters, from the different turns it makes and the irrigating canals, are brought within a convenient distance of every door. The temperature of the water is the same the year round, is neither too hot nor too cold for bathing, and a day does no pass without all the inhabitants enjoying the healthy and invigorating luxury of swimming. We say *all*—for men, women and children can be seen at any time in the river, splashing, paddling and diving about, like so many Sandwich Islanders. The women in particular are celebrated for their fondness for and skill in aquatic sports, and are excellent swimmers.

The climate is pure, dry and healthy, so much so that the old remark of "if a man wants to die there he must go somewhere else," appears specially to apply to San Antonio. During the summer months a cool and delicious breeze is blowing, bringing comfort and health. As but little rain falls, the rich and fertile bottoms of the romantic river are watered by irrigating ditches, which takes the pure waters of the San Antonio in every direction.

By far the greatest curiosities in the neighborhood of the city are the *Missions.* Before describing these immense establishments it is necessary for me to state that early after the settlement of Mexico, one of the chief objects of its policy was connected with the extension of the authority of the Catholic Church. The conversion of the Indians and the promulgation of Christianity were interwoven with the desire of wealth and an apparent religious fervor. However wanting in that true feeling of piety with which such objects should be sought, they produced some of the most remarkable incidents in the history of the country. The new doctrines were first inculcated by force and cruelty, but subsequently in a more humane temper, by allowing the superstitions of the Indians to mix with the rites introduced among them. And to this day, the anomalous consequences of this policy are to be seen in the Indian ceremonies, some of which I will describe when I shall hereafter speak of our journey through the States of Guanajuto and Mexico. For the purpose, however, of affording protection to the Roman Catholic missionaries, there were established at various times settlements which still bear the name of Missions. They are very numerous throughout California, and in Texas there are several. The Almo [sic] at San Antonio was one of much importance, and there were others hardly of less consideration in the neighborhood, called the Missions of Conception, of San Juan, San Jose and La Espada. All of them were most substantially built; the walls are of great thickness, and in their form and arrangement they were frontier fortresses. They have generally, though not always, a church at the side of a square having one entrance. On the outside they present the form of a blank square wall. In the interior they had a large granary, and the outside wall formed the back of a series of dwellings in which the missionaries and their converts lived. There was a large appropriation of the surrounding district for the purpose of cultivation, through which small canals were made for the purpose of irrigation. Such at least is the case with those Missions which I have mentioned. The Al[a]mo is now in ruins, only two or three houses of the inner square being inhabited. The gateway of the church was much ornamented and still remains, though deprived of the figures which once occupied its niches. But there is enough still to interest the inquirer of its former history, even if he could for a moment forget the scenes which have made it celebrated in the history of Texan independence.

About two miles lower down the San Antonio river is the Mission of Conception. It is a very large stone building, with a fine cupola, and, though a plain building, is magnificent in its dimensions and the durability of its construction. Here Bowie fought one of the first battles with the Mexican forces, and it has not since been inhabited. Though not so well known to fame as other conflicts, this fight was that which really committed the Texans and compelled those who thought of terms and the maintenance of a Mexican connection to see that the time for both had passed. The mission of San Jose is about a mile and a half further down the river. It consists, also, of a large square, and numerous Mexican families still live there. To the left of the gateway is the granary. The church stands apart from the other buildings in the square, but not in the centre; the west door is surrounded with most elaborate stone carvings of flowers, images of angels and figures of apostles. The interior is plain. To the right is a handsome tower and belfry, and above the altar a large stone cupola.

Behind the church and in connection with it is a long range of rooms for the missionaries, opening in a covered gallery of *portales* of nine arches.—Though the Texan troops were long quartered here the stone carvings have not been injured. The church has been repaired and divine service performed in it. About half a mile further down is the Mission of San Juan. The church forms part of the side of the square; it is a plain simple building with little ornament. The adjacent buildings are poor and out of repair. The granary stands alone in the square and on the north-west corner of the square are the remains of a small stone tower. The other Mission, that of La Espada, is also inhabited as well as the last. The church, however, is in ruins. Two sides of the square consist of mere walls; the other sides are composed of dwellings as in the other instances.

The church of San Antonio was built in the year 1717; and although it has suffered much from the ravages of time and the different sieges which the city has undergone is still used as a place of public worship. At the time San

Antonio was attacked and taken by Cole, Cooke and Milam, in 1839,[c] Gen. Cos made the belfry of this church his head-quarters. A well-directed cannon shot from the Texans struck just above the Mexican general's head, inducing him to evacuate the place with his staff immediately. The hole made by the ball is still visible, and in fact all the houses in the principal square of the town are marked more or less by shot.

At one time the city contained some twelve or fifteen thousand inhabitants; but the different revolutions, the many bloody battles which have been fought within its walls, and the unsettled state of the frontiers, have combined to lessen the number materially. It is still, however, a place of no inconsiderable trade, and should a peace be made with Mexico it will regain its former standing.

—*New Bedford Mercury*, July 1, 1842

From Philadelphia came the following brief report of yet another theatrical play depicting the battle of the Alamo.

The theatres are doing a smashing business. The circus was crowded last evening, so was Burton's theatre, and also the Ethiopian Opera House, and the Chestnut St. The Arch street had the corps of National Grays in their new and splendid uniform at the performance last evening. Texas, or the Massacre at the Alamo was the afterpiece, in which Colonel Crockett is the principal character, and is made to pile Mexican soldiers on the stage in fine style till killed off himself. Tonight Burton's piece of the "Three stages of loafing," in which the principal characters are borne by Burton himself, and Knight is to be brought, and Colonel Crockett is to die, in the afterpeice of Texas, for the last time, as is said, at this theatre.

—*New York Herald,* March 26, 1845

In his last act as president, John Tyler invited Texas into the Union on March 1, 1845. On March 4, James K. Polk took office and, anticipating war with Mexico because of the annexation, sent General Zachary Taylor with fourteen hundred troops to Corpus Christi, a Texas coastal town. While stationed there in September, an unidentified officer of Col. David Twigg's Second Regiment of US Dragoons wrote a letter describing those parts of Texas he had seen, and some of its people, extracts of which follow.

Twenty-five miles from Victoria, due west, is the town of Goliad, near which place you will recollect Fannin and his party capitulated to the Mexicans and were subsequently massacred. Goliad is a beautiful place, strongly fortified with quarters sufficient for one thousand men, and space within the walls of the fort to maneuver a regiment. The whole place is in ruins—not a soul of the 25,000 who formerly inhabited the place is left. Near the town on the opposite side of the river are the remains of a large convent. This place was abandoned in 1836; it will probably never be occupied again, as the town, as far as I can see, possesses not one single advantage to authorise it.—The soil is fertile, but the whole country looks bleak and barren for want of trees. It is somewhat strange that many of the river banks are destitute of timber. Goliad will long be remembered on account of the outrageous massacre of the 400 men, under the brave but unfortunate Fannin. . . . We buy good serviceable ponies here for $2.50, mules for $10 or $15. It is an interesting sight to see the Mexicans among their ponies and mules. A company composed this way is called a *caviad.* Their dress is the old Spanish hat, broad brim, high-pointed crown, a hirongo manufactured in the shape of a blanket by the women of the country (very costly), lower garments of leather; their legs, &c. protected by dressed goatskin, the whole fastened with a leather or hair girth, in which are stuck divers pistols, knives, &c.; their heels are armed with the most enormous spurs, around the pommel of the saddle is carried a lasso with which they catch their mustangs.

—*Macon Weekly Telegraph* (Georgia), October 21, 1845

[c] Actually in 1835.

In 1846, the first battles between US and Mexican troops broke out in Texas and thereafter south of the border. Reinforcements from the United States rendezvoused at San Antonio. One soldier stationed at "Camp Crockett, Near San Antonio," wrote a letter home to a friend in Missouri on September 2.

San Antonio is mostly upon the western side of the river, and is a singular looking place. The houses are all built for defence—heavy and low—but large, with flat roofs. It now contains about 1,200 inhabitants but formerly it contained 10,000. There are a few—and but few—Americans. We boys (as the volunteers are called) sometimes get to town and take a round. The principal amusement is the fandango. The boys go in and pay a dollar, dance with some black eyed Spanish girl, and pass the night lightly off. The [illegible] and gaming houses are well patronized by both sexes of the Mexicans, and the young Spanish girls and men, at night, when it is time will all go together to bathe in the river.

Opposite the town, and on this side of the river, stands the old Alamo, celebrated as the death place of Crocket, and one of the most bloody massacres that ever disgraced earth. A small body of Texans, 150 men under the command of Travers, took shelter at this place from 2000 Mexicans, and, after a most bloody and long fight, were overpowered, and every soul with the exception of one old negro woman, massacred. They were most cruelly murdered, and then left to rot in the vaults of the Alamo. At length the bodies were collected and burned in the largest room, and the bones are still scattered about the place—large piles of fuel are to be seen. The marks are still upon the walls, and show to the observer that the strife was dreadful. The marks of balls and axes, and the prints of bloody hands upon every part of the Alamo, tell that the slaughter was prodigious.

—*Philadelphia Public Ledger*,
October 22, 1846

One US officer, who had apparently made a point while in San Antonio of gathering together as much information about the siege and battle that he could,

penned a vivid and stirring—and at times melodramatic—account that was printed in a great number of US papers.

The Alamo.
ITS HEROIC DEFENCE BY TEXANS
IN 1836.

"Remember the Alamo!" was the war-cry of the Texans at the battle of San Jacinto, and well it might have been, for no other cry would have been so effectual in nerving their arms for the work before them. The defense of the Alamo stands preeminent among the most desperate works of bravery recorded in history, and was distinguished even in the unequal and bloody contest for Texan Independence.

Gen. Wool, of the U. S. Army, destined for Chihuahua, had his head quarters for a long time at San Antonio de Bexar, near which place stands the ruins of the Alamo. An officer of this army gives the following graphic account of the defence of the Alamo in a letter to a friend, which letter was sent to the National Intelligencer for publication. The letter is dated San Antonio de Bexar, (Texas) August 24, 1846.

On the 14th inst, I wrote you a brief letter announcing my arrival at this place.—We are so far removed from the United States that intercourse is almost prohibited. Mails are so irregular that no reliance is to be placed on them, and private expresses to La Baco, and thence to New Orleans, by any vessel that offers, form the most common means of transmission. This place is very different from any in the republic as it was, and the houses and streets are not more extraordinary than the habits and appearance of the people. The most interesting object, however, in the vicinity, is the Alamo. It is now a shapeless mass of ruins. The chapel is much defaced and broken down, and the walls of the fort are fast crumbling to decay. Time and the elements have almost completed what the Mexican artillery commenced, and the coliseum of Texas will soon form but a shattered and mournful monument of its own existence.

On the 23d day of February, 1836, Santa Anna entered San Antonio de Bexar, and took possession of the town without firing a gun. The small garrison of 130 men, under command of Wm. Barrett Travis, retired, as he had advanced to the Alamo, on the opposite side of the river, determined there to offer whatever resistance to the progress of the tyrant that God and their own energies should permit. Flushed with the conquest so easily effected, of the town, the Mexican general prepared, for an immediate attack upon the Alamo. He ordered breastworks to be thrown up on every commanding point and artillery to be planted wherever it could be made most effective. One battery was completed on the right hand of the river, by the 25th, and on this day the siege commenced.

It is a dark and gloomy morning, devoted to a dark and unholy purpose. Exulting in the work of death, upon which he is entering, Santa Anna crosses the river, the better to behold the success of his designs, and establishes his head quarters in a small stone building yet standing. The signal is given and ere the sun has risen upon the scene, the roar of artillery, from the Mexican battery awakens the echoes far and wide, and rouses from their slumber the yet sleeping inhabitants. But the defenders of the Alamo have not lost sight for a single moment of their wily and remorseless enemy; they watch the studied direction of every gun; they see the match lighted; they listen breathless, as if even at that distance they could hear the command to fire; and when it does come, and the walls of that citadel tremble under the shock of the iron hail, and the fragments of stone are whirled aloft by the sudden impulse, they send back a shout of defiance, mingled with the discharge from their own guns, almost as deafening as the thunder of their assailants. Before the smoke rolls away, and the reverberations are lost in the distance, while the shouts of the besieged still linger on the ears of the besiegers, the cannonade is renewed, and for 7 hours, fiercely continued upon the walls of the Alamo. But these walls yield no more than the spirits of their defenders. The fire is steadily returned; and though stones are shivered, around them, there are stout hearts and willing hands ready to repair every breach, and to restore from the interior whatever may have been destroyed

from without. Earth is thrown up; every crack or fissure closed as fast as created; by the eager efforts of those who will permit no evidence of success, to cheer the hopes of their enemy. The sun has almost sunk behind the western plains when there is a pause in the work of demolition. The firing ceased for the day by order of the Mexican commander, with his thirst for blood unsatiated, for not a single drop has fallen within the Alamo. Many of his own men have bit the dust, before the artillerists and riflemen of the fort; but thus far they are unavenged.— Darkness falls upon besieger and besieged; the former raise new entrenchments to prosecute the assault; the latter establish a watch for the night, and endeavor to seek that repose which shall give them fresh vigor for the contest which they know will come tomorrow.

The morning of the 26th dawns, and reveals to the occupants of the fort the effect of the midnight labors of their enemy, in the establishment of two additional batteries with the Almeda of the Alamo. The bayonets of the infantry, crossed over the river during the night, glitter in the morning beams, and the plumes of the cavalry are seen waving on the eastern hills, to intercept the expected aid, from that quarter. The contest is renewed by a slight skirmish between a few of the Texans, sent in quest of wood and water, and a detachment under the Mexican General Sesma; this is a mere overture to the grand performance of the day. The thunders of the heavy ordnance under the direction of Col. Ampudia, are soon roused into action; volley after volley is poured into the fort, and answered only except at rare intervals, by the shouts of those within. There is no pause, no cessation. Still the cannonade goes on; shells fly hissing through the air, and balls bury themselves within the ramparts; but night comes on, and the Mexican general can see no progress. Baffled, but not discouraged, he advances his line of posts, and prepares with the morning light to enter again upon his task. The north wind sweeps in Texas; a storming lullaby to the storming passions of those contending hosts. The darkness is broken only by the feeble blaze of a few huts, fired by the Texans, which have furnished a cover to their enemy. The flames curl upwards with a sickly glare, throw a fitful light for a moment upon the slumbering army and expire. The reign of darkness and of silence resumed.

On the next day, the Mexicans appear inactive. There is but little firing on either side. Those within the fort, with spirits unsubdued, and with energies weakened but not exhausted, are applying their limited resources to the purpose of defence. No heart falters; no pulse throbs with diminished power; no hand shrinks from the labor that necessity imposes; all is confidence and determination; a firm reliance springing from the holiness of the cause, and the certainty of its final triumph. Sunday follows; but brings no rest to those whom God had created in his own image, yet endowed with such unhallowed passions. Perhaps within the chapel of the Alamo, consecrated to the worship of the Almighty, and distinguished by the emblems of man's salvation which surmounts the dome, heads may be bowed in prayer to the God of battles for deliverance from their sanguinary foe; but that foe takes no heed of Sabbaths. Exclusive followers, as they claim themselves, of the true church, they doom to destruction, the very temple they have erected to its worship; and, kissing the cross suspended from their necks, and planted before every camp, they point their guns upon the image of that Saviour they once made the tutelary deity of the Alamo. The fire of their artillery keeps company with the minutes as they roll on.

Morning, mid day and evening are passed yet there is no faltering among those who are defending the Thermopylae of Texas.—Another sun rises and sets, and yet another still the indomitable hearts within quail not before the unceasing efforts of their enemy. In spite of that enemy's vindictive vigilance the little garrison receives from Gonzales a reinforcement of 33 men; additional victims for the funeral pyre, soon to be kindled by Santa Anna on the surrounding hills, as a human hecatomb to Mexican vengeance.

New batteries are erected by the besiegers; from every point around the missiles of destruction concentrate upon the Alamo.—The circles grow smaller and smaller. The final hour must come soon. Provisions are not yet exhausted, but the ammunition is almost gone. Water, for days has been supplied by the enduring efforts of a solitary Mexican woman, who, through showers of grape and musketry, has threaded her way from the castle, while her own blood has marked the path. She bears with her the spirit of her illustrious ancestor, stretched upon the racks of Cortez; and it is not the fear of death, or the torture that can swerve her from her purpose. In her presence there is hope, and joy and life. At each arrival she is hailed by the garrison as the guardian angel of the Alamo, and until it falls her efforts fail not.

The siege has continued for ten days.—The Mexican general has received large reinforcements, and his army now numbers thousands. He has been unceasing in his efforts to batter down the walls, but has thus far failed. The triumph is with Travis;—but it is written in the heart of his ruthless foe that he must die, and when the cannonade was suspended on the 6th of March, Santa Anna had determined that the hour for the assault had arrived. During ten days a blood-red flag had been streaming from the spire of the church in San Antonio, proclaiming that no quarter is to be given to the champions of the Alamo—that blood alone will appease the fury of Mexican malice. When the sun again goes down the flag is no longer seen, for the deed of which it was the sign has been accomplished.

It is midnight. Stars are smiling in the firmament, and the repose of paradise seems hovering over armed hosts, and hills, and plains which encircle the Alamo. A low murmur rises upon the air, which gradually becomes more and more distinct. Lights move to and fro in the distance, and indicate some unusual movement. The besieging army is in motion. There is no advance by columns. The force of the Mexicans is so great that the fort may be surrounded, leaving intervals only for the fire of the artillery. The plain is girded by a deep line of infantry, and these are hemmed in and surrounded by another of cavalry. If the first shrink, they must be thrust forward to the assault by the sabres and pistols of their comrades.—Suddenly the batteries are in a blaze, and from their concentric positions pour forth a radii of fire pointing to a single centre. Amid the thunders thus created, their own shouts scarcely less terrible, and the blasts of bugles, the Mexicans advance to the Alamo. A sheet of flames from rifles that never failed is the answer to the charge. The infantry recoil and fall back upon the cavalry; their ranks broken and disordered by the heavy fire of the besieged. The shouts from the fort are mingled with the groans of the dying on the plain, while the officers are endeavoring to reform their scattered masses. They return to the attack, but the leaden shower which they encounter fells them to the earth by platoons. Travis shows himself on the walls, cheering on his undaunted followers. Around him are Crocket, Evans, Bonham, roused for the last struggle, for they know their doom is sealed. In quick succession, rifle after rifle is discharged, sending hundreds to their last account. The Mexicans are again repulsed; they fall back disheartened by the dead and dying around them. The battalion of Toluca, the flower of the Mexican army, is reduced from fourteen hundred to *twenty-three.* Men have become for a moment regardless of their officers, and are almost delirious from the cries of anguish which discipline can restrain, which comes from their fallen and expiring comrades. But a breach is made at last, the disjointed forces by the aid of threats are rallied, and once more turn their faces to the Alamo. The firing in that quarter has for some time been growing slower and slower. Rifles have dropped from many a vigorous hand, now cold in death, while others cling to their weapons even in the agonies of dissolution. Ammunition, too, has been failing; one by one, the muzzles drop; the last rifle is loaded and discharged, and the Mexicans have gained the wall. Proudly conspicuous at that awful moment, Travis receives a shot, staggers, and falls. He dies not unavenged. A Mexican officer rushes upon him, and is about to plunge his sabre into the bosom of the fallen man, when, gathering all his energies for one last effort, he bathes his own sword in the blood of his enemy, and they die together.

In the meantime the battle has been raging hot and thick. The Mexicans have poured into the citadel like leaves falling before the storms of autumn. The conflict becomes hand to hand. Each man struggles with his adversary, dealing blows with rifles, sabres, or whatever missile may be within their reach. The Texans are almost buried beneath the numbers of their opponents. The massacre has been so terrible that the slain are piled up in heaps. Death stares each survivor in the face, but still he struggles on. Crocket has been conspicuous in the melee, wherever his blows fell hottest and thickest. He has forced his way over piles of the dead bodies of his enemies and has reached the door of the chapel. Here he determines to make his last stand. At one glance of his eye, he sees the fate of the Alamo rest upon his arm alone. Travis has fallen; Evans is no more; Bowie expires upon a bed of sickness; Bonham falls before his eyes, and he finds himself the only living warrior of the one hundred and sixty three who had been his comrades. Perhaps at that moment the lifeblood creeps to his heart by a natural impulse, but it is only for a moment. His foes glare on him with the fierceness of demons, & assaults him with blows from sabres, muskets and pistols. The strength of a hundred men seems concentrated in this single arm, as he deals out death to his rancorous and unsparing assailants. Their bodies have grown into a rampart before him.

Blackened with fire and smoke, besmeared with blood, and roused into phrensy, he stands, like some fabled god of antiquity laughing to scorn the malice, and the power, and the fury of his enemies. New fire flashes from his eye, and new vigor nerves his arm. On his assailants rush, but it is only upon certain death. They fall, but their places are still supplied; and so quickly, the dead seem to rise up before him, like armed men from the teeth of Cadmus. At length a ball from a distant rifle pierced him in the forehead; he falls backward to the earth in the streams of gore which curdle round him. No groan escapes him; no cry of agony gratifies the implacable rancour of his enemies; he dies, and the Alamo has fallen.

—*Vermont Gazette*, February 9, 1847

The following extract concerning the arrival of the writer and his party at San Antonio was taken from "the manuscript journal of a gentleman who has recently visited an interesting portion of the new state of Texas" and was printed in a number of newspapers as "Rambling in the South West."

An avenue of cotton woods and elms led us into town near the old ruins of the "Alamo." It was on this spot that Travis, Crockett, Bowie, and about two hundred others fell in 1836 by the massacreing bands of the Mexicans under Gen. Santa Anna: and the crumbling walls of a part of the Convent and Chapel, remain like monuments in memory of the braves who met their fate with so much patriotism and devotion to their cause. The old Mission, which takes its name of "Alamo" from the cottonwood grove in the neighborhood, was established by the Jesuits many years ago in connection with the "San Saba Fort," missions of "San Jose," "San Juan," and others, some of which are of greater antiquity and bear traces of more splendour and labor in their architecture. The ground enclosed by the outer wall was about an acre and a half, but the main defence against an enemy consisted of the Convent, with its Chapel attached, and covered only about an acre. It was built of blocks of soft limestone, the walls several feet thick, and the main entrance through the archway or portcullis in the Chapel, over the centre of which are small figures, supposed to represent saints, with Spanish coats of arms or other insignia, carved in bas relief. It was placed upon the outer curve of a bend in the San Antonio river, which latter is said to form from a hundred springs, and on the opposite side some fifty feet across stands the town, which, from the perfectly white appearance of the houses contrasts singularly with the dark foliage of the intervening oaks and elms.

—*Supplement to the Connecticut Courant*, December 11, 1847

Half a year later, the following article about San Antonio debuted in a New York newspaper, and is included in its entirety here for its rare descriptions of the Alamo, the town, its architecture, the river and its connecting irrigation system, the citizens and some of their customs—including funerals—and occasional references to the local history. Not all of it is flattering.

SAN ANTONIO

The following description of San Antonio de Bexar, Texas, appears in the N. York Journal of Commerce, over the initial H.

Were I asked, "How does San Antonio look?" I could answer with truthfulness, *"like a dilapidated city of old jails."* It does of a verity. The first object that met my eye on approaching the town, was the ruins of the church attached to the Alamo. Most of the walls are yet standing, but in a crazy condition. The roof is entirely off, so with the doors. I went inside, and found, as the only inhabitants, some fifty swine that had taken shelter for a siesta. I saw where the Texans *made their way through the walls* on first entering in possession of the city. The front of the church was handsomely embellished, with some wrought work. The figures 1758 are engraved over the arch of the main door. The side walls are of rude stone. The private cells are yet there, in all their mysteries. The walls of the Alamo inclosed five acres which embraced the barracks, parade ground, church, and dwellings for the officers, and were supposed to be impregnable, until a handful of Texans, with a determination not to be resisted, cut their way through, and became masters. The U. States have taken possession of the barracks, put on a new roof, and otherwise Americanized it for their own use. All the old Mexican houses within the bounds of defence are built one story, many fifteen feet high, with stone or adobe, the walls being from three to four feet thick, and plastered with clay and lime, actually six inches deep. The dwellings are usually made in long rows of from 100 to 200 feet, some I think 300 feet long and divided into *cells* or apartments. In many of them there is not a light of any kind, except what comes through the doorway, with occasionally a small hole that would admit a cannon's mouth, with slats across like prison bars. The roofs are covered with a sort of plaster cement, usually of the depth of two feet, making them fire, bullet, and water proof—as indeed are the centre buildings. You will remark that the only way in which the Texans could take the town, after they had taken its main defence, was to dig with the pick axe and crowbar from house to house. Beginning at one end, they cut a hole through, thrust in a rifle and the tenants would leave for the next,—so they went on literally cutting their way, with their muskets "exporting from house to house," till they some three hundred, had taken this fortified town of two thousand inhabitants. In the construction of every edifice made in early times, the first consideration was defence;—hence this strange mass of stone and mortar. The floors are all, with an occasional "American" exception, made of the rude earth. The substance is clay, lime and gravel, partly smoothed and made hard by use. The surface is uneven, except where great pains is taken to "level off." At first the sight of a ground floor to eat, sleep, drink, and live on, seems revolting, but a few days *sort of* contents one. The Mexican women and children mostly set upon the earth, few of them having sufficient seats. Besides, 'tis habit with them. The women do their washing on flat rocks in the bottom of the river, or standing knee deep in it, at the margin, or at one of the many canals or ditches running through the city.

I see only one feature to admire about this famed San Antonio—the San Antonio River. It is beautiful, lovely, inviting and useful. It runs with great strength to every point of the compass, and feeds a score of canals which pass along near every house in town. Bridges are made at each street. The river is about sixty feet wide by six deep, with a current of four miles an hour,—perfectly transparent, and affording plenty of fine fish to the angler. Its banks are low, but the stream being fed only by springs, is uniform, never disturbing by its rise anything along the banks. The water is called pure—perhaps it is, but it is most certainly highly impregnated with lime—and I am told of a rotten nature, and that one day's confinement in a tight bottle will cause a putrid smell. The springs are only three and four miles above.

These ditches or canals were constructed for the purpose of irrigating the gardens and cornfields, and but for them the crops would often fail from drought. Last year the corn crop failed almost entirely, when it was beyond the reach of irrigation. Yesterday, hearing the old broken Catholic bells toll, I felt curious to know for what, and learned 'twas for a funeral. I went and saw four Mexicans take upon their shoulders an open coffin, that is, a box the shape of a coffin with no top on. It was on a bier, and indeed made fast. They went off and in fifteen minutes returned with the same, in which was the corpse, entirely exposed to public gaze, dressed in a white shirt, cotton trousers, and suspenders, no stockings—its great toes tied together with a bit of cotton cloth. He must have been a man of fifty years. I followed into the church. The corpse was put down—the burial service was said—holy water was sprinkled and incense burned over it. It was thus taken to the grave followed apparently only by the priest, and a few idle spectators. A few words more were uttered with the rite, and the poor body was *emptied* into its last resting place, the cruel earth next moment had hidden it from mortal sight, *and the coffin returned to the church.* All very poor people are buried without cover of any kind—scarcely what decency would demand—the relations choosing rather to expend the cost with the priest for its safe transport beyond the grave. The priest in this case carried a black cross. Had the friends of the deceased been able, the cross would have been of silver, with great pomp and show attending the corpse to its grave. The whole process lasted not more than ten minutes after the corpse was brought to the church. The grave yard is literally strewed with human bones and skulls that for a half century or less have bleached and decayed in this Southern sun. Every new grave opened, reveals more or less which are thrust aside, and perchance again thrown back to help over the new corpse, or become the sport of the idle *greasers.*

—*Victoria Advocate* (Texas), July 6, 1848

The following curious report implies that a certain part of the Alamo's stone rubble was considered the identifiable result of impact by Santa Anna's artillery.

It is suggested in a Texian paper that the stone removed from the wall of the Alamo, to make the breach through which the enemy entered, is to be sent to Washington as the contribution of the State to the Washington monument. The stone still lies at the mouth of the breach, as it did on the day when Travis, Crockett, and their fellow heroes, were massacred, and is said to be a beautiful block, susceptible of a polish as fine as marble. (*Dayton Empire.*)
—*Daily Ohio Statesman*, February 9, 1850

Samuel Maverick, who had been sent by Colonel Travis in early February 1836 to Washington-on-the-Brazos to act as one of the garrison's delegates to the Convention being held there, bought property within the bounds of the Alamo compound and moved into it.

BURIED CANNON DISCOVERED.— A Mr. Maverick has purchased a building site at the old fort of the Alamo, in Texas. While digging a trench not long since, the workmen discovered 12 pieces of cannon buried deep in the ground; among them 3 18 pounders, 2 copper 12 pounders, 2 copper and 1 iron 8 pounder, and 4 swivels. They are supposed to have been buried by Col. Travis during the siege of the Alamo, to prevent their falling into the hands of the Mexicans.
—*Milwaukee Sentinel*, July 10, 1852

A related article adds some additional details.

While some laborers were digging a ditch for a fence in the Alamo, in San Antonio, Texas, recently, they came suddenly upon several pieces of ordnance, since which time thirteen pieces of cannon have already been recovered from their hiding place, four of which are copper, and nine iron pieces, from one to twenty-four pounders, and the trunnions and knobs of the cascables broken off. An old Mexican

woman says they were buried there by the brave men under the command of the noble Travis, Bowie and Crockett, at the siege of the Alamo, in 1836.
—*State Gazette* (Trenton, New Jersey), June 29, 1852

Anecdotes about James Bowie continued to appear, such as this one from a Louisiana newspaper, which also touched on the changes that had been made to the Alamo church in the 1850s.

James Bowie—The Alamo.
A correspondent, under the signature of "Jarez," writing from Bayou Terrabonne, gives us an anecdote of Col. James Bowie, the inventor of the well-known knife bearing his name. He says:
There is a great deal to interest one on this, "our Terrabonne." It was here that the celebrated Col. Bowie (he, the inventor of the knife,) resided, and carried on his daring and desperate exploits—not of rapine, but of rencounters, the like of which have never been equalled in the world's history.
By the bye—speaking of Bowie—I will narrate an anecdote of him, which was told me by old Mons. J., one of the oldest inhabitants of Southern Louisiana.
A young Virginian, of good family, (of course,) came down on the bayou to the South, and "opened a plantation." He brought with him seventy-four negroes, and eighteen thousand dollars in cash. The "sharpers," hearing of this, followed our F. F. V. down the bayou, and caught him at Houma, where they interested him with a "friendly" game of "draw." They duped the poor boy out of all his cash, and twenty-one negroes.
Our "Virginia friend" seemed to be perfectly desperate—he was almost frantic at his losses—and, in a moment of passion, accused the gamblers of cheating. This they denied—but the denial had scarcely passed their lips, before a stentorian voice cried out—*"Thieves! To Hell!"* In an instant all was confusion and uproar. The gamblers endeavored to make good their escape, but the strong arm of Bowie was

against them—they recognized the fatal knife in his hand, and he compelled them to disgorge their ill-gotten gains. This is a true type of the much-maligned Bowie.

The closing scene of the life of this strange and daring man, was in keeping with that of his early history. He met death, on a sick bed, in the little room of the Alamo, weapon in hand, and pluck to the last. The small, gloomy, thick-walled apartment, one of the strong defenses of the old mission of the Alamo, where Travis, Bowie, and Crockett died overwhelmed, but not subdued by the soldiers of Santa Anna, was, three years since, an object of much curiosity by visitors in San Antonio, as well as a glorious monument to the survivors of the independence struggle of Texas. It was at that time in a bad state of preservation, grim, blackened and perforated with cannon balls. On the walls were numerous autographs recalling the history of two weeks gallant defence of the fortress, and manifesting the interest which visitors felt in the spot. The fortress had been re-roofed, and all but this little room used as a store-house for the Federal troops quartered hard by. It is to be regretted that the old mission, with its curiously carved door and thick fortress wings, was not left in the same condition as it was after the siege—a roofless, powder-blackened monument of the desperate valor of one hundred and fifty men, who resisted for a fortnight, under serious disadvantages, the onslaught of four thousand Mexicans.

—*Daily True Delta*, January 2, 1859

A more intimate profile of Bowie, including details of his person, appeared in an 1867 Texas newspaper, reprinted from another Louisiana paper.

The Bowies.

The editor of the Concordia Intelligencer is giving a series of very interesting reminiscences of the past. In his edition of the 26th ult., we find the following:

The name of Bowie is known in every portion of this continent, and we may say over christendom. James and Resen were the two that gave notoriety to the family, and the only two of the males we ever saw. No two men ever lived that were less understood than these gentlemen, or of whom a more false opinion was formed. They lived in times when physical and moral courage was necessary to the success of every one. It is true they had not a liberal education, but were naturally of strong minds and herculean forms. They had traveled over the greater portion of the Southern States, Texas, Mexico and the West India Islands, had acquired much information, and spoke, read and wrote the French language as well as their own.

The first and only time I ever saw James Bowie—commonly known as Jim Bowie—was at Vidalia. He was walking from the clerk's office, where he had been on business, and a more perfect specimen of a human being the eye could not rest upon—combining strength and elegance, and perfect in all the proportions of a man—with head erect, shoulders thrown back, he walked the earth as if he were monarch of it, and spurned the dust under his feet. He was about six feet two inches in height, dark hair and eyes, and his complexion bronzed by exposure and travel; when in conversation, of easy and pleasant address. Vidalia was familiar to James Bowie, for after the fight on the sand bar of Natchez, some time before 1830, he was brought here covered with wounds, and remained several weeks, until his health was restored. The history of this terrible fight we got from an eyewitness, one of the surgeons who attended the occasion.

A feud had existed between parties in Alexandria for a long time, and it was determined to settle the matter by a fight. The principals, with their friends, came to Natchez, and of the party was James Bowie and Col. Wright. At the time appointed, they met on the sand bar, two or three miles above Natchez.

The fight between the principals came off; they exchanged shots without any danger to either, when an honorable settlement was made.

But here the difficulty did not terminate with the friends of the principals. The remark was made by one of them, "Here is a good time and place to settle the quarrel," when pistols were drawn and a promiscuous fight took place. It was a "free fight," every man for himself. Ten or a dozen were on the ground—some spectators—and all were armed with pistols, knives, and swordcanes; the revolver then was not known. James Bowie was looked upon as the most dangerous, and was the target; he received a pistol ball in his thigh, fired by a gentleman of Natchez, and fell.

At this stage of the fight, Colonel Wright rushed upon Bowie when he was down, and run him through the chest with his sword. Bowie had himself armed with a knife made of an old file about twenty inches long with a buckhorn handle, and when Wright thrust him through, he grappled him by the collar, and striking him in the chest about the collar bone, downward, made a wound a foot long in the chest and abdomen, Wright falling upon his adversary a lifeless man. Here ended this terrible affair. Col. Wright was brought to the side of the river and buried in the old graveyard above town. Bowie was brought here, and seventeen pistol and sword wounds dressed. He was the only one wounded, and Colonel Wright the only one killed. From this fight, and the knife used, the celebrated highly polished and deadly weapon, known as the Bowie knife, took its name. It is said Mr. Bowie would never allow any one to make the slightest allusion to this shocking tragedy. James Bowie was largely concerned in the land speculations under the Spanish grants, but he died poor.

When Mexico, under the leadership of Santa Anna, invaded Texas to hold her as a revolted province, James Bowie volunteered his services in her defense, and fell at the Alamo by the side of David Crockett, of Tennessee, and Christopher Parker, of Mississippi, a brother-in-law of Gen. Sparrow. The impression the world has of Jim Bowie is most erroneous. He was kind and benevolent, but did not seek a quarrel, and followed the advice of Polonious—

"Beware
Of entrance to a quarrel, but being in,
Bear it that the opposer may beware of thee."

He feared nothing, and was ready to fight the devil in a just cause, either for himself or a friend. He had a tender and benevolent heart for the weak, distressed and poor. Many tales

are told, of his attentions to the latter, and many extravagant stories are related of bloody and cruel adventures, of which there is no truth.

—*Dallas Weekly Herald,* June 8, 1867

An 1866 article recalling "Traditions of Old Society at the Capital," originally published in the *New York Evening Post,* included the following purported item about Congressman Crockett.

DAVY CROCKETT AT A LEVEE.

The practice, for example, of announcing in a loud voice the name and rank of each person entering the room at an entertainment, was discontinued in many elegant social circles elsewhere long before a levee at the Executive mansion was thought to admit of a breach which might be more honored than this observance, of which the last instance, as the story goes, was during the first term of Gen. Jackson's presidency. "Room for the Honorable Mr. And Mrs. George Michael Spinks, of the Senate of the United States," etc., etc. was the ponderous formula of the usher, selected for that mixture of assurance and obsequiousness so rare in this country and so requisite for the grace of such an office, and for a loud, clear voice. Crockett, with coonskin cap and linsey-woolsey hunting shirt, fringed leggings and buckskin moccasins—not unconsciously, but studiously in character, advanced to the great door to enter. "Room for the Honorable David Crockett, of the House of Representatives of the United States," cried the officious usher. "Davy Crockett will make room for himself!" exclaimed the eccentric guest in a tone of tremendous volume and gravity, as he marched into the company.

—*San Francisco Evening Bulletin,*
November 27, 1866

Four years later, a profile of Crockett made its way into a New York paper.

Col. David Crockett.

About fifty years ago, there came to the surface, in the politics of Tennessee, a new man from a new section. It was Davy Crockett, of the

Western district. He appeared in the State Senate at Nashville, a rough, uncouth, backwoodsman, of parentage and lineage so obscure that he could perhaps hardly trace them himself, but a hale, stout, athletic, fine looking hunter, without education, save in shrewd, sound, common sense and woodsman's craft. He was in the prime of life, about 34 or 35 years of age; had shot deer, hunted bear, fought Indians, skinned coons, soldiered to New Orleans under Jackson, (flatboated some we expect,) and was known to be the finest rifle shot, best hunter, and best humored rough joker on the frontier. He was the representative man of his people. (Would that our people in latter days had been as truly and honorably represented.)

This legislating was a new thing to Davy, but he had plenty of good sense; and he applied himself with effect and learned.

In 1825 he was a candidate for Congress, and came within two votes of being elected. His friends advised him to test the seat, but he told them he would never sneak into Congress. He must have the clear voice of the people, or he would not go at all. His motto was, "be sure you are right and go ahead."

In 1827 he was again a candidate, and was elected by a majority of over 2,000, and was re-elected in 1829. In 1831 he was beaten, owing to his opposition to Andrew Jackson, who was then President; but in 1833 Col. Crockett was re-elected to Congress. He was quite fond of politics and public life, and made a good Congressman. He attended regularly, and kept an eye to the business in hand, and improved every day he stayed there. When he first entered Congress he was almost as much a "curiosity" as a bear or an Indian would have been. His dialect was broad, his manners unpolished, and his general get-up decidedly awkward. But a few years later he was a pretty fair speaker, and used the language of educated gentlemen. He says himself, in a book which he wrote and published about 1834 or '35, that knowing he was "green," he at first quietly watched other men, whom he knew to be well bred, and then acted as near like they did as he could without attracting attention. (How many thousands who

have been "through the schools" want the sense to imitate Davy Crockett in this particular.)

At Washington he dressed in the usual style of other people of his position, but quite plain, and be the style what it might, he would wear his shirt collar turned down over his stock, and his hair parted in the middle.

In 1835 he made his last race for Congress, and was beaten by Adam Huntsman. The majority against him was only 230, but Col. Crockett concluded that the Western district had gone back on him. A month after the election he was on his way to Texas, where he gave his life, a few months afterward, in the struggle for independence, which the patriots of that state were then making. He was in the Alamo, which Col. Travis held with 150 men, against Santa Anna with the Mexican party. After a long siege the Alamo was carried by assault at daylight on the morning of the 9th of March, 1836. There were but six live men in the fort, Col. David Crockett was one of them. He was overpowered and taken with his trusty rifle ("Betsy," the gift of a Whig club in Philadelphia,) in his hand, and the dead bodies of no less than twenty Mexicans lying around him. He was carried before Santa Anna, who allowed him to be butchered in cold blood. Thus ended the eventful career of one of the most remarkable men that West Tennessee ever produced.

He was a citizen of Obion county, and the site of his "log cabin" is still pointed out near Crockett Station on the Mobile and Ohio railroad. We believe the debris of the "historic shanty" was removed to make room for the road bed, some fifteen or twenty years ago.

He was dead before we were born, but we have had his life and his history, his tragically heroic death and his wonderful feats in bear hunting in "the shakes" about Reelfoot Lake and the Cypress swamps and canebrakes of the bottom recounted to us, in fancy, by his old pioneer comrades and admirers, (now mostly in their graves) until to doubt them would be "a sin to Crockett." Some of these days a new county is to be made out of Haywood, Madison, Gibson and Dyer, and named after him.

—*Jamestown Journal* (New York),
September 23, 1870

Less than three months later came this tragic news for the Crockett family.

> A murder was committed at Brady's Landing, five miles from Memphis, on the Arkansas shore, a few days since. John Bell Crockett, grandson of Davy Crockett, was on Wednesday found murdered in his trading-boat at the above place, his head horribly crushed with an iron bar. The boat had been plundered, but no clue was discovered to the murderer.
>
> —*Leavenworth Bulletin,* December 30, 1870

The following article in a New Orleans newspaper contains a description of what seems to be, intriguingly, a now lost portrait of Bowie.

The Bowies.

One of Roundabout's most valued correspondents, a prominent citizen of New Orleans, and a contemporary and intimate friend of the brothers James and Rezin Bowie, sends us the following in reply to Mr. Neville Craig's letter of inquiry:

NEW ORLEANS, March 13, 1876.

COL. ROUNDABOUT—In the TIMES of the 11th inst. you have an inquiry from Brownsville, Fayette county, Pa., desiring information of the celebrated Bowie family. They were old resident planters and merchants of this State. Col. James and Rezin Bowie and family settled lands in Rapides, Big Prairie, Washita, St. Landry, Louisiana, in 1803.

Col. James Bowie, Rezin's brother, was in 1830 to 1835, a Mexican traveler to Matamoros, Mexico, etc., and with Rezin a planter in the Felicianas, where their mother resided. Col. James Bowie, one of the heroes of the Alamo at San Antonio, was a high-toned, popular and chivalrous gentleman, an intimate, social and business friend of the writer. I have a portrait of him with his hunting suit and knife, and spent the evening at a supper with him and Sterling McNeel, a planter of Brazoria, Texas, previous to their departure for the seat of war, via Red River in 1836, while the schooner Julius Caesar, Capt. Andrew Moore, belonging to our firm left New Orleans with volunteers and arms,

besides a company from Wilkinson county, etc., to assist the Texans in their struggle for independence. Previous to the battle and before the massacre at San Antonio, a misunderstanding occurred between Col. Davy Crockett and Col. James Bowie as to rank, which was amicably arranged by the intercession of the now veteran Dr. Levi Jones, aged 83 years, residing at Galveston, Texas, previous and now owner of the towns of Indianola and Bolivar, Texas, opposite Galveston. Your correspondent can get much information in regard to the Bowie family by addressing J. S. Moore, Esq., a grandson of Rezin Bowie, one of the firm of W. L. Cushing & Moore, Galveston, Texas, partner of our popular, enterprising and old resident citizen, W. L. Cushing, Esq., of New Orleans.

GILBERT

Enclosed is this notice of a portrait of Col. James Bowie:

COL. JAMES BOWIE OF LOUISIANA.— Portrait from life of the celebrated Col. James Bowie, of bowie knife celebrity. It was painted by Parker, portrait painter, of Natchez, Miss., in 1832, at his mother's plantation in East Feliciana, La., and is the only portrait of him. It was recognized by Col. Adam L. Bingamon, of Natchez, who was intimate with him. It is taken in his hunting suit, with his knife, made from a rasp, in his belt. Col. Bowie was overpowered and killed at the massacre of the Alamo, San Antonio, Texas, in 1835 or 6, with Col. Davy Crockett, Grayson and others, by the Mexican forces under Gen. Santa Anna and Gen. Cos. A portrait of Rezin Bowie (brother of Col. James Bowie) was painted by Col. T. B. Thorpe, artist, (Tom Owen, the Bee Hunter) some years afterwards, and is now in Louisiana.

—*New Orleans Times*, March 14, 1876

Once a servant to early Alamo historian Reuben Marmaduke Potter, ex–Mexican sergeant Francisco Becerra had often told his story of campaigning with Santa Anna in Texas and especially of his participation in the assault on the Alamo. This version, derived from a "careful translation" made by Texas Revolution veteran Col. John Salmon Ford, was reprinted in a number of papers.

THE MASSACRE OF THE ALAMO.

One of Santa Anna's Soldiers Tells the Story of that Bloody Day—New Statements Regarding the Dying Moments of the Famous Texan Leader.

SAN ANTONIO, Texas, March 9th.— The completion of a railway, by a Bostonian, from Houston, 200 miles, to San Antonio, in Southwestern Texas, has invested with fresh interest the memories of this ancient capital coeval with Philadelphia. Everywhere, in every city and hamlet of the United States, the play entitled, *The Alamo; or, Death of David Crockett,* has appealed to the passions of the multitude. When this railway was finished last week I went with a great throng to San Antonio and gathered the facts here detailed which give the Mexican aspect of the old familiar story. The recital as given is a careful translation by Colonel Ford, commonly known as "Old Rip," a frontier member of the Texas Senate. The old Mexican soldier the *recounter*, is named Francisco Buerra, born in Guanajuato is 1810. He became a soldier in 1828, was of the army that stormed the Alamo in 1836, and was captured by the Texans at San Jacinto. He became a citizen of Texas, served in the war of 1846-7 against his native country, and in the Confederate army in the war between the States. He is now an honored and aged citizen of Brownsville, and his recital of facts as seen by a Mexican at the storming of the Alamo has peculiar value in the eyes of your Southwestern readers.

Santa Anna was joined at Laredo, where he crossed the Rio Grande, by General Cos, who, in violation of the terms of his recent surrender at San Antonio, was forced to join Santa Anna and return into Texas. The movements of the Mexican army were greatly retarded by fires on the prairies, which rendered the horses of the whole force almost useless. Deaf Smith, a famous Texan scout, was the author of this mischief. Santa Anna halted a day at Medina, when he was met by Señor Novarro and a priest, who gave the General accurate information as to the strength—258 men in the Alamo—of the Americans in San Antonio. A sudden rain-storm and "norther" made the river impassable, and a forced march and immediate assault impossible. Next day he resumed the march, General Mora to advance with orders to seize the mission of the Concepcion, a massive stone structure deemed by Santa Anna a more defensible stronghold than the Alamo. A cannon shot was fired when the head of the column reached the cemetery. The town was not defended, and Colonel Mora was ordered to take a position north and east of the Alamo to prevent the escape of the garrison. This was late in February, 1836. Santa Anna led 4,000 men and awaited the coming of General Talza with 2,000 more. A battalion crossed the San Antonio river and took possession of houses below the Alamo to build a bridge across the river. Thirty men of two companies sent the next day to make a reconnoissance were killed. A light earth-work was thrown up above the Alamo. The firing from the fort, now invested on every side, was ceaseless. An earth-work nearer the fort was constructed at night. On the 3d day of March, General Talza arrived, and the plan of assault was defined and made known to the division commanders. On the 5th of March scaling ladders were distributed. A 3 o'clock on the morning of the 6th, ever memorable in Texan song and story, the Battalion Matamoros was moved to a point near the river and above the Alamo.

They were supported by 2,000 men under General Cos, this wing of the army being commanded by General Castrillon, General Talza leading that below the Alamo. Santa Anna spent the night in the earthworks near the Alamo. The whole force was to move silently upon the fortress at the bugle-sound and not to fire till in the trenches of the Texans. The bugle was heard at 4 o'clock. General Castrillon's division, after half an hour's desperate fighting, and after repeated repulses and unheard of losses, succeeded in effecting an entrance in the upper part of the Alamo in a sort of outwork, now a court-yard. The fighting had only begun. The doors and windows of the Alamo building were barricaded and guarded by bags of sand heaped up as high as a man's shoulders, and on the roof were rows of sandbags, behind which the Texans fought as men never fought before—muzzle to muzzle, hand to hand. Each Texan rifle-shot exhausted its force and spent itself in successive bodies of Mexicans packed together like a wall of flesh. Muskets and rifles were clubbed, and bayonets and bowie-knives never wrought such fearful carnage.

The ceaseless crash of firearms, the shouts of the defiant, desperate, beleaguered Texans, the shrieks of the dying, made the din infernal and the scene indescribable in its sublime terrors. Each room in the building was the scene of a desperate struggle with fearless men driven to desperation and conscious that escape was impossible. They fought even when stricken down, and when dying still struggled, not with death, but to slay Mexicans. In the long room used as a hospital the sick and wounded fired pistols and rifles from their pallets. A piece of artillery, supposed to be that which Crockett had used during the siege, was shotted with grape and canister and turned upon the desperate occupants of the apartment.

After the explosion the Mexicans entered and found the emaciated bodies of fourteen men, torn and rent and blackened and bloody. Forty-two dead Mexicans lay at the doorway of this room. Bowie, whose name tells of his fearful knife and deeds, lay stark and stiff on a cot in this room. He was helpless and in bed when the place was invested ten days before.

Eleven Texans fired with terrible effect from the roof of the building, where they used three or four field pieces, which they charged with nails and pieces of iron. Buerra, like all others, gives his particular version of the story that recounts the facts affecting the death of Travis and of Crockett. These two were found living, yet exhausted by death-dealing, and lying among the dead.

When Travis was discovered he gave a Mexican gold, and while conversing with him General Cos, with whom Travis had dealt most generously when San Antonio was captured by the Americans, appeared. Cos embraced Travis and induced other officers to join him in asking Santa Anna to spare Travis's life. The President-General sternly refused. Then Crockett, from among the corpses, stood up utterly exhausted,

by weary sleepless days and nights and by five hours' constant fighting.

Santa Anna was enraged beyond measure that his orders were not executed. He directed the soldiers near him to fire on the two Texans. Travis was shot first in the back. He folded his arms across his breast, and stood stiffly erect till a bullet pierced his neck. He fell upon his face, while Crockett's body was riddled with bullets. The corpses of 2,000 Mexicans were gathered and burned, a holocaust whose fires lighted the way to Texas freedom.

I have given faithfully the Mexican version of this fearful story, and hereafter will give that of the only American survivor, an aged woman who lives in Austin.—*Corr. N. Y. World.*
—*San Francisco Bulletin*, March 23, 1877

The following piece may have more truth to it than the sarcasm will allow.

One of our attorneys tells a strange, yet amusing story of a visit he received from three aged Mexicans. One of them explained that he wanted the lawyer to draw up a petition for a pension to the county court for him as a Texas veteran. "Where did you serve in the Texas army?" inquired the lawyer. "At the Alamo, with Travis and Crockett. I am the only living survivor of the massacre." "How will you prove it?" inquired the lawyer, with an incredulous smile. Pointing to his two aged companions, the old Mexican, with tears in his eyes, replied, "by these two worthy citizens. They belonged to my company, and we all three escaped together." *Valiyente Dios.* Let Paddy beat that if he can.—San Antonio Herald.
—*Boston Daily Advertiser*, April 7, 1877

Lost in the shuffle of history was Travis's slave Joe, who was mentioned in the newspapers after 1836 on only very rare occasion.

The Austin Statesman says: There are several old soldiers of the Texas revolution in Austin and in adjacent towns and counties, and these should meet on the 21st inst., San Jacinto Day. Two years ago the old colored body servant of

Gen. Travis was in this city, and his home was not far away. Why not have him brought to the capital? The only white survivor of the Alamo is here, and we do not see why the veterans should not be feted by the city government or by the citizens of the capital.

— *Times Picayune*, April 13, 1877

One of the most important accounts of the Alamo battle, by Mexican participant, Manuel Loranca, appeared forty-two years after the event in a Texas paper. It is not without occasional, and natural, errors of memory, but many key details ring true. It also includes the rare mention of a sizable body of defenders who attempted to escape the impending massacre by jumping the walls. A brief account of San Jacinto also figures in Loranca's relation.

SANTA ANNA'S LAST EFFORT.

———

THE ALAMO AND SAN JACINTO.

———

Narrative of a Mexican Sergeant who belonged to Santa Anna's Army.

[The following narrative, written for the Corpus Christi *Free Press* by an ex-sergeant in the last Mexican expedition under Santa Anna, is full of thrilling interest. It might be appropriately termed a "knapsack sketch." We are assured that the writer (ex-sergeant Manuel Loranca) has his original discharge from the expedition, and, if needed, can be sent to us. We are indebted to D. M. Hastings, Esq., Corpus Christi, who kindly made the translation.—ED FREE PRESS.]

———

Manuel Loranca, who in the year 1835, was a Second Sergeant in the Mexican army, makes the following statement of what transpired within his own knowledge after the march from San Luis de Potosi for the campaign of Texas:

On the 25th day of October, 1835, his regiment being the vanguard of the Division under the command of Senor Don Joaquin Ramires y Serna,[d] marched towards Saltillo, thence to Monterey; from Monterey in the direction of Salevias de

Victoria; from Victoria to Lampasas and thence to Laredo, meeting there the Mexican forces retiring under the Generals Vicente Filisola and Martin Perfecto de Cos. This force came for the purpose of joining the President, Santa Anna, coming from the direction of Candela, for the purpose of opening in form the campaign of Texas.

This division marched immediately as vanguard to the Rio Grande, joined President Santa Anna and the forces brought by him, and followed him to San Antonio de Bexar. We advanced a force to the river Medina, from which point the President dispatched a column of cavalry to attack the Texas forces which were in San Antonio; but these, perceiving the movement, occupied the fort of the Alamo, which being defended by eighteen pieces of artillery, was difficult of assault.

About nine in the morning, the President Santa Anna arrived and joined with his escort and staff the column which was now in the vicinity of San Antonio. We marched upon the place and were received by the fort with one or two cannon shots; those in the Alamo raised a red flag.

Santa Anna then ordered a parley to be sounded, which was answered by the chiefs of the Alamo, and the President commissioned the Mexican Colonel Batres to confer with Bowie and Travis, both Colonels of the Texan forces holding the Alamo. This was on the 26th of February, 1836.

The President Santa Anna proposed to Travis and Bowie that they should surrender at discretion, with no other guarantee than that their lives should be spared. The said Texan chiefs answered and proposed to surrender the fort on being allowed to march out with their arms and go join their government (as they had permitted the Mexican forces under Generals Cos and Filisola when they capitulated to the Texans at the Mission de la Espada and were allowed to march out with their arms, munitions of war, provisions, etc., and join the Mexican army then in the field against Texas), and if this was not willingly conceded to them, they would willingly take all the chances of war.

———

[d] Gen. Joaquín Ramírez y Sesma.

The bombardment was effectively commenced on the 27th of the same month. During this time the Mexican forces were joined by several bodies of infantry, making about four thousand men.

On the 4th of March, the President Santa Anna called a council of war to consider the mode of assault of the Alamo, and they decided to make the assault on the 6th, at daybreak, in the following manner: On the north, Col. Don Juan Baptisto Morales with the Battalion "Firmas," of San Luis Potosi; on the west, Col. Don Mariano Salas, with the Battalion of Aldama; on the south, Col. Jose Vicente Minon, with the Battalion of Infantry; on the east, a squadron of Lancers, flanked by a ditch, to cut off the retreat at the time of the assault. These Lancers were commanded by Gen. Don Joaquin Ramires y Serna.

The assault took place at 3:30 a.m. on the 6th, and was so sudden that the fort had only time to discharge four of the eighteen cannon which it had.

The Fort Alamo had only one entrance, which was on the south; and the approach was made winding to impede the entrance of the cavalry. The Mexican infantry, with ladders, were lying down at musket-shot distance, awaiting the signal of assault, which was to be given from a fort about a cannon-shot to the east of the Alamo, where the President Santa Anna was with the music of the regiment of Dolores and his staff to direct the movements. In the act of assault a confusion occurred, occasioned by darkness, in which the Mexican troops opened fire on each other. A culverin, or 16 pound howitzer, fired from the fort, swept off a whole company of the Battalion Aldama, which made the attack on the point toward San Antonio.

After that we all entered the Alamo, and the first thing we saw on entering a room on the right was the corpses of Bowie and Travis. Then we passed to the corridor which served the Texans as quarters, and here found all refugees which were left. President Santa Anna immediately ordered that they should be shot, which was accordingly done, excepting only a negro and a woman having a little boy about a year old. She was said to be Travis' cook.

Sixty-two Texans who sallied from the east side of the fort were received by the Lancers and all killed. Only one of these made resistance; a very active man, armed with a double barrel gun and a single-barrel pistol, with which he killed a corporal of the Lancers named Eugenio. These were all killed by the lance, except one, who ensconced himself under a bush and it was necessary to shoot him.

There in front of the fosse were gathered the bodies of all those who died by the lance, and those killed in the fort, making a total of two-hundred and eighty-three persons, including a Mexican found among them, who, it appears, had come from La Bahia (Goliad) with dispatches[e]; and here they were ordered to be burned, there being no room in the *campo santo* or burying ground, it being all taken up with the bodies of upwards of four hundred Mexicans, who were killed in the assault.

After a few days, a column was organized which marched on San Felipe, then the capital of the State of Texas. This column was composed of the battalions of Aldama, Morales, Matamoros and Toluca (the battalions were not numbered, as in these days). On nearing the town of Gonzales, the negro and the woman whose lives had been spared at the Alamo, and another negro who was with the Mexican troops, were sent forward with a proclamation of the President Santa Anna, offering to spare the lives and property of those who had not thrown off their allegiance to the Mexican government. But no one put any faith in it, and the people fired the town and took to the woods, taking with them the negroes and the woman. Nobody was found there.

The column marched on to the river Colorado, and then to a point called Atascoso, whence the President Santa Anna dispatched some thirty lancers to San Felipe, which they found already burned. There we remained two or three days.

Then President Santa Anna marched with the companies of Cazadores and Grenadiers of the Battalions of Morales, Matamoros, Aldama and

---

[e] Possibly a trooper of Juan Seguín's Tejano company.

Toluca and fifty dragoons, in the direction of the Brazos river, the rest of the column remaining at said river. Santa Anna arrived at the San Jacinto.

In the interval of days came a steamer from above San Felipe, in which were the most distinguished persons among the Texans, but even if we had received timely notice we could not have captured her, as she was well fortified with bales of cotton.

Having made a halt at a place called Edenburg, President Santa Anna ordered up the remaining Battalions, raising the number of the column to one thousand one hundred—the force at San Jacinto on the 21st of April.

The line of battle was then formed and arms stacked. A company of cavalry under Capt. Aguirre was then ordered to advance about two miles to reconnoitre the enemy, with orders from President Santa Anna that if they were few to retire, but if numerous to report. But this was not possible, as the enemy were advancing on the right and center, partly covered by the high grass, and Capt. Aguirre was found to be wounded in the leg and the advance retired in disorder. The enemy then charged the main body, where President Santa Anna was, and the confusion became so great that there was very little resistance, and still less when Col. Correblon fell dead under a cannon.

We then retreated with the President Santa Anna towards the Brazos, only to find the bridge burned. There we dispersed among the rushes (tule). Many were drowned, not knowing how to swim. A party of five of us—myself, Sergeant Modina, a soldier named Molino, and two soldiers whose names I do not know— arrived at the Brazos river at 7 p.m. on the 21st of April, which was the day of the action.

Gen. Filisola, who remained in command of the troops on the Brazos, would not believe our report of the defeat; but later in the night another soldier arrived afoot, bringing the same news that we did, and that he had left the President on this side of the river afoot, and that he was probably captured, as he in fact was the next day.

The Gen. Filisola marched with the rest of the forces in the direction of Columbia, to join Gen. Don Jose Urrea, coming from La Bahia, whom he met between Brazoria and Columbia, where the Generals held a council. Urrea wished to march to San Jacinto, but Filisola would not. Meanwhile a courier arrived with a note from President Santa Anna, that to save his life and the lives of the Mexican prisoners, it was necessary that the army should counter-march across the Rio Grande, and that Gen. Serna should hurry, as he was considered responsible for the deaths at the Alamo as chief of vanguard. This is all I can state.

This is what took place at La Bahia with the troops under Gen. Urrea, as told to me by an American who was among those shot, but escaped from among the corpses without knowing in what manner. Thus, when the 500 men were taken prisoners by Gen. Urrea, he guaranteed their lives until he could report to President Santa Anna, who was in San Antonio, and the answer was sent from Santa Anna by Col. Jose Vicente Minon, that they should all be shot, which was accordingly done.

MANUEL LORANCA.
—*San Antonio Express,* June 28, 1878

Mrs. Susanna Dickinson, after three failed marriages in the wake of her husband's death at the Alamo, had finally settled down in relative happiness in 1857 with German immigrant Joseph William Hannig. The following short piece concerns her meeting with actor Frank Mayo, who was the star of the play *Davy Crockett,* one of the longest-running stage productions in US history.

FRANK MAYO is quoted by the Cleveland *Herald* as saying that when in Texas he saw the Mrs. Hanig who escaped with her child from Fort Alamo, and who is now the only survivor of the massacre of which Davy Crockett was the hero. Mrs. Hanig said that Crockett was the bravest man she ever saw; that his chief occupations were fiddling and swearing, and his sole ambition was to fight Mexicans.
—*Salt Lake Tribune*, June 12, 1880

The former Mrs. Dickinson also made a number of visits to the Alamo in her later years, and newspaper reporters were generally there to cover them. This article appeared two years before her death.

The Heroine of the Alamo.
(Correspondence of the San Antonio Express.)
Texans confess keen interest in facts affecting the history and fortunes of David Crockett. San Antonio is indebted to much of its fame to that of the heroic martyr to liberty, who fell in the thickest of the fight within the Alamo. Have you listened to the simplest recital of the facts given by Mrs. Hannig, formerly Mrs. Dickenson, nee Wilkerson, in Greene county, Georgia? She went, when very young, to Bolivar, Hardeman county, Tennessee. When hardly sixteen she married Dickenson, a New England tradesman, and in 1835, went to Texas. When the revolt occurred and Mexican invasion was threatened, Dickenson removed his youthful wife to San Antonio. When Santa Anna appeared before the little city one bright spring morning in 1836, Dickenson, who was lieutenant or captain in a local company, mounted a mustang, and his wife was seated behind him with a child six months old in her lap. He entered the Alamo. He and his wife had an apartment given them in the basement of the stone church. Crockett occupied an adjoining room. Here, when not engaged in loading and firing a sort of "long Tom," a primitive eighteen-pounder, he was accustomed to saw his fiddle and abhor confinement within stone walls. He was impatient of imprisonment and especially anxious to have a fight with the Mexicans in an open field, where he might use his native weapon, "Betsy," his old-fashioned soap-stick rifle. Through ten days Mrs. Hannig was within the Alamo, encountering Crockett almost hourly till the last day of the siege, when the massacre occurred. That fatal morning Dickenson, long before the sun rose, came to his wife and bade her adieu. I have heard her tell the story with tearful eyes forty-three years after the sun went down on that terrible day. She saw Dickenson but once afterward. He was then fighting, sword in hand, at the door-way of her apartment. Men rushed into her room. There was a volley of musketry. When consciousness was restored her room was full of gunpowder smoke. A bullet had pierced her leg below the knee. She was lying on her bed, her infant, six months old, beside her, and a richly dressed Mexican officer standing near. She remembers, as I forgot to state, that simultaneously with the hand to hand fight between her husband and the Mexicans at the door-way, two little boys, sons of a German gunner, ran into her room. They were pursued by Mexicans, shot down, and bayoneted in her presence, the smoke from the guns filling her room and enabling her to escape observation. Almonte was educated in New Orleans. He interposed when the Mexicans sought to take her life, and caused her to be taken to Santa Anna. This man sought to induce her to accompany him to Mexico. When she refused, he concluded to send her to Sam Houston, that the terrible story she would tell might intimidate the little band of Texas patriots. Wounded as she was, she set out alone on a mustang, with her child in her lap, across the open prairies, for Gonzales. She, her infant, and the negro Ben, the servant of Travis, who was in command, were the sole American survivors. But San Antonio should hear Mrs. Hannig, now growing old, tell the story, as I have heard it. She would tell, too, of her flight, accompanied by the negro Ben, of the intervention of Deaf Smith who saved her when almost dying of thirst, fatigue and of pain caused by her wound. Hear her tell of her interview with Houston, and how the hero of Texan independence used the hideous story to exasperate his followers. She told him that when she was leaving San Antonio the town and country were perfumed with odors arising from the holocaust made of the bodies of those who fell within the Alamo. She beheld the flames that consumed the body of her husband and of Crockett and Travis, and was instructed by Santa Anna to describe the horrible scene to Houston and his followers. She executed the order with painstaking care. The effect was little dreamed of by the bloody Mexican leader.
—*Galveston News,* February 3, 1881

Travis's servant Joe is again called "Ben" in the following piece about the Alamo and the Texas government's apparent lack of concern regarding its preservation as a monument.

The Alamo.
American Register.

The Alamo—the old stone cathedral—of San Antonio is the Thermopylae of the new world. Its story only differs from that told of Leonidas and his devoted band in the fact that of the 165 defenders of the Alamo, against 4,000 Mexicans, there was no survivor to "tell it in Lacedaemon that we died here in obedience to her laws." The Alamo was besieged through eleven days and nights. At length, when assaulted before day dawn on every side, and when its garrison was exhausted by constant dangers and toils, the Mexicans scaled the stone wall enclosing the church. The commander of the stronghold had consulted his men. They had resolved never to surrender. Bowie's body was found pinned to his bed of sickness by bayonets. Around the spot at which David Crockett served a thirteen pounder, Mexicans were heaped up as if to constitute a fortress for the invincible Tennessean. Travis' negro body servant, Ben, was still living nine years ago. His life was spared that he might designate the bodies of the fallen chieftains. Mrs. Dickinson, whose husband was a Connecticut tradesman and lieutenant of a volunteer company of San Antonio, occupied a small apartment in the basement of the church. Dickinson fell sword in hand at the doorway of his apartment. Almonte interposed and made the infuriated drunken Mexicans spare Mrs. Dickinson and her child and this now venerable woman and the children of this daughter still live in Austin, Texas.

But we only proposed to say that The Alamo is now occupied as a grocery store. It is in the business centre of San Antonio, and its owner would sell the property, and, destroying the old church, moss-covered by time and with memories illustrative of the valor of Americans, erect new buildings on the site. There are a million and a quarter dollars in the treasury of Texas, and the state only owes a debt of four millions, fastened on it by the carpet bag oligarchy, and its failure to buy and preserve the Alamo would be a foul wrong to American fame and deeds and history. If Texas be so false to her own pride of local history and patriotism that

this proudest monument to valor must perish, even the American Union should interpose that the Alamo may tell posterity forever how brave men have fought and died for local freedom—the strongest passion, as shown in New England anniversaries, that underlies and adorns American character.

—*Plain Dealer* (Cleveland),
January 29, 1883

The year 1883 also saw the death of Susanna Dickinson.

There lately died in Texas Mrs. S. A. Hanning, one of the three non-combatant survivors of the Alamo. The two other survivors were Mrs. Alsbury and a negro body servant of Colonel Travis. It will be remembered that every combatant in the citadel perished. Mrs. Hanning was once Mrs. Dickerson, wife of Lieutenant Dickerson, of the garrison, who, in attempting to follow his wife when she left the Alamo, was riddled with bullets as he jumped out of a window of the church, babe in arms.

—*Macon Weekly Telegraph* (Georgia),
October 13, 1883

To this day, there is little agreement concerning the location of Crockett's death within the Alamo. The following article has him, breaking off a Mexican "spear" pinning him, just as John Wayne did in the 1960 movie *The Alamo*, and perishing on a second floor of the church that did not exist in 1836.

DEATH OF CROCKETT.

A Texas Correspondent's Description
of the Alamo.

San Antonio Cor. Globe-Democrat.—First the Alamo, next the $7,000 set of furniture, is the order in which the San Antonian classifies the sights to be shown the visitor. The garden wall, which formed the outer fortifications where Davy Crockett and his 140 companions held at bay a Mexican army of 10,000 is gone and the Alamo plaza extends to the doors of the ancient buildings. The nunnery portion has been transformed into a wholesale grocery and the firm sign is spread across the front of the old walls. An imitation of a mansard has been added to the two stories of the convent, and above the roof at each end rises a turret pierced with two wooden guns, the modern tribute to the structure's famous history. One can hardly go amiss on a guide for the battle cry of the second Mexican war, "Remember the Alamo!" echoes in the San Antonian's memory and the details of the massacre are as fresh in his mind as are those of the killing of Ben Thompson and King Fisher in the Vaudeville theater some time ago. A little back, but joining on the end of the convent, stands the massive building in which Crockett and his band retired and made their last fight. The door stands wide open and the floor is covered with fragments of evergreen wreaths and trimmings. A church festival was the last use to which the Alamo was put and the lumber for the tables has not yet been removed. Your guide will take you into the dungeon just to the left of the main entrance and show you the cells surrounded by solid stone walls six feet thick. This was the crematory where the Mexicans found sweet revenge in roasting the bodies of the men who had fought them so long.

Then you go up to the second story and into a little room twelve feet square with one door and one window—the same thick walls. It was through this window the Texans pointed their field-piece and, with their few remaining charges, mowed swaths through the Mexican ranks. Then, when the last grain of powder was burned, they took other positions where they could work with their long knives to the best advantage, and, as the besiegers pressed in, the foremost dropped in their tracks before the thrusts of the defenders.

"Here in this corner," said Mr. C. J. Downes, a former St. Louisan, who took your correspondent under his guidance, "when the last shots were fired from the window, Crockett took up his position with his knife. You see he was sheltered from the window and faced the door. He killed seventeen Mexicans, and their bodies lay piled up on this floor in front of him. Then they pinned him to the wall with a long spear, and he had hacked that half through with his knife before they gave him his death wounds."

In the rear of this old chapel is shown the court-yard where the single male survivor of the Alamo garrison mingled with the attacking forces and escaped to tell the story of that awful day, and then a room is shown where under a green hide a woman concealed herself and her babe when the Mexican soldiers made their first wild search intent on slaughtering every human being, regardless of age and sex. Her hiding place was not discovered until the thirst for blood was somewhat abated, and then the interference of an officer saved her.

—*Cincinnati Commercial Tribune*,
June 14, 1884

And, once again, the Bowie knife "made" the papers.

The father of all the bowie-knives is sent to the New Orleans exposition by Charles Campbell of Texas, grandson of Augusta Barrera, to whom Col. James Bowie gave it just before the siege of the Alamo. It has a deer-horn handle and a curved blade 15 inches long, much worn and somewhat rusty.

—*Worcester Daily Spy* (Massachusetts),
January 21, 1885

A writer with the byline of "A. J. S." wrote the following account of his visit to the Alamo in 1885.

THE TEXAS THERMOPYLAE
————

A recent issue of the Galveston *News* contains an interesting letter from an old Texan who recently visited San Antonio, which was the scene of so many stirring events in the struggle for Texan independence. We quote the following reminiscences:—

I also visited the Alamo, but not for the first time, however. I stood by the side of its ruined and blackened walls when a boy, and tried to imagine the fearful scene as it occurred, and how Travis, Crockett, Bowie, Bonham and Dickinson died, and how the beardless boys who composed a part of this heroic band could make such a fortress and face and attempt to beat back and hurl from its walls the fierce hordes of Santa Anna; but they did, nevertheless, as many

grief stricken mothers of DeWitt colony could attest a few days afterward. The old fortress is now open to visitors, and the Texan veteran, Mr. Rife, who has charge of it, can always be found at his post, ready to show visitors around and impart to them any information which they desire. Mr. Rife is one of the party who dug up and carried to La Grange the bones of the Mier prisoners who drew the black beans and were shot in Mexico. There were several sightseers present when I entered, and all seemed very much interested and asked many questions. In answer to one Mr. Rife said, "yes, the inclosed ground mentioned in history was just in front of the main entrance to the church, and was called the long barrack. It was there that most of the Mexicans fell, and from this room overhead Crockett descended with a few survivors and attempted to force them back from the main entrance, and when all his comrades fell, retreated into that little room there and fought them as long as life remained." In one of the rooms of the chapel is to be seen a grave which many think is the grave of Crockett, but which the inscription shows to be that of a priest who was buried there more than a hundred years ago. I saw several visitors gaze long at the window on the east side of the fortress, from which Dickinson leaped with his child in a desperate attempt to save its life, but both were killed by a volley from the Mexican cavalry as they reached the ground.
—*Texas Siftings,* October 3, 1885

The Alamo was not exempt from the occasional irrational behavior of a disturbed person.

A FOOL AND HIS FOLLY.
SAN ANTONIO, Texas, May 18, 1887.— T. T. Coyle, editor of a Catholic paper published in this city, created quite a sensation yesterday afternoon by going to the Alamo with a sledge hammer and smashing to pieces a statuette of St. Theresa. The statuette was discovered in 1867 while workmen were engaged in making excavations for a building on Houston street, and was placed in the Alamo. On the breast of the image was a Masonic emblem, consisting of a square

and compass. Coyle was arrested and was interviewed in jail. He said that the statuette was an offense to Catholics. He had written Goverenor Ross to have it removed, and that the official replied that he could not order its removal without the consent of the city of San Antonio. Coyle stated that it was his intention to blow up the Alamo with dynamite if he could not otherwise secure the removal of the objectionable image.
—*New York Herald,* May 19, 1887

The "Mrs. Alsbury" mentioned in some of the preceding accounts passed away the following year.

Death of Another Alamo Survivor.
On Tuesday afternoon a quiet funeral took place when the remains of Mrs. Juana Perez were interred in the Catholic cemetery. This lady passed away at a ripe old age, and with her was buried one more of the links to the history of the Alamo. She was a witness of the dreadful massacre, being an inmate of it at the time the Texan heroes laid down their lives on liberty's altar.

Juana Perez was the niece of Gov. Veramendi, but his daughter by adoption. When she was within the walls she was Mrs. Alsbury, the wife of Dr. Alsbury, who had placed her under the protection of Col. James Bowie when San Antonio was expecting the invasion of Santa Anna and his murderous hordes. At the time of her marriage with Dr. Alsbury she was a widow, her first husband being Ramigio Perez by whom she had a son, Alejo Perez, who is now occupying a position on the city constabulary. At the time Mrs. Alsbury was placed in the Alamo Col. Bowie was sick of typhoid fever and during his illness she often spoke to him. She passed through all the horrors of the siege and escaped barely with her life.

There are only two women survivors of that terrible fight now living. They are Madame Candelaria and Mrs. Losoya, who lives in the southern portion of the city. Mrs. Hanning (nee Anna Dickinson, the child of the Alamo) is dead. The latter years of her life were made easy by a pension paid her by the state, which amounted to $100 every three months.
—*San Antonio Daily Express,* July 26, 1888

Among the most tragic postscripts of the Alamo story was the life of Dickinson's daughter, Angelina. Fate eventually intertwined her life with that of Travis's son, Charles, and their relationship spawned unfortunate results for both, which are described in the following lengthy chronicle, first published in a Texas newspaper. Much of it reads like a tawdry historical novel. (It also implies that Angelina was born during the siege.)

BABE OF THE ALAMO.

THE SAD FATE OF A HERO'S DAUGHTER AND A STATE'S WARD.

Angelina Dicknson's Sad Career—Ruined by the Son of Travis—The Affection of Texans for Her—Incidents of Her Sad Life.

Special Correspondence of The Republic.

TEXAS BUREAU OF THE REPUBLIC, DALLAS, Nov. 15.—"The Babe of the Alamo" furnishes the saddest chapter in Texas history. Born to inherit a people's love and reverence, endowed with beauty of person and an active mind, she found her final resting place in a dishonored grave.

The story of the Alamo is familiar, or ought to be familiar, to every American. The defence of the Alamo will be told in song and story when Bunker Hill is forgotten and the charge of the Light Brigade will be a hazy reminiscence. If the Alamo happened to be in Massachusetts it would have been enwreathed in tomes of poetry long before now. If it were English troops instead of Americans that died in its defence the bards of Britain would have glorified it. Yet only one poet has sung of the Alamo in strains worth remembering. Col. R.M. Potter's "Hymn of the Alamo" deserves to live, though it is safe to say that one modern Texan in 50 never heard of it. But every Texan ought to know the lines:

"Arise! Man the wall—our clarion blast;
　　Now sounds its final reveille—
This dawning morn must be the last
　　Our fated band shall ever see.
To life, but not to hope, farewell.
　　Yon trumpets clang and cannons peal,

And storming shout and clash of steel.
　　Is *ours,* but not our *country's* knell.

"Welcome the Spartan's death—
　　'Tis no despairing strife—
We fall—we die—but our expiring breath
　　Is freedom's breath of life.

They come—like autumn leaves they fall,
　　Yet hordes on hordes they onward rush;
With gory tramp they mount the wall,
　　Till numbers the defenders crush.
The last was felled the fight to gain—
　　Well may the ruffians quake to tell
　　How Travis and his hundred fell
Amid a thousand foemen slain.

They died a Spartan's death—
　　But not in hopeless strife—
Like brothers died—and their expiring breath
　　Was Freedom's breath of life.

The author of this was a Texas veteran. He fought for Texas' independence, and subsequently served the Republic and the State. He now resides in New York, in honored old age, proud of the great commonwealth he helped to found.

* *

The Alamo is an old adobe structure, half-church, half-fortress, situated about the centre of the city of San Antonio. It is now owned by the State. Some years ago it fell into the possession of a gentleman from Jerusalem, and was used as a storehouse for his goods. The sentiment of the State revolted and the legislature authorized the Governor to buy the old building and preserve it for the State. The gentleman from Jerusalem saw that he had a chance to drive a good bargain, and the State had to fork over $20,000 before the vulgar trader would evacuate the temple of liberty. But the old structure is now owned by Texas and one of these days it will be used to shelter all the relics of the war for Texas independence in the possession of the State.

The Alamo won its glory during the war for Texas independence. On the 23rd of February, 1836, Santa Anna, Dictator of Mexico, with an army of from 3,000 to 6,000 men, well armed and equipped, invested the Alamo, then garrisoned by 145 Texans. The garrison was commanded by Lieut. Col. William Barrett Travis. Travis had been commissioned lieutenant-colonel of cavalry by the provisional government, but his corps had not been raised, and those under his command in the Alamo were volunteers. James Bowie was second in command, and the gallant and eccentric David Crockett was there as a volunteer in the ranks. There were seven women in the garrison, including a Mexican and a negress. The Mexicans bombarded the fort. The siege lasted for 12 days. On Sunday, March 6, 1836, the Alamo was stormed and all its defenders killed. On the tenth day of the siege, when Travis became convinced that succor would not arrive in time, he announced to his companions their desperate situation. He declared his intention to sell his life as dearly as possible, and drew a line in the yard with his sword. He exhorted all who were willing to fight to the death with him to form on the line. With one exception, all fell into the ranks. Even Bowie, who was dying with consumption, had his cot carried to the line. The man who declined to enter the ranks escaped from the fortress that night.

When the Mexicans stormed the fortress they killed every person in sight. The Texans sold their lives dearly. All of them were killed—144—but nearly 2,000 Mexicans bit the dust. The Mexicans had to kill every man in the fortress before they could call it their own.

Thermopylae had her messenger of defeat;
The Alamo had none.

Four noncombatants escaped the slaughter. They were a negro servant of Col. Travis, Mrs. Alsbury, Mrs. Dickenson and the infant daughter (4 days old) of the latter.

* *

Almiram Dickenson was a lieutenant of the volunteer force under Travis at the Alamo. Travis and Dickenson were not only brothers in arms battling for the same cause, but warm personal friends. Dickenson was a brave, rough frontiersman. He was a huntsman, an Indian fighter and a lover of adventure. His wife was also accustomed to the border. She could

shoot as straight as her husband, and shared in all his dangers and adventures without quailing. She had little of the polish of civilization, and no education. Dickenson and his wife and child lived at San Antonio when Santa Anna marched on the city. Dickenson immediately joined Travis' band and was chosen a lieutenant. When the Americans in San Antonio retired to the Alamo, Lieut. Dickenson took along his wife and child. When the Mexicans scaled the walls of the Alamo and the slaughter of the garrison was nearly complete, Dickenson tied his child on his back and leaped from an upper window. Scarcely had he touched the ground when himself and child were riddled with bullets. On the eighth day of the siege, or more correctly, the 2d of March, while the Mexican batteries were belching forth death and destruction and the gallant defenders of the Alamo were resisting overwhelming numbers, Mrs. Dickenson gave birth to a little girl. When the Alamo was captured and its last defender was dead, Mrs. Dickenson, still weak from the labors of maternity, was discovered with her babe in her arms in a dark and damp corner of the old church. Even the bloody Mexicans had compassion on her and her life was spared. She was cared for by some charitable people of the town.

When the fate of the defenders of the Alamo became known, the Babe of the Alamo became the pet of all Texas. She was toasted and feted and petted. Presents were sent to her from all over the United States: silks and laces were sent from Philadelphia, jewelry from New York, books from Boston and Baltimore and money from Washington. Propositions were seriously made to make her the child of the State by legislative enactment. It is a pity that the State at least did not appoint a guardian for her. Mrs. Dickenson was a coarse, vulgar woman. She grew up herself without education, restraint or object. She was quite content that her daughter should do as she had done. What was everybody's business was nobody's business. Everybody in Texas was interested in Angelina Dickenson, the Babe of the Alamo, but nobody took care of her. When the babe was 4 or 5 years old her mother moved to Houston and soon afterwards married a drayman. Angelina was as warmly petted in Houston as in San Antonio. Everybody bought sweetmeats for her. Everybody gave her presents. She had more clothes, shoes and hats than she knew what to do with. She ran around wild, and if she happened to meet someone who did not know her she would habitually introduce herself as the Babe of the Alamo and demand obeisance. The rod was spared and the child was spoiled. She became a hoiden. She was as wild as a broncho. She finally became the terror of the town. She was sent to school and the first day cut up some papers for which the schoolmaster found it necessary to correct her. It was the first time anyone struck her and she rushed from the school yelling like a Comanche. Meeting a couple of young men she complained that the teacher had whipped her severely. Of course they were indignant. What impudence! A d—— Yankee schoolmaster beating the Babe of the Alamo! They would see about it. They did. The schoolmaster received a severe trouncing and was given three hours to leave town. It is hardly necessary to say that in future teachers refrained from correcting the Babe. The whole community—the whole State, combined to spoil her. All were proud of her, devoted to her, but not one to take an interest in teaching her to be a good woman. She grew up to be 10 years old—an ignorant, wayward, hot-tempered, impulsive, handsome girl bright and merry, and as reckless and wild as a doe.

* *

In the Second Congress of the republic the condition of the Babe of the Alamo was brought before the House of Representatives, and a bill was introduced to appropriate $10,000 to educate and care for the child until she reached womanhood. The Hon. Guy M. Bryan thus in the fiery ardor of the chivalric youth supported the bill in an impassioned speech. By the way, Mr. Bryan was elected to the Lower House of the Legislature from Galveston and Brazoria counties a few days ago and the fine old boy's voice will be apt to ring again through the corridors of the new Capitol next winter. As a specimen of early Texas oratory, an extract from Mr. Bryan's speech supporting the appropriation

for the Babe of the Alamo may be interesting. It was delivered way back in the '40s:

"I intended, Mr. Speaker, to be silent on this occasion, but silence would now be a reproach when to speak is a duty. No one has raised a voice in behalf of this orphan child; several have spoken against her claim. I rise, sir, in behalf of no common cause. Liberty was its foundation, heroism and martyrdom consecrated it. I speak for the orphan child of the Alamo. No orphan children of fallen patriots can send a similar petition to this house—none, save her, can say: "I am the child of the Alamo." Well do I remember the consternation which spread throughout the land when the sad tidings reached our ears that the Alamo had fallen. It was here that a gallant few, the bravest of the brave, threw themselves betwixt the enemy and the settlements, determined not to surrender nor retreat. They redeemed their pledge with the forfeit of their lives—they fell, the chosen sacrifice to Texas freedom. Texas, unapprised of the approach of the invader, was sleeping in fancied security, when the gun of the Alamo first announced that the Atilla of the South was near. Infuriated at the resistance of Travis and his noble band, he marshalled his whole army beneath the walls, and rolled wave after wave of his hosts against those battlements of freedom. In vain he strove, the flag of liberty—the Lone Star of Texas—still streamed out upon the breeze and floated proudly from the outer wall. Maddened and persistent, he reared his batteries, and after days of furious bombardment and repeated assaults he took a blackened and ruined mass—the blood-stained walls of the Alamo. The noble, the martyred spirits of all its gallant defenders had taken their flight to another fortress, not made with hands. But for this stand at the Alamo Texas would have been desolated to the Sabine. Sir, I ask this pittance and for whom? For the only living witness, save the mother, of this awful tragedy—'this bloodiest picture in the book of time,' the bravest act that ever swelled the annals of any country. Grant the boon! She claims it as the Christian child of the Alamo— baptized in the blood of a Travis, a Bowie, a Crockett and a Bonham. To turn her away would be a shame. Give her what she asks that she may be educated and become a worthy child of the State—that she may take that position in society to which she is entitled by the illustrious name of her martyred father, illustrious because he fell at the Alamo."

The House could not resist the plea of Mr. Bryan. The bill passed almost unanimously, and was sent to the Senate. It would have passed the Senate, too, but a hard-headed old fellow named Jesse Grimes was chairman of the appropriations committee and he refused to report it back, saying that the passage of the measure would establish a dangerous precedent, and that Bryan had turned too many heads, so the appropriation failed.

* *

Miss Dickenson, or as everybody called her, the Babe of the Alamo, resided at Houston until she reached the age of womanhood. She was thoroughly spoiled. She was a handsome young woman, tall and graceful, with a clear complexion, rich brown eyes, and a great mass of wavy brown hair. She grew up as wild and untamed as if she lived on the plains miles away from a civilized being or a human habitation. She went to school when she felt like it, left when she felt like it, and remained away altogether when she felt like it. When she saw anything in the shop windows that she took a fancy to, she hailed the first passer-by, introduced herself as the Babe of the Alamo, and bade him get it for her. As a general rule she got whatever she wanted.

It is a pity that a veil cannot be drawn over Miss Dickenson's life from this time until her death. It is a mournful commentary on the frailties of human nature that the petted child of Texas, the Babe of the Alamo, should go to the bad, and that the son of William Barrett Travis should be the author of her ruin. Young Travis was a dissolute fellow. He settled in Hayes County and represented it in one session in the Legislature when he was barely of age. Like his father he was a fearless man and a soldier. He got an appointment in the United States army but was cashiered for drunkenness. He went to Houston a mature man of 35 when the Babe of the Alamo was barely 20. As the son

of the commander of the Alamo defenders he called on Miss Dickenson, the daughter of his father's friend and comrade. They became fast friends, and the dissolute man effected the ruin of the reckless, unsophisticated young girl. He deserted her after a time and she went from bad to worse. She went to New Orleans and entered a house of prostitution and led a depraved life for a number of years. Her fame as the daughter of the Alamo went with her to her degradations, and she made capital of it. But Texans ever remembered her tenderly, and several unsuccessful efforts were made to redeem her.

* *

On one occasion she made a trip on a steamboat from New Orleans to St. Louis and back in company with a dashing young man about town of New Orleans. On the return trip her escort fell into conversation with a quiet gentleman on the boat. The quiet gentleman, in answer to a question, said he was from Texas. The young man said that he was accompanied by the Babe of the Alamo, and volunteered the further information that she was the most notorious courtesan in New Orleans. At this the quiet gentleman from Texas promptly knocked the young man down. The young fellow was one of the bloods of New Orleans and he challenged the Texan. The challenge was accepted. There was no trouble in securing seconds, and when the boat stopped at Vicksburg the parties got off, went a couple of hundred yards from the river and exchanged shots. The Texan shot the young man through the head at the first fire and killed him. All parties assisted in taking the body on board and it was carried to New Orleans. The Babe of the Alamo remarked that he was a fool when she beheld his dead body. The Texan took her in charge, remonstrated with her for her evil life, and worked upon her feelings until she promised to accompany him to Texas. He promised to provide a home for her. When they reached New Orleans they boarded a boat for Galveston. When they reached Galveston the Babe met a drummer she knew in New Orleans, and giving her kind friend the slip, returned to New Orleans with him on the return trip of the boat.

* *

In the early days of the civil war Miss Dickenson, in company with some kindred characters went from New Orleans to visit a Confederate army camped in Mississippi. She fell in with some Alabama and Georgia tramps, got drunk and proceeded to have a high old time. Of course, she introduced herself as the Babe of the Alamo and told all about her birth and the affection in which she was held in Texas. After a while the soldiers became boisterous and the Babe was tossed in a blanket. This is a favorite trick of soldiers. It consists of several men grasping a blanket by the four corners, slacking it and then drawing it tight and pitching it. The person on the blanket is sometimes tossed 12 or 14 feet high. The Babe received some very rough treatment. Her clothes were torn in tatters and she bled copiously from the nose. When she escaped from her tormentors she made her way to the camp of some Texas troops, to whom she introduced herself and related her grievances. The Texans were wild. They sought the Georgia and Alabama fellows who abused the Babe, beat them into insensibility, and a first-class row between Georgia and Alabama on one hand and Texas on the other, was only prevented by the prompt action of the commanding general. The General sent the Babe and her companions out of the camp.

* *

Angelina Dickenson, the petted child of Texas, never reformed. Many Texans, individually, went to New Orleans to endeavor to rescue her, but their efforts were unavailing. She never looked upon life seriously, and until the time of her death was the untamed broncho. The late Ashbel Smith of Houston, on one occasion after vainly trying to induce her to return to Texas and reform, had her arrested in New Orleans and endeavored to have her confined in an institution. But she was of age and he could do nothing with her. She died in a brothel in New Orleans about 12 or 15 years ago. Young Travis ended almost as wretchedly as did his victim a career that dawned in promise. He

was a hopeless drunkard for a number of years before his death, and died while in the throes of delirium tremens.

O'B. M.
—*St. Louis Republic,* November 18, 1888

Naturally the discovery of any battle-related artifacts in and around the site of the old Alamo compound was major local news, and not surprisingly the reports were often reprinted in newspapers of other states.

Relics of the Alamo.

In repairing the streets of San Antonio laborers have been put to work excavating in front of the Alamo, and, although they have not gone a foot in depth, they are already turning up mementoes of the famous battle. These consist principally of cannon balls fired by the Mexicans from their smooth-bored artillery. The balls are about three inches in diameter and made of pure copper without alloy. It is supposed that when the workmen go deeper they will come upon the bones of the defenders. It is stated in history the remains of Crockett and his companions were buried by Santa Anna at some distance from the fort, but this has been disputed by many who say that the bodies were buried where they fell, and that vexed question is expected to be settled by work now in progress. Some of the unearthed cannon balls have been preserved for insertion in the foundation stone of the Alamo monument.

—*Clarion Ledger* (Mississippi),
February 14, 1889

Over the years a number of men came forth and claimed to be surviving defenders of the Alamo, some of them declaring that they had in fact made their escape during the final battle. Here is one such example.

DEATH OF COLONEL WOODS.

He Claims to Have Been at the Massacre of the Alamo.

LOUISVILLE, Ky., Feb. 7.—Colonel James A. Woods died at Bloomfield, Ky., yesterday, at the age of 74. He was in Texas in 1835, and took part in the revolution. He claimed to have been at the massacre of the Alamo, and with two others to have made his escape, although the commonly accepted story says that none escaped except a woman, a servant, and a child. Colonel Woods' statement is believed by his neighbors, and is corroborated by the fact that a native of Lincoln County, Kentucky, till recently alive in Texas, also claimed to have escaped.

—*Inter Ocean* (Illinois), February 8, 1889

Former congressman John W. Crockett, son of David, had died in 1852. Thirty-seven years later, the following notice about the passing of David's son Robert appeared in a number of papers.

NECROLOGY.

Colonel Robert Patterson Crockett,
Rucker's Creek, Tex.

GRANBERRY, Tex., Sept. 30.—Colonel Robert Patterson Crockett died at his residence, on Rucker's creek, last Thursday, in the 73d year of his age. He was one of Hood county's pioneer settlers, locating here in 1854. His death removes the only remaining son of Davy Crockett. Immediately after the fall of the Alamo and the massacre of his father by Santa Anna's brutal soldiers, he left his home in Tennessee and joined the Texas revolutionists. After peace was declared and victory achieved by the Texans, he returned to Tennessee, where he married and settled down. In 1854 he moved to Texas, bringing with him his aged mother, Elizabeth Crockett, who died here in 1860. On the evening of Aug. 11 he sustained serious injuries by a frightened team running away with the wagon and suffered intensely till his death.

—*Times-Picayune,* October 1, 1889

Back at the Alamo, laborers continued to find noteworthy items.

At San Antonio, Texas, while workmen were excavating the central Alamo plaza, with an object of preparing the ground for a park, they turned up several copper cannon balls and a number of half decayed human bones. The place is within fifty yards of the famous structure which was the death place of Crockett and Banham [sic], and some of the balls are flattened from having been fired against the stone wall, and, indeed, the venerable building bears their scars. The bones are those of Mexican soldiers who fell in the fray, some of whom were buried. The bodies of the massacred Americans were all burned up. The relics have been taken in by curiosity seekers.

—*Charlotte News,* January 18, 1890

The obituary of one man who had verifiably been one of the Alamo garrison but had missed being killed on March 6 by being sent out as a courier a few days earlier, appeared in the summer of 1890.

JOHN M. SEGUIN DEAD.

A Noted Texan Passes Away at
Nuevo Laredo, Mexico.
Special to The Republic.

AUSTIN, Tex., Aug. 27.—Gov. Ross is in receipt of a dispatch from Mrs. Seguin of Nuevo Laredo, Mexico, announcing the death of her husband, Col. John M. Seguin, in that city. The flag on the Capitol was in consequence ordered at half-mast.

Col. Seguin was a noted character in the early history of Texas. He was a son of Erasmo Seguin, known to all old settlers, and who lived 20 miles below San Antonio. The family gave the name to the present town of Seguin, in Southern Texas.

In the Texas revolution, John M. Seguin was one of the immortal garrison of the Alamo, but a few days before the massacre was sent on detached duty and thus escaped the fate of Bowie, Crockett and their doomed comrades. Capt. Seguin commanded a company subsequently at the battle of San Jacinto, where a territory larger than the empire of Germany was conquered from the government of Mexico under Santa Ana.

—*St. Louis Republic,* August 28, 1890

Another Tejano made famous by the Alamo story was Madam Candelaria. Even in her own lifetime she sparked dissension over her claim to have been inside the fort during the siege and final battle. She insisted that she had been caring for the sick Bowie when Mexican soldiers burst into his room and killed him, and she would always point to the bayonet scar on her chin as proof. Her tale was often printed in the newspapers, and as she grew into old age, that story would just as often change. But she had her champions; one of them, remarkably, was John S. "Rip" Ford, who had been a soldier of the early Texas Republic, a ranger under Captain John Coffee Hays, and had served in the Mexican War. He died five years after writing this article.

THE FALL OF THE ALAMO.

PART TAKEN BY MRS. CANDELARIA OF
SAN ANTONIO.

Events Occurring in the Historic City During
the War of the Texas Revolution Revived.

SAN ANTONIO, Tex., Nov. 5.—(TO THE NEWS.) A communication published in the Courier-Journal, as I understand, denies the facts usually believed in relation to the part taken by Mrs. Candelaria in the affair of the Alamo. The writer has taken pains to inform himself of the events occurring at San Antonio during the war of the Texas revolution. He has consulted persons in the Alamo at the time of its fall. These were ladies. Mrs. Alsbury, the wife of Dr. Alsbury, was one. She was the niece and the adopted daughter of Gov. Veramendi, the father-in-law of Col. Bowie. She was placed there in charge of her relative, Col. Bowie. Her husband had gone to the interior of Texas to procure transportation in order to remove his wife from San Antonio. Gen. Santa Anna had arrived earlier than was anticipated. Mrs. Alsbury accompanied Col. Bowie to the Alamo and carried her little sister with her. She was placed in quarters considered bomb-proof. These quarters were also occupied by Col. Bowie, Col. Travis, Col. Crockett and other officers, principally for the small period time allowed them for sleep. Col. Bowie became sick of typhoid fever, and was removed to other quarters. Mrs. Alsbury stated

that he on various occasions had men to carry him near the door of the apartment she occupied. He would assure her the parties she was with were gentlemen, and would treat her as a lady. Her son by her first husband, Senor Perez, was interpreter when she made her statement.

To the question, "Did you see Mrs. Candelaria while in the Alamo?" she replied: "There were women in the Alamo whom I did not see."

According to Mrs. Candelaria, there were ten women in the Alamo when it fell. All old Texans are sure Mrs. Dickinson was there. It is needless to give the names of the others.

In order to understand the situation at that time in Texas it is necessary to refer to events occurring previously. The consultation, the first deliberative assembly of Texas, had met in the latter part of 1835. They prepared, as well as they could, for the storm all were assured would soon envelop Texas in the turmoils of war. They elected a governor and lieutenant governor. They conferred upon Gen. Sam Houston the supreme command of the Texas army. They also left a number of their body to assist the governor in the discharge of his duties. These gentlemen differed with the governor. They finally endeavored to relieve him from duty. They announced the appointment of the lieutenant governor in his stead. They advocated carrying the war into Mexico. They were instrumental in the naming of officers to carry fire and sword to Matamoros and on the Rio Grande generally. They sent orders to military officers at Goliad, San Patricio and elsewhere. Gen. Houston only recognized the authority of the governor. He felt assured Texas would again be invaded. He did his utmost to concentrate the disjointed forces of Texas. His labors were unavailing. The divided troops of the Lone Star republic were beaten in detail by Gen. Urrea at Goliad and elsewhere. The people of Texas did not amount to 100,000. They were distracted by these wranglings, amazed and uncertain of what was right to do. At this period of time we must not judge the men left at San Felipe by the consultation harshly. They were no doubt patriotic, but mistook their duty.

Col. Bowie, in this unfortunate matter, was a firm friend of Gen. Houston. He visited different points and endeavored to induce men to listen to reason and to obey Gen. Houston. He reached San Antonio, his home. He found Col. Neill in command. This officer left soon for the purpose, his friends say, of procuring transportation to remove cannon, etc., to a less exposed point. Deaf Smith accompanied him. Col. Neill left Col. Bowie in command. He fell sick. Col. Travis of the Texas regular army reached San Antonio. He was soon induced to assume command by reason of Col. Bowie's illness.

The absence of Deaf Smith left no one the Texans would trust to give the news from the Rio Grande. Col. Juan N. Seguin was mayor of San Antonio. During the month of February, 1836, he sent his cousin to Laredo. He reported Santa Anna at that point with an army. The Texans would not believe him. Had they credited him they could have abandoned San Antonio and saved themselves. The Texan troops occupied the south side of the town.

ARRIVAL OF GEN. SANTA ANNA.

About the 23d day of February, 1836, Gen. Santa Anna reached San Antonio. The Texans retired to the Alamo. On their march they encountered twenty-five or thirty head of cattle and drove them into the Alamo. In the small houses around the fort, which had been occupied mostly by civilized Indians, the Texans found about ninety bushels of corn. They were enabled to live. It must be remembered that the Alamo at the period of time covered two or three acres of ground. It was too large to be properly manned by less than 200 men.

The army of Gen. Santa Anna consisted, at the time he arrived at San Antonio, of 4000 men. On the 3d day of March a reinforcement arrived, reported of 2000 men. If memory serves, these latter men were commanded by Gen. Tolsa. Gen. Santa Anna had awaited the coming of Gen. Tolsa and brigade in order to charge and assault the Alamo. They were met by a handful of Texans, who fought until the last man was killed—silenced in death. The Englishman Nagle, who upon a stone of the Alamo memorialized the deeds and gave a portion of the names of the immortal heroes of the holocaust made to liberty, said: "Thermopylae

had its messenger of defeat, but the Alamo had none." The Alamo stands upon the pages of history without a parallel.

The number of Mexicans who fell during the siege is variously stated at from 2000 to 2500. The roll call after the fall was one of those melancholy occurrences all can imagine but few can remember without bitter feelings when the failure to respond arises from the death of a comrade.

The Texans were piled upon layers of wood and partially consumed. Col. Seguin is credited with having collected the unburned portions of the noble dead and with having afforded them a christian burial.

Mrs. Candelaria says she had raised Col. Bowie's head with the intention of giving him water. The Mexican soldiers rushed in, bayoneted Bowie and also stabbed her on the chin by accident, the scar she still carries. Col. Bowie was well known to many Mexicans. A Mexican told Mrs. Maverick that they forced their bayonets into his body, elevated it and seemed greatly rejoiced at his death. A Mexican officer ordered them to desist.

When the Alamo fell, Mrs. Alsbury says she quit her room and went to the outer part of the building, and met a Mexican officer who treated her rather politely, but who seemed astonished to see a Mexican lady among Texas troops. By his directions she remained where she was. A Mexican who had taken part with the Texans, came running, pursued by Mexican soldiers. Upon seeing her he threw his arms round her and was bayoneted as he stood. She described her feelings as extremely painful. A number of Mexican spectators had assembled to witness these tragic scenes. To her inexpressible delight she was called. A gentleman approached her whom she recognized as the brother of her deceased first husband. He conducted her and her sister to his home and to safety.

The persons who can give evidence that Mrs. Candelaria performed the part she claims are now almost all gone. The dead cannot testify. She has her certificate of baptism and it is represented to have been given more than a hundred years since. Her accurate knowledge of events transpiring at the siege of the Alamo are almost impossible to acquire by mere hearsay. The writer knew her in 1847. It was then conceded she was at the Alamo. Such was the opinion of Col. Jack Hays, Major Chevallie and other old Texans. Creed Taylor, a Texan soldier, and at San Antonio in 1835 was rejoiced to see her. He was confident she was a friend of Texans in 1835 and since. A great many old Texans expressed similar ideas. Quite all these have gone to their long homes. Gen. Bee is yet living. He is one of Mrs. Candelaria's firm friends. Suppose some of the old class of Texans should say they did not know Mrs. Candelaria, would that invalidate the testimony of those who substantiate her claims? Assuredly not.

JOHN S. FORD.
—*Dallas Morning News,* November 12, 1892

Another article about Madam Candelaria, this time concerning her friendship with Jim Bowie, appeared in a San Antonio paper in 1893.

JIM BOWIE'S KNIFE.
A Curious Weapon Which Was Once the Property of the Noted Scout.

There is at the present time in the possession of Charles Campbell, the well known Commerce Street druggist, a weapon that was once the property of the famous frontiersman, Jim Bowie, and which was presented by him to an aged Mexican woman, now living on the west side of town and known as Madam Candelaria. The weapon is a knife of weighty proportions and curious make, the history of which is well authenticated.

The knife is a novelty of its kind and is greatly prized by its owner. About a week ago Mr. Campbell visited Madam Candelaria, who received the weapon from its famous owner and induced her to make an affidavit stating that the knife was really the property of Bowie. The certificate he is having framed and prizes second only to the dagger itself.

The knife is fifteen inches in length, blade 9 3/4 inches and handle 5 1/4 inches across the back; the thickness of the blade is 5/8 of an inch and it is 1 1/2 inches broad. For weight it surpasses any knife in common use at the present day,

weighing 1 1/2 pounds. Two pieces of deer horn constitute the handle and these are fastened with rude hand-made rivits. Undoubtedly the weapon was forged by hand as the workmanship, though good, is too crude for machinery. It bears the following inscription: "Broomhead and Thomas Celebrated American Hunting Knife." Glancing at its ugly proportions one ceases to wonder that the old settlers unhesitatingly attacked bears and other denizens of the forests with no other weapons than these hunting knives when with a single blow they could crush the skull of even the most ferocious animals.

A most interesting story was told to a STAR reporter by Madam Candelaria, the old lady who was in the Alamo during the battle and massacre. Her real name, she says, is Andrea Castanon and she was intimately acquainted with Bowie. A few days before Christmas, in the year 1835, General Bowie occupied the same house with her. This was a small adobe building and was situated on the property now covered by Wolfson's store. Prior to his departure from the house, Bowie handed her the knife referred to, another smaller one, which was forever lost, two razors, a powder-horn and a silk handkerchief, with the request that she take care of them until he should want them again. About four months after she had been entrusted with the articles, David Crockett issued an order that no Americans should leave the garrison as Santa Anna was expected daily. The greatest portion of the inhabitants of the city, chiefly Mexicans, fled from the place. The majority of the Americans however, remained and moved into the Alamo. An officer whom she calls Col. Nelson, came to her and asked her to go and attend the wants of Bowie who was lying on a sick bed in one of the corners of the Alamo, where a rude cot had been built.

She went and found the brave old soldier very ill with fever and immediately bestowed every attention upon him. She states that under the cot was a chest full of gold, which, when it became evident that the garrison was lost, Bowie told her that the she could have if in any way she could save it. He also gave her the knife and other articles he had intrusted to her care.

The old woman spoke feelingly of the golden treasure with which she failed to get off, owing to the predilections of the conquering hordes for the precious yellow metal. She was near the couch of the almost delirious hero when they swarmed into the room and witnessed his death, but the gold she never saw again.

After the massacre she was released and a fear of being seen in possession of the articles with which she had been entrusted by Bowie she turned them over to a Catholic priest, Padre Garza, who kept them a long time. Finally, however, they were returned to her by the priest and then she gave the knife to Augustin Barrera, Mr. Campbell's grandfather. Here it was used for a term of ten or twelve years in the kitchen and general house work besides being used as a hunting knife. At that time it had no history and being an exceptionally good article it was put to the best possible use.

In the course of years Mr. Barrera died and afterwards his wife presented Mr. Campbell with the famous weapon. He has kept it ever since as a relic and under no circumstance would he part with it.

The weapon can be seen at any time at his drugstore, corner of West Commerce and San Saba streets.

—*San Antonio Daily Express,* April 8, 1893

John W. Smith was another Alamo garrison member whose courier service saved him from the final annihilation. Sixty-one years later his granddaughter composed a short biography of him.

LIFE OF JOHN W. SMITH.

By Lucie J. Newton.
(A paper contributed to the Daughters of the Texas Republic, and sent to the department for "Little Men and Women," by Mrs. Looscan of Houston.)

In my estimation, my grandfather, John W. Smith, was one of the greatest heroes of the Texas revolution.

Beyond a passing notice, little is known and less said of his daring exploits as a spy, although he did much toward gaining the independence of our state.

He was born in the state of Missouri, in the year 1756[f] and died in Texas, in 1844. Of his younger life, nothing is known. He came to Texas while still a young man and married a young Spanish lady of much wealth and beauty.

He was of medium height and had long, black hair and large, blue eyes. He had a firm, well-shaped mouth and a large nose, and many people thought him very handsome.

He was a man of a great deal of deliberation and calmness at the moment of peril. Before carrying out an object he always planned and thought about the best way of doing it. After his death, plans of his house, yards, garden and orchard were found among his papers, which showed how he planned everything.

During the first part of the war the Mexican troops were stationed on the military plaza of San Antonio and John Smith acted as a spy. The Texans were camped a few miles out of the city and Smith would ride into the city in the dead of night, would visit his family, and after gaining information of the actions of the enemy would take it back to the Texan camp. His family lived on what is now called Flores street, directly back of the high school; and just on the opposite side of the ditch across from his residence, there was always a sentinel on guard.

To visit his family was a great risk to his life, and in many parts of the city where he had to pass, there were guards who would have shot him if he had been seen. When he came to his home his faithful old servant, or peon, Graviel, would muffle the horse's hoofs with blankets, and while his master was enjoying himself with his wife and children, would hide the animal in an outhouse and hold its mouth so that it could not neigh and attract the attention of the sentinel.

One night John Smith was observed by the sentinel. The spy was taking leave of his family. He was standing in the door of the cottage, with a little child in his arms. The sentinel saw that if he shot it would kill both father and child, and as he had a kind heart, he let the American escape, expecting to soon have another opportunity to kill him.

---

[f] Obviously an error because it would have made him at least 85 at the time of the Alamo siege.

On another occasion the spy was leaving the city on his way to the camp, and when just about to cross the river, he was seen by the guards, who rushed down to the ford. With great presence of mind, Smith caught up an old woman who was standing on the bank and held her on the horse behind him. The woman was well known to the guards, and not wishing to harm her, they allowed the spy to escape.

Old Graviel was of great assistance to his master. When the brave soldiers were in the Alamo, surrounded by the Mexican troops, the old Mexican would take them messages from Smith. Being a Mexican he was allowed to pass through the Mexican lines and was not suspected. He would then gain admittance into the Alamo.

The morning of the great siege of the old fort, Smith had been sent out by Travis for re-inforcements. He was accompanied by the well-known surgeon of the camp, Dr. Sutherland. When they reached the Alazan, the Mexican sentinels saw them, and began firing on them. The two men put spurs to their horses, but that of Dr. Sutherland was shot, and before its rider could extricate himself from the saddle he was caught under the falling animal, and his leg broken. The spy would not leave his friend to be killed by the enemy, so he pulled himself up on his horse, which was already almost exhausted.

They crossed the creek in safety, but owing to the painful nature of the surgeon's wound were compelled to travel very slowly. But after many weary, painful miles a farm house was reached, where the wounded man could receive the attention he so much needed. After dressing the wound of his friend, the spy proceeded on his way, but owing to the delay thus caused, was unable to reach reinforcements, and return with them, until it was too late.

When San Antonio was retaken by the Americans, John W. Smith led a few troops, who in the middle of the night, came down from their fortifications on what is now called Government hill, and waded down the bank of the river, so as not to attract attention, into the heart of the city. In the Veramendi house, which is very near the stream, were the Mexican officials, and their fortifications were all around this point.

The brave Texans tunneled all the way under this old building and came out in the street in front of it. The cowardly Mexicans were so surprised and frightened, that all fled without a show of resistance, leaving the whole city in the possession of the few Texans, whose number they took to be many times greater than it was.

Smith was held by the Mexicans as a prisoner of war once only. His companions were Calhoun and Sam Maverick. They were kept in an old building near the river called La Valleta. All arms and ammunition were taken away from them and prominent citizens in the city of San Antonio. Old records show evidence of his having held at one time eleven different commissions given him by Houston and Lamar. He died while yet in the prime of life and at the time of his death was a congressman.

The pages of Texas history are filled with the daring and noble deeds of Houston, Austin, Bowie and many others, but I will always think of my grandfather first as helping to gain the independence of our Lone Star state.

Note.—John W. Smith was the bearer of the last dispatch sent out of the Alamo by Travis, March 3, 1836.

—*Dallas Morning News,* February 21, 1897

A number of Santa Anna's soldiers had remained in Texas after the battle of San Jacinto, often becoming servants in order to survive. The passing of one of them was noted in 1900.

Death of a Veteran.

Last Saturday night at his residence in old town Francisco Ruis passed away. He was over eighty years old and has an interesting history. He was a Mexican soldier under Gen. Santa Ana, and was at the taking of the Alamo. He also served in the Mexican war, and was in several battles. After the Mexican war, he came to New Mexico and during the civil war he enlisted in the United States army and was a good soldier. Since the civil war he has lived quietly in old town, and was the well-known cannonier at fourth of July celebrations. He was so old that he did not know his own age, but he had a vivid remembrance of the Alamo and the Texas war, Peace to his ashes.

—*Albuquerque Citizen*, December 3, 1900

Among the many rifles purported to have been the property of Crockett was one described in the following 1901 article.

One of Davy Crockett's Guns.

From the Baltimore Sun:

History does not state how many guns the frontiersman David Crockett owned. Mr. C. W. Callaghan, proprietor of the Hotel Maryland, has been presented by Mr. Robert Blair, of Wytheville, Va., with a gun which his donor says was made for Davy and was his favorite weapon. Mr. Blair was lately nominated for the lieutenant-governorship of this state, but could not accept, because he is not yet 20 years old. He is a son of the late Frank Blair, a former attorney-general of Virginia.

Mr. Blair says the gun was given to his father by members of David Crockett's family. It is a flintlock of about 40 caliber. It is 5 ½ feet long, and the barrel is nearly a half inch thick. The workmanship, all by hand, is excellent. The stock is light, the wood part extending clear to the muzzle on the underside. There is a brass slide over the patch-box in the stock. In loading these rifles the ball was wrapped in a cloth patch which was greased. Then it was driven home with a ramrod. Running down the side of the barrel is a brass telescope about as heavy as a modern rifle barrel. The stock and woodwork under the barrel are decorated with brass trimmings. On one side of the stock is a brass eagle. The maker's name does not appear.

—*Duluth News Tribune*, November 4, 1901

More artifacts continued to be excavated on the Alamo grounds.

RELICS OF THE ALAMO.

A Cannon Ball, a Machette, a Sword and Bayonet Unearthed on the Herff Lot, Corner Alamo and Commerce Streets.

At East Commerce and Alamo streets, where excavations are being made for a business block to be erected by Ferdinand Herff, Sr., a number of relics have been brought to light which recall the stormy days when Texans were fighting for their freedom. From the best sources it is learned that a great deal of the hottest fighting incident to the fall of the Alamo occurred where the present work preparatory to building is being carried on.

Some time ago when excavations were being made for a sidewalk at this point a cannon ball about three and one half inches in diameter was found. It was plain to be seen that it was fired in either the defense or storming of the Alamo. This ancient cannon ball was added to the collection already in the Cradle of Texas Liberty.

Last week there was found on the lot the rusted and broken blades of a machette, and also a sword. The ravages of time had made deep inroads into the metals from which these weapons were forged, and in a few more years they would have been but a crumbling mass of rust. Tuesday a well-preserved bayonet was turned up. The weapon is now in possession of Ferdinand Herff, Jr., cashier of the San Antonio National Bank. It was given him by some of the men employed at the place of excavation.

So well preserved is the bayonet that the fine forging thereon is bound to attract attention. It is about seventeen inches in length and resembles much the bayonets used on the old Springfield rifle discarded some years ago by the army. It would still be capable of making a very ugly wound. It is a three-sided weapon and these sides are somewhat fluted. Where the weapon would be attached to the gun barrel one side is broken away as if it might have been done in a struggle.

It is thought by Mr. Herff that further excavations on the property will turn up other interesting relics. The funeral pyre on which the Texans were burned was diagonally across the street from the lot and about where St. Joseph's Church now stands. This leads to the belief that some of the bones of the martyrs may be found if they have not already moulded and turned into dust from whence they came.

—*San Antonio Daily Express*, March 28, 1902

The death of another Mexican veteran of the Alamo campaign resulted in the following obituary.

PARTICIPANT IN ALAMO MASSACRE DIES

(Associated Press by Leased Wire.)

San Antonio, May 4—Felix Rodrigues, an Aztec Indian, died here yesterday at the age of 119. He was in the Battle of the Alamo in 1836 as a teamster, in charge of the paymaster's wagon of the Mexican army. After the Texas victory he returned to Mexico, where he lived until four years ago when he came here. He died without family.

—*Bellingham Herald* (Washington),
May 4, 1907

Now and then making encore appearances were the Alamo's excavated cannon, as shown by the following articles.

DISCOVER BURIED ALAMO CANNON

Old Guns Found While Excavating for Skyscraper

Special to the Telegram.

SAN ANTONIO, July 18.—Ancient cannon used in defending the Alamo have been unearthed at the corner of Houston street and Alamo Plaza. The foundation for a skyscraper is being dug there, and when a depth of about twenty feet was reached the cannon were uncovered.

They are very large, cast iron, and there is no doubt that they are the old Alamo guns, as these relics were buried by the Texans many years ago. They are the property of the Maverick estate, but will probably be given to the state for the purpose of mounting at the Alamo in their original place.

The excavation for the new addition to the federal building will be on the site of the old graveyard of the Alamo, and many bodies will have to be reburied when the foundation is placed. When the present building was erected more than 100 skeletons were revealed.

—*Fort Worth Star-Telegram,*
July 18, 1908

Ancient Cannon to be Placed in Alamo.

From the San Antonio Express.

One of the old cannon found buried below the foundations of the building now being torn down at Avenue D and East Houston street will be added to the historical relics in the Alamo, according to the statement of William H. Maverick, interested in the estate which formerly included the lot where the guns were found.

Mr. Maverick said Saturday the date and circumstances surrounding the placing of the cannon in the ground are doubtful, and that no one is certain on these points.

Tradition says the cannon were buried there either by the Spanish or Mexicans in some of the earlier wars. It was known fifty years ago that the cannon were in the ground, and twenty years ago fifteen of the guns were unearthed, some of the number being possessed by members of the Maverick family. In that lot were several brass cannon, and it was from one of these that the bell of St. Mark's Episcopal church was made.

"It is evident," said Mr. Maverick Saturday, "that all of these guns are of Spanish make. That they were about to fall into the hands of the enemy is shown by the fact that they were spiked and otherwise rendered unfit for use."

According to Mr. Maverick, the spot where the cannon were unearthed is just outside the line of the old Alamo walls, instead of being inside the walls of the fortress, as some have said.

The largest and best preserved cannon of the five found has been chosen to be placed in the Alamo and the four remaining will be given to members of the Maverick family.

—*Kansas City Star,* July 23, 1908

POOR OLD CANNON

Envied at the columns of notice, which Dallas has been getting as a result of the Elks' reunion, San Antonio has been forced to once more dig up the old Alamo cannon in the hope that enough attention might be paid to the battle-scarred relics in order to offset some of the results of the North Texas advertising.

The cannon, therefore, were once more unearthed and the usual number of stock stories about how they came to be underground was industriously circulated. Usually the cannon have been unearthed while workmen were digging a sewer trench, but this time variety was given the story by having the workmen dig a foundation for a skyscraper.

One of the stories of the cannon detailed at great length how they had been spiked to prevent their use by Mexicans, but I. D. Affleck, a pioneer San Antonian, comes forward with a new version which rather spikes the spike story.

Mr. Affleck says the cannon belonged to Santa Anna and were left in San Antonio when that general returned to Mexico. General Andrade was left in charge of the cannon and later was instructed to destroy the Alamo and retreat to Goliad. A number of Andrade's cannon were thrown into the river, but many of them were left lying about the Alamo. Sam Maverick collected a number of these guns later and buried them at the place where they were unearthed a few days ago.

From every indication the cannon are in good condition and fit for being dug up again regularly for the next 100 years. San Antonio is to be congratulated on the possession of such an interesting relic which furnishes so much advertising at so little cost.

—*Fort Worth Star-Telegram*, July 22, 1908

Like the "poor old cannon," the Alamo epic would continue to be unearthed and revised for "advertising" as well as for a legion of other purposes—political, racial, geographical, historical, genealogical, military, archaeological, social, antiquarian, literary, artistic, cinematic, humorous—you name it. And now, in the opening decades of the twenty-first century, the unearthing seems only to have been accelerated.

The essence of the Alamo story, however, is unalterable. Despite all the freshly uncovered documentation, the rethinking, rewriting, cynical dismissal, and partisan exploitation, the Alamo has permanently embedded itself, in the words of John Myers Meyers, as "a symbol of valor in the minds of men. It can never fall again."

❧12❧
Contemporary Alamo Poetry

The fall of the Alamo kindled an immediate body of poetic works that made their debut in newspapers.[a] They are presented here largely without commentary, beginning with one of the earliest poems, printed in Mexico as an ode to Santa Anna.

Who can count, oh great Santa Anna.
The days of glory you have given the fatherland,
And the evils from which you have freed
The whole American nation.
    Your proud and noble sword
Conquers in Tampico the arrogant brow
Of the insolent Spanish tyrant
Who treads our soil and profanes it.
    You destroy York who brazenly
Declared war on the Church
And today, at last, your valor displayed
    To the ungrateful, vile, and mean foreigner;
The pillar of the Mexican nation
Is the invincible, the immortal Santa Anna.
        —*El Santanista Oaxaqueño*, April 9, 1836

From the Mississippi Christian Herald.
THE TEXIAN WAR CRY.
By S. Y. M. Forbes.
Air—Marseilles Hymn.
Ye heirs of freedom! Hear the war cry
    Now swelling from ten thousand tongues,

In shouts betokening victory,
    Blown o'er the world by trumpet lungs.

---

[a] There were also poems inspired by the Texas Revolution in general, from the taking of San Antonio in 1835 to the battle of San Jacinto, but they are too numerous for inclusion here.

Awake! awake! the drum is pealing
    On Bexar's woody hills around;
    The tread of battle shakes the ground,
And rifles keen death shots are dealing.
    Hurrah, hurrah, for war!
        The battle flag waves high;
    The rising of the Texian star
        Shall light to victory!

Shall sons of Washington not rally
    When war dogs howl on yonder plain,
And rapine stalks o'er hill and valley
    To bind us in oppression's chain?
Shall bigot violence and plunder
    On Brassos' banks infuriate roam,
    And fill with fear each peaceful home?
No! answer with the cannon's thunder!
    Hurrah, hurrah, for war!
        The battle flag waves high;
    The rising of the Texian star
        Shall light to victory!

And by that blood stained altar kneeling,
    The scathed and war torn Alamo,
We pledge our all of patriot feeling
    To hurl red vengeance on the foe.
But now the tyrant's foot is crushing
    Each gray haired sire and blooming son
    Who lifts in freedom's cause the gun.—

And shall not patriots dare his rushing?
    Hurrah, hurrah, for war!
        The battle flag waves high;
    The rising of the Texian star
        Shall light to victory!

Then, heirs of freedom! hear the war cry
    Now swelling from ten thousand tongues,
In shouts betokening victory,
    Blown o'er the world by trumpet lungs.
Awake! awake! the drum is pealing
    On Bexar's woody hills around;
    The tread of battle shakes the ground,
And rifles keen death shots are dealing.
        Hurrah, hurrah, for war!
        The battle flag waves high;
    The rising of the Texian star
        Shall light to victory!
    —*Mississippi Free Trader and Natchez Gazette*,
                                April 15, 1836

From the Natchez Daily Courier.
DAVY CROCKETT.
Friends of Freedom, you will mourn
    With unaffected grief
For him who fell in freedom's cause—
    The Tennessean chief!
His name, his deeds can never cease
    To be remembered now
For Glory's wove for him a wreath
    And placed it on his brow.

In every station he was found
    Benevolent and kind,
And all his acts through life proclaimed
    His philanthropic mind—
When Texas struggling to be free
    To freedom's sons appealed,
He bid his friends and home adieu
    And marched into the field.

With valiant arm he met the foe
    And strew'd the ground with dead
But e'er the bloody fight was o'er
    He ceased to "go a head"—
Then onward! sons of Liberty
    Shout vengeance o'er the van
Teach Mexico the price we set
    Upon this gallant man.
    —*Providence Daily Journal*, April 30, 1836

From the N. Y. Star.
CROCKETT.
Tho' sad was his fate and mournful the story,
    The deeds of the hero shall never decay—
He fell in a cause dear to freedom and glory,
    And fought to the last like a lion at bay.

When loud rang the call from a nation oppres'd,
    And her valleys, with slaughter of brave men
were red;
'Twas the pride of poor Crockett to help the
distress'd.
    And the watch word in Texas was heard,
Go ahead.

His death-dealing rifle shall no longer shower
    Its unerring balls on the proud haughty foe,
Cut down in the spring-time of life's budding
flower—
    His tombstone, alas! are thy walls *Alamo*.

Then may we not hope since valor has crown'd
him,
    And o'er him bright fame her mantle has
spread;
In the soul's parting hour good angels were round
him,
    Bid his spirit arise to the skies, "Go ahead."
                                FLASH.
    —*Memphis Enquirer*, May 18, 1836

TO THE TEXIANS.
Lift, lift, the star gemm'd banner high,
    And bid it flutter in the gale,
Bid Time's remotest hour reply,
    While children's children tell the tale—
How Texas from the tyrant's yoke
Her chain of damning bondage broke;
How glory gave her brightest wreath,
When Crockett closed his eyes in death.

Star of the brave, whose sisters glow
    In fair Columbia's flag of light,
Which Freedom, in her virgin throe,
    Gave forth, to cheer a world of night:
We bid thee gleam untarnished high,
Beneath whose light the brave can die,
We bid thee shine, while time shall last,
On ensign staff or giddy mast.

Fling wide the banner o'er the wave,
    To gleam where mortal foot has trod;
Shine out, thou glory of the brave,
    Thou last, though dearest, gift of God!
Shine out, as when on Eden's height
The mandate pealed—let there be light;
Shine out, while wondering millions gaze,
To catch young Freedom's dazzling blaze.

Thou star that gleams mid morning's light,
    We welcome thee in youthful prime;
We bid thee gleam in splendor bright,
    A new born planet of our time.
Alamo fell beneath thy fold,
While history traced thy fame in gold
(Broad as the light which glory flings),
With pinions pluck'd from Angels wings.

Shine on; thou mad'st Sant' Ana cower,
    When Mexic's slaves in panic fled,
When Coss in nature's fairest bower,
    In terror bent his bleeding head.
We bid thee live, thou dazzling gem,
A scion of a noble stem,
Till Heaven shall lose her starry host,
And shame become a nation's boast.

                                    J. E. D.
Washington, May 25, 1836.
            —*United States Telegraph,* May 26, 1836

From the Louisville Journal.
THE FALL OF THE ALAMO.

Dim—dark—and shadowy on the Alamo's walls,
The closing night had spread its raven pall;
From guard to guard low murmurs pass'd along
Like the deep echo of a funeral song,
That falls so sad, so death-like on the ear,
We breathe more freely when we cease to hear;
Or like sweet Music's melancholy tone,
Heard in the chamber death has marked his own,
Where the night-watches hear the gurgling breath—
Unequal—struggling with the chill of death.
Within the dark and barricadocd pile,
A fitful, glimmering watch-fire burned the while;
Now faintly dim, and now renewed its fire,
Like the lamp's flashing ere its beams expire.
No craven hearts with fear are sinking there;
No! Theirs is valor maddened by despair;
There every heart's enthusiastic chord
Is firm—unyielding as the trusty sword,
Whose firm-grasped hilt is starting from its sheath
As if impatient for the work of death.
They gaze unmov'd upon the entrenched lines,
Where dire oppression's lurid watch-fire shines,
From whence the shouts of revelling slaves arise,
In fiend like mockery to the echoing skies;
Nor blench to see the howitzer's sulphurous flash,
Nor start to hear the bomb's tremendous crash;
But hail with joy the blazing comet glare,
That half illumes the dreary midnight air,
Unfolds Columbia's standard to the sight;
That starry banner, which in days of yore

O'er fields of blood their patriot fathers bore.
'Tis dead of night—the exhausted watch-fires wane
The revellers sleep—the powers of darkness reign;
Deep boding silence sits amid the gloom—
Sepulchral stillness—breathless as the tomb.

The glimmering morn has streaked the dappled east,
The wreathing mist hangs on the mountain's breast,
The war-horse neighs, impatient for the strife,
While earth seems newly bursting into life.
The clanging arms—the hurried affray—
Of ranks preparing for the bloody fray;
The pealing music of the martial drum
And shrilly fife, half drown'd amid the hum
Of mingling shouts, that load the morning air.
And tell the Alamo's inmates to prepare!

They come! they come! is shouted from the wall,
They come! they come! is Echo's answering call;
The starry standard of the free and brave
Waves back defiance to the menial slave.
Tho' few the heroes that around it stand,
Each willing heart has got a faithful hand
That will not shrink in danger's trying hour,
To prove its prowess 'gainst the tyrant's power.

That hour has come! the red flag waving high
Moves swiftly forward, and the battle cry
Of Santa Annas rends the vaulted sky—
Dark lengthening lines enclose the fortress round—
They shout—they rush—upon the walls they bound—

A sheet of flame—a crash—a shriek—a groan,
Bespoke how well the work of death is done.
Flash follows flash—and shouts on shouts arise—
Here falls the patriot—there the tyrant dies—
Steel gleams on steel—and the battle's cloud,
That wraps the combatants as in a shroud.
Brave Crockett grapples with the savage foe,
While fate and death are stamped in every blow;
As round his head his viewless weapon swings,
At every stroke a despot's death-knell rings—
At every turn he foils the savage pack,
And carnage glutted, revels at his back.

Brave Travis amid the battle's fire,
Above the strugglers like a lofty spire,
Whose head has caught the livid lightning's power,
And pours to earth the devastating shower;
While desolation sweeps its bosom round,
And black'ning ruin rolls along the ground.

The living clamber o'er the heaps of dead,
At once a bulwark and a dying bed;
On—on they press—they gain—they mount the wall,
And the Alamo totters to its fall!
Brave Crockett falls! and helpless freedom weeps—
On heaps of slain the patriot-hero sleeps.
Another shaft from death's unerring bow
Has laid in death the gallant Travis low;
Oh Heaven! was there no kind protecting power,
To guard the brave at that eventful hour!
One desperate struggle—and the strife is o'er—

A deafening shout—the Alamo is no more;
The fallen fortress forms a funeral pyre
Where Freedom's spirit passed the ordeal fire.
The wreathing smoke in rolling columns rose
And pierc'd to Heaven, where Freedom's sons repose.
                                                              J. H. P.
                        —*New York Evening Star*, June 2, 1836

For the Star.
THE MASSACRE AT BEXAR.
Remember Bexar—Tennesseans!
    Be this your battle cry—
When the unerring rifle's raised
    And the deadly bullets fly—
            Remember Bexar!

Remember him who nobly fell
    'Mid tyrants overthrown,
Whose heart ne'er failed,—whose eye ne'er
quailed—
    Who proved himself your own!
            At fatal Bexar!

Ye who have shared his hours of mirth,
    Ah! think how changed the scene!
His heart is cold—his last tale told,
    Whose wit was then so keen—
            Remember Bexar!

Was he not wise, too, who, untaught
    In schools, yet unsubdued
By sounding words, forever sought
    Tennesseans for your good!

Frailties he had—for he was man—
    But who in Tennessee
While now refuse to praise and mourn
    Thy champion—Liberty?
            Martyred at Bexar!

Rise, then, ye ardent, young, and bold,
    Press on! for he paused not—
Gain freedom for earth's fairest clime,
    Or your CROCKETT's glorious lot.

Say ye of North, East, South or West,
    Friends! kindred of the slain!
Shall the blood of the murder'd brave,
    For vengeance cry in vain?
            Remember Bexar!

For every freeman butchered there,
    A hundred slaves must fall—
If ye would free that lovely land,
    From a savage tyrant's thrall.
            Remember Bexar!
                        —*New York Evening Star*, May 3, 1836

For the *National Banner.*
"SCOTS WHA HA'!"
Sons, whose fathers Washington
Led to glorious battle on,
And their Country's freedom won,
    Is that Spirit fled?

By a cruel treacherous foe,
Friends and brothers now are low,
At the glorious Alamo:
    Numbered with the dead:

Hear the suffering Texians cry;
See our land in ruin lie;
Can you still your aid deny,
    Sons of Tennessee?

No! we'll gird our armor on;
 Savage foe and haughty Don
Shall feel we're each a freeman's son,
    And Texas shall be free.

Santa Anna's pirate hordes
Soon shall fall beneath our swords;
Texas own no despot lords,
    Nor bow to slavery.

Then on, ye gallant warriors, go;
'Lay the cruel murderers low;
Be your war cry Alamo!
    Death or Liberty!!
                        CLARA.
            —*Nashville Banner & Nashville Whig,*
                                        June 10, 1836

From the *Daily Buffalo Journal.*
"GO AHEAD."
I'll "go ahead!"
The hero said
Though I should tread
On heaps of dead!
With sack upon his back,
And rifle in his hand,
He made his hasty track,
To the patriot's land.

Swiftly the forest ranging through,
He cried, 'mid scenes of danger new,
As on he led—
I'll "go ahead!"
And echo said,
"I'll go ahead!"

I'll "go ahead!"
And on he sped,
Through paths that led
To glory's bed;
Nor slacked his rapid pace,
Till on the Texian field
He saw the foeman's face;
And when the war notes pealed,
His rifle's crack the chorus rung,
And ever then the heroes' tongue,
While foemen fled
'Mid torrents red,
From those that bled,
Cried, "go ahead!"

We'll "go ahead!"
Then each one said;
"The traitor's head,
Or we are dead!"
The fatal conflict rose,
Hot grew the deadly fight!
By hundreds fell their foes,
And with a tiger's might—
'Mid Fiery bolt and burning rocket—
Hard fighting to the last, brave Crockett
Cried, "go ahead!"
The last he said
When fell his head
Among the dead!
—*Kentucky Gazette*, June 23, 1836

THE HEROES OF THE ALAMO.
Bright was their fortune, and sublime their doom,
Who perished at the Alamo—their tomb
An altar for their sons—their dirge renown!

Their epitaph nor rust shall ere efface,
Nor Time, that changes all things else debase—
Nor later ages in their pride disown!

Their tomb contains, enshrined beside the dead,
A mighty inmate.—Her for whom they bled—
Their country's unforgotten fame.

Witness the heroic Travers, who in death
Did win high valor's more than Pythian wreath,
A crown unfading—an immortal name![b]
—*New Orleans Bee*, July 25, 1836

And, finally, there was an 1836 poem by Reuben Marmaduke Potter, who would in a few years become the Alamo's first American historian:

HYMN OF THE ALAMO.
AIR. "MARSEILLES HYMN."
"Rise, man the wall!—our clarion's blast
Now sounds its final revellie;
This dawning morn must be the last
Our fated band shall ever see:---
To life but not to hope, farewell—
Yon trumpet's clang and cannon's peal,
And storming shout, and clash of steel,
Is ours, but not our country's knell:
Welcome the Spartan's death—
'Tis no despairing strife—
We fall, we die, but our expiring breath
Is freedom's breath of life."

"Here, on this new Thermopylae,
Our monument shall tower on high,
And *'Alamo'* hereafter be
In bloodier fields the battle cry."
Thus Travis from the rampart cried.
And when his warriors saw the foe,
Like angry billows move below,

Each dauntless heart at once replied,
"Welcome the Spartan's death—
'Tis no despairing strife—
We fall, we die, but our expiring breath
Is freedom's breath of life."

They come—like autumn's leaves they fall;
Yet, hordes on hordes, they onward rush;

---
[b] This poem was based on *The Patriots of Thermopylae* by the Greek, Simonides. Instead of "Alamo," substitute "Thermopylae," and instead of "heroic Travers," substitute "royal Spartan," and you have the same poem.

With gory tramp they scale the wall
    Till numbers the defenders crush.
The last was fell'd the fight to gain—
        Well may the ruffians quake to tell,
        How Travis and his hundred fell,
Amid a thousand foemen slain,
    They died the Spartan's death—
    But not in hopeless strife—
Like brothers died; and in their expiring breath
    Was freedom's breath of life.
    —*Telegraph and Texas Register*, October 4, 1836

Notes

Introduction

1. John Myers Myers, *The Alamo* (New York: E. P. Dutton and Company, Inc., 1948), 235.
2. *New York Evening Star*, May 5, 1836.
3. *New York Herald*, April 14, 1836.
4. *Washington Globe*, May 16, 1836.
5. "Letter from Matagorda, March 28," *Albany Evening Journal*, April 26, 1836.
6. *Portland Advertiser* (Maine), May 3, 1836.
7. *New York Herald*, April 14, 1836.
8. *Richmond Enquirer*, May 3, 1836.
9. *New York Herald*, April 14, 1836.
10. *Rochester Daily Democrat* (New York), May 9, 1836.
11. *Frankfort Commonwealth*, May 25, 1836. Even into the last half of the twentieth century such exaggerations persisted, often deliberately. In a lavish three-page advertisement for John Wayne's movie *The Alamo*, printed in *Life* (July 4, 1960), Russell Birdwell, Wayne's publicist, noted that the battle had pitted "185 against 7,000." Early reports of the number of troops Santa Anna had been gathering in Mexico for his Texas campaign brought the estimate as high as 10,700. *Morning Courier and New York Enquirer*, January 29, 1836.
12. *Arkansas Gazette*, April 5, 1836.
13. *Richmond Enquirer*, September 2, 1836.
14. *Arkansas Advocate*, April 22, 1836.
15. *Memphis Enquirer*, May 11, 1836. The image of Crockett wielding his rifle like a club against onrushing Mexican soldiers survives in literature, art, and motion pictures, despite the unending controversies about his manner of death.
16. *Arkansas Gazette*, April 12, 1836.
17. *New York Times*, June 29, 1836.
18. See, for example, the reports of the battle in the *New Orleans Bulletin*, March 28, 1836, and in the *New Orleans Bee* of the same date.
19. Carl G. Jung, *Man and His Symbols* (Garden City, NY: Doubleday & Company Inc., 1964), 70.
20. *New Orleans Bee*, July 25, 1836.
21. Johnson quoted in Hugh Sidey, "Deep Grow the Roots of the Alamo," *Life*, May 31, 1968, 32B.
22. Charles Fair, *From the Jaws of Victory* (New York: Simon and Schuster, 1971), 384–387.
23. Lucius Lomax, "The Plot to Hijack the Alamo Flag," *Texas Observer*, July 21, 2000; "Alamo Flag Center of Dispute," *Herald Statesman* (Yonkers, New York), September 19, 1973.
24. Charles Ramsdell, *San Antonio: A Historical and Pictorial Guide* (Austin: University of Texas Press, 1959), 52–57; "First United States Volunteer Cavalry," *The Handbook of Texas Online*, www.tsha.online.org; Theodore Roosevelt, *The Rough Riders* (New York: Charles Scribner's Sons, 1899).
25. "Kennedy Attacks Republicans for Latin-American Policies," *Dallas Morning News*, September 13, 1960; "Nixon Attacks Rival in Speech at Alamo," *Dallas Morning News*, November 11, 1960.
26. *Dallas Morning News*, October 6, 1960.
27. *Columbia Missourian*, October 24, 1968.
28. "The Kissinger Issue: Whose Alamo?" *Time*, April 19, 1976, 13.
29. *New York Times*, January 22, 1985.
30. Walter Lord, *A Time to Stand: The Epic of the Alamo Seen as a Great National Experience* (New York: Harper & Brothers, 1961).
31. *New York Evening Star*, May 3, 1836.
32. *Memphis Enquirer*, April 12, 1836.
33. *Morning Courier and New York Enquirer*, May 7, 1836.
34. Gary Brown, *Volunteers in the Texas Revolution: The New Orleans Greys* (Plano: Republic of Texas Press, 1999), 16.
35. Santa Anna to General José María Tornel, March 6, 1836, *Supplemento al Diario del Gobierno*, March 21, 1836.
36. *La Lima de Vulcano* (Mexico City), March 22, 1836, quoted in Michael P. Costeltoe, "The Mexican Press of 1836 and the Battle of the Alamo," *Southwestern Historical Quarterly*, April 1988, 537.
37. Ibid., 538–539.
38. Letter from "Bexar, March 7, 1836," *El Mosquito Mexicano* (Mexico City), April 5, 1836.
39. *La Lima de Vulcano*, March 22, 1836.
40. Ibid.
41. *El Mosquito Mexicano*, April 5, 1836.
42. Santa Anna to Tornel, March 6, 1836.
43. Costeltoe, "The Mexican Press of 1836," 537–538.
44. *El Santanista Oaxqueño* (Oaxaca), April 9, 1836.
45. *El Mosquito Mexicano*, April 5, 1836.
46. *El Nacional* (Mexico City), Supplement no. 79, March 21, 1836.
47. Invented by Richard Hoe, the double-cylinder press increased the output of printed sheets from two to four thousand an hour. Maury Klein, "A Cheap but Respectable Newspaper: The Early Years of the New York Times," *American History Illustrated*, August 1975, 18.
48. Michael Schudson, *Discovering the News: A Social History of American Newspapers* (New York: Basic Books, 1978), 17–19.

49. Paul Lancaster, "Faking It," *American Heritage*, October/November 1982, 51.
50. *Republican Monitor* (Cazenovia, New York), April 26, 1836.
51. *Boston Atlas*, April 16, 1836.
52. *Daily National Intelligencer*, April 27, 1836.
53. *New York Times*, April 7, 1836.
54. *New York Sun*, April 14, 1836.
55. Ruth R. Olivera and Lilian Crété, *Life in Mexico under Santa Anna* (Norman: University of Oklahoma Press 1991), 10, 237.
56. Costeltoe, "The Mexican Press of 1836," 533, 539–542.
57. Ibid., 541–542.
58. José Enrique de la Peña, *With Santa Anna in Texas: A Personal Narrative of the Revolution*, trans. and ed. by Carmen Perry (College Station: Texas A & M University Press, 1975), xxiv.
59. Ibid., 58–59, 60.
60. Ibid., 83–85.

Chapter 1

1. One of these frontiersmen may have been Rezin Bowie, brother of James. See William C. Davis, *Three Roads to the Alamo: The Lives and Fortunes of David Crockett, James Bowie, and William Barret Travis* (New York: Harper Collins, 1998), 44, 594, n. 36.
2. *Arkansas Gazette*, December 8, 1835; J. R. Edmondson, *The Alamo Story, From Early History to Current Conflicts* (Plano: Republic of Texas Press, 2000), 34–36; Paul I. Wellman, *Glory, God and Gold: A Narrative History* (New York: Doubleday and Company, 1954), 207–208.
3. According to a letter from "St. Antonio" dated April 23, 1813, these "Fourteen men (after reiterated assurances of protection) were clandestinely taken off, and their *throats cut from ear to ear.*" *Pennsylvania Chronicle*, July 26, 1813.
4. The fact that "Bernardo" Gutiérrez had promised his Royalist prisoners a safe escort to La Bahía, only to privately order that escort to massacre them by cutting their throats, repulsed even some diehard frontiersmen. *Bennington News-Letter* (Vermont), July 6, 1813.
5. *Franklin Gazette* (Pennsylvania), September 11, 1819.
6. Davis, *Three Roads to the Alamo*, 51.
7. Wellman, *Glory, God and Gold*, 212.
8. Ibid.
9. Edmondson, *The Alamo Story*, 56–65.

Chapter 2

1. The *Essex Register* (Massachusetts) of November 1, 1827, summarized this account under the headline, "Particulars of the Late Bloody Affair Between a Party of White Savages on the Mississippi."
2. Mark Derr, *The Frontiersman: The Real Life and the Many Legends of Davy Crockett* (New York: William Morrow, 1993), 198. See also Jim Boylston, "'Sketches' Re-Examined: The First Crockett Biography," *Crockett Chronicle* 16 (May 2007), 3–7.
3. Quoted in Boylston, "'Sketches' Re-Examined," 6.
4. Marquis James, *The Raven: A Biography of Sam Houston* (New York: Paperback Library Inc., 1966), 67–70.
5. Davis, *Three Roads to the Alamo*, 199.
6. Ibid., 201–206.
7. Ibid., 341.

Chapter 3

1. "The Fredonian Rebellion," in Francis Johnson's *A History of Texas and Texans* (New York: American Historical Association, 1914), 26–50. Over two years later a newspaper noted that Nacogdoches, "at the time evacuated by the Fredonians only contained five or six houses, and one small store.—Within less than three years about one hundred and twenty-five houses have been erected, of rough construction, many of them however are very comfortable, and the country in the vicinity is settling very rapidly with inhabitants, principally from the United States of America. The inhabitants of the town probably amount to about 650, exclusive of the military, of whom there is 250 stationed here under the command of Col. Pedras. It likewise contains 8 stores; a Post-office; 1 tannery with considerable shoe manufactory attached to it; 1 saddler's shop; 3 blacksmith shops; 1 silver and gunsmith shop; 1 hatter; 2 bakers; 1 confectioner; 2 tailors; 2 waggon makers; and two public houses."—*Daily National Intelligencer*, October 20, 1829.
2. Michael C. Meyer and William H. Beezley, eds., *The Oxford History of Mexico* (New York: Oxford University Press, 2000), 347–350. "Either the government occupies Texas *now*," warned General Manuel Mier y Terán following his surveying tours of the province in 1828 and 1829, "or it is lost forever," Johnson, *Texas and Texans*, 62.
3. Davis, *Three Roads to the Alamo*, 262–267.
4. Ibid., 347–348. The *Richmond Enquirer* (September 9, 1832) had a brief notice of Piedras's surrender but made no mention of either Bowie's role or the encounter at the Angelina River.

5. Thom Hatch, *Encyclopedia of the Alamo and the Texas Revolution* (Jefferson, N.C.: McFarland, 1999), 47, 161.

6. Davis, *Three Roads to the Alamo*, 362–363; Johnson, *Texas and Texans*, 120.

7. "Extract of a letter from S. F. Austin, dated MEXICO, June 3d, 1834," *Nashville Banner & Nashville Whig*, August 19, 1834.

8. Stephen Austin to his brother-in-law James F. Perry, January 16, 1834, in Johnson, *Texas and Texans*, 141; Austin to his cousin Mrs. M. A. Holley, April 21, 1835, in Johnson, *Texas and Texans*, 145.

9. It was reprinted in Philadelphia's *Public Ledger*, May 22, 1838.

10. See also Gary S. Zaboly, "Davy Crockett: A New Eyewitness Description—and More," *Alamo Journal*, no. 105 (June 1997).

11. Meyer and Beezley, *Oxford History of Mexico*, 330–331.

12. Johnson, *Texas and Texans*, 200–203, 206, 209.

13. Ibid, 207–208, 210.

14. *Texas Republican*, August 22, 1835.

Chapter 4

1. Stephen L. Hardin, *Texian Iliad: A Military History of the Texas Revolution* (Austin: University of Texas Press, 1994), 14–15.

2. Added the *Elyria Republican* (December 24, 1835): "Money and arms were also captured, both desirable kinds of ammunition; with some prisoners, among whom were two Mexican officers."

3. *New Hampshire Patriot*, January 11, 1836, quoting from an article in the *Telegraph and Texas Register* (November 11, 1835).

4. For Cos's signal rockets, see also "Account of the Siege and Battle of Bexar from within Bexar from the Diary of Samuel Maverick 1835," Sons of DeWitt Colony Texas website at www.tamu.edu/ccbn/dewitt/bexarmaverick .htm; for the black flag battery, see letter by veteran Charles Mason to Colonel Frank W. Johnson, dated February 4, 1874, in Johnson, *Texas and Texans*, 268.

5. This became almost a kind of sport as witnessed in the following report, which was written at Nacogdoches and published in the *Texan and Emigrants Guide* (December 25, 1835): "It is said that the Texeans besieging San Antonio delight in being shot at, the balls of the enemy serve them in turn. All anxiously watch the flash of a Mexican cannon, and throw themselves flat on the ground, and in an instant rise and give chase to the ball bounding over the field, hallooing 'stop that ball' and when unable to overtake it, 'lost ball, Captain.'"

6. Captain Almeron Dickinson (sometimes called Dickerson), one of the Texian artillery officers killed in the assault of March 6, 1836. He would be a appointed a "first lieutenant of the Artillery in the regular Army of Texas" on December 7, 1835, according to the *Telegraph and Texas Register* (January 1, 1836).

7. Davis, *Three Roads to the Alamo*, 328, 397.

8. *U.S. Telegraph*, August 22, 1835; Davis, *Three Roads to the Alamo*, 405–406.

Chapter 5

1. *New York Sun*, September 19, 1835.

2. Manley F. Cobia Jr., *Journey into the Land of Trials: The Story of Davy Crockett's Expedition to the Alamo* (Franklin, Tenn.: Hillsboro Press, 2003), 36.

3. The "Big Prairie" essentially covered the county of Prairie, in present-day Arkansas, as verified by an advertisement in the *Arkansas Gazette* (March 26, 1844), which noted the establishment of a post-coach line to carry the mail from the steamboat dock at Rockroe (present-day Clarendon) on the White River, "thro' the Big Prairie to Little Rock," a thirty-two-hour ride for a coach. This reference in the *Gazette* also proves that Crockett did not take a steamboat from Memphis to Little Rock, as some other writers have posited.

4. Many of the traditions concerning Crockett's movements in northeastern Texas are well explored and analyzed by Cobia, in *Journey into the Land of Trials*, 55–95.

5. Sixty-five years later Jesse J. Watkins—in 1835 a child of seven—would claim a "vivid recollection" of Crockett at his family's Blossom Prairie cabin, remembering that he wore "his hunting shirt and foxskin cap, with the tail hanging down behind and his long rifle, and especially his talking so much." "Early Recollections," *Dallas Morning News*, January 18, 1900.

6. In an interview with the two sons of Matthew Click, a Tennessean who had settled between today's Paris and Mount Vernon, Texas, T. J. Crooks was told of Crockett's visit to their home, and how he and their father had gone "bear hunting together, in which they were very successful." To haul the bear back "they improvised what is known as a 'lizard.' This lizard was made from the forked limbs of a bois d'arc tree, on which the bear was placed." One of Click's sons added that "the tail of Davy's horse was fastened to the lizard and the horse thus hitched pulled to the house the first bear he killed in Texas." T. J. Crooks, "Early Days in Texas," *Dallas Morning News*, July 28, 1901.

7. In 1836, Warren Abel, a young entrepreneur from

Massachusetts, established a stockaded trading post "a mile below Choctaw Bayou in what became extreme northwestern Fannin County." "Warren, Abel," *The Handbook of Texas Online*, www .tshaonline.org.

8. David Crockett to his son and daughter, San Augustine, Texas, January 1, 1836, from a photograph of the letter posted on the website of Abilene Christian University at www.acu.edu/ academics/library/govdoc/crockett.html. It is a letter of arguable authenticity only because it seems not to be in Crockett's own hand and may have been a copy penned by a scribe. In it Crockett specified, "I expect in all probability to settle on the Bodark [Bois d'Arc] or Choctaw Bayou of Red River." The "pass" for buffalo Crockett mentioned is somewhat verified in a journal kept by an officer of Col. Henry Dodge's dragoon expedition of 1834 from Fort Gibson, Arkansas Territory, southwestward into Comanche and Pawnee country. In his June 28 entry he noted that the troopers had encamped on the banks of the Bois d'Arc and had seen "a herd of buffalo this morning, some thirty or forty in number." "Journal of Col. Dodge's Expedition from Fort Gibson to the Pawnee Pict Village," *Arkansas Gazette*, February 24, 1835. This was *not* the Bois d'Arc of Fannin County, but a stream of the same name on the *Arkansas* side of the Red River, about thirty-five miles west of the Texas creek and nearly opposite Choctaw Bayou. On the Library of Congress copy of John Arrowsmith's *Map of Texas*, published in London in 1841, both streams are labeled, and handwritten notations by William Bollaert indicate "Buffaloes" between Texas's Bois d'Arc and the headwaters of the Sabine River. From a brief narrative in his 1844 journal that summarized his travels that January and February, Bollaert wrote: "Among the wild animals that roam almost undisturbed in this region, the bison, or buffalo, and wild horse are conspicuous, the former rolling onwards from our approach like porpoises at sea." See Eugene Hollon, ed., *Willaim Bollaert's Texas* (Norman: University of Oklahoma Press, 1989), 321.

9. Paul Lack, ed., *The Diary of William Fairfax Gray, from Virginia to Texas, 1835–1837* (Dallas: Southern Methodist University, 1997), 80.

Chapter 6

1. Horatio A. Alsbury to General Sam Houston, December 30, 1835, in Wallace O. Chariton, *100 Days in Texas: The Alamo Letters* (Plano, Tex.: Wordware Publishing Inc., 1990), 78.

2. Houston to Governor Henry Smith, Goliad, January 17, 1836, in Johnson, *History of Texas and Texans*, 398.

3. Natalie Ornish, *Ehrenberg: Goliad Survivor, Old West Explorer*, trans. Peter Mollenhauer (Dallas: Texas Heritage Press, 1997), 180–185.

4. *Telegraph and Texas Register*, January 16, 1836.

5. Davis, *Three Roads to the Alamo*, 504–505.

6. Placido Benavides was the *alcalde* of Victoria and an ardent anti-Centralist (Hardin, *Texian Iliad*, 28). "Colonel Gonzales, a former federal officer," had joined the Texians with "some hundred Mexican adherents" shortly after the fall of San Antonio, and promised additional support for the Matamoros expedition. "He left, after promising to keep us informed of his movements," wrote Frank Johnson, "and to establish a place of rendezvous. That was the last we heard of him." Johnson, *History of Texas and Texans*, 419.

7. José María Rodríguez noted that a path led from his father's house "through the chapparal. At the river where the Commerce Street bridge now is, a mesquite log served as a footbridge. Beyond the river the path wound on until it came to the cleared plaza about the Alamo." "J. M. Rodriguez Relates Story of Fall of Alamo," *Daily Express*, May 5, 1905.

Chapter 7

1. Col. Juan Nepomuceno Almonte was already known to some Texians and Americans. He was the son of Father José María Morelos y Pavon, a Hidalgo-era revolutionary leader who, like Hidalgo, ended up being captured by Royalist troops and executed in 1815. Fluent in English, Almonte had received an early education in the United States and later served as Mexico's representative to England. He toured Texas in 1834 and returned to warn that Mexico should either send more of its troops to garrison that province or be prepared to lose it. Hatch, *Encyclopedia of the Alamo and the Texas Revolution*, 38–39. His original journal of the campaign was sent to Washington, D.C., from the offices of the *New York Herald* on June 28, 1836, for the president to read (*New York Herald*, June 29, 1836). What happened to it afterward remains a mystery.

2. "By the 15th of March, I think Texas will be invaded, and every preparation should be made to receive them." Travis to Henry Smith, San Antonio, February 13, 1836, in Johnson, *History of Texas and Texans*, 401.

3. Lord, *A Time to Stand*, 97.

4. This is one case in which Almonte obviously, and erroneously, added information to his original journal entry long after the noted date, since Travis in his letter of March 3 wrote that the contingent of thirty-two

Gonzales men had arrived in the early morning darkness of March 1. Captain Philip Dimmitt, writing to Major James Kerr on February 28 from "Dimmitt's Point, at the mouth of the Lavaca," noted that while he was at "the Rovia" on February 24, he heard "heavy cannonading" from San Antonio, "particularly at the close of the evening," Todd Hansen, ed., *The Alamo Reader: A Study in History* (Mechanicsburg, Penn.: Stackpole Books, 2003), 600.

5. Travis's letter has been published in full in many books. See, for instance, Hansen, *Alamo Reader*, 32, and Lord, *A Time to Stand*, 14.

6. Costletoe, "The Mexican Press of 1836," 535.

7. Richard G. Santos, *Santa Anna's Campaign against Texas, 1835–1836* (Waco, Tex.: Texian Press, 1968), 67–68; see also photographic record of the actual report in Santos's appendix.

8. "Six stops per square," or "*seis paradas por plaza,*" as it reads in the original Mexican newspaper printing. "Stop per square" was a term often used by the Mexican military of the nineteenth century to denote an issuance of musket or rifle cartridges, whether in paper or cloth cartridge form or of loose ball. The number per issue, which in the case of cartridges probably came in package form, is not known. During one of the 1862 battles between the French and Mexicans, a Mexican commander bemoaned the fact that his soldiers had virtually run out of ammunition, with perhaps "two stops per square in some cartridge boxes and the major part of them nothing." Carlos de Gagera, *Apela cion de los Mexicanos a la Europa bien informada de la Europa mal informa* (Mexico, 1862), 38. Among the items in an 1841 list of equipment issued for Mexican infantry was "*paradas de cartucheos con balla,*" which translates as "stops of cartridges with ball." This was immediately followed by "*idem. sin ella,*" or "the same without it," possibly meaning a cartridge without a ball or a loose ball. *Memoria del Ministerio de Guerra y Marina Presentada a las Camares del Congreso Gen. Mexicano en Enero de 1841.* Of course Santa Anna's order does not mean that the grenadiers and cazadores carried *only* six issues of cartridge packages (or the fusiliers *only* four) into the battle, but rather that these cartridges were meant to supplement those already in their boxes. The latter, on average, held about twenty-four cartridges to begin with. If we accept Santa Anna's estimate that 1,400 *soldados* took part in the March 6 assault, that means that even before the issuance of extra ammunition they carried possibly as many as 33,600 cartridges—assuming their cartridge boxes already held twenty-four—or over 181 rounds per Alamo defender.

Chapter 8

1. Hatch, *Encyclopedia of the Alamo and the Texas Revolution*, 50.

2. In expressing his determination to hold San Antonio and the Alamo, James Bowie had noted in a February 2 letter to Governor Henry Smith that he and Col. James Neill "have come to the solemn resolution that we will rather die in these ditches than give it up to the enemy." Hansen, *Alamo Reader*, 20.

3. Daniel Cloud's letter, essentially an enthusiastic appraisal of the Texians and their revolution, can be read in its entirety in Chariton, *100 Days in Texas*, 67–69.

4. According to most of the Mexican accounts that have Crockett being executed on Santa Anna's orders, the *generalissimo* was in the Alamo's main plaza at the time surveying his conquest. But what would the Mexican general's "tent" be doing there at such a time, apparently less than an hour after the fall of the fort? If properly translated by Dolson, the Spanish word for tent is *tienta*, but this can also refer to a shop, a stall or booth, or a cover for a wagon or boat. *Neuman and Baretti's Dictionary of the Spanish and English Languages* (Boston, 1839), 664. If such a jerry-built affair had been set up, was it meant as a central storage depot for any of the enemy's valuables the Mexican officers could collect before their victorious soldiers did? The soldados had been allowed to loot, but Santa Anna's officers evidently hunted for what were, militarily and politically, the most prized articles, and before the end of the day Santa Anna had accumulated a number of defenders' items, including Travis's "bag" containing assorted documents, "official dispatches" belonging to the other officers, Crockett's rifle and accouterments, the garrison flags, including that of the New Orleans Greys, and eventually a considerable pile of arms and ammunition, not to mention money. When his army had captured San Antonio on February 23, Santa Anna had assigned Col. Juan Almonte to take charge of the enemy's stores found in town (Almonte's journal, February 23, 1836, printed in *New York Herald*, June 23, 1836). These were later sold by the commander in chief "out of his own headquarters at four times the market price after the best part of it had been picked out for the personal use of his Excellency and his favorites." Peña, *With Santa Anna in Texas*, 61–62. In his diary Sánchez Navarro wrote that "3 or 4 remnants of tent" had been seized by the army in Béxar on February 23, "and one has the label 'tent of the Government' under which expensive things are sold for money" (C. D. Huneycutt, *At the Alamo: The Memoirs of Captain Navarro* [New

London, N.C.: Gold Star Press, 1989], 67). Of course there is also the possibility that Dolson's informant merely said that the men "were marched to Santa Anna," and that Dolson added the word "tent," assuming that was what his informant had meant.

5. Dolson means that Almonte, not his "informant," was familiar with Crockett. Obviously the period in the parentheses is a printer's error—newspapers of the time were rife with them; the entirety of this article alone contains ten typographical errors—and it should have been placed after "informant." At the time of this interview, July 19, Almonte was with Santa Anna at Columbia, Texas (letter from Galveston Bay, July 21, 1836, in *Daily National Intelligencer*, August 17, 1836).

6. This does not mean that Almonte had *met* Crockett before, rather that he was familiar with Crockett's reputation. Almonte was bilingual, having received an education in the United States, and because US newspapers were regularly shipped to Mexican ports, he certainly knew something of Crockett's publicized progress both in and out of the halls of Congress. On the other hand, decades later Enrique Esparza recalled that Crockett had had conferences with Santa Anna during lulls in the bombardment (Hansen, *Alamo Reader*, 98–99). If there is any grain of truth in this, Crockett may have conferred with the English-speaking Almonte, as the latter had with Green B. Jameson on February 23.

7. It agrees to some extent with the account of Crockett's last moments given to Creed Taylor by former Mexican soldier Rafael Soldana, which was first published in James T. DeShields's *Tall Men with Long Rifles: The Glamorous Story of the Texas Revolution, as Told by Captain Creed Taylor, Who Fought in That Heroic Struggle from Gonzales to San Jacinto* (San Antonio: Naylor Company, 1935). It was reprinted in Hansen, *Alamo Reader*, 470–471.

8. Sam Houston Dixon, "Sketch of Capt. R. M. Potter," *Galveston News*, December 16, 1878.

9. A few 1836 accounts and news reports also place Santa Anna in a battery to the west of the fort, rather than north of it, during the assault. This would place him in the loop of land made by the San Antonio River. Other accounts give his position at the north battery. Mexican veteran Manuel Loranca recalled decades later that Santa Anna was "east of the Alamo . . . with the music of the regiment of Dolores and his staff to direct the movements." *San Antonio Express*, June 28, 1878.

10. By this Potter indicates that the "small gun" that had been "wheeled against the assailants within" was located on the "upper works" of the roofless Alamo

church. In his later "Fall of the Alamo," Potter places this gun on what he theorized was a high battery along the fort's west wall.

Chapter 9

1. Fascinatingly, Herman Ehrenberg, of the New Orleans Greys, noted in his memoir that Goliad had received "private letters of Travis, the commander, and letters from Bowie and Crockett," urging Fannin to send reinforcements to the Alamo. Natalie Ornish, *Ehrenberg*, 206–207. Were these letters eventually destroyed, or do they now lie bundled and forgotten in a south-of-the-border archive?

2. A psychological tactic employed by Santa Anna during the Alamo siege. See Rafael Soldana's account in Hansen, *Alamo Reader*, 470.

3. The luckless Dr. Benjamin Harrison died in North Bend, Ohio, in 1840, "very suddenly," at his father's residence. *New Bedford Mercury*, June 26, 1840.

Chapter 10

1. In fact the two cannon, six-pounders, were a gift from "the people of Cincinnati." Johnson, *A History of Texas and Texans*, 445.

2. Santa Anna to Vicente Filisola, April 22, 1836, *Richmond Enquirer*, July 15, 1836.

3. Journal of Dr. Barnard for May 22–24 in Hansen, *Alamo Reader*, 613–615.

4. Charles E. Gilbert Jr., *Flags of Texas* (Gretna, La.: Pelican Publishing Company, 1989), 74–75.

5. "It [the play] must be a bloody affair," observed the *Boston Morning Post* of June 2, 1836. San Jacinto was also deemed a fit subject for public entertainment; in New York City, the battle was recreated as an animated diorama model in a venue opposite St. Paul's Church. *Morning Courier and New York Enquirer*, August 5, 1836.

6. James Atkins Shackford, *Davy Crockett: The Man and the Legend* (Chapel Hill: University of North Carolina Press, 1986), 275.

7. Juan Seguín to General Rusk, Béxar, June 7, 1836; Seguín's commission as a lieutenant colonel, September 17, 1836; and John A. Wharton's orders to Juan Seguín, September 17, 1836, were all reproduced in Jack Jackson, *Los Tejanos* (Stamford, Conn.: Fantagraphics Books Inc., 1982), 132–133.

8. This makes it clear that the ashes of the third and largest pyre were not buried by Seguín on February 25, 1837. But in a letter he wrote fifty-two years later, Seguín did not mention any coffin burial; rather that he "ordered that the ashes deposited in an urn and that a grave be opened in the Cathedral of San Antonio, close to the Presbytery, that is, in front

of the altar railings, but very near the altar steps."
Juan Seguín to Hamilton P. Bee, March 28, 1889, in
Hansen, *Alamo Reader*, 204. Is this what he eventually
did with the ashes of the third and largest pyre, or is it
just the confused, hazy recollection of an old man?

Chapter 11

1. Travis to Governor Smith, Béxar, February 15, 1836,
   in Hansen, *Alamo Reader*, 25.
2. *Houston Telegraph*, January 9, 1839.
3. Donaly E. Brice, *The Great Comanche Raid: Boldest
   Attack of the Texas Republic* (Austin: Eakin Press,
   1987), 25.

Alamo during the Siege Essay

1. Antonio López de Santa Anna quoted in Carlos
   Castañeda, *The Mexican Side of the Texas Revolution*
   (Dallas, 1928), 202. (The orders were sent to
   Andrade by General Vicente Filisola, not Santa
   Anna.)
2. Extract from the diary of Dr. Joseph H. Barnard in
   "With Fannin at Goliad," *Dallas Morning News*,
   September 11, 1892. The pertinent extracts can also
   be found in Hansen, *Alamo Reader*, 615.
3. J. S. MaCaulay, *A Treatise on Field Fortification,
   and Other Subjects Connected with the Duties of
   the Field Engineer* (London: James Fraser, Regent
   Street, 1834), 166.
4. Letter dated "Natchitoches, June 13, 1836," in *New
   York American*, July 7, 1836.
5. *New York American*, November 25, 1836.
6. "Scenes in Texas," *Graham's Magazine*,
   January 1851, 39.
7. *The Sun* (Baltimore), February 18, 1839.
8. *New Bedford Mercury*, July 1, 1842.
9. Hollon, *William Bollaert's Texas*, 224.
10. William A. McClintock, "Journal of a Trip
    through Texas & Northern Mexico in 1846-1847,"
    Southwestern Historical Quarterly, 34, no. 1 (July
    1930): 145.
11. Comments by an unidentified Texan, "How the
    Alamo Looked Nine Years after Its Fall," *San
    Antonio Daily Express*, April 9, 1905.
12. *San Luis Advocate*, November 18, 1840.
13. Most of these plats can be seen in George Nelson,
    The Alamo: An Illustrated History (Uvalde, Tex.:
    Aldine Books, 2009).
14. Jameson to Smith and Houston, 1836, in Hansen,
    Alamo Reader, 570–573.
15. Santa Anna to the Government, and to General
    Filisola, Béxar, February 27, 1836, *El Mosquito
    Mexicano*, March 18, 1836; also in Santos, *Santa
    Anna's Campaign against Texas*, 67.

16. Huneycutt, *At the Alamo*, 63–64.
17. General Ampudia's list in Hansen, *Alamo Reader*, 377.
18. John Sowers Brooks to James Hagerty, Fort
    Defiance, Goliad, March 9, 1836, in Hansen, *Alamo
    Reader*, 606.
19. Huneycutt, *At the Alamo*, 75.
20. Ibid., 63.
21. Reuben M. Potter, "The Fall of the Alamo"
    (extracts); Hansen, *Alamo Reader*, 698.
22. *Charlotte News*, January 18, 1890. These could have
    been cannonballs fired by Austin's artillerymen the
    previous year. As Francis Johnson wrote to Robert
    McAlpin Williamson on November 18, 1835: "The
    pieces we have are too small though we will make
    the best use of them possible, but for them we have
    but few balls which we are now trying to remedy
    by collecting all the copper & bells about the old
    missions and casting it into ball for the pieces we
    have here." Available at Sons of Dewitt Colony
    website, www.tamu.edu/ccbn/dewitt/dewitt.htm.
23. Ornish, *Ehrenberg*, 134–136.
24. Joseph Field, *Three Years in Texas, Including a
    View of the Texas Revolution, and an Account of the
    Principal Battles* (Greenfield, Mass.: n.p.,1836), 18.
25. D. W. C. Baker, comp., *A Texas Scrap Book* (New
    York: A. S. Barnes and Co., 1875), 649.
26. *New London Gazette* (Connecticut), December 16, 1835.
27. Francis Johnson, "Conditions in Texas, 1826–1834,"
    in Johnson, *History of Texas and Texans*, 156.
28. Johnson to Williamson, November 18, 1835.
    Available at Sons of Dewitt Colony website, www
    .tamu.edu/ccbn/dewitt/dewitt.htm.
29. Jameson to Houston, Bexar, January 18, 1836, in
    Hansen, *Alamo Reader*, 571. Jameson's "contemplated"
    additions, however, were for the most part never built,
    as, he wrote, "the men will not labour."
30. Santa Anna quoted in Alan C. Huffines, *Blood
    of Noble Men: The Alamo Siege and Battle: An
    Illustrated Chronicle* (Austin: Eakin Press, 1999), 21.
31. "The Defence of Mexico," *New Hampshire Sentinel*,
    January 6, 1848.
32. Alwyn Barr, *Texans in Revolt: The Battle for San
    Antonio, 1835* (Austin: University of Texas Press,
    1990), 26.
33. "Account of the Siege and Battle of Bexar from
    within Bexar from the Diary of Samuel Maverick
    1835". Available at Sons of DeWitt Colony
    Texas website, www.tamu.edu/ccbn/dewitt/
    bexarmaverickhtm.
34. An undated "translation" of a message to Austin in
    Baker, *A Texas Scrap Book*, 649.
35. "William T. Austin's Account of the Siege and
    Battle of Bexar," written in 1844, in Guy M. Bryan,

A Comprehensive History of Texas (n.p.). A letter in the *New Orleans Bulletin* almost matched this number, indicating that "the garrison has 28 pieces of cannon," reprinted in the *New Hampshire Statesman and State Journal,* January 2, 1836.

36. James Ivey, *Mission to Fortress: the Defense of the Alamo* (unpublished ms.), 9, 11–12; Nelson, *The Alamo,* 36–38. The threat of Texas being invaded by US filibusters, as indeed eventually occurred, and the ebb and flow of Spanish Royalist and Mexican rebel troops in the years between 1810 and 1821, also led to additional repairs and revamping of the compound's architecture (not to mention damage).

37. James Ivey, *Estrada or Navarro? The Jose Juan Sanchez Vista and Plano of the Alamo,* manuscript in author's collection, kindly provided by Mr. Ivey.

38. Fray Lopez's 1789 description of Mission San Antonio de Valero, quoted in Anne A. Fox, Feris A. Bass Jr., and Thomas R. Hester, *The Archaeology and History of Alamo Plaza,* Archaeological Survey Report No. 16 (University of Texas, San Antonio: Center for Archaeological Research, 1976), 5.

39. Nelson, *The Alamo,* 38.

40. Jean Louis Berlandier, *Journey to Mexico during the Years 1826 to 1834* (Austin: University of Texas, 1980), 2:292.

41. James Bowie and James Walker Fannin to Stephen Austin, October 22, 1835, in E. W. Winkler, *Manuscripts and Documents of Early Texians in Facsimile* (Austin: Steck, 1937). "Unburnt bricks" referred to sun-dried adobe bricks, as opposed to kiln-dried bricks. This method of reinforcing rooftop parapets was confirmed in a letter written by Colonel Frank Johnson to General Edward Burleson, dated December 9, 1835, noting "the enemy were observed to have occupied the tops of houses in our front, where, under cover of breastworks, they opened, through loop-holes, a very brisk fire of small arms on our whole line." Chariton, *100 Days in Texas,* 15.

42. "William T. Austin's Account of the Siege and Battle of Bexar," 1844, in Bryan, *Comprehensive History of Texas,* n.p.

43. Becerra account in Hansen, *Alamo Reader,* 456. Andrea Castanon Villanueva, better known as Madam Candelaria, also testified in later years that the church's "great front door had been piled full of sand bags." Timothy M. Matovina, *The Alamo Remembered: Tejano Accounts and Perspectives* (Austin: University of Texas Press, 1995), 60. Many scholars doubt that she was in the Alamo during the battle, but in this case her statement jibes with Sergeant Becerra's.

44. Sánchez Navarro's original drawing, as well as his two plans of the Alamo, can be found in Nelson, *The Alamo,* 50–51. If the lieutenant colonel's drawing represented what he actually saw, then the Alamo as a battlemented church/compound was far from being unique. See for instance, the nineteenth-century photograph of a Santa Fe parish church and its perimeter walls, both heavily crenellated, in *The Spanish West* (New York: Time-Life, 1976), 144–145.

45. Lewis F. Fisher, *The Spanish Missions of San Antonio* (San Antonio: Maverick Publishing Company, 1998), 4–5.

46. Ornish, *Ehrenberg,* 165.

47. Potter in Johnson, *History of Texas and Texans,* 411.

48. "Death of Crockett," *Cincinnati Commercial Tribune,* June 14, 1884.

49. Potter in Johnson, *History of Texas and Texans,* 414.

50. Potter, "Attack and Defence of the Alamo," *San Luis Advocate,* November 18, 1840.

51. Potter, *The Fall of the Alamo* (San Antonio: n.p., 1860), 10.

52. Military report by General Ampudia, March 6, 1836, in Hansen, *Alamo Reader,* 376.

53. Biography of William S. Oury by Cornelius Smith, in Hansen, *Alamo Reader,* 226.

54. Potter in Johnson, *History of Texas and Texans,* 412.

55. Ibid., 415.

56. Colonel Almonte's Journal, *New York Herald,* June 22, 1836.

57. See for example, the narratives of Pablo Díaz and Juan Chavez in Matovina, *The Alamo Remembered,* 75, 96. After the battle, recalled Díaz, "I saw the red flag of Santa Anna floating from the Alamo, where the Constitutional flag had been." Herman Ehrenberg penned a speech he imagined Santa Anna had given to his soldiers before their assault on the Alamo, in which the general urged them to plant their flag on "the church instead of the star." Ornish, *Ehrenberg,* 215.

58. In November 1835, the Texas Council had approved a flag for "privateers," patterned, color-wise, after the Mexican flag, "with the figures 1, 8, 2, 4 cyphered in large Arabics on the white ground thereof." As late as April 1836, Texian naval vessels were still flying under this flag. Johnson and Grant had also carried an "1824" tricolor south from Béxar on their doomed Matamoros expedition. Johnson, *History of Texas and Texans,* 328, 369; *New Orleans Bee,* May 18, 1836.

59. Colonel Neill to the Governor and Council, Béxar, January 6, 1836, in Hansen, *Alamo Reader,* 648–649. See also pages 652, 658, 665, 670–671; Johnson, *History of Texas and Texans,* 338.

60. Almonte's journal entry, March 9, 1836, *New York Herald,* June 27, 1836.

61. Vicente Filisola, *Memorias para la Guerra de Tejas,* 2 vols. (Mexico, 1848–1849), 2:183–184.

62 Journal of Dr. Barnard in Hansen, *Alamo Reader*, 614.
63. Potter in Johnson, *History of Texas and Texans*, 411. A twelve-foot-high tereplain would have stood, in 1836 terms, about even with the top of the main door to the church, or half the height of the building's west wall: not a commanding position.
64. McClintock, "Journal," 145.
65. Peña, *With Santa Anna in Texas*, 45–46.
66. Samuel Maverick to Captain S. M. Howe, July 3, 1847, in Rena Maverick Green, ed., *Samuel Maverick, Texan, 1803–1870: A Collection of Letters, Journals and Memoirs* (New York: Augustus M. Kelly, Inc., 1952), 324.
67. Journal of Dr. Barnard in Hansen, *Alamo Reader*, 614–615.
68. For several nineteenth-century examples of flat ladders used in shipbuilding, see Alexander Laing, *The American Heritage History of Seafaring America* (New York: American Heritage Publishing Company, Inc., 1974), 120, 204–205, 250.
69. Felix Nuñez account in Hansen, *Alamo Reader*, 481.
70. Nelson, *The Alamo*, 38.
71. Rev. O. Newell, *History of the Revolution in Texas, Particularly of the War of 1835 & '36* (New York: Wiley and Putnam, 1838), 69.
72. Some of the planks used in San Antonio for rooftops, walls, and other construction projects, later cannibalized by Cos's troops for their fortifications, had been supplied to the town by the lumber mill in Gonzales. Johnson, *History of Texas and Texans*, 174.
73. Mrs. Dickinson's memoir, written by Captain John E. Elgin, circa 1876, in Hansen, *Alamo Reader*, 60. The Dickinson quarters were in the sacristy, the room immediately northwest of the cavalier battery mound. The "large trees" may indicate that saplings had grown quickly over the four months since the erection of the cavalier battery or else they were trees that had been growing in the chancel even before the 1835 campaign.
74. Potter in Johnson, *History of Texas and Texans*, 411, and facing compound plan.
75. See for instance, *Fortifications and Military Engineering* (London: The Royal Military Academy at Woolwich, 1884), 83.
76. Sutherland memoir in Hansen, *Alamo Reader*, 169.
77. Sutherland memoir in Hansen, *Alamo Reader*, 146.
78. Newell, *History of the Revolution in Texas*, 91.
79. "The Alamo," *The Sun* (Maryland), February 18, 1839. The article originally appeared in the *New Orleans Bulletin*. Just where the "chime of three bells" was located remains a mystery.
80. "Scenes in Texas," *Graham's Magazine*, January 1851, 39.
81. Macaulay, *Treatise on Field Fortification*, 83–84.
82. D. H. Mahan, *A Complete Treatise on Field Fortification* (New York: Wiley and Long, 1836), 56.
83. Bowie and Fannin to Austin, October 22, 1835, in *Manuscript Letters and Documents*.
84. Filisola, *Memorias*, 2:184.
85. Newell, *History of the Revolution in Texas*, 69.
86. Anne A. Fox, *Archaeological Investigations in Alamo Plaza, San Antonio, Bexar County, Texas, 1988 and 1989* (University of Texas, San Antonio: Center for Archaeological Research, 1992), 16.
87. Sutherland narrative in Hansen, *Alamo Reader*, 145.
88. Potter, *Fall of the Alamo* (1860), 8.
89. Sutherland memoir in Hansen, *Alamo Reader*, 175.
90. Potter in Johnson, *History of Texas and Texans*, 412.
91. Ivey, *Mission to Fortress*, 27–28. A near-contemporary depiction of a palisade with a complete earthen glacis before it can be seen in the background of Carlo Paris's circa 1834 oil preliminary for *The Battle of Tampico*, the latter intended as a celebration of Santa Anna's 1829 victory over the invading Spanish. *The Spanish West*, 111.
92. See Hansen, *Alamo Reader*, 588.
93. "Documents Published by General Andrade about the Evacuation of the City of San Antonio de Bejar in the Department of Texas," Monterrey, 25 July 1836, 131, typewritten transcript provided by Kevin R. Young.
94. Terry G. Jordan, *Texas Graveyards: A Cultural Legacy* (Austin: University of Texas Press, 2004), 75.
95. "Reminiscences of Jno. Duff Brown," *Southwestern Historical Quarterly*, 12, no. 4 (1909): 301.
96. Huneycutt, *At the Alamo*, 66.
97. Potter in Johnson, *History of Texas and Texans*, 411.
98. Ivey, *Mission to Fortress*, 9, 11.
99. Potter, *Fall of the Alamo* (1860), 10–11.
100. Ibid., 15–16.
101. William Corner, *San Antonio De Bexar: A Guide and History* (San Antonio: Bainbridge & Corner, 1890), 119.
102. Filisola, *Memorias*, 2:184.
103. Macaulay, *A Treatise on Field Fortification*, 10, 110.
104. *Aide-Memoire to the Military Sciences, Framed from Contributions of Officers and Others . . . Edited by a Committee of the Corps of Royal Engineers* (London: Lockwood & Co., 1862), 620.
105. Fox, *Archaeological Investigations in Alamo Plaza*, 21.
106. Many nineteenth-century military manuals describe tambours in their several shapes and compositions. To note just three: *Essays on the Theory and Practice of the Art of War* (London: Military Mentor, 1809), 274–275; John Michael O'Connor, *A Treatise on the Science of War and Fortification* (New York, 1817), 76–77; and Macaulay, *A Treatise on Field Fortification*, 90–91.

107. Potter in Johnson, *History of Texas and Texans*, 412. In his handwritten notes on a copy of his 1860 *Fall of the Alamo*, Potter called this position "a projecting stockade which covered a two-gun battery."

108. *Aide-Memoire to the Military Sciences*, 620.

109. Felix Salm-Salm, *My Diary in Mexico in 1867, Including the Last Days of the Emperor Maximilian* (London: n.p., 1868), 1:57. Similar Mexican works were encountered by advancing US troops near Churubusco in 1847, including this one: "a large hacienda called San Antonio, strong as a fort in itself, and doubly fortified with regular outworks and redoubts of turf and stone thrown across the causeway, and on both flanks." *The Floridian and Journal*, July 23, 1853.

110. Peter Connolly, *The Roman Army* (London: Macdonald Educational Limited, 1975), 13, 32, 39.

111. *Boston Weekly News-Letter*, March 18, 1756.

112. *Exercise of Light Infantry, with Some Instructions for Their Conduct in the Field* (Ulverston: n.p., 1804), 76.

113. *Aide-Memoire to the Military Sciences*, 620.

114. O'Connor, *A Treatise on the Science of War and Fortification*, 130.

115. Fox, *Archaeological Investigations in Alamo Plaza*, 60. Sánchez Navarro's drawing does not show pentice roofing above the palisade of the tambour; this might be explained by the fact that his viewpoint was considerably lower than the rising ground on which the Alamo sat or perhaps that the angle of the blindage was not severe enough to begin with.

116. Matovina, *Alamo Remembered*, 64.

117. Jameson's key to his plan, February 1836 in Hansen, *Alamo Reader*, 576.

118. "Fortification," *The Encyclopaedia Britannica: A Dictionary of Arts, Sciences, and General Literature* (New York, 1890), 9:438.

119. Fox, *Archaeological Investigations in Alamo Plaza*, 21.

120. Manuel Loranca interview, "Santa Anna's Last Effort," *San Antonio Express*, June 23, 1878.

121. Macaulay, *Treatise on Field Fortification*, 68.

122. Jameson key ("B") in Hansen, *Alamo Reader*, 575.

123. *Encyclopaedia Britannica*, 9:438.

124. Macaulay, *A Treatise on Field Fortification*, 73.

125. *Encyclopaedia Britannica*, 9:438; "Traverse," available at http://civilwarfortifications.com/dictionary/xgt-007.html.

126. Ivey, *Mission to Fortress*, 16.

127. Ibid., 10, 16, 21.

128. Potter in Johnson, *History of Texas and Texans*, 413.

129. Filisola, *Memorias*, 1:11.

130. Almonte journal entry, February 24, 1836, *New York Herald*, June 23, 1836.

131. Filisola, *Memorias*, 2:184. Sánchez Navarro's "Plano" shows a ditch angling around this corner, but in his key he marks it as part of a longer, outer ditch that the "colonists" had "begun, but they were unable to complete it."

132. Macaulay, *A Treatise on Field Fortification*, 67.

133. Lt. Col. C. W. Pasley, *Course of Elementary Fortification* (London: John Murray, 1822), 1:126.

134. Jameson to Houston, Béxar, January 18, 1836, in Hansen, *Alamo Reader*, 571.

135. Ivey, *Mission to Fortress*, 8.

136. Esparza interview in Hansen, *Alamo Reader*, 113.

137. Ibid., 116.

138. Peña, however, wrote that when Santa Anna entered Béxar on February 23, the Texians "had an eighteen-pounder and an eight-pounder pointing towards the town." Peña, *With Santa Anna in Texas*, 38.

139. Brown, *Volunteers in the Texas Revolution*, 11, 27–28, 34; *New Hampshire Statesman and State Journal*, January 2, 1836; Johnson, *History of Texas and Texans*, 355.

140. It is entirely possible that the gunnade had never stood within the destroyed second block of houses, that an eight-pounder did, as Peña may be suggesting, and after the eighteen-pounder was dismounted, the gunnade might have taken its place at the southwest corner. Almonte noted, on March 1, how "in the afternoon the enemy fired two 12-pound shots at the house of the President, one of which struck the president, and the other passed it." Almonte journal, *New York Herald*, June 25, 1836. The "house"—the Yturri residence on Main Plaza—contained Santa Anna's headquarters. Since the dismounted eighteen-pounder had to be replaced, and assuming that the eight-pounder remained in the second block of houses, the twelve-pound shots might well have been fired from atop the southwest corner.

141. Potter in Johnson, *History of Texas and Texans*, 414.

142. Jameson's key ("G") in Hansen, *Alamo Reader*, 584.

143. Filisola, *Memorias*, 2:184.

144. Ramon Caro, published account in Hansen, *Alamo Reader*, 383.

145. Macaulay, *Treatise of Field Fortification*, 7.

146. Ivey, *Mission to Fortress*, 25.

147. Peña, *With Santa Anna in Texas*, 175.

148. Macaulay, *Treatise of Field Fortification*, 139–140. Mahan also explains: "A hole is made through the wall to communicate with the tambour, and loop-holes are made in the wall to flank the faces of the tambour." Mahan, *Complete Treatise on Field Fortification*, 95.

149. *San Luis Advocate*, November 18, 1840.

150. *El Mosquito Mexicano*, April 5, 1836.

151. 1913 Austin (?), newspaper clipping, n.d., from Eugene C. Barker Texas History Center.

152. Peña, *With Santa Anna in Texas*, 41.
153. William P. Zuber, "Escape of Rose from the Alamo," in Hansen, *Alamo Reader*, 259.
154. Ivey, *Mission to Fortress*, 13, 14.
155. See Eastman's drawing of the Trevino block as it looked in 1848 in Nelson, *Illustrated Alamo*, 80–81. Eastman shows the doorstop of the shingled house as considerably high above the ground, obviously done to prevent flooding from the "ponds" that often formed in the compound after a rain.
156. Macaulay, *Treatise on Field Fortification*, 136.
157. Jameson plats in Hansen, *Alamo Reader*, 574, 584, 588.
158. John S. Ford, "The Fall of the Alamo," *Dallas Morning News*, November 12, 1892.
159. Sutherland narrative in Hansen, *Alamo Reader*, 154.
160. Juana Alsbury interview in Hansen, *Alamo Reader*, 87. The Maverick residence was later built where the northernmost block of mission houses stood, in the northwest corner of the compound.
161. Ford, "The Fall of the Alamo."
162. Hansen, *Alamo Reader*, 88.
163. Ivey, *Mission to Fortress*, 17.
164. Potter in Hansen, *Alamo Reader*, 699. Potter adds: "When Seguin produced the order which was to pass him and his orderly out, the sentinel at the postern began a rude comment; but a few words from the Captain, intimating that his errand was one which might bring safety, at once soothed the rough soldier, who bade him God-speed."
165. Ivey, *Mission to Fortress*, 22.
166. Filisola, *Memorias*, 2:184. Sánchez Navarro shows three guns here, but his battery is a little distance east of the northwest corner, and all three guns point north. Jameson's plats show two guns pointing north.
167. Ivey, *Mission to Fortress*, 22.
168. Filisola, *Memorias*, 2:185.
169. Maverick to S. M. Howe, July 3, 1847, Green. *Samuel Maverick*, 324.
170. Potter in Johnson, *History of Texas and Texans*, 412.
171. Peña, *With Santa Anna in Texas*, 48.
172. *The Papers of Colonel Jose Enrique de la Peña: Selected Appendices from His Diary, 1836–1839*, trans. Roger Borroel (East Chicago, Ind.: La Villita Publications, 1997), 22.
173. Peña, *With Santa Anna in Texas*, 48.
174. Ibid., 48.
175. Attack orders issued by Santa Anna, March 5, 1836, *Supplemento al Diario del Gobierno*, March 21, 1836.
176. Macaulay, *Treatise on Field Fortification*, 163.
177. "Account of the Siege and Battle of Bexar from within Bexar from the Diary of Samuel Maverick 1835," entry of November 28, 1835. Available at Sons of DeWitt Colony Texas website, www.tamu.edu/ccbn/dewitt/bexarmaverickhtm.
178. Peña, *With Santa Anna in Texas*, 48.
179. Ornish, *Ehrenberg*, 131.
180. Ivey, *Mission to Fortress*, 14.
181. Mardith K. Schuetz-Miller, *The History and Archaeology of Mission San Juan Capistrano, San Antonio, Texas,* (State Building Commission, Archaeological Program, 1968), 194.
182. Peña, *With Santa Anna in Texas*, 29.
183. Candelaria interview in Hansen, *Alamo Reader*, 298.
184. Ivey, *Mission to Fortress*, 14.
185. Peña, *With Santa Anna in Texas*, 50.
186. Macaulay, *Treatise on Field Fortification*, 146.
187. Filisola wrote that the Mexican columns attacking the east, west, and north at first "found no means of getting on tops of the flat roofs of the small rooms, whose walls formed the enclosure." Filisola, *Memorias*, 2:11.
188. Jameson to Smith, February 16, 1836, in Hansen, *Alamo Reader*, 576.
189. Ivey, *Mission to Fortress*, 18.
190. Ibid., 6.
191. Fox, *Archaeological Investigations in Alamo Plaza*, 6.
192. Enrique Esparza 1907 interview in Matovina, *Alamo Remembered*, 85.
193. Jameson key ("J" in Hansen, *Alamo Reader*, 575). The hospital had been first established by the Compania Volante in 1805; Nelson, *The Alamo*, 36. General Ampudia's postbattle inventory of the Texian armory lists "English muskets [probably Brown Besses] in usable condition, 216; Small artillery pieces (*esmeriles*), 3; Unattached bayonets, 200." Ampudia, military report, March 6, 1836, in Hansen, *Alamo Reader*, 376.
194. Hansen, *Alamo Reader*, "D."
195. For instance, he inaccurately shows an open, uncovered space where the *porteria*, or entrance into the friary patios, actually ran through the first floor of the convento. Ivey, *Mission to Fortress*, 6.
196. Potter in Hansen, *Alamo Reader*, 702.
197. Peña, *With Santa Anna in Texas*, 48.
198. Fox, *Archaeological Investigations in Alamo Plaza*, 22.
199. Nelson, *The Alamo*, 83.
200. Ibid., 95, 96.
201. Fox, *Archaeological Investigations in Alamo Plaza*, 23.
202. Almonte's journal, February 21, 1836, *New York Herald*, June 23, 1836.
203. Potter in Hansen, *Alamo Reader*, 697.
204. Esparza in Hansen, *Alamo Reader*, 106.
205. Martin Hillman, *Bridging a Continent*, vol. 8: "Encyclopedia of Discovery and Exploration" (London: Aldus Books, Ltd., 1971), 102.
206. Ivey, *Mission to Fortress*, 25.
207. Nelson, *The Alamo*, 82.

208. Sutherland narrative in Hansen, *Alamo Reader*, 178.

209. Becerra account in *San Francisco Bulletin*, March 23, 1877.

210. Adina de Zavala, *History and Legends of the Alamo and Other Missions in and around San Antonio* (San Antonio, 1917), 36.

211. Susanna Dickinson in Hansen, *Alamo Reader*, 47.

212. Map attributed to John Sutherland in Hansen, *Alamo Reader*, 160.

213. Such low parts of the compound's outer defenses may have given rise to the misconception, in one early newspaper report, that "the walls [were] only about breast high." *Mercantile Advertiser and New York Advocate*, April 26, 1836, from an article originally appearing in the *New Orleans Commercial Bulletin*.

214. "Picture of the Only Adult White Survivor of Alamo Massacre Being Offered by Retired Ranger," *Lubbock Journal*, January 16, 1933.

215. "The Real Alamo. It is Described in a Letter by Mr. A. C. Gray," Houston, Texas newspaper clipping (no title), March 4, 1907.

216. Mark Lemon, *The Illustrated Alamo 1836: A Photographic Journey* (Abilene, Tex.: State House Press, 2008), 154–161.

217. Ivey, *Mission to Fortress*, 5.

218. Potter in Hansen, *Alamo Reader*, 698.

Sources and Acknowledgments

The genesis of this book occurred in 1993, while I was engaged in research prior to illustrating Stephen L. Hardin's *Texian Iliad: A Military History of the Texas Revolution*. It had come to the point where the usual published sources relating to that conflict, both secondary and documentary, no longer satisfied, because what was so often lacking, especially for an illustrator, were the *nitty gritty details* of things. It had been my experience in previous years of researching such periods as the French and Indian War that contemporary newspapers invariably contained a bounty of such crucial little details, and in many instances details of an even greater stamp. Thus, I decided to investigate the papers of 1836.

The results exceeded my expectations: it was like unearthing an ancient monarch's tomb laden with treasures—in this case information about the Texas Revolution—that had been too long hidden away from public scrutiny. Even better, there was much that was "new" about the battle of the Alamo in particular, and as I accumulated photocopies and handwritten transcriptions of the accounts, it began to occur to me that I would *have to*, someday, compile them into book form.

The bulk of these articles and extracts were gathered in the vast depositories of the New York Public Library, sitting between Fortieth and Forty-Second streets, and between Fifth and Sixth avenues, in midtown Manhattan, and at the New York Historical Society, located on Central Park West between Seventy-Sixth and Seventy-Seventh streets, which has a smaller collection yet one quite rich in its own right. Whenever possible, the original papers were consulted, but often microfilm, micro- print cards, or photostats were the only accessible copies.

Frequently, too, an interlibrary loan was necessary to obtain a certain title. This is sometimes a long process, but it generally proved well worth the wait, and I must express my gratitude for those additional papers made available to me via libraries, museums, and other institutions across the nation. (Some of the earliest reports in this book were culled from my own personal collection of Readex Microprint newspapers.)

A number of newspaper accounts of the Texas Revolution have, of course, already been published in book and journal form. Jerry J. Gaddy's *Texas in Revolt: Contemporary Newspaper Account of the Texas Revolution* offered 137 pages worth of them, yet strangely left out date citations for each article. John H. Jenkins's *The Papers of the Texas Revolution, 1835–1836* contains many articles of value. A few are found in Francis Johnson's *A History of Texas and Texans*. Timothy Matovina's excellent *The Alamo Remembered: Tejano Accounts and Perspectives* is in its greater part composed of newspaper interviews with, or stories about, such Alamo survivors as Enrique Esparza, Juana Alsbury, the controversial Madam Candelaria, and others who had either been in the Alamo before its fall or who had witnessed the battle or its aftermath. I have purposely avoided reprinting what Matovina made available in his book and instead recommend it as a collection complementary to this one.

Todd Hansen's superb and thick compilation of firsthand (and other) Alamo accounts, *The Alamo Reader: A Study in History* includes a basic selection of newspaper accounts. Many David Crockett–related articles, dating from his years as a politician, can be found in James R. Boylston and Allen J. Weiner's authoritative *David Crockett in Congress: The Rise and Fall of the Poor Man's Friend.*

The pages of *Southwestern Historical Quarterly* have long proven a dependable and abundant resource of early Texas history, much of it in the form of extracts from contemporary newspapers. One particularly helpful analysis, from the *Quarterly*, Michael P. Costeltoe's "The Mexican Press of 1836 and the Battle of the Alamo," discusses a rarely considered side of the coin. Last but not least is *The Alamo Journal*, a quarterly published since 1986 by the indefatigable William R. Chemerka, which it frequently contains contemporary newspaper articles about the Alamo and the men who fought there, as well as its impact on today's society.

Over the years, too, a number of people have generously sent to me copies of some of the more significant published accounts. Among these are Kevin R. Young (who found the rare published letter by Dr. Joseph Barnard), Bill Groneman, the late Thomas Ricks Lindley, Joe Musso, Dorothy Black, Timothy J. Todish, and the late Jack Jackson.

Thanks to the ever-expanding Internet, many 1835–1836 articles are now available online, and these too have been perused.

I wish to also thank those members of my family who offered their encouraging words during the production of the manuscript and artwork, especially my wife Cora. Also meriting a thank you for their help are Dana Tyler and Catherine D'Agostino. For believing in the project, I am truly grateful for the enthusiasm expressed by my publishers, Donald S. Frazier and Amy E. Smith, of the Grady McWhiney Research Foundation, and by old friend and collaborator Stephen L. Hardin, Professor of History at McMurry University. To Claudia Gravier Frigo, Project Manager at State House Press, goes a big thank you for taking on a large, complex, and time-consuming task, and for shaping it into a result that is both user friendly and elegantly arranged.

To the great Phil Collins goes the credit for allowing this long-cherished project to see the light of day. His help, support, suggestions, and enthusiasm have been valuable beyond measure. And the selections included here from his incredible collection of Alamo and related artifacts have decidedly amplified the overall value of this book. In truth, all this would not have been possible without his participation.

Afterword

First off, I'd like to thank Gary Zaboly for inviting me to contribute to this book. He constantly encouraged me while writing my short essays shown in these pages.

For me, the journey started with a chance meeting with Gary, the master illustrator, and though I'd seen his work in the many books I'd read on the Alamo, we'd never met.

Then one day in 2006, I received an e-mail from Dr. Bruce Winders, curator of the Alamo. He mentioned that Gary had an oil painting that they could not afford to buy, and he thought that maybe I'd be interested in buying it.

I met with Gary in New York, and he brought the painting, "The Fight for the 18-pounder," with him. I bought the painting, and it now hangs in my Alamo basement "museum."

At that first meeting he mentioned an idea he'd had for some time: a book featuring many newspaper articles reporting on the fall of the Alamo that had not been seen since their original printings. He asked if I would I be interested in a collaboration of sorts that would include adding photos of Alamo-related relics from my collection. I was up to my eyes writing a Broadway Musical at the time, but the idea lodged in my head.

We stayed in touch; he persevered; and here we are!

Although we collaborated closely at first, Gary's book eventually became a stand-alone item, and the pieces I wrote for his book slowly expanded and became a separate book on my collection. The book on my collection will be published in 2012; Gary's, of course, you're holding in your hands! Both books, however, are companions to each other, and we consider ourselves "partners" in this endeavor.

Phil Collins

Index

A

abolitionists, 9, 247

Account of Col. Crockett's Tour to the North and Down East, in the Year of Our Lord One Thousand Eight Hundred and Thirty-Four, An, 100

acequia (irrigation canal or ditch), 81, 164, 389, 390, 397, 406, 421, S14, S43, S51, S61, S64

Acequia Madre, S64

Adams, John Quincey, 104

Adriatic, steamer, 363

Affleck, I. D., 425

Agercieno, Cadet Joaquim, 329

Agua Dulce, 232 n. 29, 309

Agualdo, Col. Francisco, 329

Aguascalientes (Mexico), 62

Aguayo, Marquis de, 19

Agustin, Capt., 74

Aguirre, Col. Marcil, 152, 329, 407

Augusta (GA), 249

Aide-Memoire to the Military Sciences, S36

Alabama, 37, 98, 128, 136, 259, 303, 323, 416

Alabama Greys, 306

Alameda (of Alamo), 157, 190, 273, 393, 396

Alameda Street, San Antonio, 274

Alamo
    abatis, 273, S31–S32
    armory, 148, S20, S60, 443 n. 193
    artillery, *see* artillery
    Artillery command quarters, S43
    Artillery quarters, S56
    as "altar," 356, 431
    as grocery store in 1883, 409
    as mission, 17–20, 21, S12, S16, S32, S33, S39, S41–S43, S62, S63
    as Spanish fort, 25, 45, 379
    as storehouse, 412
    as symbol, 1, 5
    ashes of defenders, *see* funeral pyres; Seguin, Lt. Col. Juan
    attack on, Feb. 25, 1836, 157–161, 163, 166, 167, 403, S44
    attack on, March 6, 1836, orders for, 189–190, 406
    attack on, March 6, 1836, 197–279, 350, 378, 394–395, 403–404, 406, S39–S40, S47, S51, S55
    Austin's cannon fire at, 79, S9
    autographs on walls, 384, 399
    Babe of, *see* Dickinson, Angelina
    banquette, S18. S19, S31, S 35, S62, S63
    baptistry, 253, S18, S27
    battlements, *see* crenelations
    bell towers, S16
    bells, 379, 441 n.79, S27
    blood and brain stains on walls, 254 n. 11, 392, S4, S50
    bombardment of, *see* artillery, Texian army in 1835; artillery: Mexican batteries in 1836
    bonnet (fortification), 150, S41, S51
    breach in walls, 183, 240, 393, 395, 398, S5, S8, S9, S47–S48, S55
    calabozo, S59
    canales, S14
    Castañeda House, S48, S50, S51
    casualties at, American, 2, 8, 199, 201, 216, 262, 269, 270, 309, 345, 406; casualties at, Mexican, 2, 6, 199, 200, 201, 206, 211, 216, 218, 235, 237, 238, 240, 241, 246, 267 n. 3, 269, 270, 279, 344, 350, 354, 404, 406, 419
    cattle pen, *see* courtyards
    cavalier battery, *see* Fortin de Cos
    cemetery, S32
    chamacuero, 243, S56
    chancel, 213, S21, S24, S26
    Charlis carpenter shop, S39, S41
    Charlis stone house, S39
    choir loft, S18, S19, S20
    church, cannon in, 148, 213–215, 271, 278, 410, S19–S20, S21–S26; defense works in, 276 n. 14, 278, 403, 440 n. 43, 441 n. 63, S11, S15–S28; description, 379, 390, 392, 396, 399, 410, S4, S5, S13, S16, S56; as site of Crockett's death, 266, 268, 395; occupants of, during siege, 145, 151 n. 1, 394, 399, 408, 409, 441 n. 73
    communes, S62
    confessional, 410, S18, S27

convent (convento; *see also* long barracks), 253, 396, 410, 443 n. 195, S12, S13, S32, S59–S60, S61, S64

courtyard, inner, S32, S64

courtyards, 188, 403, 444 n. 213, S4, S12, S46, S60–S61, S62–S64

crenelations (battlements), 440 n. 41, n. 44, S13, S15, S16, S17, S18, S43

description of, in late 1820s, S43; in 1828, S16; in 1835, S9–S10, S11–S12, S19; in 1836, 167–168, S21, S24; in 1839, 379, S3–S4, S27; in 1840, S5; in 1841, 384–385, S9; in 1842, 390, S4; in 1843, S4; in 1845, S4; in 1846, 392, S4, S22; in 1847, 396; in 1848, 396–397, S27, S64; in 1883, 409; in 1884, 409–410; described by R. M. Potter in 1840, 271

destroyed by Gen. Andrade, 214, 344, 345, 347,348, 349, 350, 379, 425, S2–S3, S18, S22, S35, S58, S60

ditches in buildings, *see* hide parapets and ditches inside buildings

drawbridge, S38

drawing of, by Sánchez Navarro, *S13*

"Elm Tree Fort," 167–168

excavations at, 227, 398, 416, 417, 423, 424–425, S9, S35, S37, S38, S46, S62

executions at, of surviving defenders, 211, 206, 220, 223, 234, 237, 238, 241, 262, 263–266, 267, 274–275, 278, 301, 401, 404, 406, 408, 437 n. 8-5, n. 8-6, n. 8-7

flag, *see* flags

flat ladder, 213, 347, 441 n. 68, S22, S24, *S25*, S26, S41

Fortin de Condelle, S51

Fortin de Cos, 213–214, 441 n. 73, S2, S19, S22–S26

Fortin de Teran, 230, 231, 243, S54

French language newspaper report of, 176–177

fugitives from, during battle, 199, 202, 278, 286, 406

glacis, 441 n. 91, S31, S55, S62

granary, S58, S59, S60, S62

guardhouse, S33

half moon battery, S10, S41

headquarters, 418, S50

hide parapets and ditches inside buildings, 253, 271, S5, S56

hospital, 148, 185, 252, 276, 404, 443 n. 193,

S12, S24, S33, S34, S60

hump, S18

in siege of Béxar, 1835, 74, 83, 87, 88, 92, S9, S10, S11–S12, S16, S18–S19, S22, S23, S27, S28–S29, S36, S51, S53–S55

in 1836 siege, 143–190, 192, 211, 271, 281, 288, 350, 354–355, 392–394, 403, 405–406, 408, 422, S2–S64

jacale, 173, 243, S51, S56

jail, 379, 384, S59

kitchen, S34, S56

latrines, S62

lavatorio, S64

long barracks (*see also* convent), 271, 276, 277, 278, 396, 411, S5, S9, S28, S58–S61

loopholes, 159, 220, 440 n. 41, S14, S17, S20, S31, S35, S43, S47

low barracks, 159, 253, S14, S33–S34, S50

lunette, S35

main gate, 159, 406, S12, S33, S35, S39

Mexican repossession of in 1836, rumor of, 367

Monks' Burying Ground, 151 n. 1

monument to battle dead, 367, 369, 385–386, 388–389, 398, S32

nave, S22, S23

north wall, 165, 225, 228, 230, 243, 277, S8, S9, S53–S56, S58, S61

northeastern sector, S56–S58

northwest corner, S51–S53

outside huts, S39–S40, S43

palisades, 148, 159, 165, 230, 273, 347, 441 n. 91, S8, S28–S32, S34, S35–S37, S41, S44–S46, S53, S54–S55, S58, S62

pecan tree, S13, S14, S51

pentice, S28–S29, S37, S50, 442 n. 115

pickets, *see* palisades

plan of, 1836, unknown draftsman, 249

plan of, by R. M. Potter, *S6*

plans of, by Navarro, La Bastida, Jameson, etc., discussed, S1–S64

poetry of, 3–4, 6, 412, 427–432

ponds, 443 n. 155, S61, S64

porteria, 443 n. 195

portholes, for artillery, 93, 271, 396, S5, S13, S28, S31, S33, S44, S47, S50

postern, 443 n. 164, S48, S51

powder magazine, 209, S27

quarteles, S59, S60
ramp (*see also* flat ladder), S21, S23, S24, S26, S41, S53
renovated by Gen. Andrade, 347, 348
rockets, Mexican, fired from in 1835, 88, 197–198
sacristy, 441 n. 73, S12
sallyport traverse, S39, S58
saps, S44, S46
scaffolds, S19, S20, S24, S27
shingled roof complex, S14, S48–S51, 443 n. 155
signal gun of, 150, 151 n. 23, 203, 206, 237, 287
sorties of garrison, 159, 161, 169, 173, 393–394, S43
southwest corner, 150, 151 n. 11, 171, S39–S41
statues in church niches, 379, 390, 396, 411, S18, S27, S28
suicide, reports of, 3, 231, 237, 251, 350
survivors of battle, unconfirmed, 203, 285, 381, 382, 404, 410, 416–417
tambour, 159, 441 n. 106, 442 n. 107, n. 115, n. 148, S14, S35–S38, S44, S47, S62
transept, 213, S25, S26
traverses, 231, S39, S54, S58
Trevino house, 253, 254 n. 11, 443 n. 155, S47, S48, S50
US Army occupation of, 396, S18, S32, S64
watch boxes, S33
watch tower/flagpole booth, S13, S14, S16, S19, S20
well, S61, S63
west wall, 265, 443 n. 164, S3, S13, S41–S52
Alamo Canal (or *acequia* or ditch), 81, 164, S64
Alamo de Parras, Second Flying Company of San Carlos de, 20–21, 26–27, 45, 443 n. 193, S12, S50
Alamo, or Death of David Crockett, The (play), 403
Alamo Plaza, 424, S61
Alamo Street, San Antonio, 227, 423
Alamo, The (Meyers), 1, 425
Alamo, The, (1960 movie), 409, 433 n. 11
Alazan hills (or heights), 143, 422
Alexander (LA), 57
Alexandria (LA), 376, 399

Allen, Capt., 352
Allen, Capt. (of Cincinnati), 353
Allen, Eliza, 36–37
Alley, Capt. John, 87
alligator, 301–302
Almonte, Col. Juan Nepomuceno: journal entries, 143, 149, 157, 164, 169, 171, 175, 176, 177, 180, 183, 186, 189, 199, 281, 289, 347, S20, S61; at San Jacinto, 318, 323, 328, 331, 364; as prisoner, 329, 332, 338–340, 352; journal of, captured, 345, 436 n. 7-1; description of, 332, 362–363, 364; portrait of, 362–363; mentioned, 197, 207, 236, 267, 291, 408, 409, 436 n.7-1, 438 n. 8-5, 8-6
Alsbury, Dr. Horace, 411, 418
Alsbury, Juana, 221, 409, 411, 413, 418, 419, S50–S51
Altimira (Mexico), 49
Alvarez (Mexican rebel), 168
Alzucaray, Lt. Juan, 228
Amador, Gen. Juan Valentín, 183, 189, 190, 276, S34
Amat, Col. Augustin, 183, 190, 243
American Hotel, New York City, 356
American Museum, 341
Ampudia, Gen. Pedro, 149, 176, 186 n.1, 393, S8, S20, S55
Anahuac (TX), 51–53, 63–64, 71, 142, 183, 301, 320
Anderson, Assistant Quartermaster, 210
Anderson, Capt. Bailey, 84, 194
Anderson, Pvt. C. D., 322
Anderson, Washington, 322
Andrews, Joseph, 323
Andrews, Richard, 75
Andrade, Col. Jose Juan: demolishes Alamo, 214, 344, 345, 347–349, 364, 425, S2, S18, S22, S35, S58, S60; description of, 348–349; mentioned, 188, 281, 344, S31
Angelina River (TX), 54, 58, 434 n. 1-4
antelope, 59
Apache Indians, 20, S12
Apollo Saloon, Boston, 360
Aransas Bay (TX), 71
Arabs, 1, 59
Arago, Gen. Juan, 281
Arcanzid, Lt. Raphael, 329
Archer, Col., 157

Arch Street Theatre, Philadelphia, 357, 391
Arcos, Capt. Lorenzo, 329
Arenal, Lt. Ygnacio, 329
Arenas, Gen. Jose, 329
Areos, Capt., 22
Argod, Gen., 226
Arias, Lt. Mariano, 329
Arkansas, 26, 61, 106–110, 203, 285
Arkansas River, 211
Armstrong, Robert, 38, 40
Arochos Rancho, 206
Arredondo, Gen. Joaquín de, 23
Arroyo, Dr., 344
Arroyo de Cedros River, 58
Arroyo de Chacon, 143
Arroyo de la Vaca River, 58
Arroyo Hondo, 143, 177
artillery, at Goliad in 1812, 21; in 1835, 73; in
    1836, 202, 282, 297, 303, 304; at Ft. Velasco,
    52; at Anahuac, 63; at Gonzales, 69, 87; of
    Mexicans at San Antonio in 1835, 74, 79, 82,
    88, 90, 91, 92, 93, 96–97, 127, S11–S12, S28;
    at battle of Concepción, 74, 75; of Texian
    army in 1835, 74, 75, 79, 86, 91, 93, 122, 439
    n. 22, S9, S44, S51, S56; at Alamo in 1836,
    127, 137, 145–151, 152, 159, 161, 173, 176,
    181, 199, 201, 213, 225, 227, 265, 351, 398,
    403–404, 405, 408, 410, 424–425, S2–S62; in
    Santa Anna's batteries around the Alamo, 149,
    153, 159, 164–165, 171–173, 180, 181, 183,
    188, 201, 231, 238, 243, 249, 253, 276, 393,
    403, 416, 417, 423, 424–425, S8–S9, S33,
    S51, S55, S60; with Houston's army, 203, 318,
    319, 320, 331; with Santa Anna at San Jacinto,
    319, 320, 327, 331; destroyed by Andrade at
    Alamo, 347, 351, S2, S3; in Mexican retreat
    from Texas, 349
Assieta, S31
Atacosto (TX), 406
Athens (Greece), 379, S27
Atlimeo, 24
Attakapas, 352
Augusta County (VA), S37
Austin, John, 52, 53
Austin, Moses, 26, 47, 60
Austin, Stephen: first trip to Mexico City, 26, 47;
    colony of, in Texas, 26–28, 45, 46, 47–48, 60;
    second trip to Mexico City and imprisonment,
54, 55; returns to Texas, 65, 105; commands
    Texian army, 70, 73–85, 214, 272; on rockets,
    198; spies of, S9, S12; resigns command, 86,
    91, 283; on eastern trip, 260; mentioned, 309
Austin (TX), 388, 404, 409
Austin, William T., 147, S12, S16
Autry, Micajah, 217, 295
Avalsos, Gen., 168
Avenue D, San Antonio, 424
Avica, Capt. Vicente, 329
Avoyelles Parish (LA), 377
axe, 190, 202, 205, 271, 277, 392, 397
Aysh Bayou (TX), 45, 46, 70
Aztec Indians, 424

B

Bachilla, Capt. Miguel, 329
Badgett, Jesse B., 163, 197, 226, 228, 229, 235,
    236
Badgett, William, 211, 237
Bailey, Mr., 207
Bailey's Prairie (TX), 375
Baker, Isaac, 210
Baker, Joseph, 155
Baker, Capt. Moseley, 10, 155, 193–194, 322
Baker, William Charles M., 209
Ball, Gen., 329–330
Ball, Col., see Woll, Gen. Adrian
Baltimore (MD), 22
Bananeh, Capt. Juan, 329
Bangor (ME), 121
Bank of the United States, 55, 103
Barbary, 56
Barnard, Dr. Joseph H., 253, 267, 347, 349,
    350–351, S2, S22, S24
Barra, Capt. Ygnacio, 329
Barradas, Gen. Isidro, 48–50
Barragan, Capt., 220, 221
Barragan, Gen. Miguel, 195, 293
Barrera, Augusta (or Augustín), 410, 421
Barrow, Buck, 228
Barrow, Clyde, 228
Bastrop (TX), 183, 295, 383
Batres, Col. Jose, 152, 161, 181, 325, 329, 344,
    405
bats, S3
Battle of Tampico (Paris painting), 411 n. 91
Battle of the Alamo (Gentilz painting), S18, S39

Baugh, Lt. (and Adj.) John J., 84, 163, 209, 220, 226, 235
Baxter, Col. William, 226
Bayou Boeuf (LA), 31
Bayou Terrabonne (LA), 398
bear, 32–34, 58, 59
Beard, Capt., 25
bear hunt, 32–34, 110, 376
bearskin, 20, 41, 58
Beason's Crossing (TX), 207, 236
beaver, 58, 59
Bedford, Mr., 206
Bee, Col., 363
Bee, Gen., 420
Bell's Landing (TX), 296
Bellingly, Capt. James, 322
Ben, Almonte's servant, see Harris, Benjamin
Benavides, Don Placido, 138, 436 n. 6-6
Bennett, James Gordon, 105, 244
Benton, Jesse, 211, 217, 236, 237, 249
Benton, Thomas Hart, 376
Bercerra, Sgt. Francisco, 148, 213, 214, 266, 275 n. 1; account by, 402–404; 440 n. 43, S16, S34, S62
Bergara (or Burgura), Anselmo, 206
Bermuda, 353
"Betsy," David Crockett's rifle, 34, 114, 401, 408
Bettie, slave of James Bowie, 253
Béxar (Béjar), see: San Antonio de Béxar
Big Prairie (LA), 402
Big Prairie, the (AR), 106, 435 n. 5-1
Bills, soldier at Goliad, 308
Bingamon, Col. Adam L., 402
Birch, Capt., 58
Birch, Harvey, 372, 373
Bird, Capt., 85
Bird Island (TX), 146
Birdwell, Russell, 433 n. 11
Bishop's Barroom, New Orleans, 259
"Black Flag Battery," 86
Black Hawk, 311
Black, James H., 387–388
Blair, Pvt., of Nacogdoches, 210
Blair, Robert, 423
Blair, Samuel, 161, 209, 236, 379
Blake, Lt. Edward, S15
Blakeley, Lemuel, 322
Blanchard, Alfred, 30–31

Blanchard, C. H., 30–31
blanket coat, 165, 374
blankets, 96, 123, 374, 421
Blazeby, William, 122, 209, 236, 237
blockhouse, 66
Blossom Prairie (TX), 435 n. 5-5
Blum Street, San Antonio, 275 n. 3
Bois d'Arc Creek (TX), 111, 436 n. 5-8
Bois d'Arc tree, 58–59, 132, 435 n. 5-6
Bolivar (TN), 408
Bolivar (TX), 402
Bollaert, William, 316, 436 n. 5-8, S4, S15
Bonham, Lt. James Butler, arrives in San Antonio, 127; returns to Alamo on March 3, 181, 182, 183, 240, 260; dies at Alamo, 210, 238, 295, 395; life of, 259–260; character of, 260
Bonham Street, San Antonio, 275 n. 3
Boone, Daniel, 376
boots, 314, 364
Borden, Gail, 182
Borne, Daniel, 210
Boston (MA), 56, 78, 142, 360
Bourne, Daniel, 210
Bowie, James
    and battle of Concepción, 74–77
    and Crockett, 402
    and Madam Candelaria, 252, 253, 411, 417–421
    and Texas militia, 64, 65
    anecdote, 398–399
    as land speculator, 400
    battle with Waco and Tawakoni Indians, 38–42
    black slave of, 209, 252–253
    character of, 258, 376, 386, 399–400, 402
    chest of gold, at Alamo, 420–421
    clothing of, 77, 402
    death at Alamo, 3, 7, 199, 201, 202, 206, 209, 211, 217, 219, 220, 221, 237, 238, 251–254, 258, 274–275, 350, 376, 395, 398, 404, 406, 409, S33
    death of wife, 54–55
    description of, 376, 386, 399, 402
    gun of, 387
    Houston sends to San Antonio in 1836, 127, 131, 418, 437 n. 8-2
    illness at Alamo, 153, 206, 209, 211, 217, 251, 275, 404, 411, 413, 418, 419, 420, S50
    in 1835 siege of San Antonio, 81, 131, 198
    in battle with Comanches, 386–387

in conflict of 1832, 54
in Monclova, 376
in Matamoras, 402
in second expedition against Indians, 42
knife of, see Bowie knife
marries Ursula Veramendi, 38
message to Almonte, 152, 405
Mexican criticism of, 199, 202, 203
mother of, 402
parleys with Comanches, 131–132, 137
portrait of, by Parker, 402
powder horn of, 420
profile of, 399–400
pursuit of Indians, 1835, 65
Sand Bar Duel, 12, 29–31, 376, 377, 399–400
with Long's filibuster army, 25
Bowie knife: origin, 31, 258–259, 376, 377–378,
    387–388; at Alamo, 251, 254, 365–366; at San
    Jacinto, 325, 344; articles concerning, 375–378;
    in battles with Comanches, 386–387; in James
    Bowie portrait, 402; James Bowie's own,
    410, 420–421; mentioned, 87, 361, 374, 386,
    398–399
Bowie, Rezin
    account of fight with Indians, 38–42
    and Texas army, 352
    as "inventor" of Bowie knife, 376–377
    his rifle, 386–387
    in knife fights, 258–259, 376, 377, 378
    mentioned, 434 n. 1-1
    portrait of, 132, 259, 402
    published statement of, 377–378
bows and arrows, 39, 58, 60, 132
Bradburn, Col. John ("Juan"), 51–53, 359, 360,
    S19, S34
Brady's Landing (TN), 402
Brassail, Lt. Ygnacio, 329
Bravo del Norte River, 61
Bravo, Gen. Nicholas, 293, 364
Bravo, schooner, 99, 360
Brazoria (TX), 52, 53, 73, 84, 91, 92, 127, 183,
    241, 296, 299, 317, 332, 343, 402
Brazos de Santiago River, 61
Brazos River (TX), 45, 47, 48, 52, 60, 70, 75, 126,
    156, 187, 191, 237, 249, 293, 296, 317, 321,
    330, 340, 355, 407, S44
Breece, Capt. Thomas H., 84, 306
Bridger, Capt., 352

Brigham, Maj., 332
Bringas, A. M., 177
Bringas, Col. Juan, 329
Briones, Lt. Felipe, 329
Briscoe, Andrew, 378
brogans, 123, 325
Brooks, Capt., 308
Brooks, John Sowers, S8
Broomhead and Thomas, 420
Brown Bess (see also muskets), 89, 227
Brown, Capt., 352
Brown, James, 210
Brown, John Duff, S32
Brown, John Henry, 268
Brown, Pvt., 210
Brown, Robert, 161
Brown, R. R., 232 n. 29
Brown's Hotel, Washington D.C., 100
Brownsville (PA), 402
Brownsville (TN), 114
Brownsville (TX), 168, 403
Brushy River (TX), 249
Brutus, schooner, 329, 352
Bryan, Guy M., 414–415
Buchanan, David, 38, 39, 41
Buckeye Rangers, 352
buckshot, 221, 227
buckskin clothing (see also hunting shirt), 32, 33,
    37, 42, 81, 121, 132, 135, 185, 314, 316, 325
Buena Vista, battle of, 226
buffalo, 58, 59, 60, 111, 113, 114, 115, 116, 117,
    132, 325, 357, 436 n. 5-8
buffalo coat, 165, 161 n. 11
buffalo robe and hides, 41, 58, 60, 314
Buffalo (NY), 6, 315
Buffalo Bayou (TX), 318, 320, 330, 332, 350
bullet pouch, 32, 37, 97, 359, 360, 361, 365
Bullock, Horace, 323
Bullock, U. J., 341
Bunker Hill, battle of, 245, 385, 412
Burleson, Ge. Edward, 85, 88, 91, 93, 125, 126,
    283, 318, 321, 340, 365, 385
Burnell, Assistant Quartermaster, 210
Burnet, David. G., 207, 299, 311, 351, S3
Burns, Samuel E., 210
Burton, soldier at Goliad, 308
Burton's Theatre, Philadelphia, 391
Bush, George W., 4

Bustamente, Anastasio, 51, 54
butcher knife, 31, 32, 123, 241, 258, 376
Butler, Col., 62
Butler, Pvt., 210

C
cactus, 334, S55
Caddo Indians, 38, 39, 40, 42
Caddo Lakes (TX), 58
Cage, B. P., 153
Cain, John, 210
Calatayad, Lt. Geronimo, 329
Calder, Judge R. S., 145
calico, 56
Calhoun (prisoner in Béxar, 1835), 422
California, 167, 315, 390
Callaghan, C. W., 423
Camanche, schooner, 237, 238
Campbell, Charles, 410, 420, 421
Campbell, Judge Jesse, 379, 384
Campo Santo, San Antonio, 152, 406, S20
Camp Supply, Korea, 4
Camp Travis, 263
canals, *see acequias*
Cananza, Lt. Ygnacio, 329
Canary Islands, 19
Candelaria, "Madame," 252, 253, 411, 417–421, 440 n.43, S34, S56
cane, gun (Santa Anna's), 340–341
cane, sword, 30, 31, 400
Caney Creek (TX), 71
canister, 92, 146, 159, 161, 202, 214, 304, 318, 404, S8, S23
cannon, *see* artillery
Canon de Ubalde (Uvalde) (TX), 19
canteen, 90, 123, 314, 337, 374
carbine, 73, 96, 97, 135, 202, 231, 233 n. 37, 305
Carey, Capt. William R., 131, 161, 209, 236
carretta (cart), 273
Caribbean, 145
Caro, Ramón Martínez, 190, S44
Carion, Capt. Telespero, 329
Carroll, Gov. William, 103
Carrizo (TX), 294
Carson, Col., 207
Casa Mata Antigua, San Antonio, 157
Cascades (Canada), 315, 316 n. 2
Caseres, Lt. Toribo, 329

Cash, Pvt., 228
Caspian, steamboat, 166
Castañeda, Lt. Francisco, 69, S48, S50, S51
Castilla, Lt. Rafael, 329
Castillo, Col. José María, 329
Caston, 24
Castrillón, Gen. Manuel Fernandez, 175; in March 4 Council of war, 183; in March 6 attack, 189, 271, 279, 403, S62; and Crockett, 262–265; death at San Jacinto, 279, 329, 349
Castro, Lt. Antonio, 329
Castro, Lt. José María, 329
Catholic Church and Texas, 17–18, 389–390
Catlin, George, 132
cattle, 48, 58, 61, 153, 169, 301, 303, 325, 352, 353, 364, 366, 367, 419, S60, S62, S64
Cazenovia (NY), 246
cedar, 58, 331, 334, S46
Cespedes, Col. Manuel, 329, 342
Chadwick, Joseph, 282
chamacuero, 243, S56
Chandeville, J. M., 297
Chapultepec Castle, 200, S29, S37
Charles (servant boy), 38, 39
Charlie, slave, 253
Charlis, Pierre, S39, S41
Chevallie, Maj., 420
Cherokee Indians, 37, 46, 71, 131, 132, 139, 193, 379
Cheshire, James, 97
Chester, Col. Robert I., 248
chewing tobacco, 123
Chicago (IL), 350
Chief Bowl, of Cherokees, 131
Chihuahua (Mexico), 289, 392
Childers, Col. Robertson, 109
Childress, George C., 143, 177, 178, 211, 216, 218, 219, 225–226, 229, 244, 257, 258, 295
Chisholm, Richard H., account by, 86–91, 133, 197
Choctaw Bayou (TX), 111, 436 n. 5-7, n. 5-8
Choctaw Indians, 110, 132, 139
cholera, 55
Chuly, Pvt. James, 322
Churubusco, battle of, 444 n. 109
Cibolo (Sea Willow) River, or Creek (TX), 236, 292 n. 7, 294
cigar, 348
Cincinnati (OH), 32, 56, 126, 248, 331, 335, 352, 378

Civil War, US, 403, 416, 422, S32, S53
Clarke, Mathew St. Clair, 32, 100
Clarksville (TN), 36
Clay, Henry Jr., 226
Click, Mathew, 435 n. 5-6
cloak, 135
Clopper's Point (TX), 320
Cloud, Daniel, 4, 217, 244, 261, 295, 437 n. 3
Coahuila (Mexico), 2, 22, 54, 61, 65, 66, 117, 128, 252, 289
Cochrane, James, 156
Cochran, Robert E., 210, 259
coffee, 123
Coleman, R. M., 69
Coleto Creek, battle of, 202, 228, 270, 296–297, 299, 303–305, 306, 350, 355
Collensworth, Col. 329
Collingsworth, James, 207
Collins, Major E. T., 356
Collinsworth, Capt. George Morse, 71, 73, 82, 85
Colonel Crockett's Exploits and Adventures in Texas, 357
Colorado River (TX), 47, 48, 60, 70, 146, 156, 195, 236, 239, 293, 295, 299, 330, 340, 343, 354
Columbia (TX), 343, 373, 375, 407
Columbus (GA), 298
Columbus, schooner, 145, 146, 296, S44
Comanche Indians, 18, 20, 25, 26, 27, 38, 39, 60, 81, 105, 111, 131–132, 137, 138, 311, 345, 349, 357, 379, 384, 386–387
Comargo (Mexico), 381
Commerce Street, San Antonio, 420
Commerce Street Bridge (see also San Antonio River, bridges), 436 n. 6-7
Concepción, battle of, 74–77, 268, 354, 372, 390, S11
Concepción, Mission, 74, 75, 77, 390, 403, S18
Congress, ship, 341
Congress Hall, New York City, 55
Congress, US, 32, 34, 100, 101, 103, 104, 254, 255, 316, 371, 400, 401
Connally, John, 4
Connecticut, 226, 409
Conrad, Edward, 177
Constitution of 1824, Mexican, 57, 78, 93, 97, 98, 105, 126, 138, 140, S21
Contreras (Mexico), 198

convicts (see Mexican Army, convicts in)
Cook, Captain (Texas army), 361
Cook, William G., 97
Cooksey, Dr. J. B., 340
coonskin cap, 361, 400
Cooper, Goliad survivor, 308
Cooper, James Fenimore, 372
Copano (TX), 65, 70, 71, 127, 128, 133, 136, 187, 191, 283, 288, 305, 306, 309
corn, 58, 123, 139, 142, 153, 169, 177, 191, 202, 304, 329, 331, 339–340, 352, 354, 355, 397, 419, S55
Corner, William, S34
Coro, president (Mexico), 262, 293
Corono, Capt., 308
Corpus Christi (TX), 391, 405
Correo, ship, 96, 308
Corriel, James, 38, 40, 41
Corsicana (TX), 340
Cortez, Hernando, 356
Cortinas, Lt. Juan, 54, 97
Cos. Lt. Col. Dionicio, 218, 220, 229, 230, 325, 329, 344, 345, 349
Cos, Gen. Martín Perfecto de,
    and 1835 siege and surrender of San Antonio, 7, 54, 73, 74–99, 114, 147, 172, 197, 213, 230, 288, 391, 405, S7, S10, S11, S12, S18, S27
    as brother-in-law of Santa Anna, 362
    as prisoner, 329, 332, 342, 343, 352, 362, 363
    at San Antonio in 1836, 157, 159–160, 271
    at San Jacinto, 318, 320, 323, 326, 327, 330, 331, 333
    description of, 323, 332, 343
    enters Texas in 1835, 64, 65, 70, 71, 105
    in assault on Alamo, 8, 189, 201, 205, 266, 403, 404, S23, S51, S55
    in March 4 Council of war, 183
    in return march to Texas, 138, 139, 141, 403, 405
    message to, 169
    papers of, seized at San Jacinto, 345
    parole of, 11, 93, 97, 129, 157, 186, 261, 333, 403
    portrait of, 362, 363
    saddle of, 341
    supposed horse of, 160, 167
Cosio, Lt. Manuel, 329
Cottle, George W., 210

cotton, 48, 58, 61, 62, 191, 329, 343
Couci, Mr., 59
Course of Military Fortification (1822), S41
Courtland (AL), 98
Cox, sculptor, 388
Cox's Point (TX), 191
Coyle, T. T., 411
Craig, Neville, 402
Crane (Crain), Col. Robert, 29–31
Creek Indians, 132, 139, 149
Creek Indian War, 149
Creoles, 20
Crockett, poem, 428
Crockett, Camp (San Antonio), 392
Crockett, David
    Alamo artillery and, 145–151, 404, 408, 409
    along the Red River, 110–111
    and 1835 Congressional election, 100–105, 401
    and Alamo command structure, 236
    as bear hunter, 32–34, 110, 401, 435 n. 5-6
    as Congressman, 32, 34, 254, 255, 371, 400, 401
    as Mexican mine slave, 381–384
    at Little Rock (AR), 106–110, 111, 112–113, 117
    at Lost Prairie, 111, 113
    at Nacogdoches (TX), 111, 114, 115, 117
    at San Antonio, 137, 420
    brings in 50-man relief force, 211
    bullet pouch of, 359, 360, 361
    character of, 32, 34–35, 100, 245, 254, 255–256, 260, 267, 350, 356, 357, 401, 407
    death of (*see also* execution of), 9, 199, 209, 217, 218, 220, 221, 226, 235, 238, 239, 240, 241, 244, 254–258, 262–268, 298, 350, 395, 401, 409, 410, 411, S34
    descriptions of, 55, 56, 165, 185, 255, 267, 400, 401, 435 n. 5-6
    dispute with Bowie, 402
    enters Arkansas, 106
    execution of, after battle, 238, 241, 262–267, 301, 401, 404, 437 n. 8-4, 438 n. 8-5, n. 8-6, n. 8-7
    family of, 106, 111, 352, 361, 371–372, 382, 383, 384, 402, 417, 423, 436 n. 5-8
    first death rumors of, 115, 115
    hunts buffalo, 111, 113–114, 115–117, 120
    in Boston, 56, 165
    in Feb. 25 engagement, 159, 161, 163, 168, 178
    in Memphis, 106
    in New England tour, 165
    in New York City, 55
    in San Augustine (TX), 115, 436 n. 5-8
    in War of 1812/Creek War, 149, 255
    keeps garrison's spirits up, 350, 407
    life of, 400–401
    masquerader as, 176
    opinions of, 100, 103, 104, 107, 110, 119, 356, 357
    played by actors, 357, 391, 407
    portrait of, 361
    powder horn of, 359, 360
    quarters of, during siege, 145, 151 n. 1, 407, 408, S50
    rides to San Antonio, 119
    rifles of, 34, 114, 359–361, 401, 408, 423
    sharpshooting of, 163–165, 185–186, 249, 255, S43, S63–S64
    signature on Alamo wall, 384
    survives battle, rumor of, 256–257, 311, 381–384
    travels down Ohio River, 56
    travels to Texas, 103–120, 356, 359, 401
    watch of, 111, 113
Crockett, Elizabeth (wife), 111, 113, 382, 383, 417
Crockett (grandson), 361
Crockett, John Bell (grandson), 402
Crockett, John W. (son), 371–372, 383, 384, 417
Crockett Station (TN), 401
Crockett, Robert Patton (son), 352, 417
Crockett, Thomas J. (nephew), 352, 361
Crooks, T. J., 435 n. 5-6
Crossman, Robert, 210
Cross Timbers (TX), 111
crowbar, 190, 202, 397
Cruz, Lt. Juan Santa, 329
Cuba, 5, 48, 61
Cuirassiers, proposed "Immortal Guard" of, 314
Cummings, David, 132
Cummings, William, 210
Cuney, Dr. Samuel, 29–31
Cunningham, Capt., 62
Cunningham, Robert, 210
Cushing, W. L., 402
cypress tree, S46

D

Dade, Maj. Francis, 139

Dallas (TX), 424

Darley (actor), 357

Darlington, J. W., S48

Darst, Jacob C., 210

Daughters of the Texas Republic, 421

Davila, Gen., 35

Davis, Capt. (employee of Mexican navy), 95, 359, 360

Davis, John, 211

Davis's Saloon, New Orleans, 176

Davy Crockett Almanack, 13

Davy Crockett (play), 407

Davy Crockett (poem), 428

Davy Crockett (Disney T.V. series 1954–1955), 265

Day, Pvt., 210

Dearduff, William, 210, 378

Declaration of Independence, Texan, *see* Texas, Declaration of Independence

deer, 58, 353

deerskin clothing, *see* buckskin clothing

DeKalb, schooner, 298

Delgado, Col. Pedro, 326, 329

Demill's Point (TX), 305

Denney, Dr. James, 29, 30

Dennis, Nathaniel, 211, 237

Desauque, Capt. Francis L., 210, 304, 310

Detroit (MI), 263

Despallier, Charles, 161, 210

Devault, Pvt., 210

Dewall, Lewis, 210

DeWitt's Colony, 42, 45, 69, 411

Dexter, P. B., 155

Díaz, Lt. Nicholas, 329

Diaz, Pablo, 273, 275 n. 1

Dickinson, Goliad survivor, 323

Dickinson, Capt. Almeron, 93, 159, 161, 210, 214, 236, 259, 408, 409, 413, 435 n. 4-6, S25–S26; supposed leap from height, 206, 215, 217, 236, 278, 409, 411, 413

Dickinson, Angelina, 207, 220, 291, 366, 408; post-Alamo life of, 412–416

Dickinson, Gen. Lemuel, 259

Dickinson, Susanna, accounts by, 208, 213, 220, 223, 224–225, 226, 234, 243, 291–292, 408 alleged sexual abuses inflicted on, 2, 221,

233–234, 291

and Frank Mayo, 407

character of, 413

death of, 409, 411

escorted to Gonzales by Deaf Smith, 207, 291–292, 366, 408

mentioned, 254 n. 11, 257, 263, 293, 404, 405, 409, 413, 418, S63

on cavalier battery, S25–S26

on Crockett, 145, 407–408

on rockets, 197

released by Santa Anna, 207, 217, 236, 238, 291, 406

survives battle, 206, 209, 211, 217, 219, 234, 279, 291, 406, 410, 412

wounded, 291, 292, 413

Dickson, James, 313–316

Dien Bien Phu, 4

Dimmitt, Capt. Philip, 160, 437 n. 7-4

Dimmitt's Landing, 147

Dimmitt's Point, 136

Dimmitt's proclamation, 138

Dimpkins, James, 210

Disney, Walt, 265

Dodge, Col. Henry, 81, 436 n. 58

dogs, 33–34, 88, 101, 106

Dolson, George M., 262, 266

Domingus, Capt., 22

Donalson, Maj., 104

Donaldsonville (AL), 259

Dorington, Col. J., 317

double barreled gun, 30, 39, 77, 81, 216, 225, 309, 406

Double Bayou, 301

Downes, C. J., 410

Downing, Maj., 100

Doyle, Mathew, 38, 40, 41

ducks, 59

Duffield, 310

Duncan, Capt. John, 73

Duque, Col. Francisco, 177, 183, 189, 201, 205, 243, S55

Duran, Guadaloupe Ruiz, 366, 372

Durango, brig, 343, 352

Durango (Mexico), 304

Durham, D., 217

Durham, Thomas, 217

Dutchess County (NY), 82

Duval, Capt., 303
Duvall, John, 334
Duvall, Gov. William, 334
Dyer County (TN), 341

E

Earl, Capt., 353
East Commerce Street, San Antonio, 423
East Feliciana (LA), 402
East Houston Street, San Antonio, 424
Eastman, Capt. Seth, 443 n. 155, S15, S26, S62
East Nueva Street, San Antonio, 227
Edenburg (TX), 407
Edwards, benjamin, 45–46
Edwards, Col. Haden, 45–46
Ehrenberg, Herman, 438 n. 9-1, S9, S18, S55
El Bahio (Mexico), 136
Elizondo, Col. Ignacio, 23
Ellis, Richard, 167, 177, 178
Enciso, Capt. Nicholas, 329
England, 89
Espada, Mission, San Antonio, 176, 390, 405
Esparza, Enrique, 148, 163, 228, 230, S38, S43,
    S60, S61
Espino, Lt. Basilio, 329
Espinosa, Father Ignacio, 17
esmeriles (swivel guns), 148, S20
Espiritu Santo, Bay of, 57
Estrada, Col. 201
Estrado, Lt. Martin, 329
Eugenio, Lancer Corporal, 406
Evans, Capt., 209
Evans, Maj. Robert, 209, 210, 395, S27
Everett, Edward, S15, S18, S22, S26
Ewing, A., 153
Ewing, James, 210

F

Falconer, Thomas, S15
Fall of the Alamo, 1836 play, 357
Fall of the Alamo, poem, 429–430
fandango, 88, 392
Fannin, Col. James Walker
    and 1835 siege of Bexar, 74, 75, 81, 82, 86,
        87, 198
    and battle of Coleto Creek, 228, 296–297,
        303–305, 350, 355
    and Matamoras expedition, 121, 136, 283, 288

"besieged" at Goliad, 191, 297, 217, 236, 246,
    281–282, 288, 293
clothing and personal property of, 307, 308
command of, executed, 1, 11, 228, 268, 290,
    291, 305–306, 311, 339, 350, 351
confidence in, 191, 195, 291, 293
couriers from Travis to, 153, 161, 438 n. 9-1
evacuates Goliad, 296, 303
execution of, 165, 299, 306–307, 356
family of, at Wharton's Plantation, 233, 299
letter from Houston to, 203, 206
negative opinion of, 289
reinforces Refugio, 293, 296
relief column for Alamo, 167, 175, 178, 181,
    183, 186, 187, 289
Farias, Valentín Gomez, 57
Fernandez, D. Vital, 129, 169, 174, 297, 351
fiddle, 407, 408
Field, Dr. Joseph, 159, 308, S9
Filisola, Gen. Vicente, 141, 160, 169, 170, 174,
    213, 230, 270, 281, 328, 330, 337, 344, 347,
    351, 382, 405, 407, S21–S22, S24, S26, S28,
    S41, S51, S53
First US Volunteer Cavalry Regiment (Rough
    Riders), 5
fish, 57, 289, 353, 397
Fishback, William, 211
Fisher, King, 410
Fisher, W. M., 70
Fitzpatrick, Rees, 387
flags
    Alamo flags taken, 199, 437 n. 8-4
    Coahuila and Texas, 152, *S13* (1836 drawing),
        S14, S20, S21
    Constitution of 1824, 105, 440 n. 57, n. 58
    Fredonian, 45, 46
    Independence flag, 126, 182, S21
    Mexican black flag in San Antonio, 1835, 91,
        93; in 1836, 160
    Mexican flag over the Alamo, 95
    New Orleans Greys, 4–5, 7, 200, 201, 203
    of Texas Republic, 354, 356, 368
    red banners on all Mexican entrenchments,
        192
    red flag atop San Fernando church, 152, 182,
        195, 238, 394
    red flag raised over Alamo, 1836, 405, 440 n. 57
    "regimental colors" and "general colors" for

Texian army, 123
"star" flag, 440 n. 57
Texian banner, 137
truce, 93, 95, 207, 291, 297, 304, 328
Flanders, John, 210
Flash, schooner, 296, 323
Fletcher, J., 155
Flora, schooner, 340
Flores, ranchero, 169
Flores Street, San Antonio, 421
Florida, 139
Floyd, Dolphin, 211
Forbes, Col. John, 74, 115, 166, 179
Ford, Gerald, 5
Ford, John Salmon "Rip," 402–403, 418, S50
Foster, Isaac, 362
Forsyth, John Hubbard, 209, 236
Forsythe, Dr., 24
Fortazer, Gen., 96
Fort Bend (TX), 330
Fort Carillon (NY), S31, S32
Fort Clark (ND), 316
Fort Defiance (TX; *see also* Goliad; La Bahia),
    176, 203, 207, 282, 296, 348, S8
Fort Garry (Canada), 316
Fort Gibson (AR), 436 n. 5-8
Fort Griswold (CT), 226
fortification sacks, *see* sandbags
Fort Smith (AR), 42
Fort Towson (AR), 110
Fort Travis (TX), 263, 299, 320, 323, 342, 353
Fort Velasco (TX), 52, 151 n. 8
Fort Washington (NY), 232 n. 10
Fowl, Pvt. Thomas, 323
fox, 58, 59
foxskin cap, 435 n. 5-5
France, 20
Frankfort (Germany), 378
Fredonian revolt, 45–46, 434 n. 3-1
Fremina, Maria El Garma, 25
French in "Republican Army of the North" (1812),
    21
Frenile (Mexico), 63
frogs, S61
Fulton, George W., S15
Fuqua, Galba, 211
funeral pyres for Alamo dead, 209, 211, 219,
    221, 233, 238, 241, 253, 257, 261, 273–276,

291–293, 350, 368–369, 385, 388, 392, 394,
    406, 408, 419, 423, 438 n. 10-8, S62
funeral pyres for Goliad dead, 308, 309
fur cap, 32, 176, 348, 361, 400 435 n. 5-5
fur coats, 166 n. 11
gabion, 150, 172, 231, S38, S39, S41, S54

G

Gaines, Gen. Edmund P., 355
Gaines, James, 177
Galicia, 19
Gallatin, Albert, 322
Gallegher's, Boston, 56
Galveston Bay, 48, 52, 127, 128, 146, 193, 262,
    318, 320, 342, 352
Galveston Bay and Texas Land Company, 246
Galveston Island (TX), 25, 57, 143, 145, 193, 263,
    296, 299, 301, 302, 311, 323, 327, 328, 329,
    330, 342, 345, 353, 362, 363, 402
Gaona, Gen. Antonio, 177, 180, 281, 330
Garcia, Don Francisco, 62
Garita, *see* powder house
Garrett, James Girard, 210
Garvin, John E., 210
Garza, Chaplain (Padre) Augustín, 329, 421
Garza, Gen., 49
Gay, Thomas, 156, 194
geese, 59
General Cos, schooner, 341
General DeKalb, ship, 296
Gentilz, Theodore, S18, S39
George, James, 210, 378
Georgia, 249, 323, 353, 408, 416
Georgia Battalion, 298, 299, 305, 306
Germany, 378
ghosts, 348
Giles County (TN), 381
Gloucester (MA), 345
Go Ahead, poem, 431
Goliad (TX) (*see also* La Bahia, Fort Defiance)
    anticipated Mexican attack on, 141, 236
    captured by Texians, 71–73, 82
    conditions at, 207, 295
    description of, in 1845, 391
    engagement with Indians near, 85
    evacuated by Fannin, 296, 303, 310
    execution of Fannin's men at, 1, 11, 228, 268,
    290, 291, 305–308, 309, 378, 391

Fannin at, 153, 161, 167, 174, 186, 236, 248
Filisola at, 344
Houston at, 127
letter from, 281–282
Matamoras expedition at, 121
Mexican division assigned to attack, 270, 295, 299
mission town, 20
supposed strength of, 128
survivors of massacre, 306, 308, 323, 334, 350, 359, 407
Texian prisoners at, 305, 306–308, 309
Gonzales (TX)
1835 clash at, 69–70, 71, 87
Austin at, 73
volunteers at, 74, S9
John W. Smith at, 124, 125
lumber mill in, 441 n. 72
couriers from Alamo at, 153, 161, 260
thirty-two reinforcements from, 153, 176, 181, 182, 183, 191, 192, 193, 238, 240, 350, 394, 436 n. 7-4
as rendezvous for Texian troops in 1836, 154, 156, 193–194, 288, 292, 299
rumor of enemy march on, 180
R. M. Williamson letter written at, 183
Houston arrives at, 203
reports of Alamo's fall reach, 203, 206, 207, 229, 236
burned by Houston, 236, 238, 294, 406
Mexicans march to, 281, 289, 293
Sesma's report from, 294
mentioned, 42, 45, 166 n. 11, 283, 291, 278, 379
Gonzales, Capt. Alonzo Frias, 329
Gonzales, Col. Eulogo, 138, 139, 281, 289, 329
Gonzales, Lt. Pedro, 329
Gonzales, servant boy, 38
Goode, Dr. A., 356
Gormley, 24
Gorostisa, 167
gourd canteen, 90, 337, 374
Government Hill, San Antonio, 422
Graham, Phil, 11
grape shot, 87, 92, 96. 97, 146, 159, 161, 182, 214, 228, 318, 384, 404
Granberry (TX), 417
Grant, Col. or Dr. James, 121, 138, 139, 147, 175, 194, 201, 202, 232 n. 29, 281, 283, 288, 306

"Grass Fight," 54, 85, 354, 372
Graviel, servant to John W. Smith, 421, 422
Gray, A. C., S64
Grayson, 402
Grayson, F., 198, 329
Gray, William Fairfax, 10, 219, 223–225, 231, 251
greatcoat, 374
Great Lakes, 315
Great Raft, 57–58
Greece, 2, 84, 244–245
Greene County (GA), 408
Greer, Thomas, 318
grenades, 253, S8, S29, S37, S41, S50, S56
Griffin, Peter, 308
Grimes, Jesse, 182, 415
Grimes County (TX), 274
grist, 304
Groce's Ferry (TX), 330
Groce's Retreat (TX), 219, 223, 225, 229
Guadalajara (Mexico), 382
Guadaloupe, plains of, 62
Guadaloupe River, 45, 69, 156, 195, 297, 298, 310, 366
Guadaloupe, Victoria (TX), 297, 298, 309, 330, 344
Guanzuato (Guanajuato), 136, 403
Guerrero (Mexico), 129
Guerrero, Vincente, 51
Guttierrez, see Lara, José Bernardo Guttierez
Gulf of Mexico, 20, 111, 146, 342
gunnade, 79, 150, 442 n. 140, S43–S44
Guzman, Capt. Don Nestor, 329

H
Hadden, Goliad survivor, 308
Hale, Lt. J. C., 322
Hamilton, Gov., 239
Hamilton, Mr., 216, 295
Hamm, Cephas R., 38, 39
Hannig, Joseph William, 407
Hannig, Susannah, see Dickinson, Susanna
Hannington, W. J., 356
Hardeman County (TN), 408
Hardeman, John, 177, 207
Hardway, Samuel, 323
Harris, Benjamin ("Ben"), 197, 207, 213, 236, 291, 292 n. 3, 408
Harris, Dilue Rose, 302

Harris, John, 210
Harrisburg (TX), 318, 319, 320, 327, 330, 352
Harrison, Dr. Benjamin, 309–311
Harrison, Col., 353
Harrison, Mr., 46
Harrison, William B., 209, 236
Harrison, William Henry, 104, 309, 310
Haskell, Charles, 217, 249, 295
Hastings, D. M., 405
Hatfield (MA), 259
Hathwell, actor, 357
hats, Mexican, 96, 135; Texian, 81, 353; Tejano, 82, 314, 316, 325, 391
Havana (Cuba), 377
Hawkins, Capt., 167, 352
Hawkins, Charles B., 329
Hawkins, Joseph M., 210
Hayden, Sterling, 54
Hayes County (TX), 415
Hays, John Coffee, 418, 420
Hays, John M., 210, 217, 244, 295
Healy, P. A., 132
Heiskell, Charles M., 210
Henderson, Calvin, 244
Hensley, W. R., 155
Henry Broughan, steamer, 315
Henry County (TN), 371
Hercules, 8, 203
Herff, Ferdinand, 423
Heroes of the Alamo, The, poem, 431
Heroine, steamer, 353
Herrera, Francisco, 97
Herrera, Capt. Ramon, 329
Herrera, Col., 21, 22
Hewitson, Dr. James, 26
hickory, 59
Hidalgo, Father, 21, 436 n. 7-1
Highsmith, Sam, 88
History and Legends of the Alamo and Other Missions in and around San Antonio (DeZavala), S6
History of Texas, From its First Settlement in 1685 to its Annexation to the United States in 1846 (Yoakum), S6
hobbles, iron, 73
Hocha, Capt. Ramon, 329
Hockley, Col. George W., 121, 321, 363
Hoffman, Mr., 70

Holland, Capt. Benjamin H., account of, 299, 303–306
Holland, Tapley, 210
Holloway, Samuel, 210
Holly Springs (TX), 381
Holsclau, Mr., 249
Holsinger, Lt. Col. Juan Jose, 297, 305
Holt, David I., 298, 323
Hood County (TX), 417
horses, wild, 59–60, 174, 391, 436 n. 5-8
Horton, Col., 303
Hotchkiss, A., 153
Hotel Maryland, Baltimore, 423
hot shot, 122, 172, 173, 188, S48
Hottentots, 11
Houston and His Republic (Lester), 335
Houston, Samuel
    abolitionist opinion of, 9
    and armistice with Santa Anna, 330, 334
    and Benjamin Harris, 291
    and Jameson's Alamo plan, S7
    and Mrs. Dickinson, 236, 238, 293, 408
    and Texas militia, 64, 65
    anticipated campaign of, 129
    appeal to Texas for aid, 179–180
    appointed commander of regular army, 79, 85, 86, 121
    as president of the Texas Republic, 362, 367, 373, 385
    at Goliad, 283
    at Gonzales, 194, 203, 236, 238, 285, 293
    at Nacogdoches, 139–140
    at San Felipe, 74, 75
    at San Jacinto, 318–340, 364
    at Texian convention of 1833, 54
    at Victoria, 133
    at Washington-on-the-Brazos, 1836, 177, 178, 179
    descriptions of, 36, 37, 42, 121, 332, 335
    goes to Texas, 42–43
    his report of battle, 320–323
    in New Orleans, 340
    in Washington, Texas, 70, 121
    interview with Santa Anna, 327, 328, 331, 335
    letter to Fannin, 206
    letter requesting volunteers from United States, 105–106
    made commander-in-chief of all Texian forces,

186, 193, 198, 418
   marriage to Eliza Allen, 36–37
   on Bowie's death, 251
   retreat to the Brazos, 299, 317
   retreat to Colorado River, 236, 241, 293, 294,
      295, 296, 350
   rumor of removal from command, 138
   sends Bowie to San Antonio, 127, 131
   strategy of, 121, 317, 318, 319, 330, 354
   treaty with Indians, 139–140, 179
   with army east of the Colorado, 175
Houston Street, San Antonio, 411, 424
Houston (TX), 403, 413, 415, 416
How Did Davy Die? (Kilgore), 266, 384
Howell, Dr. William D., 210
Huber, Dr. J. A., 46
Humphrey, Hubert H., 5
Hunt, Dr., 29
Hunter, steamboat, 56
hunting pouch: see bullet pouch
hunting shirt (see also buckskin clothing), 39, 56,
      82, 165, 176, 316, 352, 353, 354, 361, 400,
      402, 435 n. 5-5
Huntsman, Adam, 100–104, 401
Hurst, Capt., 303
Hurtado, Dr., 344
Huston, Gen. Felix, 218, 352, 367
Hutchinson, Pvt., 210
huts, 353
Hymn of the Alamo, poem, 431

I
Iberville (LA), 378
Illinois, 384
Independence, schooner, 329, 352
India rubber clothing, 165, 307
Indiana, schooner, 351
Indianola (TX), 402
Indians (*see also* individual tribes), mission
      Indians, 17–18; trade goods and, 58; attacks on
      settlers, 65–66, 249; stirred up by Mexicans,
      71, 193, 293; kill Lt. Collinswood, 85
Indian dress, 37
Indian trade goods, 58
Ingram, Allen, 322
Ingram, Alvia M., 361
Ingram, John, 93
Ingram, Maj. Ira, 234

Ingram, Pvt., 210
Invincible, schooner, 127, 310, 329, 352, 353
irrigation canal, *see acequia*
Isaonic, Comanche chief, 38
Israel, Capt., 308
Italians, in "Republican Army of the North," 1812,
      21
Italy, 334, 385
Iturbide, Augustin de, 26, 47, 72
Ivey, James, S30, S51
Iwonski, Carl G., S61
J
Jack, Patrick C., 51
Jackson, Andrew, 25, 36, 55, 100, 103, 104, 107,
      316, 363, 376, 400, 401
Jackson, Pvt. Thomas, 210
Jackson (TN), 249
James, Pvt. William F., 323
Jameson, Maj. Green B., 122, 147, 151 n. 11, 152,
      210, 213, 214, 236, 240, S7, S10, S27, S33,
      S38, S39, S41, S43, S44, S50, S53, S56, S58,
      S59, S62
Jeffries' Hotel, Little Rock, 106–109
jerked beef, 27
Joe (slave of W. B. Travis)
   accounts by, 12, 208, 213, 216–221, 223–226,
      227, 229, 230, 233, 243, 251, 252, 257
   and Mrs. Dickinson, 207, 291, 366
   as runaway slave in 1837, 374–375
   description, 375
   in Texas in 1874, 409
   in Texas in 1875, 404–405
   mentioned, 163, 209, 254 n. 11, 263, 293
John, Pvt., 210
Johnson, Col. Francis W., 97, 121, 125, 147, 174,
      175, 192, 194, 201, 202, 237, 238, 247, 283,
      288, 289, 298, 306, S9–S10
Johnson, Lewis, 210
Johnson, Lyndon B., 4
Johnson, Gen. S. A., 368
Johnson, William, 210
Jonesboro (TX), 110, 236
Jones, Dr. Anson, 143
Jones, Isaac N., 111, 113
Jones, Lt. John, 122, 209
Jones, John R., 155, 194, 374–375
Jones, Dr. Levi, 402
jorongo, 391

Julius Caesar, schooner, 296, 402
Juarez, Benito, S36
Jung, Carl, 3

K
Karnes, Capt., 321
Kedeson, Pvt., 210
keel boats, 58
Kemper, Samuel, 21, 22, 24
Kendall, George W., 384, 389
Kennedy, John Fitzgerald, 5
Kent, Andrew, 210
Kentucky, 10, 51, 72, 78, 118, 157, 241, 334, 354, 385, 416
Kentucky Mustangs, 303
Kerr, Maj. James, 437 n. 7-4
Khe Sanh (Vietnam), 4
Kickapoo Indians, 139
Kilgore, Dan, 266, 384
Kimball, Capt. of Mexican navy, 308, 359
Kimball, Capt., 166
Kimble, H. S., 178
King, Capt. Amon, 293, 299
King, Grey B., 301–302
King, William, 211
King, Gen., 361
Kinney, James, 210
knapsack, 173 n. 6, 314
Knoxville (GA), 341
Koch, Albert, 362
Korea, 4

L
La Baca River (TX), 298
La Bahia (*see also* Goliad; Fort Defiance), descriptions of fort at, 21–22, 71–72, 282, 391; mentioned, 18, 20, 24, 25, 26, 71, 136, 167, 175, 181, 207, 228, 260, 299, 305, 349, 406
La Bastida, Col. Ignacio (Ygancio), 213, S7, S25, S27, S28, S31, S32, S33, S35, S38, S39, S41, S43, S48, S51, S53, S58, S62, S64
Lachine (Canada), 315, 316 n. 2
ladders, scaling, 190, 201, 207, 208, 216, 220, 224–225, 234, 271, 403, 406, S47, S55
Lafayette Battalion, 288
Laffite, Jean, 25
La Grange (TN), 3, 356

Lamar, Col. Mirabeau B., 321, 323, 329, 379, 383, 384
Lamb, Lt., 322
Lampasas (Mexico), 405
lance, 73, 96, 97, 132, 135, 136, 138, 202, 234, 240, 314, 406, 410
langrage, 202
Lara, Jose Bernardo Gutirrez de, 21, 22, 23, 434 n. 1-4
Larambe, Col. Cirillo, 329
Laredo (TX), 81, 83, 98, 124, 135, 271, 288, 367, 373, 382, 383, 403, 405, 419, S56
lassadores, 136
lasso, 136, 314, 391
Last Command, The (1955 film), 54
Laura, steamboat, 146, 192
Lavaca Bay, 147
Lavaca, Port (TX), 70, 71, 309
La Villita, San Antonio, 157, 159, 168, 181, 186, 422, S44
Leaky, Mr., 286
leggings, 81, 165, 316, 325, 391, 400
Leddington, Goliad survivor, 308
Legion of Honor, Mexican Army, 129, 133
Legon, Col. 46
Leona Vicario (Mexico), 99, 129
Leonidas, 2, 216, 244, 389, 409
leopard, 58, 59
Lester, C. Edwards, 335
Levant, steamer, 237, 319
Lewis, Ira R., 207
Lewis, Pvt., of Wales, 210
Lewis, Pvt. Washington, 322
Lexington and Concord, battles of, 248
Liberty, schooner, 329
LIFE Magazine, 433 n. 11
Life and Adventures of Colonel David Crockett of West Tennessee, 32
Life of Martin Van Buren, The, 100
Lim, house of, 298
Lindley, Jonathan L., 210
Linn, Edward, 367
Linn, William, 210
Light Brigade, charge of, 412
Lincoln County (KY), 417
Lipantitlan, 129, 208, 291
liquor, 58, 123, 241, 255, 374
Little Missouri River, 203, 285, 286

Little Rock (AR), 106–110, 111, 117, 166, 203, 235, 285
Lizania, Capt. Jose, 329
lizard, travois-like device, 435 n. 5-6
Llewellen, Capt. Thomas, 283, 287
Lockhart boys, 91
log houses/cabins, 59, 401
Lomas del Alazan, Las (stream), 152
London (England), 387
Long, Dr. James, 25–27, 29
Looscan, Mrs., 421
Loranca, Sgt. Manuel, 215 n. 5, 276 n. 14, account by, 405–407, S39
Lord, Walter, 6
Los Adaes, 20
Los Almagres silver mine, 38
Los Cohates, 281
Lost Prairie (AR), 111, 114
Losoya, Mrs., 411
Louisiana, 20, 21, 23, 30, 46, 84, 128, 131, 217, 248, 257, 352, 376, 385
Louisville (KY), 56, 109, 126, 157, 248, 353, 363
Love, John, 298
Luelmo, Col. Santiago, 329
Lynchburg (TX), 332, 342
Lynch's Ferry, 318, 320, 330, 332

M

machete, 202, 423
Macon (GA), 341
Madam Garcia's, at Goliad, 282
Maddox, Dr. Thomas, 29–30
Mahan, D. H., S28
Main, Lt. George Washington, 84
Maine, 84, 113, 119, 121, 131
Main Plaza, San Antonio, 176, 442 n. 140
Mackinaw blanket, 374
MaCaulay, Capt. J. S., S3, S28, S44, S47, S48, S55, S56
Magee, Augustus, 21–22
maize, 23
Manitoba (Canada), 316
M'Arthur, Gov., 109
Manga de Clavo, 35,
Manhattan Island (NY; see also New York City), 226
Marchant, Mrs. Henry M., 361
Marines, US, 4

Martin, Capt. Albert, 69, 152, 153, 176, 211, 239
Martineau, Harriet, 110
Martínez, Gov. Antonio, 26
Martínez, Capt. (Dr.), 347
Martínez, Lt. Victoriano, 329
Masonic Hall, New York City, 260
Massachusetts, 165, 259, 345, 412
Massacre at Bexar, poem, 430
Matagorda (TX), 21–22, 71, 97, 128, 146, 160, 161, 167, 211, 246, 295, 308, 310, 352
Matagorda Bay, 47, 48, 71, 147
Matamoras (Matamoros, Mexico), 52, 96, 98, 128, 129, 138, 141, 147, 174, 269, 270, 296, 309, 351, 352, S4
Matawankeag, ship, 295
Mattepoisett (MA), 360
Maverick, Samuel, 197, 235, 398, 422, 424, 425, 443 n. 160, S11–S12, S23, S50, S53, S55
Maverick, Mrs. Samuel (Mary), 419, S15, S32
Maverick, William H., 424
Mattern, John Jacob, 378
Mayo, B., 46
Mayo, Frank, 407
Maximilian, Emperor, S36
Mazatlan (Mexico), 99
McAnneily, pleasant, 93
McCaslin, Thomas, 38, 40, 41
McLeod, Martin, 315
McClintock, William, 275, S22
McCoy, Jesse, 211
M'Cormick's (TX), 328
McGloin, James, 379
McGregor, John, 210
McKinley, William S., 5
McKinney, Collin, 177
McManaman, Capt., 303
McManus, S., 356
McMullen's house, San Antonio, 157
McNally, Samuel, 288
McNeal, Mr., 207
McNeel, Sterling, 402
McNutt, Capt., 193
McWhorter, Maj. George, 29–31
Medina River, 24, 143, 177, 403, 405
Melton, Quartermaster Eliel, 210
Memorias para la historia de la Guerra de Tejas (Filisola), S21, S39, S53
Memphis (TN), 106, 248, 249, 381, 402

Menchaca, Antonio, 143
Menchacho, Lt. Manuel, 169, 177
Menger Hotel, San Antonio, 275 n. 3
mesquite, 72, 273, 436 n. 6-7, S48, S55
Metis, 315
Mexia, José Antonio, 85, 99
Mexican army (*see also* Mexican army battalions
    and units; Santa Anna; and names of
    individual generals)
  arms and equipment of, 96–97, 423, 190, 322,
    331, 437 n. 7-8
  convicts in, 2, 73, 93, 262
  death of Alamo battle veterans, 422, 424
  drunkenness of, supposed, in March 6 attack,
    241, 409
  funding of, 96, 99, 141
  medical department, 12, 281, 344, 347, 374
  musicians of, 90, 96, 153, 189, 274–275, 276
    n. 14, 278, 304, S20
  provisions for, 128, 139, 169, 172, 344
  racial composition of, 353, 356, 424
  reconquest of Texas, anticipated in 1836, 351,
    353, 354, 364, 367
  retreats from Texas in 1836, 269, 328, 345,
    346, 347–349, 351, 352, 382, 407, 425
  servants from, 98, 271
  special military order and medal for Texas
    campaign, 129, 133
  strength of, 99, 124, 126, 270, 433 n. 11
  Texian opinion of, 342, 353, 354–357
  uniforms, 96–97, 98, 135, 172, 173 n. 6, 190,
    326, 362, 363, 364
Mexican army battalions and units
  Allende, 175
  artillery, *see* artillery, Mexican
  Aldama, 180, 183, 189, 190, 199, 201, 205,
    406
  Cavalry, regular, 69, 70, 85, 96, 126, 135–136,
    169, 190, 199, 202, 213, 240, 276, 278, 281,
    286, 294, 304, 305, 319, 347, 363, 373, 393,
    403, 405, 406, 411, S11, S26, S64
  Cavalry, irregular, 35
  Cavalry, Presidial, 20–21, 27, 135, 243, 291,
    348, S12, S43, S48, S62
  Cazadores (light infantry), 157, 165, 169, 174,
    189, 205, 227, 294, 326, 406
  Coahuila, 135
  Cuautla, 30, 270

  Dolores, 135, 169, 175, 228, 270, 271, 276 n.
    14, 293, 406, 438 n. 9
  engineers, 164, 186, 190, 213, 214, 297,
    S10–S11, S16
  Guadalajara, 270
  Guanajuato, 135, 309
  Guerrero, 4, 270, 293, 322
  Hussars, 135
  Jimenez, 157, 169, 177, 189, 190, 199, 270,
    271, S62
  La Prima Activa, 270
  Matamoros, 4, 157, 169, 183, 189, 190, 199,
    270, 271, 403, 406, S34, S62
  Mexico, 293
  Morales, 406
  Morelos (the "Invincibles"), 70, 77, 82, 93,
    270
  Nueva Leon, 95
  9th, 46
  Pioneers, 205
  Queretara, 270, 292
  San Luis Potosí, 169, 183, 189, 190, 199, 201,
    205, 270, 271, 406
  Sappers, 172, 185, 205, 265, 277
  Tampico, 135, 270, 293
  Toluca, 4, 180, 183, 189, 190, 199, 270, 271,
    395, 406, S51
  Tres Villas, 270, 292, 306
  Yucatan, 270
  Zapadores, 11, 180, 183, 190, 199, 228, 243,
    265, 270, 271, 277–278
Mexican navy, 95, 146–147, 193, 308, 341, 359,
    360
Mexican, ship, 308, 359
Mexican-American War (1846–1848), 198, 391,
    392, 418, 422, S10–S11, S27, S29, S32
Mexico, general: mission settlements by 17–19;
    early Texian unrest and, 45–47, 52, 64, 66–67;
    cholera in, 55; determination to put down
    Texian revolt, 125–126; relations with the US,
    125, 245; after San Jacinto, 340, 341, 351, 355
Mexico City, 4, 7, 11, 17, 26, 54, 55, 169, S10–S11
Michilena, Gen., 293
Mier (Mexico), 288, 411
Milam, Col. Benjamin R., 71–73, 91, 92, 97, 140,
    197, 240, 283, 356, 386, S46
Military Plaza, San Antonio, 173
Millard, Lt. Col. Henry, 179, 321

Miller County (TX), 236, 241
Miller, Maj., 305, 308
Miller, Thomas R., 210
Mills, Isaac, 211
mills, in San Antonio, 86, 87, 90, 91, 169, 180
Mina, Gen. Javier, 136, 227
mines, 38, 381–384
Minn (TX), 187
Minnesota, 316
Minon, Gen. Jose Vicente, 189, 406
missions, early Texas (see also by name), 17–20,
    389–391
Mississippi, 22, 30, 31, 217, 248, 283, 352, 372, 416
Mississippi Hotel, Natchez, 362
Mississippi River, 29, 56, 61, 106, 298, 334
Missouri, 421
Missouri River, 316
Mitchasson, Dr. Edward F., 210, 236
Mitchell, Edwin T., 210, 298
Mobile (AL), 73, 142, 245
Mobile Greys, 303, 308
moccasins, 316, 400
Modina, Sgt., 407
Mojico, Capt. Salvador, 329
Molina, Lt. Francisco, 329
Molino, soldier, 407
Monclova (Mexico), 22, 55, 129, 141, 344, 376
Money, J. H., 155
Monjarra, Capt. Juan, 329
monks, see padres
Monoga, Gen., 293
Monongahela (liquor), 255
Montano, Lt. Juan, 329
Monterey, Col., 22
Monterrey (Mexico), 25, 72, 96, 382, 405
Montezuma, 356
Montezuma, Gen., 96
Montezuma, schooner, 146–147
Montreal (Canada), 315
Moody, E. J., 3, 356
Moore, Capt. Andrew, 402
Moore, J. H., 69
Moore, J. S., 402
Moore, Pvt., 210
Moore, Robert B., 210, 237
Mora, Lt. Col. Esteban, 228, 275 n. 1, 329
Mora, Gen. Ventura, 183, 209, 220, 223–225,
    228–229, 235, 403

Morales, Gen., 362
Morales, Col. Juan, 189, 201, 297, 407
Morateas, Col., 305
Mordecai, Benjamin, 323
Morgan, Col. James, 263, 342
Moro, Dr. Don Jose Faustino, 344
Morris, Capt. Robert C., 84, 145, 202, 283, 287,
    288, 306, S44
Moseley, Dr. William, 323
Motley, David, 333
mules, 61, 83,138, 160, 314, 320, 322, 345, 349,
    351, 353, 367, 373, 374, 391
Mulhollan, Capt. Charles, 31
Murfree, David, 217
Murphy, Daniel, 334
muskets, Mexican, 71, 89, 96, 227
muskets, Texian, 122, 174, 186 n. 1, 331
muskrat, 58
mustangs (see horse, wild)
Musselman, Robert, 210
Muzquíz, Don Ramón, 95
Myers, John Myers, 1, 425

N
Nachitoches (LA), 20, 21, 22, 25, 51, 57, 61, 236,
    249, 334, 353
Nacogdoches (TX), description of, in 1829, 434 n.
    3-1; mentioned, 20, 21, 22, 24, 25, 27, 45, 46,
    54, 64, 65, 70, 74, 84, 98, 111, 139, 193, 206,
    236, 239, 285–287, 311, 319, 345
Nangle, William B., 388, 419
Napoleon/Napoleonic wars, 8, 218, 226, 277, 328,
    338, 341
Narrative of the Life of David Crockett of the State
    of Tennessee, A, 55
Nashville (TN), 37, 140, 157, 319, 376, 400
Nassau, 136
Natchez (MS), 29, 30, 74, 147, 206, 207, 218, 236,
    352, 362, 372, 387, 399, 402
Navarro, Antonio, 178, 403
Navarro, Lt. Antonio, 329
Navarro, Miss, 221
Navarro, Col. Jose Juan Sanchez
    account of Alamo assault, 201–203, 205, 228,
        231, 251, 252, 266, S9
    descriptions of Alamo fortifications, 214, S8,
        S9, S23, S27, S28, S39, S47, S54
    drawings and plans of Alamo, 442 n. 115, S7

S13, S14, S15, S16, S18, S20, S31, S32, S33, S34, S35, S36, S43, S44, S46, S48, S50, S51, S53, S55, S56, S59, S60, S62
  mentioned, 83, 95, 135, 150, 164, 171, 172
Navastota River, 58
National Museum, 361
National Theatre, Boston, 360
Navy, Mexican, *see* Mexican Navy
Navy, Texian, *see* Texian navy
Neale, William, 253
Nebel, Carl, S29
Nebraska, 5
Neches River, 58
Neggan, George, 210
Neill, Col. James C., 87, 122, 123, 127, 131, 132, 133, 137, 288, 323, 419, S21
Nelson, Annette, 378
Nelson, Col., 420
Nelson, James, 322
Nelson, Pvt., 210
Nelson, Pvt., of Austin, 210
Nelson, Pvt., of South Carolina, 210
New England, 259, 353, 408, 409
New Jersey, 269
New Mexico, 20, 422
New Orleans, 48, 57, 71, 78, 84, 85, 115, 136, 142, 156, 176, 193, 217, 245, 246, 259, 352, 388, 389, 402, 415
New Orleans, Battle of, 25, 197
New Orleans Blues, 92
New Orleans Greys
  and artillery, 145–146
  arrival in San Antonio, 74, 84
  as part of "Lafayette Battalion," 288
  at Alamo, 202, 209
  at Coleto Creek, 303
  at Goliad, 288, 289
  at Goliad massacre, 306–308
  at siege of Béxar, 84, 92, 283, S9
  at Velasco, 75, 146, S44
  composition of, 6–7, 84
  flag of, 4–5, 7, 200, 201, 203, S21
  members return to United States, 136
  mentioned, 126
Newport (OH), 126
newspapers, American, and Alamo, 1–16; and David Crockett, 13; Mexican, and Alamo, 7–8, 10–11, 12

newspapers, production of, 8–9, 14, 433 n.47
Newton, Lucie J., 421
New Washington (TX), 320, 327, 330
New York, 5, 135, 136, 142, 241, 373, 412
New York City, 55, 244, 245, 260, 345, 356, 359–360, 372, 438 n. 10-5
Nibb, Willis, 57, 133
Nieto, Lt. Juan, 329
Nixon, Maj., 152
Nixon, Richard M., 5
North Bend (OH), 310
North Carolina, 302
North Dakota, 316
Norton, Maj. B. Hammatt, 78, 353–354
Norton, George W., 261
Norway, 314,
Nueces River, 58, 142, 180, 283
Nueva Leon, 289
Nuevo Laredo (Mexico), 417
Nuñez, Felix, 273, 274, S24

O
oak tree, 59
Obion County (TN), 401
Obion River, 33
Obregon, Lt. José María, 329
Ocean, ship, 342
Ohio, 56, 263, 310
Ohio River, 56, 363
Oklahoma, 110
Olazaron, Col. Mariano, 329
Opelousas (LA), 352
opium, 339
Oregon Trail, 285
Orisnuela, Col., 183
Ortego, Lt. José María, 329
otter, 59
Ouachita, steamboat, 84
Oury, William S., S20
overcoats, Mexican, 190
Owen, Shapeley, 333
Owens, William, 22
owls, S3
Oaxaca (Mexico), 35, 36

P
Pacific Ocean, 167
Packet, brig, 311

padres, 17–18, 329, 421, S12, S16, S61, S62
Pages, Pierre Marie François de, 20
panther, 58
Pantillion, Isadore, 140, 141
Paoli, massacre at, 10, 246
Paragon, brig, 341
Paraza, Capt., 342
Parezo, Lt. Mateo, 329
Paris, Carlo, 441 n. 91
Park, William A., 322
Parker, Christopher Adams, 210, 400
Parker, Isaac, 166
Parker, William, 234
Parker, portrait painter of Natchez, 402
Parmer, Martin, 179, 182, 194–195
Parres, Gen., 63, 293
Patriots of Thermopylae, The, poem, 431
Patton, W. H., 97, 363
Peacock, Capt., 217, 283
Pearson, Capt. T., 283, 287
Pease, E. M., 123
pecan tree, 77, 90
Pedraza, Manuel Gomez, 54
Pegart, Capt., 22
Peña, Jose Enrique de la Peña, 11, 214, 231, 253, 265, 347, S22, S46, S54–S55, S56, S61
Peninsular War, 10, 246
Pennsylvania, schooner, 296
penny presses, 9
Peotillos, battle of, 227
Peralta, Lt. Don Joaquín, 329
Peralto, Gen. Augustín, 329
Perdido, plain of, 297
Perez, Gen., 262
Perez, Alejo, 411, 418
Perez, Francisco, 143
Perez, Col. Ignacio, 25, 26
Perez, Ramigio, 411
Perroes, Lt. Miguel, 329
Perry, Col., 24
Persia, 244–245
Pettus, Capt. Samuel Overton, 303
Pettus, William, 156, 194
Philadelphia (PA), 38, 67, 239, 310, 353, 357, 376, 401
Piedras, Col. Jose de la, 53, 54, 434 n. 3-1
Pierce, Capt., 379
Pike, Albert, 106, 109

Pino, Lt. Estanislar, 329
Pintos, 168
Pitkin Guards, 384
Pittsburgh (PA), 56
pivot gun, 145, 146, 147–148, 214, S12, S41
Plaquemine (LA), 352
play, based on Alamo, 357, 391, 403
poetry, 3–4, 6, 427–432
Polk, James K., 391
Polin, Mexican fifer, 274
Poland, 84, 303
Pollard, Dr. Amos, 210, 236
poncho, 135
Ponton, Judge Andrew, 208, 223
Porter, Congressman, 316
Portilla, Col. Manuel, 329
Portilla, Col. Nicholas de, 307
Portranca River, 143
Portsmouth (NH), 126, 259
Potter, Reuben Marmaduke
  "Attack and Defence of the Alamo" (1840), 231, 269–279, S5, S20, S47
  Fall of the Alamo (1860), 215, 252, 269, S5, S20, S22, S30, S34
  Fall of the Alamo (1878), 214, 215, 252, 269, S5, S9, S19, S20, S30, S31, S32, S35, S53
  life of, 269
  mentioned, 276 n. 14, 360, 388, S4–S6, S44, S62
  on Crockett's death, 265
  poetry of, 412, 431–432
  plan of Alamo, *S6*
  servant of (Sgt. Becerra), 402
Potter, Robert, 64, 65, 119, 207
powder horn, 359, 360, 365
powder house, San Antonio, 181, S64
Presidio San Antonio, 17
Presley, Elvis, 381
Preston, Congressman, 316
prostitution, 86, 139, 415, 416
Puebla (Mexico), 96
Pueblo de Valero, San Antonio, 157
Pueblo Viejo (Tampico, Mexico), 49, 50
Puellas, Lt. José María, 329
Putnam, Michael, 322
Q
Queretaro (Mexico), 83, 129, S36
Quintanas (TX), 343

R

Rabb, Capt., 193
raccoon, 58, 59, 193
Rada, Lt. Don Francisco, 95, 97
raft, 340
Raguet, Henry, 240, 251
railroad, 334, 401, 403
Ramirez, Gen., *see* Sesma, Gen. Ramirez
Ramon, Capt. Domingo, 17
Randolph (TN), 248
Rantiford, Capt., 35
Rapides Parish (LA), 31, 402
Reagan, Ronald, 5–6
Rector, Col. Elias, 42–43, 322
redan, S35
Redfish Bar, Galveston, 301
Red Lands, 75, 166 n. 11
Red River (MS), 29, 30
Red River (TX), 58, 61, 110, 111, 167, 177, 311,
    334, 402
Red Rovers, Alabama, 303, 306
Reelfoot Lake (TN), 401
Refugio (TX), 65, 127, 186
Refugio Mission, 133, 283, 293, 299, 309, 323
Regulator-Moderator War, 1842, 119
Reid, George M., 91
Reilly, Henry, 311
"Reminiscences of the Alamo," 269
Reyes, Carmel de los, 243
Reyes, Dr., 344
Reyes, Lt. Mariano, 329
Reyes, Silvestre, S56
Rice, Charles E., 211, 237
Rice, Joel C., 261
Richmond (TX), 374
Richmond (VA), 354
ricochet shot, 171, S41
Riddell, J. L., 17
Rife, Mr., 411
rifle case, 82, 132
rifles (*see also* Crockett, David, rifles of),
    Baker, 205, 227; Kentucky horse rifle, 118;
    Springfield, 423; Texas sends to New Orleans
    for, 71; Yagers, 122, 352
Riflemen Volunteers, proposed regiments of,
    313–315
Rincon, Gen., 36
Rio Frio, 18, 124, 125, 138, 143

Rio Grande, 19, 22, 23, 24, 135, 138, 139, 141,
    143, 246, 253, 288, 334, 345, 373, 374, 405
Ripley, Gen. Eleazar W., 289
Ripley, Sgt. Henry, 289, 308
Robbins, Pvt., 210
Roberts, Mr., 22
Robertson's Colony (TX), 193
Robinson, James W., 123, 124
Robinson, Sgt., 210
rockets, 86, 87–88, 197–198, 235
Rocky Mountains, 114, 119
Rodríguez, 138
Rodríguez, Ambrosio, 140
Rodríguez, Capt. Benito, 329
Rodríguez, Felix, 424
Rodríguez, José María, 140, 275 n. 3, 436 n. 6-7
Rogers, Will, 109
Roman army, S35–S37
Romero, Adj. Felipe, 329
Romero, Col. José María, 183, 189, 201, 214, 243,
    289, 329, S22, S55, S62
Roosevelt, Theodore, 5
Rose, Dilue, *see* Harris, Dilue Rose
Rose, Louis (Moses), 286–287
Rose, Pvt., of Nacogdoches, 210
Rosos, Lt. Secundino, 329
Ross, Capt., 191
Rough Riders, 5
Roundabout, Col., 402
Rountree, F. S., S63
Rowe, Elizabeth, 378
Roxbury (MA), 165
Royall, R. R., 75
Rucker's Creek (TX), 417
Ruis, Francisco, 422
Ruíz, Francisco Antonio, 213, 227, 230, 231, 252, 265
Ruíz, Col., 178
Runaway Scrape, 232 n. 2, 293, 295, 298, 299,
    301–303, 317, 345
Rusk, Jackson J., 210
Rusk, Col. Thomas Jefferson, 74, 207, 322, 349,
    341, 345, 365
Rutledge, Richard, 298
Ryan, Isaac, 210

S

Sabine River, 21, 23, 24, 25, 45, 58, 65, 174, 195,
    236, 293, 301

saddlebags, 360
saddles, 123, 341, 374, 375, 391
Salado Creek, 74, 289
Salas, Col. Mariano, 189, 297, 406
Salcedo, Gov., 21, 22
Salevias de Victoria (Mexico), 405
Salinas (TX), 98, 382
Salmon Creek (NC), 302
Saltillo (Mexico), 24, 26, 99, 129, 141, 143, 367, 405
Samson, 3
San Antonio de Béxar
    and Alamo in 1883–1884, 409–411
    and Alamo publicity, 424–425
    and Alamo siege, 143–190, 405–406
    Bowie arrives at, 1836, 133
    burial customs in, 397
    Col. Neill in command at, 122, 123–125, 131, S21
    Comanche Indians in vicinity of, 131–132, 379, 384
    condition in 1822, 27
    conditions at, 137
    Council House Fight of 1840, 379
    Crockett arrives at, 137
    descriptions of, in 1835, S28; in 1841, 384–385; in 1842, 389–391; in 1846, 392; in 1848, 396–397
    early founding and settlement, 17–21, 389–391, S56
    events in, mid-1836 through 1837, 364, 366–369
    in revolts of 1812–1813, 21–25
    Indian raid, 379, 384
    James and Rezin Bowie in, 1831, 38, 42
    Lt. Col. Juan Seguin occupies, 364, 367–369
    Matamoros expedition and, 121–122, 283
    Mexican army at, after San Jacinto, 343, 344, 347–349
    Mexican army evacuates, 344, 345, 347–349, 364, S2–S3, S18, S22
    Mexican defense works in, 1835, 74, 79, 82–83, 85, 86, 127, 147, 173, 213, 230, S11–S12, S16, S24, S27, S28
    Mexican town council, 55
    Mexican troops at, 1835, 69, 70, 73–99
    road to and from, in east, 61, 115, 119, 157, S64
    Rough Riders in, 5
    Santa Anna's army arrives at, 143, 152, 157, 350, 405
    siege and battle of, 1835, 7, 73–99, 146, 147, 191, 283, 288, 354, 372, 391, 397, 421–422, S44, 435 n. 4-5
    Stephen Austin's arrival in, 1821, 26, 47
    Travis arrives at, 137
San Antonio National Bank, 423
San Antonio River, 17, 58, 71, 72, 77, 131, 163, 167–168, 172, 282, 303, 368, 385, 389, 392, 396, 397, 422, 438 n. 8-9, S5, S9, S33, S48; bridges across, 140, 159, 168, 397, 403, 436 n. 6-7
San Augustine (TX), 84, 115, 154, 155, 294
Sanchez, Lt. Augustín, 329
Sánchez-Navarro, Col. José Juan, see Navarro, Col. José Juan Sánchez
sandals, 190
sandbags, 150, 165, 172, 187–188, 231, 403, 440 n. 43, S16, S29, S33, S37, S39, S41, S50
Sand Bar Duel, 12, 29–31, 376, 377, 399–400
San Felipe, schooner, 146
San Felipe de Austin, 47, 48, 52, 57, 64, 70, 122, 123, 128, 133, 146, 155, 156, 182, 183, 187, 191, 220, 223, 224, 289, 295, 296, 299, 301, 317, 325, 406, 407
San Fernando Church, San Antonio, 74, 70, 86, 87, 93, 147, 182, 368, 390–391, 438 n. 10-8, S11, S26, S27
San Francisco (CA), S61
San Jacinto
    animated diorama of, in NYC, 438 n. 5
    Battle of, 318–349, 330–335, 343, 345, 346, 350–351, 355, 362, 365, 407
    casualties, Mexican, 318, 319, 322, 323, 328, 331, 335, 343, 345, 350, 355
    casualties, Texian, 318, 319, 320, 322–323, 328, 332, 333, 335, 345, 350, 355
    mentioned, 6, 7, 136, 143, 266, 279, S34
    Mexican flags at, 4
    Mexican army property seized at, 320, 322, 328, 340–341 361
San Jacinto Bay, 332
San Jacinto Day, 404
San Jacinto River, 58, 331, 332
San José, Mission (San Antonio), 18, 390, 396, photograph *S17*

San Juan d' Ulloa, Castle, 35
San Juan, Mission (San Antonio), 390, 396
San Luis Potosí (Mexico), 83, 99, 351, 405
San Miguel Creek, 81
San Patricio (TX), 85, 128, 138, 174, 175, 176,
    180, 202, 208, 237, 247, 282, 283, 287, 289,
    291, 299, 309, 352
San Pedro Creek, 17, 93
San Saba district, 60
San Saba, Mission, 38, 39, 42, 396
San Saba River, 38
San Saba silver mines, 39
San Saba Street, San Antonio, 421
Santa Anna, Gen. Antonio Lopez de
    and Alamo assault, 199–205, 276, 403, 406,
      438 n. 8-9
    and armistice with Houston, 330, 334, 340,
      342, 351, S3
    and Crockett, 103–104, 263–266, 404,
      437–438 ns. 8-4 to 8-6
    and Goliad massacre, 308–309, 351, 407
    and march to Texas, 83, 96, 97, 99–100, 126,
      137, 138, 270, 271, 281, 403, 405, 419
    and Mexican newspapers, 10–11
    and Mrs. Dickinson, 207, 217, 238, 406, 408
    and special military order and medal, 129
    arrives at San Antonio, 143, 149, 152, 154,
      392, 403, 405, 419, 437 n. 8-4
    as prisoner, 323, 328–329, 332, 342, 351, 352,
      S3
    at San Jacinto, 318–349, 351, 407
    attack orders of March 5, 189–190, 271, 406
    attacks Spanish army at Tampico, 49–51
    biography of, 35–36
    cane of, 340–341
    capture of, 318, 319, 322, 323, 328, 331, 335,
      337–338
    defense of Mexican territory, 7–8, 10
    descriptions of, 35, 221, 319, 323, 331–332,
      335, 337, 338, 362, 363–364
    election as Mexican president, 54
    Feb. 17, 1836 Proclamation to troops, 142
    headquarters of, 393, 442 n. 140
    in Texas battles of 1813, 24
    interview with Houston, 327, 328, 331,
      338–340
    journey to Wash. D.C., 363
    launches Feb. 25 attack, 157, 159–160, 161

    letter of, written at Leona Vicario, 129
    "life guards" of, 235
    March 4 council of war, 183, 406
    marches east from San Antonio, 236, 239
    messages sent by, 169, 174, S7
    Mexican praise for, 8, 202, 261, 427
    mock marriage of, 168
    New Orleans Greys flag and, 7
    opinion of Alamo as fort, S10
    plans to send force into Texas, 66, 105
    portrait of, 362–363
    proclamation of, to citizens of Texas, 207–208,
      279, 291, 310, 311, 406
    puts down Zacatecan revolt, 62–63
    reconnoiters Alamo, 153, 163–164, 175, 176,
      180
    report of Alamo conquest, 199–200, 223
    saddle of, 340
    seizes control of government in 1834, 57, 72
    silverware of, 341
    strategy of, 317–318
    targeted by Texians in Alamo, 163–164, 169,
      278
    threat to march to Sabine, 313, 316
    tours captured Alamo, 218, 227, 265, 274,
      278, 437 n. 8-4, S20
    US opinion of, 78–79, 244, 245, 260, 351,
      362, 363–364
    writes protest to Burnet, 351, S3
Santa Fe (NM), 315, 440 n. 44
Santa Fe Expedition, 389
Santiano, schooner, 296
Santiesteban, Lt. Trinidad, 329
sash, 325
scalping, 38
scalping knife, 37
Schrusnecki, Capt., 303
"Scots Wha Ha'!" poem, 430
Scott, Sir Walter, 226
Scurlock, Capt. William, 267 n. 3, 308
Sea Willow River, *see* Cibolo River
Seguin, Erasmo, 417
Seguin, Capt. Juan Nepomuceno
    and ashes of Alamo dead, 273, 367–369
    as Alamo courier, 157, 159–160, 443 n. 164,
      S51
    at San Jacinto, 325, 343–344, 417
    in Texas Senate, 376

mentioned, 81, 169, 177, 198, 364, 406, 419
obituary, 417
returns to Béxar, 364, 366–369
Seguin (TX), 384
Seminole Indians, 1, 139, 245
Sesma, Gen. Ramirez, in Alamo attack, 190, 195, 286; mentioned, 83, 99, 128, 129, 135–136, 143, 167, 169, 175, 176, 177, 180, 181, 182, 183, 195, 281, 289, 293, 294, 340, 393, 405, 406, 407
Sewell, Marcus L., 210
Shackleford, Capt. (Dr.) Jack, 303, 323, 327, 348
Shain, Charles B., 334
shakos, 190
Shawnee Indians, 139
Sheffield knives, 259
Shelbyville (TN), 318
Shenandoah, schooner, 296
Sherman, Capt./Col. Sidney, 126, 318, 320, 321, 322, 325, 326, 333
shield, Indian, 39, 132
Shoupp, Sam, 87
Simms, William Gilmore, 386
Simonides, 431
Simpson, Pvt., 210
Simpson, Goliad survivor, 308
Sipican Indians, 360
Sketches and Eccentricities of Colonel David Crockett of West Tennessee, excerpts from, 32–34
slavery, 9, 18, 51, 52, 61, 220, 247, 252–253, 299, 375, 381–384, 398
Slocum, Capt. William, 21, 24
Smith, Ashbel, 416
Smith, Charles, 210
Smith, Erastus "Deaf"
    at San Jacinto, 365, 372
    burns Texas prairie in 1836, 403
    character of, 366, 372, 373–374
    death, 374
    description, 372–374
    escorts Mrs. Dickinson to Gonzales, 207, 291–292, 366
    in 1835 siege of Béxar, 81, 82, 85, 90, 93, 372, S9
    in post-San Jacinto raids, 373–374
    leaves San Antonio with Col. Neill, 419
    life of, 372

pouch, horn, and knife of, 365–366
    Tejana wife of, 366, 372, 373
    Travis and, 366, 372
Smith, Ezekiel, 365
Smith, Gov. Henry, 79, 121, 123, 127, 131, 133, 153, 235, 366, S7, S56
Smith, John W., description, 421; life of, 421–422; mentioned, 124, 140, 141, 152, 176, 183, 191, 208, 223, 286, S11
Smith, Richard Penn, 357
Smith, R., 65
Smith, William, 210
Smith, Capt., 323
Smith, soldier at Goliad, 308
Smith, Pvt., 210
snakes, S3
Snodgrass, Mr., 22
Soldana, Capt. Rafael, 185
Soledad Street, San Antonio, 92
Sombrerete (Mexico), 63
Somerville, A., 155
Souza, Lt. Jose, 329
South Carolina, 238, 385
South Dakota, 5
Southmayed, J. A., 378
Southwest Pass (LA), 342
Soviet Union, 5
Spain, 19, 35, 48
Spanish army, 17–26, 35, 48–51, 73
Sparrow, Gen., 400
Sparta, 244
Spohn, Joseph H., account of, 306–308; arrives in New York City, 359
Sprowl, J., 46
spurs, 374
Spy, The (Cooper), 372
Stael, Madam de, 27
Standish, Capt. Myles, 360
Stanley, Col., 295
Stansbury, Lt., 138
Starr, Franklin J., 133, 155
Starr, Richard, 210, 294
Statesman, steamer, 353
St. Bernard River, 349
St. Bruna, Col., 22
St. Denis, Louis Juchereau de, 17
Steele, Pvt. Alphonso, 322
Steele, Gen. William, 286

Stevens, Pvt. A. R., 322
Stevenson, R., letter of, 322
Stewart, C. B., 123, 207
St. Joseph's Catholic School, San Antonio, 274
St. Joseph's Church, San Antonio, 423
St. Landry (LA), 402
St. Louis (MO), 362, 415
St. Louis Museum, 362
St. Mark's Episcopal Church, San Antonio, 424
Stone, Capt., 56
Stony Point, battle of, 246
Storming of Chapultepec—Pillow's Attack, Nebel
    print, S29
Strange, Maj. J., 363
St. Saba River, 38
Stuart, Pvt., 210
Sublette, Col. A.S., 74, 194
sugar, 23, 48, 58
sugar maple, 59
Sulphur Fork (TX), 241
surveyors, 249
Sutherland, Dr. John, 148, 163, 191, 225, 254 n.
    11, 285, 422, S26, S30, S31, S33, S50, S62
Sutherland, Ramsay, 89
Sutherland, William De Priest, 210
swallows, S3
Sweden, 314
Swisher, Capt., 88
swivel gun, 148, 398, S20
Sylvester, Lt., 335, 338

T

Tampico (Mexico), 49–51, 57, 83, 85, 98, 99, 126,
    335, 351
Tamaulipas (Mexico), 138, 253, 283, 289, 381
tanning (hides), 60
Tapia, Lino Sanchez y, 82
Tarleton, Capt. James, account by, 332–335
Tawakoni Indians, 38–42
Taylor, Creed, 420
Taylor, Gen. Zachary, 391
Tecumseh, 311
Teran, Manuel Mier y, 434 n. 3-2, S16
Tejanos (Texas Mexicans), 127, 157, 182, 203,
    206, 207, 247, 273, 286, 316, 325–326,
    343–344, 345, 364, 366–369, 375, 389, 391,
    392, 397, 404, 406, 419, 421–422, S3, S21, S56
telescope, 123, 423

Teller, Capt. Nicholas, 329
Tennessee, 32, 34, 36, 37, 56, 103, 104, 105, 140,
    149, 157, 218, 248, 255, 258, 354, 356, 383,
    385, 400, 408, 417
tents, 122, 249, 319, 339, 372, 437 n. 8-4
Terrible, schooner, 352
Texas
    American immigration to, 27–28, 46, 51, 54,
        60–61
    annexed into Union, 391
    apathy of Texians, 157, 187, 192, 194, 221,
        288
    as Republic, 362, 379
    Austin's and other early American settlements,
        26–28, 45, 47–48, 60
    calls for US volunteers, 193, 241, 248, 282
    Civil War and, 416
    condition of, after San Jacinto, 329
    conflict at Anahuac, 51–54
    conflicts of 1812–1821 in, 21–26
    David Crockett travels to, 103–120
    Declaration of Independence Convention,
        1836, 137, 139, 140, 167, 177–179, 186, 192,
        235, 236, 244, 282, 289, 295
    description of, 26–27, 57–62, 334
    Fredonia revolt, 45–46, 434 n. 3-1
    Goliad document declaring Texas independent,
        128
    invasion of Mexico considered, 352, 356
    newspapers of, 10
    Santa Anna grants independence of, 344
    settlers in, 1835, 65–67
    Texas Consultation, 236
    US opinion, 1, 6–9, 26–28, 244, 246–247, 248,
        311
    volunteers flock to, spring-summer 1836, 315,
        352–354
Texas rangers, 155, 372–374, 418
Texian Army
    after San Jacinto, 352, 354
    arms, clothing and material needed, 122–123,
        141, 173; ditto acquired from Mexican army,
        96–97
    besieges San Antonio in 1835, 73–98, 283
    composition of, at San Jacinto, 323
    Matamoros expedition, 121, 122, 127, 147,
        174, 283, 418
    militia ordered, 141

music of, 123

provisions for, 122, 282, 305, 314, 374

regulars of, 133, 303, 331, 333, 379, S3

retreats from Gonzales, 236, 238, 293

retreats to the Brazos, 299, 317

strategy of, 195

Texian artillery (see also artillery), 133, 303, 331

Texian cavalry, 127, 133, 303, 320, 321, 333, 352, 364, 366–369

Texian navy, 128, 131, 132, 133, 145, 167, 311, 329, 440 n. 58

Texian War Cry, poem, 427–428

Thermopylae, 2, 208, –216, 221, 244, 245, 279, 356, 389, 394, 409, 413, 419, 431

Thomas of Roberston County, TN, 217, 295

Thompson, Ben, 440

Thompson, Capt., 308

Thorpe, T.B., portrait painter, 402

Three Years in Texas, Including a View of the Texan Revolution (Field), 159

Thurston, John M., 210

Ticonderoga (NY), S32

Time to Stand, A (Lord), 6

Tinaja River, 176

Tlaxcala Indians, 19, 362

Toledo y Dubois, Jose Alvarez, 19, 22, 23, 24

Tolsa, Gen. Eugenio, 289, 293, 403, 419

Tom, Pvt. J., 322

tomahawk, 123

Tomlinson, George, 210

Tom Owen, the Bee Hunter, painting, 402

Tornel, José María, decree of, 11, 99; mentioned, 129, 200

Torrices, Lt. José María, 329

To the Texians, poem, 428

trade goods, Indian, 58

Trask, Capt., 341

Trask, Pvt., 322, 345

Travels Round the World in the Years 1767, 1768, 1769, 1770, 1771 (de Pages), 20

traverse, 172, 231, S39, S54, S58

Travis, Charles, 221; and Angelina Dickinson, 415, 416

Travis, James, 227

Travis, William Barrett

    and anticipated Mexican approach, 140, 419, 436 n. 7-2

    and John Sutherland, S26

arrives at Alamo, 1836, 133, 137, 419

as lawyer, 37, 57, 133

assigns Crockett command of palisade, 148, S30

at Anahuac, 51–53, 63–64

body mutilated, 218, 220, 229, 230, 238, 274, 325, 344

character of, 260

death at Alamo, 3, 199, 201, 202, 209, 211, 216, 217, 220, 223–233, 235, 240, 243, 278, 350, 395, 404, S63

estate of, 374–375

family of, 37, 221, 415, 416

Feb. 23 message to Almonte

headquarters of, 418, S50

in 1835 raid on Mexican horse herd, 81–82, 83, 85

in planned night attack on Cos's positions, 1835, 87, 90

in San Felipe de Austin, 57

knife of, 365–366

letter of Feb. 24, 153, 154, 155, 176

letter of Feb. 25, 157, 159, 161, 163, 171, 178, 181, 182

letters of March 3, 149, 180–183, 185, 192, 195, 247, 259–260, 422, S8

letter of July 8, 1832, 52–53

letter of recommendation for Deaf Smith, 366, 372

line in the dirt, 286, 413

life of, 260

saddlebags of, 360, 437 n. 8-4

survives battle and executed, 404

Treatise on Field Fortification, and Other Subjects Connected with the Duties of the Field Engineer (MaCaulay), S3, S28, S47, S48, S55, S56

Tremont House, Boston, 165

Trevino, Capt. Alexandro, S48, S50

Trevino, Col. Don Antonio, 329

Trinidad River, 58

Trinity River, 24, 26, 65, 70, 75, 301, 302, 379

Trinity (TX), 210

turkey, 59

Troutman, Miss, 341

Tuacasite (TX), 330

tula, S43

Twiggs, Col. David, 391

Tyler, John, 391
typhoid fever, 411, 418, S50

U

Ugartechea, Col. Domingo, 69, 70, 74, 75, 77, 83, 206
Union, schooner, 352
Union Street, Natchez, 387
Urchin, schooner, 352
US Engineers, 315
US First Dragoons, 81
US Second Dragoons, 391
Ukraine, 27
Urissa, Col. Fernando, 152, 266
Urrea, Gen. Jose
    at Refugio, 293
    defeats Fannin at Coleto Creek, 296–299, 418
    destruction of Johnson and Grant, 174, 176, 180, 186, 195, 201, 202, 281
    mentioned, 169, 267, 270, 292, 308, 309, 310–311, 330, 339, 350, 407
    ordered by Santa Anna to retire, 344
    replaces Filisola, 351
Uvalde, Gen., 18–19, 20

V

Valdez, Col. Manuel, 329
Valdsquez, Col. Miguel, 329
Valejo, Lt. Luis, 329
Valentine, R. W., 210
Valiante, Capt. Ygnacio Perez, 329
Valley Forge, 6
Van Buren, Martin, 100, 101, 104, 110
Vandeveer, Logan, 322
Vaudeville Theater, San Antonio, 410
Vazguez, Col., 83
Vega, Lt. Mariano Arias, 329
Vega, Lt. Yldefonse, 329
Velasco (TX), 52, 53, 75, 148, 151 n. 9, 180, 269, 299, 328, 340, 342, 343, 350, S44
Velasco, Treaties of. 344, 345, 351
Vencas, Lt. Severiano, 329
Vencendor Del Alamo, brig, 341
Vera Cruz (Mexico), 35, 49, 50, 57, 83, 150, 306, 308, 341, 359
Vermendi, Don Juan Martín de, 38, 221, 411, 418
Veramendi, Ursula, 38, 54, 221
Veramendi House, 92, 93, 152, 386, 422, S13

Vermont, 21
Vicksburg (MS), 415
Victoria (TX), 131, 132, 133, 303, 305, 310, 327, 352, 391
Vidalia (LA), 399
Viesca, Don Augustan, 117
Vietnam War, 4
Villafranco, Capt. Jose María, 329
Villasenor, Capt. Cayentana, 329
Vince's bridge, 335
Vince's Ranch, 337
Virginia, 167
Volante, Compania, S48, S56, 443 n. 193
Voluntine, Pvt., 210
Vose, soldier at Goliad, 308
vultures, 273

W

Waco Indians, 38–42
wagons, 59, 123, 124, 139, 176, 187, 285, 286, 303, 308, 318, 351, 417, 424, 434 n. 3-1, 437 n. 84
Wake, Pvt. William S., 322
Walker, Congressman, 316
Walker, Hartwell, 126
Walker, James, S29
Walker, Martin, 322
Walker, William, 126
Walker, Col. Seth, 126
Wallace, Maj. B.C., 297, 305
Wallace, Jesse, 38
Wallace (TX), 302
Walton (actor), 357
Ward, Col. William, 293, 298, 299, 323
Wardsworth, Capt. 298
Ware, T. P., 261
Warnell, Henry, 210
Warner (executed at Alamo), 209, 210, 220, 233
Warren, Edward, 113, 119, 121, 131
Washington County (TX), 286
Washington D.C., 9, 32, 37, 100, 101, 255, 256, 311, 313, 315, 363, 398
Washington, George, 121, 317
Washington Monument, 398
Washington-on-the-Brazos (TX), 70, 113, 119, 121, 138, 167, 177, 180, 186–187, 192, 194, 223, 225, 235, 244, 282, 295, 354, 398
Washington, Pvt. Lewis, 322, 323

Washita (LA), 402
Waters, Pvt. George, 322
Watkins, Jesse J., 435 n. 5
Wavell, Gen. Arthur Goodall, 57
Wayne, Gen. Anthony, 246
Wayne, John, 409, 433 n. 11
Weakley County (TN), 105, 106
Webb, Col. James Watson, 310, 341
Wells, M., 30
Wells, Dr. Samuel, 29, 30
Wells, T. J., 30
Wells, William, 210
West Commerce Street, San Antonio, 421
Western, Maj., 369
West Feliciana (LA), 288
Westover, Capt., 303
West Indies, 61, 399
West Point (NY), 308
Wharton, John A., 70, 155, 157, 364
Wharton, Judge Advocate Gen. William Harris, 260
Wheeling (WV), 56
Wheelwright, Capt., 311
Whigs, 55, 103, 104, 106, 372
White, Judge Hugh L., 104, 107
White, Isaac, 210
White, Capt. Robert, 210
White, Gen. William A., 36
White, William C., 383, 384
Wilkinson, W. B., 24
William A. Turner, schooner, 160, 167
Williams, Col. Samuel M., 317
Williamson, Sgt. Maj. Hiram Jones, 210, 236
Williamson, Maj. Robert McAlpin, 183, 200, S10
Wilson, David, 210
Winston, Mr., 86
Winters, Pvt. William, 322
W. L. Cushing & Moore, 402
Wolfson's Store, San Antonio, 420
Wisconsin, 198
With Santa Anna in Texas: A personal Narrative of the Revolution (de la Peña), 265–266
Wood, David L., 17, 383, 384
Wood, W. P. M., letter from, 282–283, 288–289
Woodbridge (NJ), 269
Woodliff, Devereaux J., 323
Woodruff, William, 106, 107
Woods, Col. James A., 416–417

Woll, Gen. Adrian, 236, 328, 330, 345
wool, 61
Wool, Gen. John E., 392
Wright, Clairborn, 211
Wright, Judge John C., 32, 109
Wright, Maj. Norris, 30–31, 399–400
Wytheville (VA), 423

X
Xerxes, 245

Y
yellow fever, 49
Yellowstone, steamboat, 127, 191
Yoakum, Henderson, S6
Yturri House, San Antonio, 176, 442 n. 140
Yucatan (Mexico), 98, 99

Z
Zacatecas (Mexico), revolt in, 62–63, 66; mentioned, 129, 289
Zanco, Charles, 210
Zavala, Adina de, 348, S6, S62
Zavala, Lorenzo de, 78, 178, 320, 340, 354
Zempoal (Mexico), 203
Zorillo (stream), 298
Zuber, William P., 274, 286, 287